Eating
&
Drinking

2008
EDITION 1

timeoutchicago.com

Time Out Chicago Eating & Drinking 2008
Editors Judy Sutton Taylor, Margaret Littman, Heather Shouse, David Tamarkin
Copy Editors Jennifer Kester (chief), Kevin Dwire, Erin Green, Jeremy Ohmes, Bobby Reed, Kay Riley
Art Director Nicole Moulton
Photo Editor Caroline Voagen Nelson
Editorial Assistants Jake Malooley, Alice Park
Contributors Nicholas Day, Colleen Rush, Chuck Sudo

Time Out Chicago
Editorial
Editor Joel Reese
Managing Editor Amy Carr
Eat Out/Drink Up Heather Shouse (Editor), David Tamarkin, Jake Malooley

Art
Art Director Bryan Erickson
Associate Art Director Mike Novak
Designers Nadine Nakanishi, ks Rives
Photo Editor Nicole Radja
Assistant Photo Editors Donna Rickles, Martha Williams

Production
Production Manager Cheryl Magiera
Associate Production Manager Nooreen Furquan
Production Assistant Gena Bailey
Image Specialist Jamie Ramsay
Advertising Designer Chris Gallevo

Online
Online Director Amanda Meffert
Web Editor Scott Smith
Online Producer Brad Tyson

Information Technology
Technology Manager Kim R. Russell
Systems Coordinator David Gibson

Advertising
Publisher David Garland
Senior Account Manager David Wilson
Account Managers January Overton, Erik Uppenberg-Croone
Online Account Manager Aidan Enright

Marketing
Marketing Director Tony Barnett
Marketing Manager, Events, Promotions & Publicity Eva Penar
Marketing Manager Julie Sprich
Marketing and Promotions Designer Amy Betley

Circulation
Assistant Circulation Manager Karlene Sherrill
Newsstand Sales Manager T.C. O'Rourke
Retail Sales Representative Bob Matter
Partnership Coordinator Kate Lowery

Finance
Accounting Manager Patrice Mauthe
Credit Analyst Clea Coburn
Accounting Coordinator Cathrine Baltizar
Staff Accountants Yang Guo, Frances Parks, Erika Schroeder

Administration
Human Resources Manager Andy Katzman
Office Assistants Carly Mulliken, Jaclyn Wojcik

President/Group Publisher Alison Tocci
Chief Financial Officer Daniel P. Reilly
Editorial Director Elizabeth Barr
Digital Content Director Chad Schlegel
Digital Business Manager Marci Weisler

Published by Time Out Chicago Partners, L.L.L.P.
Chairman Tony Elliott
Executive Committee William Louis-Dreyfus, Joe Mansueto, Kevin S. Moore

Printed and bound in the USA
Fry Communications, Inc. Mechanicsburg, PA
ISBN 978-0-9793984-3-8 and 0-9793984-3-6

On the cover "*Elote*" at Schwa, 1466 N Ashland Ave
Photograph by Anna Knott

Street maps J.S. Graphics john@jsgarpgis.co.uk, Chris Gallevo

Contents

The lowdown

How to use this guide

Restaurants are divided alphabetically by cuisine or type of establishment (Chinese, Kosher, Steak houses). Our largest section (Classic American) is divided into two price categories, based on the average cost of an entrée: $15 and under, $16 and over. Starting on page 245, you'll find subject indexes (brunch, BYOB, outdoor seating) as well as alphabetical and neighborhood indexes. Street maps (page 291) cover the city's neighborhoods. A CTA subway map can be found on the last page of the guide.

★ **Critics' picks**
A red star next to a restaurant's name means we think the place is very good for its cuisine or category, and especially worth checking out.

▼ **Vegetarian-friendly**

☉ **Cheap eats**
This symbol denotes places where the average cost of a main course (or equivalent) is $10 or less. You'll find more than 350 restaurants with this icon in the guide.

▼ **Gay/lesbian–friendly**

⌱ **Fireplace**

☀ **Outdoor seating**

☾ **Restaurants serving after 10 pm; bars serving after 2am Sun-Fri, 3am Sat**

B **Brunch served**

BYOB **Bring your own beer/wine**

✕ **Bars serving food**

Before you set out
Although information was updated right up until this book went to press, some restaurants' hours, chefs and menus may have changed. Please call the restaurant or check timeoutchicago.com for the latest details.

Addresses
All cross streets are conveniently listed.

Business hours
We include the days and hours that the restaurant is open (though the kitchen may stop taking orders for food earlier than the closing time). Hours may change during summer and holidays.

Cash only
We've noted establishments that only take cash; otherwise, all major credit cards are accepted.

Pricing information
Not everyone orders appetizers, drinks and desserts at each meal, so we've listed the average price of each restaurant's main courses. At places that don't serve meals à la carte, we give an equivalent (e.g., pizza or typical nigiri at sushi spots).

---

timeoutchicago.com

To stay current with all the new places opening throughout the year, be sure to read the Eat Out section in the weekly *Time Out Chicago* magazine, or visit timeoutchicago.com. Complete reviews from both the magazine and the *Eating & Drinking* guide can be searched online by many criteria (such as name, neighborhood, cuisine or bar type).

Additional locations
Sister restaurants and branches are listed at the end of reviews.

Transportation
We list the nearest El stop or bus line for each restaurant. For places in the suburbs, Metra train or Pace bus information is listed where appropriate. At press time, the CTA was considering service cuts. Double-check your route at www.transitchicago.com.

2007 Eat Out Awards
Time Out Chicago magazine bestows awards annually on restaurants and bars of particular note. The awards include both Critics' Picks and Readers' Choices. We highlight the entries of each winning restaurant or bar by noting their awards in red.

This is how we do it
The establishments that appear in this guide are chosen by TOC's food critics. We visit each one anonymously and pay for our own meals and drinks in order to best evaluate the experience any diner might have when visiting the restaurant or bar.

Our advertisers
The *Time Out Chicago Eating & Drinking* guide, like the weekly TOC magazine, accepts advertising. We would like to stress that our advertisers receive no special favors and have no influence over our editorial content. No establishment has been included and/or given a favorable review because its owners have advertised in the magazine, online or in this guide. An advertiser may receive a bad review or no review at all.

BUSINESS REPLY MAIL
FIRST-CLASS MAIL   PERMIT NO 214   MT. MORRIS IL

POSTAGE WILL BE PAID BY ADDRESSEE

TIME OUT CHICAGO
PO BOX 387
MT. MORRIS, IL 61054-9907

BUSINESS REPLY MAIL
FIRST-CLASS MAIL   PERMIT NO 214   MT. MORRIS IL

POSTAGE WILL BE PAID BY ADDRESSEE

TIME OUT CHICAGO
PO BOX 387
MT. MORRIS, IL 61054-9907

Introduction

A long culinary tradition rests on these Big Shoulders.

Not just rabbit food Blackbird's confit of organically-raised Illinois spring rabbit showcases Chicago chefs' passion for local meat and produce.

Ever since the Chicago World's Fair of 1893—where America got its first taste of shredded wheat, Cracker Jack, Aunt Jemima pancakes and the hamburger—the Windy City has been making culinary history. Though these days, Chicago gets more attention for world-class meals made by chefs such as Charlie Trotter and the mind-blowing, experimental creations found at restaurants like Alinea, Moto and Schwa. If you've got money to burn, fine dining experiences here will prove that when it comes to restaurants, Chicago is no longer a piddly Second City.

If upscale isn't your thing, you'll no doubt fall in love with the plethora of cheap ethnic eats that are tucked into every far-reaching corner of the city. Given that Chicago has the second largest population of Mexicans in America (outside of L.A.), it's no surprise that the range of Mexican food available stretches from dollar tamales at Maxwell Market to bargain *mole* at Pilsen taquerias like Nuevo Leon to seasonal tasting menus highlighting various regions of Mexico prepared by celebrity chef Rick Bayless at his Frontera Grill and Topolobampo.

After you've conquered Mexican, take your tastebuds on a trip to India and Pakistan via Devon Avenue. Amidst sari shops, grocery stores and electronics outlets, you'll find revered curry houses like Hema's Kitchen and kebab havens like Chopal Kebab & Steak. Travel further east toward Lake Michigan and a bit south and you'll hit Argyle Street, otherwise known as Little Saigon. Vietnamese eats abound, and you can't go wrong with the *banh mi* at Ba Le or steaming bowls of *pho* at Tank Noodle. For another taste of Asia, hit Chinatown on the near South Side for the real

deal. Screaming hot Szechuan food doesn't get better than Lao Sze Chuan, vinegar-laced Yunanese classics can be found at Spring World and hangover-soaking dim sum is best at Shui Wah.

Other ethnic eats may not have their own neighborhood, but instead, can be found littered throughout the city. Chicago Thai restaurants have seen a surge in popularity in the last few years, thanks in part to a local foodie who took it upon himself to translate Thai-language menus at a half-dozen of the best Thai restaurants in town, including Sticky Rice and TAC Quick Thai Kitchen. Now Anglo eaters can order the same authentic dishes that once were only available to Thai-speaking Chicagoans. Just ask for the "secret menu."

Aside from ethnic food, you'll also find a noticeable increase in the use of organic and local products at many mid-level restaurants around town. Chefs at trend-setting spots like Sepia, Blackbird, Lula Café, Naha and Avec are dedicated to sourcing everything from free-range chicken to baby beets from the nearest farms available, and have been among the driving forces behind the city's popular Green City Market.

Of course, all this growth will never erase the City of Big Shoulders' roots—meat and potatoes never go out of style. Only now, in addition to old-school favorites like Chicago Chop House and Gene & Georgetti's, you'll find the over-the-top presentations of Primehouse David Burke and grass-fed beef at chef Shawn McClain's slick South Looper, Custom House. As they say, those who don't evolve will perish.—*Heather Shouse, Eat Out editor*

Enjoy
a little taste
of Heaven.

Santa Rita

Memorable Every Time

palmbay.com

Too new to review

Don't miss these noteworthy newcomers.

Setting the bar Gastro meets pub at the new Paramount Room with U.K.-style dishes like the Scotch egg (right).

Brasserie Ruhlmann SteakHouse This Chicago sibling to the Rockefeller Plaza "Parisian-style brasserie" won't have Laurent Tournedol in the kitchen but instead is bringing in Christian Delouvrier (of Ducasse, most recently). In the historic old Montgomery Ward building, they'll serve approachable rustic food, plus a raw bar with oysters, *langoustines* and lobsters. The restaurant has a 30-foot-long bar, a dining room for 200 and a banquet room for 120, not to mention an 80-seat sidewalk café. *500 W Superior St at Kingsbury St (312-494-1900). El: Brown, Purple (rush hrs) to Chicago. Bus: 8 Halsted, 66 Chicago (24hrs). Brunch (Sun), lunch (Mon–Sat), dinner. Average main counrse: $30.*

✳ **Café Bionda** Apparently, when Joe Farina left his corporate chef position at Rosebud and opened his own spot in the South Loop, his legion of family, friends and fans followed. Kisses and Bridgeport-worthy "aaayyyyy"s abound, with enough gelled hair and tanned skin on display here to make both Michael Kors *and* George Hamilton jealous. Both the mediocre Italo-American food and the '80s soundtrack scream "chain," but if you're intent on finding diamonds in the rough (that aren't on the fingers of goomahs), the *salumi* and the orrechiette with sweet sausage and rapini will do. *1924 S State St at Archer Ave (312-326-9800). El: Red to Cermak/Chinatown. Bus: 21, 29, 62. Lunch (Mon–Fri), dinner. Average main course: $16.*

Exposure Tapas Supper Club Most nightclub food is second rate, but nobody's there for the food anyway. At this new South Loop space—a small-plates restaurant, lounge and jazz club in one—food is making a play at stealing the limelight. The best bets come from the raw bar, which features a nightly ceviche (a recent shrimp special got both heat and sweetness from spicy cocktail sauce) and a crab cocktail studded with sweet corn and cilantro. The hot plates are less successful—a lobster spring roll was short on lobster; gnocchi had the consistency of clay. But head downstairs to hear some music and you'll probably forget any missteps. *1313 S Wabash Ave between 13th and 14th Sts (312-662-1060). El: Green, Orange, Red to Roosevelt. Bus: 1, 3, X3, 4 (24hrs), X4, 12, 127. Dinner. Average small plate: $8.*

❨ **La Madia** Jonathan Fox, owner of the Maggiano's empire, is opening this upscale pizzeria in the former Jazz Showcase location. Fox promises "the chew of Neapolitan-style pizza but the crispness of Roman crusts." But more enticing are promises of private pizza-tasting rooms and 4,400 square feet of wine, fancy cheeses and pizza: three of our favorite things. *59 W Grand Ave between Dearborn and Clark Sts (312-329-0400). El: Red to Grand. Bus: 22 (24hrs), 36, 65. Lunch, dinner.*

Niu Japanese Fusion Lounge Nothing says "date night" quite like dinner and a movie. Particularly if it is sushi for dinner. This new (just like its name: "niu" is pronounced "new") minimalist spot is near the mammoth AMC Streeterville theaters (in the former location of Max & Benny's). If your sweetie doesn't go for raw, there are enough

EXIGEZ DAVANTAGE DE VOTRE BIÈRE

MATILDA

WWW.GOOSEISLAND.COM

Going Dutch Pannenkoeken Café turns out seven kinds of Dutch pancakes in its sunny digs.

other options—including noodle dishes and stir fry—to keep her satisfied (not to mention a weird fusion version of chicken nuggets). A late-night cocktail lounge won't hurt your chances either. *332 E Illinois St between New St and Park Dr (312-527-2888). El: Red to Grand. Bus: 2, 29, 65, 66 (24hrs), 124. Lunch (Mon–Fri), dinner. Average main course: $12.*

(Old Town Brasserie Bob Djahanguiri used to own several Gold Coast hotspots in the '80s (including Yvette and Toulouse). Now in the new millennium he is putting that experience to good use. Hiring Chef Roland Liccioni (once at the legendary Le Francais and at Les Nomades) to create a combo French brasserie with Pan Asian influences, a takeout market and music Thursday–Saturday starting at 10pm. *1209 N Wells St at Division St (312-943-3000). El: Red to Division. Dinner (closed Sun). Average main course: $20.*

▼ **Pannenkoeken Café** A wet-behind-the-ears mother-daughter team turn out the eponymous Dutch pancakes at this bright and cheery cafe in Lincoln Square. Slightly thicker than a crêpe and 11 inches in diameter, the *pannenkoeken* come in seven varieties with baked-on toppings like thinly sliced apples with cinnamon, bacon with cheese and a chocolate-banana version topped with Dutch chocolate syrup, cocoa and hazelnuts. *4757 N Western Ave between Leland and Lawrence Aves (773-769-8800). El: Brown to Western. Bus: 11, 49, X49, 81. Breakfast, lunch. Average main course: $7.*

Paramount Room You can feast on a Scotch egg and a plate of fish-and-chips at this chic dual-level restaurant and lounge, but there's more than just U.K. fare and craft beers to be had at this gastropub. Chef Stephen Dunne elevates things with heirloom tomato salad, organic chicken and a grass-fed Argentine beef burger with complimentary bourbon-cured foie gras. *415 N Milwaukee Ave between Kinzie and Hubbard Sts (312-829-6300). El: Blue to Grand. Bus: 8, 56, 65. Lunch (Sat, Sun), dinner. Average main course: $17.*

Restaurant Takashi Chef Takashi Yagihashi (formerly of Tribute and Okada) has bought the Bucktown A-frame that formerly housed Scylla and will be offering what he calls "American-French with Japanese influence." Francois Geneve, the designer behind Spring, Green Zebra and Custom House, is in charge of the head-turning, contemporary look. Expect a cozy, 65-seat space. *1952 N Damen Ave between Homer St and Armitage Ave. El: Blue to Western. Bus: 50 Damen, 73 Armitage.*

Rosebud Prime This recent addition to the Chicagoland restaurant empire ostensibly offers more of the same to its loyal biz-cas clientele: pricey, well-portioned steaks, chops and fish in a comfortable yet elegant atmosphere. Let's just hope the burger is as delicious at Prime as at its Rosebud Steakhouse sibling. *1 S Dearborn St at Madison St (312-384-1900). El: Blue to Monroe. Lunch (Mon–Fri), dinner. Average main course: $33.*

▼ **Spertus Café by Wolfgang Puck** The Spertus Institute of Jewish Studies, the city's Jewish museum, is home to the Loop's long-awaited kosher eatery. Serving a dairy kosher menu of salmon, tuna, sandwiches and salads, Spertus Café has more than one favorite chef attached to it—executive chef Laura Frankel comes from Shallots Bistro (see kosher listing). *610 S Michigan Ave at Harrison St. El: Red to Harrison, Blue to Jackson.*

▼ **BYOB** ✳ **Su-Ra** In his take on contemporary Korean, chef Paul Choi deconstructs traditional Korean fish stew into seared monkfish with a concentrated sauce of the stew's spicy-sour flavors and douses heirloom tomatoes with soy sauce, rice wine vinegar, and slivers of ginger, garlic and green onions. Purists will find *bibimbap* and *chapchae*, but made with locally grown vegetables, prime sirloin and heirloom pork. *2257 W North Ave at Oakley Ave (773-276-9450). El: Blue to Damen. Bus: 49 (24hrs), 50, 72. Dinner (closed Mon). Average main course: $16.* ∎

FOOD
FOR
THOUGHT
MEALS ON
CHICAGO
WHEELS
$6.67
A Small Price for
Their Independence.
Meals on Wheels Chicago
MORE THAN JUST MEALS.
To find out how $6.67 can
change the life of a senior
or how you can support
Meals on Wheels Chicago,
visit mealsonwheelschicago.org

African

See also: *Eclectic*

Look, Ma, no forks
Eat with your hands at
African Harambee.

★ ▼ **Addis Abeba** An NU crowd uses spongy *injera* bread as knife, fork and spoon to sop up traditional entrées at this Ethiopian stalwart. Combo plates offer the best bang for your buck, giving you a chance to try as many as four entrées, like *yeater kit wot* (yellow split peas with garlic, cloves and cinnamon), *yesiga wot* (a spicy beef stew) and *azifa* (cold lentils with tomatoes and jalapeño). Go with someone you want to cozy up with, since food is served on a *mesob*—a single, large platter symbolizing intimacy and loyalty. *1322 Chicago Ave, Evanston (847-328-5411). El: Purple to Dempster. Bus: 201 (24hrs) Central/Ridge, 205 Chicago/Golf. Lunch, dinner. Average main course: $13.*

BYOB **African Harambee** Sisay Abebe (formerly of Edgewater's Ethiopian Diamond) is behind this African spot, where together with chef-partner Martha Yimer, he serves food "from Casablanca to Cape Town; the land of Sheba to the Ashanti Kingdom." That translates to beef dredged in seasoned pea flour, catfish in turmeric-spiked tahini sauce and lamb in dried-fruit curry. *7537 N Clark St between Birchwood Ave and Howard St (773-764-2200). El: Purple, Red, Yellow to Howard. Bus: 22 (24hrs), 97, 147, 151 (24hrs), 201 (24hrs), 205, Pace 215, Pace 290. Lunch, dinner. Average main course: $13.*

☺ **Bolat African Cuisine** Take the plunge and venture inside this Wrigleyville African restaurant. Start with fried yams: crispy, starchy slices served with a slightly spicy tomato sauce for dipping. Or get your veggie fix from dishes like sweet, caramelized plantains, savory yam porridge and

okra soup. The tilapia, immersed in yet another spicy pepper sauce, is also a good bet. *3346 N Clark St between Buckingham Pl and Roscoe St (773-665-1100). El: Brown, Purple (rush hrs), Red to Belmont. Bus: 8, 22 (24hrs), 77 (24hrs). Lunch, dinner. Average main course: $8.*

★ ▼ ☺ **Ethiopian Diamond** This Ethiopian choice stands out for consistency and punchy flavors. The ground beef in the sambusa is livened with peppers, and vegetables shine in the entrées, starring two types of split peas: the rich yet tame *alicha* and the spicy *wat*, both stewed to melt-in-your-mouth perfection and served with *injera* bread. Fat and bones abound, but don't let that stop you from gnawing on the *kay wat*, beef cubes simmered in the "diamond sauce," a gingery, cumin-laced red sauce with a nice chili kick. *6120 N Broadway between Glenlake and Hood Aves (773-338-6100). El: Red to Granville. Bus: 36, 147, 151 (24hrs). Lunch, dinner. Average main course: $9.50.*

☺ **Mama Desta's Red Sea Restaurant** Head to this 20-year-old enclave to break off pieces of flat, spongy *injera* bread to scoop up the succulent morsels of *wat* (the spicy, tender, boneless lamb stands out among the choices) and *alicha* (stewed cabbage and flavor-layered lentils are favorites). Those with a sweet tooth will enjoy the honey wine and shouldn't skip the house dessert, a delicious sweet-and-sour cream topped with tart raspberries and honey. *3216 N Clark St between Belmont Ave and School St (773-935-7561). El: Brown, Purple (rush hrs), Red to Belmont. Bus: 8, 22 (24hrs), 77 (24hrs). Dinner (closed Tues). Average main course: $10.*

Wrap it up Yams take center stage at Bolat.

⊙ **Queen of Sheba Café** Most Ethiopian restaurants in town have a good selection of beer but a poor choice of wine. That's fine if you prefer suds to quell the heat of a spicy *wat*, but for nights when you'd rather put out the fire with a Riesling, this BYOB spot does the trick. The *gomen roll*—*injera* rolled with spinach and a dry cottage cheese—has a significant bite; *shimbera fitfit* (chickpeas) are deliciously full of garlic; and *beg tibs*, juicy bits of lamb, are in an herbaceous sauce with gradual heat. *5403 N Broadway at Balmoral St (773-878-2352). El: Red to Berwyn. Bus: 36, 84, 147, 151 (24hrs). Dinner. Average main course: $8.*

★ ▼ **Ras Dashen Ethiopian Restaurant** Spinach sambusas—hot, crispy dumplings—are a fine way to start your meal at this Ethiopian spot. When you get to the main courses, be brave and try the fiery *zilzil tibs*, beef strips sautéed with peppers in *berbere* sauce, an Ethiopian specialty made with red peppers and cumin. Or go for the *doro alicha*, a fragrant, tender, milder chicken dish. This stuff is likely to induce a food coma, so snag a table with big, cushy chairs. *5846 N Broadway between Ardmore and Rosedale Aves (773-506-9601). El: Red to Thorndale. Bus: 36, 84, 147. Lunch, dinner. Average main course: $11.*

⊙ **Yassa** *2007 Eat Out Award, Critics' Pick: Best use of peanut butter since PB&J (Dakhine, lamb-peanut butter stew)* The Senegalese chef at this eatery uses slow methods of cooking mingled with the wild flavor of West African spices to make Old World, yet innovative, dishes. Signature dishes include *mafe*, a thick stew of lamb with ground peanuts and habanero peppers, and the succulent chicken *yassa*, grilled chicken that's marinated in mustard powder, vinegar and lemon juice. But we'd move mountains for the *dakhine*, seared lamb shank with onions, tomato paste, peanut butter (yes, peanut butter) and black-eyed peas

netetu, a condiment made of fermented African locust beans. *716 E 79th St between Evans and Langley Aves (773-488-5599). El: Red to 79th St. Bus: 3, 4 (24hrs), 79. Lunch, dinner. Average main course: $10.* ▣

Read 'em & eat

alitcha (ah-lih-chah) a spice blend of garlic, ginger, turmeric and onions used in mild wats

berbere (bur-bur-ee) an Ethiopian seasoning mix of garlic, red pepper, cardamom and other spices

cassava (also called *manioc* or *yuca*) a long, coarse root that is boiled and pounded to make bread and various other dishes

injera a spongy Ethiopian bread that doubles as an eating implement

kitfo an Ethiopian version of steak tartare, prepared with hot chili powder (mit'mita), spiced butter and green chili peppers

tibs (tihbz) pieces of meat or vegetable sautéed in spiced, clarified butter

wat (wuht) thick stew of slow-cooked onions and cubes of meat or vegetable that have been sautéed in a red-chili-spice blend called *berbere*

Bakeries/Cafés

See also: *Classic American $15 and under, Delis, Latin American, Italian, Vegetarian*

B ☺ **A Taste of Heaven** Baked-from-scratch goods, including cakes, cookies, cupcakes and scones are the real draw here, but the daily brunch (served until 3pm) offers favorites like buttermilk pancakes and breakfast casserole with ham, red peppers and cheese. Lunch and dinner focus on salads, sandwiches and a small selection of comfort entrees like chicken and biscuits, chicken pot pie and meatloaf–all made with reliably fresh ingredients. *5401 N Clark St at Balmoral Ave (773-989-0151). El: Red to Berwyn. Bus: 22 (24hrs), 36, 50, 92. Breakfast, lunch, brunch, dinner. Average main course: $9.*

★ B ☺ **Angel Food Bakery** Regressing back to childhood is a very good thing when you're doing it at this lively, lime-green café. Pastry chef Stephanie Samuels makes the kind of desserts you used to find in your lunch box: homespun versions of Ding Dongs, Thin Mints and superb cream-filled cupcakes. She provides nourishment, too, with seasonal soups, sandwiches on soft, housemade wheat rolls, and a breakfast and weekend brunch menu which includes powdered sugar–dusted squares of French toast with marmalade syrup. *1636 W Montrose Ave at Paulina St (773-728-1512). Bus: 22 (24hrs), 50, 78. Tue–Fri 7am–5pm; Sat 8am–5pm; Sun 9am–2pm. Average main course: $6.50.*

Argo Tea The blossoming local tea company makes trademarked concoctions like Teappuccino, Maté Laté, Smootea, Tea Sparkle and Tea Sangria, all aimed at making tea as coveted as coffee. Pastries, quiches, sandwiches and salads round out the menu, and the café has tables with Wi-Fi access. A small retail area carries a slew of tea accessories. *16 W Randolph St between State and Dearborn Sts (312-553-1550). El: Blue, Red to Washington; Brown, Green, Orange, Purple (rush hrs) to Randolph. Bus: 22 (24hrs), 29, 36, 14, 20, 56, 60 (24hrs), 124, 127, 147, 151 (24hrs), 157. 7am–10pm. Average drink: $3.* ● For additional locations, go to argotea.com.

☺ **Artopolis Bakery, Café, & Agora** This always-bustling Greek spot is popular for good reason: The food is inexpensive, you get it fast, and it tastes great. The signature artopitas—flaky puff-pastry rounds with fillings like ham and kasseri cheese, and chicken and mozzarella—take center stage, but there are also fresh salads, sandwiches and traditional Greek dishes like roasted lamb. Bonus: The front area overlooking Halsted Street is perfect for people watching. *306 S Halsted St at Jackson Blvd (312-559-9000). El: Blue to UIC-Halsted. Bus: 7, 8, 60 (24hrs), 126, 156, 157. Lunch, dinner. Average main course: $9.*

BeBoBa Bubble Tea House The kids from Lane Tech High School flock to this mod version of a neighborhood soda shop—tucked into the corner of a strip mall—to sip funky, fruity bubble teas in a rainbow of colors and flavors. Tapioca-laced teas (which originated in Taiwan) can be ordered clear, milky or frozen in flavors that run the gamut from strawberry to red bean. There's also a small menu of sandwiches, instant ramen noodles and penny candy, served by a smiley staff. *3533 N Western Ave between Cornelia and Addison Aves (773-883-2622). Bus: 49 Western (24hrs), 152 Addison. Mon–Sat 12–9pm; Sun 12–6pm. Average drink: $3.25.*

★ ☺ **Bittersweet Pastry Shop** Stop by midday for chef Judy Contino's acclaimed pastries and desserts, and chances are you'll pull up a chair for lunch. You won't go wrong with any of the handful of rotating daily menu options like carrot jalapeño soup, spinach salad with blue cheese and lemon vinaigrette, and roasted eggplant–and–goat cheese sandwiches—perfect light fare before diving into a beautiful meringue tart or ice cream scooped out into chocolate-lined Chinese takeout containers (try the intense chocolate almond). *1114 W Belmont Ave between Clifton and Seminary Aves (773-929-1100). El: Brown, Purple (rush hrs), Red to Belmont. Bus: 22 Clark (24hrs), 77 Belmont (24hrs). Breakfast, lunch (closed Mon). Average main course: $7.*

▽ ☺ **The Bleeding Heart Bakery** Pastry chef/owner Michelle Garcia puts her ethics into action at this vegan-friendly, all-organic bakery, donating to organizations like Food Not Bombs. But one sample of her scones, pecan sticky buns and fruit tarts, and you'll see this is no charity case. Punky vintage touches, plus a menu of savory sandwiches, soups and salads, add to the charm. *1955 W Belmont Ave at Damen Ave (773-278-3638). Bus: 50 Damen, 77 Belmont (24hrs). Tue–Sat 7am–7pm, Sun 8am–9pm (closed Mon). Average baked good: $3.*

★ ☺ **Bombon Café** We've often wished we could take a seat in Pilsen's Bombon Bakery and sample Laura Cid-Perea's fabulous pastries all day long. Now we can do just that in this bright, roomy space, which offers ample seating to indulge in dishes like chorizo *torta* piled with Oaxacan cheese and avocado and a mixed greens *provinciana* salad with *pepitas* and roasted corn. Don't forget Cid-Perea's signature pastries: sampling from several varieties of her incredible *tres leches* cake is the perfect way to end a meal. *36 S Ashland Ave at Ogden Ave (312-733-8717). El: Blue to Medical Center. Bus: 9 (24hrs), X9, 20 (24hrs), X20, 126. Mon–Sat 7am–7pm, Sun 8am–4pm. Average sandwich: $6. · Additional location at 170 W Washington Blvd (312-781-2788).*

☺ **The Book Cellar** See Classic American under $15 for review.

Brown Sugar Bakery Past the pink door of this South Shore spot, Stephanie Hart turns out a number of "down-home delights" that smack of her bakery's eponymous ingredient. Peach cobbler, pineapple upside down cake and sweet potato pie, as well as by-the-slice or whole cakes such as caramel, German chocolate and red velvet are just a sample of Hart's cavity-producing creations. *720 E 75th St between Evans and Langley Aves (773-723-9040). Bus: 4 (24hrs), X4, 75. Mon–Sat 10am–7pm. Average baked good: $2.*

▽ ✳ B **Café Selmarie** You might have stopped into this Lincoln Square stalwart for a croissant to go and missed the dining room hidden in back. The first-come, first-served policy means you'll have a half-hour wait for brunch, but a cup of coffee and slice of coffee cake will tide you over. For the main event, don't miss the corned-beef hash: the smoky-salty beef and potatoes are flecked with herbs and topped with two perfectly poached eggs. Lunch and dinner during the week focus on comfort foods, including a yummy grown-up mac-

Spanish revelation One sip of Angel Food's Barthelona hot chocolate, and you'll never go back to Swiss Miss.

and-cheese with leeks. *4729 N Lincoln Ave between Leland and Lawrence Aves (773-989-5595). El: Brown to Western. Bus: 11, 49 (24hrs), X49, 81 Lawrence (24hrs). Breakfast (Tues–Sun), brunch (Sun), lunch (Mon–Sun), dinner (Tues–Sun). Average main course: $13.*

⊕ **CaféNeo** You'll find more than lattes and shrink-wrapped muffins at this airy coffeehouse. The pastry spread includes croissants and cinnamon rolls, but the real draw is the sweet and savory crêpes, including Nutella and banana, and spinach and goat cheese. There are some decent quiches and salads (they hit and miss—we're not fans of strawberries on salad, whatever the season). It's all served with the nicest flatware we've ever seen at a coffee shop—supershiny and pleasantly heavy in our hands. *4655 N Lincoln Ave at Leland Ave (773-878-2233). El: Brown to Western. Bus: 11, 49 (24 hrs) X49, 78, 81 (24hrs). Breakfast, lunch, dinner. Average main course: $7.*

⊕ **Carolina Caramel** Sweets and beats are the name of the game at this late-night dessert lounge. No alcohol is on offer, but in addition to coffee and tea, oversize slices of cakes are served (six signature flavors include red velvet, German chocolate and lemon). The cakes are brought in from 75th Street's Brown Sugar Bakery, but the DJ-driven sounds—ranging from jazz to hip-hop—are homespun. *1511 S State St between 15th and 16th Sts (312-922-5007). El: Green, Orange, Red to Roosevelt. Bus: 12, 24, 21, 29, 62 (24hrs). Thu—Sun 3pm–12am. Average dessert: $5.*

Cupcakes This tiny Lakeview takeaway space makes 120 flavors of all-natural cupcakes. A handmade display shows off the sweets in varieties like chai tea latte, orange-cream cooler, German chocolate, key lime, maple cream and hot chocolate. Each day eight flavors from the collection are featured, rotating according to popularity and season, but the pupcakes, carob-based dog treats, are available anytime. Check out the flavors of the day at cupcakesacrossamerica.com. *613 W Briar St between Broadway and Orchard St (773-525-0817). El: Brown, Purple (rush hrs), Red to Belmont. Bus: 22 (24hrs), 36, 77 (24hrs). Mon–Sat 10am–7pm (closed Sun). Average cupcake: $3.*

⊕ **B Demitasse** A blend of cozy bohemian hangout and hoppin' breakfast haunt, this spot's sun-splashed walls inspire all-day coffee sipping. Try the tasty frittatas (really just open-face omelettes) and the French toast, a gooey mayhem of three-inch-thick brioche slices stuffed with sweet cream, covered with fresh strawberries and bananas, and smothered in raspberry sauce. At lunch, options include crisp panini (the pesto caprese features homegrown tomatoes and freshly picked basil), made-from-scratch tuna and egg-salad sandwiches and a few huge salads. *1066 W Taylor St between Carpenter and Aberdeen Sts (312-226-7669). El: Blue to Racine. Bus: 7, 12, 60 (24hrs). Breakfast, brunch (Sat, Sun), lunch (closed Mon). Average main course: $6.50*

Dinkel's Baking in the Lakeview neighborhood since 1922, this popular German spot reliably turns out cinnamon-raisin stollen, ornate birthday cakes, German chocolate and butter cookies and its signature "sip'n whisky cake," a moist bundt cake made with sour mash whiskey. Rumor has it that the chocolate donut is Robert De Niro's favorite treat when he is in town. The real draw, though, is the strudel, which comes in several varieties such as praline-pecan, cherry-cheese and poppy seed. *3329 N Lincoln Ave between School and Roscoe sts (773-281-7300). El: Brown to Addison. Bus: 9, 11, 77 (24hrs). Mon–Fri 6am–7pm; Sat 6am–5pm; Sun 9am–3pm. Average baked good: $3.*

⊕ **First Slice Pie Café** See Classic American under $15 for review.

⊕ **Flourish Bakery Café** See Classic American under $15 for review.

▼ ✹ ⊕ **The Grind** Lincoln Square residents love this coffee shop for its laid-back vibe, free Wi-Fi and we're-not-Starbucks sense of camaraderie. Light, Mediterranean-inspired dishes include flaky croissants split and topped with tomatoes and melty cheese, and hummus with artichoke salad on a pita. There's a rotating roster of quiche selections, as well as tasty smoothies and Italian sodas. Intelligentsia's the caffeine of choice, while desserts come from local standouts such as Southport Grocery. *4613 N Lincoln Ave at Wilson Ave (773-271-4482). El: Brown to Western. Bus: 11, 78, 145. Breakfast, lunch, dinner. Average main course: $6.*

★ ⊕ **Hannah's Bretzel** This tiny Euro-chic café bills itself as an organic carry-out restaurant, but note that the word *healthy* is nowhere to be found. Warm, whole-grain pretzels—baked throughout the day on the premises—may be good for you, and no doubt the organic salads are, too. Sandwiches, such as the Black Forest ham and Gruyère on soft "bretzel" bread, aren't exactly unhealthy, either. But our doctor probably wouldn't condone the entire wall dedicated to chocolate, stocking what must be at least 30 different bars. *180 W Washington St between Wells and LaSalle Sts (312-621-1111). El: Blue, Brown, Orange, Purple (rush hrs); Red to Washington. Breakfast, lunch, dinner (Mon–Fri) (closed Sun). Average main course: $7.*

⊕ **Humboldt Pie Café** There's not really a lot of pie here—it seems the name is purely for the pun of it—but this sunny café still has a lot going for it. Thin slices of roast beef and cheddar are piled impossibly high on rye, and the "California Pepper"—the spicy, creamy house specialty—layers turkey, cucumber, pepper-jack and avocado cream on jalapeño bread before being topped, like all sandwiches here, with the quintessential green olive. The few pies are ho-hum, so stick to a bottomless cup of Intelligentsia instead. *1001 N California Ave at Augusta Blvd (773-342-4743). Bus: 52, 66 (24hrs), 70. Mon–Thu 7am–9pm; Fri 7am–10pm; Sat 8am–10pm; Sun 8am–9pm. Average main course: $5.50.*

⊕ **Iguana Café** You can work on your novel for as long as you want in this bustling, slightly smoky European café, but eventually you'll need something besides cappuccino to sustain you. When that happens, order the *tirokafteri*, a spicy feta cheese spread in a portion big enough to feed four. A square of the spinach pie provides your greens for the day. If you're there after 3pm, finish with a dessert crêpe; before then you'll have to stick with coffee. Sip slowly—in true European fashion, refills aren't free. *517 N Halsted St at Grand Ave (312-432-0663). El: Blue to Grand. Bus: 8 Halsted, 65 Grand. Breakfast, lunch, dinner. Average main course: $6.*

⊕ **Isabella Bakery** See Latin American for review.

⊕ **Kopi, A Traveler's Café** Imagine a travel bookstore, a tiny clothing and bauble boutique, and a rock-solid vegetarian eatery all rolled up into one global handful. It's a brilliant hodgepodge of working stiffs, bookish students and colorful artists ordering up the likes of soft toast with fat smears of chèvre and juicy tempeh burgers with tart blue cheese. The menu reads like a round-the-world sampler platter, and the made-for-sharing portions are perfect when eaten while lounging on the Turkish-style pillow seating. *5317 N Clark St between Berwyn and Summerdale Aves (773-989-5674). El: Red to Berwyn. Bus: 22 (24hrs), 50, 92. Breakfast, lunch, dinner. Average main course: $8.*

Bakeries/Cafés

⊕ **Kouks Vintage Café** On an otherwise unremarkable stretch of Northwest Highway, this Jefferson Park café stands out. From the front door you'll see decades worth of vintage goods—Bakelite jewelry, retro toys and other treasures from days gone by—and it's all for sale. So, too, are the Sicilian-style pizza slices and Italian-style pastries, plus smoothies, coffee and tea. There are a few small tables where you can dine among the resale finds, but the best bet is to grab a bar stool at the counter and chat with the friendly staff. *5653 N Northwest Hwy between Seminole St and Merrimac Ave (773-594-8888). El: Blue to Jefferson Park. Bus: 56A, 68 Northwest Hwy. Metra: Metra Pacific NW to Gladstone Park. Breakfast, lunch (closed Mon). Average main course: $5.*

BYOB ☀ ⊕ **La Sera** The sensibly succinct menu at this charming café sports far more hits than misses, including a panino piled with hot, tender roast beef, gooey blue cheese and caramelized red onions; and a Caesar salad wrap in which a warm flour tortilla hugs crisp lettuce and smoky slices of chicken. Other delicious distractions include a rotating assortment of desserts (think crème brûlée and chocolate-raspberry mousse) and a large selection of coffee and loose-leaf tea (both courtesy of Julius Meinl). *1143 N Wells St between Hill and Division Sts (312-274-0442). El: Red to Clark/Division. Bus: 22 (24hrs), 36, 70, 156. Mon–Fri 7am–11pm. Sat–Sun 8am–11pm. Average main course: $8.*

Lovely Bake Shop Brooke Dailey and Gina Howie, two friends who met at the French Pastry School, are behind this homey bakery. This place is pretty damn lovely. From cakey, star-shaped muffins to flaky *pan au chocolat*, the pastries are just as sweet and delicious as they should be. And their brownies? Tinged with creme fraiche and dark chocolate, they are some of the most serious and decadent we've ever had the pleasure of savoring. *1130 N Milwaukee Ave between Thomas St and Haddon Ave (773-572-4766). El: Blue to Division. Bus: 9 (24hrs), 56, 70. Mon–Fri 7am–7pm; Sat 9am–6pm; Sun 9am–4pm. Average baked good: $3.*

Lutz Continental Café & Pastry Shop Old school in the best sense of the phrase, Lutz has rows of glass cases filled with sweets the likes of which you haven't seen since Grandma was out cutting the rug. We love anything Lutz makes with marzipan, plus the coffee cakes and traditional pastries. Delicate cookies are sold by the pound and cakes are available for special order. *2458 W Montrose Ave between Campbell St and Western Ave (773-478-7785). El: Brown to Western. Bus: 49 Western (24hrs), 78 Montrose. Cafe: Sun–Thu 11am–8pm; Fri–Sat 11am–10pm. Pastry shop: Tues–Sun 7am–8pm. Average main course: $11.*

⊕ **Marrakech Expresso** See Middle Eastern for review.

⊕ **Mekato's Colombian Bakery** Stopping by for the heavenly variety of sweet baked goods is the norm (try the flan de leche and the caramel napoleon), but we make a meal out of the rotating tins of meaty snacks that pile up in the hot case. Beef and chicken–stuffed empanadas, flavorful *palito de queso* (cheese-stuffed pretzel sticks), and wildly rich chorizo roll out of the kitchen every few hours, so arrive early so you can pluck your picks from the freshest batch while sipping turbo-strength Colombian coffee. *5423 N Lincoln Ave between Rascher and Balmoral Aves (773-784-5181). Bus: 11, 92, 93. Breakfast, lunch, dinner. Average snack: $2.*

⊕ **Mercury Café** If making a 4,500 square-foot room feel cozy and welcoming seems like an impossibility, then the owners of this massive West Town coffee shop have done the impossible. The space is littered with couches, pillows and distressed-leather chairs. The walls are covered in sunny pigments and works by homegrown artists. Intelligentsia provides the coffee beans and a few local bakeries, including Little Miss Muffin and Sweet Cakes, are responsible for the pastries as well as the vegan and dairy-free desserts. *1505 W Chicago Ave at Armour St (312-455-9924). Bus: 9 Ashland (24hrs), 66 Chicago. Mon–Fri 7am–9pm; Sat 8am–8pm; Sun 9am–7pm. Average main course: $7.*

★ B ⊕ **Milk & Honey** This sunny, friendly sandwich-and-coffee joint helps kick-start the day with countless baked goods and specialty coffees, but it's the basic sandwiches gussied up with impeccable ingredients that get us in the afternoon. Our favorites: the BLT made with extra-thick bacon and the lean, juicy, rosemary-and-thyme–encrusted housemade roast beef. The weekend crowd can be a bitch, so if that's the only time you can get here, be prepared to fight your way to the front of the line, or be prepared to just head home with bag of the cafe's signature granola. *1920 W Division St between Wolcott and Winchester Aves (773-395-9434). El: Blue to Division. Bus: 9, 50, 70. Breakfast, brunch (Sat, Sun), lunch. Average sandwich: $7. • Milk & Honey Bake Shop located at 1543 N Damen Ave (773-227-1167).*

⊕ **Mojoe's Hot House** Roscoe Village's indie coffee shop spawned this Logan Square location. Expect the same coffee, sandwiches and kitsch as the original, plus extra room for live music. There's also a room in the basement that can be reserved by any club to host meetings, so don't be surprised if you see some caffeine-high superknitters going all ballistic with their yarn. *2849 W Belmont Ave between Elston and Francisco Aves (773-596-5637). El: Blue to Belmont. Bus: 52, 77 (24hrs), 82. 7:30am–9pm. Average main course: $3.50.*

★ **Pasticceria Natalina** Start with the savory items if you must—you won't regret digging into the fantastic *arancini* or the fiercely herbal mint-and-pea *fazzoletti*. But the focus of this Sicilian bake shop is desserts like the *sfogliatelle* cookie (delicate layers of pastry encase orange-kissed ricotta); ricotta-filled cannoli; and the *barca di crema*, a square of puff pastry filled with cream and topped with amarena cherries that are so intoxicatingly delicious you'll swear they've been soaking in liquor. Beware that the shop closes early if the day's supply runs dry. *5406 N Clark St between Balmoral*

Read 'em & eat

baklava Greek sweet made with thin sheets of pastry layered with spices and nuts and coated in a honey-lemon sauce

frittata firm, round Italian omelette with ingredients mixed into the egg batter

marzipan almond paste and sugar confection that can be dyed and molded into decorative shapes, like fruit

red eye drip coffee with two shots of espresso

sfogliatelle (sfoh-lyah-tel-ee) flaky, layered Italian pastries traditionally filled with orange-flavored ricotta or almond paste

Counter productive
Sample rows of treats
at Swim Café.

and Catalpa Aves (773-989-0662). Bus: 22 Clark (24hrs), 92 Foster. Wed–Sun 9am–7pm (closed Mon and Tue). Average pastry: $3.50.

⊙ **Solomon's Kitchen & Gifts** The Solomon's cookie warehouse has been on this stretch of Elston Avenue for years, fulfilling orders for its brisk mail-order business. For its first café, it put a swingers-era spin on the place, pumping jazz into the room and selling custom-made fedoras. Start with a chunky chicken-salad sandwich or the tuna ciabatta with bacon, but be aware that it's really all about the cookies: dense raspberry brownies; rich double-chocolate chip cookies; and adorable thumbprint cookies filled with sweet jams. *2222 N Elston Ave between Webster Ave and Honore St (773-537-4214). Bus: 50 Damen, 74 Fullerton. Breakfast, lunch (Mon–Sat) (closed Sun). Average sandwich: $5.*

⊙ **Southport Grocery and Café** Go ahead and believe the hype about the cupcake: It's moist, substantial but not heavy, and the thick sugary icing hides deep flavors of chocolate and vanilla. If you're going to pick up a dozen, you may as well stick around for a meal. A bright start is the sweet and savory French toast with rosemary-roasted ham. Later, try the fillet of cod, fried up crispy and golden and plated on challah with creamy citrus-caper mayo. *3552 N Southport Ave between Eddy and Addison Sts (773-665-0100). El: Brown to Southport. Bus: 152 Addison. Breakfast, lunch (Mon–Fri). Average main course: $8.*

B ⊙ **Su Van's Café & Bakeshop** This is the sort of chipper, happy-go-lucky place that positively drips with good vibes. Start with a cup of meat-free chili and any of the oversized sandwiches—the BLT with sun-dried tomato mayo and the grilled veggie panini rock, and the house favorite is a tuna powerhouse aptly dubbed "The Cat's Meow." The little ones buzzing through with Mom can't seem to get their fill of baked goods lining the glass display case. Come to think of it, neither can the studious types digging into the free magazines in the corner. *3351 N Lincoln Ave between*

School and Roscoe Sts (773-281-0120). El: Brown to Paulina. Bus: 9, X9, 11, 77 (24hrs). Breakfast, brunch (Sat, Sun), lunch. Average main course: $6.50.

Sweet Cakes A vegan baker is like a cyclist without legs: Uncommon but not unheard of, and if Sweet Cakes is any indication–sometimes just as successful. Emily Smith, chief baker and co-owner (with her dad) of this East Village destination, presides over the ovens, and despite not eating cream or eggs or milk chocolate, she still manages to put out perfectly solid red velvet cupcakes topped with an indulgent buttercream frosting; saucer-sized chocolate chip cookies with deep brown sugar notes; and hearty corn muffins hiding a whole hardboiled egg inside, the perfect handheld breakfast—that is, if you eat that sort of thing. *935 N Damen Ave at Walton St (773-772-5771). Bus: 50 Damen, 66 Chicago (24hrs). 8am–6pm (closed Mon). Average baked good: $3.*

★ **Sweet Mandy B's** They had us at hello, those creamy, dreamy cupcakes. (Us and every other Chicagoan with taste buds.) This sweet-as-can-be little bake shop may have cornered the local market with its simple little chocolate and yellow cakes slathered in a colorful array of buttercreams, but there's much more to salivate over here. We like the puddings (butterscotch, chocolate, banana with Nilla wafers), the crispy, big-as-your cookies, the seasonal fruit crisps, the whoopie pies. Come to think of it, we haven't found a dud here yet. *1208 W Webster Ave between Magnolia and Racine Aves (773-244-1174). Sun–Thu 8am–10pm, Fri–Sat 8am–11pm. El: Brown, Purple (rush hrs) to Armitage. Bus: 73 Armitage. Average baked good: $3.*

⊙ **Sweet Thang** As its name trumpets, this French patisserie's bread and butter (so to speak) is the sweet stuff: made-daily cakes as well as countless varieties of mousses, cheesecakes, tarts and pies. There are a number of savories as well: croissants with fillings like ham, feta and spinach; quiche; and gooey panini. *1921 W North Ave between between Wolcott and Winchester Aves (773-772-4166). El: Blue to*

Take the cake Kids of all ages love the rotating roster of treats at Cupcakes.

Sweet Temptation You'll swoon for Milk & Honey's lemon-lavender cookies.

Damen; Bus: 50, 56, 72. Mon–Thu 7am–8pm; Fri and Sat 7am–9pm; Sun 8am–8pm. Average main course: $7.

★ ☺ **Swim Café** You may never want to make your own sandwich again. Using Red Hen breads and the freshest and most seasonal ingredients, Karen Gerod comes up with different creations every day (a recent creation piled turkey with cucumber, red onion, avocado, Jarlsberg and a yogurt dressing). The former caterer and wedding-cake maker also bakes scones and cookies daily (she has a soft spot for the lemon-ginger variety), and coffee drinks like the signature High Dive, a caramel-vanilla latte. *1357 W Chicago Ave between Ada and Noble Sts (312-492-8600). El: Blue to Chicago. Bus: 9 (24hrs), 56, 66 (24hrs). Mon–Fri 6am–8pm; Sat, Sun 6am–6pm. Average main course: $5.50.*

Swirlz Cupcakes With a menu of only cupcakes (flavors change daily but always include the insanely popular red velvet) and beverages, this takeout bakery bears a striking resemblance to other cupcake shops in town. But it distinguishes itself with gluten-, sugar-reduced and sugar-free options, "pupcakes" for dogs and its custom cupcake carry-out boxes, which keep the icing perfectly in place. *705 W Belden Ave between Lincoln Ave and Burling St (773-404-2253). El: Brown, Purple (rush hrs), Red to Fullerton. Bus: 8, 11, 74. Mon–Sat 9am–7pm (closed Sun). Average cupcake: $3.*

TipsyCake Despite the shop's boozy name, your blood-sugar level will be the only thing above the legal limit after a visit to this no-frills Humboldt Park bakery run by Aussie pastry chef Naomi Stepanek. She creates unforgettable delicacies from Down Under like lamingtons (small sponge-cake cubes filled with raspberry jam and covered in rich Belgian chocolate and French coconut), plus intoxicating treats such as Hungarian pancake pie and Door County cherry scones. *1043 N California Ave at Cortez St (773-384-*

4418). Bus: 70 Division. Tue-Sat 10am-7pm, Sun Noon-3pm. Average pastry: $3.

BYOB ☺ **Vella Café** The girls behind Kitchen Chicago's once-famous crêpe brunch run this daytime-only spot, a cheery, little BYOB right under the Western Blue Line stop. The weekend "blunch" menu includes a fantastic DIY soft taco with cubes of firm tofu scrambled with crumbly soy chorizo, bits of roasted zucchini, corn kernels, brown rice, smoky poblanos and scallions. For a sugar fix, go for crêpes sweetened with orange-honey cream cheese and caramel-drizzled cinnamon apples. The leaders of the lunch lineup include panini packed with tender brisket doused in a genius barbecue sauce of caramelized onion, plums and apples. *1912 N Western Ave between Cortland and Homer Sts (773-489-7777). El: Blue to Western. Bus: 49 (24hrs), X49, 56, 74. Breakfast (Mon, Wed–Fri); Brunch (Sat, Sun); Lunch (Mon, Wed–Fri). Average main course: $7.*

☺ **Victory's Banner** See Vegetarian for review.

☺ **Ventrella's Caffé** When we dream about leaving it all behind for *la dolce vita* in Italy, this is the kind of neighborhood café we picture whiling away the hours in: vintage furnishings, a great selection of Italian newspapers and magazines, and a well-chosen assortment of pastries, panini and gelati. We'd start the day with strong Lavazza coffee and a croissant, hang around till lunchtime for a grilled prosciutto, provolone and a green-apple panino, then make our way through the rich, creamy gelato (starting with pistachio). *Magnifico. 4947 N Damen Ave between Argyle and Ainslie Sts (773-506-0708). El: Brown to Damen. Bus: 50, 81 (24hrs), 92, 145. Metra: Union Pacific North to Ravenswood. 10am–8pm. Average main course: $6.* ■

Caribbean

See also: *Eclectic, Latin American*

▼ **BYOB Borinquen** The original Borinquen (it's one of three) is also the busiest. Local Puerto Ricans and Rican food lovers alike populate this authentic spot from the time the first *café con leche* is slurped down to the minute the last *jibarito* sandwich (steak between crispy pounded plantains) is consumed. Juicy onion-flecked steak, garlic-smothered plantains, crispy empanadas, yellow rice with pigeon peas and seafood salads are found on most tables in the two dining rooms. The smooth flan is ripe for seconds, and a walk-up counter does a brisk take-out business. *1720 N California Ave between Bloomingdale and Wabansia Aves (773-227-6038). El: Blue to Western. Bus: 52, 56, 72. Lunch, dinner. Average main course: $11.* ● *Additional locations at 3811 N Western Ave (773-442-8001) and 3020 N Central Ave (773-622-8570).*

▼ **BYOB** ✳ **Café Bolero** If you're into deep-fried, try the combo platter of hot, crispy, meat-stuffed potato croquettes with plantains and a moist tamale. We also like the curiously pickle-less (but nonetheless delicious) Cuban sandwich, the spicy shrimp creole and the chicken milanesa *arroz con gandules*. The vegetarian paella isn't bad for a Cuban joint. *2252 N Western Ave between Lyndale St and Belden Ave (773-227-9000). El: Blue to Western. Bus: 49 Western (24hrs), 74 Fullerton. Lunch, dinner. Average main course: $12.*

Café Central If you smell something delicious when you walk into this Puerto Rican diner, don't bother trying to figure out what it is. It could be any number of the greasy-spoon comfort foods that are dished up here daily: chunky, tomato-heavy goat stew or garlicky *mofongo*, savory balls of plantains studded with corn. Then again, it could be the oniony *jibaro* (dubbed "hee-ba-roe" on the English menu), a gooey cheese-steak–like sandwich that substitutes plantains for bread. So take a seat—looks like you've got some research to do. *1437 W Chicago Ave at Bishop St (312-243-6776). El: Blue to Chicago. Bus: 9 Ashland (24hrs), 66 Chicago (24hrs). Breakfast, lunch, dinner. Average main course: $11.*

⊙ **Café con Leche** This tiny gem is a shining star among the myriad Mexican joints populating this strip of Logan Square. Breakfast choices run heavy, with *huevos* (eggs) mentioned no less than 15 times on the menu. Get your daily quota in tortas, sandwiches or burritos that head south of the border with a twist. Cuban sandwiches and Mexican *molletes* (vegetarian pizzas) keep company with American favorites like Philly cheesesteaks and burgers. The *café con leche*, this spot's potent namesake, is a lip-smacking way to rev up for an afternoon of bargain shopping nearby. *2714 N Milwaukee Ave between Spaulding and Sawyer Aves (773-289-4274). El: Blue to Logan Square. Bus: 56, 74, 76, 82. Breakfast, lunch, dinner. Average main course: $5.*

✳ ◕ **Café Laguardia** The cocktails veer toward the fruity side at this Bucktown favorite (call us purists, but we prefer our mojitos *sin* coconut), but the Cuban food is right on target. Fried pork chops (*cerdo frito*) served with caramelized onions, yellow rice and pigeon peas,

caramelized plantains and Cuban flan feel right in the lively dining room. The Laguardia family hospitality (they're known for plying takeout customers with while-you-wait tropical shots) and live salsa bands on Tuesday and Wednesday nights make up for the sometimes slow-paced service. *2111 W Armitage Ave between Hoyne Ave and Leavitt St (773-862-5996). El: Blue to Western. Bus: 50, 56, 73. Lunch, dinner. Average main course: $13.*

✴ **B Café 28** Cuban food goes upscale at this contemporary spot. Standards are dressed up with fancy touches like saffron cream, garlic polenta and sun-dried tomato pesto, and it's all executed with competence, but with a little less oomph than the dramatic menu descriptions suggest. Pork chops arrive tender and with plenty of honey flavor, but only a trace of the advertised jalapeño. The ropa vieja, flanked by crunchy, sugary plantains, is juicy and fork-tender, but you could order it elsewhere for half the price. *1800 W Irving Park Rd at Ravenswood Ave (773-528-2883). El: Brown to Irving Park. Bus: 9, 11, 50, 80. Brunch (Sat, Sun), lunch (Tue–Fri), dinner. Average main course: $16.*

B ⊙ **Calypso Café** The food at this Caribbean spot is a lot like the Tommy Bahama–ish decor (which includes the occasional fake bunch of bananas): It's not exactly authentic, but it'll pass in a pinch. Jerk chicken wings are absolutely enormous and have an equally big, spicy flavor. Shrimp and conch fritters are crispy and golden brown on the outside, and fluffy in the middle. Plantain-encrusted tilapia is curiously bland, but the juicy *ropa vieja* sandwich on soft, house-baked Cuban bread makes up for it. *5211 S Harper Ave between 52nd Pl and E 52nd St (773-955-0229). Bus: 2, 15, X28. Brunch (Sun), lunch, dinner. Average main course: $10.*

Read 'em & eat

akee a red-skinned fruit with yellow flesh that tastes like scrambled eggs when cooked

bacalao (bah-kah-LAH-oh) salt cod

breadfruit a softball-size, green-skinned fruit with sweet, creamy flesh the texture of bread

jerk a mixture of chili and other hot spices used to marinate chicken or pork

mofongo mashed plantains mixed with meat, cheese or vegetables

picadillo (pee-cah-DEE-yo) ground meat with tomato, garlic and onion

ropa vieja a stew made with chunks of shredded beef

Now that's a sandwich
Plaintains take the place of bread
on the *jibarito* at Borinquen.

(✳ **B Coco** If this sleek Puerto Rican spot is representative of the island's cuisine and culture, we're booking a ticket to San Juan. The space's modern art and 1920s bar are an ideal setting for modernized classics like *lomo de cerdo* (pork chop in mango-rum sauce) and *escudo boriqua* (lamb chops in papaya sauce). The strong mojitos may fool you into thinking you can dance like the spiffy locals who pour in once the band starts around 10pm on Fridays and Saturdays. *2723 W Division St between Washtenaw and California Aves (773-384-4811). Bus: 49 (24hrs), X49, 52, 70. Brunch (Sun), lunch, dinner (closed Mon). Average main course: $19.*

BYOB(Cuban Island Looking for the forbidden ambience of an Old Havana nightclub? You won't find it here. Instead, you'll get straightforward Cuban chow and minty mojitos. Unlike many Cuban joints that muddle the menu with pan-Latin specialties, here the choices stay true to Cuba, including authentic *ropa vieja*, *lechon asada* and spicy seafood, served with traditional sides like *congri* (rice and beans) and *plátanos maduros* or *tostones*. The cheap weekday lunch buffet draws more crowds than you'll see at dinner and offers an opportunity to sample more of this oft-overlooked cuisine. *3446 W Peterson Ave between Bernard St and St. Louis Ave (773-588-9922). Bus: 82 Kimball-Homan, 84 Peterson. Lunch, dinner. Average main course: $12.*

⊖ **El Rinconcito Cubano** Yellowed photos of sunny Cuban beaches line the walls of this tiny storefront, a casual meeting place for the local Cuban community. Don't miss the standout *ropa vieja*, a soft pile of garlicky, tomatoey shredded beef that releases juice and flavor with every chew. Traditionalists will love the authentic *bacalao* (salt cod), the *boliche* (slow-cooked eye-of-round) and the fried pork chops. Show up early—you may walk by and see some older Cuban men smoking cigars and grunting at the television, but if it's after 8:30pm they won't let you in. *3238 W Fullerton Ave between Sawyer and Spaulding Aves (773-489-4440). El: Blue to Logan Square. Bus: 74 Fullerton, 77 Belmont (24hrs). Lunch, dinner. Average main course: $8.50.*

⊖ **Good To Go** Whether you're grabbing a meal to go or sitting down to eat at the counter of this bright storefront, expect your food to be served in a Styrofoam container. Carry-out packaging is fine by us, because the dinners—such as the tender and gamey curried goat—are so generous you'll probably want to take part of it home. No knives are needed, either, because the oxtail falls from the bone with the touch of a fork. The specialty of the house is excellent jerk chicken (sweet, hot and saucy) and juice concoctions made from fresh fruits and veggies, but the caramel cake is hot on the trail to becoming a signature standout. *1947 W Howard St between Damen and Winchester Aves (773-381-7777). El: Red, Purple, Yellow (rush hrs) to Howard. Bus: 22 (24hrs), 97, Pace 215. Lunch, dinner (closed Mon). Average main course: $7.*

⊖ **Habana Libre** Aromas of garlic assault you at the door and they don't stop there. *Tostones* (crispy plantains) and the fried yuca come with a garlic sauce so strong you'll feel it in your pores the next day. But garlic's not the only thing on offer here. *Papas rellenas* crack open to reveal silky potato, the fragile crust of the *empanada de carne* is buttery and flaky, and creamy pork *croquetas* outshine their fish and chicken counterparts. Go for the Cubano over the *pan con lechon* and get the *camarones* (shrimp) in the spicy "Cuban-Creole sauce." *1440 W Chicago Ave at Bishop St (312-243-3303). El: Blue to Chicago. Bus: 9 (24hrs), X9, 66 (24hrs). Lunch, dinner. Average main course: $8.*

Fan appreciation
The dining room at Coco is ready for business.

B ⊕ **Jamaica Jerk** The Chicago-Evanston border is a gold mine of Jamaican cuisine. Among the tried-and-true, we like this tranquil ocean-blue dining room. Conch fritters are juicy and flavorful; *channa cakes* (fried chickpea patties) are greaseless with fragrant curry notes; and the saltfish—slightly funky, salty pieces of dried fish hiding tiny morsels of bacon and peppers—is a must-try for the adventurous. Jerk chicken is deliciously seasoned and juicy, but far from spicy, so speak up if you'd like more heat. Don't skip dessert—coconut carrot cake and Grape Nuts ice cream are knockouts. *1631 W Howard St between Paulina and Marshfield Aves (773-764-1546). El: Red, Purple, Yellow to Howard. Bus: 22 (24hrs), 97, 147, 151 (24hrs), Pace 215, Pace 290. Brunch (Sun), lunch, dinner (closed Mon). Average main course: $10.*

⊖ **La Cocina de Galarza** The Puerto Rican family that runs this comfortable, mustard-colored restaurant may assume that gringos wandering in are looking for Mexican food (and they will cook it for you), but the authentic Puerto Rican specialties are the way to go. The belly-busting *guachitos*, is a delicious off-menu request that combines fried plantain with *salchicon* (salami-like sausage) and fresh guacamole. The *mofongo* (mashed, fried plantain) is easily as good as what we've had on the island. If more exotic dishes, like braised baby goat sound too risky, then the tender *carne guisada* (beef stew) is an easier route with just as tasty results. *2420 W Fullerton Ave between Western and Artesian Aves (773-235-7377). El: Blue to California. Bus: 49 (24hrs), X49, 74. Lunch, dinner. Average main course: $9.*

⊖ **La Esquina del Sabor** Forget lugging around your lunch in a picnic basket—this Puerto Rican lunch truck in

Humboldt Park lugs it around for you. As the illustration of a happily skewered pig on the side of the truck suggests, it's all about the pork here. Pulling the meat from the bone with a pair of tongs, servers pile enormous heaps on top of fluffy yellow rice (ask for lots of skin to get as much of the delicious spice rub as you can). But not everything here comes big enough for three: Baseball-size *mofongo* (savory balls of green plantain and pork) and *mini jibarito* sandwiches (pork, rather than the traditional steak, on crispy plantains) make taking the pig to go as easy as pork pie. *The northernmost intersection of Humboldt Blvd and Luis Munoz Marin Dr (no phone). Bus: 52, 70, 72. 9am–9pm. Average main course: $5.*

★ ⊙ **La Unica** Looking for great Cuban food? Wind through the grocery aisles of this "food mart" to the rear corner and you'll find a dozen tables, a friendly counterman and a wall lined with brightly colored signs touting house specialties. (Grab an English menu from the counter if your Spanish is weak.) You can find Colombian and Mexican fare, but it's the Cuban eats that have drawn regulars here for 30 years. The Cuban sandwich is the best in town; pork-filled tamales, crunchy *bacalao* (salt cod), the roasted pork dinner with yellow rice, and garlicky green and caramelized sweet plantains are all must-haves, too. *1515 W Devon Ave between Bosworth and Greenview Aves (773-274-7788). El: Red to Loyola. Bus: 22 (24hrs), 36, 151 (24hrs), 155. Breakfast, lunch, dinner (Mon–Sat). Average main course: $6.*

✳ **Marina Café** We're sure we'll regret giving up this secret, so don't hog the tables too long. This fledgling Caribbean gem is housed in a former Coast Guard building in Jackson Harbor. You won't mind the slow, somewhat rusty service a bit; the view and the vibe are meant for lazy summer evenings. Snag a prime patio table, where you can wistfully watch boats pull in around dusk. In proper seaside (okay, lakeside) fashion, the menu is twisted tropic, with standouts like pecan- and Brazil-nut–crusted prawns, sticky sweet "ramba rocking" ribs and the fruity Maui salad. Entrées are a bit pricey for the often lackluster results, so stick with spicy catfish and shrimp po' boys and burgers, or just head straight for over-the-top desserts like key-lime pound cake or pear and passion fruit mousse "cake bomb." *6401 S Coast Guard Dr between Marquette and Hayes Drs (773-947-0400). Bus: 6, 15, 28, 63. Lunch, dinner (closed Mon). Average main course: $18.*

Rhythm Nation The jerk chicken at Rhythm & Spice is addictive.

★ ⊙ **Rhythm & Spice** *2007 Eat Out Award, Critics' Pick: Best jerk (jerk chicken)* Jerk-chicken huts are as rampant on the South Side as drag queens at a Dolly Parton concert. But thanks to the smiley hospitality of owner Tasha Fisher, a spic-and-span seating area and hefty portions of unforgettable Jamaican classics, this spot shouldn't be lumped in with the rest. We like the juicy jerk chicken and tender curry goat. Adventurous eaters with a penchant for funky-salty flavors will love the *akee*, a dish of Caribbean fruit sautéed with onions, peppers and saltfish that's perfect with the hush puppy. *2501 W 79th St at Campbell St (773-476-5600). Bus: 49 (24hrs), X49, 79. Lunch, dinner (closed Mon; closes at 6pm Sun). Average main course: $10.*

▼ BYOB ⊙ **Sabor a Cuba** The Cuban vibe is alive in this pleasantly bright and tidy dining room, complete with high-backed wooden chairs and rustic cast-iron barstools. Entry-level Cuban dishes include snapper *a la criolla* with an intense garlicky red sauce and *lechon asado* (roasted pork), served with rice, black beans and sweet *plátanos maduros*. Everything is simple and authentic, though a bit lackluster. Tropical fruit *batidas* (milk shakes), Latin sodas (like Malta and Champ's Cola) and soulful desserts (try the custardy *pudín diplomatico*) perk things up a bit. *1833 W Wilson Ave between Wolcott and Ravenswood Aves (773-769-6859). El: Brown to Damen. Bus: 50, 81, 145, 148. Lunch, dinner (closed Mon). Average main course: $9.*

Sabor Latino Interested in trying Puerto Rican food, but don't know your *pastel* from your *pescado*? Use this casual little stalwart as your entry point with a *mofongo* (a pork-filled plantain fritter) to start, a *jibarito* (steak sandwich made with crispy plantains for bread) for a warm-up, and get to the main event with the sautéed steak with onions and *arroz con gandules* (pork-flecked beans and rice). Helpful photos of dishes line one wall (soups taste better than they look) and the English-speaking counter staff is good with guidance. *3810 W North Ave between Avers and Hamlin Aves (773-227-5254). Bus: 53, 65, 72. Breakfast, lunch, dinner. Average main course: $7.*

⊙ **Tropi Cuba** This bare-bones grocery store on the edge of Logan Square has a secret. Crammed in the back behind rows of provisions is a bar-stool-only Cuban dive pumping out tasty pressed Cuban sandwiches (served with paper-thin, hand-cut french fries) and wickedly strong Cuban coffee, all at bargain prices. For an even cheaper alternative, go for the dollar hotbox items up front; the *papa rellena* (a huge, crispy potato ball packed with ground beef) is a great snack on the go. *3000 W Lyndale St at Sacramento Ave (773-252-0230). El: Blue to California. Bus: 52, 56, 73, 74. Breakfast, lunch, dinner. Average main course: $5.*

★ ⊙ **Tropic Island Jerk Chicken** The Chatham residents who mill about inside this tiny, smoke-scented, Jamaican carryout spot are all waiting on the same thing: the best jerk chicken around. Members of the Grant family work in tandem, taking orders for rich, allspice-laced oxtails and having jerk-rubbed chickens out of foggy smokers before packaging them in Styrofoam containers along with sides of cinnamon-candied yams and buttery braised greens. Ask for an extra side of the lappable jerk sauce to dip your chicken in, order wings for the juicy dark-meat factor, and be prepared to either make do with one of only two rickety tables or eat in your car—the killer scents make waiting until you get home unbearable. *419 E 79th St between King Dr and Vernon Ave (773-224-7766). El: Red to 79th. Bus: 3, X3, 29, 79 (24hrs). Lunch, dinner (closed Sun, carry out only). Average main course: $7.* ∎

Chinese

See also: *Contemporary American, Pan Asian*

Bowled over The noodles at Katy's Dumpling House are worth a drive to the 'burbs.

○ **Ben Pao** The theme at this theme-parkish spot is regional Chinese, with renditions of Mongolian, Cantonese, Shanghai and Szechuan dishes, but don't let the tourist locale deter you. The menu is massive, so sip on the slusheelike, citrus vodka–spiked, frozen ginger ale while perusing. Best bets include crispy cubes of sesame-coated tofu drizzled with garlic sauce; salty-sweet star anise–braised pork with scallion pancakes for wrapping; and shrimp with wheat noodles and mushrooms in a spicy chile sauce. Skip the fried rice and beef dishes unless you want to regret not making it to Chinatown. *52 W Illinois St at Dearborn St (312-222-1888). El: Red to Grand. Bus: 22 (24hrs), 36, 65. Lunch (Mon–Fri), dinner. Average main course: $10.*

▼ ♨ **Chen's** See Pan Asian for review.

▼ **China Grill** Grilled and wok-prepared Pan-Asian fare doled out in generous portions are the specialties at this stylish, but gimicky outpost of the New York–based restaurant chain. Businesspeople on a power lunch, couples dining before heading to the Goodman and even slightly more adventurous tourists can be found gawking at the chefs behind the exhibition kitchen and squinting to read the excerpts from Marco Polo's diary that are (for better or worse) inscribed into the floor tiles. *230 N Michigan Ave between S Water and Lake Sts (312-334-6700). El: Red to Lake. Bus: 2, 3, X4, 6, 10, 26, 29, 143, 144, 145, 146, 147, 151 (24hrs), 157. Breakfast, lunch (Mon–Fri), dinner. Average main course: $25.*

○ **Dragon Court** For large groups or those seeking a late-night meal in Chinatown, this spacious place is open until 2am every night of the week and has a large and affordable menu brimming with authentic dishes. The adventurous eater seeking fresh seafood can handpick lobster, eel or clams from the front-window tank, while the squeamish can opt for the hot and sour soup or one of the many casserole entrées like short ribs in house sauce. Sharing is encouraged (hence a lazy Susan at each table) so come with friends. *2414 S Wentworth Ave between 24th Pl and 24 St (312-791-1882). El: Red to Cermak-Chinatown. Bus: 21, 24, 29. Lunch, dinner. Average main course: $8.*

○ **Ed's Potsticker House** We've found a lot of land mines on the menu here, but the winners have us hooked. The cigar-shaped potstickers are among our favorites (ask for house chile oil to stir into the dipping sauce). Sweet-and-sour fans love the crispy sticks of eggplant glazed in garlic sauce with wood ear mushrooms and flecks of red chiles. The sautéed lamb with cumin and sesame seeds, whole red chiles, onions and jalapeños is fatty, but flavorful. And the "pan-fried smoked pork cake" is a pitalike sandwich stuffed with a pancetta-ish pork, hoisin and scallion slivers. *3139 S Halsted St between 32nd and 31st Sts (312-326-6898). El: Orange to Halsted. Bus: 8, 35, 44. Lunch, dinner. Average main course: $7.*

☾ **Emperor's Choice** For two decades, this simple dining room has been the safe bet for Americanized favorites like chop suey and egg foo young. But take a cue from the smiling fish on the menu: Seafood's the real draw. Sea creatures from shrimp to lobster are fresh, especially the fish-of-the-day (largemouth bass, recently). Order it steamed whole with ginger and onion. The lobster's affordable ($33.95) and can be prepped seven different ways. Spicy salt-and-pepper prawns are huge and crispy, and go great with garlicky young pea shoots listed on the specials menu. *2238 S Wentworth Ave between 22nd Pl and Alexander St (312-225-8800). El: Red to Cermak-Chinatown. Bus: 21 Cermak, 62 Archer (24hrs). Lunch (Mon–Fri), dinner. Average main course: $12.*

No fat lady sings But dinner at Opera is still an entertaining production.

Friendship Chinese Restaurant After his father passed away, Alan Yuen completely renovated his family's Logan Square chop suey house (even installing beautiful hardwood floors himself) and set about making fresh and vibrant Cantonese-American classics, as well as somewhat contemporary takes for the neighborhood's shifting taste buds. Sesame beef, honey-walnut shrimp and beef chow fun are joined by creations like stir-fried seafood in a shredded potato "bird's nest" and boneless Peking duck with Grand Marnier sauce. Hit up the swank dining room for the Tuesday-night promotion, which offers every entrée—even the 16-ounce Hong Kong steak—for $8.95. *2830 N Milwaukee Ave between Diversey and Dawson Aves (773-227-0970). El: Blue to Logan Square. Bus: 56, 76, 82. Lunch (Mon–Sat), dinner. Average main course: $12.*

⊙ **Furama** For some, Sundays are for church. For others, it's dim sum time. This spot offers one of the largest selections in town. A mix of neophytes and lifers pack into the giant banquet hall space to settle in for the barrage of carts that wheel by brimming with a dozen different dumplings (shrimp-peanut, chive and pork stand out); fluffy buns (barbecue pork and pan-fried veggie-pork are awesome); and various fried and steamed morsels of hangover-absorbing snacks. Don't miss the taro puff, ribs, potstickers and sweet egg custard tarts. *4936 N Broadway between Ainslie and Argyle Sts (773-271-1161). El: Red to Argyle. Bus: 22 (24hrs), 36, 92, 151 (24hrs). Breakfast, lunch, dinner. Average main course: $7.*

▼ (☉ **Happy Chef** When in Chinatown, it's often hard to distinguish between the good, the bad and the General Tso's chicken. But you should do okay at this popular pick. Start with crispy shrimp dumplings (the menu says they're pan-fried, but they look dropped-in-a-vat to us), then try the pork chop in a sweet, aromatic barbecue sauce and crispy shrimp coated in a salty, spicy mix. You won't find dessert on the menu, but if you ask, you'll be served an inky black-bean soup with tapioca—it's a sweet, creamy and light ending to your meal. *2164 S Archer Ave between Wentworth and Princeton Aves (312-808-3689). El: Red to Cermak-Chinatown. Bus: 18, 21, 62 (24hrs). Breakfast, lunch, dinner. Average main course: $9.*

⊙ **Hong Huah** Locals tend to know the best spots for a bite to eat, and so do Chicago's Finest, which explains a near-constant cop presence. Every seat in this popular Chinese eatery is usually taken, and portions here are gargantuan, so it's best to share. Go old-school indulgent with a tasty eight-pack of crab rangoon and move on to a crazy-tender order of Mongolian beef loaded with scallions. The garlic eggplant has none of the sweet spark the Thais give it, so skip that and splurge for the house specialty of salt-and-pepper shrimp. *5924 W Fullerton Ave between Marmora and Mason Aves (773-889-4800). Bus: 74, 85, 91. Lunch, dinner (closed Tue). Average main course: $8.*

⊙ **House of Fortune** The lazy Susans atop each table are the first clues to this Chinatown favorite's specialty: large portions meant for sharing. Bring a big group and key in on the family dinner portion of the menu, which offers several meal options based on the size of your clan. The "family for four," for example, includes the soup of the day, shrimp, lobster, Peking duck, orange beef Chengdu, fried rice and a vegetable—so much food, you may not have enough room for that post-feast fortune cookie. *2407 S Wentworth Ave at 24th St (312-225-0880). El: Red to Cermak-Chinatown. Bus: 21, 24, 29. Lunch, dinner. Average main course: $10.*

★ ☉ **Katy's Dumpling House** City dwellers might ask, Why drive to the 'burbs for Chinese when we've got Chinatown? But we swear that you won't find noodles this fresh in the city. Start with the dumplings—ethereal pockets of noodle skin encasing scallion-flecked pork—and move on to a heaping bowl of beef noodle soup. In this Chinese version of pho, the rich beef broth is redolent of star anise, but the ginger, garlic, chiles, pickles and unbeatable long, soft noodles make this house signature stand out. *665 N Cass Ave, Westmont (630-323-9393). Lunch, dinner (closed Wed). Average main course: $6.*

☉ **Ken-Kee Restaurant** Located in the Chinatown Square mall, the booths and tables at this Cantonese spot are usually filled with a mix of longtime Chinatown residents and chatty tourists who come for traditional dishes like fried spaghetti, curried ox tongue and a variety of congee. Among the signature dishes is the surprisingly cheap ($6.95) Ken-Kee special, which features, among other things, squid, chicken and pork skin. *2129 S China Pl between Wells St and Princeton Ave (312-326-2088). El: Red to Cermak-Chinatown. Bus: 18, 21, 24, 29. Lunch, dinner. Average main course: $8.*

KS Seafood With so much fuss being made over this spot's Taiwanese specialties (by expats and chowhounds alike), we haven't made it past the picture menu to try much else. Of those Taiwanese options we found so-so results. Sweetly glazed baby eels were overfried on two visits but pork belly steamed buns and wok-seared clams with thick, gingery soy clinging to their shells fared better. The two best bets are clams in a delicate broth with razor-thin slivers of ginger and crunchy skin-on shrimp covered in a pile of puffy fried garlic. *2163 S China Pl, Chinatown Mall (312-842-1238). El: Red to Cermak-Chinatown. Bus: 21 Cermak, 62 Archer (24hrs). Lunch (Mon–Fri), dinner. Average main course: $10.*

★ ☉ **Lao Sze Chuan** Chinatown gurus know this menu by heart, so we'll speak to the novices peering into windows wondering where to go: This place is the best spot for

Read 'em & eat

bao (bow) a sweet, steamed bun, typically filled with pork

bok choy a cabbage with white stalks and green leaves

congee (CAHN-jee) rice porridge garnished with meat, seafood or pickled vegetables

hoisin (also known as Peking sauce) a thick, piquant-sweet dark-brown sauce of garlic, soybeans, chilies and spices, served as a condiment or as an ingredient in dishes

huo guo (hwoh gwoh) a "fire pot" of simmering broth in which thinly sliced meats, seafood and vegetables are cooked (think: Chinese fondue)

lychee (also spelled litchi) a small, juicy, sweet fruit

ma po tofu (mah poh toh-foo) Szechuan dish of tofu and minced pork in spicy chili sauce

Sumthing old

Dim sum is the original small-plates dining experience.

Chinese

Steamed-dumpling gang
Feast on little pockets of tastiness at Shui Wah.

Before wine bars started serving teeny plates of carpaccio and tapas restaurants hit it big outside of Spain, the Chinese were making meals out of dim sum—appetizer-size portions of dumplings, filled buns and other snack-size foods. A Cantonese specialty, dim sum is served with tea for breakfast, lunch or brunch in China, but it's most popular in the States for weekend brunch, when big groups gather round and pass steamer baskets and plates filled with small treats.

Some things to know before you go
Some restaurants will provide small cards, like the lists at sushi spots, where you can check off the dishes you'd like. But you won't get a menu or have your order taken at other places, where part of the fun is eyeing the carts filled with goodies that are pushed past your table, and simply pointing to what you want. There's a fixed price per plate (usually just a few dollars), and a tally is kept on a check left on your table.

Expect lots of steamed and fried dumplings with meat, vegetable and seafood fillings. Popular varieties include *har cheung* (long, flat glutinous rice pancakes wrapped around shrimp) and *fun gau* (half moon–shaped pockets filled with minced pork and shrimp). Other choices you might see are *char siu bao* (doughy steamed buns filled with bits of barbecued pork), *luo buo gao* (fried turnip cakes) and *pai gwat* (pork sparerib pieces in black-bean sauce).

When your teapot needs refilling, tip or open the lid as a signal to your waiter. Double tap your index and middle fingers on the table to say thank you.

Places to try
Furama, 4936 N Broadway between Ainslie and Argyle streets, 773-271-1161
Phoenix Restaurant, 2131 S Archer Ave, between Wentworth Ave and Cermak Rd, 312-328-0848
Shui Wah, 2162 S Archer Ave between Wentworth and Princeton Aves, 312-225-8811
Three Happiness Restaurant, 209 W Cermak Rd between Wentworth and Archer aves, 312-842-1964

Szechuan cuisine in town. It uses plenty of Szechuan pepper, dried chiles, garlic and ginger to create flavors that are incredibly addictive. Our favorites are Chengdu dumplings, crispy Chinese eggplant with ground pork, "chef's special" dry chile string beans, twice-cooked pork, *ma po tofu*, Szechuan prawns and "chef's special" dry chile chicken. Trust us or choose at random—you won't be disappointed. *2172 S Archer Ave between Wentworth and Princeton Aves (312-326-5040). El: Red to Cermak-Chinatown. Bus: 21 Cermak, 62 Archer (24hrs). Lunch, dinner. Average main course: $10.*

⊖ **Lee Wing Wah** Getting a good meal in Chinatown takes some trial and error, but looking around at other diners' plates can tip you off to specialties. Here, every table is brimming with the pan-fried "salt and spice" shrimp, giant shell-on beauties with a thin layer of crispy crunch. (Ask for chile oil for dipping.) Go family-style and feed four with the shrimp, a heaping bowl of curry-laced Singapore noodles, a plate of garlicky Chinese spinach and a roasted duck with tangy hoisin sauce for dipping. Fresh fruit smoothies make for the perfect ending. *2147 S China Pl, Chinatown Square (312-808-1628). El: Red to Cermak-Chinatown. Bus: 21 Cermak, 62 Archer (24hrs). Lunch, dinner. Average main course: $10.*

⊖ **Mandarin Kitchen** At this Shanghai-style Chinese restaurant, the *xiao long bao*, or soup dumplings, are a magical creation of hot soup broth and pork or crab encased in dough. The restaurant also offers Beijing specialties like cumin-coated grilled lamb skewers, and the classic Chinese hot pot, which has been somewhat successful in luring diners seeking the wonders of the fonduelike, do-it-yourself meal. Whether it's the soup dumplings that tempt you—or the chewy homemade noodles in spicy sesame oil—you'll wonder how you've gone without for so long. *2143 S Archer Ave between Wentworth Ave and Cermak Rd (312-328-0228). El: Red to Chinatown. Bus: 18, 21, 62 (24 hrs). Lunch, dinner. Average main course: $10.*

▼ **Moon Palace** Shanghai cuisine is what Moon Palace is all about, and that means distinctly sweet flavorings and alcohol-based soups and sauces. Standouts are *xiao long bao* (soup-filled dumplings) and five-flavor beef (a toothsome and flavorful Chinese take on cow meat) and fans of the pig will be pleased with the shank. Wood paneling, a few prints on the wall and a well-stocked bar make this perhaps Chinatown's most sedate room (though prices are a touch higher than most). *216 W Cermak Rd between Archer and Wentworth Aves (312-225-4081). El: Red to Cermak-Chinatown. Bus: 21 Cermak, 62 Archer (24hrs). Lunch, dinner. Average main course: $12.*

▼ (✳ **Opera** Chef Paul Wildermuth is the only guy in town who could get us to pay double Chinatown prices for Chinese food on steroids. His intensified Chinese classics go hand in hand with owner Jerry Kleiner's trademark over-the-top, carnival-of-colors decor. Sticky soy-chile Mongolian lamb ribs are killer; basil-and-mint–laced minced chicken makes for tasty lettuce wraps. Peking duck comes in three expertly prepared forms: The crispy-skinned breast gets moo shu pancakes, leg and thigh are roasted to juicy perfection and extra bits are stir-fried with shiitake, oyster sauce and chow fun noodles. The decor is not to be missed either. *1301 S Wabash Ave at 13th St (312-461-0161). El: Green, Orange, Red to Roosevelt. Bus: 1, 3, X3, 4 (24hrs), X4, 12, 127. Dinner. Average main course: $20.*

✳ **P.F. Chang's China Bistro** Far more Michigan Avenue than Cermak Road, this double-decker outpost of the chain restaurant lures hungry bag-toting shoppers and tourists with contemporary, simplified (some would say bastardized) versions of what one would find in Chinatown in a sleek, modern setting. A nod to the low-carb craze, the lettuce wraps, available with chicken and vegetarian fillings, are a popular item. Standards like wonton soup, lo mein and mu shu pork are also on offer. *530 N Wabash Ave at Grand Ave (312-828-9977). El: Red to Grand. Bus: 29, 36, 65. Lunch, dinner. Average main course: $12.*

⊙ **Saint's Alp Teahouse** Hailing from Hong Kong (where there are 40 locations), Saint's Alp probably doesn't raise an eyebrow among anybody back in the homeland. Here in the States, however (where only three locations exist), this fast-food teahouse is a novelty. The teas here are great (we particularly liked the creamy and full-flavored sesame-milk variety) but the food lacks excitement. At least there's a view: Sucking down a bowl of vermicelli noodles while taking in the sights of bustling Chinatown is this spot's strong suit. *2131 S Archer Ave between Wentworth Ave and Cermak Rd (312-842-1886). El: Red to Cermak-Chinatown. Bus: 18, 21, 62 (24hrs). Lunch, dinner. Average small plate: $3.50.*

✳ **Shanghai Terrace** Normally we don't condone paying through the nose for Chinese food when Chinatown options abound, but this gorgeous fourth-floor terrace, brimming with fresh flowers and offering a view of the historic Water Tower, is hard to beat. And the elevated takes on five-spiced duck, drunken baby chicken and wok-baked lobster mostly surpass expectations. *The Peninsula Chicago, 108 E Superior between Michigan Ave and Rush St (312-573-6744). El: Red to Chicago. Bus: 3, X4, 10, 26, 29, 66 (24hrs), 143, 144, 145, 146, 147, 151 (24hrs), 157. Lunch, dinner (closed Sun). Average main course: $20.*

▼ ✳ **Shine & Morida** See Pan Asian for review.

★ ⊙ **Shui Wah** To feed your dim-sum cravings during the week, this spot serves Chinese breakfast every day. Check off your order on the provided paper (no rolling carts here) and soon you'll be stuffed with all the classics, from Chiu Chow–style (meaning, hailing from Hong Kong and its surrounding region) dumplings to memorable salt-and-pepper squid. Come 4pm, the dim-sum menu is replaced by dinner offerings; best bets include clams in slightly spicy black-bean sauce, salty egg tofu with four types of 'shrooms, green beans with dried fish slivers and minced pork, and Japanese-ish eggplant with beef. *2162 S Archer Ave between Wentworth and Princeton Aves (312-225-8811). El: Red to Cermak-Chinatown. Bus: 21 Cermak, 62 Archer (24hrs). Breakfast (dim sum 8am–3pm), lunch, dinner. Average main course: $9.*

BYOB ⊙ **Silver Seafood** If the name doesn't tip you off, seafood's the name of the game at this modest, banquet hall–like Chinese staple. So start off right with crispy salt-and-pepper calamari dotted with crunchy onion and jalapeño bits or opt for the land portion of the menu with crispy chicken—a half or whole bird with golden, crackly skin and fresh lemon and spiced salt to add simple zing. The huge menu spans from kung pao chicken and pineapple fried rice to shark-fin soup and stir-fried abalone with sea cucumbers. *4829 N Broadway St between Lawrence Ave and Gunnison St (773-784-0668). El: Red to Lawrence. Bus: 22 (24hrs), 36, 81 (24hrs), 92, 148, 151 (24hrs). Lunch, dinner. Average main course: $10.*

★ ⊙ **Spring World** If the gloopy, corn-starch-heavy dishes of traditional Cantonese restaurants aren't doing it for you, try this place. The owners are from Yunan, so the food has touches of puckery vinegar and spicy red chiles. Try the

Soup for you Shanghai- and Beijing-style soups are good food at Mandarin Kitchen.

hand-shredded chicken with spicy sesame vinaigrette dotted with peanuts, garlic, sesame seeds and scallion slivers or the crispy whole tilapia topped with tangy garlic-ginger-chile paste. Other favorites include spicy baby chicken with ginger, cold noodles in sesame-chile-vinegar sauce and crispy scallion cakes, perfect for dipping in the chile sesame oil on the table. *2109-A S China Pl between Wells St and Princeton Ave (312-326-9966). El: Red to Cermak-Chinatown. Bus: 21 Cermak, 62 Archer (24hrs). Lunch, dinner. Average main course: $10.*

⊙ **Sun Wah Bar-B-Q Restaurant** This no-frills joint tempts passersby with lacquer-skinned roast ducks hanging by their necks in the steamed-up window. The menu is expansive but inexpensive: The Pei Par BBQ duck and the Hong Kong–style barbecued pig are sublime in their simplicity, savory and slick with fat. Chinese broccoli arrives jade-green and crisp, and the beef chow fun (from the pan-fried noodles section of the menu) comes out charred and tasting of the properly smoking wok. Even the egg rolls are notable, dotted with bits of roasted pork. *1132–34 W Argyle St between Broadway and Winthrop Ave (773-769-1254). El: Red to Argyle. Bus: 22 (24hrs), 36, 81, 92, 151. Breakfast, lunch, dinner (closed Thu). Average main course: $6.*

★ ⊙ **Three Happiness Restaurant** The first thing to know before heading to this Chinatown gem is that it's not the giant Three Happiness on the corner of Wentworth Avenue, and we stress this because the difference is monumental. Regulars toss "little" before the name to avoid confusion, pack the tables nightly, ignore the far-from-spotless decor and know to skip the so-so appetizers in favor of black pepper beef with rice noodles (ordered "crispy"), stir-fried Dungeness crab in chile-seafood XO sauce, crispy salt-and-pepper shrimp and Cantonese-style crispy-skin chicken. *209 W Cermak Rd between Wentworth and Archer Aves (312-842-1964). El: Red to Cermak-Chinatown. Bus: 21 Cermak, 62 Archer (24hrs). Breakfast, lunch, dinner. Average main course: $8.* ▪

Not your mother's kitchen The decor and menu at Dine are retro, but not old fashioned.

Classic American

See also: *Contemporary American*

$16 and up

✳ ♦ **Atwater's** Located inside the Harrington Inn & Spa, this intimate, ten-table dining room has three atrium-style window walls that look out onto the banks of the Fox River. At breakfast, plenty of sunlight pours in as diners start their day with soufflé pancakes, frittatas and basics like bacon, eggs and hash browns. In the evening hours, classics like beef tenderloin, duck and filet are served in flickering light from the towering stone fireplace. *Herrington Inn, 15 S River Ln, Geneva (630-208-8920). Breakfast, lunch, dinner. Average main course: $25.*

▼ **B Atwood Café** Chef Heather Terhune's food draws mobs of tourists and local ladies seeking nourishment after a particularly grueling shopping session at Macy's. For them, her seasonal menu of updated American classics is perfect— sophisticated and unintimidating. Case in point: dishes like thyme-and-mace–roasted duck breast with pea tendrils and crispy potato cakes; rock shrimp pappardelle with garlic cream, spring peas and basil pesto; and a warm strawberry-rhubarb and almond tart with vanilla-bean ice cream. *1 W Washington St at State St (312-368-1900). El: Blue, Red to Washington. Bus: 56, 60 (24hrs), 124, 127, 157. Breakfast (Mon–Sat), brunch (Sun), lunch (Mon–Sat), dinner. Average main course: $23.*

✳ ♦ **Bad Dog Tavern** If you're looking for an outdoor patio for a night of drinking and a few bites of sustenance to keep you from getting entirely sloshed, head here. The tree-lined patio, with views of guitar heroes marching into Old Town School of Folk Music, is tough to beat for a lazy summer's night. The Bad Dog Black Angus burger is a safe bet, but steer clear of the sickeningly sweet mango and tequila glazed pork ribs. Go when you have time to settle in; the service can be just as leisurely as the night. *4535 N Lincoln Ave between Sunnyside and Wilson Aves (773-334-4040). El: Brown to Western. Bus: 11, 49 (24hrs), X49, 78, 81 (24hrs). Lunch (Tue–Sun), dinner. Average main course: $18.*

▼ **B Chalkboard** Chef Gilbert Langlois's upscale comfort-food spot has personality galore. Go for the grilled blue cheese with roasted tomato bisque; the aggressively seared halibut balanced by a light pea puree and salty dark-meat chicken confit; and the creamy mac and smoked Gouda. Ever-changing entrées are a bit hit or miss, but the fish and beef are typically cooked well, if not spectacularly composed. The room is soothing and refined and the wine is fairly priced. *4343 N Lincoln Ave between Cullom and Montrose Aves (773-477-7144). El: Brown to Western. Bus: 11, 49 (24hrs), X49, 50, 78. Dinner (closed Tue). Average main course: $20.*

❨ **Cordis Brothers Supper Club** Dan and Mike Cordis set out to create a modern-day supper club, and quite frankly, they failed—their restaurant feels so authentically homey, old-school and nourishing that there are few modern things about it. But this is a good thing: It means you get a complimentary relish tray to start your meal (though the hummus on it would be the exception to the aforementioned authenticity); a buttery crab cocktail and a well-dressed

Caesar salad as appetizers; and a hefty slice of lasagna, redolent of nutmeg, for an entrée. *1625 W Irving Park Rd at Marshfield Ave (773-935-1000). El: Brown to Irving Park. Bus: 9, X9, 80, X80. Dinner (closed Sun). Average main course: $20.*

▼ ✳ **Dine** This retro hotel restaurant promises to bring you back to the 1940s, which loses its appeal when you're forced to eat meatloaf and wedges of iceberg lettuce. But all is not lost: Chef Christopher Turano sneaks a bit of modernity into his wonderfully juicy pork chop, and he puts out a decent roasted chicken. Desserts like red velvet cake, rice pudding and house-baked pie won't send you to the '40s, but they will give you flashbacks to childhood. *733 W Madison Ave at Halsted St (312-602-2100). Bus: 8, 20 (24hrs), 126. Breakfast, lunch, dinner. Average main course: $20.*

★ **B erwin** Chef Erwin Drechsler has been delivering American standards to hungry Chicagoans for almost two decades, and since 1994, he's been doing it at this simple, comfortable dining room. There's no fusion, no complicated techniques or piled-high presentations, just good, solid food. Expect seasonal soups, classic salads, pan-roasted fish and wood-grilled meats, with standouts like pan-seared Pyrenees cheese, sea bass in a pool of chunky clam chowder and what's surely in the running for the best roasted chicken in town, flanked by mashed parsnips and apple cider–and–andouille sausage pan sauce. *2925 N Halsted St between George St and Oakdale Ave (773-528-7200). El: Brown, Purple (rush hrs) to*

Burger bonanza Seasonal and local ingredients boost the burger at Erwin's.

Get comfy Comfort food like chicken pot pie is on the menu at Chalkboard.

Diversey. Bus: 8, 22 (24hrs), 76. Brunch (Sun), dinner (closed Mon). Average main course: $17.

❊ **B Four Farthings** This family-owned neighborhood pub does beer, wine and food better than most . The beer selection–around 15 on tap and 13 in bottles–is only surpassed by the wine list–100 are available by the bottle and 12 by the glass. Those looking to dine can take a seat on the patio in the warmer months and pick from a lengthy menu featuring gorgonzola ravioli with parmesan cream sauce, black olives and tomatoes; blackened flank steak and mushroom salad; and a selection of poultry and chops. *2060 N Cleveland Ave at Lincoln Ave (773-935-2060). El: Brown, Purple (rush hrs) to Armitage. Bus: 11, 22 (24hrs), 36, 73. Brunch (Sun), lunch, dinner. Average main course: $20.*

Gale Street Inn From the second you take your seat and a manager asks, "Howyadoin?" in her thick Chicago accent, you know this place is about as classically Chicago as they come. And judging by how crowded it is, it may be one of the main culprits behind the city's obesity problem: Enormous entrées are like tender baked ribs and juicy barbecue chicken come with bread, salad and big, hearty sides like the twice-baked, cheesy gratin potatoes. A *real* Chicagoan, however, should have no trouble cleaning their plate. *4914 N Milwaukee Ave between Gale St and Higgins Ave (773-725-1300). El: Blue to Jefferson Park. Bus: 56, 56A, 81 (24hrs), 85, 85A. Lunch (Friday), dinner. Average main course: $22.*

▼ ▼ **Jack's on Halsted** Awash in underwater blue-green hues and pulsing with ambient techno (lest we forget we're in Boystown), this spot is a neighborhood draw for older gay couples and even older Lakeview lifers. While the solid menu offers few surprises, what Jack's does, it does well: a grilled calamari starter with spicy tomato-pesto that's as simple as it is delicious; and a four-inch-high ice-cream turtle pie that's a gut-busting ender. Or make like a bona fide Boystowner and finish with a sweet-as-candy martini from the 14-strong list. *3201 N Halsted St at Belmont Ave (773-244-9191). El: Red, Brown, Purple (rush hrs) to Belmont. Bus: 8, 22 (24hrs), 77 (24hrs). Dinner. Average main course: $19.*

L. Woods Tap & Pine Lodge We were briefly fooled into thinking that this old-school-looking lodge truly was old-school. Nevertheless, it seems to have gotten some parts of a Wisconsin lodge experience right (for one thing, bacon cheeseburgers are listed as "light dinners"). The signature tomato soup is creamy and sweet, and crusted whitefish is flaky and buttery. Stick around for dessert—the shakes, made with frozen custard, are some of the best outside of the Dairy State. *7110 N Lincoln Ave , Lincolnwood (847-677-3350). Bus: Pace 290. Lunch (Mon–Sat), dinner. Average main course: $18.*

Lawry's The Prime Rib Old-school doesn't begin to describe this Chicago landmark. Though not the original (which opened in 1938 in Beverly Hills), the Lawry empire's second notch has stood its downtown ground since 1974. When we need a break from the fancy cheeses and foams, we head here for comforting nostalgia, order the Lawry cut medium-rare, use the crispy Yorkshire pudding to sop up the mahogany gravy, go for the lobster tail add-on, finish with a dense, simply delicious slice of chocolate cake and savor every last minute in our favorite time warp. *100 E Ontario St at Rush St (312-787-5000). El: Red to Grand. Bus: 29, 65, 145, 146, 147, 151 (24hrs). Lunch (Mon–Sat), dinner. Average main course: $30.*

$16 and up Classic American

(B Mike Ditka's Decades ago, Da Coach helped the Bears shuffle to a Superbowl, but currently the only bowls Iron Mike is associated with are the piping-hot "souper bowls" of corn chowder and crab bisque coming out of his restaurant's kitchen. Predictably, the memorabilia-rich decor and the menu reference Ditka's former sports glories: "Kickoffs" include fried calamari, chicken wings and crab cakes, and the half-pound Fridge Burger is appropriately, if gratuitously, large. *Tremont Hotel, 100 E Chestnut St at Rush St (312-587-8989). El: Red to Chicago. Bus: 3, X4, 10, 26, 66, 125, 143, 144, 145, 146, 147, 151 (24hrs). Brunch (Sun), lunch, dinner. Average main course: $20.*

✻ Park Grill Overlooking the Millennium Park Ice Rink has its pros and cons: Watching flailing skaters is transfixing, but with food this good, you want to focus on your meal. Seasonal offerings might include whisper-thin beef carpaccio sprinkled with Parmesan and juicy capers or flat iron steak encrusted with porcinis. We can think of no better last meal than the Kobe burger: melted Gorgonzola topping thick-as-your-fist beef between buttery brioche, served with a heap of thin, crispy fries. Skip the defib—strap on some skates to get your heart pumping again. *11 N Michigan Ave at Madison St (312-521-7275). El: Brown, Purple (rush hrs), Orange, Green to Madison; Red, Blue to Monroe. Bus: 3, 4 (24hrs), X4, 14, 26, 127, 145, 147, 148, 151 (24hrs). Lunch, dinner. Average main course: $19.*

★ B Prairie Grass Café If you ever ate Sarah Stegner's food during her much-lauded tenure as chef of the Dining Room at the Ritz-Carlton, you understand how happy we are that we don't have to sell a kidney to eat her food anymore. We'll even endure the drive to the 'burbs to dig into garlicky, vinegary skirt steak topped with sautéed 'shrooms; her housemade lamb sausage with sweet fennel and warm goat cheese; and her mom's banana-cream pie. Incredible food we can eat while wearing jeans—perfect. *601 Skokie Blvd, Northbrook (847-205-4433).. Brunch (Sat, Sun), lunch (Tue–Fri), dinner (Tue–Sun). Average main course: $17.*

♨ TABLE fifty-two Chef Art Smith (you may know him as Oprah's chef) is behind this spot, which may be small and dainty but the menu is big and unabashedly country. Squash-onion casserole, three-cheese mac, chile-crusted pork chops with pickled peaches, plus buttermilk-fried chicken made from the recipe of Smith's mama are some of the rib-sticking offerings. *52 W Elm St between Clark and Dearborn Sts (312-573-4000). El: Red to Clark/Division. Bus: 22(24 hrs), 36, 70. Dinner (closed Mon). Average main course: $25.*

Tavern at the Park Chef John Hogan of Keefer's Restaurant is catering to the tourist clientele of Millennium Park with updated standards such as a barbecue-chicken sandwich (completed with a cherry-cola barbecue sauce), double-cut pork chops, chicken potpie, housemade shredded onion rings and shoestring fries served with white-truffle aioli. *130 E Randolph St between Beaubien Ct and Stetson Ave (312-552-0070). El: Brown, Green, Orange, Pink, Purple (rush hrs) to Randolph. Dinner. Average main course: $20.*

▽ (✻ B Tavern on Rush Full of worn brown leather couches and dark, polished wood, this room exudes an Ivy League kind of pomp. Yet when there's a football game on, it quickly becomes about as dignified as a locker room. Artichoke dip and pizzas appease the fans, but the real finds are old-school staples like juicy, mushroom-topped London broil. Those football fans may come in handy if you order the chocolate cake for dessert—it's so ridiculously huge, you'll need at least a few of them to help you finish it. *1031 N Rush St at Bellevue Pl (312-664-9600). El: Red to Clark/Division. Bus: 22 (24hrs), 36, 66 (24hrs), 70. Brunch (Sat, Sun), lunch, dinner. Average main course: $30.*

★ ▼ ✷ **B Tweet** Michelle Fire's theory for her restaurant is "good food for nice people." Her popular brunch is constantly evolving, and recent specials include "Bib im Bop," a play on bibimbap, the Korean casserole of rice, veggies and egg; organic corn arepas topped with organic eggs and avocado; and biscuits and gravy made with Amish sausages from Michigan and Indiana. As dedicated to art as she is to organic ingredients, Fire features brunch dishes made from recipes from artists, whose work covers the walls. *5020 N Sheridan Rd between Carmen and Argyle Sts (773-728-5576). El: Red to Argyle. Bus: 81 (24hrs), 92, 151 (24hrs). Breakfast, brunch (Sat, Sun), lunch (closed Tue). Average main course: $16.*

✷ **Twin Anchors** Nothing's changed much in the 75 years since this Old Town rib institution first started packing in the crowds, and that's okay with us. Once in a while, we'll still cram our way into the old tavern to wait among the masses (no reservations are taken) for the falling-off-the-bone, baked-then-grilled babybacks with a side of the "zesty" (really tangy) sauce. Add a side of the pork-flecked baked beans and an Old Style, and it's a perfect Chicago meal. *1655 N Sedgwick St between Concord Pl and Eugenie St (312-266-1616). El: Brown, Purple (rush hrs) to Sedgwick. Bus: 72 North, 156 LaSalle. Lunch (Sat, Sun), dinner. Average main course: $20.*

✷ **Weber Grill** We're not going to pretend that this place isn't tourist hell. But if you can deal with the long waits and the T.G.I. Friday's vibe, you'll be rewarded with surprisingly delicious grill fare. Steak skewers are sweet, succulent and plated atop an enormous heap of addictive fried onions. Golden "beer can chicken" get its intense flavor from loads of garlic and an herbal spice rub. And thick Black Angus burgers are dripping with juices. All of which begs one question: Why are we letting tourists have the run of this place? *539 N State St at Grand Ave (312-467-9696). El: Red to Grand. Bus: 22 (24hrs), 36, 65. Breakfast, lunch, dinner. Average main course: $19.*

★ ✷ **West Town Tavern** We wish every neighborhood had a cozy spot like this—unfussy food, fun wines, and jeans and suits mingling sans attitude. Chef-owner Susan Goss and her husband, Drew, not only are pillars in the local food community, but also they keep us coming back for different nightly specials, like Monday's buttermilk biscuit–and–fried chicken platter, made with Goss's great-grandma's recipe. Other nights, the staple menu—antipasto plate, skillet-roasted mussels and "campfire s'mores"—is supplemented by seasonal specials. *1329 W Chicago Ave at Throop St (312-666-6175). El: Blue to Chicago. Bus: 9 (24hrs), 56, 66 (24hrs). Dinner (closed Sun). Average main course: $18.*

Wildfire The only thing that's wild about this place is how insanely popular it is—even on a sleepy Tuesday night, you'll need a reservation. Other than that, though, the menu will be familiar (think upscale T.G.I. Fridays). Steaks seem to be a favorite among regulars, but we found that the seafood fared better: Meaty swordfish "London Broil" is topped with juicy roasted tomatoes and sweet roasted red onion, and crab-crusted shrimp are the epitome of guilty pleasures. *159 W Erie St between LaSalle and Wells Sts (312-787-9000). El: Blue, Brown, Orange, Pink, Purple (rush hrs) to LaSalle. Bus: 1, 7, 22 (24hrs), 24, X28, 125, 151 (24hrs). Dinner. Average main course: $20.*

Side dish

Dog days
The best hot dogs in town come with a side of history.

Did you know there are more than 1,800 hot-dog stands in Chicago? Say all you want about deep-dish pizza, the all-beef, Chicago-style hot dog is the one food export inexorably linked with our city.

Hot dogs came our way via a couple of Austro-Hungarian immigrants at the 1893 World's Fair. And dogs dressed with the seven required toppings—mustard, bright green relish, tomato, chopped onion, dill pickle, celery salt and sport peppers—have been around since the '30s. This tradition of "dragging it through the garden" was initially a matter of economics. Each of the components came from combining the offerings of competing immigrant street vendors: The Germans provided the hot dog, bun and mustard; German Jews introduced the pickle; relish came from Czech traditions; Greeks contributed the onion and tomato; celery salt is arguably a French concoction; and the sport pepper is an Italian thing. Enough history; time to dig in.

Hot Doug's *(3324 N California Ave at Roscoe St, 773-279-9550)* The self-described "encased-meat emporium" is known for its gourmet sausages made from game meats, but Doug also delivers when it comes to an old-fashioned Chicago dog.

Murphy's Red Hots *(1211 W Belmont Ave between Lakewood and Racine Aves, 773-935-2882)* Owner Bill Murphy was recently inducted into the Vienna Beef Hall of Fame, so he's doing something right. Dogs are charred or steamed, and the superfresh toppings are proudly displayed behind the Plexiglas counter.

Superdawg *(6363 N Milwaukee Ave at Devon Ave, 773-763-0660)* The owners have used their own exclusive product (as opposed to Vienna dogs) since 1948, served steamed and with a tart green tomato and no celery salt.

The Wiener's Circle *(2622 N Clark St between Wrightwood Ave and Drummond Pl, 773-477-7444)* This late-night institution's rep as the place to go for verbal bitch slaps can overshadow the fact that it serves a damn fine Chicago dog.

Suck it up Enjoy all the diner classics at Salt & Pepper Diner.

$15 and under

A & T Restaurant The letters in its name stand for "Abundant and Tasty," an apt description of the food at this classic neighborhood diner. Large omelettes filled with fresh veggies, cheese and meat and other breakfast favorites like hash browns can be ordered all day long, while steaming bowls of chicken soup and solid sandwiches are offered in the afternoon and evening. *7036 N Clark St at Greenleaf Ave (773-274-0036). Bus: 22 (24hrs), 96, 155. Metra: Union Pacific North to Rogers Park. Breakfast, lunch, dinner. Average main course: $7.*

A Taste of Heaven See Bakeries/cafés for review.

Al's Italian Beef Unwrap your Italian beef sandwich (you ordered peppers on it, right?) and spread out the paper like a tablecloth. Grab your sandwich with both hands and hold it in front of you, keeping your elbows on the table. To take a bite, lean toward the sandwich; do *not*, under any circumstances, move the sandwich toward you. Doing so will only lead to juices spilled onto your clothes—and if you're simultaneously working on a messy side of cheese fries (which you should be), you don't need the added risk. *169 W Ontario St between Wells St and LaSalle Blvd (312-943-3222). El: Brown, Purple (rush hrs) to Chicago; Red to Grand. Bus: 22 (24hrs), 125, 156. Lunch, dinner. Average main course: $4.*

Artist's Café You'll be lured in by the bright vintage sign, the novelty of eating in the Fine Arts Building and the cute art-school servers. Inside, you'll find chrome counters, tattered booths, a bakery case full of pie. Take advantage of the sidewalk dining in warmer months and order a no-frills breakfast of eggs and bacon or a generous grilled cheese on thick multigrain with hot, Parmesan-sprinkled chips. Avoid the lean burgers and opt to calorie-load with desserts trucked-in from Bucktown's Sweet Thang. *412 S Michigan Ave between Van Buren St and Congress Pkwy (312-939-7855). El: Brown, Green, Orange, Purple (rush hrs) to Adams. Bus: 1, 3, 4 (24hrs), X4, 7, 26, X28, 126, 127, 145, 147, 148, 151 (24hrs). Breakfast, lunch, dinner. Average main course: $9.*

Augie's Unlike some (okay, most) diners, the retro vibe here is not manufactured. This place actually dates back to the '50s, and it shows. Fountain sodas, milkshakes and malts get served by pleasant gals who won't hesitate to call you "hun," and the menu is dotted with mom-approved comfort food like meatloaf, mostaccioli and steak. *5347 N Clark St between Summerdale and Balmoral Aves (773-271-7868). El: Red to Berwyn. Bus: 22 (24hrs), 36, 50, 92. Breakfast, lunch, dinner. Average main course: $7.*

Bombacigno's J and C Inn The J is for Joe, the C for Claudette, and if the battered bar and nostalgia-covered walls haven't tipped you off already, they've been at this for a while. Since 1972 she's worked the register while he's churned out house specialties like Italian Beef Pizziola, a big, wet, mess of an Italian beef with mozzarella and tomato sauce that's so flavorful it reminds us why this sandwich became famous in the first place. The signature cold pasta—angel hair tossed with romano, basil, garlic and olive oil—is a side we can't pass up. *558 W Van Buren between Clinton and Jefferson Sts (312-663-4114). El: Blue to Clinton. Bus: 56 Milwaukee, 125 Water Tower Exp. Lunch (Mon–Fri) (closed Sat, Sun). Average main course: $7.*

The Book Cellar This is more than a bookstore; think wine bar with tasty bites in a spot that just happens to be filled with books. Soups—sweet onion tomato and carrot ginger bisque—are tasty and filling. The vegetarian sandwich is a cool combo of tomato, cucumber, provolone and mixed greens on slices of *ciabatta* spread with herbed cream cheese. Bookworms can enjoy 1/2 price wine and beer at the store on book club nights, the first Wednesday of each month. *4736 N Lincoln Ave between Leland and Lawrence Aves (773-293-2665). El: Brown to Western. Bus: 11, 49 (24hrs), X49, 81 (24hrs). Lunch, dinner (Mon, Wed–Sat). Average main course: $6.*

Breakfast Club Holding strong in the middle of an industrialish residential 'hood is the mother of all breakfast haunts. It's like Granny's cozy kitchen but with the morning news flowing via a stream of chatty city employees, laptop-wielding businessmen and convivial construction workers. They fuel up for the day on whole wheat pancakes, football-size omelettes and biscuits with sausage-packed gravy. Lunch stays on the heavy side with bowls of beef stew and thick, delicious sandwiches. Since everything is made from scratch, doors close promptly at 3pm so the staff can prep the next day's fare. *1381 W Hubbard St between Noble and Ada Sts (312-666-2372). El: Green, Pink to Ashland. Bus: 9 (24hrs), X9, 65. Breakfast, lunch. Average main course: $8.*

Brett's Kitchen It's worth a trek to this gallery-district lunch counter no matter where you work. The Pyrenees sandwich takes the eponymous cheese and pairs it with tabouli, tomato and lettuce for a creative, light lunch. Likewise, the chicken sandwich goes Mexican with creamy avocado and a hint of hot sauce. Daily soups, such as mushroom barley, are fresh, light and simple, and a glass case in the front of the store is stocked with freshly-baked quickbreads and cakes, all sliced big enough to feed two. *233 W Superior St at Franklin St (312-664-6354). El: Brown, Purple (rush hrs) to Chicago. Bus: 66 Chicago (24hrs), 156 LaSalle. Breakfast, lunch (closed Sun). Average sandwich: $6.*

Brisku's Bistro This somewhat amorphous place has a bar feel, but the food is far better than any mere watering hole could dish out. Plates of curried chicken, bacon-wrapped scallops, drunken calamari and pizzas are not only killer and generously sized but cheap to boot. Brisku's is also very active in its Irving Park neighborhood, providing an outlet for local bands (Saturday nights bring out the headbangers), supporting local softball teams, dance troupes and indie filmmakers on the hunt for reasonable catering. *4100 N Kedzie Ave between Belle Plaine Ave and Irving Park Rd (773-279-9141). Bus: 80, X80, 82. Lunch, dinner. Average main course: $7.*

The Brown Sack Locals cram in to this West Logan Square sandwich-and-shake shack and eat everything in sight. That means that not everything on the chalkboard menu will be in stock, but if you're lucky you'll snag a bowl of thick, peppery, housemade minestrone. Sandwiches (such as the Reuben, filled with thick slices of beef and mercifully light on Thousand Island dressing) and hand-dipped shakes are the stars of the show, but it wasn't until we tried the superb sweet-potato pie that we truly understood what all the fuss was about. *3706 W Armitage Ave between Lawndale and Ridgeway Aves (773-661-0675). Bus: 53, 73, 82. Lunch and dinner (closed Mon, closes at 7pm daily). Average sandwich: $5.*

Buffalo Joe's Who would have guessed that pure nirvana comes in three varieties: mild, hot and suicide? Chicken wings are the only reason to walk into this grungy

NU dive: plump and double-fried, the wings are coated with one of three housemade sauces. Harcore types go for either the hot sauce or the vinegary jalapeño suicide version, which packs a hint of sweetness with its heat. Newbies may scoff at the ranch dressing served for dipping instead of blue cheese, but we think it cools the palate just enough to ready us for the next round. *812 Clark St, Evanston (847-328-5525). El: Purple to Davis. Bus: 205 Chicago. Lunch, dinner. Average main course: $5.*

⊕ **Café Penelope** It's slim lunch pickings on this stretch of Ashland, so this wholesome food is worth the sometimes-slow service. The simply decorated room (okay, it's just undecorated) retains a feeling of coziness, and the straightforward menu follows suit. Crispy, thin-crust pizzas, crisp Greek salads and sandwiches stacked with everything from turkey to curried eggplant will make you think your mom is in the kitchen. The exception is the soft, plate-size oatmeal cookie with white chocolate, dark chocolate and raisins. Unless your mama was Betty Crocker, she never made cookies like this. *230 S Ashland Ave between Adams St and Jackson Blvd (312-243-6655). Bus: 9, 20 (24hrs), 126. Breakfast, lunch, dinner. Average main course: $6.*

⊕ **Chicago Bagel Authority** This Ohio-loving, toaster-shunning shop steams every bagel it serves, and if that sounds weird, you obviously haven't had one of its warm, soft sandwiches yet. Steaming the bagels (or, if you must, wraps and sub rolls) makes ambitious sandwiches like the "Bacon Boat to Turkey Town" (stuffed with turkey, bacon, chive cream cheese, red onion, banana peppers and spicy mustard) and "Mikey's Munch" (roast beef, pepperjack, avocado and peppercorn dressing) manageable. If it's a crisp bagel you prefer, though, you're out of luck. *953 W Armitage Ave between Bissell St and Sheffield Ave (773-248-9606). El: Brown, Purple (rush hrs) to Armitage. Bus: 8 Halsted, 73 Armitage. Breakfast, lunch, dinner (Mon–Thu). Average main course: $6.*

▼ ✳ ⊕ **Chicago Diner** See Vegetarian for review.

⊕ **Clarke's** Goths, mall punks and the Halsted Street crowd have a monopoly on the booths at this diner's Lakeview location (*930 W Belmont Ave, 773-348-5988*), but this older, brighter location, where '50s decor meets an '80s soundtrack, belongs to stressed out DePaul students, hungry cops and a sprinkling of staff from the nearby Children's Memorial Hospital. Burgers, burritos, sandwiches and salads are available, but the fluffy omelettes and even fluffier pancakes are what really make this gem shine. *2442 N Lincoln Ave between Fullerton Pkwy and Montana St (773-472-3505). El: Brown, Purple (rush hrs), Red to Fullerton. Bus: 8, 11, 74. Breakfast, lunch, dinner. Average main course: $8.*

⊕ **Cobblestones Bar & Grill** For many Sox fans this bare-bones, wood-paneled room is the best place to catch the game. A couple of beers and a few home runs are all these guys need to nourish them. You, on the other hand, need a muffaletta (an enormous sandwich stuffed with salami, cappicola and provolone, topped with a tapenade) or the "CB&G" sandwich, which piles on succulent roast beef soaking in its own juices. Hoping for something fancier? What are you, a Cubs fan? *514 W Pershing Rd between Normal and Parnell Aves (773-624-3630). Bus: 39 Pershing, 44 Wallace. Lunch (Mon–Fri), dinner (Tue–Fri). Open on weekends during Sox games. Average main course: $7.50.*

Classic American $15 and under

⊕ **Dagel & Beli** An infatuation with spoonerisms (the transposition of the initial consonants of two words) inspired this sandwich shop's moniker, and also led to some interesting names for its steamed bagel sandwiches, such as fart smella (roast beef and blue cheese on an onion bagel) and royola lubin (corned beef, sauerkraut and Swiss on a rye bagel). Owner Dan Sullivan, whose great-grandfather built the space in 1915, also owns the new next-door coffeehouse Charmers Café, which is linked to the Dagel by a corridor. *7406 N Greenview Ave between Jarvis and Fargo Aves (773-743-2354). El: Red to Jarvis. Bus: 22 (24hrs), 147, 151 (24hrs). Breakfast, lunch, dinner. Average sandwich: $6.*

⊕ **Daily Bar & Grill** Bright yellow walls, gray slate floors and flowers blooming everywhere make this sun-drenched 18-table patio on bustling Lincoln Avenue the perfect spot for a great burger. This place has two: the Daily burger, a half-pound of Black Angus beef on a toasted bun with lettuce, tomato and onions; and the belt-busting Sunday Edition, which piles on bacon, cheese and grilled mushrooms and onions. *4560 N Lincoln Ave at Wilson Ave (773-561-6198). El: Brown to Western. Bus: 11, 49 (24hrs), X49, 78, 81 (24hrs). Lunch, dinner. Average main course: $10.*

⊕ **The Depot American Diner** Everything on the Depot's menu is simple and excellently seasoned: Golden breakfast potatoes get a sprinkling of paprika, big bowls of chili have enough bite to wake your taste buds up (but not burn them off) and the juicy pieces of turkey on the open-faced sandwich are covered in thick, peppery gravy—so much that you may have trouble finding the bread underneath it all. Housemade desserts tempt from behind the counter; sadly, they look better than they taste, so stick with coffee. *5840 W Roosevelt Rd between Mayfield and Monitor Aves (773-261-8422). El: Blue (Forest Park branch) to Austin Lombard. Bus: 12, 91, Pace 305, Pace 315. Breakfast, lunch, dinner. Average main course: $7.*

Kitsch'n sink They serve a little bit from a lot of decades at Kitsch'n on Roscoe.

B ☺ **Dunlay's on the Square** When Sunday morning finds you cranky and in desperate need of coffee (read: hungover), the wait for a table at nearby Lula can seem like cruel punishment. That's when this handy standby comes in. The grace and sophistication of Lula's food might be missing, but the thick and hearty oatmeal pancakes become surprisingly dreamy with a slathering of maple butter; the salmon (smoked in-house) is thick, meaty and smoky-sweet; and the Irish breakfast pairs delicious sausage with a pint of Guinness. The best part: There's no wait—at least not yet. *3137 W Logan Blvd at Milwaukee Ave (773-227-2400). El: Blue to Logan Square. Bus: 56 Milwaukee, 74 Fullerton. Brunch (Sat, Sun), dInner. Average main course: $10.*

★ ☺ **Edgebrook Coffee Shop** People go to other diners for greasy bacon and eggs, fatty hamburgers and limp french fries. But they come to this one, a tiny, charming room with '50s-era nostalgia, for food they can watch being made to order in the open kitchen. Sitting at the long counter, you can witness the eggs being cracked for your fluffy omelette, the batter being stirred for your thin and airy pancakes, and, if you're there on the weekend, the sausage-studded gravy being spooned over dense, buttery biscuits. *6322 N Central Ave between Caldwell and Devon Aves (773-792-1433). Bus: 85A North Central. Breakfast, lunch (Mon–Sat). Average main course: $6.*

☺ **Evanston Chicken Shack** Regulars at this roadside dive know to call in their orders ahead of time so they don't have to drool for 20-plus minutes waiting for their fresh-from-the-fryer, juicy birds. You'll find a few tables next to the pop machines, but this is mostly a takeout joint that caters to a steady stream of NU students and fried-chicken fanatics who go bonkers for the slightly peppery, battered chicken

dinners, complete with fries, cole slaw and bread for sopping the grease. *1925 N Ridge Ave, Evanston (847-328-9360). El: Purple to Central. Lunch, dinner (closed Sun). Average main course: $7.*

★ ☺ **Feed** There's a fine line between kitsch and authenticity, and this homely chicken shack sits right in the middle. Because despite the crowds of gay Moby-look-alikes, Starter jacket–clad teenagers and yuppie moms sneaking in cigarettes after devouring whole birds, this place still looks and feels the way we imagine a rural Kentucky chicken shack does. And that's a good thing, since it means juicy rotisserie chickens flanked by tortillas, salsa, sides like sweet corn pudding, plus banana pudding and a rotating roster of freshly made fruit pies. *2803 W Chicago Ave at California Ave (773-489-4600). Bus: 52, 65, 66 (24hrs). Lunch, dinner (closed Sun). Average main course: $7.*

☺ **Feed the Beast** This bar and grill may just look like your average cozy neighborhood joint, but there are a few hidden gems on the menu for adding a belly buffer so that you can have one more (or three more) beers. The "Nachos con Fusion" is a huge, gluttonous portion, so share them or suffer tomorrow. Mini–tenderloin sandwiches were juicy and oozing with herbed butter and the house salad is a garden of perfectly dressed crisp veggies. *4300 N Lincoln Ave at Cullom Ave (773-478-9666). Bus: 11, 50, 78. Dinner. Average main course: $9.*

☺ **First Slice Pie Café** You might expect to walk into Lillstreet Art Center and be assaulted by fumes from paint and clay. But with First Slice Café residing in the corner, you'll instead inhale the aroma of fresh-baked pie (red wine and poached pear, peanut butter and chocolate, plus standbys like apple). First Slice uses part of its profits to help feed the hungry, using local and organic ingredients so you won't feel like you're making a sacrifice. In fact, we'd come back for the hot chicken–and–blue cheese sandwich and the not-too-sweet chocolate-ginger scones no matter who was benefiting from our tab. *In the Lillstreet Art Center, 4401 N Ravenswood Ave at Montrose Ave (773-506-7380). Bus: 50, 78, 145. Lunch, dinner (closed Sun). Average main course: $6.*

B Flourish Bakery Café Midwesterners who pine for old-fashioned salads, sandwiches and baked goods like Mom used to make will find a good selection (macaroni, pea and pearl-onion salad, anyone?) at this sunny Edgewater bakery/café. We like the more modern panini—especially the caprese with prosciutto—as well as the rotating assortment of fresh-baked breads, including multigrain and hearty deli rye. The Metropolis coffee—a special blend brewed exclusively for the bakery—may not be as retro as a packet of Ma's Sanka, but we like it that way. *1138 W Bryn Mawr Ave between Winthrop Ave and Broadway (773-271-2253). El: Red to Bryn Mawr or Berwyn. Bus: 22 (24hrs), 36, 50, 84, 151 (24hrs). Breakfast, brunch (Sat, Sun), lunch, dinner (Mon–Sat). Average main course: $8.*

B ☺ Flying Saucer Don't be fooled by the 1950s greasy spoon atmosphere. That's just retro decor; this Humboldt Park diner focuses on local ingredients and healthy options. Hormone-free meat is the name of the game here, so eat your breakfast sausage without guilt. And breakfast is served until 3pm, so you don't even have to get up early. Order up the sweet potato and tofu hash or the Flying Tofu Bowl. The menu can change depending on what's in season, but there are always a number of solid standard egg dishes and Mexican-inspired options. *1123 N California Ave between Thomas St and Haddon Ave (773-342-9076). Bus: 49 (24hrs), X49, 52, 70. Breakfast, brunch (Sat, Sun), lunch. Average main course: $7.*

☺ Gaslight Bar & Grill Believe it or not, the cult item on this pubbish menu is the salads. The $5 salad special on Tuesday nights (stereotypically dubbed "girls' night out") has made the big bowls of greens topped with avocado and portobello mushroom the hottest dish on the block. But bar-food aficionados need not worry: A trio of soft pretzels (two of which are filled, respectively, with marinara sauce and mozzarella) and the deep-fried Reuben rolls (a heart attack waiting to happen) fill that niche nicely. *2426 N Racine Ave at Montana St (773-929-7759). El: Brown, Purple (rush hrs), Red to Fullerton. Bus: 74 Fullerton. Lunch (Sat, Sun), dinner. Average main course: $9.*

☺ Gene & Jude's Red Hot Stand Do not ask for ketchup when you order one of the legendary slender, snappy hot dogs that come topped with a fistful of fries at this SRO institution that's been serving 'em up since 1951. The scowling, surly types behind the counter don't go for sissy stuff like that. Claim your place at the end of the perpetually long line and entertain yourself by watching potatoes being cut and fried into perfect greasy strips while you wait. Once it's your turn, order your dog with everything, then count your blessings for the wax paper–wrapped bliss that lies before you. *2720 N River Rd, River Grove (708-452-7634).. Lunch, dinner. Single dog with fries: $1.80.*

☺ Glenn's Diner All-you-can-eat cereal. Blackboard fresh catch tilapia specials. Huge salads (no iceberg lettuce here). Red Hot pancakes. (Yep, that's pancakes with Red Hots cinnamon candies baked inside.) Any place with that varied of a menu is going to have some hits and misses. Needing a steak knife to eat our stuffed bell pepper makes

All-night filling stations

Chicago's dying breed of 24-hour diners fights to hold onto a little piece of Americana.

"Home Depot offered me a million dollars for this corner," George Liakopoulos insists, standing where **White Palace Grill** (*1159 S Canal St at Roosevelt Rd, 312-939-7167*) has stood since 1939. But Liakopoulos declined, saying diners are in his blood: His father owned a handful, and he once presided over Lincoln Avenue's Golden Apple.

After taking over the legendary White Palace in 2000, Liakopoulos cleaned up the weathered spot. The cops, hard-hats and third-shift coffee drinkers don't seem to notice; they order "the usual" just the same.

Farther south at **Don's Humburgers** (*1837 S Western Ave at 18th Pl, 312-733-9351*), regulars cluster at the Formica counter sipping coffee, debating the pointlessness of decaf and the price of gas. Don Wageman opened his counter-only grill in 1955, misspelled *hamburger* to turn heads, and tells stories of suing McDonald's for introducing a "Humburger" toy. Legend has it that the Happy Meal trinket was renamed Hamburglar, but story aside, it's the grilled onion–topped, double humburger that keeps Don's going despite the looming golden arches across the street.

The regulars who resist modern fast-food spots are the lifeline of these old-school diners, and here they've found common ground. "We're the place the lonely can come talk to somebody, the insomniac can come when they can't sleep," Frank DiPiero says of **Jeri's Grill** (*4357 N Western Ave at Montrose Ave, 773-604-8775*), which he took over in 2000 when his father, the owner since '63, passed away. "Here, what you see is what you get," DiPiero says, motioning to signs on the wood-paneled wall that beckon with BONE-IN HAM and BISCUITS AND GRAVY.

At Arnold DeMar's **Diner Grill** (*1635 W Irving Park Rd at Marshfield Ave, 773-248-2030*), minijukes line the counter, a TV sputters out *The Three Stooges*, and a grease-splattered sign reads HOME OF THE SLINGER, DON'T ASK, JUST EAT.

that dish a miss. But the salads, grilled sandwiches and enormous omelettes are all made with fresh veggies, and there's no greasy-spoon feel. Plus, there's never anything wrong with a big bowl of Cocoa Puffs. *1820 W Montrose Ave at Honore St (773-506-1720). Bus: 50, 78, 145. Breakfast, lunch, dinner (Mon–Sat). Average main course: $8.*

(☉ **Goose Island Brew Pub** The beer selection alone is enough of a draw at this local brewery, where we can happily while away an afternoon nursing a crisp 312 Urban Wheat Ale or malty Smoked Porter. But pair our drinks of choice with a Paulina Market sausage sampler of locally made links or a baked Bavarian pretzel, and things look even better. If we throw caution to the wind and indulge in a stilton burger, a hearty, black-pepper crusted patty smothered in stinky cheese and roasted garlic cloves atop a pumpernickel roll, we know we'll be rolling home. But we'll be rolling home very happy. *1800 N Clybourn Ave at Willow St (312-915-0071). El: Brown, Purple (rush hrs) to Armitage; Red to North/Clybourn. Bus: 8, 72, 73. Lunch, dinner. Average main course: $10. • Additional location at 3535 N Clark St (773-832-9040).*

☀ ☉ **Hackney's on Harms** Want to escape to a simpler life this weekend? Head to this 60-something-year-old hideaway. Before it was a restaurant, it was a farmhouse with a porch where friends would stop in for cold beer and corned-beef sandwiches. Pan-fried burgers served on house-baked black rye came along soon after (as did a full-fledged business), and are still the spot's signature. Friday night's lake perch fish fry is also a hit. *1241 Harms Rd, Glenview (847-724-5577). Lunch, dinner. Average main course: $9. • Additional location at 733 S Dearborn St (312-461-1116).*

☉ **Hamburger Mary's** Could anything be more fabulous than a gay hamburger chain? Not if you're into fried food and burgers so over-the-top that they border on obnoxious. Sandwiches here are less about the meat and more about the toppings: "Buffy (the Hamburger Slayer)" packs in big flavors of red wine and aioli; the "Barbra-Q Bacon Cheeseburger" has so much on it (onion rings, barbecue sauce, bacon) it can hardly be held. If big burgers aren't your thing, head straight for the fried Twinkies; they're universally appealing, no matter what team you bat for. *5400 N Clark St at Balmoral Ave (773-784-6969). El: Red to Berwyn. Bus: 22 (24hrs), 50, 92. Lunch, dinner. Average main course: $10.*

Read 'em & eat

black and white large sugar cookie with white frosting on one half, chocolate on the other

corned-beef hash chopped corned beef mixed with chunks of potato and onion

phosphate (fahs-FAYT) hand-mixed fountain drink made with carbonated water or club soda and flavored syrup, such as cherry or vanilla

shoofly pie molasses pie commonly associated with the Pennsylvania Dutch

S.O.S. toast smothered in creamed chipped beef, a.k.a. "shit on a shingle" in Army lingo

▼ (☀ **Hard Rock Café** The rock & roll memorabilia at this shiny, over-the-top pseudo-museum might've gone to our heads, but we're seeing band homages everywhere. Okay, the "Joe Perry of Aerosmith Quesadilla" is shamelessly overt, but do Paul and Linda have anything to do with the "Classic Wings?" Does Jeff Tweedy know about his "Tupelo Chicken Tenders?" And why the hell would "Creamed Spinach" be on the menu if not to reference Eric Clapton's psych-blues trio? *63 W Ontario St between Clark and Dearborn Sts (312-943-2252). El: Red to Grand. Bus: 22 (24hrs), 65, 156. Lunch, dinner. Average main course: $12.*

▼ ☀ **B Harmony Grill** If you're into comfort food, huge portions and supporting local farmers, this casual folk art–filled dining room is for you. Seasonal specials sure to please meat-eaters might include a grilled grass-fed sirloin with wild mushroom-leek ragout. Vegetarians get plenty of love with dishes like edamame hummus, smoked tofu-veggie chili, a Southwestern falafel burger and killer mac and cheese. Brunch favorites include kid-friendly peanut butter and jelly pancakes. If you're finishing up with a show at the adjacent Schubas, prepare to hear the music from a food coma. *3159 N Southport Ave at Belmont Ave (773-525-2508). El: Brown to Southport. Bus: 9, X9 11, 77 (24hrs). Brunch, lunch, dinner. Average main course: $12.*

☉ **Harold's Chicken Shack #24** For years, outposts of this empire have multiplied like rabbits, making it tough to go five blocks without bumping into another shack turning out the best fried chicken around. Why highlight this one? We believe it's the best. Order the four- or six-wing plate, ask for it "fried hard" (extra crispy) with pepper (lemon-pepper if you want zing) and get both mild and hot sauce on the side for dipping. (It's 27 cents for sauce on the side, but do it unless you want your chicken drenched.) *407 E 75th St between Vernon Ave and King Dr (773-488-9533). El: Red to 79th. Bus: 75 74th-75th. Lunch, dinner. Average main course: $5. • Additional locations include 1361 N Milwaukee Ave (773-252-2424).*

☉ **Hashbrowns** The smooth service and easy-going atmosphere are thanks to the Italian family who runs the joint. The Ruffolos have extended the most important meal of the day to cater to late-risers, serving their hangover-helpers until 3pm. Whether it's dressed-up omelettes or straight-up bacon and eggs, all breakfasts come with the namesake hash browns. But our vote goes to the "killer" hash browns, a massive attack of potatoes topped with cheese, onions, sour cream and cornflakes that's baked to bubbly perfection. *731 W Maxwell St between Union Ave and Halsted St (312-226-8000). El: Blue to UIC-Halsted. Bus: 8, 12, 168. Breakfast, lunch. Average main course: $6.*

▼ (☀ **Heartland Cafe** Heartland is as much a playground for twenty- and thirtysomethings as it is a restaurant. Local music acts ranging from folk to rockabilly to jazz flock to its stage as frequently as the local art on the walls changes. Top billing, however, belongs to the menu. To the delight of vegans, vegetarians and the cholesterol conscious, organic whole wheat breads, salad plates, seitan fajitas and black bean burgers are offered, but red meat–seekers won't be disappointed when the turkey alternatives to bacon and ham arrive plated next to their generously-sized omellettes. *7000 N Glenwood Ave at Lunt Ave (773-465-8005). El: Red to Morse. Bus: 22 (24hrs), 147, 96, 155. Breakfast, lunch, dinner. Average main course: $12.*

★ ▼ ☉ **Hot Doug's** Doug Sohn's homage to encased meat is packed with suits, students and blue-collar lunch breakers. They stand together in longer-than-ever lines and put up with

Top o' the morning
Ina's knows a good breakfast.

limited hours to get classic Chicago dogs and brats served with Doug's untouchable flair for flavor. There are veggie dogs for vegetarians, bagel dogs for kids, specialties like cranberry-and-cognac chicken sausage for high-brow hot-doggers and, of course, the famous fries cooked in duck fat (available only on Fridays and Saturdays). *3324 N California Ave between Henderson and Roscoe Sts (773-279-9550). Bus: 52, 77 (24hrs), 152. Lunch (closed Sun). Average dog: $2.50.*

B ⊙ Hot Spot Breakfast and lunch items (such as the rich biscuits in a thick vegetarian mushroom gravy and the tuna melt on marble rye) at this popular Logan Square spot are available all day, and a rotating list of specials (chicken piccata, stuffed peppers) round out the menu for dinner. Breakfast and brunch is also available on the weekends, but with ever-present long lines, you may be better off getting your bacon-and-egg fix on Monday night. *2824 W Armitage Ave at Mozart St (773-770-3838). El: Blue to California. Bus: 52, 56, 73. Mon 11am–9pm; Wed–Fri 11am–9pm; Sat, Sun 8am–2:30pm (closed Tue). Average main course: $6.50.*

⊙ Huey's Hotdogs It's hard not to like a mustard- and ketchup-hued hot dog joint with its own foosball table and a menu of artery cloggers named for the owner's family members. Try Kali's Killer chili cheese dog or Pokey's grilled Polish with all the trimmings and a free side of fries to boot. The menu also offers burgers, a smattering of sandwiches, veggie dogs and some salads, but why bother? A dog and one of Huey's thick "rockstar" milk shakes are the best way we can think of to load up on nitrates and saturated fat. *1507 W Balmoral Ave at Clark St (773-293-4800). El: Red to Berwyn. Bus: 22 (24hrs), 92, 147. Lunch, dinner. Average main course: $4.*

★ ⊙ **Ina's** Judging from the long lines on the weekends, people seem willing to wait forever for the Scrapple (a crispy, slightly spicy polentalike dish flanked by eggs and chorizo) and Heavenly Hots (sour cream pancakes with fruit compote) on the breakfast menu. But that same comfort-food theme can be found at dinner as well, when Ina cooks her famous fried chicken (made with trans-fat–free soy oil that allegedly lowers cholesterol) and serves her "Friday night in Brooklyn" special—matzo-ball soup and brisket—on the weekends. *1235 W Randolph St between Racine Ave and Elizabeth St (312-226-8227). Bus: 20 Madison (24hrs). Breakfast, lunch (Mon–Sat), dinner (Tue–Sat). Average main course: $8.*

⊙ **Jeri's Grill** There is a bevy of 24-hour greasy spoon diners in this city, but none of them offer anything as curious as Jeri's "jailhouse special," a plate of fried bologna, eggs, hash browns and toast. Kind of makes you wonder what Jeri was up to before the grill, doesn't it? Get there before 2pm for the biscuits and gravy; the rest of the cheap eats are served all day and include fries and patty melts. *4357 N Western Ave between Pensacola and Montrose Aves (773-604-8775). Bus: 49 (24hrs), X49, 78. 24 hrs. Average main course: $6.*

★ ⊙ **Jerry's Sandwiches** If this design-your-own-sandwich bar—with its selection of eight breads, 28 fillings and 25 sauces—doesn't make you slip into a coma of indecision, then, we're sorry, but you're probably one of the most boring people on Earth. A list of suggestions is on hand to help indecisive lunchers, but with 100 selections, all of them as tempting as the Diego A. (steak, avocado, cilantro, cheddar, chipotle chutney and adobo sauce), it doesn't really help. So when you're here, grab a menu to study from at home. .*1045 W Madison St between Carpenter and Aberdeen Sts (312-563-1008). Bus: 8 Halsted, 20 Madison (24hrs). Lunch,*

Fries with that? Black Angus burgers are Patty Burger's signature.

dinner (Mon–Fri). Average main course: $7. • Additional location at 1938 W Division St (773-235-1006).

(☺ **Jimmy's Red Hots** Jimmy's is a purist's hot-dog stand. No seating, no char-anything, and for crissakes, no ketchup. You'll find nothing but tasty Vienna Beef hot dogs and Polishes served on steamed buns, and rolled up into paper with a load of greasy, hand-cut fries. As a consolation for the much-maligned ketchup-lover, Jimmy's sells a decent housemade habanero hot sauce to dip your fries in, or to pour on your "supreme tamale." It's open late-night, which is the best time to catch sketchy parking-lot antics. *4000 W Grand Ave at Pulaski Rd (773-384-9513). Bus: 53 Pulaski (24hrs), 65 Grand. Lunch, dinner. Average main course: $2.*

(**Ken's Diner and Grill** See Kosher for review.

☺ **Kevin's Hamburger Heaven** In the wee hours of the morning, the industrial laborers at this 24/7 stainless-steel–dominated diner just south of the Cell fill up on steak and eggs platters, pancakes and hash browns to tide themselves over until noon. When the lunch whistle blows, however, it's Kevin's eponymous burger, "the One and Only," that the hardhat crew favors. You can order the hand-formed patty, seasoned with a secret blend of spices, with or without cheese. *554 W Pershing Rd between Normal Ave and Wallace St (773-924-5771). Bus: 8, 39, 44. 24 hrs. Average main course: $6.*

B (**Kitsch'n on Roscoe** Packaging timeless diner fare in the kitsch of the'70s helps this candy-colored eatery draw large crowds. Rays of retro sunshine pour from the flower power interior: Bright-orange Formica tables sit on linoleum floors, and the yellow walls are dotted with memorabilia from Me Decade stars like David Cassidy.

The menu playfully follows suit with items like "Green Eggs and Ham" (spinach pesto, scallions, smoked ham, Texas toast and hash browns) and "Not Your Mom's Meatloaf," served with rosemary-garlic mashed potatoes. *2005 W Roscoe St between Damen and Seeley Aves (773-248-7372). Bus: 11, 50, 77, 152. Breakfast (Mon–Sat), brunch (Sun), lunch, dinner (Tue–Sat). Average main course: $7. • Additional location at 600 W Chicago Ave (312-644-1500).*

(**Kroll's South Loop** Cheeseheads reserve most of their enthusiasm for pigskins, but they can muster some excitement over curds once in a while, too. At this offshoot of a Green Bay staple, you can do both: Flat screens show football and other sports, and the kitchen puts out authentic dairyland fare. Butter burgers—topped with ketchup, pickles, raw white onions and, of course, a buttered, grilled bun—are cutely wrapped up in butcher paper. Otherwise, thin-crusted pizzas and chewy, golden fried curds make good beer accompaniments. *1736 S Michigan Ave at 18th St (312-235-1400). Bus: 3, X3, 4 (24hrs), X4, 29, 62 (24hrs). Lunch, dinner. Average main course: $13.*

★ ☺ **Lou Mitchell's Restaurant** Thinking of spending your Sunday morning at this classic Chicago diner? Better check the weather: The line snakes out the door and onto Lou Mitchell Way well into the afternoon. Customers are treated to fresh, sugar-dusted doughnut holes (and, if you're a woman, Milk Duds) while they wait, but the real feast starts when you sit down. Stacks of "meltaway" pancakes are perfectly browned, omelettes come in hot skillets (try the sweet, rich apple-and-cheese variety) and juicy, gooey patty melts seem too big to finish. *565 W Jackson Blvd between Jefferson and Clinton Sts*

(312-939-3111). El: Blue to Clinton. Bus: 7, 60 (24hrs), 124, 125, 126, 156. Breakfast, lunch. Average main course: $9.

▼ **The Lucky Platter** There's always a wait for a table at the Lucky Platter. All three squares are favorites with both locals and NU students, who crowd into the small booths and tables. Peruse the extensive collection of paint-by-numbers art while you wait, and once you're seated, try the veggie-potato hash at breakfast, the jambalaya at lunch and jerk chicken at dinner. The sides are fantastic: Mashed potatoes and gravy, sweet-potato fries and gratis corn bread are all equally tasty. *514 Main St, Evanston (847-869-4064). El: Purple to Main. Bus: 200, 201 (24hrs), 205. Breakfast, lunch, dinner. Average main course: $11.*

★ (✳ ♨ **Lux Bar** When this Gibson's offshoot calls itself "Lux," it means it in an old-school way. Both the food and space seem to be imported from a simpler era, with dishes like luscious filet mignon "sliders" and impossibly crispy, impeccably juicy fried chicken presented without fanfare. Sometimes the straightforward approach can backfire (like with the bland turkey burger) but for the most part this spot's a gem. Especially for those who appreciate well-made cocktails and solid food. *18 E Bellevue Pl at Rush St (312-642-3400). El: Red to Clark/Division. Bus: 22 (24hrs), 36, 70. Breakfast, lunch, dinner. Average main course: $15.*

★ B ☺ **m. henry** At this sunny, daytime-only café, health food is tasty enough to eat. The owners are committed to organics and offer meat-free options, but they're okay with a little cheese, butter and sugar every now and then. Case in point: thick, dense blueberry pancakes (chose maple or pomegranate syrup) and a heaping breakfast sandwich of fried egg, gorgonzola, applewood-smoked bacon and fresh thyme. If that's too good and gooey for you health nuts, there's always the Vegan Epiphany, an organic tofu scramble that just may live up to its name. When the lines are winding, as they often are on weekends, opt for tasty bakery items from the takeout counter. *5707 N Clark St between Hollywood and Edgewater Aves (773-561-1600). El: Red to Bryn Mawr. Bus: 22 (24hrs), 50, 84, 147. Breakfast, brunch (Sat, Sun), lunch (closed Mon). Average main course: $8.*

✳ B **Mac's** If you tried to explain to the posthipsters at this Division Street staple that the menu is more carefully thought out than it is at most bars around town, you'd be greeted with little more than a puff of cigarette smoke in your face. Luckily, the kitchen musters more enthusiasm about their hearty, no-frills comfort food. Opt for a round of beers and a platter of cheesy, jalapeño-spiked nachos; an impressive slice of onion-studded meatloaf; salty, hand-cut fries; and a fat slab of ribs painted with a dark, full-flavored sauce. *1801 W Division St at Wood St (773-782-4400). El: Blue to Division. Bus: 9 (24hrs), 50, 56, 70. Brunch (Sat, Sun); lunch (Mon–Fri); dinner. Average main course: $11.*

☺ **Manny's Coffee Shop & Deli** See Delis for review.

B ☺ **Medici** Bring a Sharpie and an appetite for burgers and pan pizza when you hit this University of Chicago hangout. Patrons have left poetry and political rants on the Med's booths since it opened in 1963. Among the surprisingly good takes on typical student fare are specialty burgers and shakes, as well as great late-night salads. Go for the simple but classic Ensalada Kimba—blue cheese, apples and pecans over crisp romaine. The restaurant also serves freshly baked pastries from its sister bakery next door. *1327 E 57th St between Kenwood and Kimbark Aves (773-667-7394). El: Red to 55th. Bus: 2, 6, 15, 28. Brunch (Sat, Sun), lunch, dinner. Average main course: $7.*

Metro Klub See Kosher for review.

▼ (**Minnies** This concept from Jonathan Segal—a partner in Japonais, Le Passage and P.J. Clarke's—offers a menu of nothing but mini portions. All of the eats—from cheeseburgers to a cucumber-dill "high tea minnie"—are teeny-tiny and served in quantities of three, six or a dozen, and the retro decor is going for a '40s feel. Cue the models and the guys who love them. *1969 N Halsted St between Willow St and Armitage Ave (312-943-9900). El: Brown, Purple (rush hrs) to Armitage. Bus: 8 Halsted, 73 Armitage. Lunch, dinner. Average main course: $11.*

☺ **Mr. Beef** You're here for one thing: the Italian beef sandwich. Get it as "wet" and "hot" as you can (that is, ask for extra gravy and an extra spoonful of the crunchy giardiniera). The thin strips of beef are tender and flavorful enough as it is, but the sandwich doesn't really sing until it's got a little kick of spice. Alternatively, you could order the combo, which seasons your beef sandwich with a crackly skinned Italian sausage. But come on—you couldn't possibly hate yourself that much, could you? *666 N Orleans St between Erie and Huron Sts (312-337-8500). El: Brown, Purple (rush hrs) to Chicago, Red to Chicago/State. Bus: 65, 66 (24hrs), 156. Mon–Thurs 8am–5pm, Fri 8am–5am, Sat 10:30am–3pm and 9:30pm–5:30am (closed Sun). Average main course: $6.*

☺ **New Life Vegetarian Restaurant and Health Food Store** See Vegetarian for review.

B ☺ **Nookies Tree** We'll admit it: We've never really considered trying the food here when we were sober enough to taste it. No. 3 in the local "chain" of straightforward diners has always been a 3am favorite of Boystown barhoppers, so we were pleasantly surprised to find that in the light of day,

Love (this) shack
Feed your craving for finger-lickin' food at Feed.

Whip it good Breakfast staples get over-the-top treatment at A & T Restaurant.

this place can cook. Fruit filled pancakes and fluffy French toast are hits, as are the frittatas (try the combo of bacon, mushroom, Gouda cheese and caramelized onions). It's a great way to start the day—or end the night. *3334 N Halsted St at Buckingham Pl (773-248-9888). El: Brown, Purple (rush hrs), Red to Belmont. Bus: 8, 22 (24hrs), 77 (24hrs). Breakfast, brunch, lunch, dinner (24 hrs Fri–Sat). Average main course: $7.* ● *Additional locations at 1746 N Wells St (312-337-2454) and 2112 N Halsted St (773-327-1400).*

B ☻ **Orange** This popular brunch spot earned its rep with "frushi" (fruit and coconut milk-laced rice) and pancake flights. Brunch is served daily until 3pm, pastries are baked on-site, the signature juice machines are in place at the bar. Lunch and dinner are solid options, too, with fancy grilled cheese sandwiches (think pesto and blue cheese) and salads on offer, plus sophisticated but comfy fare like rack of lamb. *3231 N Clark St between Belmont Ave and School St (773-549-4400). El: Brown, Purple (rush hour only), Red to Belmont. Bus: 22 Clark (24hrs). Brunch (Tue–Sun), dinner (Tue–Sun). Average main course: $8.* ● *Additional locations at 2011 W Roscoe (773-248-0999) and 75 W Harrison St (312-447-1000).*

☻ **The Original Pancake House** The subterranean outpost of this Portland, Oreg.–based chain (so much for it being "original") typically has less of a wait than its Gold Coast sibling. This is a good thing because watching people partake in that enormous apple pancake—a mountain of caramelized cinnamon apples—can be torture. It's foolish not to at least try the buttermilk pancakes when you're here, even if you're more in the mood for the salami scramble; luckily almost everything comes with a short stack. *2020 N Lincoln Park West between Clark St and Dickens Ave (773-929-8130). Bus: 11, 22 (24hrs), 73, 151 (24hrs). Breakfast, lunch. Average main course: $7.* ● *Additional locations include 22 E Bellevue Pl (312-642-7917).*

★ ✷ **B Parlor** The retro-food trend may come and go, but, so far, Parlor remains. That's probably because ever since opening summer 2005 they've built a maniacal following for their hot, greasy, buttery chicken and waffles. Other mouthwatering options include a turnover filled with pumpkin, squash, sage and goat cheese, and a Cobb salad made with house-smoked bacon and Maytag bleu cheese, and at brunch, malted waffles with cherries. *1745 W North Ave between Hermitage Ave and Wood St (773-782-9000). El: Blue to Damen. Bus: 9 (24hrs), 50, 72. Brunch (Sat, Sun), dinner. Average main course: $14.*

☻ **Patty Burger** Started by CEO Gregg Majewski—a man who was instrumental in the Jimmy John's sandwich chain—this local burger shack hopes to bring its Black Angus burgers, soft brioche buns and thick chocolate-peanut-butter shakes to all corners of the country. Maybe that accounts for the streamlined menu—burgers, fries, shakes, chili and breakfast egg sandwiches are the only items on offer. But the things they're cooking they're cooking well: Burgers are thick and juicy, piled with fresh toppings and flanked by tasty (if McDonald's-ish) fries. *72 E Adams St between Wabash and Michigan Aves (312-987-0900). El: Brown, Green, Orange, Pink, Purple (rush hrs) to Adams. Breakfast (Mon–Fri), lunch (Mon–Sat), dinner (Mon–Fri) (closed Sun). Average main course: $4.*

☻ **Pauline's** The portions are as big as the personality of this breakfast-and-lunch institution that's packed with tchotchkes, mismatched chairs and tablecloths. Blueberry-studded pancakes the size of dinner plates are dense with fruit; and giant chunks of flaky salmon, white and green

Lounge act Sit and sip a craft beer or stay for one of 100 sandwiches at Jerry's.

asparagus, and goat cheese stuff a five-egg omelette served with crispy potatoes. Of the sandwiches, the turkey Reuben stands out, thick with 1/3 pound of turkey, kraut and gooey cheese, with double-battered fries and housemade soup on the side. The only thing scaled back here? The prices. *1754 W Balmoral Ave between Paulina and Ravenswood Aves (773-561-8573). El: Red to Berwyn. Bus: 22 (24hrs), 50, 92. Breakfast, lunch. Average main course: $6.75.*

B Polo Café Catering Once a neighborhood candy store, Polo remains a local gathering place in close-knit Bridgeport. Lunch is the main meal, starring charred Angus beef burgers slathered with garlic aioli, salads and giant bowls of pasta. Kill Friday night's debauchery with the Saturday Bloody Mary brunch that offers stick-to-your-ribs fare like Da Mare's steak and eggs and housemade biscuits with gravy. The joint oozes with South Side history (an oversize photo of Richard J. Daley grinned over our booth), and features Bridgeport's own Filbert's fruit sodas and root beer. *3322 S Morgan St at 33rd Pl (773-927-7656). El: Red to Sox-35th. Bus: 8 Halsted, 35 35th. Brunch (Sat), lunch (Mon–Fri), dinner (Fri, Sat). Average main course: $12.*

☻ **R.J. Grunts** The man behind TRU and Everest started his Lettuce Entertain You empire with this shabby joint? Opened in 1971—with, we're assuming, much of the same look it has today—this tightly packed hamburger shack is where to get the thick, juicy "Gruntburger," topped with addictive fried onions and blue-cheese dressing; sloppy buffalo wings and spoonable milk shakes with thick whipped cream. You can also check out the world's first salad bar, since this is where it all began. *2056 N Lincoln Park West between Clark St and Dickens Ave (773-929-5363). El: Brown, Purple (rush hrs) to Armitage. Bus: 11, 22 (24hrs), 36, 73. Lunch, dinner. Average main course: $8.*

☻ **Riverview Tavern** Stick to the basics at this neighborhood watering hole, and you'll be rewarded with $3 microbrews and enormous portions of delicious pub grub. Pizzas come from the adjoining Robey Pizza Company, where the crackerlike crust and spicy sausage on the eponymous pie make an addictive meal. Ditto for the "silver flash," a thick Black Angus burger spilling over with sweet grilled onions, melted Swiss and crisp curls of bacon. Skip the bland hummus and boring quesadillas. *1958 W Roscoe St between Wolcott and Damen Aves (773-248-9523). El: Brown to Paulina. Bus: 50 Damen, 77 Belmont (24hrs). Lunch, dinner. Average main course: $8.*

★ ☺ **Salt & Pepper Diner** There's more chrome and grease here than a motorcycle repair shop, but that's how you know a diner is worth its spit. The decor's no retro throwback—the original Lincoln Avenue location has been around since '65. Our favorites from the standard diner menu include gooey, juicy cheeseburgers; hot, crispy fries; thin omelletes overstuffed with sauteed vegetables; and appropriately famous milk shakes. We also love the fact that you can eat your heart out (or at least enough to give yourself heart disease) for less than ten bucks a person. *3537 N Clark St between Cornelia Ave and Eddy St (773-883-9800). El: Red to Addison. Bus: 8, 22 (24hrs), 152. Breakfast, lunch, dinner (Mon–Sat). Average main course: $6.* ● *Additional location at 2575 N Lincoln Ave (773-525-8788).*

☺ **Silver Cloud Bar and Grill** Busy sipping on the tasty tropical-teaser cocktails and gazing at all the pretty passerby down Damen Avenue from one of the 20 sidewalk tables, it never dawned on us to try the burgers. Good thing we did, because they're the best on the block. The half-pound of Black Angus beef is cooked perfectly medium-rare and served on a buttered and grilled bun, which is key. We're torn between the blue cheese and the brie with caramelized onions. *1700 N Damen Ave at Wabansia Ave (773-489-6212). El: Blue to Damen. Bus: 50, 56, 72. Brunch (Sat, Sun), lunch (Mon–Fri), dinner. Average main course: $10.*

(✲ **The Silver Palm** If you've been in a train's dining car recently, you know the menu ranges from Doritos to Ruffles and most of the clientele is passed out with cans of Bud Light at their feet. Thankfully, this dining car is nothing like that. The menu includes gems like light, crispy calamari and a club sandwich with sliced duck breast and prosciutto. Skip the jumbo shrimp and beware that service can be slow, but the caramelly apple pie is a must. Perfectly made, classic cocktails come from the attached bar, Matchbox. *768 N Milwaukee at Ogden Ave (312-666-9322). El: Blue to Chicago. Bus: 56 Milwaukee, 66 Chicago (24hrs). Dinner (closed Mon). Average main course: $11.*

☺ **Soupbox** You can take Emergen-C, pop Tylenol and swig DayQuil all you want, but you're never going to get over that cold without some chicken-noodle soup. This location also features everyday made-to-order salads, but when you get sick, go for one of the 12 daily soups on offer. We like the delicious (but slightly thin) vegetarian chili and hearty Southwestern bean. Additional locations at 500 W Madison St (312-993-1019) and 2943 N Broadway (773-938-9800). *50 E Chicago Ave between Wabash Ave and Rush St (312-951-5900). El: Red to Chicago. Bus: 3, 4 (24hrs), X4, 10, 26, 66 (24hrs), 125, 143, 144, 145, 146, 147, 151 (24hrs). 11am–10pm. Average bowl of soup: $5.50.*

B **Stanley's Kitchen & Tap** This Southern-style comfort food isn't the best in town, but it still has enough cream, grease and sugar to keep you happy. Especially when you're hanging out at a comfy bar with a beer and a basket full of corn bread, hush puppies and apple butter. You could also take a seat in the dining room and clog your arteries with the fat, french-fried shrimp and creamy chicken shortcake. Don't leave your liver out—there's a list of more than 70 domestic whiskeys. *1970 N Lincoln Ave at Armitage Ave (312-642-0007). Bus: 11, 22 (24hrs), 36, 72, 73. Brunch (Sat, Sun), lunch, dinner. Average main course: $8.* ● *Additional location at 324 S Racine Ave (312-433-0007).*

☺ **Stella's** This diner's long been a neighborhood favorite for it's super-friendly service (especially from owner Gus who renamed the joint a few years ago to honor his mom), thick milkshakes and all-day breakfast. The massive menu is all over the map, from *penne di portabella* to teriyaki chicken. But we stick with the diner staples that Stella's does best: massive 1/2-pound burgers, gargantuan egg skillets and fun takes on fried foods, like Tabasco-spiked onion rings. *3042 N Broadway St at Barry Ave (773-472-9040). El: Brown to Wellington. Bus: 22 (24hrs), 36, 76, 77 (24hrs). Breakfast, lunch, dinner. Average main course: $8.*

★ ☺ **Superdawg Drive-In** Despite a renovation in 1999, this hot dog drive-in is still as old-fashioned as ever, with uniformed servers bringing your order directly to your car window. The owners have trademarked almost every dish, the main draw being the "Superdawg," an all-beef frank so plump it's hard to remove it from its cartoon-covered box. After a meal of hot dogs, fries, burgers (try the delicious, double-decker "Whoopercheesie") and "Supershakes" (actually not very super), expect to literally roll yourself home. *6363 N Milwaukee Ave at Devon Ave (773-763-0660). Bus: 56A North Milwaukee, 91 Austin. Lunch, dinner. Average main course: $5.*

☺ **Tempo** Somewhere along the line, this unassuming Gold Coast diner picked up a few celebrity endorsements and became a destination for locals and tourists alike. Is it worth dealing with the mobs on the weekend? Well, we don't know

Model train Silver Palm's owners nailed down the dining car theme.

The hole picture Donuts and coffee are signature staples at Lou Mitchell's.

another place that serves egg skillets like this. Portions are enormous, the eggs are soft and fluffy, and they're served with thick, doughy slices of Texas toast. So if you're into that—or equally massive plates of pancakes and French toast—go for it. *6 E Chestnut St at State St (312-943-4373). El: Red to Chicago. Bus: 22 (24hrs), 36, 66 (24hrs). Breakfast, lunch, dinner. Average main course: $7.*

B ☉ Toast Brave enough to fight the crowds at this adorable brunch spot? Bring a snack, it'll be awhile before you eat. But as fans have found, the cobb salad sandwiches, buckwheat-blueberry pancakes and decadent French toasts (an "orgy" puts three varieties on one plate) are worth the wait. *2046 N Damen Ave at Dickens Ave (773-772-5600). El: Blue to Western. Bus: 49 (24hrs), 50, 73. Breakfast, brunch, lunch. Average main course: $9.* ● *Additional location at 746 W Webster Ave (773-935-5600).*

★ **B ☉ Twisted Spoke** When you begin brunch by showing your ID at the door, you know you're in the right place for a Bloody Mary. Spicy and sweet, garnished with salami and completed with a beer back, it's practically a meal in itself. Don't let that distract you from the food, however. Breakfast tacos are a good way to spice up your egg intake. And the Spoke's signature "fatboy" burgers are thick, juicy and perfectly tender. *501 N Ogden Ave at Grand Ave (312-666-1500). El: Blue to Grand. Bus: 8, 9, 65. Brunch (Sat, Sun), lunch, dinner. Average main course: $8.*

☉ **U Lucky Dawg** See Ice cream/sweets for review.

▼ ☉ **Vegetarian Fun Foods Supreme** See Vegetarian for review.

▼ (✷ ☉ **The Wiener's Circle** The sassy hot dog girls behind the counter at this classic roadside shack have had

enough of drunk yuppies' crap. Enough so that they've developed their own brand of smack-talking that's now synonymous with a late-night dog run here. Get your Chicago red hot with the traditional fixings—mustard, onion, neon green relish, pickle spear, tomato, celery salt and sport peppers—an order of thick-cut fries and a big, fat lemonade. If meat's not your thing, don't worry—they've got veggie burgers on-hand, too, pansy-ass. *2622 N Clark St between Wrightwood Ave and Drummond Pl (773-477-7444). El: Brown, Purple (rush hrs) to Diversey. Bus: 22 (24hrs), 36, 76. Lunch, dinner. Average hot dog: $2.50.*

▼ ✷ **B Winston's Market Everyday** When we don't have time to cook, the idea of stopping someplace where we can have healthy, inspired meals is consoling. For this, Winston's is a good choice. Sandwiches are a bright spot—turkey and fig compote with blue cheese and grilled chicken with smoked Gouda on pretzel roll stand out. A rotating selection of prepared foods like beet salad with goat cheese and a savory bread pudding with bacon and caramelized onions stand up to other gourmet markets. *3440 N Southport Ave between Roscoe St and Newport Ave (773-327-6400). Bus: 9 Ashland, 152 Addison. Brunch (Sat, Sun), lunch, dinner. Average main course: $12.*

Wolfy's In the pantheon of Chicago hot-dog stands, Wolfy's deserves a seat on the dais. The room is sparkling clean and the staff is sweet—think of it as the anti–Wiener's Circle. Though it offers a lot more, take a cue from the iconic signage that features an impaled hot dog on a sparkling fork and stick to the sausages. The Vienna Beef char-grilled Polish is near-perfect, but it's Wolfy's hot dog, one of the best in the city, that will make even the most jaded hot-dog eater smile. *2734 W Peterson Ave at Fairfield Ave (773-743-0207). Bus: 11, 84, 93. Lunch, dinner. Average main course: $3.50.* ■

Pretty little things Lula Café roasts baby beets and serves them with mini toasted brioche sandwiches.

Contemporary American

See also: *Classic American, Eclectic, French, Italian*

Aigre Doux *2007 Eat Out Award, Critics' Pick: The You-Scream-We-Scream Best Ice Cream Award (honeycomb ice cream)* If you've heard conflicting reports about this restaurant from husband-and-wife team Mohammad Islam and Malika Ameen, they're probably all true. But don't give up on the place. The last time we ate there the oxtail ravioli exploded with juicy meat, the seared turbot came with an addictive pile of buttery "melted" baby leeks, and the ice cream practically put us into a coma—that's just how creamy and luscious it was. The more you put off going, the better it's likely to be—but the harder it will be to get a reservation. *230 W Kinzie St between Wells and Franklin Sts (312-329-9400). El: Brown, Purple (rush hrs) to Merchandise Mart. Bus: 65, 125, 156. Lunch, dinner. Average main course: $28.*

★ **Alinea** *2007 Eat Out Award, Critics' Pick: Best chemistry experiment (Hot Potato, Cold Potato); Readers' Choice: Best upscale dining Gourmet* magazine anointed Alinea the No. 1 restaurant in the country. What's all the fuss? Chef/mastermind Grant Achatz serves food the likes of which you've never seen. Sit back and enjoy the show, a well-orchestrated ride that plays with textures, temperatures and notions of "normal" cuisine, while somehow remaining grounded in season, flavor and flawless execution. Past menu stunners have included squab with peppercorn custard, sorrel and strawberries) and "Hot Potato, Cold Potato:" a warm potato ball skewered on a thin needle with pieces of black truffle, parmesan, chive and butter over a translucent bowl of chilled potato soup. But you never know what dish will steal the show when you're in the audience. *1723 N Halsted St between North Ave and Willow St (312-867-0110). El: Red to North/Clybourn. Bus: 8 Halsted, 72 North. Dinner (Wed–Sun). Average degustation: $125.*

★ **Avec** *2007 Eat Out Award, Readers' Choice: Best small-plates spot* Owner Donnie Madia and chef Paul Kahan's tiny space looks like a sauna, has communal seating, doesn't take reservations and is loud as hell. But it is also the must-eat spot for foodies in the know. Small mainstays like chorizo-stuffed dates and salty brandade are unbeatable. Wood oven–roasted curried pork shoulder with sweet dumpling squash and housemade smoked–black-pepper pasta tossed with garlic sausage, cavolo nero and shaved Parmesan, are other favorites, but the menu changes with the season. You'll like Kahan's picks, no matter the time of year. *615 W Randolph St between Jefferson and Desplaines Sts (312-377-2002). El: Green to Clinton. Bus: 56 Milwaukee, 125 Water Tower Exp. Dinner. Average small plate: $10.*

★ ▼ **Avenues** Chef Graham Elliot Bowles dishes up some culinary magic at this restaurant in the Peninsula Hotel, but he's a bit more grounded and seasonal than the whimsical chef-wizards with whom he is compared. On his ever-changing seasonal menu, he pairs spring peas with grilled Meyer-lemon rind and eucalyptus marshmallows; wild king salmon confit with crispy pork belly and merlot risotto; and red and golden beets with hazelnut brittle and Roquefort foam. The formal dining room glows golden with a view of the Mag Mile below—a perfect setting to splurge, sit back and let the sumptuous experience unfold. *108 E Superior St between Rush St and Michigan Ave (312-573-6754). El: Red to Chicago. Bus: 3, X3, 4 (24hrs) X4, 10, 26, 125, 144, 145, 146, 147, 151 (24hrs). Dinner (Tue–Sat). Average degustation: $70.*

★ **Backstage Bistro** This culinary student–operated restaurant in the Illinois Institute of Art surprised us with every course. An heirloom-tomato salad offset the bright, juicy tomatoes with three flavored goat cheeses. Pan-roasted chicken came with a distinctly Southern slant, paired with warm corn fritters, a peppery barbecue sauce and smoky Hoppin' John (a mixture of pork and black-eyed peas). And just in case we ever worried about the next generation of Chicago chefs, the supermoist citrus cake and miniature cookies are the proof we need that the future looks very bright. *180 N Wabash Ave between Benton Pl and Lake St (312-777-7800). El: Brown, Green, Orange, Pink, Purple (rush hrs) to Randolph. Bus: 3, 4 (24hrs), X4, 10, 26, 143, 144, 145, 146, 147, 151 (24hrs). Lunch. Average main course: $11.*

Bandera A mega-rotisserie serves as the heart and hearth of this cozy Mag Mile restaurant, where the simple, quality American food has a dash of Tex-Mex flavor. Rotisserie chicken and lamb find their way into many of the oversized sandwiches and salads. It's popular with the suits during lunch, and in the evening tired shoppers looking for a substantial dinner stop in for a meal that won't challenge their palates or their purses. The veggie burger is a favorite of vegetarians and carnivores alike. *535 N Michigan Ave, second floor between Grand Ave and Ohio St (312-644-3524). El: Red to Grand. Bus: 3, 65, 145, 146, 147, 151 (24hrs), 157. Lunch, dinner. Average main course: $20.*

(♿ **B Bella Lounge** Chef Brian Jupiter has come up with a menu of upscale bar snacks for his heavily sequined clientele of celebrities, celebrity wanna-bes and celebrity stalkers. His beef tenderloin skewers could be something out of T.G.I. Friday's if they weren't so tenderly prepared. His thin-crust buffalo-chicken pizza, while tasty, can't escape that stigma. But Jupiter's game is elevated with his "tuna two ways:" tangy tartare and a seared filet on a bed of risotto sweetened with corn and lobster. Yet no matter how good the food is, the cocktails will never be worth $14. *1212 N State Pkwy between Division and Scott Sts (312-787-9405). El: Red to Clark/Division. Bus: 22 (24hrs), 36, 70, 156. Dinner. Average main course: $25.*

★ ▼ (B ❋ ⊕ **bin wine café** *2007 Eat Out Award, Critics' Pick: Best new cooking "show" (watching the action from the back counter)* Sometimes great things come in small packages. That's the idea behind this cozy storefront by the folks behind BIN 36, where the focus is on wine—36 are offered by the glass—and chef John Caputo's global cuisine. Nab a seat at the back counter for a perfect view of all the slicing, dicing and plating going on in the open kitchen. Then, get a load of the dinner menu, which is full of hard-to-resist seasonal plates, such as slow-roasted pork ribs with blood-orange barbecue sauce and pan-roasted mahi mahi with sweet potatoes. It's the brunch that's really making us fat, though. With must-trys like chocolate-chip pancakes, housemade granola, and blue crab–and–spinach quiche,

you'll probably be too full to eat dinner. *1559 N Milwaukee Ave between Honore St and North Ave (773-486-2233). El: Blue to Damen. Bus: 50, 56, 72. Brunch (Sat, Sun), dinner. Average small plate: $13.*

★ ▼ ✳ **Blackbird** *2007 Eat Out Award, Readers' Choice: Best midscale dining* Paul Kahan's James Beard Award–winning, minimalist chic restaurant is as popular as ever, with chef Mike Sheerin (from NYC's WD-50) feeding the way too-cool-for-school crowd and pastry chef Tim Dahl (formerly of Naha) indulging their sweet tooth. You'll find evidence of the duo's handiwork at this creative, contemporary stunner in dishes like crispy veal sweetbreads and cool Meyer-lemon mousse flanked by nibs of dehydrated olive, fennel and grapefruit bits. *619 W Randolph St between Jefferson and Desplaines Sts (312-715-0708). El: Green to Clinton. Bus: 8, 56, 125. Lunch (Mon–Fri), dinner (Mon–Sat) (closed Sun). Average main course: $28.*

★ **Bluprint** Blue Plate Catering has the first full-service restaurant in the Merch Mart, with a focus on highly stylized design and eclectic cuisine. Power lunchers should opt for shortrib potstickers followed by a pulled pork sandwich topped with housemade bread-and-butter pickles. For dinner, dig into the hamachi tartare-topped banana cake with cinnamon-soy emulsion. Also try any of the fish on offer (the kitchen does well with seafood); pancetta-dotted polenta, greens and violet mustard keep things interesting. Same for the potent cocktails, and slick bar and lounge menu of small bites. *222 Merchandise Mart Plaza, suite 135, at Wells St (312-410-9800). El: Brown, Purple (rush hrs) to Merchandise Mart. Bus: 65, 125, 156. Lunch (Mon–Fri), dinner (Mon–Sat). Average main course: $24.*

★ ✳ **BOKA** Giuseppe Tentori, a Trotter's alum with a gentler, more sophisticated touch, works magic at this Lincoln Park hot spot. Succulent salmon, paired with green tea–infused soba noodles, stands out, followed closely by the tender veal cheeks and the duck breast flanked by herb-packed semolina gnocchi. Dessert fans can indulge in pastry chef Leticia Zenteno's famous cookie plates. *1729 N Halsted St between North Ave and Willow St (312-337-6070). El: Red to North/Clybourn. Bus: 8 Halsted, 72 North. Dinner. Average main course: $24.*

B ⊙ **Bongo Room** Hungover rock stars, early-rising soccer moms and everybody in between seem to flock to this bright, cheery spot for fancy morning cocktails and a hearty bite. Some dishes are worth the often-very-long wait. The chocolate tower French toast—no doubt the menu's piece de resistance—is a creamy, luxurious pile of chocolate bread smothered in what is essentially melted banana crème brûlée. It's definitely more dessert than breakfast, but sweet tooths won't complain. *1470 N Milwaukee Ave between Evergreen Ave and Honore St (773-489-0690). El: Blue to Damen. Bus: 50, 56, 72. Breakfast (Mon–Fri), brunch (Sat, Sun), lunch (Mon–Fri). Average main course: $10.* ● *Additional location at 1152 S Wabash Ave (312-291-0100).*

★ BYOB ✳ **Bonsoiree** After trying to be a combination take-out shop, grocery and restaurant, this tiny gem finally put the focus on what it does best: dinner. Case in point: a $20 three-course tasting menu. Pick a first course such as an asparagus-and-oyster-mushroom salad with vanilla-guava vinaigrette, an entrée such as pan-roasted Hawaiian moonfish with braised taro root or Grand Marnier–seared salmon, and finish with the signature banana-bread pudding. Want more? Sign up to get invited to the Saturday-night "Underground Dinner Parties," where select guests get an exclusive five-course dinner for around $50. *2728 W*

Be my honey Honeycomb ice cream makes for a sweet ending at Aigre Doux.

Armitage Ave at Fairfield Ave (773-486-7511). El: Blue to California. Bus: 52 Kedzie/California, 73 Armitage. Dinner (closed Sun, Mon). Average main course: $11.

Butter Chef Lee Wolen, a Moto alum, took the reigns at Butter's kitchen, turning this hip night spot into a chic eatery with dishes that are lighter and brighter than those for which the restaurant was once known. Expect small plate creations such as a maple glazed pork belly, seasonal risotto (such as asparagus) and crab salad. In addition to fabulous wine lists, sample the martini, vodka and champagne flights. Desserts like the coffee-glazed donuts with chocolate-banana pot au crème, however, show Wolen can be just as indulgent as the next chef. *130 S Green St between Adams and Monroe Sts (312-666-9813). Bus: 8 Halsted, 20 Madison (24hrs). Dinner (closed Sun). Average main course: $28.*

▼ **Café Absinthe** A decade ago, it was considered daring to venture down the alley into this restaurant's almost hidden entrance. Now that the neighborhood is fully gentrified, it's a little harder to snag a table on weekends. What hasn't changed is the cuisine: simple, seasonal ingredients brought together without too much fuss. Duck breast is moist inside, crisp outside and comes with tasty duck confit ravioli on a bed of caramelized onions, wilted arugula and Asian mushrooms. *1954 W North Ave between Winchester and Damen Aves (773-278-4488). El: Blue to Damen. Bus: 50, 56, 72. Dinner. Average main course: $24.*

▼ BYOB ✳ B **Café Too** As part of the Inspiration Corporation's 13-week program (the same group that runs Inspiration Café), refugees and the recently homeless shadow paid pros at this full-service, contemporary American restaurant. They'll be gaining experience and a city-issued food service and sanitation certificate, working toward a fresh start on life, but chef Jenny Urban is making sure you don't just visit once as a charitable good deed. Baked goods and coffee kick-start your day; brunch brings omelettes and more; lunch features global belly-fillers like curried-chicken–

Wonder dome Sepia casts its diners in a cool glow.

salad sandwiches; and the dinner crowd gets classics like chicken roulade with wild rice. *4715 N Sheridan Rd between Lakeside Place and Leland Ave (773-275-0626). El: Red to Lawrence. Bus: 81 (24hrs), 145, 151 (24hrs). Breakfast (Mon–Fri), brunch (Sat, Sun), lunch (Tue–Fri), dinner (Thu–Sat). Average main course: $13.*

Caliterra Chef Anthony Scelzo's playful Tuscan-influenced menus are updated monthly and are marked by his dedication to incorporating organic produce and other seasonal ingredients with fresh seafood and meat. The amber-tinted dining room, which resides inside the Wyndham Hotel, owes much of its elegance to the tables readied with bright, starched linens and caramel-colored wood chairs that match the large exposed ceiling beams overhead. *633 N St. Clair St between Ontario and Erie Sts (312-274-4444). El: Red to Grand. Bus: 2, 3, X4, 10, 26, 65, 143, 144, 145, 146, 147, 151 (24hrs), 157. Breakfast, lunch, dinner. Average main course: $25.*

★ ▼ **Charlie Trotter's** Trotter remains one of the best chefs in the country, proving nightly that not only did he train the younger talent in town, but he can still school them. À la carte doesn't exist here, so go full throttle with the impeccable, contemporary eight-course tasting menu and tack on wine pairings; this team hits them out of the park. A vegetable-focused (but not vegetarian) tasting menu and nonalcoholic beverage pairing are also on offer for you health nuts. *816 W Armitage Ave between Halsted and Dayton Sts (773-248-6228). El: Brown, Purple (rush hrs) to Armitage. Bus: 8 Halsted, 73 Armitage. Dinner (Tue–Sat). Average degustation: $125.*

▼ ✻ **Chef's Station** Train enthusiasts and kitsch lovers will adore the ultracutesy decor of this restaurant in the Davis Metra station: The flatware and napkins are tucked into jeans pockets; diners sit in armchairs; and copper pipes serve as light fixtures. We groaned, but once we looked at the wine list (handily categorized by flavor profile) and tried some dishes (don't miss the rich goat cheese–and–artichoke tart or the velvety braised short ribs with blackberry-mint sauce), we would have been on board even if our server wore engineer's overalls and gave us our change from his belt. *915 Davis St, Evanston (847-570-9821). El: Purple to Davis. Bus: 93, 205, 206, Pace 208, Pace 212, Pace 213. Dinner (closed Mon). Average main course: $25.*

BYOB **CHIC Café** Students at CHIC (Cooking & Hospitality Institute of Chicago) test out their chops here, both in the kitchen and in the dining room. But trust us, CHIC Café ain't no standard lunchroom. Most still need to practice their waitressing skills, but the menu rarely disappoints. And, because the students are still learning the ropes, the meal's always a bargain. *Cooking and Hospitality Institute of Chicago, 361 W Chestnut St at Orleans St (312-873-2032). El: Red to Chicago. Bus: 66 Chicago (24hrs). Breakfast, lunch, dinner (closed Sat–Sun). Average main course: $20.*

★ ✻ **copperblue** *2007 Eat Out Award, Critics' Pick: The Stick-It-to-the-Man Award ("duck liver," a.k.a. foie gras)* Chef-owners Michael Tsonton and Victor Newgren keep their atmosphere and service down-to-earth. The pair also have a sense of humor: their "duck liver" dish ("It Isn't Foie Gras Any Moore" is a poke at Alderman Joe Moore, who authored Chicago's foie ban. First and second courses are now divided into "Work" (featuring "humble" dishes such as roasted pork shoulder and grilled shrimp with blue crab salad) and "Play" ("whimsical and fun" dishes like organic duck two ways and braised rabbit empanadas). But if you're all business (or all play), don't worry: A database keeps track of customers' likes and dislikes, ensuring that the experience is tailored to your preferences. *580 E Illinois St, Lake Point Tower (Illinois Ave entrance) (312-527-1200). Bus: 2, 3, 29, 65, 66 (24hrs), 124. Lunch, dinner (closed Mon). Average main course: $26.*

▼ **Crofton on Wells** Hopefully, Suzy Crofton likes the clean, contemporary look of her restaurant, because as owner, manager, sommelier and chef, she spends a lot of time here. Her seasonal American cooking has inspired a couple of dishes that regulars won't let her take off the menu, like the jumbo lump crabmeat crab cake and the smoked-apple chutney–topped Gunthorp Farms pork belly. But for spring she's managed to sneak in some new cultworthy dishes, such as halibut cheeks with pickled ramps, Kobe skirt steak with Tuscan bread salad and a smoked-salmon tartare with American sturgeon caviar. *535 N Wells St between Grand Ave and Ohio St (312-755-1790). El: Red to Grand. Bus: 65 Grand, 125 Water Tower Exp. Dinner (closed Sun). Average main course: $23.*

▼ ✻ **B Deleece** There's new life being breathed into this Lakeview standby. Gone is the artwork that gave the place its outdated, *Blossom*-style funkiness; in its place is a new awning, new logo and a newfound sleekness. Even the comfort food manages to branch out: Salmon is given an Asian treatment by plating it over black sticky rice and a rack of lamb is stuffed with creamy cambozola. *4004 N Southport Ave between Irving Park Rd and Cuyler Ave (773-325-1710). El: Brown to Irving Park, Red to Sheridan. Bus: 9, 22 (24hrs), 80, X80. Brunch (Sat, Sun), lunch (Tues–Fri), dinner. Average main course: $16.*

★ ☉ **Dodo** *2007 Eat Out Award, Critics' Pick: Best chef to wake up to (Kim Dalton)* Since this folk art–plastered café decided to expand into nights, recent dinner specials have included zucchini purée with bacon; pan-seared tilapia with tea-smoked tomato sauce, fresh corn and fried plantains; and seasonal desserts like mango kulfi, a combination of frozen cream and mangoes served with raspberry and mango purées. Still, we return for the breakfast standbys that got us hooked in the first place, including the veggie-packed tofu scramble and the thick Greek yogurt topped with housemade granola and berries. *935 N Damen Ave at Walton St (773-772-3636). Bus: 50 Damen, 66 Chicago (24hrs). Breakfast, lunch, dinner (Mon–Fri). Average main course: $7.*

Read 'em & eat

emulsion liquids blended together to form a thick, silky sauce (think: oil+vinegar=vinaigrette)

foam an ingredient that has been liquefied, mixed with gelatin and dispensed through a whipped-cream canister

heirloom native, nonhybrid fruits and veggies grown by replanting seeds year to year

sous vide (soo VEED) a process of cooking vacuum-sealed food in a low-temperature water bath, a technique said to better preserve the food's natural flavor and texture

sweetbreads a delicacy made with veal, lamb or pork pancreas or thymus glands, usually fried or sautéed

♦ Entourage on American Lane *2007 Eat Out Award, Readers' Choice: Best suburban restaurant* The dramatic two-story steel-and-mahogany entryway is the first hint you're in for something big. With the exception of the cocktail waitresses' skirts, everything here is huge. A virtual mountain of calamari is served Asian-style with a light hoisin–serrano chili coating, and a tender lavender-and-honey–glazed pork chop is four inches thick, yet perfectly cooked. With desserts like the triple-chocolate cake—served in two ginormous wedges with housemade raspberry sauce and a petite dollop of whip cream—it's easy to see why doggy bags here are full-size shopping bags. We needed two. *1301 American Ln, Schaumburg (847-995-9400). Brunch (Sun), lunch (Mon–Fri), dinner. Average main course: $28.*

▼ ✳ B Fiddlehead Café Traces of Square Kitchen, which used to occupy this space, can be found in this new joint's brunch—which is just as dependable (and boring) as ever. Dinner, however, is a different story: Chef Robert Levitt's quail, paired with housemade chorizo and sweet dates, arrived beautifully golden brown and perfectly juicy, and his slow-roasted Berkshire pork fell apart the moment it met a fork. It's clear that Fiddlehead is serious about its food—which is a lot more than we can say about its predecessor. *4600 N Lincoln Ave at Wilson Ave (773-751-1500). El: Brown to Western. Bus: 11, 49 (24hrs), X49. Brunch (Sat, Sun), dinner. Average main course: $17.*

Fixture Fixture is a small plates place with a big appetite. The tapas-style dishes include Prince Edward Island Mussels sautéed with *guajillo* peppers, garlic, shallots and white wine and a dessert of cinnamon donuts complemented by an apple cider shooter. The entrée-sized items like beer-battered fish and chips and hanger steak with crab, asparagus, fingerling

Attention to detail
Guiseppe Tentori creates edible art at Boka.

potatoes and béarnaise fill bigger appetites. The cozy environs are perfect for date night...or look-for-your-next-date night. *2706 N Ashland Ave between Wrightwood Ave and Diversey Pkwy (773-248-3331). Bus: 9 Ashland, 76 Diversey. Dinner (closed Mon). Average small plate: $9.*

✳ Green Dolphin Street Eating in this quasi-fancy dining room gets you free admission into the adjoining jazz club, but there's no reason why dinner here shouldn't be an attraction all by itself. Chef Hal Lascano takes his work seriously. Silky strips of smoky salmon and tender, pan-roasted scallops are a good way to start, and his Asian-influenced tuna, brushed with a soy glaze and plated on vermicelli noodles, is a delicious second act. But it's really the world-class wine list, which has a fair share of bottles around $30, that steals the show. *2200 N Ashland Ave at Webster Ave (773-395-0066). Bus: 9 Ashland, 74 Fullerton. Dinner (Wed–Sat) (closed Sun–Tue). Average main course: $27.*

▼ Green Zebra See Vegetarian for review.

✳ The Grill on the Alley If the plethora of newspaper clippings in the lobby are any indication, this import from Beverly Hills was *the* restaurant in 2000. Now that the buzz (and, as a result, the crowds) has died down, the effect is just the opposite: You can sink into one of the roomy leather booths, put down a few well-executed classic cocktails, tear into a citrus-marinated skirt steak (or, if you're feeling a little heart-healthy, the cedar-planked barbecue salmon) and relax, knowing that nobody will ever find you. *909 N Michigan Ave at Delaware Pl (312-255-9009). El: Red to Chicago. Bus: 143, 144, 145, 146, 147, 151 (24hrs). Breakfast, lunch, dinner. Average main course: $20.*

★ ▼ BYOB B HB Home Bistro The Food Network hype surrounding the Hearty Boys has died down a little, so grab a table in this funky-cozy Boystown BYOB. Seasonal dishes from chef Joncarl Lachman might include artichoke fritters, , a bread salad with asparagus and balsamic butter that's served with pan-roasted chicken, and red-curry halibut on a bed of crawfish tails tossed with chickpeas and green beans. Sweets fiends won't want to miss the cupcake flight. *3404 N Halsted St between Roscoe St and Newport Ave (773-661-0299). El: Brown, Purple (rush hrs), Red to Belmont. Bus: 8, 22 (24hrs), 77 (24hrs), 135, 145. Brunch (Sat, Sun), dinner (Wed–Sun). Average main course: $16.*

❨ Hop Haus Riding on the growing appreciation for craft beers, the owners have invested heavily in fantastic beer pairings for each of the 20 burgers on offer. The burgers themselves are mediocre (although the ground lamb patty with feta, cukes and smashed kalamatas is mighty tasty) and the dining room is corporate-feeling. But with cocktails from stellar (though already departed) mixologist John Kinder, 25 great bottles under $35 and the best beer list in River North, we'll deal with a few missteps. *646 N Franklin St between Erie and Ontario Sts (312-467-4287). El: Brown, Purple (rush hrs) to Chicago. Bus: 65 Grand, 66 Chicago (24hrs). Lunch, dinner. Average main course: $11.*

★ ▼ B HotChocolate *2007 Eat Out Award, Readers' Choice: Best desserts* Don't let the name fool you—it's not just desserts here; the seasonal, savory menu is just as tempting. Seasonal dinner highlights include a hearty steak salad and brined, bone-in pork chop with sautéed spaetzle and porkbelly with braised endive. Eat up, of course, but leave room for dessert: owner/pastry chef Mindy Segal whips up perfection ranging from the Black and Tan (that would be a drink of hot chocolate and hot fudge layered together) and seasonal offerings such as her "Thoughts On Cherries," a

Contemporary American

Nice stack Chef Koren Grieveson works magic via clever combinations at Avec.

tasting plate of the fruit done four ways. *1747 N Damen Ave at Willow St (773-489-1747). El: Blue to Damen. Bus: 50 Damen, 56, 73 Armitage. Brunch (Sat, Sun), lunch (Tue–Fri), dinner (closed Mon). Average main course: $14.*

▼ ✳ B **Jane's** This crowded neighborhood favorite's menu changes seasonally, with an emphasis on locally grown ingredients, and the results are typically good. The goat cheese, vegetable and tofu burrito isn't something you'll find elsewhere, and the burger with grilled onions and bacon is one of the best around. Don't bother with the pasta dishes—you can do just as well at home. Brunch favorites include the banana-nut-bread French toast and the apple and apricot pancakes. Plan ahead: Service can be spotty. *1655 W Cortland St between Marshfield and Hermitage Aves (773-862-5263). Bus: 9 Ashland, 73 Armitage. Brunch (Sat, Sun), lunch (Mon–Fri), dinner. Average main course: $17.*

▼ ✳ **Karyn's Cooked** See Vegetarian for review.

(**La Pomme Rouge** Chef Jeffrey Mauro isn't a stranger to contemporary American cooking: He tops his house-baked English muffins with scrambled eggs, caviar and potato-bacon foam; pairs Amish chicken breast with a lone tortellini stuffed with a creamy mixture of foie gras and shallots and infuses spicy ginger into the tapioca that arrives with the pear tart. It's solid—if slightly precious—food, creative and for the most part perfectly delightful to eat. Pity, then, that since this place has more satin and silk than a upscale 19th-century brothel, it will always be outshadowed by the decor. *108 W Kinzie St between Clark and LaSalle Sts (312-245-9555). El: Brown, Purple to Merchandise Mart. Bus: 11, 125, 156. Dinner (closed Sun). Average main course: $17.*

★ ▼ ✳ B **Lula Café** This funky restaurant has one of our favorite seasonally driven menus. For a sunny brunch or breakfast, vie for a seat at a small table indoors or on the sidewalk cafe, where planters spill over with the same herbs you'll find in your eggs Florentine or red-pepper strata. Local organic eggs and sausage pair perfectly with the black sambal Bloody Mary or blackberry Bellini. At night, expect dishes like artichoke-and-Meyer-lemon soup with a dollop of caviar and bits of roasted squab breast for added interest or raw striped marlin with pickled ramps. *2537 N Kedzie Blvd between Linden Pl and Logan Blvd (773-489-9554). El: Blue to Logan Square. Bus: 56 Milwaukee, 74 Fullerton. Breakfast, brunch (Sat, Sun), lunch, dinner (closed Tue). Average main course: $13.*

★ ▼ ✳ B **Magnolia Café** Exposed brick walls and black-and-white photography give this casual, contemporary café the feeling of an unpretentious gallery. The straightforward approach carries through to the food, where a range of flavors are done well. Menu items change based on what's in season, but this neighborhood eatery always gets it right with possibilities like grilled shrimp over lemon-chive-sweet-pea risotto and miso black cod with a zippy lemongrass-ginger reduction. Don't worry about hailing a cab home—the staff will call you one, and shake a mean nightcap for you while you wait. *1224 W Wilson Ave between Racine and Magnolia Aves (773-728-8785). El: Red to Wilson. Bus: 22 (24hrs), 36, 78, 145, 148. Brunch (Sun), dinner (Tue–Sun), (closed Mon). Average main course: $18.*

★ ▼ **May Street Market** Chef-owner Alex Cheswick makes standout dishes like pistachio-crusted venison and lemongrass-carrot soup studded with black mussels. The bar menu shows off Cheswick's talent with burgers (a trio

At ease Parrot Cage makes sure diners are nice and comfortable.

offers tastes of the duck, beef and venison versions) as well as some shareable noshes, such as his blue-cornmeal calamari and a Spanish and American cheese plate—both of which should make that wait for a table more tolerable. *1132 W Grand Ave at May St (312-421-5547). El: Blue to Grand. Bus: 8, 9 (24hrs), X9, 65. Lunch (Mon–Fri), dinner (closed Sun). Average main course: $27.*

▼ ✳ **B Meritage Café and Wine Bar** Even after all its years as a cozy wine bar with better-than-average food, this spot still manages to seem insidery. The all-American wine list is packed with perfect pairings (all available by the glass) for the signature menu of French-American favorites like crab cakes, raw oysters and duck confit. Seasonal flavors show up randomly—white asparagus with the halibut, spring garlic with the pork loin—and the brunch menu is consistently droolworthy. Choices include biscuits with boar-bacon gravy, banana-chocolate French toast, peppered skirt steak with eggs, and eggs Benedict with spicy *capocollo* and poached shrimp. *2118 N Damen Ave at Charleston St (773-235-6434). El: Blue to Western. Bus: 49 (24hrs), 50, 73. Brunch (Sat–Sun), dinner. Average main course: $26.*

★ ▼ **mk** Chef Erick Simmons keeps season at the forefront at Michael Kornick's upscale American spot. The rotating roster of menu items might include roasted rack of Berkshire pork with grilled radicchio and panzanella salad, or housemade fettucine with tomato, basil and Parmigiano-Reggiano cheese. Not hungry for a full meal? Stop in for a classy nightcap in the beautiful dining room and one of the deceptively simple desserts like amaretto zabaglione with raspberry jam, seedling fruit raspberries and an almond biscotti. *868 N Franklin St at Chestnut St (312-482-9179).*

El: Brown, Purple (rush hrs) to Chicago. Bus: 66 Chicago (24hrs), 156 LaSalle. Dinner. Average main course: $28.

Moto The buzz on chef Homaro Cantu has been reaching fever pitch: He's working with the government to "end world hunger" with edible paper, cooking with military-issued lasers. But what's going on in the mad scientist's restaurant? More of the same, and always something new. It's anybody's guess what the night's tasting menu holds, but current trickery includes a play on Vietnamese egg-drop soup in which frozen egg- and microgreen-pellets are dropped tableside into steaming soup, and triple-seared beef is paired with "caramelaserized wine." Yes, a laser is involved in a wine pairing. *945 W Fulton Mkt between Sangamon and Morgan Sts (312-491-0058). El: Blue to Grand. Bus: 8 Halsted, 65 Grand. Dinner (Tue–Sat). Average degustation: $100.*

★ ✳ **Naha** Chef Carrie Nahabedian delivers an upscale experience minus the pomp, courtesy of a snazzy room, great service and a seasonal menu that reads like a who's who in regional, sustainable foods. (The menu changes daily.) Seasonal veggies—French wild asparagus, spring peas and sugar-snap peas—accompany the wild Copper River Alaskan salmon. The whole-roasted ranch squab and duck liver arrive with a slew of fresh picks: summer red cherries and plums, local rhubarb puree, crisp potato cake, apple mint, pink peppercorns and licorice. *500 N Clark St at Illinois St (312-321-6242). El: Red to Grand. Bus: 22 Clark (24hrs), 65 Grand. Lunch (Mon–Fri), dinner (Mon–Sat). Average main course: $30.*

▼ ✳ ◆ **B North Pond** *2007 Eat Out Award, Critics' Pick: The annual Farmers' Friend Award (Bruce Sherman)* When you're only a few feet from a pond in the middle of

Lincoln Park you are as close to nature as it gets in the city. Even more so when you sample chef Bruce Sherman's latest elevated contemporary menu that's concocted with as much locally grown organic food as the Green City Market advocate can get his hands on. Sherman's ever-changing offerings include a housemade merguez sausage link and grilled black cod with sweet-potato puree and balsamic-roasted raddichio. And although it's unlikely that you'll have anything left on your plate at meal's end, if you do, eco-conscious Sherman will make sure it gets composted. *2610 N Cannon Dr between Fullerton Pkwy and Lake Shore Dr (773-477-5845). Bus: 76, 151 (24hrs), 156. Brunch (Sun), dinner (Tue–Sun). Average main course: $30.*

Oak Park Abbey There are only a couple of ways to explain the crowd that gathers around this bar drinking cocktails and beer (despite the fact that this *is* a wine bar): Either Oak Park has a lack of good bars or everyone's here for the food. It's probably the latter. A trio of hummus is spiked with herbaceous spinach and spicy red pepper. Pizzas' cracker-like crust is a vehicle for savory flavors of onion and feta. And earthy hay-smoked beef tenderloin is smoked (yes, over hay) in the yard by the chef himself. *728 Lake St, Oak Park (708-358-8840). Dinner (closed Sun, Mon). Average small plate: $9.*

★ **one sixtyblue** Martial Noguier (our pick for most underrated chef in the city) creates contemporary French fare grounded by seasonal American products, hitting all the right buttons: sweet, sour, salty, bitter and savory. Dishes might include chilled ahi tuna tartare with mango; skatewing with puree of artichoke and a red-wine anchovy sauce; and free-range Indiana chicken flanked by tempura crayfish. Sweets like wood-oven strawberry-and-rhubarb pie are tasty endings, but we prefer to relax in the lofty dining room with a port and a cheese plate starring a hunk of America's finest, bubbling in a cast-iron crock from time spent in the wood oven. *1400 W Randolph St between Ada St and Ogden Ave (312-850-0303). El: Green to Ashland. Bus: 9 Ashland (24 hrs), 20 Madison (24hrs). Dinner (closed Sun). Average main course: $25.*

Otom This is Moto backwards—literally and figuratively—a casual take on the on the hyper-modern creative-cum-scientific restaurant that makes headlines every time it introduces a new dish. Otom is more casual and laid-back, but still not staid. Yes, there is mac and cheese on the menu, but it is andouille sausage with anise mac and cheese. You don't get the full Moto experience here, but you don't pay the full Moto prices either. *951 W Fulton Mkt between Sangamon and Morgan Sts (312-491-5804). El: Green to Clinton. Bus: 8 Halsted, 20 Madison (24hrs). Dinner. Average main course: $18.*

B ⊖ Over Easy Café *2007 Eat Out Award, Readers' Choice: Best new brunch* Ravenswood locals can wave good-bye to Toast, Orange and all those other funky brunch spots in town. Because, thanks to Jon Cignarale—himself a veteran of m. henry and Uncommon Ground—they have their own. Dishes like oversize pancakes stuffed with blackberries and topped with orange butter, eggs served "sassy" (atop chorizo hash) and spicy vegan chilaquiles (who knew tofu could be greasy?) are carried through this bright, cheery dining room by the tray-full during the busy weekend brunch. But with the good comes the bad: The wait for tables spills out onto the sidewalk. *4943 N Damen Ave between Ainslie and Argyle Sts (773-506-2605). El: Brown to Damen. Bus: 50, 81 (24hrs), 92. Breakfast (Tue–Sun), brunch (Sun), lunch (Tue–Sun). Average main course: $7.*

BYOB Parrot Cage We'll admit there's a somewhat amateurish edge to the service in this ornate dining room. But at least these servers have an excuse: They're students from Washburne Culinary Institute who are learning how to run a restaurant under the direction of chef Steven McAfee. Luckily the food makes up for any service missteps: *Frito misto de mar*—fried tilapia, calamari and shrimp—is crisp and greaseless; falafel-crusted salmon is offset perfectly by the fennel fattoush salad on which it's served; and tender braised lamb shank is rich, succulent and doubles your pleasure with two juicy lamb chops. *7059 S Shore Dr between 70th and 71st Sts (773-602-5333). Metra: Elec S Chicago to South Shore. Bus: 6, 26, 71. Dinner (Wed–Sat). Average main course: $17.*

(* **Phil and Lou's** Don't come to this classic family restaurant looking for light fare; there is little to none. What you will get is Italian-American comfort food in large portions with no frill. Pastas on offer include lobster ravioli, baked lobster macaroni and cheese and rigatoni with spicy sausage. And like any true family restaurant, Phil and Lou's offers a ribeye steak (this one's 18 ounces), brown sugar–brined pork chops and meat loaf and mashed potatoes. *1124 W Madison St at Aberdeen St (312-455-0070). Bus: 20 Madison. Dinner. Average main course: $18.*

★ (B **The Pump Room** If you're a local, you may have forgotten all about this place, or you never really had it on your radar. But this regal dining room, sparkling chandeliers and all, was once the place where celebs rubbed elbows in the Windy City. Now it is waking up and hoping to return to the top of Chicago's restaurant scene. To that end, the menu includes creative, seasonal dishes such as pan-roasted halibut with rhubarb puree, pickled ramps and candy-striped beets;

Classic combo Tomato soup and grilled cheese help diners get comfy at Fixture.

and confit of roasted salmon with avocado puree and a citrus emulsion. *1301 N State Pkwy at Goethe St (312-266-0360). El: Red to Clark/Division. Bus: 22 (24hrs), 36, 70. Breakfast, brunch (Sun), lunch (Mon–Sat), dinner. Average main course: $26.*

★ ✳ **Rhapsody** With its built-in clientele of symphony fans, this place could get away with subpar food and rushed "preshow" meal deals. Luckily, it doesn't, so you don't have to be down with Mahler to be down with its new seasonal menu. Appetizers like orange-infused Peking-duck gnocchi and cured yellowfin tuna make choosing what to eat here difficult; entrées like oven-roasted spring rack of lamb with caramelized artichokes don't help matters. And as if giving the Loop a decent place to dine weren't sweet enough, the roasted hazelnut–and–pineapple cake is. *65 E Adams St between Wabash and Michigan Aves (312-786-9911). El: Red to Chicago, Orange, Pink, Purple (rush hrs) to Adams. Bus: 1, 7, X28, 126, 151. Lunch, dinner. Average main course: $22.*

▼ **Ritz-Carlton Café** The Dining Room has ended its era (banquets and private affairs may still be held there), so chef Mark Payne has shifted his focus to the Café. Winners abound on the menu: Roasted Vidalia onion soup is sweet from caramelized onions and rich from beef shank braised in the broth,and there's a fantastic ricotta gnocchi tossed in duck *ragù* with briny olives and aged pecorino shards. Compared to these gems, desserts are a bit lackluster. Ingredients are top notch and execution is nearly flawless, but it's the high prices that keep us from making the Café a regular spot. *160 E Pearson St between Michigan Ave and Mies van der Rohe Way (312-573-5223). El: Red to Chicago. Bus: 3, 4 (24hrs), X4, 10, 26, 125, 143, 144, 145, 146, 147, 151 (24hrs). Breakfast, lunch, dinner. Average degustation: $75.*

(✳ **B Rockit Bar & Grill** Most of the guys who go to this sporty, sceney homage to stainless steel don't seem to care what the food tastes like—it's more of a tits and beer thing for them. But if they'd pay attention, they'd find that most of the menu is much better than the chewy, cardboardish pizzas. As counter-intuitive as it may seem, the antibar food is where the gems are, like the mildly spicy braised lamb lettuce wraps and the perfectly golden roasted chicken. *22 W Hubbard St between State and Dearborn Sts (312-645-6000). El: Red to Grand. Bus: 29, 36, 65. Brunch (Sun), lunch, dinner. Average main course: $17.*

★ ▼ **BYOB Schwa** *2007 Eat Out Award, Critics' Pick: Best head-scratcher (black truffle–buffalo milk shake with bittersweet chocolate cake)* Fewer than 30 diners can fit in this tiny storefront restaurant at one time and all of them must have had reservations weeks in advance. The menu is more of a suggestion: Schwa serves what it wants and doesn't get into too many descriptions of what those dishes are. But as a 2006 *Food & Wine* best new chef, chef-owner Michael Carlson is allowed to call the shots. Let him. You may be treated to a take on pad thai, with marinated slivers of jellyfish standing in for noodles, or zucchini pudding topped with naan puree, rosewater-pickled cucumbers and hummus-stuffed zucchini flowers. But the most stunning dish we tried blended buffalo ricotta with house-made black-truffle ice cream for an earthy milk shake, a perfect complement to a moist slab of bittersweet Venezuelan chocolate cake. *1466 N Ashland Ave at Le Moyne St (773-252-1466). El: Blue to Division. Bus: 9 (24hrs), 50, 70. Dinner (closed Sun, Mon). Average degustation: $75.*

♨ **Seasons Restaurant** Far above the hustle and bustle of Michigan Avenue lies the serene tranquility and decadence that is Seasons. Chef Kevin Hickey's creative dishes might include garden pea and young coconut bisque with Vietnamese mint Prosciutto dumplings and roast Colorado lamb served with grilled Greek lamb sausage,feta gnocchi and kalamata olive jus. It's the stuff power lunches and dinners are made of, but Seasons makes an effort to be family-friendly, too, with children's and tween menus for proper little ladies and gents. *Four Seasons Hotel, 120 E Delaware Pl between Michigan Ave and Rush St (312-649-2349). El: Red to Chicago. Bus: 10, 143, 144, 145, 146, 147, 151 (24hrs). Breakfast (Mon–Sat), brunch (Sun), lunch (Mon–Sat), dinner. Average main course: $27.*

★ **B Sepia** Restaurant vet Emmanuel Nony is behind this swank West Looper, where the emphasis is on luxe hospitality and seasonal cuisine. The gorgeous dining room strikes a unique balance between classic and contemporary, offering a perfect setting for chef Kendal Duque's stellar menu. Crispy-skinned wild sea bass is a perfect contrast to heirloom tomatoes and tender young leeks while spice-rubbed roasted chicken gets cool pea shoots and citrus-spiked wax beans. No time for dinner? Opt for the lounge, a gingery Sepia Mule cocktail and the sweet-salty-smoky flatbread of fresh peaches, creamy blue cheese and bacon. *123 N Jefferson St between Washington Blvd and Randolph St (312-441-1920). El: Green to Clinton. Bus: 8, 56, 125. Dinner (closed Sun). Average main course: $23.*

★ ▼ **Spring** Chef Shawn McClain may be more well known for his contemporary steak spot Custom House or his veg-head haven Green Zebra, but this upscale dining room is really where his solo career in the city took root. Here, he combines Asian elements and locally sourced ingredients to subtle results. A few signatures dot the menu, but the seasonal specials are the strength. Possibilities include yellowfin tuna tartare with avocado foam; spring garlic-potato soup; and Meyer-lemon mousse chiffon cake with grapefruit parfait. *2039 W North Ave between Damen and Hoyne Aves (773-395-7100). El: Blue to Damen. Bus: 50, 56, 72. Dinner (closed Mon). Average main course: $25.*

▼ ✳ **Townhouse** Located in a sleek corner of a Loop office building, this contemporary restaurant by the Bar Louie folks is bustling with pin-striped professionals who require a glass of wine to go with their office gossip. Like their attire, the food is safe but it works. Big, juicy shrimp are wrapped in bacon and topped with jalapeño sauce; short ribs get a tangy crust of mustard, herbs and bread crumbs. But while you don't necessarily need to be a banker to eat here, you do need to keep bankers' hours: The kitchen closes at 7pm. *111 S Wacker Dr at Monroe St (312-948-8240). El: Brown, Pink, Purple (rush hrs), Orange to Quincy. Bus: 1, 7, X28, 56, 60 (24hrs), 124, 126, 127. Lunch, dinner (closed Sat, Sun). Average main course: $17.*

▼ **TRU** Locals in the habit of splurging are familiar with Rick Tramonto and Gale Gand's contemporary creations at special-occasion prices. Depending on the season, you'll find offerings such as prime beef tartare, seared orange marlin and Swan Creek Farm suckling pig. Or if you really want to indulge in the freshest offerings, go for the seasonal collection. A recent summer collection (nine tastes for $195) included green asparagus with coconut pearls, trout roe, frog leg and a finish of rhubarb consommé. *676 N St Clair St at Huron St (312-202-0001). El: Red to Chicago. Bus: 3, 66, 151 (24hrs), 157. Dinner (closed Sun). Average three-course prix fixe: $95.*

Say cheese The Maytag blue cheesecake at May Street Market is served on a crispy pecan crust.

▼ ⟨ ✳ ♿ **B Uncommon Ground** You might expect that a place that has a 70% vegetarian menu and was completely nonsmoking before it was the law would serve boring dishes made with soy milk and flaxseeds. But this coffee shop/bar/restaurant/performance space will surprise you with dishes like the Jamaican jerk pork chop served with citrus-celery slaw. During brunch, the winners keep coming: The *huevos rancheros* are gooey, cheesy and substitute black-bean cakes for tortillas; and the fruit plate sometimes comes with passion-fruit sorbet and a slice of white-chocolate banana bread. *3800 N Clark St at Grace St (773-929-3680). El: Red to Addison. Bus: 22 (24hrs), 80, 152. Breakfast, brunch (Sat, Sun), lunch, dinner. Average main course: $11.*

✳ **Viand** Chef Steve Chiappetti is working on a more upscale experience for diners at this tourist standby. Overall, it's working: A carrot-curry-crab soup is a beautiful dish, each ingredient distinct yet in harmony with the others, and "Chiappetti's Lamb" arrived at our table so tender it could barely be moved from tagine to plate. Still, Chiappetti's whimsical approach to plating—entrées arrive in big wooden boats; the "junk food cart" of housemade marshmallows and brownies arrives in a mini-shopping cart—keeps the experience from getting too haughty. *155 E Ontario St between Michigan Ave and St Clair St (312-255-8505). El: Red to Grand. Bus: 65, 146, 147, 151 (24hrs). Breakfast, lunch, dinner. Average main course: $14.*

★ ▼ **Vie** Rent a car, con a friend into driving or take Metra—do whatever it takes to get to this classy,

Something old, something new
Rustic digs meet contemporary cuisine at HB Home Bistro.

comfortable restaurant that's as delicious as anything within the city limits. Chef Paul Virant's (named a *Food & Wine* magazine best new chef) penchant for old-school canning makes for a jam-packed pantry through winter, but other times of year he pairs local produce with farm-fresh cheeses and meats. You might find halibut treated with cranberry beans; herb mayo and pickled asparagus; and "warm gooey" butter cake topped with Traders Point frozen yogurt, cinnamon and poached plums. *4471 Lawn Ave, Western Springs (708-246-2082). Metra: Burlington Northern Santa Fe to Western Springs. Dinner (closed Sun). Average main course: $25.*

▼ ⟨ ✳ ♿ **Vintage Wine Bar** This sleek, slightly clubby spot has chef Ian Swope in the kitchen, who avoids typical wine-bar fare (think hummus-and-olive platters) and offers up inspired dishes such as a subtle scallop carpaccio. We're also fans of the succulent slice of braised pork belly offset by a tangy white-bean puree; salmon filet flanked by irresistible brussels sprouts; and a trio of dessert wontons, one sweet, one bitter and one salty. We couldn't figure out how we were supposed to share these dishes—they seemed plated for one. Then again, who'd want to share? *1942 W Division St between Winchester and Damen Aves (773-772-3400). El: Blue to Division. Bus: 50 Damen, 70 Division. Dinner. Average share plate: $16.*

✳ ♿ **Volo** Owner Jon Young of Kitsch'n on Roscoe and Kitsch'n River North has teamed up with chef Stephen Dunne (formerly chef de cuisine at mk) at this cozy small-plates wine bar. Dunne's best dishes are the rich ones—intense duck confit leg with sweet garlic puree, seared diver scallops topped with caviar and crispy leeks, and roasted veal marrow bones with toast—but seasonal specials like peekytoe-crab salad with preserved lemon and avocado suit us just fine, too. The eclectic wine list is well thought out with plenty of food-friendly flights available. *2008 W Roscoe St between Damen and Seeley Aves (773-348-4600). Bus: 50, 77 (24hrs), 152. Dinner (closed Sun). Average small plate: $10.*

✳ **B Yoshi's Café** The room is reminiscent of a retirement-home cafeteria, and the menu has multiple personalities, but somehow Yoshi pulls it all together. Considering his 20-plus years in the game putting out mishmashed food long before the term *fusion* was coined, it's no shock to see yellowtail with guac or a Wagyu burger topped with a huge chunk of Brie. Thanks to Yoshi's former gig as a fish guy, seafood sings here, especially seasonal items like fat, juicy mussels in lemongrass curry. Desserts, on the other hand, were disappointing. *3257 N Halsted St at Aldine Ave (773-248-6160). El: Brown, Purple (rush hrs), Red to Belmont. Bus: 8 Halsted, 77 Belmont (24hrs). Brunch (Sun), dinner (Tue–Sun). Average main course: $25.*

★ ▼ **Zealous** After more than 14 years in business, Michael Taus's baby remains as innovative as ever. His creative menu, offset by the minimalist decor, showcases seasonal ingredients in new ways. Look for vegetarian-friendly dishes such as truffled sweet potato risotto, Asian crab cakes with mango-basil emulsion and macadamia nut–crusted grouper with rock shrimp–taro root hash. Pair your meal with one of the 750 wines from the breathtaking wine cellar. *419 W Superior St between Sedgwick and Kingsbury Sts (312-475-9112). Bus: 66 Chicago (24hrs). Dinner (Tue–Sat). Average main course: $30.*

⊙ **Zia: A New Mexican Café** See Eclectic for review. ▪

Delis

See also: *Classic American, Kosher*

Lox of love Eppy's Deli serves the quintessential Sunday morning sandwich.

⊕ **Ashkenaz Deli** The Chicago versus New York debate will never cease. Those who yearn for true Big Apple tastes can get a taste of home at this Gold Coast storefront. The pastrami here comes from New York, and diehards find the lox, herring, corned beef and gefilte fish up to their standards. Like all good delis, Ashkenaz puts its efforts into food, not decor. Deal with it. *12 E Cedar St between State St and Lake Shore Dr (312-944-5006). El: Red to Clark/Division. Bus: 22, 36, 70. Breakfast, lunch, dinner (open until 6pm Fri-Sun). Average main course: $8.*

⊕ **The Bagel** Restaurants may come and go, but The Bagel never closes...it just changes locations. In its current spot (the third since 1950), the deli has managed to bring a little Jewish curmudgeonliness to Boystown. So, when you're at the take-away counter ordering your potato knish, or sitting in one of the booths with your housemade chicken soup, you might have a brusque comment thrown your way. But this is to be expected. After all, the Bagel hasn't survived by being nice. *3107 N Broadway between Barry Ave and Briar Pl (773-477-0300). El: Brown, Purple (rush hrs), Red to Belmont. Bus: 36, 77 (24hrs), 145, 146, 152. Breakfast, lunch, dinner. Average main course: $8.*

⊕ **Bari Foods** See Italian/pizza for review.

⊕ **Cold Comfort Café & Deli** The name seems to suggest that no matter how thoroughly you stuff your face with the Jewish deli goods on offer, stress release will still elude you. But we beg to differ: Sitting in the bustling space

on a weekend afternoon, drinking a Dr. Brown's and noshing on the "Katfish" (a perfectly executed tuna melt on fragrant, toasted rye) and the warm Reuben oozing with Russian dressing, we couldn't feel more at ease. *2211 W North Ave between Leavitt St and Bell Ave (773-772-4552). El: Blue to Damen. Bus: 49 (24hrs), X49, 50, 56, 72. Tue–Fri 7:30am–4pm; Sat 8am–4pm; Sun 9am–3pm (closed Mon). Average main course: $7.*

⊕ **Deli Boutique** Jana Buchtova knows that Chicagoans are well-traveled people and her Euro-style deli

Read 'em & eat

***kneidl* (k-NAY-dl) (also *kneidlach*)** matzo ball (traditional Jewish dumplings made with matzo meal, served in soup)

***knish* (kuh-NISH)** baked or fried savory pastry filled with potato, meat or cheese that is a common Eastern European Jewish snack

***latke* (LAHT-kuh)** fried potato pancake, popular at Hanukkah

***matzo* (MAHT-suh)** crackerlike unleavened bread eaten during Passover

Side dish

The wandering Jew
It may take a little schlepping, but you can get good Jewish deli.

Stop wandering Find what you crave at Tel Aviv Bakery.

A Jew without a bagel shop is like a Rockette without her feathers. And yet so many Chicago Jews—and the gentiles here who love Jewish food—have trouble finding a good nosh.

To them we say: Oy! Stop your kvetching! If it's bagels you want, head west on Devon Avenue and keep going until the curry stops and the kugel begins. A small Orthodox community calls this strip home, and you can find the most authentic goods. Start with dessert first by hitting **Tel Aviv Bakery** *(2944 W Devon Ave between Richmond St and Sacramento Ave, 773-764-8877)* which offers big, yeasty rugalach in dark chocolate and nutty cinnamon varieties; cakey black-and-white cookies; and, of course, tender loaves of challah. Next door at **Good Morgan Fish** *(2948 W Devon Ave between Richmond St and Sacramento Ave, 773-764-8115)* you'll find savories to precede your sweets: smoked salmon, housemade gefilte fish and, during Hanukkah, legendary latkes. And though **BB's Bagels** *(2835 W Touhy Ave between California and Francisco Aves, 773-761-8805)* isn't on Devon, the big, sweet bagels are worth the walk. What are you, lazy?

But Devon can't help you when it comes to delis, which are scattered haphazardly all over the city. If you can only hit one, make it **Ashkenaz Deli** *(12 E Cedar St at State St, 312-944-5006)*. You'll know you're there when you see the big sign outside touting New York pastrami. The hot corned beef is tender and bursts with flavor; the pastrami is well spiced, with hints of cracked pepper. (Skip the soup, though, and go to **The Bagel** *(3107 N Broadway at Barry Ave, 773-477-0300)* for bright gold chicken stock with puddles of schmaltz and a matzo ball as big as a fist.) What, you have too much pride to eat New York meat? Go to **Eppy's Deli** *(224 E Ontario St between St. Clair and Fairbanks Ct, 312-943-7797)* if it makes you happy—it has a killer Reuben. And if you're *really* hungry, head to **Manny's** *(1141 S Jefferson St at Grenshaw St, 312-939-2855)*. There, the corned beef spills out from the sandwich and covers the entire plate, hiding a pickle and a greasy potato pancake. So it may not be a Jewish deli per se. Eat it anyway. Really, *boychik*, you're too skinny...

reminds them of where they've been. Her formula for success? Her breads are imported, par-baked, from Europe, and she's using them on her panini, including one that layers prosciutto, pepper salami, fresh mozzarella and an olive tapenade. She also has imported meats and cheeses, and serves Italian coffee drinks. *2318 N Clark St between Belden Ave and Fullerton Pkwy (773-880-9820). El: Red to Fullerton. Bus: 22 (24hrs), 36, 74. 8am–8pm. Average main course: $7.*

☉ **Eleven City Diner** Owner Brad Rubin scoured the country to research this Jewish deli/diner. His pastrami is tender, fatty and full of flavor; the milk shakes are thick and oversized; matzo balls are enormous; and the brisket is good enough that any grandmother would want to claim it, Jewish or not. Rubin holds his own as the charming/obnoxious host, giving this place enough character to become a neighborhood fixture. *1112 S Wabash Ave between 11th St and Roosevelt Rd (312-212-1112). El: Green, Orange, Red to Roosevelt. Bus: 1, 3, X3, 4 (24hrs), X4, 12. Breakfast, lunch, dinner. Average main course: $8.*

☉ **Eppy's Deli** "Larry the Jew" is at the helm of this slick underground operation, which has all the chutzpah of a New York Jewish deli, but none of the grittiness. Ordering your sandwich on the marbled rye is your best bet, and whether you go with thinly sliced turkey or celery-flecked tuna salad, the goods are piled on thick and high. Sides like tangy potato salad and an assortment of mustards will keep you happy, but it's the grilled Reuben that will keep you coming back. *224 E Ontario St between St. Clair St and Fairbanks Ct (312-943-7797). El: Red to Grand. Bus: 2, 3, 66, 145, 146, 147, 151 (24hrs), 157. Breakfast, lunch, dinner. Average sandwich: $6.*

Sweet surprise Eleven City Diner brings Jewish deli to the South Loop.

What ails you? No matter, The Bagel's matzo ball soup is the cure.

Pastrami story At Ashkenaz, the iconic meat is brought in from New York.

⊕ **JB's Deli** This counter—like every good Jewish deli—is manned by workers who are gruff, efficient and impatient. The food is equally no-frills: Thinly sliced corned beef is piled on high; lox platters include red onion, cream cheese and tomato, but lettuce stands in for capers (available for an extra charge); housemade blintzes are small pockets of creaminess served on paper plates. Chicken soup is on the menu, too, but this place is situated in a pharmacy, so if that doesn't do the trick, the cold meds are just a few feet away. *5501 N Clark St at Catalpa Ave (773-728-0600). El: Red to Bryn Mawr. Bus: 22 (24hrs), 36, 50. Breakfast, lunch, dinner. Average main course: $6.*

⊕ **Manny's Coffee Shop & Deli** Chicago's most quintessential restaurant is not a steakhouse or a laboratorylike kitchen putting out cutting-edge cuisine. It's a cafeteria. Before you get in line at this 65-year-old institution, decide what you want. You'll pass plates of Jell-O and chicken salad, but this line moves too quickly to decide on the spot. We'll make it easy: Grab an oversize corned beef or pastrami sandwich (there really is bread under all that meat), a potato pancake and a packet of Tums for dessert. *1141 S Jefferson St at Grenshaw St (312-939-2855). El: Blue to Clinton. Bus: 8 Halsted, 12 Roosevelt. Breakfast, lunch (closed Sun). Average main course: $7.*

⊕ **Panozzo's** We'd like to romanticize that a good Italian deli is one that's been up and running for years, where the mozz and *salumi* are made in-house, and the accents thick. But in the newly built-up South Loop, exceptions are made for the *only* Italian deli around. None of the ingredients piled onto the Italian sub are housemade, but the imported salami, capicolla, mortadella and prosciutto are good quality and are generously layered onto fresh LaBriola bread. Fist-size meatballs are flavorful and a good add-on to a pasta. *1303 S Michigan Ave at 13th St (312-356-9966). El: Green, Orange, Red to Roosevelt. Bus: 1, 4 (24hrs), 12. Tue–Fri 10:30am–7pm; Sat 10am–5pm; Sun 10am–4pm. Average sandwich: $6.*

⊕ **Perry's** The closest thing Chicago has to the "soup Nazi," Perry's is a lunchtime institution with random trivia questions barked over a loudspeaker and a strict no-cell-phones policy. The wait is rewarded with deli classics like matzo ball soup (only served on Mondays); juicy pastrami; and "Perry's Favorite"—corned beef, Jack cheese, coleslaw and Russian dressing piled on fresh rye. It's also one of the only places in the area to get a real chocolate malt, and a tasty one at that. *174 N Franklin Ave at Couch Pl (312-372-7557). El: Blue, Brown, Green, Orange, Pink, Purple (rush hrs) to Clark/Lake. Bus: 22 (24hrs), 24, 152. Lunch (closed Sat, Sun). Average sandwich: $6.*

⊕ **Samuel's Deli** These folks have been providing weekend noshes for three decades. They've made some concessions to a nonkosher crowd: Several sandwiches commit crimes against deli purists, such as pairing pastrami and corned beef with melted cheese. Still, great bagels from Skokie's New York Bagels provide a chewy base for smoked-whitefish salad, thick slices of lox, and thinner slices of Vienna corned beef and pastrami. *3463 N Broadway between Stratford Pl and Cornelia Ave (773-525-7018). El: Red to Addison. Bus: 8, 36, 152. Breakfast, lunch, dinner (Mon–Fri). Average main course: $6.* ■

Borscht belt Old-school Ukrainian favorites are what keep the crowds coming to L'Viv.

Eastern European

See also: *German, Polish*

⊙ **Beograd Meat Market** If you don't blend in with the demographic at this Serbian market/café—that is, if you aren't a young, beefy Eastern European guy—this place can be a little intimidating. Get over it. Flaky, housemade pies are filled with either meat or cheese and have a chewy, buttery crust. Slow-roasted beef is succulent with a crisp, charred edge. Housemade baked goods include soft rounds of white bread and *krofna*—puffy, sugar-dusted doughnuts. Besides, these guys are much too interested in watching football (that's soccer to you) to pay you any notice. *2933–39 W Irving Park Rd at Richmond St (773-478-7575). Bus: 80, X80, 82. Breakfast, lunch, dinner (Mon–Sat). Average main course: $7.*

⊙ **Bobak's** There aren't many ironclad rules for dining out, but "avoid buffets" and "don't eat near the airport" are practically set in stone. Bobak's, a few blocks from Midway, is a notable exception to both. Famed for its sausage factory and its Eastern European grocery, Bobak's also features a rich, filling buffet. It's not particularly vegetarian-friendly (any given day features at least a dozen pork dishes), but a fresh fruit bar, massive dessert table and some of the finest pierogi in town make up for it. Offerings change daily; don't miss the near-perfect prime rib most Sundays. *5275 S Archer Ave between 51st and 52nd Sts (773-735-5334). El: Orange to Midway. Bus: 47, 54B, X54, 62, 62H. Lunch, dinner. Average buffet: $10.*

⊙ **Café Effe** Because it sports a façade that blends right in with its busy comic-store neighbor, this place can be easy to miss. So keep your eyes open—we've discovered that within the serene pink-striped walls is some of the most delicious café fare around, all made with a heavy Bosnian hand. Make like the Bosnian construction workers on their lunch break and chow down on the made-from-scratch chevapi, something like an Eastern Euro cross between sausage and hamburger. All of the sandwiches are plunked down on fat rounds of crumpetlike bread. *2030 W Montrose Ave between Damen and Seeley Aves (773-334-3436). Bus: 11, 50, 78, 145. Breakfast, lunch, dinner. Average main course: $9.*

★ ⊙ **Deta's Pita** Among the regulars huddled over cups of coffee and packs of cigarettes at the worn wooden tables is an older lady with the Midas touch. Some of her breads may already be made, but if you're lucky she'll have to bake some from scratch, which takes about 30 minutes. Order one meat and potato, one spinach and cheese, and soon she'll flip a hot pan over a paper plate, coaxing out a round of steaming, fragrant bread that resembles a stuffed Danish. She calls it pita, we think it's more like *boerek*, but the buttery, flaky pastries are so luscious we don't really care what they're called—we just know we can never make it home with anything left in the bag. *7555 N Ridge Blvd between Birchwood Ave and Howard St (773-973-1505). Bus: 49B, 97, 201, Pace 215. Breakfast, lunch, dinner. Average main course: $6.*

⊙ **Duke's Eatery and Deli** Behind Duke's nondescript façade, you'll discover what seems to be the wild fantasy of some hunting enthusiast/interior

Nice to meat you Treat yourself to traditional Bosnian fare at Café Effe.

designer—as well as Chicagoland's "fanciest" Lithuanian dining. In a room of dark wood, sturdy beams, heraldry and portraits of medieval nobility, diners enjoy hearty sausages, sauces and pickles favored in Baltic states. The "fried bread hill" is a perfect drinking buddy: a bready Lincoln Log–like construction coated with garlicky cheese. For an entrée, the ground boar wrapped in bacon is a flavorful blend of both wild and domestic porkers. Visit the well-stocked deli for cheeses, meats and housemade salads to take a piece of Lithuania home with you. *6312 S Harlem Ave, Summit (708-594-5622). Bus: 62H, 62W, Pace 307. Breakfast, lunch, dinner. Average main course: $10.*

⊙ **Healthy Food** As delicious as the heavy Lithuanian food at this diner is, its name is about as far from the truth as possible. You can get the diner fare anywhere, so don't bother with pork chops and tuna salad. Instead, focus on Lithuanian specialties like *kugelis*, a pan-fried square of potato pudding that's rich with the flavors of bacon and onions, and sweet, crêpelike pancakes called *blynai*, topped with fruit (order them unfilled rather than stuffed with the dry and spongy cheese). Pork lovers will flip for the fresh bacon buns, served on Friday only, which are exactly what they sound like and the *koldunai*, fat dumplings stuffed with meat and sprinkled with—you guessed it—more bacon *3236 S*

Old country You'll get Old World service—and dishes—at the Loop's Russian Tea Time.

a seat to dig in to tender beef goulash wrapped in an enormous potato pancake, the *hortobágyi húsos palacsinta* (a crêpe filled with addictive, creamy chicken paprikash) and the housemade cherry strudel, all of which, despite the shiny new space, still taste like they're straight from the Old World. *602 W Northwest Highway, Arlington Heights (847-253-3544). Lunch (Tue–Fri), Dinner (Sat–Sun), closed Monday. Average main course: $16.*

★ **Russian Tea Time** A classy choice for the symphony set and couples looking to indulge, this institution proves excess is best. Slide into a cozy booth and start the assault with classic borscht, sour cream-slathered dumplings and caviar blini. Follow up with creamy beef Stroganoff or oniony, nutmeg-laced, ground-beef-stuffed cabbage rolls. Finish with hot farmer's cheese blintzes or Klara's apricot-and-plum strudel, a family recipe from the restaurant's matriarch. Skip the wine and order a flight of house–infused vodkas (pepper, pineapple, ginger, coriander and more). *77 E Adams St between Michigan and Wabash Aves (312-360-0000). El: Brown, Green, Orange, Pink, Purple (rush hrs) to Adams. Red, Blue to Jackson. Bus: 3, 4 (24hrs), X4, 6, 7, 14, 26, X28, 127, 145, 147, 148, 151. Lunch, dinner. Average main course: $20.*

⊙ **Sak's Ukrainian Village** Past the dark bar (where regulars smoke and pour tall bottles of beer into frosted glasses) is a dining room, heavily decorated with oil paintings and plastic flowers. Once you're here, remember you're not here for burgers and steaks, so stick to the Ukrainian side of the menu. Dense stuffed cabbage is topped with a thick mushroom gravy, and potato pancakes are thin and crisp (eat them while they're hot). But it's all just a vehicle to get to dessert: powdered sugar–dusted blintzes whose browned and crisp exterior gives way to sweet, decadent cheese. *2301 W Chicago Ave at Oakley Blvd (773-278-4445). Bus: 49 (24hrs), X49, 50, 66 (24hrs). Lunch, dinner (closed Mon). Average main course: $8.* ∎

Halsted St between 32nd and 33rd Sts (312-326-2724). Bus: 8, 35, 39, 44. Breakfast, lunch, dinner (Fri, Sat) (closed Mon). Average main course: $8.

⊙ **Nelly's Saloon** Pearls? Check. Cigarettes? Check. Bright pink lipstick? Check. All of owner Nelly's essentials are in order and she's officially open for business. Expect handsome, loaded Romanian imports chowing down on the earthy cuisine of Romania: platters of *mititei* (grilled sausages); fried kraut with bits of bacon fat; heaping bowls of polenta with feta; and pan-fried chicken wings. Other than weekends when there's live music or anytime a soccer game's on, it's likely to be just you and Nelly, the queen of amaretto stone sours. *3256 N Elston Ave between between Belmont Ave and Henderson St (773-588-4494). El: Blue to Belmont. Bus: 77 (24hrs), 82, 152. Average main course: $10.*

⊙ **Old L'Viv** If there's one thing at Old L'Viv you definitely don't want to make a choice among, it's the selection of soups. Before digging into this old-school Ukrainian restaurant's buffet, you'll have to decide between the silky and gorgeous borscht, the chicken soup sprinkled with fresh dill, or cabbage soup that's tart with housemade sauerkraut. Can't call it? Go crazy and order all three. You're going to gorge yourself on the oniony potato pancakes (Mondays and Fridays only), tender *schnitzel* and blintzes anyway...why not get a head start? *2228 W Chicago Ave between Leavitt St and Oakley Blvd (773-772-7250). Bus: 49 Western (24hrs), 66 Chicago (24hrs). Lunch, dinner (closed Mon). Soup and buffet: $8.50.*

Paprikash Vegetarians, dieters and anyone not fond of cabbage should steer clear of this Hungarian staple, which recently moved to the northwest suburbs after a long stint in the city. The rest of you, however, should scramble to get

Read 'em & eat

beluga the most prized and expensive of caviars, the large, soft, silver-to-black eggs come from beluga sturgeon in the Caspian Sea

blini pancakes made from yeast-raised buckwheat flour, often served with caviar

borscht (bohrsht) beet soup, served hot or cold, with a dollop of sour cream

cevapi (che-VAHP-ee) small ground beef and lamb sausage, usually served with white bread, chopped raw onions and cottage cheese

kasha a sticky, nutty roasted buckwheat

osetra: caviar that is second after beluga in terms of highest quality and price; medium-size and ranges in color from brownish-gray to gray

schnitzel (shniht-SUHL) thin cutlet of meat coated in egg and bread crumbs, and fried, such as wiener (veal) schnitzel

sevruga caviar that is maller than osetra, and gray in color

Eclectic

See also: *Contemporary American, French, Latin American, Pan Asian, South American, Vegetarian*

Seat yourself There are more than six kinds of seating options at Landmark.

⊙ **Aloha Eats** There's enough starch and Spam in this casual little Hawaiian café to keep you set through a weeklong power outage, but don't wait for one to dive into the Big Island classics. The best of the rice-packed menu includes the curry-chicken katsu (crispy panko-breaded, boneless chicken with subtly spicy curry gravy) and the kalua pork (perfectly tender pulled pork tossed with stewed cabbage). The "seafood-BBQ" platter comes with crunchy fish and shrimp, plus sweet, sticky, grilled short ribs, chicken or beef. Value-junkies will love the massive portions and easy-on-the-wallet prices. *2534 N Clark St between Deming and St James Pls (773-935-6828). El: Brown, Purple (rush hrs), Red to Fullerton. Bus: 11, 22 (24hrs), 36. Lunch, dinner. Average main course: $7.*

B ⊙ **Ann Sather** Ann Sather is not the best dinner in town. It's not the best lunch, or the best breakfast. It may not even be the best diner food. But that doesn't matter, because Ann Sather has the sweetest cinnamon rolls in the Midwest. If you must, you can order some "real" food off the menu—crab cake benedicts for brunch won't disappoint you; neither will Swedish specialties such as the roasted duck with lingonberry glaze. But let's get real: You're only after those fluffy cinnamon rolls, which arrive too big for the plate they're on and submerged under warm icing. Lucky for you, they come with almost every order. *929 W Belmont Ave between Sheffield Ave and Clark St (773-348-2378). El: Red*

to Belmont. Bus: 8, 22 (24hrs), 77 (24hrs). Breakfast, lunch, dinner. Average main course: $10.*

Aria It's a concept that's almost impossible to pull off: Serve dishes from India, Brazil, and China, tone it down for "American" palates and charge anywhere between $20 and $45 an entrée. So it's no surprise that things here are hit or miss. The tastiest dishes are free: the basket of warm nan to start with, and an indulgent trio of potatoes (sweet, fingerlings, gratin) that arrives with the entrées. We like the crab-stuffed sweet-and-sour shrimp, and roasted cod. But steer clear of the chewy duck and lobster chow mein. *200 N Columbus Dr at Lake St (312-444-9494). Bus: 4 (24hrs), 20 (24hrs), 60 (24hrs). Breakfast, brunch (Sat–Sun), lunch, dinner. Average main course: $30.*

✳ **BB's** The menu is more comfort-food than gastropub, but with prices this low we're not inclined to let semantics get in the way. Tiny pulled-pork sandwiches (called, in overly cute fashion, "BBites") are tender and sweet and the bar steak, while a little plain, is flavorful and juicy (just ignore those limp fries). Beer is pushed as the drink of choice here, but the real draw is the wine list, which has 25 bottles—only one of which exceeds $30. *22 E Hubbard St between State St and Wabash Ave (312-755-0007). El: Red to Grand. Bus: 29, 36, 65. Lunch, dinner (closed Sun). Average main course: $13.*

Aloha Sola's unagi timable with avocado, jasmine rice and banana brings a taste of Hawaii to Chicago.

Eclectic

▼ ✱ **Broadway Cellars** Neighborhood restaurants are tricky things, and Broadway Cellars is a good example why: The friendly, neighborly service and living-roomish ambience are precisely what every neighborhood wants; but the food only sometimes lives up to the environment. Our advice is to order the rich duck lasagna, the hearty and well-spiced coffee-rubbed pork loin and, if you can stomach the name, the Mmmmini burgers. This place might just be the neighborhood joint you've been waiting for. *5900 N Broadway at Rosedale Ave (773-944-1208). El: Red to Thorndale. Bus: 36 Broadway, 84 Peterson. Dinner, brunch (Sun) (closed Mon). Average main course: $12.*

B ▼ ☉ **Café Aorta** An adorable, hip coffee shop in Pilsen that's not on 18th Street? But wait, there's more: It's vegetarian-friendly and cheap. Sides like veggie Puerto Rican rice with *gandules* (pigeon peas) and green olives, sweet potatoes boiled with raw sugar, and *sazon* (seasoned) hash browns showcase chef Papi Perez's Caribbean roots. But the hearty comfort food is universal: Brunch includes French toast (order the thick slabs "crunchy") and a "gypsy skillet" (two eggs on a bed of vegetables and potatoes). Both include OJ or coffee and a pastry. *2002 W 21st St at Damen Ave (312-738-2002). El: Pink to Damen. Bus: 21 Cermak, 50 Damen. Mon–Thu 7am–8pm; Fri 7am–8pm; Sat 9am–7pm; Sun 9am–3pm. Average main course: $10.*

☉ **Catedral Café** This place is decked out with so much Catholic imagery it looks like a garage sale thrown by the pope. But as long you don't have an aversion to angels, this is one of the most comfortable spots in Little Village. Upscale café grub—crêpes stuffed with slices of smoked salmon on fresh greens; a chicken-breast panino with layers of sweet, silky mango—is balanced by pastas and breakfast fare. Earnest service and endorsements from Will Ferrell and Maggie Gyllenhaal (who filmed scenes from *Stranger Than Fiction* here) will make you a believer. *2500 S Christiana Ave at 25th St (773-277-2233). Bus: 52 Kedzie/California, 60 Blue Island/26th (24hrs). Breakfast, lunch, dinner. Average main course: $7.*

☉ **Chowpatti** See Vegetarian for review.

▼ **BYOB Dorado** The concept is Mexican-French (chef Luis Perez spent 18 years cooking French food before opening this spot in 2004), but at first glance this menu seems pretty straight-up Mexican. A closer read reveals that the nachos are topped with juicy, smoky morsels of duck and the *chiles rellenos* are stuffed with plump shrimp and tiny bay scallops. So seek out the fusion and don't look back—until dessert, that is. The *tres leches* doesn't have an ounce of French in it, but it's the right way to end. *2301 W Foster Ave at Oakley Ave (773-561-3780). El: Brown to Western. Bus: 49 (24hrs), X49, 92. Lunch, dinner (closed Mon). Average main course: $14.*

▼ ✱ ♨ B **Feast** When the appetizers hit your table, you know you're in for a meal not meant for a delicate palate. Neighborhood regulars gobble up the penne mac and cheese, its richness cut with scallions and bacon, and the wonton napoleon, stacked with wasabi-spiked slices of tuna sashimi and tartare. The butternut-squash ravioli incorporates goat cheese, balsamic and brown butter for extreme decadence. Mondays and Tuesdays are BYOB, a great way to start the week. *1616 N Damen Ave between North Ave and Concord Pl (773-772-7100). El: Blue to Damen. Bus: 50, 56, 72. Breakfast, brunch, lunch (Mon–Fri), dinner. Average main course: $14.*

▼ B **Flo** Folk-art collectors Renee and Rodney Carswell's funky, casual dining room is an all-day draw for those looking for an interesting meal at a reasonable price. The brunch and breakfast menu standouts include New Mexico–influenced tongue-scorchers like green-chile enchiladas and *huevos rancheros*—perfect when balanced with fresh-fruit smoothies and strong coffee. At dinner, local and often organic produce appear as salads and sides for comforting classics like fish tacos, chorizo meatloaf and roasted chicken *mole*. *1434 W Chicago Ave between Greenview Ave and Bishop St (312-243-0477). El: Blue to Chicago. Bus: 9, 66 (24hrs), brunch (Sat, Sun), lunch (Tue–Fri), dinner (Tue–Sat). Average main course: $13.*

▼ **foodlife** To say there's something for everyone at this expectation-defying food court in Water Tower Place is an understatement. You won't find any outposts of greasy chains here; instead this Lettuce Entertain You entity runs its own show with upmarket stalls including an Asian noodle bar, rotisserie, soup station, and even a healthy eats area (a partnership with *Cooking Light* magazine). Most of the stalls turn out surprisingly tasty fare, so expect longer-than-life lines on busy shopping days. *Water Tower Place, 835 N Michigan Ave between Chestnut and Pearson Sts (312-335-3663). El: Red to Chicago. Bus: 66 (24hrs), 143, 144, 145, 146, 147, 151 (24hrs). Lunch, dinner. Average main course: $7.*

B **Fornetto Mei** An upscale hotel dining room with a menu that's two-thirds Italian and one-third Asian would normally send us running. (So would the atrocious upholstery on the banquettes.) But this place surprised us at every turn. We watched as a pizza maker rolled out the dough for our deliciously sweet, creamy, salty pie of grapes, goat cheese and sausage and baked it to perfection in a wood-burning oven. And believe it or not, a trio of plump seafood dumplings were tasty little things that could have come out of any Chinese kitchen. *107 E Delaware Pl between Ernst Ct and Michigan Ave (312-573-6300). El: Red to Chicago. Bus: 22 (24hrs), 143, 144, 145, 146, 147, 151 (24hrs). Breakfast, brunch (Sat, Sun), lunch, dinner. Average main course: $22.*

▼ **Geja's Café** This dimly-lit fondue spot is a reliably romantic date destination. The four-course Prince Geja Combination ($44.95 per person), while pricey, allows couples a chance to get cozy while experimenting with various dips. A salad starter is followed by the cheese fondue appetizer with bread, grapes and apples. Then, beef tenderloin, chicken breast, lobster tail, jumbo shrimp and sea scallops are brought out to be cooked in the tableside hot oil pot. Save room for the flaming chocolate fondue dessert, served with cake, marshmallows and several kinds of fruit. *340 W Armitage Ave between Orleans and Sedgwick Sts (773-281-9101). Bus: 11, 22 (24hrs), 36, 73, 151 (24hrs), 156. Dinner. Average fondue dinner: $35.*

☺ **Icosium Kafé** *2007 Eat Out Award, Critic's Pick: Best way to drop a ten-spot* This Algerian crêpe place makes the standard French crêperie pale in comparison. You'll find typical butter-and-sugar or banana-and-Nutella combos, but savory crêpes are where Icosium lets its Algerian flag fly. Fillings include mostly organic vegetables, halal meats (including *merguez*, a lamb sausage) and even escargot. Those who are watching their carbs can opt for the same ingredients in salads. Even everyday tea seems special here, served in a

Room with a view Look down on those not lucky enough to dine at NoMI.

charming teapot with a teacup rimmed in gold with fresh mint leaves on request. *5200 N Clark St at Foster Ave (773-271-5233). El: Red to Berwyn. Bus: 22 (24 hrs), 50, 92 Foster. Breakfast, lunch, dinner. Average main course: $8.50.· Additional Location at 2433 N Clark St (773-404-1300).*

★ **Kevin** The man behind the name on the door creates meals that are mostly interesting and sometimes incredible. We forgive chef Shikami's Wagyu ribeye (unexciting despite white truffles and balsamic) because the tuna tartare is so creamy and has a gentle wasabi kick and spicy hoisin-glazed lamb is so tender, it feels like cream in our mouths. Don't overlook desserts like the decadent banana madeline cakes with chocolate pot de creme, sour cream sorbet and chocolate banana walnut chutney. *9 W Hubbard St between State and Dearborn Sts (312-595-0055). El: Red to Grand. Bus: 22 (24hrs), 29, 36, 65. Dinner (closed Sun). Average main course: $32.*

▼ (☀ **Kit Kat Lounge** If you don't know who Marilyn and Joan are, don't bother. Come to this slick nightspot to be entertained by classic movies and performances by sexy, sophisticated female impersonators. The 100-martini drink list is also a draw. The menu plays runner-up to the entertainment, but there are some pleasant surprises, like the eponymous salad, full of crunchy pumpkin seeds and the filet mignon rubbed with eye-opening espresso beans. It's not haute cuisine, but you didn't actually come here for the food, did you? *3700 N Halsted St at Waveland Ave (773-525-1111). El: Red to Addison. Bus: 8, 36, 152. Dinner (closed Mon). Average main course: $20.*

▼ (**Landmark** Scene reigns supreme at this venture from the owners of down-the-block neighbor BOKA. Take your pick of a half-dozen seating choices (including an elevated "catwalk" and comfy bar booths) and start with a stellar cocktail like the Asian pear martini or Cherry Blossom. Opt for the dining-room menu over the hit-and-miss bar menu for a melange of American and Mediterranean flavors: wood-grilled ribeye encrusted in herbs with roasted root vegetables; brioche-crusted Alaskan halibut with braised collard and smoked ham broth; and a lobster club on earthy walnut toast. *1633 N Halsted St between North Ave and Willow St (312-587-1600). El: Red to North/Clybourn. Bus: 8 Halsted, 72 North.. Dinner (closed Mon). Average main course: $23.*

▼ ☀ **Le Lan** See Pan Asian for review.

▼ (☀ B **Morseland** This Rogers Park restaurant/concert venue/bar could have ventriloquists "entertaining" diners and a menu composed solely of Hot Pockets and it would still bring in business—there aren't many restaurants in the immediate area. Yet it overachieves with favorites like the Creole-spiced crab cakes; fried mac-and-cheese wedges with a chipotle-cumin dipping sauce; and nod to area hippies with the vegan Moroccan veggie tagine and vegan burger. *1218 W Morse Ave between Glenwood Ave and Sheridan Rd (773-764-8900). El: Red to Morse. Bus: 147 Outer Drive Express. Brunch (Sun), dinner (Tue–Sun). Average main course: $16.*

☺ **Moxie** The bartenders here whip up some of the tastiest cocktails in the city, and it's hard to drink just one. That's why it's vital to fill up on the small plates from Moxie's eclectic menu, such as the jerk pork or "mammoth wings," which aren't that mammoth, but pack tongue-tickling spice. Heavier dishes include gnocchi sprinkled

Eclectic

with toasted garlic and lobster rangoon, which is light on lobster, heavy on cream cheese, and just the thing to offset a few lemon martinis. *3517 N Clark St between Cornelia Ave and Eddy St (773-935-6694). El: Red to Addison. Bus: 22 (24hrs), 77 (24hrs), 152. Dinner. Average small plate: $9.*

★ ✳ **B NoMI** *2007 Eat Out Award, Readers' Choice: Best hotel restaurant* Like the good Frenchman he is, chef Christophe David takes where his food comes from very seriously. Options include an appetizer of morels (served with Virginia ham) from Washington State, veal paired with creamy polenta and chanterelle mushrooms, and lamb with artichokes and a natural jus. Desserts include a pineapple-coconut panna cotta and a citrus Napoleon, but you may want to end your meal with something from the restaurant's vintage tea list instead. *800 N Michigan Ave between Chicago Ave and Pearson St (312-239-4030). El: Red to Chicago. Bus: 3, 10, 26, 66, 125, 143, 144, 145, 146, 147, 151 (24hrs). Breakfast, brunch (Sat, Sun), lunch (Mon–Fri), dinner. Average main course: $36.*

▼ BYOB ✳ **Rick's Café** Plenty of restaurants have the class to light the kind of regal, skinny candles that reach a full foot above your table. This is the way things are done at this old-school Lakeview storefront. Go all the way and order the luscious chicken-and-duck pâté to start. From there, choose between a thick fillet of tuna with crème fraîche sauce and the daily housemade pasta in sweet marinara. Be sure to bring enough wine—those candles take a while to burn down. *3915 N Sheridan Ave between Byron and Dakin Sts (773-327-1972). El: Red to Sheridan. Bus: 36, 80, 151 (24hrs). Dinner (closed Mon). Average main course: $18.*

▼ (**B Rodan** It's easy to dismiss this place as a scenester sipping spot, but the South American/Southeast Asian menu from co-owner Maripa Abella is worth a visit even if slick digs aren't your bag. We advise gliding past the line of lemmings at Bongo Room, grabbing a seat here, and starting off with the Vietnamese coffee with powdered sugar–topped, beignetlike doughnuts and the coconut milk rice pudding with fresh fruit. Pan-Latin classics like black bean *arepas* and *huevos rancheros* are delicious, too. *1530 N Milwaukee Ave between Damen Ave and Honore St (773-276-7036). El: Blue to Damen. Bus: 50, 56, 72. Brunch (Sat, Sun), dinner. Average main course: $13.*

✳ **Roy's** One of three dozen restaurants in the Hawaii-born Roy's empire, this spot boasts a seafood-heavy menu that offers both classic dishes you could find at any location and original creations from the executive chef Kevin Dusinski. Hawaiian swordfish (*shutome*), snapper and butterfish are among the main-event picks, and they're nearly always cooked well, but it's the butter-based sauces and gluttonous sides like Chinese sausage fried rice that provide the can't-stop-eating-it appeal. Don't pass up the lobster ravioli starter or the simple yet tasty chocolate soufflé. *720 N State St at Superior St (312-787-7599). El: Red to Chicago. Bus: 36, 66 (24hrs), 125, 156. Dinner. Average main course: $25.*

Saltaus Chef Michael Taus may have departed from this swank Randolph Row spot, but it's plugging along just as well. It's the "Sal" of Saltaus—owner Nader Salti—who's responsible for the stunning space. Enjoy it best by requesting an upstairs table with a view of both the skyline and the DJ booth (which is manned after 9pm). Dishes like mandarin-marinated hamachi, chorizo-stuffed

"C" before "h" The chefs at Shikago cook better than they spell.

calamari and a risotto of favas, peas, asparagus and pecorino in mint cream are as dependable as the pomegranate-driven cocktail list. *1350 W Randolph St at Ada St (312-312-455-1919). El: Green to Ashland. Bus: 9, 19, 20 (24hrs). Dinner (closed Sun). Average main course: $21.*

★ **Shikago** Okay, okay—it's a terrible name. Luckily, the food doesn't follow suit. Brothers Kevin and Alan Shikami (who also own Kevin on Hubbard St) are serving great food, such as Vietnamese spring rolls stuffed with delectable Korean-style short ribs; Vietnamese-style "shaking" beef tenderloin; and luscious scallops paired with a vibrant coconut risotto. And Catherine Miller's desserts, such as an insanely pleasurable pineapple trio (think pineapple doughnuts) are just as beautiful a thing to look at as they are to eat. *190 S LaSalle St at Adams St (312-781-7300). El: Brown, Orange, Pink, Purple (rush hrs) to Quincy. Lunch (Mon–Fri), dinner (Mon–Sat). Average main course: $17.*

▼ **Slice of Life/ Hy Life Bistro** See Kosher for review.

▼ ✳ **Socca** If you could see the classy, airy space this Mediterranean restaurant takes up, you'd never guess it used to be the infamous pick-up joint Buddies. This incarnation is named for the chickpea crêpe that hails from Provence, a dish always present on the menu. But for our money, we like to start with the loaded antipasto board, move on to housemade pastas and end with rich, tasty comforts like beef short ribs. *3301 N Clark St at Aldine St (773-248-1155). El: Brown, Purple (rush hrs), Red to Belmont. Bus: 8, 22 (24hrs), 77 (24hrs). Dinner. Average main course: $18.*

★ ▼ ✳ **B Sola** It always feels like a warm, sunny day when we eat chef Carol Wallack's Hawaiian-influenced food. Dishes such as pan-seared pork chops with pineapple-rosemary risotto, lemongrass-crusted mahi mahi with coconut jasmine rice and ginger-glazed grilled salmon with edamame puree beg to be eaten outside on the restaurant's patio, but in winter, you'll do just as well to take a few bites, close your eyes and dream of brighter days. *3868 N Lincoln Ave at Byron St (773-327-3868). El: Brown to Irving Park. Bus: 11, 50, 80, X80. Brunch (Sat, Sun), lunch (Thu, Fri), dinner. Average main course: $19.*

▼ **The Stained Glass Wine Bar, Bistro & Cellar** All signs point to wine bar: exposed brick and beams, a wall devoted to wine storage, 250 by the bottle and 32 by the glass. But as our waitress said, "Wine is the gimmick; the food is the selling point." Case in point: the melt-in-your mouth beef carpaccio surrounding a salad of baby bok choy and greens. Knockouts include a perfectly cooked rack of lamb with mint pesto and white-truffle crème brûlée, and filet mignon with shallot cabernet butter. *1735 Benson Ave, Evanston (847-864-8600). El: Purple to Davis. Bus: 93, 205, 206, Pace 208 , Pace 212, Pace 213. Dinner (closed Tue). Average main course: $25.*

⊖ **Svea** Fancy-shmancy breakfast food—the kind with goat cheese in the omelettes and too much fruit in the pancake batter—is a bit much on mornings when we want to quietly nurse away the night before. That's when we head instead to this Andersonville diner, a neighborhood mainstay cluttered with Swedish folk art and plates packed with hearty, no-nonsense food. The Viking Breakfast— two eggs, three Swedish pancakes with lingonberry compote, *falukorv* sausage and toast—is our favorite hangover cure, but we're just as happy with rib-sticking potato pancakes or Swedish meatballs later in the day. *5236 N Clark St at Farragut Ave (773-275-7738). El: Red to Berwyn. Bus: 22 (24hrs), 36, 50, 92. Breakfast, lunch. Average main course: $7.*

◉ **Swirl Wine Bar** Because drinking on an empty stomach is a one-way ticket to drunk-dialing your ex, falling asleep in the bathroom or other embarrassing drama, this wine bar thankfully puts just as much focus on the food. The housemade empanada hides earthy mushrooms inside its flaky crust; hefty crab cakes get a golden exterior of panko crumbs; a caprese salad gets a twist by using blue cheese instead of mozz; and a pizza topped with caramelized onions and pears goes perfectly with an off-dry riesling. *111 W Hubbard St between Clark St and LaSalle Blvd (312-828-9000). El: Brown, Purple (rush hrs) to Merchandise Mart; Red to Grand. Bus: 22 (24hrs), 36, 62 (24hrs), 65. Dinner (Tue–Sat). Average main course: $10.*

❨ ✳ **Tarascas International** The "international" part of the name comes from the fact that this Lincoln Park spot serves both Mexican and Caribbean fare, but you'll do best forgoing anything tropical-sounding and sticking with traditional, well-executed South-of-the-Border staples. Creamy guacamole, enchiladas in smoky mole sauce and nicely grilled carne asada somehow seem fancier served in the candlelit dining room. But beware of potent margaritas that can make the meal seem a little out of focus. *2585 N Clark St at Wrightwood Ave (773-549-2595). Bus: 22 (24hrs), 36, 74, 76, 151 (24hrs). Breakfast (Sat, Sun), dinner. Average main course: $14.*

◉ **Tre Kronor** The children depicted in the murals of this quaint café scare the hell out of us, so we turn to the weekend brunch of Scandinavian comfort food to ease our minds. We love the flaky danishes filled with apples and pecans, thin Swedish pancakes with lingonberry preserves and omelettes bulging with *falukorv* sausage and dill. For lunch, try the meatball sandwich, served open-faced on limpa—Swedish rye bread—and topped with hard-boiled egg and tomato. *3258 W Foster Ave between Sawyer Ave and Spaulding Ave (773-267-9888). El: Brown to Kedzie. Bus: 81 (24hrs), 92, 93. Breakfast, lunch, dinner (Mon–Sat). Average main course: $6.*

Ⓑ ◉ **Treat** The small menu on this hip eatery is heavy on sandwiches, and the few entrées —café staples like pan-seared salmon mingle with disappointing Indian dishes—don't stand out for their creativity. But the kitchen has a way of sneaking in surprising flavors. Case in point: spicy, creamy and endlessly flavorful *harissa aioli* that covers an otherwise predictable pile of hot, crispy calamari. Get the peppercorn ice cream if it's available. *1616 N Kedzie Ave between North and Wabansia Aves (773-772-1201). Bus: 52, 72, 82. Brunch (Sat, Sun), lunch and dinner (closed Tue). Average main course: $10.*

❨ ◉ **V.I.C.E.** Vivo's sister spot is very much a lounge, with ottomans, banquettes and coffee tables standing in for traditional dining-room furnishings. But even while trying to figure out the best way to dine from a square stool, we can appreciate the hors d'oeuvres–size dishes. The mini Kobe burgers—juicy and topped with crispy pancetta, Camembert, fresh arugula and a ripe little slice of tomato—are the best of the bunch, but duck confit flatbread is a strong second. The DJ gets booty-rific around 10pm, so plan accordingly. *840 W Randolph St between Green and Peoria Sts (312-733-3379). El: Green to Clinton. Bus: 8*

Halsted, 20 Madison (24hrs). Dinner (closed Mon). Average small plate: $8.

Ⓑ Viand See Contemporary American for review.

✳ **Wave, W Chicago Lakeshore** Hotel lobbies aren't our dining rooms of choice, but we make an exception for the sultry vibe of this low-lit Mediterranean spot with a lake view from the patio. Many of the small plates are overpriced, so avoid buyer's remorse with standouts like the watermelon salad, which pairs cool cubes of melon with fiery spice-cured beef and creamy feta; and a *crudo* (slivers of raw scallops and tuna) packing big, sprightly flavors. Ignore the waiter's hard sell; three small plates and two large feed a group of four just fine. *644 N Lake Shore Dr between Ontario and Erie (312-255-4460). Bus: 134, 135, 136. Breakfast, lunch, dinner. Average small plate: $11.*

✳ **Yoshi's Café** See Contemporary American for review.

◉ **Zia: A New Mexican Café** If New Mexicans eat like this every day, they either possess superhuman tolerance for spice or they don't have any taste buds left. The *carne adovada*—shredded pork topped with a red chile sauce—has a, juicy texture and a flavor dominated by the chile's tongue-searing heat. Less masochistic eaters can go with the *sopaipillas* (fried bread) stuffed with mildly spiced ground beef. Just make sure to save the basket of plain sopaipillas for dessert; filled with honey, they're a hard act to follow. *340 W Armitage Ave between Orleans and Sedgwick Sts (773-525-6959). Bus: 11, 22 (24hrs), 36, 73, 151 (24hrs), 156. Lunch, dinner (closed Sun). Average main course: $10.* ■

Share alike Wave links hotel dining with small plates.

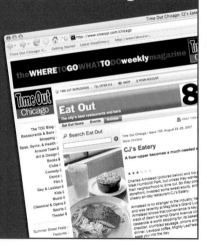

French

See also: Contemporary American, Eclectic, Vietnamese

His goose is cooked
Cyrano's chef Didier Durand
has figured out ways around
Chicago's foie gras ban.

smoked salmon; and tasty *coq au vin*, a straight-from-the-oven crock of chicken roasted with bacon, onions and copious amounts of red wine. Lest anybody think the French too serious, the dining room features photos of the chef-owner's young daughter, Margot, posing as a painter, a dancer and, of course, a chef. *1437-39 N Wells St between Schiller St and Burton Pl (312-587-3660). El: Brown, Purple (rush hrs) to Sedgwick. Bus: 72 North. Brunch (Sat, Sun), lunch, dinner. Average main course: $18.*

✳ **Bistro 110** Weary shoppers have long escaped the Mag Mile for respite in a glass of *vin* and a heaping bowl of steamed mussels at this solid bistro. Comfy banquettes, brass accents and a lengthy bar add to the Frenchie flair of it all. The menu sticks to standards, of which the roasted chicken, steak frites and crème brûlée. scratch that Right Bank itch. A sidewalk patio offers prime people-watching, and a nice spot for weekend brunch. *110 E Pearson St between Michigan Ave and Rush St (312-266-3110). El: Red to Chicago. Bus: 10, 66 (24hrs), 125, 143, 144, 145, 146, 147, 151 (24hrs). Lunch, dinner. Average main course: $20.*

B Bistrot Zinc Amid tony Gold Coast restaurants is this surprisingly authentic Paris-style bistro, complete with the day's paper dangling from wooden rods and a menu that delivers all the classics in reliable fashion. Wine-steamed mussels and butter-drenched escargots sate shellfish-lovers, while the onion soup's beefy broth and gobs of Gruyère satisfy comfort-food cravings. The steak frites is fine, but the meat is thin. Opt instead for the peppercorn-crusted New York strip. *1131 N State St between Cedar and Elm Sts (312-337-1131). El: Red to Clark/Division. Bus: 22 (24hrs), 36, 70. Brunch (Sat, Sun), lunch, dinner. Average main course: $20.*

✳ **Brasserie Jo** Chef Jean Joho is best known for the jacket-required dining style of Everest, but this brasserie is casual both in design and spirit. The menu of simple Alsatian food matches: The classic salad lyonnaise, rife with chewy *lardons*, is a solid starter, but it can't compete with the crispy, onion-filled *tarte flambé* (free at the bar on Tuesdays). The chicken in the creamy riesling *coq au vin* was a little overdone,

✳ **Bank Lane Bistro** The ride up Sheridan Road along the North Shore to this cozy, tranquil French bistro is a good excuse to expand your horizons. The menu—a rotating list of carefully executed seasonal dishes and tasty standards like steak frites and roasted duck breast—isn't anything you won't find within city limits, but the location overlooking Lake Forest's historic Market Street sure beats an urban landscape of snarled traffic and dumpsters. Be sure to save room for fancy housemade s'mores for dessert. *670 Bank Ln, Lake Forest (847-234-8802). Lunch (Mon–Fri), dinner (Mon–Sat). Average main course: $29.*

★ ✳ **Bistro Campagne** Translated as "countryside bistro," this restaurant is so warm and inviting we could stay all night. Ingredients are organic across the board and meld into French bistro classics with unforgettable flavors. There isn't a bad thing on the menu, but if we had to limit ourselves, we'd go with onion soup, mussels steamed in Belgian ale, roasted chicken and pan-seared flatiron steak flanked by amazing frites. Oh, and all of the day's ice creams. *4518 N Lincoln Ave between Sunnyside and Wilson Aves (773-271-6100). El: Brown to Western. Bus: 11, 49 (24hrs), X49, 78, 81 (24hrs). Dinner. Average main course: $18.*

✳ **B Bistrot Margot** The only way this bistro could get more French is if Gerard Depardieu were cancan dancing on a table. Until then, Francophiles will have to make do with a menu of French onion soup brimming with soft, sweet onions;

Read 'em & eat

béarnaise a sauce made from a reduction of vinegar, tarragon, shallots, egg yolks and butter

cassoulet (ka-soo-LAY) slow-cooked dish of white beans and meats, traditionally sausage, duck and pork

confit a method of cooking and preserving meat in its own fat

coq au vin (kohk oh VAHN) chicken (customarily rooster), mushrooms, onions and bacon cooked in red wine

but it worth it for the accompanying pile of doughy, salty *kneffla. 59 W Hubbard St between Dearborn and Clark Sts (312-595-0800). El: Red to Grand. Bus: 22 (24hrs), 36, 65, 156. Dinner. Average main course: $20.*

▼ ✳ **Café Bernard** This Lincoln Park classic has a popular, less-expensive dining room in the back of the building (Red Rooster). That just means you can get a table at this French spot that has been dishing it since 1973. Get your hands on the housemade duck pâté (immensely improved with the proper amount of mustard), plump scallops drizzled with balsamic and a rare, peppery filet mignon flanked by soft, creamy potatoes. Finish off with a classic creamy crème brûlée. *2100 N Halsted St at Dickens Ave (773-871-2100). El: Brown, Purple (rush hrs) to Armitage. Bus: 8, 73, 74. Dinner. Average main course: $20.*

✳ **B Café des Architectes** It's a far cry from the warm, bustling bistros around town, but that doesn't make this mod Sofitel hotel restaurant any less French. Classic touches are found in the attentive service and the bubbling French onion soup. We wouldn't miss the scallop tart, piled with leafy greens and golden-brown scallop slivers over a puff-pastry base. And it's hard to resist the three coins of duck, each wrapped in bacon, stuffed with kumquat, and paired with a vegetable puree (broccoli, potato, carrot)—they're so pretty you'll coo, "ooh la la." *20 E Chestnut St at Wabash Ave (312-324-4000). El: Red to Chicago. Bus: 36, 66 (24hrs), 143, 144, 145, 146, 147, 148, 151 (24hrs). Breakfast, brunch (Sat, Sun), lunch, dinner. Average main course: $24.*

✳ **Café Le Coq** The inspiration for this authentic French bistro came from the rooster lamp on the corner of the bar, which the owners picked up in France. But it's chef Jim August who makes sure that every dish on his classic French menu pays homage to tradition, particularly the buttery escargot, handmade pâté, marvelous steak frites and herb-crusted rack of lamb. The best thing about this place is that it offers French charm without any stereotypical French pretension. Daily specials, like Tuesday night's $22 three-course prix fixe, turn reasonable prices into downright bargains. *734 Lake St, Oak Park (708-848-2233). El: Green to Oak Park. Dinner (closed Mon). Average main course: $15.*

▼ ✳ **Café Matou** The ever-changing menu of rich French flavors at this Wicker Park staple include venison "scallops" in a Syrah sauce and a grilled pork chop in lemon-sage cream sauce—dishes that are simple, hearty and get the job done. A three-course prix-fixe menu—offered Sunday, Tuesday, Wednesday and Thursday evenings for only $23— changes as often as the regular menu, but recent offerings have included grilled asparagus with chive vinaigrette and Pacific rockfish in Chardonnay-thyme cream sauce. *1846 N Milwaukee Ave between Bloomingdale Ave and Moffat St (773-384-8911). El: Blue to Western. Bus: 49 (24hrs), X49, 56, 73. Dinner (closed Mon). Average main course: $20.*

✳ **Café Simone** It's appropriate that chef Didier Durand would name his new venture after his daughter, Simone, because the café/cabaret is the offspring of his restaurant Cyrano's Bistrot. Housed in Cyrano's basement, the energetic space features musicians and entertainers performing nightly. The menu is composed mostly of half-portions from the restaurant upstairs: mussels with curry sauce, cones of frites and hearty charcuterie plates. As good as the food is, nothing tops Durand taking the mike singing a ditty about *coq au vin. 546 N Wells St between Grand Ave and Ohio St (312-467-0546). El: Brown, Purple (rush hrs) to Merchandise Mart. Bus: 65 Grand, 125 Water Tower Express. Dinner (Fri, Sat). Average small plate: $15.*

▼ ✳ **Chez Joël** Little Italy is not just about red-sauce joints. Another option is this quaint spot, where the walls are the color of buttercream and the pâté is just as smooth. The mushroom quiche is thick with earthy 'shrooms and crunchy bread crumbs, and the steak frites come with a particularly herbal maître d'butter and habit-forming shoestring fries. Don't miss lavender/blueberry desserts when available. *1119 W Taylor St at May St (312-226-6479). El: Blue to Racine. Bus: 7, 12, 60 (24hrs). Lunch (Tue–Fri), dinner (closed Mon). Average main course: $20.*

BYOB ✳ **Côtes du Rhône** This is the nice guy of Chicago's restaurant scene: dependable and pleasant if a bit milquetoast. The menu of French classics is executed with results varying from solid (a beefy French onion soup) to lovely (a decadent duck confit) and all the way down to miserable (a mushy cassoulet). For dessert, try the chocolate bread pudding—some nights the only other option is a store-bought Bailey's cheesecake, and there's nothing nice about that. *5424 N Broadway St between Balmoral and Catalpa Aves (773-293-2683). El: Red to Berwyn. Bus: 36, 84, 147, 151 (24hrs). Dinner (closed Tue). Average main course: $17.*

✳ **Cyrano's Bistrot & Wine Bar** *2007 Eat Out Award, Critics' Pick: Best culinary crusader* Via vintage movie posters, Cyrano de Bergerac's long, obtrusive nose pokes its way into every corner of this charming bistro—just as the town of Bergerac's cuisine fills every part of the menu. Chef Didier Durand has built a loyal following for his southwestern French fare, like crisp-skinned rotisserie duck with orange sauce, succulent skirt steak with a hot pile of frites and the most adorable cheese plate known to man. He's revered for thumbing his nose at Chicago's foie gras ban as much as he is for his bread pudding, made with kumquat preserves and Grand Marnier. *546 N Wells St between Grand Ave and Ohio St (312-467-0546). El: Brown, Purple (rush hrs) to Merchandise Mart; Red to Grand. Bus: 65 Grand. Lunch (Mon–Fri), dinner. Average main course: $16.*

Everest For years Everest has lived up to its name, becoming the pinnacle of high-end French dining in the Windy City. Atop the Chicago Stock Exchange, it is still the height of elegance, with views of the rooftops that made the city famous. Chef Jean Joho's seasonal menu hasn't changed much in years, but one could argue, if it ain't broke, don't fix it. His Alsacean menu specialties include boneless rabbit with horseradish, frog legs and black cod. But the real specialty is the sense of elegance you feel just from having dined at this level. *440 S LaSalle St at Van Buren St (312-663-8920). El: Brown, Orange, Pink, Purple (rush hrs) to LaSalle. Dinner (closed Sun–Mon). Average main course: $27.*

✳ **Gabriel's** See Italian/pizza for review.

B Hemmingway's Bistro This traditional French bistro takes its name from the famous author (albeit spelled with an extra "m"), whose birthplace is just up the street. Tucked into the 1920s-era Write Inn, this spot has little signage. But once you find it, the ambience is everything a Francophile could want: cozy banquettes, soft lighting and French music. Chef Christopher C. Ala's menu doesn't push the envelope. However, bistro staples like escargot, cassoulet and beef Wellington are well executed. *211 N Oak Park Ave, Oak Park (708-524-0806). Bus: Pace 311to Ontario. Metra: Union Pacific W to Oak Park. Breakfast, brunch (Sun), lunch, dinner. Average main course: $22.*

✳ **Jacky's Bistro** While the man behind the moniker (Jacky Pluton) has since split from this cozy French bistro, he didn't take the charm with him. It's tough to go wrong here if

French couture Chef Michael Lachowicz puts his personal spin on French classics at Michael.

French

Créme of the crop
Koda Bistro puts a fresh
spin on créme brûlée.

you're prepared to forget calorie counting and dig into dishes like the indulgent pan-seared foie gras with duck rillette. Onion soup is a cheesy, crunchy-crouton–studded dream and the sirloin that makes up half of the ubiquitous steak frites is juicy, flavorful and well cooked (though the frites are so-so). Skip the ho-hum desserts in favor of the imported cheese plate. *2545 N Prairie Ave, Evanston (847-733-0899). Metra: Union Pacific N to Central. Bus: Pace 201, 206, 213. Lunch (Mon–Fri), dinner. Average main course: $21.*

▼ B **Jilly's Café** It's definitely the food that puts this unassuming Evanston bistro high on the date night list. Nothing's more of a turn-on than superb French-American chow for cheap. Meals start with fantastic sourdough bread, impossibly creamy butter and silky pâté. Refreshing pinot noir sorbet follows the appetizers, leading to notable entrées such as New Zealand venison with Door County cherries and delicate wild mushroom risotto. If your date is a day-sipper, this is the place to come for a posh Champagne brunch, served Sundays from 10:30am to 2pm. *2614 Green Bay Rd, Evanston (847-869-7636). El: Purple to Central. Bus: 201 (24hrs), 206, Pace 213. Brunch (Sun), lunch (Tues–Fri), dinner (closed Mon). Average main course: $19.*

✳ **Kiki's Bistro** A good French bistro never gets old— even as it ages. This charming standby still packs in customers every night, sending them off happier and fatter than they were when they arrived. The seasonal menu may include irresistibles like *navarin d'agneau printanier* (lamb stew) or oven-roasted pork tenderloin with apple-Calvados sauce. Kiki's proves getting older doesn't mean losing your touch. *900 N Franklin St at Locust St (312-335-5454). El: Brown, Purple (rush hrs) to Chicago. Bus: 36 Broadway, 66 Chicago. Lunch (Mon–Fri), dinner (closed Sun). Average main course: $20.*

Koda Bistro *2007 Eat Out Award, Critics' Pick: Best Alsatian creation (tarte flambé)* Chef Aaron Browning earned his Franco stripes in the revered local kitchens of Le Vichyssoise and Everest. At this Beverly bistro, his menu gives classic French dishes a dose of seasonal and contemporary flair, such as skate with a caper and brown butter sauce. We love the rich and savory pizza-like tarte flambé, topped with a smear of cottage cheese blended with sour cream and nutmeg, then slices of Brie, toasted walnuts and Bosc pear slices.. *10352 S Western Ave between 103rd and 104th Sts (773-445-5632). Bus: 49A, 103, Pace 349. Dinner (closed Mon). Average main course: $20.*

☺ ✳ **La Creperie** With its dim, smoky bar, weathered posters of Paris and battered leather banquette, it's no wonder this mainstay is a draw for bohemians who seem content to sit for hours eating, drinking and typing on their laptops. The atmosphere is so comfortable that it almost overshadows the food. Almost. Once you try the trio of pâtés, the simple steak flanked by crispy frites or any of the namesake crêpes (we like the crème brûlée for a sweet ending), you'll understand how it's weathered more than three decades. *2845 N Clark St between Diversey Pkwy and Surf St (773-528-9050). El: Brown, Purple (rush hrs) to Diversey. Bus: 8, 22 (24hrs), 76. Lunch, dinner (closed Mon). Average main course: $7.*

La Petite Folie With a list of tasty wines and a menu with venison pâté, trout almondine and Alsatian *choucroute garni*, you'd expect to drop some dough. But chef Mary Mastricola knows she's not quite Jean Banchet, and prices dishes accordingly. Still, the packed dining room of older theatergoers (Court Theatre is nearby) gobble up the early $32 three-course prix fixe (5–6:30pm), while younger couples take the last reservations (8pm). *1504 E 55th St, Hyde Park Shopping Center (773-493-1394). Bus: X28 SB, 55, X55. Metra: Electric Line to 55-56-57th St. Lunch (Tue–Fri), dinner (Tue–Sun), closed Mon. Average main course: $21.*

La Sardine Devotees of Wicker Park's Le Bouchon might tell you otherwise, but the bistro essentials at this sibling spot are just as tasty as those at the homebase. The setting is much more open and airy than Bouchon, but the rest of the package is the same: plump mussels drenched in white-wine broth, onion soup that tests even serious cheese-lovers' thresholds, juicy grilled hanger steak with bordelaise and bouillabaisse jam-packed with seafood. *111 N Carpenter St between Washington Blvd and Randolph St (312-421-2800). Bus: 8, 9, 19, 20 (24hrs). Lunch (Mon–Fri), dinner (closed Sun). Average main course: $18.*

▼ **B La Tache** This Andersonville eatery is the place to go if you're looking for classic French bistro with a little something different. Highlights of this dependable menu are the trout, paired with celery-root puree and a pomegranate drizzle; Berkshire pork chops come with mushroom-bread pudding; and burgers are served with your choice of four sauces or compound butters. Wednesday is "Grilled Cheese Night." Try the Grilled Cheese La Tache (Gruyère, tomato, balsamic onions) with frites for a night of melted, cheesy bliss. *1475 W Balmoral Ave between Clark St and Glenwood Ave (773-334-7168). El: Red to Berwyn. Bus: 22 (24hrs), 36, 92. Brunch (Sun), dinner. Average main course: $18.*

★ **Le Bouchon** Yes, it's crowded, smaller than most studio apartments, and you'll have to wait at the bar for a bit even with a reservation. But it's the closest thing Chicago has to that adorable little bistro in Paris. Regulars have their never-fail favorites: the flaky, caramelly onion tart; the robust onion soup with a gluttonous amount of Gruyère; the feeds-two duck l'orange; and the simple profiteroles. Only snootier waiters could make for a more French experience. *1958 N Damen Ave between Homer St and Armitage Ave (773-862-6600). El: Blue to Damen. Bus: 50 Damen, 73 Armitage. Dinner (closed Sun). Average main course: $16.*

Le Petit Paris Even those who know the local food scene may not have heard of Le Petit Paris. That just means you are more likely to get a seat at this little-known, but excellent French bistro. The menu is full of classics, like mushroom-laden beef bourguignonne and luscious veal "Marengo," but chef Michael Foley sneaks in creative dishes (like artichoke fritters served with a tart lemon mayonnaise) on a regular basis. *260 E Chestnut St between De Witt Pl and Lake Shore Dr (312-787-8260). El: Red to Chicago. Bus: 10, 125, 157. Dinner. Average main course: $20.*

✳ **Marché** You'd think that in Randolph Row's ever-evolving restaurant climate, the block's old-timer either would have become obsolete or changed with the times. It's done neither. The decor still looks like a drag queen catfish; the bistro menu remains intact; and the crowd fills every single seat in the house. The onion soup, spit-roasted chicken, steak frites and unbeatable apple tarte Tatin continue to satisfy. *833 W Randolph St at Halsted St (312-226-8399). El: Green to Clinton. Bus: 8 Halsted, 20 Madison (24hrs). Lunch (Mon–Fri), dinner. Average main course: $20.*

Michael Chef Michael Lachowicz made a name for himself at other local French eateries. He made such a name, in fact, that he christened this venture after himself. He's not reinventing the wheel here, but the man can cook. Classics abound: gooey cheese puffs, an impossibly tender filet–and–short rib duo, and a rich hot chocolate–and–soufflé combo. Lachowicz proves that no matter whose name is on the door, the draw is what's on the plate. *64 Green Bay Rd, Winnetka (847-441-3100). Metra: Union Pacific North to Hubbard Woods. Dinner (closed Mon). Average main course: $24.*

◖ ✳ **B Miramar** Chef-owner Gabriel Viti took more than a cue from New York's famed Pastis (the subway tiles, the

hard-boiled eggs at the bar, the menu) but just the same, he did for the 'burbs what Pastis did for the Meatpacking District—got people to go there. Copycat or not, the food is great. We love any shellfish he cracks open. Ditto for the pâté and garlicky brandade. *301 Waukegan Ave, Highwood (847-433-1078). Brunch (Sun), lunch (Mon–Sat), dinner. Average main course: $17.*

✳ **Mon Ami Gabi** They say practice makes perfect, and the pitch-perfect bistro dishes here show years of rehearsal. The Epcot Center feel of some other Lettuce Entertain You restaurants is missing. Instead you get a cozy and bustling bistro serving steamed mussels in a white ale broth and mega caramelized apple tart tatin. Nightly *plats du jour* like duck à l'orange and steak tartare are consistently delicious as menu stalwarts like seared skate wing. *2300 N Lincoln Park West at Belden Ave (773-348-8886). El: Brown, Purple (rush hrs), Red to Fullerton. Bus: 22 (24hrs), 36, 134, 143, 151 (24hrs), 156. Dinner. Average main course: $19.*

✳ **NoMI** See Eclectic for review.

✳ **Pierrot Gourmet** In the morning, these communal dining tables are packed with those fueling up on cappuccinos and buttery croissants. In the evening, however, you're likely to have the place to yourself. Which is curious, because we love the simple French fare: rustic charcuterie plates and crunchy Alsatian tarts resembling thin-crust pizzas. The pride of Pierrot are the pastries, and we like to take them one step further by dipping them in the Valrhona chocolate fondue. Be warned of the non-Parisian close time: 7 pm. *108 E Superior St at Rush St (312-573-6749). El: Red to Chicago. Bus: 3, 66, 145, 146, 147, 151 (24hrs). Breakfast, lunch, dinner. Average main course: $13.*

✳ **Red Rooster** This bistro has a side-street entrance that is tough to spot. Keep your eyes peeled because there's nothing like warming up with hearty French provincial food such as tender beef bourguignonne on a bed of egg noodles or duck confit ladled with berry sauce when it's numbingly cold. Even in mild temps, the meaty snails in bubbling garlic butter and inexpensive wine list—many bottles are $29 or less—make Red Rooster worth cozying up to. *2100 N Halsted St at Dickens Ave (773-929-7660). El: Brown, Purple (rush hrs) to Armitage. Bus: 8, 73, 74. Dinner. Average main course: $14.*

✳ **Shallots Bistro** See Kosher for review.

▼ **Sweets & Savories** David Richards knows you. He knows that you want big flavors, big portions and not a lot of fuss. So he packs his ever-changing menu full of decadent French fare like fragrant asparagus risotto drizzled with white-truffle oil; oversize duck-fat frites; and an incredibly indulgent burger topped with truffle mayonnaise and pâté. Desserts—like the dense brown-sugar cake infused with cardamom—are exactly how we like them: simple, comforting and without a trace of pretension. *1534 W Fullerton Pkwy between Bosworth and Ashland Aves (773-281-6778). Bus: 9 Ashland, 74 Fullerton. Brunch (Sun), dinner. Average main course: $20.*

◔ **B Vive la Crêpe** This cozy little bistro has "cute date spot" written all over it. The menu is a mix of mostly French-inspired salads and sandwiches, along with crêpe standards (think ratatouille and bananas Foster for fillings) that are bright instead of boring. Weekend brunch is served until 2pm, so you can linger over a late eggs Benedict with your sweetie. *1565 N Sherman Ave, Evanston (847-570-0600). El: Purple to Davis. Breakfast (Sat, Sun), brunch (Sat, Sun) lunch, dinner (closed Mon). Average main course: $8.* ■

Gastropubs

See also: *Classic American, Contemporary American*

Working lunch The Gage gives Loop diners the kind of meals they've been fishing for.

* **BB's** See Eclectic for review.

* **Black Duck** The stretch of Halsted Street that lays claim to this classy tavern is packed with upscale eateries and the buttoned-up crowd dining at them. This spot keeps the scene grounded. Grab one of the tables that surround the beautiful, dark-wood bar and start with a Black Duck martini and plate of scallops wrapped in salty bacon. Move on to the New York strip seasoned simply with salt, pepper and rosemary. It's not Alinea, BOKA or Landmark. But then again, it's not supposed to be. *1800 N Halsted St at Willow St (312-664-1801). El: Red to North/Clybourn. Bus: 8 Halsted, 72 North. Dinner. Average main course: $17.*

The Bluebird Tom McDonald (of Webster's Wine Bar) and Paul Johnston didn't plan for their Bucktown tavern to be such a food destination. It's not that the wine and beer selection isn't great—on the contrary, the list (organized by climate, one of the most pretentious moves we've seen in a long time) is full of gems. But with a menu full of tempting bites such as meaty braised rabbit over pasta and flatbreads topped with serrano ham and manchego cheese, it's hard not to see this place as a spot where drinking is merely a warm-up (and possibly a cool-down) for the dinners that can be had. *1749 N Damen Ave at Willow St (773-486-2473). El: Blue to Damen. Bus: 50, 56, 73. Dinner. Average small plate: $10.*

⊙ **Cullen's Bar and Grill** With the waitresses brandishing brogues along with the shepherd's pie and Guinness pints, you know this Lakeview Irish pub is the real deal. Everyone from neighborhood families to tipsy Cubs fans stop in for above-par bar grub. You can't go wrong with

the char-grilled skirt-steak sandwich, turkey-and-corned-beef Reubens, and Bass Ale–battered onion rings the size of your head. *3741 N Southport Ave between Addison St and Irving Park Rd (773-975-0600). El: Brown to Southport. Bus: 9, 22 (24hrs), 152. Lunch, dinner. Average main course: $10.*

(**English** With high-top tables and a bar that runs the length of the room, it's clear this Britishish spot is putting its pounds on the pub scene. New and old come together on both the cocktail list and the menu: Drinks include a traditional Pimm's Cup and an Earl Grey–mint martini, while classic fish-and-chips and a turkey burger topped with mushrooms and goat cheese are among the food choices. The mussels are puny, but the Newcastle-battered cod is crispy, fat and flaky, and the DIY meatball sandwich comes with a comforting mushroom gravy. *444 N LaSalle St at Hubbard St (312-222-6200). El: Brown, Purple (rush hrs) to Merchandise Mart. Bus: 65, 125, 156. Lunch, dinner. Average main course: $13.*

★ * **The Gage** Owner Billy Lawless and chef Dirk Flanigan have a hit on their hands with this downtown stunner. Beer options reach beyond the basics and wines are accompanied by clever, straightforward descriptions. Flanigan's food is aggressively flavorful, from the perfect-for-snacking Scotch egg to the Gage burger, served with melted onion marmalade and gobs of stinky Camembert. We're not as wowed by the fish and chips, but with little else along the Mag Mile that compares, we'll dodge a couple of bullets. *24 S Michigan Ave between Monroe and Madison Sts (312-372-4243). El: Brown, Green, Orange, Pink, Purple (rush hrs) to Madison. Bus: 14, 20 (24hrs), X20, 56, 60 (24hrs), 124, 127, 157. Lunch, dinner. Average main course: $24.*

★ ▼ (♨ Hopleaf Thought this was just a bar to belly up to with a Belgian brew in hand? One bite from the seasonal menu and you'll know there's much more. Carnivores can exercise their organic options with the smoky brisket sandwich or grilled Dakota beef flank steak. Other highlights might include roasted spring chicken with oven-roasted artichokes, spring onions and mashed potatoes; veggie meatloaf (made with spring veggies covered in tangy red-pepper sauce); and CB&J, a grilled sandwich of housemade cashew butter, fig jam and morbier cheese on sourdough bread. *5148 N Clark St between Winona St and Foster Ave (773-334-9851). El: Red to Berwyn. Bus: 22 Clark (24hrs), 92 Foster. Dinner. Average main course: $16.*

♨ B Mrs. Murphy and Sons Soda bread? Black-and-white pudding? Not so much. This Irish bistro serves food you'd find in modern-day Dublin, which means Guinness isn't just on the epic beer list, but also in a rich onion–and–white cheddar soup. You'll also find it in the beef stew, along with chunks of parsnips and carrots. Other creative takes include orange-marmalade glazed lamb with goat cheese, dried cherries and pistachios served on a bed of arugula. If a full meal isn't in the cards, stop by for a great Irish whiskey at the gorgeous bar. *3905 N Lincoln Ave between Byron St and Larchmont Ave (773-248-3905). El: Brown to Irving Park. Bus: 11, 50, 80, 152. Brunch (Sat, Sun), dinner (closed Mon). Average main course: $20.*

⊙ Pepper Canister Ever wonder what it'd be like to feel years being taken off your life with a single meal? The Irish-ish pub menu here will kill your curiosity. Go greasy with the Irish Breakfast, with fat slabs of fried ham and soft, meaty sausages, or the "toastie special," a buttery, oniony, cheesy mess of a grilled sandwich. Both are perfect for the drunk, the hung over and anybody trying to pack on the pounds. *509 N Wells St between Illinois St and Grand Ave (312-467-3300). El: Brown, Purple (rush hrs) to Merchandise Mart, Red to Grand. Bus: 65 Grand, 125 Water Tower Express. Lunch (Mon–Fri), dinner (Mon–Sat). Average main course: $10.* ■

Mining for gold Mrs. Murphy and Sons' beef stew is laced with Guinness.

Side dish

Patty time
The city's best burgers.

Easy does it An egg tops the eponymous burger at Kuma's Corner.

Nothing satisfies like a good burger. For the true connoisseur, we've tracked down the city's best burgers—from tiny to tremendous, plain to posh. Dig in with both hands.

Best classic Naha *(500 N Clark St at Illinois St, 312-321-6242).* Whether you're eating it over a white tablecloth or on a stool at the front bar, this Angus beef burger—liberally seasoned, with a bed of caramelized onions tucked under your choice of fancy cheeses—is the perfect partner for the fresh, hand-cut parsley fries alongside it.

Best steakhouse burger Rosebud *(192 E Walton St between Michigan Ave and Mies van der Rohe Way, 312-397-1000).* The tuxedoed waiters aren't too jazzed about diners taking up their tables to eat a $12 burger, but we endure whatever they dish out just to get at this superjuicy, 12-ounce bastion of beef and all its buttery, grilled–pretzel roll glory.

Best dressed-up burger Sweets & Savories *(1534 W Fullerton Pkwy between Bosworth and Ashland Aves, 773-281-6778).* This hefty Kobe beef patty is topped with a slab of foie gras pâté and truffle mayo. Now that foie has become contraband, eating this burger has an element of excitement that we haven't experienced since…well, since we ate it the first time.

Best nonbeef burger May Street Market *(1132 W Grand Ave between May St and Racine Ave, 312-421-5547).* Once we tasted the duck (with oven-roasted figs and Maytag blue cheese) and venison (with poached pears, pancetta and aged Spanish goat cheese) burgers, our only complaint was that their small stature doesn't even begin to satiate our appetite for them.

Best pub burger Kuma's Corner *(2900 W Belmont Ave at Francisco Ave, 773-604-8769).* Long before the menu boasted burgers named after metal bands, there was only one: the "Kuma Burger," a half-pound Black Angus patty perfectly grilled to order and topped with bacon, cheddar and a dribbly over-easy egg.

German

See also: *Eastern European, Polish*

Chicago Brauhaus Lincoln Square may have lost many of the Germans who settled there over the first half of the 20th century, but this bastion of oompah fun, baron-sized beers and heaping platters of carb-tastic classics remains. The plastic, feather-stuck alpine hats passed out to patrons Disney-fy the experience a bit, but long wooden tables built for big groups add to the campy party atmosphere. The lederhosen-clad Brauhaus Trio performs nightly, packing the raucous dining hall with duos who ditch their *rouladen* to jump up and dance *zwiefacher*-style (think polka with quick turns). *4732 N Lincoln Ave between Leland and Lawrence Aves (773-784-4444). El: Brown to Western. Bus: 11, 49 (24hrs), X49, 81 (24hrs). Lunch, dinner (closed Tue). Average main course: $14.*

⊙ **Edelweiss** Thirty years old and still ticking, this German-American party hall really gets going on the weekends, when crowds raise steins to the traditional tunes of live bands. Strands of white lights and greenery are up year-round, adding to the festive feel of the cozy space. Meat and potatoes fill the menu, with the best bet being the combo platter of smoked pork chop, roasted pork loin, bratwurst, rouladen, griddled potatoes and spaetzle. The thin, flavorful veal cuts with perfect, crispy breading are great with your pick of nearly two dozen German beers. *7650 W Irving Park Rd, Norridge (708-452-6040). Bus: 80 Irving Park, Pace 326. Lunch, dinner. Average main course: $10.*

Glunz Bavarian Haus Before you get schnitzel-faced at this friendly German restaurant, sample the dozen or so ales and lagers on tap. Don't know your Weizen from your Dunkel? The cute, German-accented waitresses are happy to make recommendations in between doling out soft pretzels with mustard and platters of sausages, cheese, pickles and olives. Stick-to-your ribs entrees include *saurbraten*, red wine–braised beef served with cheesy *spaetzle* that's dotted with marjoram and onions. Before you roll out the door, have a bite or two of the house-made *sacher torte* or apple strudel. *4128 N Lincoln Ave at Warner Ave (773-472-0965). El: Brown to Irving Park. Bus: 11 Lincoln, 80 Irving Park. Lunch, dinner (closed Mon). Average main course: $16.*

★ (☀ **Laschet's Inn** If you were to wander in off the street, you might think this gem is little more than a charming German pub. It is, and it has been since '71, but since '91 it's also been one of the best spots in town for *rouladen*, thin beef rolled with bacon, onions and pickles. The German comfort food is served with tasty brown gravy, sweet braised cabbage and perfect, fluffy *spaetzle* dumplings. Try other authentic offerings like *hackepeter* (rich, fresh steak tartare on rye with capers and onions) and the *wiener schnitzel* (pounded-thin veal breaded and fried crispy). *2119 W Irving Park Rd between Hoyne and Hamilton Aves (773-478-7915). El: Brown to Irving Park. Bus: 11, 50, 80. Lunch, dinner. Average main course: $13.*

Mirabell The cozy side room and larger dinner-hall are the kind of authentic you usually associate with tourist brochures. But there's nothing contrived about the food; a carnivore's delight, the menu features tremendous sauerbraten, an outstanding sausage sampler and some of the best goulash in the English-speaking world. Mirabell may be best known for its bar—featuring a staggering array of heady German beers—but the restaurant shouldn't be overlooked. *3454 W Addison St between Bernard St and St. Louis Ave (773-463-1962). El: Blue to Addison. Bus: 82 Kimball, 152 Addison. Lunch, dinner (closed Sun). Average main course: $12.*

Resi's Bierstube From the shingled roof to the oompah music, this North Side fave is the place to get your Teutonic eat on. Many trundle in for the extensive collection of German beer but the food is *sehr gut*, too. The butter-soft smoked Thuringer sausage has a great mellow taste, while the Sheboygan brat makes a delicious mess with mustard and a heaping pile of sauerkraut. Try the hearty *rahmschnitzel*, a breaded pork loin swimming in mushroom gravy—a meal that will stick to your ribs for days. *2034 W Irving Park Rd between Seeley and Hoyne Aves (773-472-1749). El: Brown to Irving Park. Bus: 11, 50, 80. Dinner. Average main course: $11.*

⊙ **17 West at the Berghoff** For those of you who waited in those ridiculously long lines in 2006 thinking it was your last chance to get this German institution's famous corned beef sandwiches, you've been had. After only about a week of darkness, the 100-year-old restaurant reopened under the name 17 West, but not a thing about the place changed. Well, technically the legendary space is now owned by the Berghoffs' daughter, who's added a few modern dishes such as stuffed portabella and herb-crusted tilapia, but the carving station still serves up sandwiches, the bar still pours Berghoff beer and rootbeer, and the kitchen still slings *weiner schnitzel, sauerbraten* and the like. *17 W Adams St between State and Dearborn Sts (312-427-3170). El: Blue, Red to Monroe. Bus: 1, 2, 6, 7, 10, 22 (24hrs), 24, X28, 36, 62 (24hrs), 126, 151 (24hrs). Lunch, dinner (closed Sun). Average main course: $4.50.* ∎

Read 'em & eat

palatschinken crêpelike pancakes either sweet or savory

sauerbraten a marinated beef roast

schnitzel breaded and pan-fried cutlet of veal or pork

spaetzle dumpling or noodle dish made from eggs, flour, water or milk, salt and occasionally nutmeg

strudel pastry made of thin layers with sweet or savory fillings

wurst sausage; blutwurst (blood sausage), bratwurst (sausage made with pork and veal)

Brew ha ha The joke's on you if you thought the Berghoff was closing for good. It's alive and well as the renamed 17 West at the Berghoff.

See also: *Middle Eastern*

▼ ✳ ◖ **Athena** The massive outdoor patio with a close-up view of the city skyline is the main draw of this Greektown spot in the warmer months, but there are reasons to dine inside, too. The restaurant's signature dish—lamb and artichokes in lemon sauce—is tender and nicely tangy, and other menu standbys, like creamy *taramasalata* (fish roe spread), char-broiled octopus and well-seasoned gyros, are up to neighborhood standards. Skip the same old baklava for dessert and opt for the dreamy *galaktibouriko*. *212 S Halsted St at Adams St (312-655-0000). Bus: 8 Halsted, 20 Madison (24hrs). Lunch, dinner. Average main course: $14.*

★ ◖ **Artopolis Bakery, Café & Agora** See Bakeries/cafés for review.

◖ **Athenian Room** The theory goes like this: The first time you eat at this unassuming Greek spot you may try the gyro salad and think: "Not bad." Next time, you'll try the creamy *taramasalata* on warm rounds of pita, and say: "Pretty good." But according to the cultish customer base, it's on your third visit—when you order the juicy chicken kebabs, the vinegary Greek fries or the flaky *spanakopita*—that the spell is cast and you become one of them. *807 W Webster Ave between Halsted and Dayton Sts (773-348-5155). El: Brown, Purple (rush hrs), Red to Fullerton. Bus: 8, 11, 22, 74. Lunch, dinner. Average main course: $8.*

▼ **Costa's** All Greektown restaurants are not created equal, and when it comes to *taramasalata, tzatziki* and *htipiti* (a spicy feta spread), this elegant stalwart rises above the rest. From there you can go one of many routes: two thick, juicy lamb chops; the "Shrimp Costas," big, garlicky crustaceans piled atop angel-hair pasta; or the gyros. No matter which route you take, make the simple, cinnamony, housemade rice pudding your final stop. *340 S Halsted St at Van Buren St (312-263-9700). El: Blue to UIC-Halsted. Bus: 7, 8, 126. Lunch, dinner. Average main course: $20.*

◖ **Greek Corner** You could walk right by this spot and think it's nothing more than a greasy spoon. You'd almost be right. But once you head to the cute, often-barren patio, open up a bottle of your own wine and check out the modest prices, you'll become much more forgiving. Start with the huge Mediterranean salad with tasty *dolmades*, feta, peperoncini and more. Also tasty are the flaky, peppery *spanakopita* and the Spartan pizza, which swaps spicy hummus for tomato sauce and is topped with grilled chicken, spinach, feta and olives. *958 N Damen Ave at Augusta Blvd (773-252-8010). El: Blue to Division. Bus: 50, 66 (24hrs), 70. Lunch, dinner (closed Sun). Average main course: $7.*

▼ ✳ **Greek Islands** Half the joy of eating at this Greektown stalwart is seeing how many times you can get your server to say "*Opa!*" (We found that with a little nudging, he'll do it every time he fills your water glass.) The other half comes in the form of the savory *saganaki* (Opa!) and the *keftedakia*—small, luscious meatballs simmered in tomato sauce. The sea bass lacks punch, so choose the rich and flaky spinach-cheese pie or the fantastic *loukanico* sausage instead. Honey-laden desserts are solid across the board, so order with confidence. *200 S Halsted St at Adams*

St (312-782-9855). El: Blue to UIC-Halsted. Bus: 8 Halsted, 126 Jackson. Lunch, dinner. Average main course: $13.

◖ **9 Muses** Do the young Greeks who pack this trendy restaurant know something you don't? Yes. And they probably want to keep this place to themselves. But we crash on nights when we want Greek munchies like Florina peppers (two roasted red peppers stuffed with creamy feta), loukanika (a pork-lamb sausage), "toasts" (essentially panini) and huge gyro platters. If you stop yourself from talking by shoveling in food, nobody will know you don't belong. *315 S Halsted St between Jackson Blvd and Van Buren St (312-902-9922). El: Blue to UIC-Halsted. Bus: 7, 8, 60 (24hrs), 126. Lunch, dinner. Average main course: $7.*

▼ ✳ **Pegasus** The name of this joint makes you think that the food here will be so good you'll sprout wings and fly. That didn't *quite* happen when we dug in to the *loukaneko* or the smooth, tangy *taramasalata*, but it got our meal off to a good start. Skip the chewy scallops and typical spanakopita and go right from apps to dessert. Baked in-house and brought in from sister restaurant Artopolis Bakery, sweets include *milopita* (flaky apple pie spiked with cinnamon and honey). *130 S Halsted St between Adams and Monroe Sts (312-226-3377). El: Blue to UIC-Halsted. Bus: 8 Halsted, 20 Madison (24hrs). Lunch, dinner. Average main course: $13.*

★ ✳ ◖ **Santorini** If Greektown makes you feel like you're drowning in a sea of bad food and obnoxious tourists, here's your life jacket. The Kantos family serves food that is impeccably fresh, importing organic olive oil and oregano from the family farm in Sparta. Look for starters like sprightly spanakopita to hit your palate with fresh herb flavor. Like most of the seafood, the whole, grilled red snapper needs nothing more than a squeeze of lemon to show off its subtle flavor. *800 W Adams St at Halsted St (312-829-8820). El: Blue to UIC-Halsted. Bus: 8 Halsted, 126 Jackson. Lunch, dinner. Average main course: $17.* ∎

Read 'em & eat

galaktoboureko (ghal-lahk-toh-BOO-reh-ko) a phyllo pie filled with farina-based custard

loukanika (loo-KAH-nih-kah) fresh lamb and pork sausage spiked with orange rind

pastitsio a type of lasagna with layers of macaroni, ground beef and seasonings

saganaki kasseri cheese (made from sheep or goat's milk) fried in butter or oil and sprinkled with lemon juice; usually served as an appetizer

taramasalata (tah-rah-mah-sah-LAH-tah) appetizer dip made with fish roe, lemon juice, olive oil, garlic and onions, and sometimes bread crumbs and milk

Ice Cream and Sweets

See also: *Bakeries/Cafés, Classic American*

What's the scoop? At Flamingo's, it could be exotic flavors that range from tequila to sweet corn bread.

Anna Held Florist & Fountain Café Flora may be its bread and butter, but this quaint fixture sticks to its tradition of serving shakes, malts, ice-cream sodas and sundaes, as it has since 1927. Stop into the charmingly old world shop for a seasonal bouquet and it's difficult to resist being seduced into snacking—if not on ice cream, then on a piece of pie and a cappuccino. *5557 N Sheridan Rd between Catalpa and Bryn Mawr Aves (773-561-1940). El: Red to Bryn Mawr. Bus: 84, 136, 147, 151 (24hrs). Mon–Sat 10am–6pm. Average ice-cream cone: $2.*

(Annette's Homemade Italian Ice Bellying up to the sidewalk window is the easy part. Deciding on a cool treat from the lengthy menu—therein lies the rub. While soft-serve frozen yogurt, ice-cream sundaes and shakes are available, it's the more than 20 flavors of homemade Italian ice (a simple corn syrup–free combo of fruit, sugar and ice) on offer that are the real draw. From strawberry and peach to passion fruit and coconut-banana, you can beat the heat here with virtually any fruit under the sun. *2011 N Bissell St at Armitage Ave (773-868-9000). El: Brown, Purple (rush hrs) to Armitage. Bus: 8 Halsted, 73 Armitage. Open Apr–Oct., noon–11:30pm. Average cup: $3.*

★ **(* Bobtail Ice Cream Company** Late-night hours (till 11pm weekdays, midnight weekends) mean you can get a postdinner jolt from the caffeinated "cream espress" milk shake (vanilla and espresso) at this soda fountain. Or grab a scoop of the Lakeview Barhopper (chocolate ice cream with Jack) to get a jump on the night's festivities. *2951 N Broadway at Wellington Ave (773-880-*

7372). El: Brown, Purple (rush hrs) to Wellington. Bus: 22 (24hrs), 36, 76, 156. Sun–Thu 11am–11pm; Fri–Sat 11am–midnight. Average ice-cream cone: $3.50.
● *Additional location at 3425 N Southport Ave (773-248-6104). Seasonal kiosk at Buckingham Fountain.*

★ * **Canady Le Chocolatier** It's always encouraging to find little ice-cream shops that make their own products, so you can imagine how psyched we were to find that this gelato gem also makes dozens of varieties of filled chocolates and truffles. Go for broke and get a cup of gelato for now (the pistachio and the tiramisu are our favorites) and a custom-selected box of sweets for later (try the ginger truffle and the dulce de leche chocolate). The shop also does custom gelato cakes that would reduce the folks at Baskin-Robbins to tears. *824 S Wabash Ave between 8th and 9th Sts (312-212-1270). El: Red to Harrison. Bus: 1, 3, 4 (24hrs), 29, 62 (24hrs). Mon–Fri 11am–9pm; Sat, Sun Noon–9pm. Average ice-cream cup: $2.50.*

(Chocolate Shoppe Ice Cream The bright, ever-changing decorations at this retail outlet for the Wisconsin ice-cream company of the same name are matched only by the more than three dozen flavors of ice cream that rotate in and out of its freezers. At any given time, flavors can include cinnamon, cherry chocolate chip and horchata, a take on the Mexican rice-milk beverage. A selection of soft-serve yogurt, sorbet, sherbet, sugarless and soy-based flavors are also available. *5337 W Devon Ave at Minnehaha Ave (773-763-9778). Bus: 84 Peterson, 85A North Central. 10am–11pm. Average ice-cream cone: $3.*

Chocoholic You'll feel like a kid in a candy store at Sarah's Pastries & Candies.

Dairy Queen As far as soft-serve ice cream is concerned, the Queen is king. Sure, it's an international chain, but this location, with its windowside booths packed with smiling faces and outdoor seating along a family-friendly stretch of Southport, retains the feel of a neighborhood original. Besides cones, sundaes and their famous "Blizzard" mash-ups, this DQ also offers hot dogs and barbecue sandwiches. *3811 N Southport at Grace St (773-857-7004). Bus: 9, 77 (24hrs), 80, X80, 152. Mon–Thu 11am–10pm; Fri–Sun 11am–10pm. Average ice-cream cone: $3.*

Dairy Star The crowds line up on the rainbow sprinkle–coated blacktop outside this ice-cream shack just north of the Lincoln Village movie theater to get a soft-serve ice cream dipped in chocolate, cherry or myriad other flavor hard-shell coatings. Grab a spot on one of the benches for people-watching that reflects a great cross-section of city types—blue-collar working stiffs stealing a quick break, large Orthodox Jewish families who love that some of the ice cream is certified kosher, high schoolers on first dates. If you're feeling indulgent, try the Buddy parfait, made with vanilla ice cream, hot fudge and salted peanuts. *3472 W Devon Ave at St Louis Ave (847-679-3472). Bus: 11, 96, Pace 210. Open Apr–Oct, noon–10pm. Average ice-cream cone: $3.*

Flamingos Owner Guadalupe Lopez uses 14 percent cream from the local Elgin Dairy and a wild imagination to create 118 flavors of her amazing ice cream. Adding as little sugar as possible, she captures the essence of each flavor—even exotic ones like Parmesan cheese or sweet corn bread. Don't miss the jalapeño, tequila, mamey, avocado and coconut options. Lopez also makes popsicles for sale in the store. *6733 W Cermak Rd, Berwyn (708-749-4287). Bus: 21, X21, 25, Pace 304, Pace 311, Pace 322. Mon–Thu 11am–10pm; Fri–Sun 11am–10:30pm. Average ice-cream cone: $2.50. ● Additional location at 2635 W 51st St, Chicago (773-434-3917).*

Gertie's Ice Cream/Lindy's Chili The original Gertie's location at 55th and California started serving ice cream in 1901. Lindy's launched its famed chili biz in 1924, and in the mid-'70s, a local entrepreneur purchased both businesses and put them under one roof. The chili is supposedly still made from the original recipe, and it's a tasty one at that. But we go for ice cream, which is about as creamy as it gets this side of gelato. *7600 S Pulaski Rd at 76th St (773-582-2510). Bus: 53A South Pulaski, 79 79th. Lunch, dinner. Average ice cream cone: $3.50. ● Additional locations include 3685 S Archer Ave (773-927-7807) and 11009 S Kedzie Ave (773-779-7236).*

Ghirardelli Chocolate Shop & Soda Fountain What sets San Francisco–based chocolate specialists Ghirardelli apart from other sweet shops is that you can usually choose your poison in either bar or ice cream form. The Intense Dark sundaes, spawned from the chocolate bar series of same name, mix cocoa-heavy chocolate with flavors such as espresso, raspberry and mint chip. The parlor's '50s-era decor, which includes wood pretzel-backed chairs and white marble–topped tables, is a fun spot to sip milk shakes, root beer floats and coffee, but you can also take your treat out to the tables in front in warm weather. *830 N Michigan Ave at Pearson St (312-337-9330). El: Red to Chicago. Bus: 66 (24hrs), 125, 151 (24hrs). Sun–Thu 10am–11pm; Fri and Sat 10am–midnight. Average ice-cream cone: $5.*

Hartigan's Ice Cream Shoppe The Hartigans took a sizable risk when, in 1996, they decided to transform their Baskin-Robbins franchise store into a family owned-and-operated ice-cream shop. It seems the gamble has paid off, though. The store now carries more than 50 flavors from Wisconsin-based ice creamery Cedar Crest, and everyone from Northwestern students to stroller-pushing moms and dads can be seen coming in for a double-dip cone or a cup of joe. *2909 Central St, Evanston (847-491-1232). Bus: 201 Central/Ridge (24hrs). Open Feb–Dec, 11am–11pm. Average ice-cream cone: $3.50.*

Icebox Once the cold days are behind us, this store transforms from Soupbox (where a dozen soups are on offer) into Icebox and starts scooping out 20 flavors of "icyfruit." Cantaloupe and honeydew are among our favorites, and we love digging into the watermelon and coming up with chunks of fruit, proof that this place favors the real deal over fruit syrups. *2943 N Broadway (773-935-9800). 11am–11pm. Average cup: $2.50. ● Additional locations at 50 E Chicago Ave (312-951-5900) and 500 W Madison St (312-993-1019).*

Margie's Candies More so than the ice cream and chocolates, it's nostalgia that draws people out in droves to this kitschy diner/ice-cream parlor. Fancy silver trays with paper doilies and saucers filled with chocolate and caramel sauces bring back fond memories for many, whose families have made this place a tradition since it opened in 1921. Equally as reminiscent of the good old days are the display shelves crowded with memorabilia from the Beatles, who just had to have some Margie's ice cream after they played Comiskey. *1960 N Western Ave at Armitage Ave (773-384-1035). El: Blue to Western. Bus: 49 (24hrs), 56, 73. Sun–Thurs 9am–midnight; Fri, Sat 9am–1am. Average ice-cream cone: $3. ● Additional location at 1813 W Montrose Ave (773-348-0400).*

Miko's Italian Ice This quaint Bucktown take-out window is an offshoot of the original Miko's in Logan Square. Passersby find it hard to resist the refreshing watermelon, the fresh strawberry (with seeds and pulp galore) and the sweet, creamy mango (how Miko makes the ice so creamy without dairy is beyond us). The banana with chocolate chips is a more acquired taste, but it's one that, luckily, more people now have the opportunity to try. *2236 N Sacramento Ave between Lyndale St and Belden Ave (773-988-9664). Open Apr–Oct. El: Blue to California. Bus: 56, 76, 82. Mon–Fri 2–10pm; Sat, Sun noon–10pm. Average cup: $2.50. ● Additional location at 1846 N Damen Ave (773-645-9664).*

Oberweis In business for almost a hundred years now, it's doubtful that any Chicagoan hasn't had this dairy farm's milk or ice cream at some point in his or her life—if not every Friday night. The ice cream, proudly touted as being 18% butterfat, is already rich and sweet enough on its own. But that doesn't stop this shop from pairing it with warm brownies and hot fudge, or with coffee to create frozen lattes. *1293 N Milwaukee Ave between Ashland Ave and Paulina St (773-276-9006). El: Blue to Division. Bus: 9, 70, 72. Mon–Sat 11am–11pm; Sun 11am–10pm. Average ice-cream cone: $3. ● For additonal locations go to oberweis.com.*

Original Rainbow Cone For 81 years, the awning-covered picnic tables of this Far South Side ice-cream shop have been packed with locals feeding their sweet tooth. It recently added smoked brisket and pulled-pork sandwiches to the menu, but the classic Rainbow Cone is what keeps us coming back. The five-flavor cone features slices of chocolate, strawberry, Palmer House (vanilla with cherries and walnuts), pistachio and orange sherbet stacked one on top of the other for an unbeatable classic.

Side dish

Try it, you'll like it
Restaurants cater to kids with menus that move beyond McNuggets.

Dr. Spock and those *What to Expect* books never mentioned that the mere act of procreating meant resigning yourself to a decade or more of nothing but PB&J and chicken fingers.

But you *can* have your curry (or steak tartare) without springing for a sitter, says Dan McGowan, president of Big Bowl, the pan-Asian chain with four Chicago-area restaurants. "If you only feed kids mac and cheese and pizza, that's what they'll want and they will be less likely to eat much of anything else," he says. "When a kid has the chance to experience new flavors, they are more open to new things."

McGowan is among a growing number of local restaurateurs applying creativity to kids' cuisine.

Sola (*3868 N Lincoln Ave at Byron St, 773-327-3868*) **Menu** Roasted chicken breast with glazed carrots and mashed potatoes; ice-cream sundae with gummy bears **Pint-size perks** No games or puzzles here—the kids' menu looks like a miniversion of the regular menu, so kids get to feel grown-up for the night.

Big Bowl (*6 E Cedar St at State St, 312-640-8888; 60 E Ohio St at State St, 312-951-1888; and suburban locations*) **Menu** Grilled chicken satay (who can resist chicken on a stick?); stir-fry with jasmine rice and a drink for kids; teriyaki baby back ribs with rice **Pint-size perks** The menu comes with games that go beyond the usual mazes and word seek.

Tsuki Japanese Restaurant and Lounge (*1441 W Fullerton Ave between Greenview and Janssen Aves, 773-883-8722*) **Menu** Chicken teriyaki bento box, tofu nuggets with rice, California sushi bento box with California and cucumber rolls **Pint-size perks** Hello Kitty bento boxes for girls, bus-shaped ones for boys.

Brasserie Jo (*59 W Hubbard St at Dearborn St, 312-595-0800*) **Menu** Tomato tarte, grilled ham and cheese on brioche with pomme frites, filet of salmon. All kids' items include petite chocolate mousse for dessert. **Pint-size perks** The menu is attached to the back of an Etch A Sketch (with Velcro). Kids' entrées are served first, often with the adult appetizers.

9233 S Western Ave between 91st St and 92nd Pl (773-238-7075). Bus: 49A, X49, 95W. Open Mar–Dec.,11am–10:30pm. Average ice-cream cone: $2.50.

★ **Petersen's** These folks have been making their rich, fatty ice cream since 1910, and they haven't survived all this time on summer business alone. The hot-fudge sundaes—two mounds of luscious vanilla flanked by a pitcher of the viscous sauce, the tall root-beer floats and the infinitely creamy milk shakes make this spot worth the trip anytime of year. 1100 Chicago Ave, Oak Park (708-386-6131). El: Green to Harlem/Lake. Bus: Pace 305, Pace 307, Pace 309, Pace 313, Pace 318. Sun–Thu 11am–9pm; Fri, Sat 11am–10pm. Average ice-cream cone: $3.50.

✳ **Sarah's Pastries and Candies** Sarah Levy's popular candy store/bakery features crunchy clusters of chocolate and nuts and decadent baked goods like chocolate-raspberry brioche. Her menu also includes pressed sandwiches, such as a grilled cheese with truffle oil, and a gelato selection, with flavors like fresh blueberry. We'd scream at her for making our bodies decidedly not swimsuit ready, but, alas, when we're here, our mouths are always full. 70 E Oak St between Rush St and Michigan Ave (312-664-6223). El: Red to Chicago. Bus: 36, 66 (24hrs), 143, 144, 145, 146, 147, 148, 151 (24hrs). Tue–Thu 8am–7pm; Fri, Sat 8am–9pm; Sun 10am–6pm. Average ice-cream cone: $2.50.

▼ (✳ **Scoops** Aromas of fresh waffles pervade the air of this Bridgeport parlor, evidence of their signature, housemade waffle cones. Dipped in chocolate and adorned with various brightly colored candies, these deep cones are indulgent carriers for one or both types of chocolate ice cream they offer here (though our preference is for the darker variety). Should the ice cream get to be too rich, you're in luck: Like all good Italians, these guys focus on espresso, the perfect antidote to your forthcoming sugar crash. 608 W 31st St between Wallace St and Lowe Ave (312-842-3300). El: Orange to Halsted. Bus: 8 Halsted. 11am–midnight. Average ice-cream cone: $2.50.

★ **Scooter's Frozen Custard** Here's how it's going to go down: You'll walk into Scooter's and disregard the hot dogs, Italian ice and anything else that doesn't contain the words *frozen* and *custard*. You'll order a Boston shake, and you'll quiver in awe as the towering milk shake topped with hot fudge and whipped cream is handed over. You'll tell yourself you can't possibly finish it. But as you taste how dense, thick, buttery and rich the custard is, you'll soon be on your way to a full stomach and an ice-cream headache. And it'll be worth it. 1658 W Belmont Ave at Paulina St (773-244-6415). El: Brown to Paulina. Bus: 9, 11, 77 (24hrs). Open Apr–Oct., Mon–Fri 2–10pm; Sat 1–10pm, Sun 1–9pm. Average cup: $4.

Susie's Drive-in Though this tiny 24-hour shack with a three-seater counter only serves two flavors of soft serve—vanilla and chocolate—it's the 54 flavors of milk shakes that draw out folks at all hours. By throwing candy, cookies and flavored syrups into the blender, they create flavors like "baboon" (chocolate and banana), Oreo and strawberry shortcake—thick shakes that pair well with an order of chili-cheese fries and a burger at 4am. 4126 W Montrose Ave between Elston and Keokuk Aves (773-283-6544). El: Blue to Montrose. Bus: 53 Pulaski, 78 Montrose. 24 hrs. Average ice-cream cone: $3.

Sweet Treats Thanks to this sweet shop, you no longer have to cross state lines to get your hands on a scoop

Sweet corner
Imagine the soda jerk days of someone else's youth at Bobtail Ice Cream Company.

of Mackinac Island Fudge or other craveworthy flavors from Sherman's, the renowned ice-cream purveyor from South Haven, Michigan. We're particular fans of Caramel, Caramel, Caramel: caramel ice cream dotted with chocolate-caramel pieces and swirled with ribbons of—you guessed it—more caramel. You'll find fun twists on sundaes (Everyday's Your Birthday is made with yellow-cake-batter ice cream and served atop a cupcake) plus other baked goods from nearby Sensational Bites. *2207 W Montrose Ave at Lincoln Ave (773-539-3044). El: Brown to Western. Bus: 11, 49 (24hrs), 78. Mon–Fri 2–11pm; Sat–Sun 11am–11pm. Average ice-cream cone: $2.50.*

Tom and Wendee's Homemade Italian Ice
Stroller-pushing Lincoln Park moms loves this corner Italian ice spot, probably because the all-natural, nonfat ices are nice to their waistlines. We hear them on that, but we also appreciate the classic lemon ice for its full flavor and the bits of lemon rind sprinkled throughout. Ditto for the watermelon with its sweet juiciness and, to our surprise, the chocolate ices, which are made with cocoa and packed with deep, rich chocolate flavor. You'd swear something like the "chocolate toffee crunch" is bad for you—and let's be honest, the sugar in it probably is—but we'll continue to eat it in semi-ignorant bliss. *1136 W Armitage Ave at Clifton Ave (773-327-2885). El: Brown, Purple (rush hrs) to Armitage. Bus: 8 Halsted, 73 Armitage. Open Mar–Oct, noon–10pm. Average cup: $3.*

Treats The soft-serve here isn't your average belt-busting stuff. Treats prides itself on offering servings of ice cream with only one gram of fat, which is good because

you're probably going to want to eat a lot of it. Along with chocolate and vanilla, four featured flavors are on offer daily, including varieties like caramel fudge éclair and chocolate marshmallow. *3319 N Broadway at Aldine (773-525-0900). El: Brown, Purple (rush hrs), Red to Belmont. Bus: 8, 22 (24hrs), 36, 77 (24hrs). Mon–Thu 11am–10pm; Fri–Sat 11am–midnight. Average ice cream cone: $4. ● Additional location at 2224 N Clark St (312-472-6666).*

✻ **U Lucky Dawg** You can't miss this establishment's towering sign beaming a bright, anthropomorphized hot dog down Western Avenue. Obviously, the dogs are the main event here, along with a few other greasy options. But after you've had your fill of Vienna Beef, top things off with a scoop or two of their hand-dipped ice cream, which comes in eight flavors including Superman, rainbow sherbet, and cookies and cream. *6821 N Western Ave between Pratt Blvd and Farwell Ave (773-274-3652). Bus: 49B, 96, 155. 6am–11pm. Average ice-cream cone: $2.*

Windy City Sweets There's a large selection of novelty gift items and homemade candies here (truffles, chocolate-covered pretzels and fudge), but the nightly post dinner rush comes for the ice cream. Standouts among the more than 30 flavors include blueberry cheesecake and green tea. Employees are generous with the scoops, which they plop down onto everything from plain cake cones to hulking chocolate- and candy-dipped sugar cones. *3308 N Broadway at Aldine Ave (773-477-6100). El: Brown, Purple (rush hrs), Red to Belmont. Bus: 8, 22 (24hrs), 36, 77 (24hrs). 11am–11pm. Average ice-cream cone: $3.* ■

Mixed grill Indian-meets-Bengali
at Radhuni Indian Kitcken

Indian/Subcontinental

See also: *Middle Eastern, Pan Asian, Vegetarian*

▼ **Ankh** See Vegetarian for review.

▼ **BYOB** ☺ **Arya Bhavan** Vegetarians and vegans hit pay dirt with this meat-free spot. During the week, they go for popular South Indian dishes like *dosas* (thin, crispy, rice-lentil crêpes filled with potatoes and onions) and *uttappam* (thicker like pancakes, with onions dropped into the batter). On the weekends (Friday through Sunday), the main attraction is the buffet—a massive spread North Indian dishes. The selection rotates, but you'll typically find gingery lentils, eggplant mashed up with mushrooms, and potatoes with cauliflower in an oniony gravy. *2508 W Devon Ave between Campbell and Maplewood Aves (773-274-5800). Bus: 49B Western, 155 Devon. Lunch, dinner. Average main course: $8.*

☺ **Bhabi's Kitchen** The owner-waiter is Mr. Syed (who goes by Bobby), the cook is his lovely wife and the name Bhabi means "sister-in-law." What's not confusing about this color-splashed Indian treasure is the food. You might just rub elbows with some of the area's top chefs digging into the best vegetable samosas in the city and incredibly flavorful entrées including pureed rapini, baby eggplant, oniony beef (dubbed frontier *gosht*), butter chicken in spicy tomato-cream sauce or whatever else Bobby suggests that night. Be warned: The spice level is definitely not Americanized. *6352 N Oakley Blvd between Devon and Rosemont Aves (773-764-7007). Bus: 49B Western, 155 Devon. Lunch, dinner. Average main course: $8.*

☺ **Chopal Kabab & Steak** You'll often find members of the local Indo-Pak community sitting on the ornately carved, brightly colored wooden furniture, discussing what appear to be important matters. We think they're chatting about how incredibly good the food is: yellow lentils rife with roasted garlic; silky smooth lemon-kissed rapini (Italian broccoli); fiery chunks of chili chicken; and delicious, tender goat chops (which the menu calls "champs"). Quell the heat with the amazing Chopal lassi, and refrain from bringing wine or beer out of respect for the devout Muslim staff and diners. *2240 W Devon Ave between Bell and Oakley Aves (773-338-4080). Bus: 49B Western, 155 Devon. Lunch, dinner. Average main course: $7.*

☺ **Ghareeb Nawaz** The large crowd at the counter of this bare-bones Indo-Pak spot seems chaotic, but the diners are really just waiting for their postmeal chai. So push your way through, and order a bowl of delicious *daal*, loaded with bay leaves and chile peppers. Ask for the chili chicken and spoon the greasy, delicious, fiery red chunks on to the dense *paratha* bread. No matter what you order, you'll get your money's worth; most things here only cost about four bucks. *2032 W Devon Ave at Seeley Ave (773-761-5300). Bus: 49B Western, 155 Devon. Breakfast, lunch, dinner. Average main course: $4.*

★ ▼ **BYOB** ☺ **Hema's Kitchen** Since culinary gem Hema Potla opened up her second location in Lincoln Park, we haven't been able to determine which has better food—we just know we love them both. You'd be hard-pressed to find an Indian restaurant that creates dishes with such distinction. After rounds of chicken masala, lamb vindaloo, *mataar baneer* (peas and cheese) and chickpea curry, we promise you won't be lost in a sea of sameness. *6406 N Oakley Ave at Devon Ave (773-338-1627). Bus: 49B Western, 155 Devon. Lunch, dinner. Average main course: $9. • Additional location at 2411 N Clark St (773-529-1705).*

▼ **Indian Garden** This is the Devon Avenue spot you take your spice-phobic parents or grandparents to while still managing to get good grub and throw back an Indian beer or two. With locations in Schaumburg, Westmont and downtown, this place's accessibility is pretty obvious, but thanks to personable service, your requests for various heat levels will be met. Go for the vegetarian *thali*, a combo platter of mashed, roasted eggplant, creamy spinach, simmered black lentils, rice and nan. Meat-eaters should try the *murg methi chaman*, a fenugreek chicken dish bursting with fresh herb flavor. *2548 W Devon Ave between Maplewood Ave and Rockwell St (773-338-2929). Bus: 49B, 93, 155. Lunch, dinner. Average main course: $13. • Additional location at 247 E Ontario St (312-280-4934).*

▼ **India House** The dinner prices reflect this spot's downtown address and swank decor, so we like to take advantage of the daily lunch buffet ($14.95 Thurs–Sun; $13.95 Mon–Wed) that's one of the best in town. The hot line has around ten flavorful choices, and usually includes creamy chicken tikka masala, cardamom-flavored lamb rogan josh, silky spinach with fresh cheese cubes and spicy coconut-flecked fish goa curry. Tender, smoky chicken vindaloo and

---

Read 'em & eat

biryani (also biriani) rice dotted with spiced meat or vegetables

cacik yogurt-cucumber spread with garlic and dill

dolma stuffed grape leaves (often filled with a spiced lamb-and-rice mixture)

dosa (or dosai) a very thin, lightly fried pancake, usually made of rice flour and lentil flour

gosht (also goshi or josh) meat, usually lamb

kofta a meat or vegetable dumpling

korma a mild, creamy yogurt-based curry, often enriched with nuts

masala (or masaladar) literally "blend of spices" in Hindi

mezes hors d'oeuvres; also the time preceding a meal during which they are served

nan (or naan) a flatbread cooked in a tandoor (clay oven)

Spice it up Date night heats up at Marigold.

fresh nan come straight from the kitchen rather than sitting on the buffet. *59 W Grand Ave between Dearborn and Clark Sts (312-645-9500). El: Red to Grand. Bus: 22 (24hrs), 36, 65. Lunch, dinner. Average main course: $15.*

▼ **BYOB Indian Grill** Chef-owner Shri Tikka Ram Sharma has spent the last 35 years cooking Indian fare in kitchens across Chicago and now runs this spot with the help of his son. We've yet to find any disappointing dishes on the vast menu, but our favorites are the masala-marinated pomfret (Indian Ocean butterfish) and juicy lamb chops and yogurt-marinated chicken, all smoky and slightly charred from the tandoor. Amazing meatless dishes include oniony chickpeas and the creamy, tomato-based *dal makhani*, made from kidney beans and both yellow and black lentils. *2258 N Clark St between Belden Ave and Grant Pl (773-477-8000). Bus: 11, 22 (24hrs), 36. Lunch (Wed–Sun), dinner. Average main course: $11.*

★ ☺ **Khan B.B.Q.** After a fire at the original Khan sent fans of this smoky kebab house into fierce withdrawal, the owners set up shop in the former Jewel of India space. We're happy to report our favorites are just as tasty: the spicy, marinated, char-grilled chicken chunks (*boti*), the juicy sausage-shaped ground-beef patties (*seekh kebab*), and veggie dishes like creamy spinach with potato chunks (*aloo palak*) are all as great (and cheap) as before. Service is slower, but the trade-off is that the air isn't *quite* as thick with the charcoal smoke that ultimately destroyed the previous location. *2401 W Devon Ave at Western Ave (773-274-8600). Bus: 49B Western, 155 Devon. Lunch, dinner. Average main course: $6.50.*

▼ **Klay Oven** This semi-upscale Indian restaurant takes its name from the cylindrical clay ovens that make possible

its best offerings. Out of these ovens, called "tandoors," come 10 varieties of piping-hot fresh bread, as well as meat dishes like *tandoori murg* (chicken marinated in yogurt and spices), lemon-garlic lobster tail and the seekh kebabs, seasoned ground lamb on a skewer. Also popular is the keema samosa, an appetizer which includes a pastry shell filled with lamb, peas, ginger and fresh coriander. *414 N Orleans St at Hubbard St (312-527-3999). El: Brown, Purple (rush hrs) to Merchandise Mart. Bus: 125 Water Tower Express, 156 LaSalle. Lunch, dinner. Average main course: $11.*

★ ▼ ✷ **Marigold** *2007 Eat Our Awards: Readers' Choice, Best new restaurant* This is a haven for those seeking modern, upscale Indian eats. The jewel-toned room is date-worthy, the wine list is pairing-friendly, and contemporary dishes such as *garam masala*–dusted scallops, duck leg confit with blistered green beans, and seared peppercorn-crusted thick yogurt with orange-coriander dressed greens are worth the extra dough you'll drop eating here rather than on Devon. Don't miss the expertly grilled *kalonji* chicken with almond and raisin–studded rice *pulao*. *4832 N Broadway St between Lawrence Ave and Gunnison St (773-293-4653). El: Red to Lawrence. Bus: 22 (24hrs), 36, 81 (24hrs). Dinner (closed Mon). Average main course: $16.*

☺ **Mazza BBQ** This tandoor-focused Indian spot specializes in *boti* and kebabs. Stick to the back page of the menu, where the barbecue items are listed (plus a few puffy *paratha* breads to mop up everything): The crimson-stained chicken boti is tender, and fantastic when drizzled with mint-green cilantro-yogurt sauce; fish filets are rubbed with a cumin-paprika blend before being grilled to juicy perfection; but the minced lamb and beef *seekh* kebabs don't get much of a char and instead arrive a bit mushy. Still, it's impossible to

Peek at the peak
Nepalese cuisine climbs to new heights at Mt. Everest.

wrapped in a whole-wheat flour casing and deep-fried. Skip the confusing Radhuni special salad, but don't miss the juicy tandoori chicken, delicious nan, and housemade mango and pistachio *kulfi* (ice cream). *3227 N Clark St between Belmont and Aldine Aves (773-404-5670). El: Brown, Purple (rush hrs), Red to Belmont. Bus: 8, 22 (24hrs), 77 (24hrs). Lunch, dinner. Average main course: $12.*

⊙ **Sabri Nehari** Be warned that the namesake dish, *nehari*, a spicy Pakistani pot roast, will induce craving so strong you'll consider relocating to Devon. First-timers should know that the half-inch oil slick atop the gingery gravy is supposed to be there; it's ghee (clarified butter) and should be stirred in before ladling the comfort food onto fluffy rice. For a nice contrast, order the frontier chicken, which pops with ginger, garlic and fresh cilantro. For a complete meal, use garlicky nan to sop up the cumin- and chili–laced yellow *dal. 2502 W Devon Ave at Campbell Ave (773-743-6200). Bus: 49B Western, 155 Devon. Lunch, dinner. Average main course: $8.*

⊙ **Tiffin** Don't let the lack of Indian patrons make you skeptical—they're staying away because this place serves alcohol (which many Eastern religions forbid), not because the food isn't good. The meat-loving sibling of Udupi Palace, this white-tablecloth spot is one of the classier restaurants on the block, so entrées are about a buck more than elsewhere. Try the crispy vegetable *pakoras*, massive rounds of bubbly garlic nan, a fiery *bhindi masala* (okra sautéed with onions and tomatoes) and a chicken *tikka masala* dripping in a rich, creamy and, if you request, spicy sauce. *2536 W Devon Ave between Maplewood and Rockwell Aves (773-338-2143). Bus: 49B, 93, 155. Lunch, dinner. Average main course: $9.*

★ ⊙ **Udupi Palace** Carnivores seem to think that without meat on their plate they'd starve. But this 100% vegetarian South Indian spot puts an end to that theory with its famous *dosai*—a gigantic cumin- potato- and onion-filled rice and lentil crêpe that comes in nearly a dozen varieties. Like most veg spots, lentils abound, but other good bets include vegetable *pullav* (a cardamom, clove and cinnamon-laced rice dish with fresh carrots and green beans) and the "Madras-style" okra curry that regulars swear by. *2543 W Devon Ave at Maplewood Ave (773-338-2152). Bus: 49B Western, 155 Devon. Lunch, dinner. Average main course: $8.*

⊙ **Usmania** Formerly a dingy dive that served up some great Indo-Pak food, Usmania now resides in a swankier spot. Luckily, the food is the same. The menu yields well-executed versions of Pakistani standards like *nehari* and kebabs, and the rice biryanis are great, particularly the one made with mutton. The warm staff earnestly tries to live up to its claim of being "the finest family restaurant in Chicago," and it's not far off. *2253 W Devon Ave between Bell and Oakley Aves (773-262-1900). Bus: 49B Western, 155 Devon. Lunch, dinner. Average main course: $8.*

▼ ✳ **Vermilion** It's no surprise to find a sleek black-and-red dining room decorated with beautiful contemporary photography in River North. It *is* surprising to find Indian food on the menu. The female owner-and-chef team (both of Indian descent) isn't doing Devon; it's attempting to elevate Indian cuisine for the swank set that wouldn't venture north of Belmont Avenue. The dishes that weave in Latin American flair are more interesting and flavorful than the straight-up Indian; try the empanada with lychee-jalapeño salsa, the tandoori skirt steak with plantain chips and the mint-ginger ceviche. *10 W Hubbard St between State and Dearborn Sts (312-527-4060). El: Red to Grand. Bus: 22 (24hrs), 29, 36, 65. Lunch (Mon–Fri), dinner. Average main course: $25.* ∎

argue with the prices and fresh flavors. *2226 W Devon Ave at Bell St (773-338-5566). Bus: 49B, 93, 155. Lunch, dinner. Average main course: $7.*

▼ **Mt. Everest Restaurant** Fans of Indian food can get their fixes while also trying Nepalese fare here. Among the Nepalese offerings (no dairy, milder spices, and less oil than Indian food), go for *khasi ko maasu*, goat meat on the bone stewed in a gentle, savory broth; and *jhane ko dal*, mashed yellow lentils sautéed with cumin and cilantro. Of the Indian dishes, the *palaak paneer*, spinach with tart cubes of curdled milk, and lamb vindaloo with potatoes and a smooth tomato sauce stand out. *630 Church St, Evanston (847-491-1069). El: Purple to Davis. Bus: 201 (24hrs), 205, Pace 208, Pace 213. Lunch, dinner. Average main course: $11.*

▼ **Mysore Woodlands** For review, see Vegetarian.

⊙ **The Olive Mountain** It could be the *mosabaha*—creamy hummus with an extra dose of tahini and dotted with whole chick peas and sumac—or the savory, fava bean–based *foul* that make young families, professors and undergrads willing to endure the long (but quickly moving) line for a table here. But after tasting the *shish taouk*, big hunks of infinitely moist chicken; the juicy, parsley-flecked *kefta*; and the expertly prepared cubes of filet that are as juicy as berries, we're pretty sure it's the kebabs. *610 Davis St, Evanston (847-475-0380). El: Purple to Davis. Bus: 96, 201 (24hrs), 205. Lunch (Mon–Fri), dinner. Average main course: $9.*

▼ BYOB **Radhuni Indian Kitchen** The word *radhuni* translates roughly from Bengali to "home cook," and this Indian-with-a-Bengali-twist restaurant seems to have a few of those in the kitchen. Must-try starters are the slurpable tomato soup, and the "Bengol" kebab, chicken chunks

See also: *Classic American, Contemporary American, Eclectic, Kosher*

That's amoré Readers fell in love with Spacca Napoli's Neopolitan pizzas.

▼ ✳ **A Tavola** This tiny Ukrainian Village dining room is tight on tables and menu items—there are about a dozen of each—but what it lacks in size is made up for with charm. The simple Italian fare has no bells or whistles, but most dishes don't need any. A duo of meaty mushrooms—perfectly roasted portobello and sautéed oyster—is dressed only with balsamic and thyme, and the roasted chicken gets by on its golden, crispy skin alone. Of course, there's a fine line between simple and bland—the housemade tagliatelle bolognese teeters toward the latter. *2148 W Chicago Ave between Hoyne Ave and Leavitt St (773-276-7567). Bus: 49 (24hrs), 50, 66 (24hrs). Metra: Milwaukee North Line to Western Ave. Dinner (closed Sun). Average main course: $20.*

▼ BYOB ✳ **B Adesso** There's a lot to love about this casual Italian Boystown eatery: It's BYOB; it's bustling without being a clubby mob scene; the design is sleek but comfortable; and the simple Italian dishes are much-needed in this Italian-bereft 'hood. Dishes to try include the *pollo al mattone*, a Tuscan herb–rubbed half chicken; *trota rosso*, ruby-red trout stuffed with braised fennel, olives, capers and garlic; and *pesce e patate*, a cornmeal-crusted skate wing flanked by garlic fries and red-pepper aioli. *3332 N Broadway at Buckingham Pl (773-868-1516). El: Brown, Purple (rush hrs), Red to Belmont. Bus: 36, 77 (24hrs), 145, 146, 152. Brunch (Sat, Sun), lunch, dinner. Average main course: $14.*

▼ **B Angelina** You know those Italian places you see in the movies? Those charming neighborhood joints where the walls are lined with empty bottles of wine (most of them baring messages of thanks from customers past) and the room has a constant candlelit glow? The kind where the menu isn't a revelation, but the big portions of food are hearty and delicious? Where herbaceous spinach lasagna and savory eggplant parmigiana pull in regulars who've been coming "for years"? Yeah, this place is exactly like that. *3561 N Broadway between Brompton Ave and Addison St (773-935-5933). El: Red to Addison. Bus: 36, 146, 151 (24hrs), 152. Brunch (Sun), dinner. Average main course: $16.*

▼ **Anna Maria Pasteria** This Italian stalwart has retained all of the charm it had when it made Wrigleyville home: The exposed brick, rustic, frescoed walls and flickering candlelight could warm even the residents of the cemetery across the street. The menu features traditional pasta and meat dishes that, while not earth-shattering, are satisfying. All your marsalas, piccatas and parmigianas are represented, but don't miss the delicate, lemony grilled calamari starter or the *rigatoni al pomodoro secco*, with its fat mushrooms and just-heavy-enough Gorgonzola sauce. *4400 N Clark St at Montrose Ave (773-506-2662). Bus: 22 (24hrs), 78, 145, 148. Dinner. Average main course: $15.*

▼ ✳ **Anteprima** It's cute, it's bustling, service is helpful, and the food borders between good and great. What's not to like about this Andersonville bistro? Well, the veal meatballs aren't too hot but other than that, we're big fans of this small plates eatery. Don't miss the balsamic and honey–laced quail—perfectly roasted so that the crispy skin gives way to juicy, well-seasoned meat—the tender, lemon-kissed, grilled octopus or the salumi plate. Save room for vanilla bean–speckled lemon panna cotta and chocolate tart lined with a

buttery hazelnut crust. *5316 N Clark St between Berwyn and Summerdale Aves (773-506-9990). Bus: 22 Clark (24hrs), 92 Foster. Dinner. Average main course: $19.*

▼ **Apart Pizza** Designer pizza's all the rage, but we still long for a simple, no-frills Neapolitan pie—the kind that's cut into perfect triangular slices, not kiddy-size squares. Salvation has come by way of this immaculate Lincoln Square storefront, where the industrial-size mixer is a cue that this place takes thin crust seriously. Add a perfect sauce to topping ratio, a smattering of fresh salads and house-made dressing options, and the result is the perfect little takeout pizza joint. Bonus: Delivery's free. *2205 W Montrose Ave at Lincoln Ave (773-588-1550). El: Brown to Western. Bus: 11, 49 (24hrs), 78. Lunch (Wed–Sun), dinner. Average pizza: $13.*

▼ BYOB **The Art of Pizza** It's the sauce. Don't get us wrong; we love the fresh toppings, including meaty chunks of mild sausage and fresh vegetables that are crisp and crunchy when you bite into them. But it's really the sauce—full of fresh tomato flavor, speckled with oregano, basil and the faintest hint of red pepper—that's made this pizzeria a Chicago institution. Both the deep-dish and the (not very thin) thin-crust lack the flakiness of other local pies, but they resist sogginess after a night in the fridge, making them the breakfast of champions. *3033 N Ashland Ave at Nelson St (773-327-5600). El: Brown to Paulina. Bus: 9 (24hrs), X9, 11, 77 (24hrs). Lunch, dinner. Average pie: $13.*

Bacchanalia Ristorante Though named after a hedonistic festival, this is a quaint, family-owned restaurant that has been serving up what it calls "recipes from the Old Country" in the Heart of Little Italy for more than 25 years. Nouveau Italian cuisine takes a backseat to over 20 pasta dishes and a long list of classics like chicken parmigiana and veal scaloppine. Bacchanalia is not nearly as sinful or risky as its name implies, but it is certainly satisfying. *2413 S Oakley Ave between 24th and 25th Sts (773-254-6555). El: Blue (rush hrs), Pink to Western (54th and Cermak). Bus: 49 (24hrs), X49, 60. Lunch, dinner. Average main course: $11.*

(✳ **Ballo** This spot from the Rosebud empire looks at lot more like Jersey circa 1977 than Italy: A disco ball spins overhead and flat-screen televisions flicker with a repertoire of classic disco films and gangster pics. But it's not all gimmicks. An extensive antipasi array of succulent meats and cheeses are sliced to order, "Grandma's Gravy" tops rigatoni with juicy slices of braised pot roast, and the excellent trio of "Mama's Meatballs" are so addictive you'll start looking for opportunities to marry into the family. *445 N Dearborn St between Hubbard and Illinois Sts (312-832-7700). El: Red to Grand. Bus: 22 (24hrs), 36, 65. Lunch (Mon–Fri), dinner. Average main course: $18.*

☺ **Bari Foods** If you're anywhere near the West Loop, you *have* to make a stop at this Italian grocery. Work your way through the tiny aisles with jam-packed shelves offering imported pastas, olive oils and biscotti galore and head for the deli counter in back. You'll find the best Italian sub in town: a crusty sub loaf (baked next door at D'Amato's) brimming with cappocollo, Genoa salami, mortadella, provolone, oregano, tomato and housemade giardiniera. Grab a San Pellegrino and a pint of Ciao Bella gelato and you've got the best lunch in town for less than a ten spot. *1120 W Grand Ave between Aberdeen and May Sts (312-666-0730). Bus: 65 Grand. Lunch. Average sandwich: $5.*

▼ ✳ **Basil Leaf Café** This tiny, one-room restaurant doesn't stand out. But don't discount the allure of a place where you can get good pasta and where the waitstaff treats

everyone like a ten-year regular. Waiters offer to sprinkle fresh Parmesan over everything, from the calamari and mussels appetizer, to the Alfredo-sauce–laden cheese tortellini, to the chicken breast topped with asparagus. We pass on the extra *formaggio*, but when we're asked if we want more of the thick, crusty bread, we say, "hell yes." *2460 N Clark St at Arlington Pl (773-935-3388). El: Red, Brown, Purple (rush hrs) to Fullerton. Bus: 22 Clark (24hrs), 74 Fullerton. Lunch, dinner. Average main course: $14.*

▼ **Bella Notte** People generally seem to love gargantuan portions (for the value), but when the heaps actually taste good, it's a win-win. Couples linger over decent bottles of wine and specialties like garlicky housemade sausage links with blistered bell peppers, fresh cavatelli and rapini swimming in white wine garlic butter sauce, roasted chicken oreganato and the juicy New York strip with sweet and vinegary peppers. The marble and mahogany bar and handful of café tables up front are perfect for a stop-in drink or dessert. *1374 W Grand Ave between Ada and Noble Sts (312-733-5136). El: Blue to Chicago; Green to Ashland. Bus: 9 Ashland (24hrs), 65 Grand. Lunch (Mon–Fri), dinner. Average main course: $20.*

▼ ✳ **Bice Ristorante** You don't hear much about this big, bilevel restaurant in the Gold Coast. And there's something to be said about an Italian spot that's outlasted countless other restaurants in the nearly two decades it's been open. We think its secret is keeping things simple: The warm and inviting dining room and curvaceous bar entice diners, and the food doesn't disappoint. There's the impeccably fresh buffalo mozzarella; hearty bowls of cheesy, housemade gnocchi; and a wine list that—like everything else—is nothing if not dependable. *158 E Ontario St between Michigan Ave and St. Clair St (312-664-1474). El: Red to Grand. Bus: 3, 10, 26, 125, 143, 144, 145, 146, 147, 148, 151 (24hrs). Lunch, dinner. Average main course: $20.*

☉ **Big Cheese** Chicago's in love with Naples-style thin-crust pizza. But this joint takes its inspiration from somewhere a little closer to home: New England. An outpost of this pizza parlor has been in Rhode Island since 1965, and despite the neon-green interior giving us rave flashbacks, we like this location's simple salads tossed in sprightly housemade dressing, soft and savory meatballs, and pizzas that pile fresh vegetables on crispy crust that's thicker than the Neapolitan stuff, thinner than deep-dish and a good option for when you just can't decide between the two. *2554 W Diversey Ave at Rockwell St (773-227-1122). Bus: 49 (24hrs), X49, 76. Lunch, dinner. Average main course: $8.*

☉ **BoJono's** In a city known for its deep-dish pizza, this hideaway is churning out tasty slices of super-thin, cheese-heavy goliaths to the hungry masses craving a taste of the NYC wedge. Mostly a storefront delivery/takeout joint, BoJono's menu is loaded with simple, mob-friendly selections that fill the belly and appease those hard-core greasy cravings (we like the garlic, oil and tomato). The juicy steak sandwich—topped with bubbly, melting cheese on toasted garlic bread—is a meatlover's dream. Finish off with a slice (or two) of the tangy cheesecake. *4185 N Clarendon Ave between Buena Ave and Gordon Ter (773-404-9700). El: Red to Sheridan. Bus: 36, 80, 135, 145, 146, 151 (24hrs). Lunch, dinner. Average main course: $8.*

▼ **Brick's** Should the thick-crust theorists and thin-crust connoisseurs ever stop their quarreling for a night, this is where they'll come together. Because here, the bubbly crust fits somewhere in between those two camps. Whether piled with feta and spinach (like the garlicky Popeye pie) or housemade meatballs and fresh mozz, the simultaneously crispy and fluffy crust never buckles. Nor does it get in the way, so purists on both sides should be satiated. And if they're not, the well stocked beer list (including Fat Tire and the entire Anchor Brewing lineup) can be tapped to calm things down. *1909 N Lincoln Ave at Wisconsin St (312-255-0851). Bus: 11, 22 (24hrs), 36. Dinner. Average pizza: $15..*

▼ **Bruna's** This old-school favorite opened its doors in the Heart of Italy neighborhood in 1933, which almost explains the faded travel posters and weary saloon decor. But the kitchen is far from tired, going beyond typical pastas and parmigianas to specialize in rustic dishes from Siena. Tucked between the chicken Vesuvio and the stuffed shells are a rich ravioli filled with porcini mushrooms and a spirited rendition of penne alla puttanesca. For the complete Oakley Avenue experience, stop at the bar for a digestif with the locals. *2424 S Oakley Ave between 24th Pl and 24th St (773-254-5550). El: Blue, Pink to Western (54th/Cermak). Bus: 21, 49 (24hrs), X49, 60 (24hrs). Lunch, dinner. Average main course: $18.*

▼ **Bubamara Pizza & Pasta** This pale green Ravenswood pizza joint looks like just another neighborhood hole-in-the-wall. But like any good delivery/takeout spot, the pie is more important than in-store ambience. And the coolest thing about this place is that in addition to its regular menu, from May–November an organic menu includes 100% organic pizzas, pastas and salads. And we're not talking one or two items. Pizza toppings include loads of veggies, chicken, beef, sausage and even bacon. The organic goods cost about double the conventional dishes, but taste even better. The pizzas arrive at your door in a white box affixed with the little organic-produce stickers. *4607 N Wolcott Ave between Leland and Wilson Aves (773-334-2633). El: Brown to Damen. Bus: 50, 78, 81 (24hrs), 145. Dinner. Average organic pizza: $18.*

▼ ✳ **Buona Terra Ristorante** The urban Italian food served here ranks a significant notch above standard spaghetti-house fare. The exposed brick dining room exudes as much warmth and charm as the T-shirt-clad servers. Panzanella Toscana, though presented more like a bruschetta than the true bread salad, is juicy and balanced. Pastas, including an admirably clammy version of linguine alle *vongole*, are served properly al dente and generously sauced. You'll never see pesto mashed potatoes in Italy, but they sure taste fine sitting next to a chicken breast adorned with smoky mozzarella, bacon and tomatoes. *2535 N California Ave between Altgeld St and Logan Blvd (773-289-3800). El: Blue to California. Bus: 52 California, 74 Fullerton. Dinner (Tue–Sun). Average main course: $12.*

☉ **Café Ciao** This bright storefront cafe has won the hearts of the neighborhood—residents of the surrounding condo buildings can spend hours here with a cappuccino. Any West Loop workers looking for a low-key, down-to-earth lunch will become fans, too. The limited, carb-loving menu is full of hearty Italian-American classics like garlicky linguine with clams, rigatoni mixed with spicy sausage and doused in a creamy tomato sauce, and a portobello mushroom and artichoke panini. Food this basic makes for a disappointing dinner, however, so in the evening, stick to visiting for a postmeal coffee. *939 W Madison St at Sangamon St (312-850-2426). Bus: 8, 19, 20 (24hrs). Lunch, dinner (closed Sun). Average main course: $8.*

BYOB ✳ **Café Luigi** The only way this old-school slice shop could get more New York is if Woody Allen was rolling the dough, Sarah Jessica Parker was tending the sauce and Michael Bloomberg was working the register. Big, foldable slices are thin and can be piled with spinach, artichokes,

ricotta and fresh tomato—though real New Yorkers know that plain is the way to go. Housemade sausage and pepperoni-stuffed "New York rolls" and thick Sicilian slices round out the menu, and the BYOB status keeps things cheap. *2548 N Clark St at Deming Pl (773-404-0200). El: Brown, Purple (rush hrs) to Diversey. Bus: 8, 22 (24hrs), 36, 76. Lunch, dinner. Average main course: $4.*

▼ **Café Spiaggia** If you want to dine at Spiaggia but just can't foot the bill, your solution is this adjacent sibling café. The ingredients come from the same kitchen, so they're just as impeccable, and the attention to regional Italian tradition is just as detailed. The room is more casual, prices are lower and service is less formal, making it a perfect lunch escape from Mag Mile shopping. Save room for incredible pastas like gnocchi pillows in perfect wild-boar ragù or strands of *perciatelle* tossed with *guanciale*, Calabrian peppers, garlic, onion and fresh basil. *980 N Michigan Ave between Oak St and Walton Pl (312-280-2750). El: Red to Clark/Division. Bus: 143, 144, 145, 146, 147, 151 (24hrs). Lunch, dinner. Average main course: $17.*

☉ **Calo Ristorante** Tucked between the Swedish stalwarts and shiny new bistros and sushi houses in Andersonville is this red-sauce Italian spot, which has been serving up can't-go-wrong classics to the locals since 1963. A much-needed recent remodel modernized the dining room, but the menu remains solidly old-school, with dishes like crisp chicken parmigiana and shells stuffed to the hilt with fresh ricotta. Feeling fancy? Try the fluffy gnocchi filled with Gorgonzola and served under a blanket of tomato cream sauce. *5343 N Clark St between Summerdale and Balmoral Avenues (773-271-7725). Bus: 22 (24hrs), 50, 92. Lunch, dinner. Average main course: $10.*

▼ ✳ **Campagnola** The chef may have changed (the kitchen is now helmed by Vince DiBattista) at this popular upscale storefront, but the focus remains sophisticated Italian food made with organic ingredients here, including a simple pappardelle bolognese that gets a boost from its delicate veal, pork and pancetta *ragù*. Though limited, the mostly Italian wine list offers some exciting choices, especially the dark, velvety Liveli *negro amaro*. *815 Chicago Ave, Evanston (847-475-6100). El: Purple to Main. Bus: 205 Chicago/Golf. Dinner. Average main course: $22.*

▼ ✳ ☉ **Caponies Trattoria** Irony doesn't exist at this red-sauce joint, so take a cue from the name and the Sopranos mobile dangling over the cash register and behave yourself. It'd be a crime to get yourself banned from this place because while it might not be doing anything new, its brand of Italian classics is impeccably executed. Thin-crust Margherita pizzas shimmer with olive oil and explode with the flavors of basil, garlic and fresh mozzarella; enormous portions of chicken parmigiana are greaseless and immersed in a chunky, fresh tomato sauce. *3350 N Harlem Ave between School and Roscoe Sts (773-804-9024). Bus: 77 (24hrs), 90, 152. Lunch (Tue–Sun), dinner. Average main course: $12.*

▼ BYOB **Caro Mio** The deep-red walls and friendly service make this charming Ravenswood spot as warm and comforting as the food. And because it's BYOB, it's hard to beat the value. Bring a bottle of Sangiovese to match with the soft grilled polenta topped with the chunky house *ragù*. The housemade tricolored rotolo is our favorite of the pastas, stuffed with ricotta and spinach, then baked to hot, hearty perfection. Specials like chicken parmigiana baked in a cream-based red sauce are winners—as are most of the dishes on the menu. *1827 W Wilson Ave between Ravenswood and Wolcott Aves (773-275-5000). El: Brown to*

Mix master Perfectly poured drinks—not just pizza—are on the menu at Crust.

Fare well Mouth-watering antipasto (pictured, left) is served up in a mod setting at Francesco's Forno.

Damen. Bus: 50 Damen, 145 Wilson/Mich Exp. Lunch (Mon–Fri), dinner. Average main course: $15.

▼ ⟨ **Chicago Pizza and Oven Grinder Co.** Since 1972, this underground institution has been luring Chicagoans with the promise of famous sandwiches and pizzas. Its "Pizza Pot Pies" are in no way, shape or form actual pizza—they're more like bread bowls filled with pizza sauce and melted cheese. But the grinders, such as the Italian combination that piles on Genoa salami and smoked ham, are so mammoth, crispy and warm, and the salads topple with such insane quantities of artichoke hearts, olives and peppers, that we'll forgive the false advertising. 2121 N Clark St between Dickens and Webster Aves (773-248-2570). El: Brown, Purple (rush hrs) to Armitage. Bus: 11, 22 (24hrs), 36. Lunch (Sat, Sun), dinner. Average main course: $11.

▼ **Club Lago** Yuppies may come and go from this ever-changing neighborhood, but Club Lago always remains the same. Now in the hands of Guido and Giancarlo Nardini (grandsons of the original owner) the food is as basic and hearty as it was in 1952. The manicotti is overstuffed with ricotta and piled with the meaty, signature red sauce; the baked clams are crusted in golden bread crumbs, and veal is prepared in every way you can imagine (we like the simple lemony bracioline all'agro). History never tasted so good. 331 W Superior St at Orleans St (312-337-9444). El: Brown, Purple (rush hrs) to Chicago. Bus: 66 Chicago (24hrs). Lunch, dinner (closed Sun). Average main course: $11.

▼ ⟨ ✳ **Club Lucky** The nearby condo dwellers with kids in tow may be a different crowd than the Polish regulars who once frequented the joint post-Prohibition, but the owners have gone out of their way to restore the original cocktail-culture look of the '50s. The place is always packed, thanks to a dependable, old-school, family-style Italian menu with

standouts like grilled calamari, chicken Vesuvio, and escarole with sausage and beans. But if you're kidphobic, go late for the lounge vibe of Sinatra standards and signature martinis. 1824 W Wabansia Ave at Honore St (773-227-2300). El: Blue to Damen. Bus: 50, 56, 72. Lunch (Mon–Fri), dinner. Average main course: $16.

▼ BYOB **Coal Fire** East Coast–style pizza in Chicago? Finally! Right down to the namesake oven, the pies these guys are turning out are immensely impressive, with slightly charred bubbles. We're fans of the sweet-heat combo on the Fiorentino, a marriage of red peppers and hot salami. The housemade sauce incorporates canned tomatoes, but they're high quality and taste fresh and bright. Fans of ricotta could skip red pies altogether and go with either the white pizza or the pesto (salty black olives combine with the fresh ricotta for perfect balance). 1321 W Grand Ave between Elizabeth and Ada Sts (312-226-2625). El: Blue to Chicago. Bus: 9 (24hrs), X9, 65. Dinner (closed Mon). Average pizza: $13.

★ ▼ **Coco Pazzo** The soft focaccia and fruity olive oil delivered to your table at this popular Gold Coast mainstay are good indicators of what's to come. Start with some antipasti—it's not on the menu, but on your way in you probably passed by a table stocked with the wonderful chunks of Parmesan, white beans slick with olive oil and herbs, and thin slices of tender prosciutto. The garganelli pasta dish is doused in lamb ragù; and housemade gelato are decadent endings. All of which, we promise, are worth dealing with the lazy service. 300 W Hubbard St at Franklin St (312-836-0900). El: Brown, Purple (rush hrs only) to Merchandise Mart. Bus: 65 Grand, 125 Water Tower Express. Lunch (Mon–Fri), dinner. Average main course: $17.

★ ▼ ⟨ ✳ **Crust** The motto of Crust, Michael Altenberg's certified-organic pizzeria, is "Eat Real." Eat simple and good is more like it, as that's the general take on straightforward salads composed of impeccably fresh vegetables; tender pulled pork topped with crunchy slaw on soft housemade brioche and flanked by sweet beet chips; and the pizza (appearing on the menu as "flatbreads"), which has a bubbly, half-inch–thick crust that is slightly, pleasantly chewy. When it is topped with béchamel, caramelized onion, bacon and caraway seeds—like the "Flammkuchen" is—it can be very good. *2056 W Division St at Hoyne Ave (773-235-5511). El: Blue to Division. Bus: 50 Damen, 70 Division. Lunch, dinner. Average main course: $12.*

▼ **Cucina Paradiso** Walking into this swank space, you won't think "pizza," but you should: The Gorgonzola-and-pear–topped pie with balsamic drizzle is delicious. To sustain your high, knock back a three-wine flight priced at only $8.25. You could stop right there and be happy, but if you must proceed, go with the signature pistachio chicken with herbaceous polenta. Skip the veal medallions; they're overwhelmed by pancetta and fontina. Instead, carbo-load with popular pastas (including several all-veggie options) and a stellar version of bread pudding. *814 North Blvd, Oak Park (708-848-3434). El: Green to Oak Park. Lunch (Fri), dinner. Average main course: $16.*

▼ **BYOB** (☺ **Da'Nali's** See Kosher for review.

☺ **Dave's Italian Kitchen** In lots of ways, eating here is like going to your Italian grandmother's house for Sunday dinner. It's loud, a little dysfunctional and the decor is pretty worn, but all that fades into the background at your first taste of that housemade red sauce. Northwestern students and neighborhood families allow Dave's to be the grandma they never had, crowding the basement-level eatery for mega portions of mostaccioli, eggplant parmigiana and half-moon calzones. Wine snobs dine here, too, to see what new bottles oenophile Dave is serving up from his global collection. *1635 Chicago Ave, Evanston (847-864-6000). El: Purple to Davis. Bus: 201 Central/Ridge. Dinner. Average main course: $9.*

▼ ✳ **Dinotto Ristorante** Comfy digs and an accommodating waitstaff draw a casually dressed crowd from the nearby Piper's Alley and Second City theatres to this family-owned Italian restaurant. Starters include fresh clams and mussels in white wine garlic sauce and a signature salad of mesclun lettuce, Gorgonzola cheese, pine nuts and tomatoes topped with warm balsamic vinaigrette dressing. Besides the requisite selection of pasta, chicken and veal, the restaurant features two fresh fish entrées and a grilled duck breast tossed with portobello, field mushrooms and fettuccine. *215 W North Ave at Wells St (312-202-0302). El: Brown, Purple (rush hour only) to Sedgwick. Bus: 72 North. Lunch (Mon–Sat), dinner. Average main course: $15.*

☺ **Enoteca Piattini** This trusty Italian spot lures locals into its sunny dining room with its extensive wine list and keeps them there with its solid menu. Tender meatballs simmering in marinara seem the perfect mate for a medium-bodied Italian red, while entrées like saltimbocca Siciliana—veal topped with savory prosciutto and fontina—seem made for a lemony glass of white. End dinner with the watermelon sorbet. It may taste more like watermelon candy than the actual fruit, but it's a refreshing ending nevertheless. *934 W Webster Ave at Bissell St (773-935-8466). El: Brown, Purple (rush hrs), Red to Fullerton. Bus: 8, 73, 74. Dinner (closed Mon). Average main course: $10.*

☺ **Enoteca Roma** From the family behind Letizia's Natural Bakery comes one of the best back patios in the Ukie Village/Wicker Park area. Cop a seat among the greenery and dive into the wine list (not limited to Italian wines); it's playful, varied and built for food. The bruschetta varieties—topped with toothsome ingredients like Brie and honey, cannellini beans and black olive puree—are the favorite son of the extensive menu, but don't overlook the Roman-style pizzas and Letizia's soft, salty focaccia with spicy mustard. *2146 W Division St between Hoyne Ave and Leavitt St (773-342-1011). El: Blue to Division. Bus: 49 (24hrs), X49, 70. Dinner. Average main course: $8.*

▼ ✳ **Erba** Yes, this small, contemporary Lincoln Square Italian spot lists "fancy olive oil" on its menu, but that's not the only thing you should consider. The menu includes dishes such as mussels steamed in Moretti beer, herbed polenta with morel mushrooms and thyme, and pan-roasted chicken breast with Parmesan pudding are begging for your attention. The menu is divided into antipasti, primi and second; don't skip the housemade pastas, such as the goat-cheese gnocchi with fingerling potatoes, green beans and pesto, and the pappardelle with slow-roasted duck. *4520 N Lincoln Ave between Sunnyside and Wilson Aves (773-989-4200). El: Brown to Western. Bus: 11, 49 (24hrs), X49, 78, 81 (24hrs). Dinner (closed Mon). Average main course: $16.*

Filippo's We've seen couples linger over dinner here, head to a nearby movie, and come back later for dessert. The draw of the place is dishes such as the housemade salmon-and-ricotta–stuffed *ravioli neri*; the creamy, perfectly al dente risotto with peas, ham and asparagus. But the meal doesn't end there: Just when you think you can't eat anything else, the friendly owner comes over and pours a shot of housemade limoncello. *2211 N Clybourn Ave between Webster and Greenview Aves (773-528-2211). El: Brown, Purple (rush hrs) to Armitage.Bus: 9 (24hrs), X9, 73, 74. Lunch (Tues–Sat), dinner. Average main course: $12.*

★ ✳ ✳ **Follia** Chef-owner Bruno Abate has decorated his high-style Italian restaurant with a wall of simulated grass and mannequins dressed in flashy couture, but the diverse crowd here comes for the food, not the fashion. We love the crispy, paper-thin pizzas from a wood-burning oven (try the napoletana, topped with oregano and anchovies) and the pastas (a simple but spectacular risotto bolognese was a recent special). Entrées are hit-or-miss—on one visit, the veal Milanese was limp and underseasoned—but the personable servers make reliable recommendations. *953 W Fulton Ave at Morgan St (312-243-2888). El: Blue to Grand. Bus: 8 Halsted, 65 Grand. Dinner. Average main course: $15.*

B ☺ **Francesca's Forno** This Wicker Park outpost from the Francesca's chain packs in the hungry and hip for small plates of simple Italian fare for bunch, lunch and dinner. The BLT goes above standard with pancetta, arugula and a lemon mayo, plus a handful of pecorino and truffle oil–laced fries and their signature Traviata pizza comes stuffed with herbed robiola cheese, mixed greens and sea salt. *1576 N Milwaukee Ave at North Ave (773-770-0184). El: Blue to Damen. Bus: 50, 56, 72. Brunch (Sat, Sun), lunch (Mon–Fri), dinner. Average main course: $8.*

▼ **Francesca's on Taylor** The portions are generous, the room is comfortable and the food is reliable. This, plus the place's ability to glide from family-friendly pasta joint to romantic trattoria as the night progresses, is what packs 'em in every night. Good bets are crispy calamari, *quatro stagioni* pizza, rosemary-laced roasted chicken and housemade sorbetti. The food isn't going to conjure any memories of travels to Italy, but in Little Italy's gradually less-Italian landscape, this is a safe venture. *1400 W Taylor St at Loomis St (312-829-2828). El: Blue to Racine. Bus: 12 Roosevelt, 60*

Blue Island/26th (24hrs). Lunch (Mon–Fri), dinner. Average main course: $15.

✷ **Franco's** Don't waste your time searching for the crudo and antipasto. This is Bridgeport, where locals eat thick, roasted pork chops (how one person could eat the order of two is beyond us) and big bowls of penne tossed with spicy pesto, capers and succulent nibs of prosciutto. The kitchen can get overzealous with its fire sometimes—an order of lemon-kissed grilled octopus came charred and the chops a bit dry—so request it toned down. But don't be surprised if your waiter tells ya to get lost. Like we said, this is Bridgeport. *300 W 31st St at Princeton Ave (312-225-9566). El: Red to Sox-35th. Bus: 35 35th St. Lunch (Tue–Fri), dinner (closed Sun, Mon). Average main course: $16.*

▼ ✷ **Frasca Pizzeria and Wine Bar** With wood-fired pizza spots opening faster than a Cubs pitcher can throw, it looks like thin-crust pizza has replaced sushi as Chicago's trendiest cuisine. This is the swankiest of the bunch, with arches reminiscent of a Tuscan wine cellar and sexy red leather banquettes. The cavernous space is packed to conversation-inhibiting capacity with twentysomethings chomping on chewy thin-crust pizzas—we like the fennel sausage, onion and mozz Capone—and tossing back reasonably priced wines. *3358 N Paulina St between School and Roscoe Sts (773-248-5222). El: Brown to Paulina. Bus: 9 (24hrs), 11, 77 (24hrs), 152. Lunch (Sat, Sun), dinner. Average main course: $16.*

▼ ✷ **Fresco** A better name for this place might be Alfresco, because the wine garden in back—with its walls covered with murals depicting provincial Italian life—is the restaurant's most sought-after asset. Sitting here, it's nearly impossible not to take advantage of the restaurant's wine list (or its considerably un-Italian pitchers of sangria) while noshing on tender grilled calamari with feta and roasted red peppers, or light, crispy artichoke fritters. *1202*

Chicago classic Harry Caray's scores a win with it's chicken Vesuvio.

W Grand Ave between Racine and Ogden Ave (312-733-6378). El: Blue to Grand. Bus: 8, 9 (24hrs), X9, 65. Lunch, dinner. Average main course: $12.

✷ **Gabriel's** For more than a decade chef-owner Gabriel Viti has been the culinary darling of the North Shore. His eponymous restaurant is the flagship of his restaurant empire and it is easy to see why. The white tablecloths are offset by the mahogany interior, and the service and food are equally elegant. Expect seasonal French and Italian cuisine, a large selection of pasta and an impressive wine list. *310 Green Bay Rd, Highwood (847-433-0031). Dinner (closed Sun–Mon). Average main course: $28.*

▼ **Gino's East** This Chicago-style pizza institution is no longer at its original Superior Street location (opened in '66), but tourists still flock in droves, so skip weekends. The famous deep-dish has a cornmeal crust that's void of the butter glaze others give the pan, so it's not greasy (but also not very flavorful). Luckily, the punch comes from the sauce, which is tangy and ripe. Try half spinach–half sausage (let it sit for a minute when it arrives to avoid a runny mess). *633 N Wells St at Ontario St (312-943-1124). El: Brown, Purple (rush hrs) to Chicago. Bus: 37, 65, 125. Lunch, dinner. Average pizza: $20.*

BYOB **Gio's Café & Deli** From the street, Gio's looks like any other Chicago corner store. But Gio's packs a tiny, red-checkered tablecloth restaurant plus an array of imported Italian groceries into a space the size of a deli counter. The food is unspectacular (though the *arancino* is a nicely fried risotto ball packed with meat sauce and peas), but the cast of characters kept us amused. Our waitress did everything short of pulling up a chair to make us feel at home, and we love the frozen lemon flute, a tart limoncello-and-cream concoction. *2724 S Lowe St between 26th and 28th Sts (312-225-6368). El: Orange to Halsted. Bus: 8, 44, 62. Lunch, dinner (closed Sun). Average main course: $11.*

▼ ✷ **B Gioco** Chef Fred Ramos excels at hearty, unfussy pastas like the penne with prosciutto, spring peas and mushrooms in Parmesan cream sauce and gnocchi with mushrooms, leeks and shrimp in a truffle cream sauce. Seasonal produce shows up in several salads; we like the combination of arugula, pears, candied hazelnuts, pancetta and ricotta. The kitchen typically nails classics like the huge 40-ounce porterhouse. Go ahead and try to finish it; there's no need to save room for the skippable desserts. *1312 S Wabash Ave at 13th St (312-939-3870). El: Green, Orange, Red to Roosevelt. Bus: 12, 29, 62 (24hrs). Brunch (Sun), lunch (Mon–Fri), dinner. Average main course: $28.*

▼ **Giordano's** Way before the Windy City got all fancy with its 'zas, Giordano's was here. Serving up hefty deep-dish goodness to Chicagoans since the '70s, this chain is still pleasing masses with no-frills gut-busters topped with sausage, spinach and other classics. The chain also serves salads and red-sauce dishes likes lasagna and chicken parmesan, but why waste your time? *135 E Lake St at at North Beaubien Ct (312-616-1200). El: Brown, Green, Orange, Pink, Purple (rush hrs) to State. Lunch, dinner. Average pizza: $18.*

☉ **Golden Crust Italian Pizzeria** Sometimes you don't want artisanal ingredients manipulated by globe-trotting chefs. Sometimes you want the stuff of your childhood memories—actual comfort food—not nuevo comfort food. This is where you go when you want those absurdly large portions of lasagna, pizza and other Italian classics, topped with almost too much Parmesan and red sauce. You'll dine in a dated booth, on paper place mats emblazoned with a map of Italy. Take leftovers home for lunch tomorrow. *4620 N Kedzie Ave between Wilson Ave and Eastwood Ave (773-539-5860). El: Brown to Kedzie. Bus: 78, 81 (24hrs), 82. Lunch (Sat, Sun), dinner. Average main course: $8.*

▼ (✳ **Gulliver's** The decor of this Rogers Park restaurant—with Victorian and Art Nouveau antiques hanging on every square inch of wall and ceiling space (including the bathroom stalls)—is like a lighting store exploded in a Bennigan's. The menu's just as eclectic as the ambience. Skip the mediocre apps and entrées for the pan pizza—a gooey, melty mess of cheese, fresh veggies, oregano and basil on a thick, crispy crust—that's perfect with a frosty mug of beer. *2727 W Howard St between Washtenaw and California Aves (773-338-2166). Bus: 97 Skokie, Pace 215. Lunch, dinner. Average main course: $15.*

✳ **Harry Caray's** The legendary Cubs announcer may be gone, but his spirit lives on at his popular namesake eatery. These days Caray's widow, Dutchie, greets patrons who continue to crowd the place during Cubs games as well as the off-season for gargantuan steaks (23-ounce porterhouse, anyone?) and classic Italian dishes like chicken Vesuvio, sausage and peppers and veal picatta. The walls are awash in memorabilia that will keep sports fans entertained for ages. Go to harrycarays.com for suburban location info. *33 W Kinzie between State and Dearborn Sts (312-828-0966). El: Red to Grand. Bus: 22 (24hrs), 36, 65. Lunch (Mon–Sat), dinner (Mon–Thu). Average main course: $35.*

▼ ⚄ **Ignotz's Ristorante** Head for this homestyle cucina in the Heart of Italy for feather-light, spinach-stuffed gnocchi in cream sauce; juicy chicken *à la tippi* (pounded breasts fried in a Parmesan, egg and basil batter, then smothered with a tart lemon butter sauce); and whitefish Vesuvio. The small waitstaff seems frantic (this place gets packed early), but it still manages to coerce the crowd into entire-room birthday sing-alongs. Save room for the freshly made tiramisu—it's a legend in its own right. *2421 S Oakley Ave between 24th and 25th Sts (773-579-0300). El: Blue to Western. Bus: 21, 49 (24hrs), 60. Lunch, dinner (closed Mon). Average main course: $14.*

▼ BYOB **Il Covo** With its hit-or-miss Italian-Australian fusion menu, the original incarnation of this Bucktown joint never gelled. But there's still hope: Chefs Nino Coronas and Giovanni Carzedda have overhauled the menu in favor of Sardinian signatures such as the *involtini di pollo alla sarda* (oven-baked chicken breast rolled with *prosciutto di parma*, finished with Vermentino wine sauce) and the penne *alla sarda* (penne with white wine, clam juice, bottarga and tomatoes). Dessert also goes Sardinian with the *sevada*, fried sweet dough filled with pecorino cheese and lemon zest, drizzled with honey. *2152 N Damen Ave between Shakespeare and Webster Aves (773-862-5555). El: Blue to Western. Bus: 50, 73, 74. Dinner. Average main course: $20.*

✳ ⚄ **Il Mulino New York** Years of fending off the Zagat-clutching crowds at their Greenwich Village flagship gave the brothers behind this New York classic the confidence to expand, which is exactly what they've done: to Tokyo, Las Vegas and now, the Gold Coast's Biggs Mansion. Every meal here starts with complimentary antipasto, fried zucchini and garlic bread sticks, followed by entrées such as saltimbocca (veal sautéed with sage and prosciutto) and spaghettini bolognese—with a healthy slice of New York attitude on the side. *1150 N Dearborn St between Elm and Division Sts (312-440-8888). El: Red to Clark/Division. Bus: 36, 70, 151 (24hrs), 156. Lunch, dinner. Average main course: $35.*

Be a cheap date…
…or not. Spend whatever you want on wooing another.

Woo moves The dishes at Hot Chocolate can make any date seem sweet.

The $25 date The key for a successful $25 date? *Lunch.* If you try to stretch that money on dinner, you're going to end up at Boston Market. And that's not sexy. Lucky for you, **Fan Si Pan** *(1618 W Chicago Ave between Ashland and Marshfield Aves, 312-738-1405)* is cheap and delicious: Two sandwiches (we like the *bahn mi* and the five-star beef) and two honeydew limeades will set you back $17 (plus tax and tip). That leaves you with enough to stroll up Milwaukee Avenue until you reach **Lovely Bake Shop** *(1130 N Milwaukee Ave between Thomas St and Haddon Ave, 773-572-4766)*. There you can shower your date with cupcakes ($2.50) or minipies ($4). While you're at it, shower her with compliments, too—you can't afford booze on this date, so you'll have to intoxicate her with your charm.

The $50 date All right, so you might not be the richest guy in the world. Show your date that you've at least got a conscience by choosing dinner at the all-organic **Crust** *(2056 W Division St at Hoyne Ave, 773-235-5511)*. One salad (split between the two of you—tell your date it's more romantic that way) and two pizzas should set you back about $30. That gives you $20 more to impress her, which can be done pretty easily at **HotChocolate** *(1747 N Damen Ave at Willow St, 773-489-1747)*, where a couple of milk shakes ($5 each) and an order of doughnuts ($8) will end any date, no matter how disastrous, on a sweet note.

The $100 date Okay, big spender: Time to show your date what you're made of (which, apparently, is lots of crisp dollar bills). Start with an *amuse-bouche* of juicy pancetta-and-Camembert–topped mini Kobe burgers ($10 for two) and two glasses of bubbly ($12-$18 each) at **Vice** *(840 W Randolph St between Green and Peoria Sts, 312-733-3379)*. Then head down the street to **Avec** *(615 W Randolph St between Jefferson and Desplaines Sts, 312-377-2002)*. Sixty dollars' worth of small plates later, finish things up at the **Violet Hour** *(1520 N Damen Ave between LeMoyne St and Wicker Park Ave)*. Sure, two drinks here will put you back an extra $22. But since when do you care about money?

▼ ❋ **Il Vicinato** Loosely translated, *vicinato* is Italian for neighborhood, and though this corner tavern may not be in yours, it's worth a trip to eat good in the Heart of Italy. Expect big plates of traditional fare, including *bianco nero* ("black white"), a wide bowl of tasty mussels and clams in garlicky broth, and pillowy potato gnocchi made in house and topped with a meaty *ragù*. For dessert, share a dark chocolate ice cream *tartufo* the size of Tony Soprano's fist. *2435 S Western Ave at 24th Pl (773-927-5444). El: Blue to Western (54th/Cermak). Bus: 21, 49 (24hrs), X49. Lunch (Mon–Fri), dinner (Mon–Sat) (closed Sun). Average main course: $16.*

❋ **Jay's Amoré Ristorante** Jay Emerich, who ran a handful of Rush Street supper clubs during that trend's golden age, has taken over this once-empty Italian spot. The tasty penne *Abbruzzese*, though a tad overcooked, gives pork top billing with both pancetta and Italian sausage starring in the light tomato sauce. The classic Vesuvio treatment takes a thick bone-in pork chop to the next level. Thanks to a crowd from central casting, this trattoria feels like it's been here for years. *1330 W Madison St between Ada and Loomis Sts (312-829-3333). Bus: 9 (24hrs), 19, 20 (24hrs). Dinner (closed Sun). Average main course: $17.*

★ ▼ ❤ **La Bocca della Verita** The simple rooms at this Roman-style tratorria are matched by an authentically simple menu. We love the *caprese* (the mozz is so good we

Read 'em & eat

baccalà (bah-kah-LAH) dried salt cod

bolognese (bole-OH-nase) rich meat sauce for pasta; wine, milk or cream may be used

bruschetta bread slices rubbed with garlic and olive oil, then toasted

caponata a cooked mixture of anchovies, capers, eggplant, olives, onions, pine nuts, tomatoes, vinegar and olive oil

carciofi artichokes

fagioli beans, usually the white kidney variety

frutti di mare seafood

involtini (ihn-vohl-TEE-nee) thin slices of meat (traditionally veal) or fish rolled around a seasoned cheese filling and baked, grilled or fried

Margherita (mahr-gur-EE-tah) pizza with tomato, mozzarella and basil

mozzarella di bufala mozzarella cheese made from the milk of water buffalo (American mozzarella is made from cow's milk)

osso buco braised veal shank in a rich onion-tomato sauce

tartufo a truffle, or chocolate ice cream in the shape of a truffle

vitello tonnato veal with tuna-anchovy sauce, served cold

order it even when tomatoes aren't in season) and the tart green apple and celery salad dressed only with olive oil, fresh lemon and shavings of delicious Parmesan. Couple these starters with the warm, crusty bread and follow up with the *guanciale*-dotted spaghetti alla carbonara and the sage-, shallot- and duck breast–filled ravioli in tomato cream, and you can skip main courses altogether. *4618 N Lincoln Ave between Wilson and Eastwood Aves (773-784-6222). El: Brown to Western. Bus: 11, 49 (24hrs), X49, 81 (24hrs). Lunch, dinner. Average main course: $12.*

▼ **B La Donna** The pasta menu at this Andersonville staple allows you to choose a housemade pasta and pair it with a sauce of your choice. While you may feel qualified to make such a choice, some of the delicious sauces, like the carbonara, don't work with every pasta. Play it safe and order from the entrée menu, where combos are already paired for you. There, *misto di pesce* (grilled seafood) gets the calamari, octopus and shrimp cooked perfectly and tender (if fatty) osso buco comes with a delicious side of saffron cavatell. *5146 N Clark St between Winona St and Foster Ave (773-561-9400). El: Red to Berwyn. Bus: 22 (24hrs), 36, 92. Brunch (Sun), lunch, dinner. Average main course: $12.*

☺ **La Gondola** It looks like just another anonymous pizza joint in a strip mall. But venture inside and you'll find a homey, five-table restaurant that is one of the tiniest—and most charming—Italian spots in town. Crispy thin-crust pizza is what the place is known for (we like the puttanesca with briny anchovies), but pasta fans should go for the housemade *agnelotti mezzaluna* stuffed with spinach and ricotta. Is everything a hit? No—the bologna on our antipasto platter had to be Oscar Meyer—but we're not the type to pick on the little guys. *2914 N Ashland Ave at Wellington Ave (773-248-4433). Bus: 9 Ashland (24hrs), 76 Diversey. Dinner. Average main course: $10.*

▼ ❋ **La Luce** It's hidden under the El tracks on a dark, deserted corner in the West Loop, but that doesn't keep this historic room from being a destination for Northern Italian fare. Of all the appetizers, the fried, housemade gnocchi will likely tempt you the most, but we suggest heading face-first into the entrées. Between the housemade ravioli (filled with ricotta and topped with brown butter and crunchy bits of fried sage) and the enormous portion of juicy grilled, stuffed pork chops, you won't have room for much else anyway. *1393 W Lake St at Loomis St (312-850-1900). El: Green, Pink to Ashland. Bus: 9 (24hrs), X9, 20 (24hrs). Lunch (Mon–Fri), dinner. Average main course: $19.*

❋ ❤ **La Mora** Consistency is not La Mora's strong suit. But what it lacks in being always dependable, it makes up for with amenities. This neighborhood eatery offers warm, crusty bread and delicious fried calamari. And you can't beat the nightly specials, like penny-wine Wednesdays (glasses of house wine for one red cent) sipped at the stained glass bar. If only they'd lose the blaring techno music. *2132 W Roscoe St at Hamilton Ave (773-404-4555). El: Brown to Paulina. Bus: 49 (24hrs), X49, 50, 77 (24hrs), 152. Dinner (closed Mon). Average main course: $17.*

▼ ❤ **La Scarola** It's okay to splash a little red sauce on the butcher-paper-topped tables in this raucous storefront. Old friends and big families admire the autographed celebrity photos and shots of the owner's family tacked to the walls. Smiling waiters squeeze between tables juggling huge plates of eggplant parmigiana and decent bottles of Italian red. Order any of the appropriately garlicky pastas and a plate of escarole and beans for the table; the leftovers will warm up just fine tomorrow. *721 W Grand Ave between Union Ave*

Hamming it up Executive chef John Coletta gets up close and personal with the prosciutto at Quartino.

and Halsted St (312-243-1740). El: Blue to Grand. Bus: 8, 56, 65. Lunch (Mon–Fri), dinner. Average main course: $17.

▼ * **La Tavernetta** Expect "homestyle" fare (think housemade doughy delights with rich gravies typical of an Italian grandma). The lost art of complimentary starters lives on with a choice of a fresh mesclun salad or a cup of minestrone. Both starch-o-phobes and the carb-indulgent can leave well fed: The vast menu includes archetypal Italian treasures such as eggplant *parmigiana*, gnocchi with sausage, portobellos with Gorgonzola and roasted red peppers, and rigatoni smothered in a creamy tomato sauce. 3023 N Broadway between Wellington and Barry Aves (773-929-8787). El: Brown, Purple (rush hrs), Red to Belmont. Bus: 22 (24hrs), 36, 77 (24hrs), 156. Dinner. Average main course: $14.

▼ * **Leonardo's** Don't expect plain old pasta at this contemporary Tuscan storefront, which bills itself as a simple neighborhood bistro. Chef Nick Van Wassenhove left for Extra Virgin but soon realized his mistake: He returned, reuniting with his signature "18-hour ravioli," among others. The housemade pasta squares filled with veal osso buco and goat cheese are always a solid choice. You might opt for your own helping of the ravioli, but plan on sharing the enormous Gorgonzola and sausage–stuffed pork chops. Don't be afraid to fill up on dinner; desserts are uninspired. 5657 N Clark St at Hollywood Ave (773-561-5028). El: Red to Bryn Mawr. Bus: 22 Clark (24hrs), 50. Lunch (Sat, Sun), dinner (Tue–Sun). Average main course: $20.

⊙ **Lou Malnati's Pizzeria** There are two kinds of Chicagoans. No, not North Siders and South Siders. We're talking Giordano's people and Lou Malnati's people. Lou Malnati's deep-dish is the pinnacle of cheesy Chicago-style goodness. Everything else on the menu—like pastas and salads—is passable, but not worth passing on the 'za. Get the butter crust. And, no worries, about where you are when the

Malnati's munchies hit you: They Fed-Ex pizza anywhere in the country. 439 N Wells St at Hubbard St (312-828-9800). El: Brown, Purple (rush hrs) to Merchandise Mart. Bus: 65 Grand, 125 Water Tower Express. Lunch, dinner. Average main course: $7. ● Additional locations include 958 W Wrightwood (773-832-4030) and 3859 W Ogden Ave (773-762-0800).

▼ **Luna Caprese** You've seen it all before: the white tablecloths, the oversize wine posters, the empty bar in need of a liquor license. But Pietro Cristillo's nod to his native Capra deserves more than a cursory look. The antipasto plate includes thin, grilled slices of garlic-topped zucchini and tender, meaty folds of prosciutto and salami. Housemade, perfectly cooked pappardelle is paired with a rich and subtle mushroom cream sauce that's even better when you add a pinch of salt. Finish with the Caprese cake, rich with fudgy chocolate and ground almonds. If you don't live close by, this spot may not be worth a special trip, but it's heaven-sent for those already in the 'hood. 2239 N Clybourn Ave between Janssen and Greenview Aves (773-281-4825). Bus: 9 (24hrs), 73, 74. Dinner (closed Mon). Average main course: $15.

▼ * **Maggiano's Little Italy** Sure, there's a lot that's Disney-esque about this Lettuce Entertain You red sauce spot, from the fake black-and-white family photos to the red-checkered tablecloths. But, as much as we hate to admit it, we find ourselves wanting to get our hands on those family-sized platters of puffy gnocchi, dense eggplant parmesan and juicy chicken marsala. But what we don't crave—or understand, in this city of so many fine Italian options—are the never-ending mob scenes. 516 N Clark St at Grand Ave (312-644-7700). El: Red to Grand. Bus: 22 (24hrs), 65, 156. Lunch, dinner. Average main course: $12.

⊙ **Marie's Pizzeria & Liquors** Contrary to most of the country's opinion, Chicago does not exist on deep-dish alone. The other kind of pizza unique to the city is sometimes called

Sliced right Neapolitan-style pizza comes from state-of-the-art ovens at Sapore di Napoli.

"bar pizza," a pie with cracker-thin crust topped with bubbled, almost crispy, cheese that's square-cut rather than pie-cut. Since 1940, this liquor store/bar/restaurant has been serving this style, and it's quite a tasty version. Sausage is the preferred topping among the just-off-work construction dudes sucking down beers at the bar, and we agree that the fennel-seed–flecked Italian sausage is great, especially with diced onions. You'll be disappointed by the rest of the menu—deep-fried stuff and iceberg lettuce galore—so stick with the signature pizza. *4127 W Lawrence Ave between Karlov and Kedvale Aves (773-685-5030). Bus: 53 Pulaski (24hrs), 81 Lawrence (24hrs). Lunch, dinner. Average pizza: $10.*

★ ✳ **B Merlo Ristorante** There's no doubt that the Gold Coast location of this upscale Italian favorite is more quaint and intimate (housed in a turn-of-the-century walk-up), but for some reason, the food's a bit better at this locale. Authentic Bolognese recipes reign, so stick to signatures like housemade tagliatelle pasta with rich, nutmeg-kissed meat sauce; and long, paper-thin tagliolini noodles with prosciutto and veal *ragù*, quail eggs and truffle oil. *2638 N Lincoln Ave between Sheffield and Kenmore Aves (773-529-0747). El: Brown, Purple (rush hrs) to Diversey. Bus: 11 Lincoln, 76 Diversey. Brunch (Sun), dinner. Average main course: $22.* ● *Additional location at 16 W Maple St (312-335-8200).*

▼ ✳ **Mia Francesca** Clearly the business minds behind this Italian concept have figured out a formula for success: approachable, Northern Italian cooking for the masses, with suburban outposts seemingly opening every week. At this location, loyalists from the neighborhood dig in to huge oval platters of cool, caper-studded carpaccio; pastas tossed with lemony cream and asparagus; and what's surprisingly the

best garlic spinach in town. Couples and families happily wait at the bar, somehow oblivious to the chaos of the always-packed room and the obligatory wait even for those with a reservation. *3311 N Clark St between Aldine Ave and Buckingham Pl (773-281-3310). El: Brown, Purple (rush hrs), Red to Belmont. Bus: 22 (24hrs), 77 (24hrs), 152. Lunch (Sat, Sun), dinner. Average main course: $13.*

☉ **Nonno Pino's** This cavernous space's ambience is a bit spartan, but it's comfortable, family-friendly, and the staff is always welcoming. Expect a fairly quiet office crowd midday, but at night the joint is packed with young professionals at the bar up front, while families sit at tables in the back. Notables from the cross-section of satisfying, if standard, pasta dishes and entrées include pasta with *besciamelle* sauce and chicken breast encrusted with pistachios. Numerous specials are posted on boards for those who get bored with the regular menu. *6718 N Northwest Hwy between Oshkosh and Oliphant Aves (773-594-1155). Metra: Union Pacific NW to Edison Park. Bus: 68 NW Hwy, Pace 209. Lunch (Mon–Sat), dinner. Average main course: $9.*

☉ **O'Famé** After a quarter century of churning out Italian food to Lincoln Park locals, this family-run restaurant has become a dependable spot for solid, simple food. Start with the vinegary tomato and move on to the signature "specialty pizza"—garlic, olive oil and tomato on thin or pan crust (we like the thin). The pizza may not look like much, but it packs a powerful punch of flavor. For a quicker bite, the hot, crusty Italian sub (packed with salami, capicolla and Fontinella) pairs perfectly with a cold glass of Peroni. *750 W Webster Ave between Burling and Halsted Sts (773-929-5111). El: Brown, Purple (rush hrs), Red to Fullerton. Bus: 8, 11, 74. Lunch (Tues–Sat), dinner. Average main course: $10.*

★ ▽ Osteria di Tramonto *2007 Eat Out Awards, The Annual Worth-the-Trip Award* Wheeling's hottest destination restaurant is the cavernous rustic Italian restaurant from TRU vets Rick Tramonto and Gale Gand. Belinda Chang handles the wine list, which is packed with good finds and decent deals. The meat lasagna, inspired by Tramonto's mother's recipe, is housemade, and the freshly made cavatelli is tossed with crumbly lamb sausage, softened rapini and roasted garlic (a similar combo can be had on a tasty, cheesy, hand-tossed pizza). Fish and steak entrées are usually stellar. *601 N Milwaukee Ave, Wheeling (847-777-6570). Breakfast, lunch, dinner. Average main course: $19.*

★ ▽ ✷ Osteria Via Stato *2007 Eat Out Awards, Readers' Choice: Best Italian* The masterminds behind TRU have done it again, but this time think Italian share plates for a nice price. Servers will steer you toward the $35 three-course table tasting, but remember that anything can be ordered à la carte. For the fixed price, seasonal tastes arrive in waves, and you choose only your entrée. Marinated olives in herbed oil with warm focaccia are followed by antipasti like veal meatballs. Hearty pastas rotate but may include a tasty bolognese pappardelle. *620 N State St at Ontario St (312-642-8450). El: Red to Grand. Bus: 22 (24hrs), 36, 65. Lunch (Mon–Sat), dinner. Average main course: $18.*

▽ ✷ Pane Caldo The authentic Northern Italian eats at this tony Gold Coast mainstay are luscious enough to make you forget their over-inflated price tags. (Come on, half-orders of pasta for $27?) But if you can swing it, go all the way, dahling. Order up a bottle of Barolo and buttery risotto sprinkled with slices of black truffles. Follow up with organic chicken stuffed with spinach, mozzarella and wild mushrooms. Dessert shifts gears by heading for France, with bombes and financiers as dolled up as most of the patrons. *72 E Walton St between Ernst Ct and Michigan Ave (312-649-0055). El: Red to Chicago. Bus: 36, 66 (24hrs), 143, 144, 145, 146, 147, 148, 151 (24hrs). Lunch, dinner. Average main course: $33.*

☉ Pasta Palazzo At first glance, you might think this tiny storefront is nothing more than a yuppified Italian spot, but dig a little deeper and you'll find some truly tasty pastas. A dense, nicely spiced bolognese sauce is a perfect accompaniment to housemade ricotta gnocchi, but slightly more souped-up dishes like *penne alla melanzane* with eggplant and tomatoes come together well, too. Everything from meatballs to pine nuts to shellfish are offered as add-ons for customizing. There's a small beer and wine list, plus daily dessert specials. *1966 N Halsted St at Armitage Ave (773-248-1400). El: Brown, Purple (rush hrs) to Armitage. Bus: 8, 11, 73. Lunch, dinner. Average main course: $9.*

▽ (Pequod's Pizza Exposed brick and plasma-screen TVs have taken the place of worn pool tables and dart boards after a fire forced a redesign of this neighborhood dive. But while the digs may be snazzier, the signature pan pizza—in all its glory with a ring of caramelized cheese around the crust—remains the same. Skip flavorless fried-vegetable appetizers and sandwiches and save your appetite for a ginormous slice of a sausage pie, dotted with perfectly spiced, Ping-Pong ball–size pieces of seasoned ground pork. *2207 N Clybourn Ave at Webster Ave (773-327-1512). Bus: 9 (24hrs), X9, 74. Lunch, dinner. Average pizza: $13.*

✷ Petterino's It's 6pm, we're going to an 8pm play and we're in the middle of an assholes-to-elbows crowd at this theater-district restaurant. Wait for a table? Hell, no—we'll sit at the bright, window-filled bar, where we can order from the full menu and ask the busy bartenders to keep the sidecars

coming. We'll skip right to the main course: The New York strip steak *au poivre* is ridiculously tender and even better topped with caramelized onions. With service this fast, we have time to linger over the baked-in-house desserts and still catch the show. *150 N Dearborn St at Randolph St (312-422-0150). El: Red to Lake; Blue, Brown, Green, Orange, Purple (rush hrs) to Clark/Lake. Bus: 22 (24hrs), 156. Lunch (Mon–Sat), dinner. Average main course: $19.*

▽ ✷ Piazza Bella We're always on the hunt for another affordable rustic Italian restaurant, and this one fits the bill perfectly. Looking like it was imported straight from the boot, this eatery packs the house every night of the week and dishes up Tuscan country fare like platters of soft ricotta-stuffed tortellini in a sage and brown butter–heavy-cream sauce (the first bite could stop time). With a glass of fruity Sangiovesi, an *insalata de cannelloni* (with shrimp) and a breeze on the patio, Italy never seemed closer. *2116 W Roscoe St between Hoyne and Hamilton Aves (773-477-7330). El: Brown to Paulina. Bus: 50, 49 (24hrs), X49, 152. Brunch (Sat, Sun), lunch (Mon–Fri), dinner. Average main course: $16.*

▽ ☉ Piccolo Chef Ed Navar has nailed more than half of the 20 gelato creations at this casual counter-service gelato/panini spot. Play the odds and sample to find your own favorite; we loved the roasted pistachio, malty "jivara" milk chocolate, sprightly chopped mint and ridiculously rich peanut butter (the latter is fantastic with extra bitter "manjari" chocolate). For sustenance before the main attraction, salads won't help much, but a plate of bruschetta will—try the tart anchovy and the honey-drizzled Brie and prosciutto. Ten perfectly-pressed panini are available. *859 N Damen Ave at Rice St (773-772-3355). Bus: 50 Damen, 66 Chicago (24hrs). Lunch, dinner. Average main course: $7.*

Piccolo Mondo The chintzy decor of the ground-floor dining room of the Windermere, one of Hyde Park's architectural grand dames, leaves something to be desired. Luckily, floor-to-ceiling windows offer views of the majestic Museum of Science and Industry. The kitchen turns out quality Italian dishes, including a sage-spiked sausage appetizer and tangy veal Marsala. You can't go wrong with the fresh, housemade pasta dishes, and a separate takeout counter does a brisk business in classic Italian subs at lunchtime. *1642 E 56th St between Hyde Park Blvd and Cornell Ave (773-643-1106). Bus: 15, 55 (24hrs), X55. Lunch, dinner. Average main course: $15.*

▽ (Pie Hole Like almost everything Twisted Spoke's owners (the Einhorn brothers) do, this tiny pizza joint has unexpected details of excellence that betray its machismo, carefree atmosphere. Fresh garlic and pristine basil (free for the asking), bacon, French olives and more all add up to some pretty delicious pizza. The red pesto pie has two standout features: the meaty and brilliantly spiced sausage and the chewy crust. *737 W Roscoe St between Halsted St and Elaine Pl (773-525-8888). El: Brown, Purple (rush hrs), Red to Belmont. Bus: 8, 36, 152. Dinner. Average pizza: $15.*

▽ Piece Two things keep this place from going the route of sports-bar-beer-bong culture: excellent house brews and expertly executed pizzas. The crispy pies hold a lot of weight, so after you choose your pizza style—red, white or New Haven–style "plain" (red sauce, no mozzarella)—start piling on the toppings. (If you're really going New Haven–style, try one with clams and bacon.) Wash it down with a pitcher of the crisp Golden Arm, and you'll never disparagingly say "pizza and beer joint" again. *1927 W North Ave between Wolcott and Winchester Aves (773-772-4422). El: Blue to Damen. Bus: 50, 56, 72. Lunch, dinner. Average pizza: $13.50.*

Italian/Pizza

Perfect pair Appetizing looking
starters are a prelude to more
good things at Adesso.

☺ **Pizza Art Café** This candlelit room and wood-burning oven with 14 types of pie—between Chicago-style bar pizza and the relatively spare Neapolitan varieties—has made us fans of the Pugliese pizza with onion and pecorino cheese. There's also strong representation from Italy's Dalmatian coast neighbors; some Bosnian specialties show up on a "secret" menu. We were impressed with the *cevapcici*, sausage dressed with a creamy cheese and raw onions, cushioned in fresh-cooked pita. Our favorite of the lot is the must-have house-cured smoked beef: dense, chewy, salty and, like most great works of art, complex. *4658 N Rockwell St between Eastwood and Leland Aves (773-539-0645). El: Brown to Rockwell. Bus: 49 (24 hrs), X49, 81 (24 hrs). Dinner (Tue–Sun). Average main course: $10.*

★ ▼ **Pizza D.O.C.** This Lincoln Square spot fills up in the early evenings with families diving into crispy, thin, dinner-plate–size pizzas. Baked in a wood-burning oven and served uncut in true Italian style, pizza toppings range from the simple (a Margherita dressed with fresh mozzarella and basil) to the intoxicating (a Quattro Stagioni with quadrants of artichoke, olive, prosciutto and mushrooms). Later, neighborhood couples slurp up pastas and appetizers (try the *suppli*, crispy rice balls oozing with cheese) that live up to local authenticity standards. *2251 W Lawrence Ave between Bell and Oakley Aves (773-784-8777). El: Brown to Western. Bus: 11, 49 (24hrs), X49, 81 (24hrs), 145. Lunch (Sat, Sun), dinner. Average main course: $15.*

▼ ◖ ✳ **Pizzeria Due** This crowd-pleasing sister to the original Uno's pizza institution features a cozy, below-street-level dining room/bar that reeks of that "old Chicago" feel, complete with black-and-white tiled floor, historical photos, and plenty of Ditka and Butkus memorabilia. Knife-and-fork, deep-dish pizza is its sole *raison d'être*, with a rich crust that gets crisp from its time in a traditional black iron pan. Our tasters preferred the bright-green fresh spinach and broccoli (your perky waiter calls it "spinoccoli") over the bland sausage. Tourists love it, but, secretly, jaded locals do, too. *619 N Wabash Ave between Ohio and Ontario Sts (312-943-2400). El: Red to Grand. Bus: 29, 36, 65. Lunch, dinner. Average main course: $15.*

☺ **Pizzeria Uno** Drawn by tales that this pizzeria originated Chicago deep-dish, tourists and new transplants often flock here for their first Windy City meal. Around lunchtime, a crowd can be found in the lobby ordering their pizza while waiting for one of eighteen tables. Each pizza takes at least 45 minutes to cook, but it's worth the wait when your steaming pan with cheese-heavy slices arrive. If you've got a larger party or just can't stand the wait, head down the street to Pizzeria Due (619 N Wabash Ave, 312-943-2400), Uno's more spacious sister. *29 E Ohio St at Wabash Ave (312-321-1000). El: Red to Grand. Bus: 29, 36, 65. Lunch, dinner. Average main course: $7.*

☺ **Pompei on Taylor** The thin-versus-thick debate means nothing at the original Pompei, which has been making traditional thickish, square, Italian bakery–style pizza since 1909. Pompei has fancier digs and a gussied-up menu this century, luring healthy types from the nearby medical centers for crisp salads with addictive housemade dressings. Scoot through the long cafeteria lines with the diehards who come in for slices of sausage, hand-cut pastas with gargantuan meatballs, and classic pepper-and-egg sandwiches. *1531 W Taylor St at Ashland Ave (312-421-5179). El: Blue to Polk. Bus: 9 Ashland (24hrs), 12 Roosevelt. Lunch, dinner. Average main course: $8. ● Additional locations include 2955 N Sheffield Ave (773-325-1900) and 212 E Ohio St (312-482-9900).*

Quartino The Gibsons go rustic Italian with this cavernous dining room decked out with reclaimed wood and subway tiles, vintage mirrors and mismatched chairs. To ensure authenticity on the plate, they've enlisted chef John Coletta, who doesn't disappoint with housemade salumi like beef bresaola, spicy soppressata and duck prosciutto served with housemade giardiniera and *mostarda*. The pizza is among the better thin-crust versions in town. Living up to the name, the affordable, half-Italian, half-global wine list is offered in quarter, half and full liters. *626 N State St at Ontario St (312-698-5000). El: Red to Grand. Bus: 22 (24hrs), 36, 65, 156. Lunch, dinner. Average small plate: $5.*

▼ ◖ ✳ **Renaldi's Pizza** Chicago-style pizza joints are a dime a dozen, but New York–inspired takes are harder to come by. Grab a booth in the dim, casual, somewhat shabby room (it's not bad, but the place does much more takeout biz) and dig into the flavorful meatballs, tangy tomato sauce and toasted bread that make for one great meatball sandwich. . But pizzas rule the roost—the thick-crusted, square-cut pan is a good base for hearty toppings like Italian sausage, but we prefer the thin crust for delicate classics like spinach, tomato and garlic. *2827 N Broadway between Diversey Pkwy and Surf St (773-248-2445). El: Brown, Purple (rush hrs) to Diversey. Bus: 8, 22 (24hrs), 36, 76. Lunch, dinner. Average pizza: $15.*

★ **Riccardo Trattoria** *2007 Eat Out Awards, Critics' Pick: The Try It, You'll Like It Award (tripe florentine)* One of the best Italian restaurants in town isn't tucked away on some corner in Little Italy. Surprisingly, it's smack-dab in vanilla Lincoln Park. Chef Riccardo Michi's family founded the Bice restaurant empire in Milan, so he knows a thing or two about regional Italian food. Don't miss the bacon-topped roasted quail with crispy polenta cake, the orecchiette with wild-boar sausage, garlicky rapini and pecorino cheese or the rack of lamb. Or trust us and throw caution to the wind with an order of tripe florentine—we promise veal stomach lining never tasted so good. *2119 N Clark St between Dickens and Webster Aves (773-549-0038). El: Brown, Purple (rush hrs), Red to Fullerton. Bus: 22 Clark (24hrs), 74 Fullerton. Dinner (Tue–Sun). Average main course: $18.*

▼ **RoSal's** Typically we'd tell the server to save the speech, but here it's somehow still charming when the bubbly girl "from da neighborhood" explains how the namesake owners Roseanne and Salvatore came to open their Little Italy spot. Cozy cuteness aside, the food's among the best on the Taylor Street strip. Start with the lightly charred but tender grilled calamari; get a pasta course of big, fat garlicky shrimp tossed with shells and broccoli; and go for the veal saltimbocca with a side of spinach for the main event. *1154 W Taylor St between May St and Racine Ave (312-243-2357). El: Blue to Racine. Bus: 7, 12, 60 (24hrs). Dinner (Mon–Sat). Average main course: $18.*

▼ ✳ **Rose Angelis** Lincoln Park locals seem to head to this adorable Italian eatery at least once a week, so there's always a wait, especially for the garden tables. The cozy-cute surroundings inspire foodies to let the spotty menu slide, but we enjoy the *mezzalune al burro*, a subtle yet hearty preparation of ricotta-and-spinach–stuffed pasta in brown butter; *raviolini alla Maria*, salmon-filled ravioli in a creamy pesto sauce; thin, whole-wheat pizzas; and manicotti preparations that change daily. *1314 W Wrightwood Ave between Lakewood and Wayne Aves (773-296-0081). El: Brown, Purple (rush hrs), Red to Fullerton. Bus: 11, 74, 76. Dinner (Tue–Sun). Average main course: $13.*

❋ The Rosebud In Chicago Rosebud is not a sled. It is a local chain of classic—yet tasty—Italian restaurants. There's nothing particularly innovative about the rigatoni alla vodka, clam linguini and other baked and tossed pasta dishes. But they always arrive in large portions, tasting like you expect and you'll walk away full. There's no real reason to choose one location over another other than convenience. *1500 W Taylor St at Laflin St (312-942-1117). El: Blue to Polk. Bus: 9 Ashland (24hrs), 12 Roosevelt. Lunch (Mon–Fri), dinner. Average main course: $20.* • *Additional locations include 70 W. Madison St (312-332-9500) and 720 N Rush St (312-266-6444).*

▼ Sabatino's A dark and cozy date-friendly ambience, seasoned servers and old-school Italian dishes—what's not to like about this place? Couples should snag a booth, the perfect spot for sipping a well-priced bottle of Chianti and kicking the night off with the signature cheesy garlic bread. *Shrimp de jonghe* is fresh (and garlicky as hell, so don't forget the mints), ricotta-filled manicotti and gnocchi in meat sauce won't disappoint, and the extrathick New York strip is seasoned only with salt and pepper before hitting the grill for a spot-on medium-rare. *4441 W Irving Park Rd between Kenneth and Kilbourn Aves (773-283-8331). El: Blue to Irving Park. Bus: 53 (24hrs), 54A, X54, 80, X80. Lunch (Mon–Fri, Sun), dinner. Average main course: $12.*

▼ BYOB Sapore di Napoli One of the members of the legion of Chicago's Neapolitan pizza joints is good enough to become your favorite neighborhood spot. The *quattro stagioni* piles big cuts of prosciutto, fat artichokes, mushrooms and olives onto perfect, bubbly crust, and the *verdure*, with its heaps of asparagus, peppers, eggplant and zucchini, nearly takes care of your daily veggie requirements in one bite. Panini, served only at lunch, are pretty tasty, and the *gelati* are as smooth and creamy as any we've had in European *gelaterias. 1406 W Belmont Ave at Southport Ave (773-935-1212). El: Brown to Southport. Bus: 9 (24hrs), X9, 77 (24hrs). Lunch, dinner (closed Mon). Average pizza: $12.*

▼ ❋ Sapori Trattoria As Lincoln Park's go-to Italian joint for all occasions—witness the awkward Internet date in one corner, the anniversary celebration in another—it's easy to get the impression that people are coming here out of habit. In fact, the throngs of people are attracted to the warm, homey room and the housemade pastas like spaghetti with veal meatballs and fennel-flecked Italian sausage, or sumptuous gnocchi paired with a lively pesto sauce. *2701 N Halsted St at Schubert Ave (773-832-9999). El: Brown, Purple (rush hrs) to Diversey. Bus: 8, 22 (24hrs), 76. Dinner. Average main course: $17.*

▼ ❋ Scoozi! It's not the hot spot it was when it put River North on the map in the early '80s, but this cavernous Italian mainstay still keeps the crowds coming. The flatbread pizzas are a good bet, especially the Yellow Tomato *Bianca* with housemade mozzarella and aged provolone. The wine list is as big as the dinner menu, with more than 30 by-the-glass options. Expect a huge family crowd on Sundays, when kids 12 and under get to don chef gear and make their own pizzas at no charge. *410 W Huron St between Sedgwick St and Hudson Ave (312-943-5900). El: Brown, Purple (rush hrs) to Chicago. Bus: 66 Chicago. Dinner. Average main course: $20.*

★ ▼ ❋ Spacca Napoli *2007 Eat out Award, Readers' Choice: Best new pizzeria* This place is serious about Neapolitan pizza: A custom-built, oak-stoked oven kicks out bubbling beauties with perfectly charred peaks in less than ten minutes. The hand-formed crust is paper-thin at the center, thicker toward the edges and, in contrast to the cracker-crunch of Roman pizzas, has the unmistakable chew of a true Neapolitan pie. Aside from the simple marinara or Margherita, toppings run the gamut from fennel-flecked sausage to bitter rapini. Add a humble Italian wine-and-beer list, after-dinner options such as limoncello, and you've got our new favorite haunt. *1769 W Sunnyside Ave between Hermitage and Ravenswood Aves (773-878-2420). El: Brown to Damen. Bus: 50, 78, 145. Lunch and dinner (Wed–Sun) (closed Mon and Tues). Average main course: $12.*

★ Spiaggia Want to skip rent this month and have the best Italian fine-dining experience in town? Splurge here. Executive chef Missy Robbins and her culinary partner-in-crime Tony Mantuano marry imported Italian foodstuffs with top-notch American ingredients and a deep understanding of cuisine from the north end of "the boot." Wood-roasted filet mignon with marrow and herb crust is served with hen of the woods mushrooms, roasted red pearl onions and purple potato puree. Pastas like gnocchi (served with ricotta and black truffle sauce) are made fresh every day. Toss in a two-dozen–choice cheese cave and perfect service, and you've got a night that's worth dodging the landlord. *980 N Michigan Ave between Oak St and Walton Pl (312-280-2750). El: Red to Clark/Division. Bus: 143, 144, 145, 146, 147, 151 (24hrs). Dinner. Average main course: $37.*

❋ Tarantino's If the name makes you think Quentin, think again. This corner neighborhood spot is a lot less about hit men and kung-fu Uma than it is about seductive, oversize polenta fries served with tomato chutney, and thin pizzas piled with arugula and prosciutto. Pork chops are paired with red wine-and-vinegar–soaked grapes and creamy rosemary mashed potatoes. While it may not have anything to do with the star filmmaker, this place is still a blockbuster. *1112 W Armitage Ave at Seminary Ave (773-871-2929). El: Brown, Purple (rush hours) to Armitage. Bus: 8 Halsted, 73 Armitage. Dinner (closed Mon). Average main course: $16.*

▼ ☉ Tel Aviv Kosher Pizza See Kosher for review.

☉ Teena Mia You'll think Sbarro. But if you look past the Kraft parmesan on the tables you'll find that this West Loop lunch spot can put out some solid, made-to-order Italian food. Bruschetta is sharp with red onions and garlic, and eggplant parmigiana—served as a portion as big as your head—is smothered in a hearty red sauce. The pasta primavera is flavorful but as soupy as minestrone. Skip it and save room for the housemade Italian cheesecake and tiramasu (but ask them to hold the cheap chocolate syrup). *564 W Washington Blvd between Clinton and Jefferson Sts (312-441-9577). El: Green, Pink to Clinton. Bus: 8 Halsted, 20 Madison (24hrs). Lunch. Average main course: $10.*

★ ▼ BYOB ❋ Terragusto Theo Gilbert has a master plan for his customers: They're going to sit down and eat a four-course Italian meal made with local, organic, sustainable ingredients. And they're going to like it. And you *will* like the food: *Ripiene* (filled pasta) are delicate and delectable; pan-fried polenta is a luscious base for bitter rapini and sweet onions; and roasted chicken is plump and juicy inside, salty and crispy on the outside. But do you really need four courses? No. Save yourself the stomachache—and the cash—and settle for three. *1851 W Addison St between Lincoln and Wolcott Aves (773-248-2777). El: Brown to Addison. Bus: 11, 50, 152. Dinner (every other Tue, Wed–Sun). Average main course: $16.*

▼ ❋ B 312 Chicago Chef Dean Zanella combined his many generations of at-home family Italian cooking knowledge with his modern interest in sustainability to come

Pro choice Deciding what to dine on at Anteprima isn't easy.

up with a menu for this hip pre-theater Italian eatery. Housed in the Hotel Allegro, adjacent to the Cadillac Palace, the restaurant is bright and energetic. The classic Italian dishes, including veal meatballs and gnocchi, are combined with more modern options including sea bass and seared ahi tuna. *Hotel Allegro, 136 N LaSalle St at Randolph St (312-696-2420). El: Brown, Pink, Orange, Purple (rush hrs) to Washington/Wells. Bus: 14, 20 (24hrs), X20, 56, 60 (24hrs), 124, 127, 157. Breakfast, brunch, lunch, dinner. Average main course: $20.*

❋ **Timo** Formerly of Thyme, chef John Bubala has gone the Italian route, putting out dishes like a grilled romaine salad (creamy and warm with an anchovy-caperberry bite) and a perfectly cooked risotto hiding flavorful bits of sausage at his new haunt. The main cooking instrument is still the wood-fired rotisserie, and that's a good thing, with pork dishes, such as roasted pork loin with bacon, roasted onions and red wine sauce, rotating on and off the menu. *464 N Halsted St at Grand Ave (312-226-4300). El: Blue to Grand. Bus: 8, 56, 65. Dinner (Tue–Sun). Average main course: $23.*

★ ▽ ❋ **Trattoria D.O.C** This bright space houses a wood-fired oven that churns out 29 varieties of the original Lincoln Square location's signature thin-crust, uncut 12-inch pizzas. Don't miss the *spaghetti alle vongole e bottarga*, a perfectly seasoned plate of pasta and clams with a nice crunch from dried roe. If you're trying to limit your carbs, the flaky oven-baked bass redolent of garlic and rosemary won't seem like a sacrifice at all. *706 Main St, Evanston (847-475-1111). El: Purple to Main. Bus: 200, 201 (24hrs), 205. Lunch, dinner. Average main course: $14.*

▽ ❋ **B Trattoria Gianni** Theatergoers needing an Italian fix before the show have a few options on Halsted Street, but

none as classically red-sauce-and-Chianti as this. *Melanzane del pecaraio*—roasted eggplant topped with tomato sauce, goat cheese and black olives—packs in endless sweet, salty and tangy flavors, while the *conchiglie del mercante* tosses the shell-shaped pasta with spicy Italian sausage. If the housemade pappardelle doused with truffle oil is on offer, get it; the housemade tiramisu you can leave alone. *1711 N Halsted St between North Ave and Willow St (312-266-1976). El: Red to North/Clybourn. Bus: 8 Halsted, 72 North. Brunch (Sun), dinner (closed Mon). Average main course: $16.*

▽ **Trattoria No. 10** Despite numerous reviews that heaped on the praise when it first opened, this basement dining room remains somewhat of a secret after-work spot. Guys tuck their ties into their shirts so they can dig into the signature ravioli, such as delicious butternut and acorn squash, with abandon. The seasonal sweet-potato gnocchi, fragrant with orange rind, comes in a brown-butter sauce, and the veal scaloppine is drizzled with a delectable porcini-sage-veal reduction. Take a cue from the businessmen and protect your clothes: You'll want every last drop to land in your mouth. *10 N Dearborn Ave between Madison St and Calhoun Pl (312-984-1718). El: Brown, Green, Pink, Purple (rush hrs), Orange to Madison; Blue, Red to Washington. Bus: 14, 20 (24hrs), X20, 124, 127, 157. Lunch (Mon—Fri), dinner (Mon–Sat) (closed Sun). Average main course: $23.*

▽ **Trattoria Porretta Ristorante & Pizzeria** Neighborhood types in Portage Park wouldn't dream of going anywhere else for their 'za, and after tasting the pizza *di casa*—topped with a heavenly combo of sausage, bacon, onions and Parmesan—we understand why. We'll stick with the standbys on the rest of the gussied-up menu: a simple mixed seafood grill studded with calamari, shrimp, mussels and octopus, and eggplant parmigiana and baked rigatoni

Italian/Pizza

New York state of mind
The addictive dishes at Il
Mulino New York spawned
a Chicago offspring.

that both get a red sauce worthy of every last crumb of bread on the table. *3656 N Central Ave between Waveland and Patterson Aves (773-736-1429). Bus: 85 Central, 152 Addison. Dinner. Average main course: $14.*

▼ ✱ **Trattoria Roma** Rome it ain't, but this place can get so packed you'd think the pope was in the kitchen. It's been like this since 1985, and here's why: a carpaccio salad comes with thin slices of beef, arugula and shaved Parmesan; soft morsels of veal sidled by sharp, garlicky, wilted spinach; and tricolor pasta in sweet and nutty four-cheese sauce. For dessert, try housemade tiramisu and cheesecake—authentic touches amid the faux Roman-ruin decor. *1535 N Wells St between Burton Pl and North Ave (312-664-7907). El: Brown, Purple (rush hrs) to Sedgwick. Bus: 11 Lincoln/Sedgwick, 72 North. Lunch, dinner. Average main course: $18.*

▼ ✽ **Trattoria Trullo** Chef-owner Giovanni DeNigris brought his Pugliese dishes with him when he relocated his Evanston trattoria to Lincoln Square. Portions are hefty: Prosciutto with melon arrived with half a shaved pig on the plate. Pasta dishes include ziti with fava-bean puree and chicory tomato stew, and *cavatelli crudaiola*, corkscrews with tomato pulp, basil, arugula and ricotta. The lunchtime café menu lists comfort food choices, including *arancini* and grilled sausage and peppers, while a deli area sells imported olive oils, dry pastas and cured meats. *4767 N Lincoln Ave between Leland and Lawrence Aves (773-506-0093). El: Brown to Western. Bus: 11, 49 (24hrs), X49, 81 (24hrs). Lunch, dinner. Average main course: $15.*

Tucci Benucch A chain Italian restaurant inside a shopping mall is not exactly our idea of fine dining. But this Lettuce Entertain You restaurant inside the 900 N Michigan shops serves its intended purpose well. If you're exhausted from a day at Barney's and Bloomie's, you can stop here for a salad or something more substantial and not feel like you compromised with fast food, nor feel like you

overspent on an average meal. The simpler dishes, like the pizzas and chopped salads, tend to be best. *900 N Michigan Ave at Walton St (312-266-2500). El: Red to Chicago. Bus: 3, X4, 10, 26, 66, 125, 143, 144, 145, 146, 147, 151 (24hrs). Lunch, dinner. Average main course: $11.*

▼ ✽ **Tufano's Vernon Park Tap** This old-school Italian joint is holding strong in its ever-changing 'hood. The chalkboard menu rarely changes, and regulars never even glance at it before ordering the house specialty: the rosated, citrus-spritzed lemon chicken Vesuvio is among the best around. After a couple of bites, you'll get caught up in the tradition of the place, enough to overlook iceberg salads, standard pastas and carafes of jug wine. *1073 W Vernon Park Pl between Carpenter and Aberdeen Sts (312-733-3393). El: Blue to Racine. Bus: 7, 12, 60. Lunch (Tue–Fri), dinner (Tue–Sun). Average main course: $14.*

▼ ✽ **Tuscany** You don't usually hear the words sophisticated and Wrigleyville in the same sentence, but the dining room of this trattoria is just that: warm, comfortable and, despite its proximity to Wrigley Field, completely free from Old Style–fueled antics. *Raviolli Pera alla Giorgio*, stuffed with pear and Parmesan, is slightly sweet, using pine nuts and walnuts to make it savory enough for dinner. Pork chops are adorned with a white-wine sauce sporting thick slices of garlic. *3700 N Clark St at Waveland Ave (773-404-7700). El: Red to Addison. Bus: 8, 22 (24hrs), 36, 152. Lunch (game days only), dinner. Average main course: $16. ● Additional location at 1014 W Taylor St (312-829-1990).*

★ ▼ ✽ 👍 **Va Pensiero** This quiet restaurant on the first floor of the Margarita European Inn may be Evanston's best-kept secret. In addition to the extensive, all-Italian wine list, there's also a list of well-executed, appetite-inducing apertivos. And there's even food to go with it—dishes like stalks of spring asparagus paired with a nutty Parmesan and lively tomato *fonduta*; housemade ravioli stuffed with a sweet-and-savory combination of caramelized onions, pancetta and spring peas; and juicy slices of lamb lined with dark, char marks from the grill. *1566 Oak Ave, Evanston (847-475-7779). El: Purple to Davis. Bus: 93, 201 (24hrs), 205, 213. Dinner. Average main course: $28.*

Ventoso This upscale Italian option in the Marriott offers antipasti like little neck clams; a salad of heirloom tomatoes, mozzarella, bocconcini, fresh basil and sea salt; and a selection of steaks and chops. The standard breakfast buffet, offered seven days a week along with the à la carte menu, features made-to-order eggs, waffles and pancakes. *540 N Michigan Ave between Grand Ave and Ohio St (312-836-6336). El: Red to Grand. Bus: 2, 3, X4, 10, 26, 29, 65, 125, 143, 144, 145, 146, 147, 151 (24hrs), 157. Breakfast, lunch, dinner. Average main course: $23.*

▼ **Via Carducci** A few things to keep in mind while visiting this popular Lincoln Park eatery: The cabonara, made the real way (with an egg) is excellent; the gnocchi, outsourced from an Italian-grandmother type, is rich and fluffy; and the *salsiccia alla calabrese*, with soft, sweated peppers and succulent sausage, is a good bet. The wine list is surprisingly decent for a restaurant at this price level. And the rest of the food…well, it passes muster. Thin pizzas, bulging panzerotti and a somewhat mushy eggplant parmigiana are fine but nothing special. *1419 W Fullerton Ave between Janssen and Southport Aves (773-665-1981). El: Brown, Purple (rush hrs), Red to Fullerton. Bus: 9, 11, 74. Lunch (Mon–Fri), dinner. Average main course: $13.*

▼ ✹ **Via Carducci la Sorella** This sister to the popular Carducci in Lincoln Park, with its hint of a Goodfellas feel, seems a tad out of place amid the other, trendier-than-thou spots on Division. But crowds pour in to listen to an old-school crooner play "Volare" on an electric keyboard while they dig into red-sauce favorites. Some dishes miss, like paper-thin eggplant overloaded with goat cheese and marinara. But others are right on the mark: Linguini *frutti di mar* has a garlicky bite and is studded with plump shrimp, clams, mussels and calamari. *1928 W Division St between Wolcott and Damen Aves (773-252-2244). El: Blue to Division. Bus: 9, 56, 70. Lunch, dinner. Average main course: $13.*

BYOB ▼ ✹ **Via Veneto** From the outside, this place looks like it was held over from the '50s. But get inside and you'll find a contemporary, family-friendly restaurant. Serving a classy version of Italian-American red-sauce fare, the kitchen puts out *melanzane stuzzicante* (garlicky discs of fried eggplant), *petto di pollo alla senape* (juicy chicken breast in a shallot-mustard sauce) and big squares of cheesy lasagna at record speed; but a nice selection of grappa is on hand should you want to linger. *6340 N Lincoln Ave at Drake Ave (773-267-0888). Bus: 11, 82, 155. Lunch (Mon–Fri), dinner. Average main course: $15.*

▼ ❨ **The Village** This windowless red-sauce joint is more tourist attraction than restaurant. In fact, it's a downright theme park, the entire room designed to look like an Italian village (hence the name), complete with businesses, a perpetually-revolving water wheel and a mischievous black cat in the corner. Like most theme parks, the focus is more on the experience than the food. Take advantage of the hearty lasagna and the extensive wine list. *71 W Monroe St between Clark and Dearborn Sts (312-332-7005). El: Blue, Red to Monroe. Bus: 1, 2, 6, 7, 10, 14, 20, 22 (24hrs), 24, 28, 29, 36, 56, 60 (24hrs), 62, 124, 126, 127, 144, 146, 151 (24hrs), 156, 157. Lunch, dinner. Average main course: $14.*

▼ ✹ **B Vinci** Most people visit this corner Italian stalwart and go to Steppenwolf afterward. Turns out you don't need

the theater as an excuse to visit, because the *ortolano* pizza—piled high with spicy arugula and a sticky balsamic reduction—is an attraction in its own right. *1732 N Halsted Ave between North Ave and Willow St (312-266-1199). El: Red to North/Clybourn. Bus: 8 Halsted, 72 North. Brunch (Sun), dinner (closed Mon). Average main course: $16.*

✹ ♨ ☉ **Vines on Clark** This Italian-focused restaurant in the heart of Cubs territory serves up a large selection of panini—including the Italian, a meat-lover's dream piled high with pepperoni, salami, ham, provolone, lettuce and tomato. Like any Italian joint worth its sauce, it also has pizzas including the spinach, bacon, mozzarella and pesto pie. Pasta additions include eggplant parmigiana, shrimp primavera and blackened steak Alfredo. *3554 N Clark St at Eddy St (773-327-8572). El: Red to Addison. Bus: 8, 22 (24hrs), 77 (24hrs), 152. Mon–Fri 11am–1am; Sat 11am–3am; Sun 11am–1am. Average main course: $10.*

☉ **Vito & Nick's** Serving pizza to the Southwest Side since 1949, Vito and Nick's is the king of thin-crust pizza done Chicago-style. With Old Style on tap and the Bears on TV, surly waitresses shuffle bubbling-hot pies to a full room of revelers. The crispy but pliant crust, tangy sauce and top-quality sausage separate this pizza from other Chicago thin crusts. Sure, the place has other things on the menu, like spaghetti, but it's the pizza that keeps customers loyal through the generations. *8433 S Pulaski Rd at 84th Pl between Clark and Dearborn Sts (773-735-2050). Bus: 53A Pulaski, 87 87th. Lunch, dinner. Average main course: $10.*

Vivere The best of the three restaurants that make up the multilevel Italian Village, Vivere boasts a menu as contemporary as its decor. That's quite a feat when your dining room looks like an Italian baroque version of Alice's Wonderland. The menu is a balance of classics and interesting twists to housemade pastas, seafood stews and grilled game. The best part about the kitchen offering half-orders of pasta is that you can get two. Try the pheasant-filled agnollotini and the rigatoni alla bolognese. *71 W Monroe St between Clark and Dearborn Sts (312-332-7005). El: Red, Blue to Washington; Orange, Brown, Green, Purple (rush hrs) to Adams. Bus: 1, 7, X28, 126, 151. Lunch (Mon–Fri), dinner (Mon–Sat) (closed Sun). Average main course: $20.*

✹ **Vivo** This sexy eatery was the first to brave Randolph Street back when it was, er, a little less gentrified. More than 15 years later, the food still holds up. Golden housemade gnocchi is doused in a creamy, earthy truffle sauce; tuna fillet is dressed up with a lively combo of balsamic and mint; and the pistachio gelato with merengue and hot fudge is almost as utterly unshareable. *838 W Randolph St between Green and Peoria Sts (312-733-3379). El: Green to Clinton. Bus: 8 Halsted, 20 Madison (24hrs). Lunch (Mon–Fri), dinner. Average main course: $22.*

▼ **Zia's Trattoria** This upscale Edison Park Italian spot is a big hit with the trendy neighborhood types, who pack the expansive, rustic-feeling rooms until you feel like you're part of one big, noisy party. They come for the signature tenderloin stuffed with garlic and herbed cheese and covered in wine sauce, plus well-executed pastas like penne tossed with sausage, rapini and ricotta—all giant portions served on platters. If you drive, take advantage of the complimentary valet—something tough to find in other 'hoods. *6699 Northwest Hwy at Oliphant Ave, Edison Park (773-775-0808). Metra: Union Pacific NW to Edison Park Bus: 68 Northwest Hwy. Lunch (Tue–Fri), dinner. Average main course: $15.* ∎

Japanese and Sushi

See also: *Chinese, Korean, Pan Asian, Seafood, Vietnamese*

▼ (❋ **Agami** It looks like someone at this sushi spot took decorating tips from the Mad Hatter and color cues from a Life Savers roll, warping them into an LSD-influenced underwater scene. Somehow, the decor, along with equally wild takes on artistic maki rolls, works. In addition to eye-crossingly delicious nigiri, try the Ocean Drive, a refreshing roll of tuna, yellowtail, avocado, green peppers, spicy mayo and cilantro. Also excellent is the Dragon Festival, an amalgam of flavors and textures like soft-shell crab, cucumber, avocado, eel and tobiko. *4712 N Broadway St at Leland Ave (773-506-1854). El: Red to Lawrence. Bus: 22 (24hrs), 36, 78, 81 (24hrs). Dinner. Average nigiri: $2.50.*

Blu Coral This slick sushi den stands out amidst its budget-bin neighbors, but when stacked up against other similar spots, it's really the creative small plates that are worth a second glance. The menu is massive and overwhelming, but go right for the Dragon Fire (crispy softshell crab, eel and asparagus bound together by thin slices of raw tuna). The bacon-wrapped scallop–and–blue crab cake maki is almost good enough to overlook poor service, detracting music and industrial dungeon look. *1265 N Milwaukee Ave at Ashland Ave (773-252-2020). El: Blue to Division. Bus: 9 (24hrs), X9, 56, 72. Dinner. Average nigiri: $3.*

▼ **Bluefin** Locals return to this sexy, dimly lit space for the reliably fresh, generous cuts of fish and the inventive maki (don't miss the perfectly crunchy Hot Night), most of which stop just short of ridiculous (with exception of the Shiroyama, a goopy, mayo-soaked mess topped with baked scallops). Chef's specials change monthly, but we're praying the creamy Brazilian lobster sashimi sticks around forever—it's so sweet and smooth you won't mind that there's only ice cream for dessert. *1952 W North Ave at Milwaukee Ave (773-394-7373). El: Blue to Damen. Bus: 50, 56, 72. Lunch, dinner. Average nigiri: $3.*

★ ▼ (❋ **Bob San** Think sidewalk spots along Division are divey hangs for local hipsters? This high-quality sushi star debunks that myth. We've always had good luck asking servers what's freshest, and we're not ashamed to admit that they hooked us on their nontraditional rolls, like the House Crunch. Added bonus: When the weather warms up, the outdoor seating is a refuge from the ubiquitous sushi-bar house music. *1805 W Division St between Wood and Honore Sts (773-235-8888). El: Blue to Division. Bus: 9 Ashland (24hrs), 70 Division. Dinner. Average nigiri: $2.50.*

BYOB ▼ ❋ **Café Blossom** With only a smattering of tables and stools, this tucked-away sushi house is ideal for folks who like their fish with a dose of intimate, family-run personality. Begin with *ika sansa*, a wildly flavorful marinated squid, and the snappy tatiki salad of mixed greens topped with flame-seared tuna. The bright and fresh maki rolls come with whimsical names like Granny Smith, Smoky Bear, and our favorite, Winter Blossom (salmon, yellowtail and Japanese mint muddled with black tobiko). *608 W Barry Ave at Broadway (773-935-5284). El: Brown, Purple (rush hrs), Red to Belmont. Bus: 8, 22 (24hrs), 36, 77 (24hrs), 156. Dinner (closed Sun). Average nigiri $1.75.*

▼ **Chiyo** The fish is supremely fresh at this sushi and hot pot restaurant, but don't stop there: The more social, and fun, option is either the shabu-shabu or sukiyaki. Both are self-cooked, one-pot meals of either sirloin or Wagyu beef and a heaping array of tofu and veggies, including onions, cabbage, mushrooms, chrysanthemum leaves and leeks. But while the meat is simmered in seaweed broth for shabu-shabu, it's seared in melted pork fat for sukiyaki before a sugary mirin-soy broth is added. *3800 W Lawrence Ave at Hamlin Ave (773-267-1555). El: Brown to Kimball. Bus: 53 (24hrs), 81 (24hrs), 82. Dinner (closed Tue). Average main course: $15.*

BYOB ▼ (**Coast** This place knows how to exploit sushi's sex appeal while maintaining a low-key, neighborhood-favorite vibe. Slippery, curvaceous morsels of tuna, yellowtail, salmon and more are served in a dark, sultry dining room full of slick minimalist furniture and tableware. The main focus is great-quality raw fish, but a few liberties are taken, and with success. The ceviche maki pairs lime-marinated scallop with mango, cilantro and jalapeño and salmon gets stuffed in a spring roll, fried and served with green curry dipping sauce. *2045 N Damen Ave between McLean and Dickens Aves (773-235-5775). El: Blue to Western. Bus: 50 Damen, 73 Armitage. Dinner. Average nigiri: $2.50.*

BYOB ▼ **Green Tea** Sometimes you want a good piece of sushi without the black-clad servers, hip house beats, triple-digit bill and lighting so dim you can't tell your toro from your tako. This tiny, no-frills sushi cafe slices up fresh, meaty cuts of all the standards, including tasty salmon, fatty tuna, mackerel and yellowtail. For starters, try the housemade pickles and the soy-sesame-ginger-marinated, grilled baby octopus. If you're into Americanized, everything-but-the-kitchen sink maki rolls, the Chicago Spicy Crazy is the one to try. Lazy? They deliver for a small fee. *2206 N Clark St between Webster Ave and Grant Pl (773-883-8812). Bus: 22 Clark (24hrs), 74 Fullerton. Lunch (Tue–Sat), dinner (Tue–Sun). Average nigiri: $2.*

▼ ❋ **Hachi's Kitchen** Chef Jim Bee's loyal followers are not limited to catching his cuisine at Lincoln Park's legendary Sai Café thanks to this sister spot in Logan Square. Sleek decor is sophisticated but not sceney, the sake and wine lists are packed with ideal sushi partners, and the creative starters and maki steal the show from the thick, glossy cuts of expected fish varieties. Try the crunchy-creamy tuna *masako*, the citrus and sesame oil–kissed chilled octopus, and the slick miso-glazed black cod. *2521 N California Ave between Altgeld St and Logan Blvd (773-276-8080). El: Blue to California. Bus: 52, 56, 74. Dinner. Average nigiri: $2.50.*

BYOB ▼ **Hama Matsu** This spot claims to be a Korean/Japanese restaurant, but its nods to Korean cuisine include a few bibimbaps and complimentary banchan. The specialty is sushi, and it's done well. The house roll takes a kitchen-sink approach, combining asparagus, smoked salmon, unagi, crabmeat, avocado, green onion and teriyaki sauce into one bloated, delicious bite. The Low Carb Maki's lettuce, zucchini, avocado and crab was bland (no shock there), but the Dragon roll (unagi, avocado, shrimp tempura) was crunchy, sweet

Sliced and diced
Wakamono's sushi chefs
give tuna a new treatment.

and artfully plated. *5143 N Clark St at Winona St (773-506-2978). El: Red to Berwyn. Bus: 22 Clark (24hrs), 92 Foster. Dinner. Average nigiri: $1.95.*

▼ **Itto Sushi** If double-headed dragon rolls and ginger soy–tinis are what you expect from your sushi experience, go elsewhere. This old-school sushi den has been offering Japanese standards in a no-frills setting for 25 years. It's got a solid sake list, fresh nigiri (don't miss the buttery toro or the tender baby hamachi) and traditional maki. Fish-haters can sample housemade gyoza or choose from a huge list of appetizers, noodle dishes and tempuras. Judging by the autographed photos of Japanese pro-baseball players, this place is a homesickness cure for at least a few jocks. *2616 N Halsted St at Wrightwood Ave (773-871-1800). El: Brown, Purple (rush hrs), Red to Fullerton. Bus: 8, 11, 74. Lunch, dinner (closed Sun). Average nigiri: $2.50.*

▼ (✳ **Izumi Sushi Bar and Restaurant** The volume of the *doont-doont-doont* beats at this overlooked spot on Randolph Row is tolerable enough that we can focus on our friends and our food. The best of the latter includes thick squares of sashimi (fresh salmon, superwhite tuna and yellowtail are all fresh and flavorful) and the punch-packing Lion maki roll (yellowtail, tuna, avocado, cilantro and jalapeño rolled tight and drizzled with chile sauce). Wash it all down with the value-priced sake; two people can sip for around $12. *731 W Randolph St at Court Pl (312-207-5299). El: Green, Pink to Clinton. Bus: 8 Halsted, 20 Madison (24hrs). Lunch (Mon–Fri), dinner. Average nigiri: $3.*

▼ BYOB (**Jai Yen** Once you get used to the musty smell in this cute-as-a-mochi spot, you'll be able to concentrate on the mostly sushi menu. Until then, breathe through your mouth and think about peonies. Ready? Okay, start with the tuna tataki (chunks of cool tuna, avocado and red onion in a lemon-soy sauce) or the chive dumpling, perfectly pan-fried until lightly crisp and bulging with fresh chives. Avoid maki with unagi sauce: The chef has a heavy hand when it comes to ladling, and the rolls become a soggy mess. *3736 N Broadway between Grace St and Waveland Ave (773-404-0555). El: Red to Addison. Bus: 8, 36, 152. Lunch, dinner. Average nigiri: $2.*

★ ▼ ✳ **Japonais** We're not sure what distant land we're supposed to be transported to when we come to this swank spot on the Chicago River, but the Ian Schrager–esque space is sexy, vibrant and, incredibly, she ain't just nice to look at— she can cook, too. The modern Japanese food centers around superb-quality raw fish, presented simply as sashimi or whacked out into tasty rolls. Don't leave without having the Kobe carpaccio, Tokyo drums, kani nigiri, yukke toro or "Le Quack Japonais." *600 W Chicago Ave at Larrabee St (312-822-9600). El: Brown, Purple (rush hrs) to Chicago. Bus: 8 Halsted, 66 Chicago (24hrs). Lunch (Mon–Fri), dinner. Average main course: $25.*

▼ (✳ **Kamehachi** Long before Chicago's great sushi boom, this Old Town stalwart (opened in '67) taught us how to tell nigiri from sashimi and miso from udon. It's still packing in the crowds: Old-timers who sit at the sushi bar, funky types who dig the lounge upstairs, and everyone who can squeeze onto their pretty, flower-filled garden patio out back., plus the suburbs. *1400 N Wells St at Schiller St (312-664-3663). Bus: 11 Lincoln, 72 North. Lunch (Mon–Sat), dinner. Average nigiri: $2.* ● *Additional locations at 240 E Ontario St (312-587-0600), 20 N Dearborn St (312-744-1900) and 311 S Wacker Dr (312-765-8701).*

▼ BYOB **Katachi** Sushi and BYOB go together like Matthew McConaughey and crap movies, which explains

why this cozy, unassuming raw-fish emporium gets packed to the gills with folks looking for reliably good sushi to pair with their Trader Joe's pinot grigio. All the maki standbys are present and accounted for, but signature rolls like the tuna, salmon and yellowtail–packed Triple and the unagi-topped, shrimp tempura–stuffed Dragon allow the chef's creativity to shine. *3911 N Sheridan Rd between Byron and Dakin Sts (773-880-5340). El: Red to Sheridan. Bus: 36, 80, X80, 145, 151 (24hrs). Dinner. Average nigiri: $2.*

★ **Katsu** The best raw fish in town is at this small, unassuming West Rogers Park hideaway. Here, you'll find incredibly fresh, melt-in-your-mouth, super-premium yellowtail, bluefin, mackerel and fatty tuna. Beyond the raw, Katsu's crew has skills on the grill, turning out a tasty marinated duck breast and a crispy yellowtail collar (great with a dab of shaved, pickled daikon, a sprinkle of sea salt and a squirt of lemon). *2651 W Peterson Ave between Talman and Washtenaw Aves (773-784-3383). Bus: 49B Western, 84 Peterson. Dinner (closed Tue). Average nigiri: $5.*

★ ▼ ✳ **Kaze** Gifted with the hands of a warrior, chef Macku slays fish instead of dragons at his sophisticated Japanese storefront. The Chan clan (chefs Kaze and Hari round out the family) makes yearly sojourns around the globe for inspiration. The result is a form of fusion that dresses up slick cuts of nigiri with seasonal, cooked toppings and includes creations like whitefish tempura wrapped in shrimp and drizzled with a parsley butter. Menus change with the seasons, and Tuesday nights are a steal: Four courses with wine pairings goes for $45. *2032 W Roscoe St at Seeley Ave (773-327-4860). El: Brown to Paulina. Bus: 49 (24hrs), 50, 77 (24hrs). Dinner. Average main course: $15.*

▼ **Kohan** The construction dust has settled from the University Village neighborhood, unearthing this casual

Read 'em & eat

dashi (DAH-shee) basic stock for miso and ramen soup made with kombu (kelp) and dried fish flakes

gyoza (gee-OH-zah) dumplings commonly filled with meat, then fried or steamed

mirin (MEE-reen) a sweetened rice wine

omakase (oh-mah-KAH-say) the chef's choice of a series of dishes

shabu-shabu a dish of thinly sliced raw beef and vegetables prepared in a hot broth at the table

shiso perilla, a rough-edged, leafy herb of the mint and basil family

tonkatsu (tawn-kaht-soo) Breaded, deep-fried pork cutlet

udon soft, thick wheat noodles, typically served in a soup

yakitori: a dish of chicken marinated in soy sauce, sugar and sake, placed on skewers and broiled or grilled

Japanese spot where the service is warm and welcoming enough to fool diners into believing it's an old favorite. Half of the menu is dedicated to teppan (Benihana-style open grill), and the teriyaki-glazed shrimp, steak and veggies are tasty enough, but the sushi offerings impress more. Stick with the specials board for interesting and supremely fresh catches like shaved ginger-topped *aji* (horse mackerel), meaty bluefin and rich, grilled yellowfin collar. *730 W Maxwell St between Union Ave and Halsted St (312-421-6254). El: Blue to UIC-Halsted. Bus: 8, 12, 168. Lunch (Mon–Fri), dinner. Average nigiri: $2.25.*

▼ **Kuni's** Many old-school sushi lovers—the kind who scoff at new-age maki—consider this two decades-old Evanston spot the best sushi place around. We wouldn't go quite that far, but we do love the generous pieces of superfresh nigiri (especially the melt-in-your-mouth toro). The simple maki—yellowtail with scallions, salmon skin—are satisfying, too, but other Japanese standards are a little ho-hum. Still, prices are reasonable, service is friendly and the atmosphere is no-frills—a perfect combination for indulging sushi cravings without breaking the bank. *511-A Main St, Evanston (847-328-2004). El: Purple to Main. Bus: 205 Chicago/Golf. Lunch (Mon, Wed–Sat), dinner (Mon, Wed–Sun) (closed Tues). Average nigiri: $2.50.*

▼ **Kyoto** Over the years this garden-level Japanese spot has become overlooked. We found the sashimi to be up to par (especially the buttery *maguro*), but we were more intrigued by the cooked dishes. The *agadashi* tofu is battered and fried, rendering the tofu creamy and warm, and the *oyako don* takes a bowl of rice and tops it with a fluffy omelette and crispy chicken. The solid food and friendly owner will tempt you to spread the word, but you may want to keep it all for yourself. *2534 N Lincoln Ave at Lill Ave (773-477-2788). El: Brown, Purple (rush hrs), Red to Fullerton. Bus: 8, 11, 74, 76. Lunch, dinner (closed Mon). Average main course: $11.*

★ ▼ ✳ **Mirai Sushi** Signatures like *yukke toro* (fatty tuna tartare with quail egg and housemade soy sauce) and *kani nigiri* (seaweed filled with baked spicy crab) aren't exclusive to this restaurant (Mirai shares its head chef with Japonais), but the funky neighborhood and surrounding postdinner bar choices are. A closer look at the menu reveals that diners pay an extra $2 to $5 per item at Japonais, so when here, use that extra dough to attack the specials sheet, which often offers supremely fresh flights of tuna and whitefish of varying fattiness. *2020 W Division St between Damen and Hoyne Aves (773-862-8500). El: Blue to Division. Bus: 50 Damen, 70 Division. Dinner (closed Sun). Average nigiri: $4.*

▼ ◖ **Mizu** If you can overlook indifferent service and bad music, give this place a shot. Skip apps and go straight for the goods: generous sushi that tastes flown-in fresh (especially the buttery salmon) and the *yakitori*, grilled skewers of guilty pleasures like crispy chicken skin and meaty gizzards, good-for-you eats from asparagus to eggplant and unusual finds of bacon-wrapped tomato and chicken-stuffed portobello. Bonus: You can use the pointy skewers to end your misery when Tupac's "Dear Mama" is played. *315 W North Ave between North Park Ave and Orleans St (312-951-8880). El: Brown, Purple (rush hrs) to Sedgwick. Bus: 72 North. Dinner. Average nigiri: $2.50.*

Noodles by Takashi Good ramen is hard to find, especially in the Loop. And while we're grateful for chef Takashi Yagahashi's return to Chicago (after successful runs in Detroit and Vegas), we have to try hard to shrug off the $9 price tag for a bowl of noodles in broth. To avoid buyer's remorse go with a friend, split the *shio* ramen (typical noodles boosted by a soy-miso broth, ground pork, baby bok choy,

ground ginger and sesame seeds) and supplement with starters like the steamed bun stuffed with glistening braised pork. *Macy's on State Street, 111 N State St, seventh floor, at Washington St (312-781-1000). El: Blue, Red to Washington; Brown, Green, Orange, Purple (rush hrs) to Randolph. Bus: 3, 4, X4, 14, 20, 26, 60 (24hrs), 127, 145, 147, 148, 151 (24hrs). Lunch (Mon–Sat). Average main course: $8.*

▼ **Osaka** The sushi here isn't going to change your life, but we love this carry-out spot as an easy Loop lunch option. Zippy chefs concoct daily specials like eel rainbow rolls on the fly, while the refrigerated case is stocked with just-made combos (Cali, Philly and spicy tuna is a good one). But our favorite thing about the place is the "wall of fruit": It's the sign that true fresh-fruit smoothies are being made (in flavors like watermelon, lychee, mango and avocado) instead of drinks with that grainy, premade powder, tapioca drink crap. *400 S Michigan Ave at Van Buren St (312-566-0118). El: Brown, Green, Orange, Purple (rush hrs) to Adams; Red, Blue to Jackson. Bus: 1, 3, 4 (24hrs), X4, 6, 7, 14, 26, X28, 126, 127, 145. Lunch, dinner (closed Sun). Average nigiri: $1.75.*

▼ ✳ **Oysy Sushi** Sashimi is the way to go at this popular South Loop spot—big, thick cuts of very fresh, cool standards are dependable and tasty, and richer indulgences like fatty tuna and sea urchin are equally good and almost always available. Interestingly, the cooked menu is offered as small plates, making it easy to try a handful of unique dishes like roasted chicken-stuffed lotus root in crispy tempura batter and baked sesame-crusted scallops with wasabi mayo. *50 E Grand Ave between Wabash Ave and Rush St (312-670-6750). El: Red to Grand. Bus: 29, 36, 65. Lunch, dinner. Average nigiri: $2.*

▼ **BYOB Ringo** This neighborhood spot underwent a face lift to get rid of tangerine walls, industrial carpeting, a low drop ceiling and the unsettling walk through the kitchen to reach the restroom. Now, there's a giant space (it expanded into the next-door storefront) with soaring ceilings, eclectic artwork, a new "kushi bar" (skewered meats and veggies) and, thankfully, the same great sushi. Still reliably delicious are the crunchy dragon roll and the spicy sweet potato maki. *2507-09 N Lincoln Ave between Lill Ave and Altgeld St (773-248-5788). El: Brown, Red, Purple (rush hrs) to Fullerton. Bus: 8, 11, 74. Dinner (closed Tue). Average nigiri: $1.75.*

▼ ✳ **Rise** This neighborhood sushi spot is often packed to the gills with chic SoPo types giving off a too-cool-for-school vibe, and there are a few head-scratchers on the maki menu (a "fire roll" made with salmon, jalapeño and melted provolone). But sometimes the chef's creativity works, like with the Mexican maki filled with yellowtail, avocado, cilantro, jalapeño and a squeeze of fresh lime juice. Non–sushi eaters have plenty of good options to choose from, including gingery beef tenderloin and crispy crêpe–wrapped duck breast. *3401 N Southport Ave at Roscoe St (773-525-3535). El: Brown to Southport. Bus: 9, X9, 77 (24hrs). Dinner. Average nigiri: $3.*

Ron of Japan Like the popular Benihana restaurant chain, Ron of Japan's chefs prepare your food in the *teppanyaki*-style—on a sizzling iron plate set into each table. Each grilled meal (choices include filet mignon, lobster tail, chicken breast and tofu) is served with two shrimp kogane-yaki (an appetizer topped with an egg-yolk sauce), chicken soup, a salad, veggie rice, green tea and dessert. Not only do you get a meal, but, as with all *teppanyaki*-style dining, you get a table-side performance from knife-wielding chefs. *230 E Ontario St between Fairbanks Court and St Clair St (312-644-6500). El: 2, 3, X4, 10, 26, 66, 125, 143, 144, 145, 146, 147, 151 (24hrs), 157. Dinner. Average main course: $25.*

Roll with it Maki doubles as art at Blu Coral.

RT Lounge This slick little spot is perfect for getting to know chef Rick Tramonto's sexier side (insert lewd joke here). Belinda Chang's wine list (not to mention the full bar) is the focus, but it's augmented by Tramonto's pristine, Asian-inspired snacks—bites like rock shrimp tempura with lemongrass aioli; tuna tartare dressed in soy-sesame sauce; and a pristine selection of maki, nigiri and sashimi. The execution is excellent, but these dishes are small—if it's dinner you're after, head downstairs, where two other Tramonto restaurants wait to fill you up. *601 N Milwaukee Ave, Wheeling (847-777-6575). Mon–Thu 5pm–midnight; Fri, Sat 5pm–1am; Sun 5–11pm. Average nigiri: $8.*

▼ (✻ **Sai Café** For two decades, this traditional Japanese spot has offered more of a steakhouse atmosphere—with low lights, jazz tunes and TVs at the bar—and keeps the focus on food. Sushi is best ordered as sashimi; you'll get thick, meaty cuts, and you should ask for a side of the perfect, warm rice for contrast. Standards are all great, but try some not-so-common choices like sea urchin and escolar, a firm, oily fish with full flavor. Aside from sushi, try the *kani su*, a salad of cucumbers and crab in tangy vinegar dressing. *2010 N Sheffield Ave between Armitage and Dickens Ave (773-472-8080). El: Brown, Purple (rush hrs) to Armitage. Bus: 8 Halsted, 73 Armitage. Lunch (Sat, Sun), dinner. Average nigiri: $2.50.*

▼ **BYOB South Coast** The owners of Wicker Park's most popular BYOB sushi spot Coast expanded their biz with the opening of this South Loop sibling. You'll find the same stellar quality of sashimi and nigiri, cult-worthy signatures like the white tuna ponzu and the south scallop rolls, plus new dishes like teriyaki ribeye steak and seared sesame scallops on spinach with toasted yolk sauce. *1700 S Michigan Ave at 17th St (312-662-1700). Bus: 3, X3, 4 (24hrs), 18. Dinner. Average nigiri: $2.*

Starfish The competition's stiff on Randolph Row's strip of global eats, but this place stands out for its classy-not-clubby vibe and creative concoctions. Skip traditional maki and go with the Dragon Fire, a roll that swaps yellowfin tuna for nori, wrapping the fish around softshell crab and teriyaki-glazed eel. Or try the Jazz Spring, a soybean sheet–encased combo of both super white and fatty tuna, freshwater eel, and a bright ohba (Japanese mint) leaf. Skip the $30 lobster tail from the entrée menu and go for a $4 grilled lobster skewer instead. *804 W Randolph St at Halsted St (312-997-2433). El: Green to Clinton. Bus: 8 Halsted, 20 Madison (24hrs). Lunch (Mon–Fri), dinner. Average nigiri: $3.*

▼ (✻ **SushiSamba Rio** See Pan-Asian for review.

▼ **Sushi Luxe** Andersonville must be swimming with sharks—the amount of raw fish being consumed in the neighborhood is phenomenal. The owners of this one (the folks behind New Tokyo) have gone chrome-crazy, with zig-zag track lighting, a shiny chrome wall, a curvy chrome and chocolate-toned bar and a shiny-framed TV monitor in the bathroom playing random movies. Surprisingly, the sushi menu is standard. *5204 N Clark St between Foster and Farragut Aves (773-334-0770). El: Red to Berwyn. Bus: 22 (24hrs), 36, 92. Dinner. Average nigiri: $2.*

▼ ✻ **Sushi Naniwa** If you've ever found your girlfriend's younger sister hot but realized your girlfriend is more dependable, less flighty and doesn't treat you like you're a dork, you're a Naniwa kinda guy. The older sibling to the trendy Ukie Village Bob San, this old-school sushi house hasn't changed much during its 10 years. Straight-up sushi (luscious salmon, slick mackerel and bass with ponzu are standouts) and classics like Japanese pickles and boiled-spinach apps hold their ground. *607 N Wells St between Ohio and Ontario Sts (312-255-8555). El: Red to Grand. Bus: 65, 125, 156. Lunch (Mon–Fri), dinner. Average nigiri: $2.25.*

Japanese and Sushi

Side dish

Get more from your maki

Tired of the same old toro? Try these tips to really spice up that tuna.

Heck of a job, brownie
Sushi made with brown rice packs a nutrional punch.

It's time to demand more from your sushi. Let's start with the rice: White rice is not only bad for your health (all that refined flour) but also for your attention span. Our first suggestion is to seek out sushi with brown rice. But be warned: While brown rice may be healthier for your body—it is less processed than its white counterpart, so it retains more of its nutritional values—it's slightly less healthy for your wallet. At **Sushi Wabi** *(842 W Randolph St between Green and Peoria Sts, 312-563-1224)*, brown rice can be substituted for white in maki and nigiri for 50 cents extra per order; at Whole Foods *(locations throughout the city)*, an eight-piece tuna roll made with brown rice will set you back $8.75. And when brown rice loses its luster? You can still go one shade darker: **Starfish** *(804 W Randolph St at Halsted St, 312-997-2433)* serves black rice (also touted for its alleged health benefits) for an upcharge of $1 for maki and 50 cents for nigiri.

Maybe you're more into presentation. In that case, we suggest escaping your tired old maki routine and trying the chirashi at **South Coast** *(1700 S Michigan Ave at 17th St, 312-662-1700)*. In this traditional dish, sashimi is fanned over vinegar-doused rice in an artful way, stimulating your eyes and, eventually, your mouth.

If none of that does the trick, remember that the Japanese aren't the only ones who know how to roll stuff up in seaweed. The Koreans have *kim bop*, and at **BBop** *(3952 N Sheridan Rd between Dakin St and Irving Park Rd, 773-868-0828)* these makilike rolls are stuffed with fish cake, egg, spinach, cucumber, carrots and rice.

And if you're still bored after all that? Well, we hate to be the ones to tell you, but maybe it's not the food that's so boring...

★ ▼ (**Sushi Wabi** We could be snarky and say that it's all about the scene here, but the sushi is so damn good, we won't. Countering the aloof, black-clad servers, the Sade-remix–loving DJ and the throngs of clubgoers filling up on preparty snacks are incredibly fresh sushi and creatively cooked dishes. Flash-cooked, citrus-tinged shrimp tops cool green-tea–soba noodles; spicy, vinegar-tossed slaw is topped with tempura softshell crab that's drizzled with wasabi honey; impeccable grilled salmon gets earthy plum sauce and seared mizuna greens; and crunchy, gooey maki like the Ecuador, Godzilla and Tarantula overload our senses and stand in for dessert. *842 W Randolph St between Green and Peoria Sts (312-563-1224). El: Green to Clinton. Bus: 8 Halsted, 20 Madison (24hrs). Lunch (Mon–Fri), dinner. Average nigiri: $3.*

Sushi X Face it: The Japanese are just cooler. If you've seen the way young Japanese hipsters trick themselves out, you know what we're talking about. But if you need a reminder, this tiny, minimalist sushi shop should jog your memory. There's no sashimi served here, so check out the creative honey roll—which flavors tuna with mustard, wraps it in crunchy tempura flakes and adds just a touch of honey—or more traditional rolls like a creamy spicy scallop or a simple *hamachi* roll. Too boring? Sides like wasabi mashed potatoes kick things up. *1136 W Chicago Ave at Milwaukee Ave (312-491-9232). El: Blue to Chicago. Bus: 8, 56, 66 (24hrs). Lunch (Mon–Fri), dinner. Average maki: $7.*

T Spot Sushi & Tea Bar Sample your way through dozens of loose-leaf teas at this sushi restaurant (the dragon well and the magnolia oolong are amazing), then nibble on the marinated squid salad and pay attention when the server rattles off the maki specials: These are the kitchen's best bets. If the "Hot Spot maki" is still around, get it. Honey-drizzled mushrooms come in spicy crab, shrimp and eel with slivers of jalapeño for addictive results. Sushi snobs be warned: The sashimi is mediocre, so stick with maki and tea. *3925 N Lincoln Ave between Byron St and Larchmont Ave (773-549-4500). El: Brown to Irving Park. Bus: 11, 50, 80, X80. Lunch, dinner (closed Sun). Average nigiri: $3.*

☺ **Takumi** This slick little Japanese spot aims to bring a bit of class to your lunch hour. Sit down at a table (or the sushi bar) and indulge in a bento box full of crisp and sweet tempura shrimp, plump California rolls and a salmon fillet topped with a creamy mushroom sauce. Sushi is influenced by the Loop, with maki named "Monroe," "Randolph" and "Jackson." Thankfully the "Lake" roll—golden fried oysters with ginger and mayo—tastes nothing like its namesake. *555 W Madison St at Clinton St (312-258-1010). El: Green, Blue to Clinton. Bus: 14, 20 (24hrs), 56, 60 (24hrs), 124, 125, 157. Lunch (Mon–Fri), dinner. Average main course: $9.*

▼ **Tampopo** Film buffs and food geeks know Tampopo as one of the best—and most overtly erotic—food flicks ever made. This cute sushi spot may not be as, um, *intense* as the film, but the thick cuts of fresh salmon and yellowtail on offer are hard to argue with. Delicious "Caterpillar" rolls (sweet unagi, cucumber and avocado) and "French" rolls (shrimp, cucumber, Japanese mayo) will satiate maki fans, while a steaming bowl of noodles and shrimp in a salty broth makes a rich, flavorful sushi alternative. *5665 N Lincoln Ave between Washtenaw and Fairfield Aves (773-561-2277). Bus: 11, 92, 93. Lunch, dinner (closed Mon). Average nigiri: $2.*

▼ ✳ **Tank Sushi** *2007 Eat Out Awards, Readers' Choice: Best sushi* This Lincoln Square hot spot distinguishes itself with consistently fresh ingredients and perfectly seasoned rice. Delicate cuts of salmon and white tuna rival the best places in town, though sometimes at prices to match. Seasonal small plates, like refreshing sesame-watermelon salad, can be as good as the sushi. The energetic staff turns up the techno come late night, but guests who can't handle the din can book a private tatami room, which seats up to eight. Bonus: Early-bird half-price maki specials on Saturdays and Sundays may just be the best deal in town. *4514 N Lincoln Ave between Sunnyside and Wilson Aves (773-769-2600). El: Brown to Western. Bus: 11, 49 (24hrs), X49, 78, 81 (24hrs). Lunch (Sat, Sun), dinner. Average nigiri: $3.*

BYOB ▼ ◖ Tanoshii Look for the loyal following of Mike-heads: sushi foodies who've followed chef "Sushi Mike" from Hama Matsu and San Soo Gap San to his new post at this small, casual sushi bar. If you try the cooked items, you're likely not to go back. If you order your own sushi, you're likely to offer up a "So what." But if you make like the regulars and put yourself in Sushi Mike's hands (name your price and he creates a combo), you might just become a believer. *5547 N Clark St between Gregory St and Bryn Mawr Ave (773-878-6886). El: Red to Bryn Mawr. Bus: 22 (24hrs), 50, 84, 147. Lunch (Mon, Wed–Fri), dinner (Wed–Mon). Average nigiri: $2.50.*

Tokyo 21 The flashing pachinko machines, the oversize "lucky cats" and the glowing bar of ever-changing colors are supposed to make this dining room seem like a Tokyo-away-from-Tokyo. But it's hard to think "Japan" when the menu says "Mexican" (tacos with "Asian guacamole"). So stick with the sushi: Kamehachi vet Toku Iwamoto turns out quality cuts of fresh *hamachi* and *tai*, not to mention fabulous "tumiki blocks," rectangular maki made without nori. It may not look like the maki you're used to. Then again, few things at this place are supposed to be familiar. *901 W Weed St at Fremont St (312-337-2001). El: Red to North/Clybourn. Bus: 8 Halsted, 72 North. Dinner (closed Sun–Tues). Average nigiri: $3.*

BYOB Tokyo Marina Don't go to Tokyo Marina if you're looking for fancypants feng shui seating arrangements or marvelous maki creations. This is a basic raw fish emporium where chefs acquit themselves yeoman-like, churning out fresh stuff for decent prices. You won't be wowed, you won't be bummed, but if you get a combo platter or *chirashi*, you will be quite content. *5058 N Clark St at Carmen Ave (773-878-2900). El: Red to Argyle. Bus: 9, 22 (24hrs), 92. Lunch, dinner. Average main course: $11.*

BYOB ▼ Toro This place had us at the premeal hand towels: aspirinlike tablets that grow into towelettes when servers pour hot water over them. But this spot offers more than just gimmicks. Sushi man Mitch prides himself on serving oversized pieces of nigiri (he says that's how he was taught, and he's not changing) and creative rolls (we particularly like the Crazy Horse combo of tuna, salmon, yellowtail and avocado topped with tobiko). Nonsushi eaters can opt for traditional dishes (teriyakis, tempura, udon). *2546 N Clark St at Deming Pl (773-348-4877). El: Red, Brown, Purple (rush hrs) to Fullerton. Bus: 22 (24hrs), 36, 151 (24hrs). Lunch (Fri, Sat) and dinner (Tue–Sun). Average nigiri: $2.*

▼ Triad Luckily, these slick, contemporary digs are more than just a pretty face. The *kaki* shooter—oysters, scallion, quail eggs and a lemon-soy sauce—is a tangy, salty tongue teaser. Another solid but simple starter is the "dynamite"—shellfish and mushrooms baked with spicy mayonnaise. For entrées, the green-tea shrimp is a subtle choice—light, fresh and perfect for summer—or you can go the raw route with the luscious sushi. Karaoke in the lounge and a private room for

parties add to the draw. *1933 S Indiana Ave at Cullerton St (312-225-8833). El: Red to Cermak/Chinatown. Bus: 1, 3, 4 (24hrs), 62. Dinner. Average sashimi: $2.50.*

☺ **Tsuki** The dim, sultry, candlelit dining room features modern, white-on-white tableware and an eccentric, sexed-up Japanese menu. Chef Hemmi (singularly named on the menu) drops sweet clusters of crab atop greens, oranges and avocados for a tasty starter. The pricey nigiri and sashimi deliver, with fresh, clean flavors and meaty cuts. The smoky, sweet and tender duck nigiri is delicious. But skip the spicy tuna sampler—toppings like pine nuts, caviar and avocado add interest but little flavor. *1441 W Fullerton Ave between Janssen and Greenview Aves (773-883-8722). Bus: 9 Ashland, 74 Fullerton. Dinner. Average main course: $8.*

▼ ✳ ◖ Tsunami This is where the neighborhood's beautiful people come to feast on just-as-pretty (and tasty) maki. Try one-of-a-kind rolls like the "White Tiger" (spicy salmon and asparagus with honey mayo, topped with white tuna) and the "Tuna 4-way" (spicy ahi tuna with layers of yellow fin, *shiro* and *toro* tuna and an orange-mango sauce). Carnivores can dig into juicy beef tenderloin with lobster mashed potatoes, a dish almost as rich as the "Tsunami Tower" dessert—chocolate Florentine cookies layered with vanilla ice cream and berries, then topped with chocolate mousse. *1160 N Dearborn St at Division St (312-642-9911). El: Red to Clark/Division. Bus: 22 (24hrs), 36, 70. Dinner. Average nigiri: $3.*

★ **Wakamono** *2007 Eat Out Award, Critics' Pick: Sounds Bad, Tastes Good ("Japas," Japanese tapas)* This cool-conscious place focuses on small plates of dishes like fresh tofu sprinkled with chili oil and peanuts, and prosciutto topped with ponzu sauce, crunchy toasted shallots and charred asparagus are a brilliant, unexpected combination of flavors. And the sushi (never frozen) is simply impeccable. Yet the biggest surprise is the service: The servers here actually smile. *3317 N Broadway between Aldine Ave and Buckingham Pl (773-296-6800). El: Brown, Purple (rush hrs), Red to Belmont. Bus: 36, 77 (24hrs), 152. Dinner. Average small plate: $5.* ■

Chef for a day
Customers cook their own shabu shabu at Chiyo.

Korean

See also: *Pan Asian*

⊕ **Alice & Friends' Vegetarian Café** See Vegetarian for review.

⊕ **Amitabul** See Vegetarian for review.

BYOB ⊕ **Bbop** Owner Okcha McDonald wants to ease locals into appreciating Korean, and to that end she's succeeding: Her BBop Mandoo (savory beef dumplings), BBop (a.k.a. *bibimbap*, a casserole of rice, vegetables and egg) and kimchi pancake are all good, if basic, introductions. Sometimes the food is too simple—we wished the *kalbi* and *bulgogi* were more aggressive in flavor. We're looking forward to the day McDonald puts Korean Food 201 on the menu. *3952 N Sheridan Rd between Dakin St and Irving Park Rd (773-868-0828). El: Red to Sheridan. Bus: 36, 80, 151 (24hrs). Lunch, dinner. Average main course: $7.*

★ ⊕ **Cho Sun Ok** The intoxicating aromas of soy sauce, sugar, rice vinegar and garlic tell you this place is good before you walk in the door. Try to talk the server into letting you cook your own sliced beef because the salty-sweet marinated meats (from beef tenderloin to octopus) we cooked tableside were more tender than the kitchen's version. Of the giant wave of little side dishes that accompany the barbecue, don't pass up the moist fish cake. *4200 N Lincoln Ave at Berteau Ave (773-549-5555). El: Brown to Irving Park. Bus: 11, 50, 78, 80, X80. Lunch, dinner. Average main course: $10.*

▼ (**Hae Woon Dae** Korean barbecue joints distinguish themselves by the quality of their meat, marinades and accompanying side dishes (*banchan*). This mainstay nails all three. Tender beef (*kalbi*) gets a garlic-soy-sesame oil marinade, while slices of pork (*bulgogi*) are saturated with a spicier mixture. While your meat sizzles on the charcoal grill inset in your table, sample *banchan* like pickled turnips, kimchi, eggy potato salad and tofu skin with green chile and a bottle of Korean beer. *6240 N California Ave between Granville and Rosemont Aves (773-764-8018). Bus: 84, 93, 155. Lunch (Sat, Sun), dinner. Average main course: $12.*

▼ (**Jin Ju** When we tell you that this spot is slick, sexy and seductive, we're referring to the servers, the space and the food. Unlike most Korean barbecue houses, there's no tabletop grilling here, but the kitchen does it better than you could. Opt for *o jinga bokum*, strips of squid with the heat and flavor of chiles, or the *kalbi*, beef short ribs that are sweet, salty and tasty. *5203 N Clark St between Foster and Farragut Aves (773-334-6377). El: Red to Berwyn. Bus: 22 (24hrs), 36, 92. Dinner (closed Mon). Average main course: $16.*

★ **Kangnam** The *dolsot bibimbap* at this quiet, strip-mall Korean joint has garnered a cult following over the years. The steaming classic *is* delicious, but don't ignore the other treats: sweet and garkicky *bulgogi*, spicy yet cooling cucumber kimchi and a flavorful soup with tofu. *4849 N Kedzie Ave between Lawrence Ave and Ainslie St (773-539-2524). Bus: 81 (24hrs), 82, 93. Lunch, dinner. Average main course: $13.*

B **Koryo** Korean classics you'd cook yourself on tabletop grills at other spots arrive already prepared on sizzling platters here. That reminds us of bad fajita experiences. We opt to get our *bulgogi* (beef) fix in the *so go-ki guk*, a rich beef broth packed with vermicelli noodles and tender pieces of beef. Some dishes, such as the flour pancake, border on bland, but *dolsot bibimbap*, the toasted, veggie-laden, egg-topped rice bowl, is exactly how it should be. *2936 N Broadway between Oakdale and Wellington Aves (773-477-8510). El: Brown to Wellington. Bus: 22 (24hrs), 36, 76, 151 (24hrs). Brunch (Sat, Sun), dinner. Average main course: $11.*

★ (**San Soo Gap San** The smoking ban has taken effect for barless restaurants like this one, but you'll still leave here with the essence of ash wafting from your clothes. That's no reason to stay away from the charcoal-fueled Korean barbecue, however: The *wang kalbi* and *dai ji kalbi* are marinated, not saturated, in their sauces, which gives the high-quality meats a chance to speak for themselves. Or, try the *bibim naeng Myun*, cold buckwheat noodles and beef topped with spicy chili sauce. *5247 N Western Ave between Farragut and Berwyn Aves (773-334-1589). Bus: 11, 49 (24hrs) X49, 49B, 92. 24 hrs. Average main course: $15.*

Solga The sweet smell of grilled short ribs emanated so strongly from this unsuspecting spot that we abandoned our previous plans and swerved into the parking lot. From our first bite of the flat seafood pancake rife with scallions and squid, we knew it was a good decision. Skip the bowls of slippery noodles for the *kalbi*, whose soft layers of fat melted on our tongues. *5828 N Lincoln Ave between Francisco Ave and Richmond St (773-728-0802). Bus: 11, 84, 93. Lunch, dinner. Average main course: $14.*

▼ (**Woo Chon** Korean food is all about the barbecue for us, so imagine our surprise when the *kalbi* here took a backseat. We gladly forgo it for the rich *dolsot bibimbap*, a fantastic version of the classic, the seafood pancake or the *doeji kimchi bokkum*, slices of pork mixed with kimchi. Then there's the best surprise of all: tofu soup, which gets props for its deep flavor, and also for being free. *5744 N California Ave between Ardmore and Lincoln Aves (773-728-8001). Bus: 11, 84, 93. Lunch, dinner. Average main course: $12.* ▪

Read 'em & eat

banchan small side dishes of pickled, chile-sauced, or marinated items, like tofu, glass noodles or vegetables, including the spicy cabbage kimchi.

bibimbap rice topped with a variety of vegetables

bulgogi boneless, grilled and marinated beef

kimchi (also kimchee) various pickled vegetables and chiles

mandoo steamed or deep-fried dumpling filled with ground beef, pork, cabbage or kimchi

Kosher

See also: *Middle Eastern*

Back in the loop Metro Klub in the Crowne Plaza Metro brings kosher dining back downtown.

▼ **BYOB (☉ Da'Nali's** Da'Nali's is hidden in a Skokie strip mall, but that's only the first of its many surprises. This yummy family-friendly pizza place is the only brick-oven, kosher vegetarian restaurant around. It is also one of the only restaurants with a kosher pastry chef. Save room for the great cheesecakes. Like many kosher restaurants, post-Shabbat evening hours are busy, with lots of live music. *4032 Oakton St., Skokie (847-677-2782). Bus: 97 Skokie. Closed sundown Fri–sundown Sat. Average main course: $10.*

☉ **(Ken's Diner and Grill** This is the Johnny Rockets of kosher eating. Head to this old school soda fountain for fat, messy, tasty burgers and perfectly-seasoned fries. Also on the menu are bison burgers, pie and homemade cookies. The shakes, of course, are strictly non-dairy. *3353 Dempster St, Skokie (847-679-2850). Bus: Pace 250. Closed sundown Fri–sundown Sat. Average main course: $8.*

Metro Klub To get to Metro Klub you need to walk through the Crowne Plaza Chicago Metro hotel or its Dine restaurant. If you are looking for a Glatt kosher restaurant downtown, it is worth the slight maze, as this is the only current option for dining with the kosher crowd in the 312 area code. The upscale-ish eatery serves up turkey clubs, skirt steak, salmon and other non-dairy lunch dishes. *733 W Madison at Halsted St (312-602-2104). Bus: 157. Mon–Thu 11am–3pm. Average main course: $7.*

✳ **Shallots Bistro** This kosher, clubby French bistro is a hit with the locals in Skokie—the waitstaff and diners schmooze like one big happy family. The melt-in-your mouth steaks rival many pricier steakhouses (the bordelaise, in a red-wine reduction topped with crispy onions, was our

favorite). Other standouts include hearty seasonal stews and the house special Black Hat dessert, a molten Belgian chocolate cake with sorbet that somehow tastes fresh and new in the sea of chocolate lava cakes served all over town. *4741 Main St, Skokie (847-677-3463). El: Yellow to Skokie. Bus: 54A, 97, Pace 254, Pace 250. Lunch (Mon–Thu), dinner (Sun–Thu) (closed Fri, Sat). Average main course: $25.*

▼ **Slice of Life/ Hy Life Bistro** These restaurants are a one-two kosher punch. Slice of Life is the dairy half of this building, with big booths and a substantial menu. The dairy kitchen serves up a mock chicken cacciatore that is large enough for leftovers the next day. The spinach citrus salad is a treat, with a wine vinaigrette instead of the standard bacon dressing that ruins so many spinach salads. Hy Life is the meat restaurant, with a darker vibe and a more substantial menu. Choose from beef riblets, fried chicken and more. *4120 W Dempster St, Skokie (847-674-2021). Bus: Pace 215, Pace 250. Sun 10:30am–9pm; Mon–Thu 11:30am–9pm; Fri 11:30am–2pm; Sat sunset–12:30am. Bistro: Sun–Thu 5pm–9pm (closed Fri–Sat). Average main course: $20.*

▼ **Spertus Café by Wolfgang Puck** See Too new to review.

B ☉ **Taboun Grill** Named for the traditional clay oven used for baking pita, Taboun Grill is one of the city's kosher hot spots. Tables at this Israeli grill fill quickly, as families and couples come from as far as Milwaukee for tasty rib-eye kabobs, lamb chops, schnitzel and shwarma. Unlike some other kosher eateries, the service here is friendly, and sure to make you feel comfortable, regardless of whether or not you're a regular. *6339 N California Ave between Devon and Rosemont Aves (773-381-2606). Bus: 93, 155. Closed sundown Fri–sundown Sat. Average main course: $9.*

▼ ☉ **Tel Aviv Kosher Pizza** This laid-back neighborhood hang-out has far more than pizza (thick and thin crust) on its kosher (including dairy and fish, but no meat) menu. Other options include egg salad sandwiches, Mexican entrees, Chinese food, chili, salads, Middle Eastern treats. Even the dense chocolate brownies are good. *6349 N California Ave between Devon and Rosemont Aves (773-764-3776). Bus: 93, 155. Mon–Thu 11am–11pm; Fri 11am–2pm (winter), 11am–3pm (summer); Sat two hours after sundown–1am. Average main course: $4.* ▨

Read 'em & eat

kishka (KISH-kah) (also called *stuffed derma*) beef intestine stuffed with matzo meal, chicken fat and spices

kreplach (KREHP-lahk) meat-filled dumplings served in soup

plov rice dish with lamb, carrots and onions

Latin American

See also: *Eclectic, South American*

BYOB ⊕ Café las Delicias Why there isn't a *pupuseria* on every corner is a mystery to us—the El Salvadorean cornmeal pancakes filled with savory ingredients such as beans, pork and cheese can hold their own against hot dogs any day. But until the humble *pupusa* gets more attention, we'll head here for our fix. The zucchini and cheese variety is why we come, but we also snag a luscious sweet-corn-and-cream tamale; an order of hot, crispy and hearty pork-stuffed *pastelitos*; and a bowl of honey-soaked *nances* (a small, somewhat grapelike tropical fruit). *3300 W Montrose Ave at Spaulding Ave (773-293-0656). El: Brown to Western. Bus: 78 Montrose, 82 Kimball. Lunch, dinner. Average main course: $7.*

(⊛ Carnivale When a restaurant this size is this busy (it seats 400, but an hour wait is typical), it must be making somebody happy. Jerry Kleiner's colorful—if slightly dated—design *can* make a person smile, and the mojitos and margaritas don't hurt, either. On the pan-Latin menu you'll find all sorts of variations on traditional fare, like oxtail pupusas and mini whitefish tacos. Some of them, like the juicy *ropa vieja*, raise this restaurant's bar, but it's the crowd here that entertains the most. *702 W Fulton St at Union Ave (312-850-5005). Bus: 8 Halsted, 65 Grand. Lunch (Mon–Fri), dinner. Average main course: $20.*

BYOB Col-ubas Steak House Pedro Navarrete ran his own restaurant in his homeland of Colombia, but when he asked his family to pitch in and help him start a restaurant stateside, his half-Cuban daughter wanted to be fully represented on the menu. The result is a list of dishes just like her—both Cuban and Colombian. Traditional mixed grills with skirt steak with fried egg, corn bread and chimichurri appear alongside *ropa vieja* (shredded beef), *lechon asado* (roasted pork) and braised oxtail. *5665 N Clark St between Hollywood and Edgewater Aves (773-506-1579). El: Red to Bryn Mawr. Bus: 22 (24hrs), 36, 50, 84. Breakfast, lunch, dinner (Wed–Mon). Average main course: $13.*

▼ (⊛ B Coobah Given the neighborhood and decor this pan-Latin joint could be written off as akin to Chi-Chi's. But it takes only a promising pair of subtle *lumpia*—Filipino egg rolls stuffed with duck, peppers, red cabbage and onions—to realize that this spot deserves a closer look. Tilapia arrives dredged in blue corn flour and served on a rice paper tostada; Chicken Negra Modelo is glazed in its namesake beer and flanked by spinach and cheese chilaquiles; and the Sandwich Coobah is as solid a Cuban sandwich as any other—despite the misspelling. *3423 N Southport Ave between Roscoe St and Newport Ave (773-528-2220). El: Brown to Southport. Bus: 9, 22 (24hrs), 152. Brunch (Sat, Sun), lunch (Mon–Fri), dinner. Average main course: $18.*

★ DeLaCosta *2007 Eat Out Award, Critics' Pick: Best mash-up (muddled cocktails)* Take in the Suhail-designed room (think Tim Burton–esque, Rio-style Carnivale) while starting with one of the killer muddled cocktails like vodka-drenched watermelon smashed with fresh lime. Ceviches may be signature, but we had better luck with hot apps like the watercress-topped duck confit flatbread. For the main event, don't miss the suckling pig with glistening, crackly skin, perfectly sweet plantains and black-bean puree. *River East Arts Center, 465 E Illinois St between Peshtigo Ct and Lake Shore Dr (312-464-1700). Bus: 2, 29, 65, 66 (24hrs), 124. Lunch (Mon–Fri), dinner. Average main course: $28.*

★ BYOB El Llano This small, cheery room is packed with Colombian tchotchkes (as well as an stuffed armadillo hanging on the wall) which gives the place a festive vibe. What are they celebrating? Chicken, and the fact that they turn this blank-slate-of-foods into a dinner that's plump, juicy, golden, perfectly charred and endlessly flavorful. Tender brisket immersed in mild tomato sauce, crisp and starchy fried yuca, and a strip steak with fresh and lively chimichurri grace this menu. But they're just back-up. For once, the lowly chicken is the star of the show. *3941 N Lincoln Ave between Larchmont Ave and Irving Park Rd (773-868-1708). El: Brown to Irving Park. Bus: 11, 50, 80, 152. Lunch, dinner. Average main course: $11.*

⊕ El Salvador Restaurante This cozy Brighton Park Salvadorean restaurant is our favorite for *empanadas de leche* (sugary fried plantain pockets stuffed with thick condensed milk), *pupusa chichurrones* (pork-filled cornmeal pancakes) and chunks of deep fried yuca. The *panes con pavo* is also an interesting find: housemade bread smothered with gravy-laden turkey. The back of the menu is saved for Mexican offerings (try the ground-beef tacos), just in case you can't find Mexican anywhere else in the city. *4125 S Archer Ave at Francisco Ave (773-579-0405). El: Orange to 35th/Archer. Bus: 35, 62 (24hrs). Lunch, dinner. Average main course: $10.*

⊕ El Tinajón It's not the only Guatemalan spot in town, but with two decades under its belt, it might just be the oldest. Start off with the bright pink tamarind-and-rum cocktail, and you'll blend right into the cozy room's color scheme. The menu is heavy on seafood, with standouts that include grilled tilapia, grilled shrimp and seafood soup. The excellent *chuchitos* (Guatemalan tamales) are something like a loose lettuce wrap, and the burritos aren't your standard Mexican variation but instead emphasize fresh vegetables and black beans. *2054 W Roscoe St at Hoyne Ave (773-525-8455). El: Brown to Paulina. Bus: 50, 77 (24hrs), 152. Lunch, dinner. Average main course: $10.*

BYOB Gloria's Café Colombian chef-owner Gloria Santiago and her Puerto Rican husband, Jaime, have put their heart into this casual eatery. The colorful space is modest, but the food is complex and belly-busting. The steaming bowl of herb-flecked *sancocho* (hen stew), makes for a great lunch, packed with yuca, plantains and corn. For a dinner for two, go with the brown-skinned rotisserie chicken and the *bandeja paisa* (country plate), an assortment of tender skirt steak, fantastic housemade pork sausage links, a dense corn cake, crispy chicharron, avocado and beans. *3300 W Fullerton Ave at Spaulding Ave (773-342-1050). El: Blue to Logan Square. Bus: 56, 74, 82. Lunch, dinner. Average main course: $11.*

⊕ Irazu Never tried Central American food? Here's your safe entry. It's simple, authentic, cheap, supercasual and friendly. Start with the hearts of palm salad—huge, tangy stalks on a bed of shredded cabbage that's been tossed in a

Lovely 'rita Seductive cocktails at Nacional 27 include the signature El Corazón margarita.

lime vinaigrette, along with radishes, cilantro, cucumber, pickled beets and ripe avocado. Make it a meal by adding a side of perfect white rice, soupy black beans and sweet plantains. Bring a bottle of Malbec to match, and end the meal with one of the shakes (oatmeal and tamarind are our favorites). *1865 N Milwaukee Ave between Oakley and Western Aves (773-252-5687). El: Blue to Western. Bus: 49 (24hrs), 56, 73. Lunch, dinner. Average main course: $8.*

★ ☺ **Isabella Bakery** Do whatever it takes to snag one of the three tables in this tiny Guatemalan café—you don't have enough hands to take away everything you'll want to try. Don't miss the *chile relleno* sandwich, a delicious spread of peppers and onions on soft, housemade bread. Tamales are served in the banana leaves they're steamed in and hold a tender chunk of bone-in pork. Desserts are a must—take sips of the especially smooth cappuccino in between bites of strawberry empanada and tall, moist chocolate layer cake. *1659 W Foster Ave at Paulina St (773-275-5237). El: Red to Argyle. Bus: 22 (24hrs), 50, 92. Average main course: $3.*

☺ **La Brasa Roja** If you can walk by this place and not be drawn in by the sight of plump, juicy rotisserie chickens rotating over smoldering coals just on the other side of the window, you're either a vegetarian or devoid of tastebuds. Assuming you're neither, get into this Colombian eatery, order the droolworthy chicken and don't stop there. Try the cheesy corncakes, meat-filled turnovers, tangy marinated skirt steaks topped with bright green chimichurri (think Latin American pesto), sweet plantains and fresh fruit drinks. *3125 W Montrose Ave at Troy St (773-866-2252). El: Brown to Francisco. Bus: 78 Montrose, 82 Kimball. Breakfast, lunch, dinner. Average main course: $10.*

▽ ✳ **La Fonda Latino Grill** Perhaps not worthy of the fawning praise lauded during an episode of local PBS show *Check, Please!*, La Fonda is nevertheless a solid Latin American option. Start with the small, but tasty, beef and spinach-mushroom empanadas with spicy avocado sauce. Red snapper, shrimp, squid, scallops and clams swim in the *cazuela de mariscos'* creamy tomato sauce, and the flank steak (*sobrebarriga a la criolla*) is so tender, chewing is almost a formality. Savor it, though, just as you should the delicious margaritas—shaken and poured into martini glasses tableside. *5350 N Broadway between Berwyn and Balmoral Aves (773-271-3935). El: Red to Berwyn. Bus: 36, 92, 147. Lunch and dinner (closed Mon). Average main course: $15.*

▽ **La Humita** In the bustling Avondale neighborhood, earth-toned walls, hardwood floors, colorful artwork, gracious service and occasional live music qualify as an upscale dining experience. At this Ecuadorian/pan-Latin spot, appetizers (such as the signature piping-hot, tamalelike *humita*) and desserts (like spongey, sweet corn cake wrapped in a banana leaf) steal the show. Seafood dishes are a bit overpriced for what you get (the $5.95 tilapia lunch special is a better bet), but the juicy churrasco steak is tasty and filling with sides of avocado, fries and eggs. *3466 N Pulaski Ave between Cornelia and Newport Ave (773-794-9672). El: Blue to Irving Park. Bus: 53 (24hrs), 60 (24hrs), 80. Lunch, dinner (Tue–Sun), (closed Mon). Average main course: $11.*

❨ ✳ **La Pena** Weekends are popular at this Ecuadorian spot—that's when Ecuadorian bands take to the stage in the dining room, and apparently some people like their dinner with a side of pan flute. Us? We'll take the quieter weeknights, when we can really focus on the *pinchos*, three skewered and perfectly grilled shrimp drizzled with a sprightly chimichurri, and the *llapingacho*, your choice of sausage, steak or chicken (go for the thick, grilled steak) flanked by potato pancakes

topped with a rich, savory peanut sauce. *4212 N Milwaukee Ave between Berteau Ave and Hutchinson St (773-545-7022). El: Blue to Montrose. Bus: 54, 56, 78. Lunch (Sun), dinner (closed Mon). Average main course: $15.*

La Sierra Deciding between the Mexican and Ecuadorian specialties at this Ravenswood is almost impossible, so you'll probably end up choosing both. Make sure to try the *llapingachos*, two savory potato pancakes paired with a peanut sauce and a fried egg (mix the runny yolk with the sauce for maximum creaminess); oversize spicy pork sopes; and tender goat stew, cooked with beer and laced with a trace of cumin. *1637 W Montrose Ave between Ashland Ave and Paulina St (773-549-5538). Bus: 22 (24hrs), 50, 78, 145. Breakfast, lunch, dinner. Average main course: $10.*

★ BYOB ✳ **Las Tablas** By most standards the *arepa chorriada* (pseudo-polenta smothered in melted cheese and onion-and-tomato *criolla* sauce) at this Colombian steak house is dense, greasy and unattractive. But the combination is such a simple pleasure that before you know it, you've scraped the plate clean. That's the theme here: Before you can exclaim how enormous the *bandeja paisa* combination is, you've already sliced into the juicy New York strip, torn off a crisp piece of fried pork and broken the fried egg and mixed the yolk with the beans. *2965 N Lincoln Ave between Wellington Ave and George St (773-871-2414). El: Brown, Purple (rush hrs) to Diversey. Bus: 9 (24hrs), 11, 76, 77. Lunch, dinner. Average main course: $16.*

▽ ✳ **Mambo Grill** Mambo Grill's dark room, Latin sounds and around-the-world rum flights add up to a sexy singles scene. Best bets include the flaky mushroom-and-roasted-corn empanadas, *tres queso* chile rellenos, crisp Latin cobb salad in a refreshing *mojo de mango* rum vinaigrette, coconut-curried tilapia and a tequila-marinated skirt steak that's tempting enough to drag us back on a weekday for

Hot plate Creative takes on Latin comfort food keep the crowds coming back to Mas.

Latin American

another helping. In the light of day, and when we're not-so-under-the-influence, lunch is a bit lackluster. *412 N Clark St between Hubbard and Kinzie Sts (312-467-9797). El: Brown, Purple (rush hrs) to Merchandise Mart. Bus: 22 Clark (24hrs), 65, 156. Lunch (Mon–Fri), dinner (closed Sun). Average main course: $17.*

★ ▼ ✱ **Mas** Chef John Manion's nuevo Latino spot offers an ever-changing menu of addictive food like a flaky empanada oozing with goat cheese, mushrooms and walnuts, and tilapia and shrimp ceviche in a tequila-spiked citrus-coconut–milk blend. Shrimp-crusted halibut is sinfully rich, with a buttery, vanilla-laced saffron-lobster sauce, and vegetarians will love the roasted acorn squash filled with wild mushrooms and *boniato* (tropical sweet potato). A tropical cocktail list is the perfect excuse to linger longer to soak up the hot preclubbing weekend crowd. *1670 W Division St at Paulina St (773-276-8700). El: Blue to Division. Bus: 9 (24hrs), X9, 72. Dinner. Average main course: $22.*

★ ▼ **BYOB May Street Café** It takes a lot to brighten a corner as industrial as this, but we challenge anybody to visit this pan-Latin mecca and not feel a little bit sunny. Chef-owner Mario Santiago drops dried cranberries into a perfectly balanced butternut-squash soup, pairs juicy mangos and plump shrimp in a quesadilla and gives chicken fajitas a kick with gobs of cinnamon and chipotle. Three little coins of mango flan make for an insanely decadent ending—but it's only truly insane if you forgo it. *1146 W Cermak Rd between May St and Racine Ave (312-421-4442). Bus: 8 Halsted, 21 Cermak. Dinner (Tue–Sun). Average main course: $15.*

⊙ **Mekato's Colombian Bakery** See Bakeries & Cafés for review.

❨ **Mitad del Mundo** The owner of this Ecuadorian-Cuban spot is a gregarious sort who wants everybody to have

a good time; and on weekends, when the DJ starts mixing beats and the place fills up with the Central and South American clientele from around the area, the lovely room can get pretty rowdy. Stick around for well-prepared seafood dishes, including an elaborate paella and a giant mixed seafood plate that's perfect to share with friends (or a small army). *2922 W Irving Park Rd at Richmond St (773-866-9454). Bus: 80, X80, 82. Dinner. Average main course: $15.*

★ ✱ **Nacional 27** *2007 Eat Out Award, Readers' Choice: Best cocktail menu* DJs spinning and customers dancing in the dining room may not be for everyone, but if you're into the nightclub scene, the food is an added bonus. Chef Randy Zweiban takes his inspiration from 27 Latin American countries and turns out luscious eats. Seasonal ceviches might include ahi tuna with watermelon in a spicy rice wine viniagrette, while main courses include creative takes on Latin comfort food like spice-crusted duck breast with morel mushroom flan. Seductive, expertly made cocktails like the El Corazon, a passion fruit and pomegranate margarita, mean you'll find plenty of people here happily drinking their dinners. *325 W Huron St between Franklin and Orleans Sts (312-664-2727). El: Brown, Purple (rush hrs) to Chicago. Bus: 66 Chicago (24hrs). Dinner (closed Sun). Average main course: $19.*

❨ **Pueblito Viejo** Plan for a late weekend dinner for the full experience at this Colombian steakhouse, crammed with an assaulting array of artificial flora and fauna, and waiters dressed à la Juan Valdez. Once the music starts playing, crowds young and old hit the dance floor, but stay put and take in the action while feasting on *arepas*, fried white-corn pancakes filled with cheese and sausage. Also try one of the Colombian combo plates, most of which include fried flank steak, pork or pork rind, plus melt-in-your-mouth plantains and cassava. *5429 N Lincoln Ave at Rascher Ave (773-784-9135). Bus: 11, 49 (24hrs), X49, 49B, 92, 93. Dinner (closed Mon). Average main course: $15.*

❨ **Rumba** Latin fusion is the name of the game at this upscale River North restaurant where Cuban, Puerto Rican and Peruvian influences mingle on the dance floor as well as the kitchen. The glammed-up, mojito-sipping clientele is usually loud and lively. If you're looking for a little more privacy, the six-seat, reservation-only chef's room gives front-row seats to chef Benjamin Soto's culinary show. Latin bands and DJs perform on weekends and complementary salsa lessons are held Thursday through Sunday. *351 W Hubbard St at Orleans St (312-222-1226). El: Brown, Purple (rush hrs) to Merchandise Mart. Bus: 125 Water Tower Express. Dinner (closed Sun–Mon). Average main course: $28.* ■

Read 'em & eat

chuletas pork chops

maduros sweet plantains, similar to banana but thicker and starchier

mofongo mashed green plantains stuffed with pork or shrimp

pupusa stuffed cornmeal tortilla

tostones green (savory) plantains

Mexican

See also: *Latin American, South American*

Mexx it up Mexx Kitchen at the Whiskey combines smooth drinks with modern Mexican eats.

★ ▽ ✳ **B Adobo Grill** They call them *las señoras cocineras*—"the cooking ladies"—and every morning they're the first people here. They use their own recipes to make the rich *mole poblano* for the wood-roasted chicken and the handmade tortillas that wrap up light, crispy skate wing. An ex-server named Max supplied many of the colorful paintings on the wall, and the rotating cast of bartenders makes great margaritas (go for the "smoky floater" of mezcal). And while the cooking ladies could make a killer guacamole, they leave that gimmicky tradition to the servers. *2005 W Division St at Damen Ave (773-252-9990). El: Blue to Division. Bus: 50 Damen, 70 Division. Brunch (Sun), dinner. Average main course: $17.*

☉ **Amelia's Bar and Grill** Head down to this Back of the Yards storefront for generous platters of comforting Mexican-American food. Get the most bang for your buck with a combo plate like enchiladas sauced three ways—with *guajillo*, *tomatillo* and *mole*. (Each is equally flavorful, but the guajillo is the tastiest.) The cheerful servers positively beam when presenting dessert, and the big slabs of tres leches cake prove they have something to smile about. Stop in for the weekday lunch specials—smaller, but still ample, portions from the best of the menu. *4559 S Halsted St between 45th and 46th Sts (773-538-8200). El: Red to 47th. Bus: 8, 44, 47. Breakfast, lunch, dinner. Average main course: $10.*

BYOB ✳ **Caliente** *Muy caliente* is more like it— *enchiladas del mar*, packed with shrimp, scallops and crab, sounded innocent enough, but the *guajillo* pepper sauce crept up on us, and pretty soon we were sweating bullets. *Puerco en chile verde con nopales*, which paired luscious pork with cactus, proved a much more mild choice. The Fullerton Avenue location has a larger menu with mini Cuban sandwiches and "Argentine" burgers. *3910 N Sheridan Ave between Dakin St and Sheridan Rd (773-525-0129). El: Red to Sheridan. Bus: 36, 80, 151 (24hrs). Dinner (closed Sun, Mon). Average main course: $15.* • *Additional location at 2556 W Fullerton Ave (773-772-4355).*

B Caoba Mexican Bar & Grill In the people-watching mecca where Wicker Park and Bucktown collide, offering margarita pitchers in a breezy, open-front restaurant nearly guarantees a packed house, regardless of what's on the plate. That's why we were surprised by these better-than-average Mexican eats. 'Ritas are ripe, chips are fresh, salsa is complex and smoky, and sizzling platters of seafood are downright scarfworthy, brimming with perfectly seared, fat scallops; spice-rubbed *langoustines*; and tender calamari tubes. Just skip the pedestrian stuff—especially the rock-hard *sope* and enchilada starters—and stick with the *parrilladas*, or mixed grills. *1619 N Damen Ave between North Ave and Concord Pl (773-342-2622). El: Blue to Damen. Bus: 50, 56, 72. Brunch (Sat, Sun), dinner. Average main course: $12.*

Cuernavaca What you'll find at this delightful hacienda-size Mexican institution are *chiles rellenos con queso*, two snappy ancho chiles stuffed with *queso anejo*, smothered in butter, cheese and *mole* and plated with simmered beans and golden rice. Others opt for the *sopes*—griddled *masa* patties topped with chorizo, beans and *picadillo*—and a tequila-bombed margaritas. *1160 W 18th St at Racine Ave (312-829-1147). El: Blue, Pink to 18th St. Bus: 18, 60 (24 hrs), 168. Breakfast, lunch, dinner. Average main course: $11.*

▼ ✳ **de cero** This taqueria fancies itself as edgy and upscale. We don't know if battered fish tacos fit the bill, but they make for a delicious guilty pleasure. More refined tacos include the ahi tuna, coupled with a mango salsa and bursting with bright, fresh flavors, and the chorizo, whose kick is tempered by cool *crema*. Fresh corn tamales shine with straight-off-the-cob flavor that goes perfectly with one of the tart hibiscus margaritas. The fresh berries in lime honey (the least fussy dessert on the list) is worth every penny. *814 W Randolph St between Green and Halsted Sts (312-455-8114). El: Green to Clinton. Bus: 8 Halsted, 20 Madison (24hrs). Lunch (Mon–Fri), dinner (closed Sun). Average main course: $13.*

★ **Delicioso y Sabroso Restaurant** Chef Geno Bahena takes on two concepts in one at his restaurant just off the Chicago Skyway. Delicioso is an upscale Mexican concept featuring a delicious scallop ceviche and seven different kinds of *mole* (go on a Wednesday for the *mole manchamanteles* special). But we prefer Sabroso—it's more casual, the food (such as the chicken in *mole roja* and the gooey *chile relleno* tacos) is the same Bahena quality and the prices give Taco Bell a run for its money. *10468 S Indianapolis Blvd between 104th and 105th Sts (773-374-6089). Bus: 30 South Chicago. Dinner. Average main course: $15.*

▼ ◖ ✳ ◉ **El Cid** This cozy Mexican mainstay has everything you could want from a neighborhood joint: an amazing back patio complete with soft-strumming guitarists; potent and fruity margaritas; sweet-as-pie servers; and reliably tasty dishes for a nice price. We've sampled our way through the menu to narrow down some favorites: garlicky tilapia tacos; inky black beans with perfect white rice; skirt steak; plantains with crispy edges; giant red snapper with crispy coating, smothered in tart tomato-and-olive Veracruz sauce; potato tacos that keep vegetarians happy. *2645 N Kedzie Ave between Milwaukee and Wrightwood Aves (773-395-0505). El: Blue to Logan Square. Bus: 56 Milwaukee, 76 Diversey. Breakfast, lunch, dinner. Average main course: $9.*

◉ **El Jardin** While there are Mexican restaurants with better menus and better margaritas, it's hard to compete with El Jardin's outdoor area in the warmer months. There's a good deal of sunshine seating–the front patio seats 40 and the spacious garden in the back seats 100–but the wait for a table can sometimes be rather lengthy, especially on game days at Wrigley Field (located just three blocks north). *3335 N Clark St at Buckingham St (773-528-6775). El: Brown, Purple (rush hrs), Red to Belmont. Bus: 8, 22 (24hrs), 77 (24hrs). Lunch, dinner. Average main course: $10.*

◉ **El Norte** You can get the same atmosphere—or lack thereof—at any of the *taquerias* that pepper this intersection of Ridge and Broadway. But you can't get this gem's fantastic housemade *horchata* redolent of cinnamon and nutmeg. You probably couldn't find a *mole* as complex, with its sweet, long finish. A *carnitas* taco anywhere else probably won't be as overstuffed or juicy. And you'd be hard-pressed to get such food any time you crave it: On the weekends, this place is open 24 hours. *5600 N Ridge Ave at the intersection of Bryn Mawr Ave, Broadway and Ridge Ave (773-728-0182). El: Red to Bryn Mawr. Bus: 36, 84, 136, 147, 151 (24 hrs). Breakfast, lunch, dinner. Average main course: $7.*

▼ ✳ **El Nuevo Mexicano** How does a seemingly typical Mexican restaurant survive Lakeview's changing landscape

for 25 years? By being consistent with the simple stuff and throwing in a few specials every now and then to keep things interesting. The regular appetizer menu is Anglo-ized and boring, so ditch that and go for the flaky beef empanadas from the specials list. Stick to that list for the delicious pomegranate margarita (made with real lime, not a mix) and the chicken enchiladas in smoky red *mole*. If there's room, finish with the perfectly rich flan. *2914 N Clark St between Wellington and Oakdale Aves (773-528-2131). El: Brown, Purple (rush hrs) to Diversey. Bus: 8, 22 (24hrs), 36, 76. Lunch, dinner. Average main course: $12.*

◉ **El Potosi** This tiny taco shanty gives a splash of psychedelic color to an otherwise sober and gray stretch of Elston Avenue. Heroes of the Mexican Revolution peer at you from photos as you chow on made-to-order guacamole, unique *barbacoa* beef tacos and breakfast (egg and chorizo) burritos. On the weekends, folks flock here for restorative bowls of *menudo* and *pozole*. *3710 N Elston Ave between Kimball and Christina Aves (773-463-2517). Bus: 82 Kimball-Homan, 152 Addison. Breakfast, lunch, dinner. Average main course: $5.*

◉ **El Presidente** The rather average offerings at this late night Mexican restaurant are made more attractive by both their value and their round-the-clock availability. From 11pm until 5am, six entrees ranging from burritos to burgers to seafood are offered for the paltry price of $6.75 apiece. And from 5–11am, you can plop down into a colorful booth and partake of huevo-heavy breakfast items and Mexican sausage. *2558 N Ashland Ave at Wrightwood Ave (773-525-7938). Bus: 9 Ashland, 74 Fullerton. Open 24 hrs. Average main course: $7.*

◉ **El Salvador Restaurante** See Latin American for review.

◉ **El Tapatio** We'd hit this small spot just for its frothy, boozy margaritas (particularly the tamarind). The key to avoiding hangovers is filling up on the fantastic food, but skip the chips and salsa and instead start with the *coctel de camaron*—plump shrimp, avocado and sweet tomato sauce on Saltines. We love the plantain-stuffed enchiladas slathered in chocolaty *mole*, and carnivores will swoon over the *revoltijo ajijic*, a plank of plantains topped with diced steak, onion, peppers, mushrooms and Chihuahua cheese. The flan or the dulce de leche–stuffed crêpes are fine finishes. *3400 N Ashland Ave at Roscoe St (773-327-5475). El: Brown to Paulina. Bus: 9, 11, 77 (24hrs), 152. Lunch (Mon–Fri), dinner. Average main course: $9.50.*

▼ BYOB **Fajita Grill** This souped-up Mexican spot is a welcome addition to a boring stretch of Foster Avenue, with salsa and guacamole made tableside and a waitstaff that seems eager to please. The menu is a combination of traditional items like tamales, plus organic salads and sophisticated seafood dishes. Standouts include filet mignon topped with chipotle sauce and melted cheese and sautéed salmon with shrimp, mussels and scallops, brightened up with salsa *verde*. The namesake fajitas are nothing extraordinary. *1706 W Foster Ave at Paulina St (773-784-7455). Bus: 9, 22 (24hrs), 92. Lunch, dinner. Average main course: $16.*

◉ **Fernando's** Look, if you order one of the more sophisticated dishes—the bland white fish, perhaps?—you're missing the point. This place is all about the stuff you really want: juicy chicken tacos, cheesy nachos, deep-fried stuffed peppers. Don't want to eat for a few days? Get the gigantic fajita quesadilla, an oversize tortilla bulging with

Bowled over The *molcajete* at Zapatista makes for a hearty meal.

grilled slices of steak or chicken, bell peppers and onions that'll fuel you for weeks. The house margaritas are so big and potent that you won't remember a thing. *3450 N Lincoln Ave at Newport Ave (773-477-6930). El: Brown to Paulina. Bus: 9, 11, 152. Dinner. Average main course: $9.*

★ ★ **B Fonda del Mar** Raul Arreola's menu is a nod to traditional Mexican fish houses known as *marisquerías*, and the man *can* work aquatic magic. Firm white fish chunks get tossed with jalapeño, cilantro and lime juice for lively ceviche, whole red snapper mojo de ajo, and the fish tacos are flanked by a bowl of smoky squid and octopus-laden *guajillo* broth. But Arreola's greatest achievement—and the dish that is the restaurant's signature—is from the land: the *borrego en mole negro*, four petite lamb chops paired with a *mole. 3749 W Fullerton Ave between Ridgeway and Hamlin Aves (773-489-3748). El: Blue to Logan Square. Bus: 53 Pulaski, 74 Fullerton, 82. Milwaukee North to Healy. Brunch (Sun), lunch (Sat), dinner. Average main course: $12.*

★ ☺ **Frontera Fresco** Macy's brought celeb chef Rick Bayless into the fold with this foodcourt counter offering tortas, huaraches, quesadillas, tamales, salad and soup, but with fillings that counter most fast-food notions. Smoked pork loin and applewood bacon top the torta Cubana, Amy's All-Natural Chicken Chorizo shows up in a quesadilla, and steak joins garlicky mushrooms and chipotle sauce for an earthy huarache. And at $7 for a creative Loop lunch, don't be surprised if the lines rival Frontera's weekend queues. *111 N State St, seventh floor at Washington St (312-781-1000). El: Blue, Red to Washington; Brown, Green, Orange, Purple (rush hrs) to Randolph. Bus: 3, 4, X4, 14, 20, 26, 60 (24hrs), 127, 145, 147, 148, 151 (24hrs). Lunch (Mon–Sat). Average main course: $7.*

★ ▽ ✳ **B Frontera Grill** Most chefs behind culinary empires branch to other cities, leaving the original back home to suffer. Rick Bayless kept close to the kitchen and chose to expand in other ways (packaged food line, cookbooks, TV shows). Lucky us. For two decades, this has been the spot for

Read 'em & eat

caldo largo de alvarado chili-spiced fish soup

carnitas (kahr-NEE-tahs) chunks of slow-roasted pork (sometimes boiled in its own fat), served with chopped onions, cilantro, salsa, limes and tortillas

cecina (seh-CHEE-nah) thin slices of salted and smoked or air-dried beef, similar to Italian *bresaola*

chilaquiles(chee-lah-KEE-les) tortilla chips baked in a casserole with shredded chicken, sour cream, *queso fresco* and tomatillo sauce

mole (MOH-lay) sauce made with dried chili peppers, spices, nuts

pozole (poh-SOH-lay) soup made with large dried, hulled kernels of corn (called hominy) and shredded pork, garnished with cabbage, radishes, avocado, lime, oregano and cilantro

salpicón de res chilled beef salad

intensely flavorful, impeccably fresh Mexican food. We like the upscale sister Topolobampo, but Frontera offers a vibrant slice of Mexico City, a place to chow down on ceviches, earthy *mole*, wood-grilled steak tucked into housemade tortillas, and of course, insanely good margaritas. *445 N Clark St between Hubbard and Illinois Sts (312-661-1434). El: Brown, Purple (rush hrs) to Merchandise Mart; Red to Grand. Bus: 22 (24hrs), 29, 36, 65. Brunch (Sat), lunch (Tue–Fri), dinner (Tue–Sat). Average main course: $15.*

☺ **La Cantina Grill** Chef Juan Carlos Lopez ran a Mexico City restaurant El Famoso ("The Famous") 13 years ago, and brought his straightforward menu here. That means you can expect the usual suspects, like ceviche, tacos, fajitas, chicken *mole* and grilled skirt steak, along with summery dishes like the "El Jardinero" salad topped with fresh tomatoes, avocado and tortilla strips and rotisserie chicken rubbed with 14 spices. That menu, plus a dozen tequilas, Mexican beers, fruity sangrias and margaritas, might just make him *famoso* in Chicago. *1911 S Michigan Ave between 18th and Cullerton Sts (312-842-1911). El: Red to Cermak-Chinatown. Bus: 3, X3, X4, 18, 21. Lunch, dinner. Average main course: $10.*

★ **La Casa de Samuel** If you haven't explored Little Village, this would be a good starting point. The owner's regional heritage shows up in the food, and in this case, the inspiration is the state of Guerrero. This means you can expect a few exotic options, including bull's testicles, rattlesnake, wild boar and alligator. We go with house specialties like fried smelts; thin, cured venison *cecina*; and tender baked goat served with chunky guac, warm housemade tortillas and a smoky *pasilla* chili sauce. *2834 W Cermak St between California Ave and Marshall Blvd (773-376-7474). El: Blue (54th/Cermak branch during rush hrs), Pink to California. Bus: 21 Cermak, 94 South California. Breakfast, lunch, dinner. Average main course: $12.*

BYOB ☺ **La Cazuela** It's tough to choose among the many Mexican spots hawking specialties via window signs around these parts, but if you're in the mood for an outdoor setting to sip 'ritas (bring your own tequila) and enjoy decent eats, head here. Seafood is the house focus, and most of it is pretty tasty, particularly the sauteed garlic shrimp (crunchy skin and all) with lard-rich beans and tomatoey rice. Meat-eaters should try the tangy-spicy pastor pork tacos. *6922 N Clark St between Farwell and Morse Aves (773-338-5425). El: Red to Loyola. Bus: 22 (24hrs), 151 (24hrs), 155. Metra: Union Pacific North Line to Rogers Park. Lunch, dinner. Average main course: $10.*

☺ **La Encantada** Mexican cuisine in Humboldt Park is as commonplace as fireworks on Puerto Rican Independence Day. But beyond *taquerías* and take-out burrito joints, options are fairly limited, which is why this spot is so welcome. The menu is full of refreshingly different, modern Mexican dishes like plantain-filled enchiladas with *mole* sauce; side salads topped with guava dressing; and *chile en nogada*—a poblano pepper filled with ground beef, fruit and nuts. Not to mention, the decor is attractive and the waitstaff is eager to please. *3437 W North Ave at St Louis Ave (773-489-5026). Bus: 56 North, 82 Kimball. Lunch, dinner. Average main course: $10.*

✳ ☺ **La Finca** A hodgepodge menu of from-scratch regional dishes from central Mexico has customers feasting on food such as orange roughy bathed in white wine, tomatoes and onions, and spicy chicken *mole*. Tucked behind the building is a spacious patio that's utterly magical on a summer night, and most evenings you'll find a handful of diners relaxing under the stars enjoying one of the

Toast of the town La Finca's ginormous Cazuela cocktail contains five shots of tequila.

Fiesta time The El Jardinero salad at La Cantina Grill makes a festive start to a meal.

restaurant's specialties: a humongous Cazuela, a potent elixir composed of fresh-squeezed juices and five shots of tequila. *3361 N Elston Ave between Sacramento Ave and Roscoe St (773-487-4006). Bus: 52 Kedzie/California, 77 Belmont (24 hrs). Lunch, dinner (closed Sun). Average main course: $10.*

❋ ⊙ **La Justicia Restaurante** We recommend this colorful Little Village spot, even though it has a haunted jukebox. A few minutes after we dug into the juicy chicken with peppery *mole*, the juke suddenly lit up and started belting Spanish-language soft rock. Thirty seconds later it stopped, so we continued eating the platter of small, crispy grilled onions and a savory chorizo taco. After about 15 minutes, we thought we were in the clear, but then the jukebox started again. This time, however, we hardly noticed—we were too immersed in the nicely charred *carne asada* to care. *3901 W 26th St at Springfield Ave (773-522-0041). Bus: 53 Pulaski (24hrs), 60 Blue Island/26th St (24hrs). Breakfast (Sat, Sun), lunch, dinner. Average main course: $8.*

❋ ⊙ **La Michoacana** This melt-in-your-mouth pork haven is the kind you stumble upon down a seedy back alley in Mexico. Lucky for you, this 19-year-old stalwart is right in Pilsen. Whole pigs are cooked for hours in giant tubs filled with lard, chopped to smithereens and sold by the pound as delicious *carnitas*. Most of the locals in the chaotic line streaming out the door take their *carnitas* to go, but we like them with a mound of corn tortillas, fresh cilantro and lime wedges to scarf on the spot. *2049 W Cermak Rd between Damen and Hoyne Aves (773-254-2970). El: Blue (rush hrs), Pink to Damen (54th/Cermak). Bus: 21 Cermak, 50 Damen. Breakfast, lunch, dinner (Mon–Fri). Average main course: $6.*

❋ **La Perla Tapatia** When there's a tiny Mexican storefront on nearly every corner in the city, how do you figure out which deserve your cash? Go to places like this, where the scent permeates and the dollar stretches for miles. This two-person crew doles out crispy, meat-stuffed tortas; king-size *Suiza* (Swiss cheese) burritos packed with grilled steak, crumbly ground beef or pulled chicken; and big bowls of fresh seafood *caldos* (soup). The chile rellenos tacos and the Mexican gyros torta are packed with flavor but lack spice, remedied with one of the housemade salsas. *3251 W North Ave between Sawyer and Spaulding Aves (773-486-3120). Bus: 52, 72, 82. Lunch, dinner. Average main course: $8.*

⊙ **La Sierra** See Latin American for review.

▽ ❋ **Lalo's** Want to eschew authenticity? No problem. Head to this local chain to wash down chunky guac in a bowl the size of your head, add shrimp to your bulging fajita and inhale that pork taco with an electric-blue margarita. *733 W Maxwell St between Union Ave and Halsted St (312-455-9380). El: Blue to UIC-Halsted. Bus: 8, 12, 168. Lunch (Mon–Fri), dinner. Average main course: $14.* ● *Additional locations include 1960 N Clybourn Ave (773-880-5256).*

★ ⊙ **Las Islas Marias** Las Islas Marias is turning into a Mexican seafood empire. The chef-owners are from Nayarit, Mexico, and just like their two spots on south Pulaski, this place specializes in *langoustines* and ceviche. Plates heaped with the lobsterlike crustaceans head to almost every table (the three restaurants bring in around 1,200 pounds from the Indian Ocean each week). Coated in a secret garlicky, salty, fiery "seven-spice" mixture, they're known to inspire die-hard fans. *6635 N Clark St between Wallen and North Shore Aves (773-973-4752). El: Red to Loyola. Bus: 22 (24hrs), 36, 151 (24hrs), 155. Lunch, dinner. Average main course: $10.* ● *Additional locations include 4770 W Grand Ave (773-637-8233) and 5401 S Pulaski Rd (773-767-0908).*

Mexican

Side dish

Cart attack

Start eating a la cart with out beginners guide to Chicago street food.

Bagful o' fun You can never have too many chicharrones (those are pork rinds to you and me).

Many people wonder about those vendors making their way up and down Chicago's streets but never dive in because their Spanish is limited or they're skeeved out by the concept of a restaurant on wheels. Relax: Vendors are licensed by the city and inspected regularly. And with this handy guide, the most tongue-tied taster can orderilke a pro.

Agua de tamarindo
How to order it "AH-gwa day tah-mah-REEN-dough"
What it is Water flavored by tamarind pulp that tastes like a very sour cross between apricots and dates
Champurrado
How to order it "cham-poo-RAH-dough" **What it is** A warm, chocolate drink thickened with masa (cornmeal) seasoned with cinnamon and piloncillo (dark-brown sugar)
Chicharrones
How to order it "chee-cha-ROHN-es" **What it is** Fried pork skins, sprinkled with chile powder and fresh lime juice (con chile y limón, "kohn CHEE-lay ee lee-MOHN").
Elote
How to order it "eh-LOW-tay" **What it is** Boiled corn (or grilled, if you're lucky), served skewered and on the cob or with the kernels sliced off the cob and into a cup. Traditional toppings are margarine, mayo, Parmesan-like cheese called cotija, chile powder and lime juice. For the works, order it con todo ("kohn TOE-doe").
Fruta mixta
How to order it "FROO-tah MEEKS-tah" or "pep-EEN-oh" **What it is** Sliced-up fresh fruit (or cucumber) in a cup or plastic container. Traditionally, it's eaten with liberal sprinkles of chile powder and a squeeze of lime.
Horchata
How to order it "or-CHA-tah" **What it is** Rice water with cinnamon and sugar. Think liquid rice pudding.
Nieve
How to order it "nee-EH-vay" **What it is** Nieve translates to "snow," and it describes a snow cone–like concoction. Most of the carts hawk shaved ice that you can customize with squirts of bright, flavored (read: fake) syrups, but some use real fruit like coconut, strawberry and lime for sorbetlike results. For the latter, try the Milwaukee-Kimball-Diversey intersection.

▼ ✳ **B Las Palmas** We're dubious of a Mexican joint where the servers push mojitos as their favorite drink. But it made sense when we saw a menu that started somewhere in Mexico and took cues from around the world. The lamb is laced with cinnamon and wrapped in banana leaves. Skip the empanadas but don't miss the crêpes filled with cream cheese and caramel; they're tart, sweet and delicious. Like the food, the mariachi goes global, singing traditional Mexican ditties only to segue into tunes like "Ruby Tuesday" and "Cecilia." *1835 W North Ave at Honore St (773-289-4991). El: Blue to Damen. Bus: 50 Damen, 72 North. Brunch (Sat, Sun), lunch, dinner. Average main course: $14.*

☺ **Las Piñatas** Old Towners' loyalty lies with this sea-blue burrito-and-margarita shack. The main ingredient here is cheese: It's melted on the *suiza* overfilled with spiced beef and the sweet *mole* enchiladas (but not, thankfully, on the hearty chorizo tacos). Not everything here is tailored for the American palate, though: The salsa on the table packs a good amount of heat—the perfect pairing for one of the famous margaritas. *1552 N Wells St between Burton Pl and North Ave (312-664-8277). El: Brown, Purple (rush hrs) to Sedgwick. Bus: 72 North, 156 LaSalle. Lunch, dinner. Average main course: $10.*

☺ **Lobos al Fresco Tacos** Mexico native Yebel Shlimovitch (the Russian name comes courtesy of Grandpa) is a vet of area restaurants (including Frontera Grill and Chilpancingo), the chef-owner clearly knows his way around the kitchen: The pork in his *cochinita pibil* is exquisitely cooked, and his *pozole* comes alive with a squeeze of lime and a handful of cilantro. However, much of his food lacks punch, so choose carefully (avoid chicken dishes) and hope Shlimovitch becomes more familiar with his spice rack soon. *1732 N Milwaukee Ave at Wabansia Ave (773-486-3101). El: Blue to Western. Bus: 49 (24hrs), X49, 56. Lunch, dinner. Average main course: $9.*

☺ **Los Dos Laredos** Yeah, you can get your taco fix here, whether you prefer steak, chicken or tripe. Same goes for burritos. But if you're not ordering the "meat lover's" platter for two at this Little Village spot, you're missing out. The sizzling plate is piled so high with steak, bacon, chorizo, sweet grilled onions and peppers, and whole jalapeños that it can barely be carried to your table. If it's fish you're after, whole red snapper comes many ways, including topped with a *veracruzana* sauce packed with sweet, softened carrots and onions. *3120 W 26th St between Albany Ave and Troy St (773-376-3218). El: Blue (54th/Cermak branch during rush hrs), Pink to Kedzie. Bus: 21, 52, 60. Breakfast, lunch, dinner. Average main course: $10.*

☺ **Los Nopales** The chef-co-owner here is a former cook at the Palmer House Hilton and Heaven on Seven, and he's capable of elevating typical taqueria fare. Standouts include the *caldo de pollo*, a gargantuan serving of Mexican chicken soup served with rice and tortillas (perfect for a chilly night); the ceviche with citrus-spiked tilapia and shrimp; and cactus salad dotted with jicama, avocado and mango-chipotle dressing (perfect for a sweltering night). Expect weekend queues. *4544 N Western Ave between Wilson and Sunnyside Aves (773-334-3149). El: Brown to Western, Bus: 11, 49 (24hrs), X49, 78, 81 (24hrs). Lunch, dinner (closed Mon).* Average main course: $10.

★ ☺ **Maiz** This is one of our favorites for feeding our need for every type of corn creation under the sun. The banana leaf–steamed tamale is delicious, with a feather-light exterior of incredibly smooth masa hiding tender shredded chicken kicked up with green chiles, and the empanadas

Taco time De Cero is a sophisticated answer to the neighborhood taquería.

are the lightest and flakiest in town. The *sopes* (lightly griddled, dense corn patties) can be topped with everything from *pastor* (roasted pork) to *huitlacoche* ('shroomlike corn fungus) to spinach. Skip dessert and finish with a "bull"—a blend of rum, lime juice and beer. *1041 N California Ave between Cortez and Thomas Sts (773-276-3149). Bus: 53, 66 (24hrs), 70. Dinner (closed Mon). Average main course: $6.75.*

★ ✳ **Mexx Kitchen at the Whiskey** This Nuevo Mexican spot shares the same owners and address as Gold Coast hot-spot the Whiskey, but the vibe in this tiny dining room could not be more different. In fact, under the dim lights, it's the food that creates the most fuss. The guacamole is uncommonly creamy; the shrimp in the tacos are plump and toothsome; and carnitas sport an impressively crispy crust. Skip the lackluster pomegranate margaritas and belly up to the Whiskey for an after-dinner drink instead. *1015 N Rush St between Oak St and Bellevue Pl (312-475-0300). El: Red to Clark/Division. Bus: 22 (24hrs), 36, 70, 151 (24hrs). Breakfast (Sat, Sun), lunch (Mon–Sun), dinner. Average main course: $20.*

BYOB ☺ **Nuevo León** Since 1962, the Gutierrez family has been running this mecca of Mexican food, starting every dinner with an unexpected amuse-bouche. Taste, but don't fill up—there's a lot more where that came from, like roasted chicken pieces covered in a thick, dark, intense *mole*, and tacos de chorizo (housemade chorizo scrambled into an egg and wrapped in one of the famous housemade tortillas). The waitresses hustling back and forth between two smoke-free rooms are cheerfully brisk but will bring you anything you ask for. Except alcohol—you've gotta bring the mezcal yourself. *1515 W 18th St between Laflin St and Ashland Ave (312-421-1517). El: Blue, Pink to 18th. Bus: 9 Ashland (24hrs), 18 16th-18th. Breakfast, lunch, dinner. Average main course: $10.*

B ☺ **Papacito's Mexican Grille** Eating at this casual Lakeview spot is like hanging out in the kitchen while Dad whips up another one of his delicious meals. Sip a from-scratch limonada or *horchata* while the kitchen cooks *huevos rancheros* and mango pancakes at breakfast, light fish tacos studded with tilapia at lunchtime and hearty enchiladas for dinner. The heaping $8 carne asada dinner entrée, perfectly grilled and served with creamy guacamole and rice and beans, may just be the best deal in town. *2960 N Lincoln Ave between Wellington Ave and George St (773-327-5240). Bus: 11, 76, 77 (24hrs). Breakfast, lunch, dinner. Average main course: $7.*

☺ **Perez Restaurant** A little west of Pilsen's main strip, this long room starts off narrow and then opens up into a large dining area, complete with a stage for the band in the corner. Throw in a couple of the heavily touted "best margaritas" and you have an instant party. But that's not to say this place won't work for a lunch or early dinner, too: Chicken tostadas are piled high; tamales are stuffed with deliciously spicy shredded pork; and burritos are stuffed with succulent beef and creamy refried beans. *1163 W 18th St between May St and Racine Ave (312-421-3631). El: Blue (rush hrs), Pink to 18th. Bus: 18, 60 (24hrs), 168. Breakfast, lunch, dinner. Average main course: $9.*

Picante Grill We've had bowls of soup smaller than the margaritas at this upscale Pilsen option, but that's not a complaint. The bilevel space is lively and colorful (we particularly love the James Dean painting on the wall), the

Holy *mole* Delicioso makes seven different kinds of mole sauce.

Mexican

service is attentive and friendly, and the Mexican menu updates classic dishes with delicious success. We'll be back for the mild pan-fried tilapia flanked by delicious roasted zucchini and the flank steak paired with three enormous grilled shrimp in bright white wine sauce. *1626 S Halsted St between 16th and 17th Sts (312-455-8500). Bus: 8, 18, 168. Lunch, dinner. Average main course: $15.*

▼ ✳ ♿ **B Platiyo** Let's cut to the chase: On Sundays, the perfect house margarita is yours for $3. All day. That alone makes for a festive atmosphere, but the Mexican folk art (from local designer Nancy Warren) lining the walls does a good job, too. And you really can't go wrong with the food: The ceviche is tangy, the masa that makes up the black-bean and mushroom sopes smooth, the *mole rojo* rich, the tilapia fresh and the chocolate pecan pie sweet. We'll drink to that. *3313 N Clark St between Aldine Ave and Buckingham Pl (773-477-6700). El: Brown, Purple (rush hrs), Red to Belmont. Bus: 22 (24hrs), 77 (24hrs), 152. Brunch (Sun), dinner. Average main course: $15.*

B ☺ Rique's Regional Mexican Food "All over the map" isn't usually a compliment, but Rique's takes pride in giving diners tastes of unfamiliar dishes from Mexico's diverse regional cuisine. Namesake Enrique Cortes moved on, but Victor Arellano, a veteran of Chicago kitchens Bertucci's Corner and Café Central, promises not to change a thing. Strong menu staples remain, such as achiote-marinated grilled chicken in a tomatillo–pumpkin-seed sauce. Visit on Saturday nights for the $20, four-course prix-fixe menu that showcases food from a single Mexican state. *5004 N Sheridan Rd between Argyle St and Carmen Ave (773-728-6200). El: Red to Argyle. Bus: 36, 81 (24hrs), 92, 147, 151 (24hrs). Brunch (Sat, Sun), lunch (Wed–Fri), dinner. Average main course: $10.*

✳ **B ¡Salpicon!** This swanky Mexican spot is known for perfect margaritas, a Wine Spectator–recognized wine tome, and chef Priscila Satkoff's traditional salsas, queso fundido and earthy *mole* served with handmade tortillas. These classics are served in a lively, art-splashed dining room that's pretty close to the contemporary restaurants you'd find in the chef's hometown of Mexico City. Authentic Mexican flavors from blue-marlin ceviche to lacy crepas filled with goat's milk caramel are explained by the warm and friendly staff. *1252 N Wells St between Scott and Goethe Sts (312-988-7811). El: Red to Clark/Division. Bus: 11, 36, 70, 156. Brunch (Sun), dinner. Average main course: $20.*

▼ (✳ **Salud** If you're looking for interesting tequilas, contemporary Mexican snacks and an under-30 crowd, this spot will work. The back room has more of a dining-room feel, but we prefer the front lounge, with its illuminated tables and Tim Burton–style metal tree sprawled out over the bar. Skip the so-so entrées in favor of *antojito* menu picks like bright ceviche made with huge chunks of tilapia, scallops, shrimp and octopus; fish tacos, with plump pieces of barely battered tilapia wrapped in warm tortillas. *1471 N Milwaukee Ave between Honore St and Evergreen Ave (773-235-5577). El: Blue to Damen. Bus: 50, 56, 72. Dinner. Average main course: $11.*

☺ **Taquería El Asadero** It's not going to win any awards for most welcoming decor, but look past that and you'll find some of the freshest tacos in town. Meats are grilled on the spot (our favorite is the perfectly spiced *carne asada*), then sprinkled with fresh cilantro and onion and served up with a fiery, take-no-prisoners *salsa verde*. Wash it down with a *horchata* and a side of creamy, made-to-order guac—served with a mound of fresh-from-the-fryer chips—that rivals the fancy tableside preparations you'll find at upscale Mexican spots around town. *2213 W Montrose Ave at Lincoln Ave (773-583-5563). El: Brown to Western. Bus: 11, 49 (24hrs), X49, 78. Lunch, dinner. Average main course: $5.*

☺ **Taquería Los Gallos 2** On the weekends this popular *taquería* is packed to the rafters with families enjoying steaming bowls of *menudo* and *carne en su jugo*—the house specialty. (This version of the primordial beef soup doesn't come with grilled knob onions; order them separately.) Not into soup? Order the *carne apache*, essentially *carne en su jugo* without the broth—steak, beans, radish, avocado and bacon served with tortillas. *4252 S Archer Ave at Whipple St (773-254-2081). Bus: 52, 62, 94. Breakfast, lunch, dinner. Average main course: $7.*

☺ **Taquería Puebla** This primarily Spanish-speaking restaurant specializes in the authentic street food of Puebla, the central Mexico town credited as the birthplace of *mole poblano*. Because Puebla has a large concentration of Lebanese immigrants, you'll find tacos *arabes*, pork tacos with thick, pitalike wrappers. These chipotle-spiked beauties and their friend the *cemita milaneza* (a sesame-studded, breaded beef, cheese and avocado sandwich) are among the best of the menu. *3619 W North Ave between Monticello and Central Park Aves (773-772-8435). Bus: 72 North, 82 Kimball. Lunch, dinner. Average main course: $6.50.*

☺ **Taquería Tayahua** This Little Village restaurant distinguishes itself by its location off the main strip and with its food, which is a step above the standard 26th Street fare. *Camarones a la diabla*, shrimp in a fiery red sauce, are flanked by buttery, corn-studded rice; *caldo de res* (beef soup overflows with corn on the cob and a succulent, savory slice of beef; and tacos come with sweet grilled onions. Don't worry about getting addicted—thanks to its late-night hours (open 24 hours on the weekends), you'll never have to go without a fix. *2411 S Western Ave between 24th St and 24th Pl (773-247-3183). El: Blue (54th/Cermak branch during rush hrs), Pink to Western. Bus: 21, 49 (24hrs), X49. Breakfast, lunch, dinner. Average main course: $7.*

★ **Topolobampo** The more sophisticated side of Rick Bayless is no less delicious than his lively Frontera Grill side—it's merely more exquisite. His careful attention to seasonal, authentic flavors can be seen throughout offerings that in colder weather might include slow-cooked duck "*carnitas*" with wild arugula and sunflower shoots, roasted rock hen with fennel stew and toasted almonds, and roasted pork loin with *pasilla* chile-fig sauce and red-chile bread pudding. A chef's tasting is on offer for $75; add paired wines for $45. Be sure to make reservations. *445 N Clark St between Hubbard and Illinois Sts (312-661-1434). El: Brown, Purple (rush hrs) to Merchandise Mart; Red to Grand. Bus: 22 (24hrs), 29, 36, 65, 156. Lunch (Tue–Fri), dinner (Tue–Sat) (closed Sun, Mon). Average main course: $33.*

(✷ **Twisted Lizard** Nothing's better than kickin' back at this spot with a potent pitcher of margaritas and baskets of thick chips and homemade salsa. If it weren't for the big, fat Starbucks sign next door, you might even think you were in a roadside cantina in the Mexican outback. Think tender, flame-grilled steak fajitas, with piles of warm tortillas and a stack of limes; Baja-style beer-battered fish tacos, with tangy chipotle–sour cream sauce; and sides of firm black beans and chewy Mexican rice, peppered with little bits of veggies. *1964 N Sheffield Ave between Armitage and Maud Aves (773-929-1414). El: Brown to Armitage. Bus: 8 Halsted, 73 Armitage. Lunch, dinner. Average main course: $12.*

☉ **Wholly Frijoles Mexican Grill** The hour-long wait is laborious, but in the case of this blink-and-you'll-miss-it Mexican grill, it's worth it. Usually, the word rustic is saved for earthy European fare, but that's the only way to describe the flavor of piping hot tortilla soup thickened with blended tortillas; buttermilk-tinged, slawlike house salad; and caramel-colored, char-grilled chicken perched on a pile of smoky chipotle mashed potatoes. We'll be back, especially for the mango cheesecake (a breathtaking mix between flan and mousse) topped with fresh mango and raspberry puree. *3908 W Touhy Ave, Lincolnwood (847-329-9810). Bus: 11 Kedzie, Pace 290. Lunch, dinner (closed Sun). Average main course: $10.*

★ B ☉ **Xni-Pec** The name (pronounced "shnee pek") refers to the runny nose–inducing, housemade habanero salsa, but everything is worth a mention. Must-haves include Yucatecan specialties like *tacos de cochinita*, rich pork tacos cut by pickled onions, and *papadzules*, housemade tortillas stuffed with egg and topped with sprightly pumpkin-seed sauce. If the *relleno negro* tacos are available, order as many as you can—the shredded pork-chicken-beef mixture is immersed in a midnight-black sauce with endless flavor. You won't have room for the chilled, citrus-kissed, roasted pumpkin slices, so take them to go. *5135 W 25th St, Cicero (708-652-8680). El: Blue (54th/Cermak) (rush hrs), Pink to Cicero. Bus: 54 Cicero, 54B South Cicero. Lunch and dinner (Tues–Sun), (closed Mon). Average main course: $9.*

☉ **Zacatacos** Warm tortillas overflow with succulent meat, onions and cilantro at this homey corner spot. The housemade chorizo isn't half bad but the *al pastor* is not to be

missed. It's more than tacos that keeps this place consistently packed, though: The weekend special of *mole poblano* with chicken is a steal, and if you're still recovering from the night before, a big bowl of *menudo*—a traditional Mexican hangover cure—should nurse you back to health. *6224 W Cermak Rd, Berwyn (708-484-8443). Bus: 21 Cermak. Pace 304, 315, 322. Breakfast, lunch, dinner. Average main course: $6.*

★ ▼ ✷ B **Zapatista** Big, packed and loud, this is the type of place strong cocktails are made for, and their takes are stellar (particularly the *bigote*, a mojito-'rita-colada combo). The meal starts off as promising with mini tacos that pop with flavor (we particularly love the pork roasted with chile peppers). Entrées like chicken breast smothered in a sweet *mole* are solid, but the fajitas are much more of a show: They're served in a hot, mortar-like *molcajete* where the peppers and scallions sizzle until you stuff them into housemade tortillas. *1307 S Wabash Ave at 13th St (312-435-1307). El: Green, Orange, Red to Roosevelt. Bus: 1, 4 (24hrs), 29, 62 (24hrs). Brunch (Sat, Sun), lunch, dinner. Average main course: $14.*

Zocalo There's a lot to choose from on this small-plates menu, which owners Edgar and Marcos Castañeda very much want to be different from Lalo's, their family's chain of Mexican spots. Our advice is to go crazy with the *cazuelas*, small bowls of meats simmering in their sauces (soft, shredded beef steamed in banana leaf; shrimp, scallops and calamari served in an excellent guajillo-garlic sauce) and served with housemade blue-corn tortillas. Go for the trio of guac appetizer, too, and if you fancy a ceviche, try the *camarones*. *358 W Ontario St between Orleans and Kingsbury Sts (312-302-9977). El: Brown, Purple (rush hrs) to Chicago. Bus: 65 Grand, 125 Water Tower Express. Dinner. Average small plate: $8.* ■

Face off Zocalo serves artfully prepared small plates.

Mexican

Middle Eastern

See also: *Kosher, Indian/Subcontinental*

▼ (**A La Turka** Modern-day Turkey isn't the idea here. This dining room hearkens to times of eating on luxurious floor cushions and sucking on hookahs like they're Tic Tacs. You can make a meal out of the hot appetizer platter—thin zucchini pancakes, tangy rolls of feta-stuffed phyllo and the Turkish pizza, a housemade pita piled with perfectly seasoned ground lamb. Or fill up on the A La Turka special: sauteed beef and grilled vegetables served with a slightly sweet eggplant puree. Portions are sized for big appetites, so you won't leave hungry. *3134 N Lincoln Ave between Barry and Belmont Aves (773-935-6101). El: Brown to Paulina. Bus: 9, 11, 77 (24 hrs). Dinner. Average main course: $15.*

▼ ⊙ **Afghan Restaurant** The walls here have been made into a makeshift variety store—glassware sets, Afghani DVDs and pressure cookers hang, readied for purchase—but the real draw is the amazing Afghani food. After tasting your way through the bargain menu, you'll be convinced this place was opened to satiate your vegetable cravings. Big bowls of slurpable curried lentil soup, stewed eggplant with garlicky yogurt sauce (*borani badinjan*) and all-day-simmered spinach with tender chunks of lamb (*sabzi chalow*) make for veggie nirvana. Hefty, marinated kebabs are served with an addictive side of buttery basmati rice. *2818 W Devon Ave between California Ave and Mozart St (773-262-8000). Bus: 93 California/Dodge, 155 Devon. Lunch, dinner. Average main course: $7.*

⊙ **Al Khayameih** It gets overlooked among the many Middle Eastern restaurants that dot Kedzie Avenue, but the exceptionally fresh fare puts this Lebanese spot at the head of its class. Pita bread—baked next door at the bakery/grocery store of the same name—makes for a soft and warm utensil to scoop up *moutabal*, a spread of eggplant mashed with onions and peppers. *Kibbeh* is made to order, and is one of the most greaseless and flavorful versions in the city. Unlike it's popular neighbors, there's never a long wait to get inside. *4748 N Kedzie Ave between Leland and Lawrence Aves (773-583-0999). Bus: 81 Lawrence (24 hrs) El: Brown Line to Kedzie. Breakfast, lunch, dinner. Average main course: $10.*

⊙ **Aladdin's Eatery** Health food that doesn't taste like health food, fast food that doesn't taste like fast food: and those are both compliments. Lemony *fool* (fava bean puree) arrives at the table just moments after it is ordered. The "rolled pitas"—essentially Middle Eastern burritos stuffed with grilled chicken *shistawook* and a slathering of *toum* and then grilled—aren't far behind. Housemade juices like the sweet carrot-apple provide an extra dose of nutrients. If your mental health requires something stronger, an interesting wine list featuring many Lebanese bottles is on hand. *614 W Diversey Pkwy between Clark St and Lehman Ct (773-327-6300). El: Brown, Purple (rush hrs) to Diversey. Bus: 22 (24 hrs), 36, 76. Lunch, dinner. Average main course: $7.*

▼ (**Alhambra Palace** This opulent, 24,000-square-foot space was supposed to be Eric Aubriot's new home, where he would combine French and Moroccan cuisine in sophisticated ways. But, in a turn that surprised nobody, Aubriot didn't last but a few weeks, leaving behind a restaurant that serves a limited menu of kebabs, hummus,

lentil soup and a few tagines. Everything is cooked appropriately, but it all needs salt and other flavor enhancers. Still, it's worth it to go once, if only to gawk at the amazing tilework, fabrics and belly dancers (who are more than happy to let you get a good look). *1240 W Randolph St between Racine Ave and Elizabeth St (312-666-9555). El: Green to Ashland. Bus: 20 Madison (24 hrs) Lunch, dinner. Average main course: $26.*

▼ **Amira** The food at this Mediterranean spot isn't going to change your life, but the service might. Should anything go wrong while you munch on crisp pizzas, garlicky hummus, a perfectly fine steak, say the word. Servers will tend to you with honest concern. And that, more than anything, is why you'll come back. *455 N Cityfront Plaza between Water and Illinois Sts (312-923-9311). El: Red to Grand. Bus: 2, 3, 4 (24 hrs), X4, 10, 26, 29, 65, 143, 144, 145, 146, 147, 148, 151 (24 hrs), 157. Lunch (Mon–Fri), dinner (closed Sun). Average main course: $14.*

▼ BYOB✻ **Andalous** With countless Moroccan specialties on the menu, it's easy to forgive a few pitfalls. But order right and you won't have to. The briwates (Moroccan egg rolls) are fine, but the Andalous appetizer combo is sublime. The "famous couscous" left us wondering how it earned its moniker, but the chicken in the Meknès tagine falls from the bone, crusted in crispy skin. A steaming cup of Moroccan tea gives you a good excuse to linger at meal's end. *3307 N Clark St between Aldine Ave and Buckingham Pl (773-281-6885). El: Brown, Purple (rush hour only), Red to Belmont. Bus: 22 Clark (24 hrs), 77 Belmont (24 hrs). Lunch (Sat, Sun), dinner. Average main course: $11.*

▼ (🍴 **Andies Restaurant** Andersonville's *other* Mediterranean spot (located next door to its competition, Reza's) heavily touts the health benefits of its food. But you're likely to stuff yourself so silly that the health benefits will be canceled out. The gluttony starts with complimentary rounds of warm, thick pita served with red-pepper hummus and incredible, half-off deals on wine daily. It continuea with Moroccan chicken buried under toothsome couscous and juicy kebabs. Don't stop until the last spoonful of Tunisian housemade hazelnut pudding is gone. *5253 N Clark St between Berwyn and Farragut Aves (773-784-8616). Bus: 9, 22 (24 hrs), 92. Lunch, dinner. Average main course: $11.*

▼ BYOB ✻ **Café Orchid** The Middle Eastern crowd at this Turkish spot should tip you off that it isn't another watered-down outlet for hummus and pita chips. If you aren't convinced, the menu reveals its authenticity. It's filled with dishes that are largely unfamiliar in these parts, such as *balik sarma*, grape leaves stuffed with sardines and crisped around the edges for an aggressively flavorful, crispy starter; *cig borek*, a savory, deep-fried pastry stuffed with ground lamb; and *manti*, dumplinglike "Turkish ravioli" stuffed with more lamb and topped with a garlic-yogurt sauce. *1746 W Addison St at Hermitage Ave (773-327-3808). Bus: 9, 11, 50, 152. Lunch, dinner (closed Mon). Average main course: $11.*

▼ BYOB (**Café Suron** Sometimes we have to pinch ourselves just to remember that this tranquil café isn't a

The slice is right *Lahmacun* stands in for pizza at Nazarlik.

Arabian nights Explore 24,000 square feet of French-inspired Morocco at Alhambra Palace.

mirage. The sunny room feels so much like a courtyard that you won't mind that there's no outdoor seating. "Fresh" doesn't even begin to describe the *borani*, bright spinach studded with sweet almonds and topped with tangy yogurt, the herbal ground lamb or the *dolmeh*, stuffed, surprisingly, with raisins. But nothing tops the cubes of tenderloin. Marinated overnight in olive oil and saffron, they're so tender they have the consistency of a marshmallow. *1146 W Pratt Ave between Sheridan Rd and the lake (773-465-6500). El: Red to Loyola or Morse. Bus: 96, 147, 155. Dinner (Tue–Sun), (closed Mon). Average main course: $12.*

☺ **Carthage Café** In-the-know cabbies and hungry hoodies alike have transformed this Middle Eastern hookah café into a lively late-night spot. The sun-blasted dining room is long and lean, with a smaller, more private room tucked to the side (best for long tokes off the hookah). Gently priced platefuls of tender beef and lamb kebabs show up on tables as often as the made-daily hummus and smoky baba ghanoush. Vegetarians take notice: The spinach appetizer is a garlicky delight. *3446 W Foster Ave between Bernard St and St. Louis Ave (773-539-9004). El: Brown to Kimball. Bus: 81 (24hrs), 82, 92. Lunch (Mon–Sat), dinner. Average main course: $6.*

☺ **Cedars Mediterranean Kitchen** Cedars' falafel, hummus, baba ghanoush, lentil soup—pretty much everything that goes with its delicious, warm pita bread—have us hooked. We could fill up just on appetizers and salads here, but should you venture into the entrées, be prepared for huge portions and bring friends. The family-style special for parties of four or more gets you ten dishes for dinner ($12.95 per person) and seven for lunch ($10.95). Service can be unpredictable, but the potent house coffee and three kinds of baklava (traditional, pistachio or walnut) will help you to

overlook it. *1206 E 53rd St at Woodlawn Ave (773-324-6227). Bus: 2, 6, 15, 28, 55, X55, 171, 172. Lunch, dinner. Average main course: $10.*

▼ ✳ ☺ **Couscous** The real draw of this small, Little Italy storefront is the Maghrebin food. Taking influences from Moroccan, Algerian and Tunisian fare, it's a mash-up of cuisines resulting in delicious tajeens, cheesy soufflés stuffed with beef or chicken that aren't cooked in tagines but are tasty nonetheless. Or go for the comforting plates of couscous sporting huge chunks of potatoes, carrots and zucchini surrounding flavorful cuts of lamb. *1445 W Taylor St between Bishop and Laflin Sts (312-226-2408). El: Pink, Blue to Polk (54th/Cermak). Bus: 7, 12, 60 (24hrs). Lunch, dinner. Average main course: $9.*

☺ **Cousin's** The dining room is frumpy at this family-owned Turkish kitchen, but what's always in fashion are the terrific prices for generous servings of tasty eats. Even a simple *eza gelin* (lentil soup) is layered in flavors. A third of the nearly 40 main dishes are vegetarian (check out the sweet-potato crust on the amazing vegetable moussaka or the chili-hot *ezme*, a snappy appetizer of peppers, tomatoes and walnuts). Relax on plush, Arabian Nights–style pillows at four stout tables along the south wall. *2833 N Broadway between Diversey Pkwy and Surf St (773-880-0063). El: Brown, Purple (rush hrs) to Diversey. Bus: 22 (24 hrs), 36, 76. Lunch, dinner. Average main course: $10.*

▼ **BYOB Cousin's I.V.** See Vegetarian for review.

★ ▼ **BYOB Fattoush** The dining room is full of tables dressed with blinding white linens that are, most of the time, empty. But don't let that give you pause. The maza we tried—

a creamy bowl of hummus, a steaming spinach pie and a crunchy, eponymous salad—were all potent with sharp, tangy lemon juice, while the aromatic kibbeh was packed with cinnamon. The kebabs are more like thin steaks than cubes, but juicy nonetheless. We'd rather save room for the four kinds of sticky, flaky baklava. *2652 N Halsted St between Wrightwood and Schubert Aves (773-327-2652). El: Brown, Purple (rush hrs) to Diversey. Bus: 8 Halsted, 76 Diversey. Lunch, dinner. Average main course: $12.*

▼ **BYOB** ✳ **Kan Zaman** Slipping off your shoes and curling up on cushions at low tables is a royal way to eat, even if your meal doesn't start off that way. The pita is of the thin, tough, store-bought variety, and the olive oil is flavorless. But once you dig into the vegetarian combo, with its tart feta, zesty tabouli and hummus you'll know that you're eating like a prince, not just sitting like one. Now dig into the meaty kibbeh and you'll be on your way to becoming king. *617 N Wells St between Ohio and Ontario Sts (312-751-9600). El: Brown, Purple (rush hours) to Chicago; Red to Grand. Bus: 65 Grand. Lunch, dinner. Average main course: $14.*

⊙ **Kebab House (formerly Sahar Pita)** The nondescript strip-mall location and blinding fluorescent lights won't likely draw you in, but this new Middle Eastern take-out joint makes it worth overlooking the unsavory surroundings. Kedzie Avenue is lousy with falafel joints, but Sahar—an offspring of the renowned Sahar Meat Market just a few doors down—stands out for its spicy *kefta* beef, delicious steak shish kebab, soft chicken (all halal meat) and pillowy rice. And don't miss the smoky baba ghanoush, heaped on warm pita bread. *4835 N Kedzie Ave between Lawrence Ave and Ainslie St (773-583-6695). El: Brown to Kedzie. Bus: 81 Lawrence (24hrs), 82 Kimball. Lunch, dinner. Average main course: $9.*

⊙ **Larsa's** Give a Middle Eastern chef a pizza oven (left by the previous owners) and what you get is *laham ajeen*—a crispy, paper-thin, pizzalike starter topped with parsley-kicked, finely ground beef; tomatoes; onions; and peppers. The fresh-flavor train keeps rolling with the entrées: The juicy marinated chicken kebabs, kefta kebabs, beef shawarma and charbroiled catfish stand out. Each comes with a veggie soup–like stew that's meant to be spooned over the fluffy white rice for added oomph. *3724 W Dempster St, Skokie (847-679-3663). Bus: Pace 215, Pace 250. Lunch, dinner (closed Mon). Average main course: $8.*

▼ **BYOB Marrakech** Snake your way past the Moroccan lanterns and rugs in the bazaar beyond the door and into the simple dining room to try specialties like *briwates*, lemon chicken egg rolls; *zaalouk*, a smoky mix of eggplant and tomatoes; and Fez tagine, a tender lamb shank in an eggy sauce studded with prunes. Generous pieces of dense, syrupy baklava may satisfy a certain sweet tooth, but we preferred the sweet and savory chicken pastille, a flaky, sugar-dusted, phyllo pie. It's reserved for important people so puff out your chest and pretend. *1413 N Ashland Ave between Blackhawk St and Beach Ave (773-227-6451). El: Blue to Division. Bus: 9 Ashland (24hrs), 56 Milwaukee. Dinner. Average main course: $11.*

⊙ **Marrakech Expresso** It started out as a coffee shop, a place to sip the strong, sweet, spicy coffee and teas for which Morocco is known. But once owner Boucheib Khribech started whipping up batches of his couscous, his customers got hooked. With your pots of tea, order Khribech's thick hummus, juicy kefta kebabs and signature lamb tagine (with a big shank that falls apart before your fork even touches it). Order a hookah and smoke one of the flavored tobaccos while

finishing up those last drops of tea. *4747 N Damen Ave between Giddings St and Lawrence Ave (773-271-4541). El: Brown to Damen. Bus: 11, 50, 81 (24hrs). Lunch (Sat, Sun), dinner. Average main course: $8.*

★ ▼ **Maza** We're usually too busy stuffing our mouths with this tasty Middle Eastern grub to talk. If we could, we'd tell you that the *fool modamas* are warm fava beans simmered in mouth-puckering herbs, lemon juice and olive oil. We'd tell you that the crispy, salty, juicy whole red snapper has addictive powers. And we'd tell you that the dining room is warm and romantic, and that you shouldn't leave it until you've had the flaky, buttery, housemade baklava, made on the premises nightly. *2748 N Lincoln Ave between Schubert Ave and Diversey Pkwy (773-929-9600). El: Brown, Purple (rush hours) to Diversey. Bus: 11 Lincoln, 76 Diversey. Dinner. Average main course: $12.*

⊙ **Nazarlik** The name Nazarlik refers to the eye-shaped beads rumored to ward off bad luck. You won't need any of those at this Turkish restaurant, because the food is prepared with lots of care. We had the greatest success with the *mujver*, a crispy and ethereal pan-fried zucchini patty; the gooey spinach-and-cheese pie; and the *lahmacun*, a pizzalike concoction that was rolled out, baked to order and flanked by fresh, smoky baba ghanoush. With so much success, we decided to brave *ayran*, a drink composed of yogurt, ice and salt; we were pleasantly pleased—and refreshed. *1650 W Belmont Ave between Ashland Ave and Paulina St (773-327-5800). El: Brown to Paulina. Bus: 9, 11, 77 (24hrs). Lunch, dinner. Average main course: $8.*

⊙ **The Nile** Unless you're lucky enough to have a grandparent sitting at home frying up fresh batches of falafel, this may be the freshest Middle Eastern food you'll find in Chicago. The refrigerated case is filled with rows of plump, glistening, marinated chicken and just-formed kefta kebabs waiting to be grilled-to-order. Freshly baked savory pies, bursting with spinach and big chunks of onion, sit on the counter. Behind that, a man pushes falafel into a pool of bubbling oil. We don't care who your grandma is, she's not making anything like this. *3259 W 63rd St between Kedzie and Spaulding Aves (773-434-7218). Bus: 52, 63, 67. Lunch, dinner. Average main course: $5.*

★ ⊙ **Noon O Kabab** If the city were flooded with Persian joints tomorrow, this spot would still be our favorite. There's something about the casual room brightened with colorful tile murals, the smoky baba ghanoush, the cinnamon-and-tomato braised lamb shank and those kebabs—mmm, the kebabs. Marinated filet cubes, tender chicken breast hunks and oniony ground beef wrapped around skewers and charred outside but still juicy inside, plopped down on fluffiest rice alongside charbroiled tomatoes and onions. *4661 N Kedzie Ave between Eastwood and Leland Aves (773-279-8899). El: Brown to Kedzie. Bus: 81 Lawrence (24hrs). Lunch, dinner. Average main course: $10.*

⊙ **Oasis Café** This take-out joint has saved many a vegetarian stuck in the burger-heavy Loop. Best bets are smoky baba ghanoush, tabouli studded with mint and daily specials, especially Friday's Moroccan couscous with sweet potatoes, eggplant and spinach. Carnivores shouldn't miss Monday's Moroccan chicken pastille: flaky phyllo stuffed with saffron-ginger-cinnamon-laced chicken. *17 S Wabash Ave between Madison and Washington Sts (312-558-1058). El: Brown, Green, Orange, Pink, Purple (rush hrs) to Madison; Red, Blue to Washington. Bus: 2, 6, 10, 29, 26, 56, 60 (24hrs), 124, 127, 157. Lunch (closed Sun). Average main course: $5.*

⊙ **Old Jerusalem** For more than 20 years, this Old Town spot has dished out good-quality, reasonably priced Middle Eastern food in a neighborhood not exactly known for bargains. With a few exceptions the menu's not terribly adventurous, but they do a great job with standards like hummus, flavorful falafel and well-seasoned kefta kebab. The rickety old chairs don't inspire diners to linger over their Arabic coffee, but desserts, like warm honey cake, can always be taken to go. *1411 N Wells St between Schiller St and North Ave (312-944-0459). El: Brown, Purple (rush hours) to Sedgwick. Bus: 72 North, 156 LaSalle. Lunch, dinner. Average main course: $8.*

⊙ **The Olive Mountain** See Indian/Subcontinental for review.

▼ ✳ **Reza's** When a restaurant is so big it practically takes up the whole block, and the menu's as big as a book, there's bound to be a few blunders. But if you stick to the basics, you'll be happy. The *kashkeh bodemjan* blends eggplant with sweet caramelized onions, garlic and mint for an addictive spread. The chicken *koubideh* is a delicious, herbal kebab, and the fattoush is full of clean, sharp flavors. Skip the mass-produced cakes and go for the housemade baklava and Turkish coffee to finish the meal. *432 W Ontario St between Orleans and Kingsbury Sts (312-664-4500). El: Brown, Purple (rush hours) to Chicago. Bus: 22 Clark (24hrs), 65 Grand. Lunch, dinner. Average main course: $13.*
● *Additional location at 5255 N Clark St (773-561-1898).*

▼ ✳ ⊙ **Roti** There's a disorienting flurry of activity going on inside this riverside joint, which has tapped the Loop's feverish hunger for Middle Eastern food. First timers should just get in line and pick a bread ("hand-stretched" flatbread), a filling (we like the juicy fire-roasted chicken) and then sauces and toppings. The line moves quickly, and workers exhibit

Read 'em & eat

borek pastry (often phyllo) stuffed with cheese, meat, parsley and spinach

branzini Mediterranean sea bass

foul moudammas (fool moo-DAH-mahs) fava-bean salad seasoned with lemon and garlic, eaten with pita bread

harissa Tunisian chili paste used as a meat rub, or, when mixed with oil or water, as a condiment

kofte (kof-TEH) a dish of ground or minced meat (usually lamb), flavored with spices and mixed with rice, bulgar, or bread crumbs, then shaped into balls and fried, grilled or skewered

shish tawook (also shish taok) chargrilled chicken that has been marinated in garlic, lemon juice and olive oil

toum (toom) pungent dip or sauce of pureed garlic, oil and lemon, similar to aioli

za'atar a tart, flavorful spice blend that varies across the Middle East, but commonly includes thyme, sesame seeds and marjoram

little patience, so you won't have much time to think. Luckily, with options such as kalamata olives, a cool yogurt-cucumber sauce and roasted red pepper aioli, it's hard to go wrong. *10 S Riverside Plaza between Madison and Monroe Sts (312-775-7000). El: Brown, Pink, Purple (rush hrs), Orange to Quincy. Bus: 14, 20 (24hrs), 38, 60 (24hrs), 124, 125, 157. Breakfast, lunch (closed Sat, Sun). Average main course: $7.*

⊙ **Salam** First of all, there's the 21-cent falafel with a crisp, browned crust that cracks open to reveal a fluffy green center. But a trip to this dingy storefront wouldn't be complete without also trying a bowl of *mossabaha*, hummus studded with whole chickpeas and pools of olive oil, or a plate of the rich beef shawarma. Daily specials, such as Wednesday's stuffed lamb, typically run out around lunchtime, so if you want some you'll need to take the day off. Trust us, it's worth a vacation day. *4636 N Kedzie Ave between Eastwood and Leland Aves (773-583-0776). El: Brown to Kedzie. Bus: 78 Montrose, 81 Lawrence (24hrs). Breakfast, lunch, dinner. Average main course: $8.*

▼ **Sayat Nova** It may be a magnificent mile for shopping, but when it comes to dinner, Michigan Avenue often disappoints. If you're looking for something other than burgers and Italian, head for the only Armenian restaurant in town. Sink into a booth and recharge with flaky spinach-stuffed phyllo triangles (called *boereg*) and flavorful kebabs. The lone server can make the experience slow, but that's nothing like the *mahalabeya*, a creamy milk pudding topped with walnuts and lemon syrup—can't make you forget. *157 E Ohio St between St Clair St and Michigan Ave (312-644-9159). El: Red to Grand. Bus: 2, 3, 10, 26, 125, 143, 144, 145, 146, 147, 148, 151 (24hrs), 157. Lunch (Mon–Sat), dinner. Average main course: $13.*

▼ ⊙ **Semiramis** On a sunny day, this Lebanese café is warm and full of light. On darker days, the food provides such pleasures. The *fattoush* salad provides forkfuls of bright, tart flavors, and the basket of warm pita begs to be slathered with *ful*—fava beans cooked with olive oil and garlic. Sandwiches, like a chicken wrap, and tender kebabs are prepared skillfully, and everything benefits from a slather of the housemade garlic sauce, *toum*. Pair the *mamoul* cookies with a cup of rich cardamom-laced coffee for dessert. *4639 N Kedzie Ave between Eastwood and Leland Aves (773-279-8900). El: Brown to Kedzie. Bus: 78 Montrose, 81 Lawrence (24hrs). Lunch, dinner (closed Sun). Average main course: $7.*

▼ ◖ **Shiraz** If the chandeliers and Persian rug–upholstered banquettes in this dining room don't make you swoon, just wait. Soon you'll swoon over the focaccia like bread with a block of crumbly feta cheese, tart pickles and ripe tomatoes. Enjoy, but don't go too crazy—you'll want to leave room for the *kashk-e-bademjan*, a savory eggplant puree with a tang of yogurt; the *sotani*, juicy prime-rib kebab alongside another kebab of ground beef, lamb and veal; and the *gormeh sabzi*, a sprightly beef stew. *4425 W Montrose Ave between Kenneth and Kostner Aves (773-777-7275). El: Blue to Montrose. Bus: 53 (24 hrs), X54, 78. Lunch (Sat, Sun), dinner (closed Mon). Average main course: $11.*

⊙ **Sinbad's** Tucked away in a below-sidewalk-level strip mall, this Mediterranean spot is easy to miss. Popular Middle Eastern staples like smooth hummus, smoky baba ghanoush and spinach pies (which are cooked on the grill, lending them a nice charred flavor) share center stage with Moroccan specialties. Lamb shank arrives so tender it's falling apart all by itself, but it lacks the delicious flavor of the juicy chicken and kefta kebabs. Judging from the flavorful, affordable menu options, this place won't likely stay underground. *444*

Food for thought Vegetarians have mounds of options at Afghan Restaurant.

W Fullerton Pkwy at Clark St (773-525-2233). El: Brown, Purple (rush hrs), Red to Fullerton. Bus: 22 (24hrs), 36, 74. Lunch, dinner. Average main course: $9.

Taboun Grill See Kosher for review.

◑ **Taste of Lebanon** For quick, dependable Middle Eastern grub, this tiny restaurant makes perfect sense. The lentil soup has an addictive peppery flavor, but leave room for creamy baba ghanous, hummus, and especially the lamb kebab wrap, a thin pita stuffed with a full-flavored ground-lamb patty, parsley and tahini. (You can skip the overly thick beef shawarma.) *1509 W Foster Ave between Clark and Ashland Aves (773-334-1600). Bus: 22 Clark (24hrs), 92 Foster. Lunch, dinner (closed Sun). Average main course: $4.*

◑ **Taza** Loop lunchers flock to this Mediterranean café, which touts itself as serving "fresh and healthy, low fat and low cholesterol" food. We can't get enough of their hearty kefta kebab, daily specials such as the Moroccan chicken and anything having to do with the fluffy, dill-flecked rice. *176 N Franklin Ave between Couch Pl and Randolph St (312-201-9885). El: Blue, Brown, Green, Orange, Pink, Purple (rush hrs) to Clark/Lake. Bus: 22 (24hrs), 24, 156. Lunch (closed Sat, Sun). Average main course: $6.*

▼ ✳ **Tizi Melloul** The Moroccan-themed, Suhail-designed space that was deemed *the* date destination upon opening in '99 is still warm, cozy and lush—exactly how you'll feel after downing one of its potent cocktails. Take it easy: You're going to want to remember the simple, warm, flaky feta crisps and the cinnamon-kissed currants and almonds in the chicken *bisteeya*. The lantern-filled "crescent room" is tête-à-tête perfect any night; on Sundays you'll encounter belly dancers. A few of those cocktails and you may do a little swiveling yourself. *531 N Wells St at Grand Ave (312-670-4338). El: Red to Grand. Bus: 65 Grand, 125 Water Tower Express. Dinner. Average main course: $17.*

★ ◑ **Turkish Cuisine and Bakery** Typically we try to not fill up on bread before our food arrives, but at this comfortable Middle Eastern joint, that's practically impossible. When the basket of housemade bread arrives, we go through it in hyperspeed, slathering slices with rich baba ghanoush and cool, creamy, yogurt-based *cacik*. From there it's on to the savory pies stuffed with cheese and eggs. We might take a break from the carbs with the chicken-thigh kebabs, but then it's back to the baked goods for baklava, an ideal ending. *5605 N Clark St between Bryn Mawr and Olive Aves (773-878-8930). El: Red to Bryn Mawr. Bus: 22 Clark (24hrs), 50 Damen. Lunch, dinner. Average main course: $9.*

▼ **BYOB** ✳ **B Turquoise Café** We can't rave enough about this stylish Turkish spot. We wolf down the *manti* (Turkish ravioli stuffed with bits of lamb in a creamy yogurt and chili oil sauce), whole slabs of juicy, salt-crusted sea bass and some of the best hummus around. Savvy regulars skip the filling entrées to fuel up on apps and sides like fried zucchini pancakes with yogurt dip and char-grilled calamari with diced tomatoes and garlic. *2147 W Roscoe St between Hamilton Ave and Leavitt St (773-549-3523). El: Brown to Paulina. Bus: 49 (24hrs), X49, 50, 77 (24hrs), 152. Brunch (Sun), lunch, dinner. Average main course: $16.*

★ ▼ ◑ **Zad** The menu at this Middle Eastern spot doesn't contain anything you haven't tried before—there's the usual assortment of falafel, hummus and kebabs. The surprise comes when you taste the bright, fresh flavors in dishes that can be ho-hum elsewhere. The appetizer combo for two is the best place to start—the enormous platter of smoky baba ghanoush, greaseless falafel, creamy hummus and *dolmas* easily makes a meal. Don't miss the shawarma—both the chicken and lamb/beef varieties of marinated, rotisserie-cooked meat had us planning a return visit. *3112 N Broadway between Briar Pl and Barry Ave (773-404-3473). El: Red, Brown, Purple (rush hrs) to Belmont. Bus: 8, 22 (24hrs), 36, 76, 77 (24 hrs). Lunch, dinner. Average main course: $10.* ∎

Globalization Expand your horizons with Thai-inspired tapas at Sura.

See also: *Chinese, Eclectic, Japanese, Korean, Thai, Vietnamese*

⊕ **Adobo Express** Knowing what you want goes a long way at this chic (for a stripmall) Filipino joint. There's no menu for any of the meals other than breakfast, and the guys behind the steam table aren't good at answering questions. But push them to talk or you could end up with a bowl of pig ears. Try the mongo beans, a stew that resembles lentil soup and includes chunks of beef. Chicken curry is a good choice for timid eaters—the chicken is fried before the spicy (but not hot) curry is added. *5343 N Lincoln Ave between Summerdale and Balmoral Aves (773-293-2362). Bus: 11, X49, 49 (24hrs), 92. Breakfast, lunch, dinner. Average main course: $5.*

▼ **Big Bowl** After local chain Lettuce Entertain You sold this Pan-Asian money-maker to the folks behind Chili's, the restaurant slacked on quality. So LEYE bought it back and revamped the food. Thanks to freshly roasted peanuts, fiery blistered chilies and made-to-order sauces, it's better than ever. In addition to authentic Chinese specialties that include Mongolian beef and Thai curries like a scallop and shrimp combo, Niman Ranch pork is used in the fried rice, and local produce has found its way onto the impressive stir-fry bar. *6 E Cedar St at Rush St (312-640-8888). El: Red to Clark/Division. Bus: 36 Broadway, 70 Division.. Lunch, dinner. Average main course: $12.*

⊕ **Butterfly** Thailand native Apidech Chotsuwan used to own Bangkok Thai, but after a trip to Japan, he sold his stake to ready this half-Thai, half-Japanese restaurant. Chotsuwan trained the Thai chef to handle standards from noodles to curries, while he mans the sushi bar, serving up nigiri and maki for the budget-conscious, as well as teriyaki and katsu for fans of cooked Japanese fare. Pulling double duty as interior decorator, Chotsuwan decked out the space in an orange-and-black color scheme, an homage to his favorite butterfly hues. *1156 W Grand Ave between May St and Racine Ave (312-563-5555). El: Blue to Grand. Bus: 8, 9 (24hrs), X9, 65. Lunch, dinner. Average main course: $7.*

▼ 🍴 **Chen's** Surrounded by all the boisterous Clark St Cubs bars pushing pub grub, this upscale Chinese restaurant and sushi bar—specializing in crispy duck, whole red snapper and a variety of stir-fry dishes—stands out like a sore thumb. The tables are nicely spaced in the sleek, minimal dining room, which is given a splash of color by a variety of potted floor plants. *3506 N Clark St between Cornelia Ave and Eddy St (773-549-9100). El: Red to Addison. Bus: 8, 22 (24hrs), 152. Dinner. Average main course: $11.*

▼ **China Grill** See Chinese for review.

⊕ **Cid's Ma Mon Luk** Named for (but no relation to) the famed Filipino-Chinese restaurant in Manila, this no-frills restaurant dishes out a highly satisfying egg noodle–and–roasted pork soup called *mami*. Slow-cooked, fall-apart–tender pork or chicken adobo arrives in dark, slurpable gravy, perfect for soaking up with *puto*, a fluffy rice-flour cake. *Siopao*, steamed pork buns, are airy-light with mild, meaty fillings. Wash dinner down with a sweet-tart calamansi juice (from the citrus fruit), or top it off with halo-halo, a shaved-ice concoction of chewy flan, red-bean paste, coconut jelly and jackfruit. *9182 W Golf Rd, Niles (847-803-*

3652). El: Blue to Jefferson Park. Bus: Pace 270, Pace 208. Lunch, dinner (closed Mon). Average main course: $8.

▼ ✳ **Dee's** There's a clear dichotomy at this often-overlooked spot: Older neighborhood folks come for the well-executed, if dull, Chinese dishes; and the younger crowd devours the fresh, delicious sushi. The ambience is a nod to the old-school patrons—floral carpeting, white tablecloths, smooth jazz and a roaring fire. But we'll overlook the hotel-lobby decor as long as the flavor-packed maki keep coming: Dee's maki, a giant roll packed with lettuce, tuna, salmon, yellowtail, avocado and sprinkled with tobiko, and the guilty-pleasure Mexican maki, a tuna roll spiced up with cilantro, jalapeno and lime. *1114 W Armitage Ave at Seminary Ave (773-477-1500). El: Brown, Purple (rush hrs) to Armitage. Bus: 8 Halsted, 73 Armitage. Dinner. Average nigiri: $2.50.*

▼ **BYOB** ⊕ **Dharma Garden** The Thai owners of this blissed-out spot are self-described "biospiritualists," which means that they don't serve "land animals" (only veggies and seafood), they aim to use the freshest ingredients possible and the bar serves only but freshly squeezed juices. Housemade, garlic-flecked, potstickers are delicate wraps with spinach-carrot-cabbage filling, and the Dharma Garden spring rolls are the epitome of fresh, with bright flavors of Thai basil and mint. Save room for restorative entrées like steamed lime salmon over a mound of fresh garlic, ginger and chilies. *3109 W Irving Park Rd between Albany Ave and Troy St (773-588-9140). El: Blue to Irving Park. Bus: 80, X80, 82. Lunch, dinner (closed Mon). Average main course: $9.*

▼ **BYOB dib** This upscale spot on a seedy strip of Uptown sticks out like a little sore thumb, all bright and shiny amid its tired surroundings. It's just as chipper inside, with the decor and music keeping things lively. Starters like grilled avocado salad with minced spicy tuna are tasty, but heavier on style than substance. Creative maki include a *tom yum* roll made with shrimp paste and topped with ponzu sauce, and a crispy shellfish roll. You'll find the standard array of Thai noodle dishes, but your best bets are from the sushi bar. *1025 W Lawrence Ave at Kenmore Ave (773-561-0200). El: Red to Lawrence. Bus: 36, 81 (24hrs), 151 (24hrs). Lunch, dinner. Average nigiri: $2.50.*

▼ **BYOB Grande Noodles and Sushi Bar** Rogers Parkers craving everyday, affordable Asian opt for this adorable lavender-and-orange storefront. From the Thai

Read 'em & eat

goreng Southeast Asian fried rice dish, flavored with chilies, garlic, cumin, coriander, egg, chicken and shrimp

pancit Filipino rice noodles

sambal condiment made with chili peppers, salt and brown sugar typically found in Malaysia

Side dish

Make me a match
Use this cheat sheet before you hit a BYOB.

African Match African meat 'n' heat with light-bodied reds, which are low in alcohol with gobs of fruit. Try 2005 Georges DuBoeuf's Beaujolais Fleurie; it will allay the ouch. *$12 at Binny's (3000 N Clark St between Barry and Wellington aves, 773-935-9400).*

Chinese Sugar is everywhere in Asian cooking (sweet marinades, oyster sauce). Sweet needs sweet, so go with a versatile and juicy Riesling like 2005 Loosen's "Dr. L." *$13 at Whole Foods (1000 W North Ave at Sheffield Ave, 312-587-0648).*

Indian Choose a crisp white wine as a backdrop to the flavors and aromas of your many courses. Try 2006 Santa Julia's Torrontes. *$11 at Sam's Wines & Spirits (1720 N Marcey St at Willow St, 312-664-4394).*

Korean The *banchan* (those innumerable side dishes) can be mighty salty. Use a pinot noir that's high in acidity, such as 2004 Chanson's Bourgogne Rouge. *$13 at Whole Foods.*

Mexican Everyone brings beer. You want wine. Bring the wine world's "beer"—fizzy, off-dry Spanish cava. We like NV Aurelio Cabestrero's "1+1=3" Brut. *$12 at Wine Discount Center (1826 N Elston Ave between Cortland and Willow sts, 773-489-3454).*

Middle Eastern Perk up those chickpeas and cut the fat of olive oil and meat with a Loire Chinon, a fruity red made of cabernet franc. We're partial to 2004 Charles Joguet's "Cuvée Terroir." *$16 at Binny's.*

Sushi Sushi's badass sidekick is Austrian Grüner Veltliner. Is it the flavor of green fruits? The white-pepper finish? Either way, 2005 Loimer's "Lois" Groovee has it all. *$13 at Whole Foods.*

Thai Pair the five Thai flavors of spicy, sour, sweet, salty and bitter with white wines—those low in alcohol, high in acidity and with a hair's breadth of sweetness—that can take anything, such as 2005 Viña Nora's Albariño. *$15 at UnCork-It! (393 E Illinois St at McClurg Ct, 312-321-9400).*

Vietnamese Unorthodox but delicious is NV Alvear Fino Sherry, a fortified, dry white. The extra hooch works with broths, but finos also complement vegetables, fish and noodles. *$12 at Howard's Wine Cellar (1244 W Belmont Ave at Lakewood Ave, 773-248-3766).*

portion of the menu, go with the crunchy spring roll and the panang curry packed with heat. Of the Japanese options, the deep-fried spicy tuna roll is delicious, nigiri cuts are generous and fresh, and maki are tasty though standard. One exception: Sweet-potato maki, usually bland, is pimped out with green onions, cream cheese and tempura crunch, and slathered in wasabi mayo and eel sauce. Not so authentic but, oh, the creamy goodness. *6632 N Clark St at Wallen Ave (773-761-6666). El: Red to Loyola. Bus: 22 (24hrs), 36, 151 (24hrs), 155. Metra: Union Pacific North Line to Rogers Park. Lunch, dinner. Average nigiri: $2.*

▼ **BYOB Indie Café** This small Thai-Japanese spot in Edgewater packs in crowds who come for the artfully prepared dishes that stand out from typical neighborhood Asian. Gems include the Massaman curry made with lemongrass, coriander and garlic; chicken- and prawn-studded smoked chili combo; and "Metallica" maki made with scallops, spicy mayo and black tobiko. If the higher-than-average prices are off-putting, try the lunch specials, which include three-course deals for just $6 to $12. *5951 N Broadway St between Thorndale and Elmdale Aves (773-561-5577). El: Red to Thorndale. Bus: 36, 147, 151 (24hrs). Lunch, dinner (closed Mon). Average main course: $11.*

☉ **Joy Yee's Noodles** The Joy Yee miniempire took root in Evanston back in 1993 and continues to pack in everyone from students to local office stiffs who loosen up with platter-size portions of pan-Asian food. The menu's a bit less adventurous here than at the Chinatown outpost, but we still stop in for mussels with black-bean sauce, garlicky chicken with string beans and gargantuan bowls of udon-noodle soup. And it wouldn't seem right to leave without a pastel-colored bubble tea from the spot that claims to have introduced them to Chicagoland. *521 Davis St, Evanston (847-733-1900). El: Purple to Davis. Bus: 201 Central/Ridge, 205 Chicago/Golf. Lunch, dinner. Average main course: $9. ● Additional locations at 1335 S Halsted St (312-997-2128) and 2159 S China Pl (312-328-0001).*

▼ ♨ **Koi Chinese & Sushi** Even though this isn't the place for a Chinese or Japanese cuisine purist, the food can be unexpectedly good, especially the Szechuan red snapper, lemon chicken and mu shu wraps. If you dig unpredictability, go for a sushi special plate, a selection of fish compiled on the chef's whim, starting at $40. Don't overlook the selection of specialty teas, which includes rare varieties like *miteag genmaicha*, a mix of *sencha* and brown rice. *624 Davis St, Evanston (847-866-6969). El: Purple to Davis. Bus: 93, 201 (24hrs), 205, Pace 208, Pace 212, Pace 250. Lunch, dinner. Average nigiri: $2. Average main course: $11.*

▼ ✳ **Le Lan** *2007 Eat Out Award Critics' Pick, Best play on surf-and-turf (Wagyu beef carpaccio with trout roe)* Co-owners Roland Liccioni and Arun Sampanthavivat may have reputations that precede them, but their chef de cuisine at this upscale Asian spot, Bill Kim, has proved his merit as one of Chicago's brightest new(ish) talents. Kim cooked under Charlie Trotter and Susanna Foo, which might account for his talent for balancing flavors, especially evident in the Wagyu carpaccio starter, razor-thin slices of buttery beef with dollops of trout roe and a drizzle of thick, soy-spiked balsamic vinegar, and spring rolls packed with briny pink shrimp with smoky pork belly. *749 N Clark St between Superior St and Chicago Ave (312-280-9100). El: Red to Chicago. Bus: 22 Clark (24hrs), 66 Chicago (24hrs). Dinner (closed Sun). Average main course: $26.*

☉ **Lulu's** The dim sum's not really dim sum (dishes are too big and too expensive), but some items, like the moist, steamed *bao* (buns) (essentially *char siu* pork doughnuts), and the one-dimensional but tasty sesame noodles make good appetizers. The Mongolian pork stir fry is sweet but not cloying, spicy but not hot. *804 Davis St, Evanston (847-869-4343). El: Purple to Davis. Bus: 93, 205, Pace 208, Pace 212, Pace 213. Lunch, dinner. Average main course: $9.50.*

(Mulan The central conceit of the Asian-inflected menu at this slick Chinatown spot is that all of the entrées are some variation of surf and turf. Sometimes it works—thin, rare cuts of Wagyu beef are paired with lobster mashed potatoes—but often the combos seem arbitrary (duck breast comes with wonton noodles, enochi mushrooms and krill shrimp). Apart from a watercress and pea shoot salad, the menu offers no meatless options. Save room for stellar desserts like green-tea cheesecake with panko-coated fried bananas, wasabi-spiked simple syrup and diced cucumber. *2017 S Wells St between 18th St and Cermak Rd (312-842-8282). El: Red to Cermak-Chinatown. Bus: 21 Cermak, 62 Archer (24hrs). Dinner. Average main course: $23.*

▼ Paradise Japanese This Japanese-Korean restaurant's decor is a metaphor for the kitchen's food: nothing too flashy. The flavors of the many turns on fish are subtle, and the presentations are easy on the eyes. Fish is fresher than tomorrow (the sea urchin is especially tender), but the Korean dishes—such as *bi bam nang myun*, cold, fiery noodles—are the menu's thunderclap. Service brings a happy mix of wizened sushi chefs and youthful servers. The restaurant is attached to next door's Paradise Beauty Shop & Sauna—a rubdown makes for a fine dessert. *2916 W Montrose Ave between Francisco Ave and Richmond St (773-588-1989). El: Brown to Francisco. Bus: 78 Montrose. Lunch (Mon–Sat), dinner. Average nigiri: $2.50.*

▼ Penang This national chain is a dependable pick when dining with a group with varied tastes. The menu spans Asia, including esoteric Malaysian specialties such as oyster omelette and water spinach stir-fried in spicy shrimp paste. Other tasty takes include the Indian *roti* pancake with curry dipping broth, Chinese-style onion duck, *ayam rendang* (chicken chunks simmered in an Indianish coconut curry) and crispy red snapper done Thai-style with tangy tamarind lemongrass sauce. There are also Japanese offerings, from *udon* noodle soup to grocery store–quality sushi. *2201 S Wentworth Ave at Cermak Rd (312-326-6888). El: Red to Cermak-Chinatown. Bus: 21 Cermak, 62 Archer (24hrs). Lunch, dinner. Average main course: $11.*

BYOB ▼ ✳ ☺ Penny's Noodle Shop Purists may scoff at the ho-hum offerings, but this long-time favorite continues to pack in crowds who may prefer their *pad se eu* come a little more Anglofied than authentic. You'll find perfectly fine versions of standard noodle and rice dishes like *lad nar* (crispy wide noodles sauteed with veggies and topped with gravy) and Chinese fried rice. Vegetarians will do well choosing from inspired sides like watercress with garlic bean sauce and chilled steamed broccoli with dijon-soy dressing. *3400 N Sheffield Ave at Roscoe Ave (773-281-8222). El: Red, Brown, Purple (rush hrs) to Belmont. Bus: 22 Clark (24hrs), 77 Belmont (24hrs). Lunch, dinner. Average main course: $6. ● Additional locations at 1542 N Damen Ave (773-394-0100) and 950 W Diversey Pkwy (773-281-8448).*

BYOB ☺ Ping Pong A lone goldfish in a bowl is the only decoration the art-gallery-esque room has—that is, if you don't count the tricked-out, fashionista-boy servers. The pan-Asian fare is just as stylish, but thankfully more complex. The lettuce cups pair spicy chicken with ginger, peanuts and a spark of lime. Other delectable choices include the golden

calamari, gently spiced with chilies, and a perfectly tender Chilean sea bass in a soy-riesling sauce that was a tad too sweet. *3322 N Broadway between Aldine Ave and Buckingham Pl (773-281-7575). El: Brown, Purple (rush hrs), Red to Belmont. Bus: 36, 77 (24hrs), 152. Dinner. Average main course: $10.*

▼ (✳ Red Light The only problem at this pan-Asian West Loop stalwart is what to order; the vast menu is packed with tempting options. We love starting with the five-spice ribs, the octopus-and-avocado kimchi salad and the crunchy calamari-tangerine salad. Next, we go for the fisherman's stew (it's the miso-lobster chili broth that makes it), the pork chop with thick black-vinegar demi-glace and the peanut-studded panang-beef curry. *820 W Randolph St between Halsted and Green Sts (312-733-8880). El: Green, Pink to Clinton. Bus: 8 Halsted, 20 Madison. Lunch (Mon–Fri), dinner. Average main course: $21.*

(Republic Restaurant & Lounge Sushi purists no doubt will haggle about the finer points of the sashimi. But even the biggest cynic will give props to Republic for one thing: With its sleek white bar, curved banquette and oversize flat-screen airing anime, this restaurant has succeeded in making the Four Points Sheraton—believe it or not—sexy. Stick with signature maki (like the namesake that balances sweet unagi sauce with pungent cilantro) and cooked dishes such as the lemongrass shrimp; ours was perfectly cooked and packed plenty of bite. *58 E Ontario St at Rush St (312-440-1818). El: Red to Grand. Bus: 22 (24hrs), 66 (24hrs), 125. Lunch, dinner. Average main course: $16.*

▼ ✳ Shine & Morida Combination Chinese-sushi restaurants are like '80s band reunions: They rarely work. As if to detract from this universal truth, the folks behind this Lincoln Park favorite have designed a room that's so slick it steals all the attention away from the food. However, the thick

Rosy glow You don't have to put on the Red Light to enjoy these Pan Asian eats.

Full plate Minimalism meets the South Loop at Tamarind.

Generous sushi cuts are tasty and the signature duck soup is a standout. *614 S Wabash Ave between Harrison and Balbo Sts (312-379-0970). El: Red to Harrison. Bus: 2, 6, 10, 29, 36, 146. Lunch, dinner. Average main course: $13.*

⏱ **Tatsu** A Thai-sushi spot might seem like a welcome change of pace across a stretch of Italian red-sauce joints. And it is—just so long as you stick to the Thai food. The sushi we tried here was mediocre at best. But the chicken satay in the sampling platter was perfectly tasty. Ditto for the curry fried rice, which arrived with plump cubes of tofu. The extensive cocktail list may tempt you to end your meal with a nightcap—a fine choice, but Mario's Italian Ice is right next door. *1062 W Taylor St between Carpenter and Aberdeen Sts (312-733-8933). El: Blue to Racine. Bus: 7, 12, 60 (24hrs). Lunch (Mon–Fri), dinner. Average main course: $8.*

⏱ **Tien Giang** Skip the Chinese side of the menu and dive into Vietnamese specialties like young papaya salad with pork, shrimp and a bright *nuoc cham* dressing. The famous fish sauce-chili-lime-garlic-ginger blend also makes an appearance on various bun or rice-noodle plates, including peanutty, grilled, lemongrass beef. *Banh xeo* (often called "happy pancake") is extracrispy here, and should be wrapped in the lettuce leaves and herbs. *1104–06 W Argyle St at Winthrop Ave (773-275-8691). El: Red to Argyle. Bus: 36, 81 (24hrs), 92, 147, 151 (24hrs). Lunch, dinner (closed Thu). Average main course: $9.*

▼ ❬ **Viet Bistro and Lounge** Chef-owner Daniel Nguyen, formerly of Uptown's Pasteur, says he's "taking ideas from all over the world but using what I know about Vietnamese food." The results: specials such as Japanese-tinged lobster-avocado roll, seaweed salad with baby shrimp, and label-defying dishes like pinot noir–marinated beef shish kebabs skewered with fresh pineapple, bell peppers and cherry tomatoes. *1344–46 W Devon Ave between Wayne and Glenwood Aves (773-465-5720). Bus: 22 (24hrs), 36, 147, 151 (24hrs), 155. Dinner. Average main course: $12.*

⏱ **Wow Bao** The "wow" factor at this take-out joint dedicated to *bao* (steamed Asian buns) could be anything: It could be the fluffy *bao* stuffed with sweet, dark-red barbecue pork, spicy Mongolian beef or Thai curry chicken. It could be the pomegranate ginger ale spiked with sharp slivers of fresh ginger. But it's probably the mere fact that you're eating so well at a fast-food restaurant in a mall. *Water Tower Place, 835 N Michigan Ave between Pearson and Chestnut Sts (312-642-5888). El: Red to Chicago. Bus: 66 (24hrs), 143, 144, 145, 146, 147, 148, 151 (24hrs). Lunch, dinner. Average main course: $3. • Additional location at 175 W Jackson St (312-334-6395).* ∎

slices of yellowtail flavored with fresh cilantro that make up the hamachi carpaccio are good enough to bring your focus back. *901 W Armitage Ave at Fremont St (773-296-0101). El: Brown, Purple (rush hrs) to Armitage. Bus: 8 Halsted, 73 Armitage. Dinner. Average main course: $12.*

Sura The Thai owners behind New York's Peep, Spice and SEA have a flair for slick and stylish dining rooms and cheap and tasty eats. This *Jetsons*-esque Chicago outpost seems no different. Small plates of Asian-fusion creations average around five bucks a pop, making it easy to go nuts with a menu that includes coconut-crusted shrimp, duck crêpes and crispy ginger calamari. *3124 N Broadway between Barry Ave and Briar Pl (773-248-7872). El: Brown, Purple (rush hrs), Red to Belmont. Bus: 22 (24hrs), 36, 77 (24hrs). Lunch, dinner. Average small plate: $5.*

▼ ☀ **Sushisamba Rio** Not only is the plush rooftop patio with a 40-foot bar, sharp sound system, sofas and stools perfect for a nightcap (or night-starter) but it's great for sashimi as well. We're not crazy about the rice, so skip the nigiri in favor of slick cuts of the day's fresh catch. For a break from the mundane happy hour rituals that abound downtown, the $10 bento box promo offered from 5-7pm is a good deal, but it's Wednesday nights after 10pm that this slick spot turns booty-rific for "Favela nights," a weekly party driven by Rio rhythms and performance artists. *504 N Wells St between Illinois St and Grand Ave (312-595-2300).El: Brown, Purple (rush hrs) to Merchandise Mart. Bus: 65, 125, 156. Lunch, dinner. Average main course: $20.*

▼ **Tamarind** This cute South Loop spot is part slick, part casual, with soothing bamboo-decked green walls and a staff that's eager to please. Jump around the massive, multicultured menu and you'll find great dishes across the board, from Chinese soup dumplings to ponzu-drizzled sashimi to Vietnamese-style grilled lemongrass beef.

Wow factor Expect more from your fast-food lunch at Wow Bao.

Polish

See also: *German*

Everything's better with bacon... even the hearty pierogi studded with onions from Pierogi Factory.

⊙ **Andrzej Grill** If you're still living at your mama's house for her home-cooked meals, then this tiny family-run Polish hideaway is for you. Navigate your way through gargantuan dishes of crispy fried potato pancakes, soft potato dumplings and pierogi, all of which are made more incredible when slathered with sour cream. (What isn't?) Pork and veal dishes rule the dinner menu, but don't miss the shaved beet salad or crêpes filled topped with powdered sugar. Plus, with the TV blaring and family feuds in the kitchen, you'll feel right at home. *1022 N Western Ave between Augusta Blvd and Cortez St (312-489-3566). El: Blue to Division. Bus: 49 (24hrs), X49, 66, 70. Lunch, dinner (closed Sun). Average main course: $7.50.*

⊙ **Angelica's** You may find it daunting to sit under paintings of severe Polish street scenes, but suck it up and savor Angelica's tasty chow at Perestroika-era prices. Start with the excellent $2 soup (cucumber, white borscht, etc.), all house-made and served with serious bread for sopping. Hand-wrapped pierogi are sauced with warm bacon fat while "Beef Roll with Pickle and Bacon Inside" is a hunk of toothsome meat, drowned in gravy and served alongside full-flavored buckwheat. Of the many Polish brews, Browar Lomza proves a decent match for this satisfying comfort food. *3244 N Milwaukee Ave between Belmont Ave and School St (773-736-1186). El: Blue to Belmont. Bus: 56, 77 (24 hrs), 82. Lunch, dinner. Average main course: $8.*

BYOB Halina's Polish Delights This Polish staple's simple, superb soups include creamy mushroom and borscht in a teacup, delivering a blast of beet and an unexpected "egg roll" of liver paste on the side. The Polish Plate features the greatest hits of comfort foods: cabbage rolls, pork cutlet, tangy *kielbasa*, pierogi and dumplings. Surveying neighboring tables manned by Polish-speakers inspired us to order a delicious meaty pork shank with horseradish and sides of housemade pickles and sauerkraut. If you choose not to BYOB, sip a glass of *kompot*, a traditional Polish drink made by boiling dried

Read 'em & eat

***borscht* (also *borsch*)** Polish or Russian beet soup; it can contain meat or other vegetables, and is served hot or cold

***paczki* (PUNHCH-kee)** marmalade- or cream-filled doughnuts traditionally eaten on Fat Tuesday before Lent

***pierogi* (peer-OH-gee)** noodle dumpling filled with finely chopped ingredients, like pork and onion or mushroom and cabbage

Comfy cozy Hearty food is served in ski lodge-esque digs at Smak-Tak Restaurant.

fruits with sugar and water. *5914 W Lawrence Ave between Marmora and Mason Aves (773-205-0256). El: Blue to Jefferson Park. Bus: 81 Lawrence (24hrs), 91 Austin. Lunch, dinner. Average main course: $11.*

⊙ **Pierogi Factory** Stand-outs among the dozen varieties of pierogi at this Lakeview eatery include hearty potato and cheese, tangy sweet cabbage and desserty plum. All can be either boiled or deep-fried, and the savory options taste even better topped with optional bacon, sour cream and grilled onions. Other traditional Polish treats— pyzy (potato dumplings) with ground beef and pork, stuffed cabbage, and borscht—are nearly as satisfying. You can eat with plastic utensils at a handful of tables or opt for fast take-out, plus bring home frozen pierogi, chocolates and tea. *1034 W Belmont Ave at Kenmore Ave (773-325-1015). El: Red, Brown, Purple (rush hrs) to Belmont. Bus: 77 Belmont (24hrs), 22 Clark (24hrs). Lunch, dinner. Six-piece order of pierogi: $5 .*

⊙ **Smak-Tak Restaurant** *Smak tak* translates to "delicious, yes!" in Polish, and we're not about to disagree after sampling sauerkraut pierogi flecked with tint pieces of mushroom, crispy potato pancakes that rival our grandma's, and stuffed cabbage rolls with tangy tomato sauce. It's all served up in a Jefferson Park spot with a vibe that's more ski lodge than diner—just the kind of cozy place to warm up in when the weather turns nippy. *5961 N Elston Ave between Mason and Austin Aves (773-763-1123). Bus: 56A Milwaukee, 68 Northwest Highway, Pace 270. Lunch, dinner. Average main course: $10.*

Staropolska From the looks of it—booths, a counter/bar, coffee cups upturned on saucers—this bright, homey spot could pass for an all-American diner. That is, if the Polish words on the menu and coming from the TVs don't tip you off otherwise. If you're not dining in, visit the deli next door and stock up on the full-flavored, crackly-skinned housemade sausage. Throw in some herring (served with crisp apples in cream) and pillowy potato pierogis. Most of this stuff can be found on the "Polish plate" served in the dining room, piled together with mashed potatoes and drowned in a tomatoey sour cream sauce that's the best part of the dish. *3028 N Milwaukee Ave between Ridgeway and Lawndale Aves (773-342-0779). El: Blue to Belmont. Bus: 56, 76, 77. Breakfast, lunch, dinner. Average main course: $8.*

🔥 **Szalas** Packed with kitschy decorations, this massive A-frame building is like some kind of Polish theme park, with everything from a working water wheel to a stuffed elk head. Most of the building materials and decorations were brought directly from the Polish highlands, a place that serves as the inspiration for the menu. Stick with delicious, hearty dishes like wild rabbit in chardonnay cream sauce or the Highlander's special (potato pancake topped with beef goulash). Attempts at contemporary twists, like a Polish pizza bread with ketchup instead of tomato sauce, are downright weird. *5214 S Archer Ave between Kenneth and Kilbourn Aves (773-582-0300). El: Orange to Pulaski. Bus: 62 Archer (24hrs). Lunch, dinner. Average main course: $14.* ∎

Seafood

See also: *Contemporary American, Classic American, Japanese, Pan Asian*

✳ B **Blue Water Grill** Joel Dennis, Rick Tramonto's right-hand man at TRU for three years, is the executive chef at this New York transplant. Keep an eye out for signs of Dennis's affection for sustainable foods and farmers' market finds with dishes like line-caught halibut with morels and fava beans; and cod covered with chickpea puree, chorizo, tomato and dusted with espelette pepper. *520 N Dearborn St between Illinois and Grand Aves (312-777-1400). El: Red to Grand. Bus: 22 (24hrs), 29, 36, 65. Brunch (Sun), lunch (Sun–Fri), dinner. Average main course: $28.*

Bubba Gump Shrimp Co. This tourist-packed, Disneyland-like version of a rickety New Orleans shrimp shack sports all the proper decorative contrivances like chipping paint and seafaring kitsch, a zydeco soundtrack and the requisite menu of shrimp dishes and other "Dixieland favorites" like baby back ribs and barbecue pork. Clothing, stuffed shrimp dolls and "Run Forest Run" license plates are sold in the gift shop. *Navy Pier, 700 E Grand Ave at Lake Shore Dr (312-252-4867). Bus: 2, 29, 65, 66 (24hrs), 124. Lunch, dinner. Average main course: $20.*

☉ **Calumet Fisheries** This seafood smoke shack was born when the steel industry was thriving and the area was populated by hungry day laborers. Set at the base of the famous "Blues Brothers" (95th Street) bridge, this little white box is still smoking and frying up some great seafood. Loyal customers come from all over for the smoked shrimp, but leave room for the smoked fish available by special order only. Usually you'll see folks sitting in their cars eating fried shrimp and fish out of paper bags, a quintessential part of the experience. *3259 E 95th St between Chicago and Ewing Aves (773-933-9855). Bus: 26 South Shore Express. Metra: Electric Line to 93rd/South Chicago. Lunch, dinner. Average main course: $7.*

Cape Cod Room This seafood restaurant has been the flagship of the Drake Hotel's dining program since 1933. Red-checkered tablecloths, uniformed waiters and nautical paraphernalia are all presented without a hint of irony, which is why it may be the only restaurant in Chicago where you can, and should, order throwback dishes like lobster Thermidor or Dover sole prepared tableside. *140 E Walton Pl at Michigan Ave (312-787-2200). El: Red to Chicago. Bus: 3, X4, 10, 26, 66 (24hrs), 125, 143, 144, 145, 146, 147, 151 (24hrs). Lunch, dinner. Average main course: $25.*

✳ B **Davis Street Fishmarket** It's critical to scan the giant chalkboards for fishmonger and chef Charlie Raygoza's extensive list of new arrivals from the coasts, Alaska and Lake Superior. His faithful takes on Louisiana Cajun and breaded Calabash standbys deliver, but everything from Florida is a good bet, too. The rosemary, whole pan-fried red snapper and grilled red grouper are exceptional. Add the raw bar and eclectic beer selections, and it's nearly impossible to leave room even for the delectable, buttery bread pudding with whiskey caramel sauce. *501 Davis St, Evanston (847-869-3474). El: Purple to Davis. Bus: 93, 201 (24hrs), 205, Pace 208, Pace 212, Pace 250. Brunch (Sun), lunch, dinner. Average main course: $18.*

Jumbo shrimp
Calumet Fisheries packs
the portions high.

Hagen's Fish Market This old-school, full-service fishmonger has flair that's a little bit country and a little bit Scandinavian. Inside there's a fish counter (half fresh, half smoked), and a small grocery featuring Scandinavian staples like *lutefisk* and herring. Indulge your yen for deep-fried eats with the juicy sea scallops, spicy popcorn shrimp, hush puppies and clam strips. Don't even try to resist the allure of the elusive deep-fried cheese curd. There's no seating inside, but orders are packed in specially designed bags to keep your fish crispy and hot until you get home. *5635 W Montrose Ave at Parkside Ave (773-283-1944). Bus: 78 Montrose, 85 Central. Breakfast, lunch, dinner. Average main course: $5.*

✳ **Half Shell** "We close when we feel like closing" and "Nothin' but cash, no exceptions" are among the oh-so-perfect-for-the-setting sayings we overheard in just one night at this 39-year-old, subterranean spot. Grab a table in the tiny Christmas light–strewn room and start out with the "Mulligan stew" and an order of crispy calamari. For more fried goodness, order the "Thirty-Two Pointer" for an entrée—a crunchy pile of smelts, perch, frog legs, clam strips and fat shrimp. And if you're looking to crack some crab, splurge on the massive, meaty king legs. *676 W Diversey Pkwy between Orchard and Clark Sts (773-549-1773). El: Brown, Purple (rush hrs) to Diversey. Bus: 8, 22 (24hrs), 36, 76. Lunch, dinner. Average main course: $15.*

✳ **Hugo's Frog Bar** This seafood fave not only shares the kitchen of Gibson's Steakhouse but also the slick tie-and-blazer crowd. The boardroom–meets–Rat Pack decor is full of dark wood, leather booths, and career servers hoisting huge trays with succulent and sweet Alaska king crab legs, giant Australian lobster tails and massive porterhouses. Old-school classics are prepared well; a few even qualify as addictive. We like the clams casino (baked clams topped with bread crumbs and bacon), the frog legs with garlic butter and the smoked salmon—which is heat-smoked rather than cured. *1024 N Rush St between Oak St and Bellevue Pl (312-640-0999). El: Red to Clark/Division. Bus: 36 Broadway, 70 Division. Lunch, dinner. Average main course: $25.*

Crustacean infatuation
Shellfish is king at Shaw's Crab House.

★ B **Joe's Seafood, Prime Steaks and Stone Crab** You should feel like a king when you're paying through the nose for a steakhouse experience. The service should be top-notch, the atmosphere classy and the food stellar. This place hits each mark. Start with one of the signature stone crabs, the sugar prawns and a delicious chopped salad that could easily feed two. Go straight to the bone-in New York strip, perfect when ordered charred medium-rare. Blackened mahi mahi is juicy and just spicy enough. Key lime pie is puckeringly sweet for those who like a hit-you-over-the-head finish. *60 E Grand Ave at Wabash Ave (312-379-5637). El: Red to Grand. Bus: 29, 36, 65. Brunch (Sat, Sun), lunch, dinner. Average main course: $30.*

✳ **King Crab** If you can stand the cheesy '80s rock and crowds that love coupling those tunes with mai tais, this seafood stalwart is worth a visit. Weekly deals include a pound of meaty king crab legs for $18.95 on Sundays and Mondays, but you can get daintier snow crab, massive Dungeness crab, and shrimp or fish prepared every conceivable way for decent prices any day of the week. Skip table service as well and grab a stool at the bar to fill up on beer and oysters. *1816 N Halsted St at Willow St (312-280-8990). El: Red to North/Clybourn. Bus: 8 Halsted, 72 North. Lunch, dinner. Average main course: $16.*

Nick's Fishmarket Peanut butter and jelly. Romance and…fish. At least that's the vibe at this upscale Chase Plaza–level institution, where the only thing that could get in the way of a couple's canoodling is the single long-stemmed rose that's artfully placed on their table. It's common to see couples feeding each other forkfuls of crispy and bright citrus-ginger salmon, deep-red slices of seared tuna and clams casino, a tasty dish even if the clams only serve as a vehicle for garlicky slabs of bacon. *1 Bank One Plaza at Monroe St (312-621-0200). El: Blue, Red to Monroe; Brown, Green, Purple (rush hrs), Pink, Orange to Madison. Bus: 3, 4 (24hrs), 14, 20, 26, 60 (24hrs), 124, 127, 145, 147, 148, 151 (24hrs), 157. Lunch (Mon–Fri), dinner (closed Sun). Average main price: $28.*

✳ **Oceanique** It's tough to keep a comfortable, laid-back vibe while serving upscale food, but this Evanston favorite does it. Chef-owner Mark Grosz didn't bring with him the pretension of former employer Le Francais, but he did bring the skill with classic (albeit pricy) Euro dishes. Close to ten different seafood entrées are offered on any given night, and while the multi-ingredient preparations border on overwhelming, Grosz somehow manages to balance flavors while completely flipping off subtlety. Big portions means you may not be tempted to follow the delicious savory fare with dessert. *505 Main St, Evanston (847-864-3435). El: Purple to Main. Bus: 200, 201 (24hrs), 205. Dinner (closed Sun). Average main course: $28.*

▼ (**Raw Bar** If we were psychologists, we'd diagnose this place as being bipolar. The front room is a boisterous bar; the dining room is a serene, candlelit venue for local cabaret acts. But whichever vibe you prefer, the menu is the same: Meaty crab legs are a standout from the raw bar, chunky crab cakes are topped with a sharp chive mayo, and juicy salmon filets are flanked by perfectly grilled shrimp. The menu also contains some Middle Eastern dishes, of which the Egyptian chicken is juicy and flavorful. *3720 N Clark St between Waveland Ave and Grace St (773-348-7291). El: Red to Addison. Bus: 22 (24hrs), 36, 152. Lunch, dinner. Average main course: $14.*

Shaw's Crab House There are so many seasonal seafood choices here, flown in from Atlantic, Gulf and Pacific coasts, it is hard to go wrong. Those with large appetites should opt for "Rocky's Lobster Deal" ($34.95), a traditional East Coast lobster broil, which includes a cup of lobster bisque, Maine lobster, corn on the cob, red bliss potatoes, a side of coleslaw and a slice of key lime pie. You'll also find oysters, sushi and sashimi, and—naturally—a bevy of seasonal crab selections, all in a clubby, sophisticated atmosphere. *21 E Hubbard St between State St and Wabash Ave (312-527-2722). El: Red to Grand. Bus: 29, 36, 62 (24hrs), 65. Lunch, dinner. Average main course: $22.* ∎

Read 'em & eat

chubs small, smoked, oily, white-fleshed lake fish

John Dory a delicately flavored fish with a flat body and spiny head found in European waters

mignonette sauce (meen-yawn-AY) condiment made of finely chopped shallots, sherry vinegar and white wine served with raw oysters

sablefish a mild-tasting, white-fleshed fish from the Pacific Northwest

sea bream (known as *orata* in Italian and *daurade* in French) a firm, low-fat fish

skate (also called *ray*) a kite-shaped fish whose fins yield mild sweet flesh

skookum a plump oyster from the Skookum Inlet or Puget Sound that has a smoky-sweet taste

* **Brazzaz** This Brazilian *churrascaria* that's offering an all-you-can-eat onslaught of more than a dozen cuts of spit-roasted meats and endless trips to a veggie-packed salad bar for close to $50. Obligatory caipirinhas and mojitos anchor the cocktail list, but specialty martinis and slick plasma TV screens hint that they're aiming at a style-conscious crowd. *539 N Dearborn St between Grand Ave and Ohio St (312-595-9000). El: Red to Grand. Bus: 22 (24hrs), 36, 65. Lunch (Mon–Fri), dinner. Rodizio service per person: $48.50.*

BYOB * **Buenos Aires Forever** This Argentine grill and sandwich shop is pretty casual for a date (tin ceiling, mustardy walls, original art), but adequate for a laid-back summit of meat lovers. The open kitchen makes the tiny dining room a bit saunalike, but with the heat comes top-notch empanadas and hearty *milanesa* sandwiches. Carnivorous couples should share the *parrillada*, a mixed-grill platter of steak, ribs, sausage and sweetbreads. Solo diners would do well with the Vacio steak, a perfect vehicle for the deep green chimichurri sauce with which this cuisine is synonymous. *939 N Ashland Ave between Augusta Blvd and Walton St (773-486-8081). El: Blue to Division. Bus: 9 (24hrs), X9, 66 (24hrs), 70. Breakfast, lunch, dinner. Average main course: $14.*

(* **Carnivale** See Latin American for review.

▼ (* **Coobah** See Latin American for review.

BYOB **El Llano** See Latin American for review.

▼ ☉ **El Nandu** Order a basket of the crispy, stuffed, savory empanadas and a bottle of Malbec to transport yourself to the owner's homeland of Argentina. Our favorites are the *criolla*, an aromatic blend of ground beef, onions and golden raisins, and the *maiz*, plump with corn, peppers and hard boiled eggs. If you have room, finish off with the *dulce de batata*, a slice of sweet potato paste toned down with a slice of mild cheese. A live band plays tango and bolero music Thursday through Saturday evenings. *2731 W Fullerton Ave between Fairfield and California aves (773-278-0900). El: Blue to California. Bus: 52 Kedzie/California, 74 Fullerton. Lunch (Mon–Sat), dinner. Average main course: $14.*

☉ **Latin Sandwich Café** Sandwiches are the name of the game here, and for good reason: The Chilean versions are assembled on crusty, housemade white bread and feature addictive fillings (such as the pork, avocado and mayonnaise in the creamy "*pernil con palta*"). But we're really smitten with the empanadas, two-handed affairs filled with beef, onions, olives and hard-boiled eggs. If all those carbs put you into a food coma, a full lineup of espresso drinks are on hand to perk you right up. *4009 N Elston Ave between Irving Park Rd and Ridgeway Ave (773-478-0175). El: Blue to Irving Park. Bus: 53 (24hrs), 80, 82. Lunch, dinner. Average main course: $5.*

▼ (* **ñ** A visit to this clubby, dimly lit sister to Tango Sur is a lot like escaping to Buenos Aires—without the

Sea of love Fans of shellfish dig in to hearty platters at Taste of Peru.

airefare. An unconsciously chic gang of international exiles sip mojitos and flirt to tropical grooves at either the tile shard–covered front bar or tables for two. The best of the *picadas* (apps) are the simple, garlicky eggplant and the mixto plate of the lauded empanadas. Soak up the booze with substantial fare like the *vacio*, a grilled skirt steak with chimichurri, or *dos tiras*, tender short ribs. *2977 N Elston Ave at Rockwell St (773-866-9898). Bus: 9, X49, 76, 77 (24hrs). Dinner (Tue–Sat). Average main course: $12.*

BYOB **Rinconcito Sudamericano** Those looking for a more casual Peruvian experience pile in for the sprightly ceviche, big platters of mixed marinated fish brimming with the tart, fresh flavors of lime and jalapeño. Cooked seafood doesn't fare as well (the plump shrimp we ordered arrived in a rich walnut sauce, but it wasn't enough to cover up the overly fishy taste), so focus on the beer-marinated duck instead. *1954 W Armitage Ave between Damen and Winchester Aves (773-489-3126). El: Blue to Western. Bus: 50 Damen, 73 Armitage. Lunch (Tue–Sun), dinner. Average main course: $14.*

BYOB * **Rios d'Sudamerica** Dino Perez's parents have run Peruvian stalwart Rinconcito Sudamericano for

Meating of the minds
Gauchos brandish skewers of prime cuts at Brazzaz.

25 years. His own spot is just a block away. But Perez claims to be moving beyond "old school" Peruvian in favor a "fusion of Peruvian, Argentinean and Brazilian" as well as stylized presentations of classics like *lomo al pisco* (sautéed steak with onions, tomatoes and fried potatoes. Bartenders armed with juices and mixers turn BYO liquors into cocktails. *2010 W Armitage Ave at Damen Ave (773-276-0170). El: Blue to Western. Bus: 50 Damen, 73 Armitage. Dinner (closed Mon). Average main course: $19.*

B ⊙ Ritz Tango Café We don't know what's cuter: the Golden Years couples taking tango lessons five nights a week, or the *de migas*—two-bite ham-and-cheese sandwiches on paper-thin slices of bread. Empanadas are filled with raisins and chicken, heraty *milanesa* sandwiches fit veal between slices of warm focaccia, and a *hojaldre* cake—seven cookie layers held together with caramel— had us doing the tango in our seats. *933 N Ashland Ave between Walton St and Agusta Blvd (773-235-2233). El: Blue to Division. Bus: 9 (24hrs), X9, 66 (24hrs), 70. Breakfast, lunch, dinner. Average main course: $5.*

(Rumba See Latin American for review.

BYOB Taste of Peru Seafood is king at this cozy, casual Peruvian spot, so start with the hefty mixed ceviche of fresh calamari rings, big shrimp, baby octopus and huge mussels and move on to the family-size paella studded with every creature from the sea. Meat eaters will love the *lomo saltado* (tangy, tender, marinated beef strips) sautéed with tomato and onion and topped with a heap of crispy fries to sop up the steak juice. End with sweet, crispy plantains and amazing dulce de leche cookies. *6545 N Clark St between Arthur and Albion Aves (773-381-4540). El: Red to Loyola. Bus: 22 (24hrs), 36, 151 (24hrs), 155. Lunch, dinner. Average main course: $12.* ∎

Read 'em & eat

caipirinha (kai-pee-REEN-ya) a cocktail made of cachaça (a Brazilian sugarcane liquor), lime and sugar

chimichurri a pestolike mixture of oil, garlic, onion and herbs (typically basil and parsley)

entraña skirt steak

farofa seasoned, fried yuca flour

feijoada (fey-ZHOO-ah-dah) a traditional black-bean stew with pork, beef and sausage

moqueca (MO-ke-ka) seafood stew

papas rellenas (pa-PAS ray-ANE-as) deep-fried mashed potatoes stuffed with beef

parrillada (pa-REE-ah-da) an entrée of grilled meats (*parrilla* means "grill") or a restaurant that serves parrillada

peruano tamales cornmeal stuffed with meat, seafood or vegetables, and steamed in banana leaves

rodizio all-you-can-eat restaurant service with an emphasis on skewered meat

Southern

See also: *Classic American*

⊕ **Army & Lou's** More than 60 years old, this Chatham tablecloth spot still serves dependable comfort food. Servers are as sweet as the peach cobbler. Start with the seafood platter, a crispy combo of fried scallops, shrimp and oysters, battered with a cornmeal-flour mix. The "Southern specialties" side of the menu is the way to go. The light brown pan gravy is tasty when poured over tender short ribs and pan-fried pork chops, but the fried chicken should be ordered without it. For sides, go with black-eyed peas and sweet-potato pie. *422 E 75th St between King Dr and Vernon Ave (773-483-3100). El: Red to 79th. Bus: 3, X3, 75. Breakfast, lunch, dinner (closed Tue). Average main course: $9.*

(⊕ **Barbara Ann's BBQ** The sage- and fennel-flecked sausage is custom-made by a local sausage maker, and gets significant smoke time over the smoldering hickory and cherry wood. Rib tips remain the juiciest pork option (over the often drier spare ribs), and also the best value. Skip the beef ribs; spend the dough on "Miss Winters'" outsourced 7UP, sour-cream and chocolate cakes instead. *7617 S Cottage Grove Ave between 76th and 77th Sts (773-651-5300). El: Red to 79th. Bus: 4 (24hrs), X4, 75. Lunch and dinner (Tue–Sat) (closed Sun, Mon). Average main course: $9.*

⊕ **BJ's Market & Bakery** Designed like some sort of cross between Denny's and Burger King—only with a soul-food slant—this South Side minichain may be the only fast-soul-food joint in town. But while the food takes only minutes to arrive at your table, it tastes like it was slowly and carefully cooked over a home stove. With its crispy, golden crust, the mustard-fried catfish is clearly the restaurant's standout dish, but don't discount the juicy smoked chicken, collared greens, pork-studded black-eyed peas or delicious peach cobbler, which puts those other fast-food pies to shame. *8734 S Stony Island Ave at 87th St (773-374-4700). Bus: 28 Stony Island Express, 87 87th. Breakfast, lunch, dinner. Average main course: $7.50.*

B **Blu 47** Don't look for any signs marking this Bronzeville lounge and restaurant. Just follow the train of cars in line for valet. This upscale eatery is hidden on the second floor of a nondescript commercial complex, but the eclectic menu and vibe make this a spot worth seeking out. This is soul food transcended. You'd be hard-pressed to find anything elsewhere like chef David Blackmon's signature bayou catfish, a tasty dish of two crispy filets stuffed with Cajun spiced crabmeat on a bed of grilled vegetables. Reservations are key. *4655 S King Dr at 47th St (773-536-6000). El: Green, Red to 47th. Bus: 3, X3, 47. Brunch (Sun), dinner. Average main course: $18.*

BYOB B ○ **CJ's Eatery** Humboldt Park's cozy, local art–filled spot merges the traditions of Southern cooking with touches of Latin American cuisine. Southern comforts like buttermilk biscuits with gravy, pulled pork and fried catfish dominate. Fresh blueberry lemonade and sweet tea are also offered, as well as the classic combo of chicken and waffles for brunch. *3839 W Grand Ave at Avers Ave (773-292-0990). Bus: 53, 65, 70. Breakfast, brunch (Sat, Sun), lunch, dinner. Average main course: $8.*

⊕ **Dixie Kitchen & Bait Shop** The tin Coca-Cola signs and hanging rusty red wagons come close to gimmickry, but from the time they set down your first basket of Johnnycakes to when you polish off the last bite of peach cobbler, you'll hardly notice. Huge portions of authentic Southern dishes include deep-fried baby catfish, spicy jambalaya studded with andouille sausage and addictive crawfish-corn fritters. And although the place isn't swarming with U. of C. students, most dishes would fit within their budgets. *5225 S Harper Ave between 52nd and 53rd Sts in Harper Court Shopping Center (773-363-4943). Bus: 2, 15, 28, X28 SB, 55 (24hrs), X55. Lunch, dinner. Average main course: $11.* ● *Additional location at 825 Church St, Evanston (847-733-9030).*

⊕ **Edna's** This West Side institution has been serving up stick-to-your-ribs soul food for 30 years. The crispy, black pepper-laced fried chicken is made to order, so expect a 20-minute wait. For sides, go for the biscuits, greens, mac and cheese, candied yams, and black-eyed peas. If you spy glass cake stands on the diner counter filled with triple-layer caramel, chocolate or coconut cake, don't leave without snagging a slice. *3175 W Madison St between Albany and Kedzie Aves (773-638-7079). El: Green to Kedzie. Bus: 20 Madison (24hrs), 52 Kedzie. Breakfast, lunch, dinner (closed Mon, closes 7pm nightly). Average main course: $8.*

✳ **Fat Willy's Rib Shack** Can good barbecue exist on the North Side? Yep. But instead of the South Side tradition of cash 'n' carry, here there's a dining room—a comfy no-frills spot with a beer and wine list, and a house cocktail called the Hogarita (think cran-citrus margarita). For starters, go for the smoky, greasy rib tips and an insanely rich mac and cheese. Move past salads to a slab of baby backs and the beef brisket sandwich with horseradish. *2416 W Schubert Ave between*

Read 'em & eat

chitlins (or chitterlings) fried pig intestines that are eaten alone or added to sauces and soups

étouffée (eh-too-FAY) a spicy shellfish-and-vegetable stew thickened with roux, served over white rice

fricassee a chunky stew made with vegetables and either chicken or veal that has been sautéed in butter; served with rice

gumbo okra soup thickened with roux or filé (powdered sassafras leaves) and filled with tomatoes, onions, and game, poultry or seafood

hot links spicy pork sausages

jambalaya (juhm-buh-LI-yah) Creole dish of rice, tomato, onion, green pepper and other seasonings mixed with chunks of chicken, sausage, ham or seafood

Western and Artesian Aves (773-782-1800). Bus: 49 (24hrs), X49, 76. Lunch, dinner. Average main course: $9.

B ☺ **5 Loaves Eatery** We were picking up the catfish po' boy, wondering how we were going to fit the two-handed affair in our mouth, when it happened: A gentle breeze actually blew the door open, confirming the fact that this is the most charming cafe in South Shore. The main attraction is the crispy po' boys, the tender filets of pan-seared tilapia and the creamy sides of horseradish-and-dill-packed coleslaw. Not up for a full meal? Enjoy coffee and dense slices of lemon pound cake. *2343 E 71st St between Oglesby and Crandon Aves (773-363-0393). Bus: 6, 26, 71. Breakfast, brunch (Sun), lunch, dinner (closed Mon). Average main course: $7.*

Heaven on Seven This homegrown minichain of Creole food is the closest you'll get to New Orleans in Chicago. Bottles of hot sauce take up as much tabletop room as the food—unless you order one of the po' boys (the shrimp is a good bet), which are piled so high they necessitate a knife and fork. Soups like the hearty gumbo stick to the theme. Order one of the margaritas served in a tall, curvy glass, and you'll start feeling like you're on Bourbon Street. *111 N Wabash Ave between Washington and Randolph Sts (312-263-6443). El: Blue to Washington; Red to Lake; Brown, Green, Orange, Pink, Purple (rush hrs) to Randolph. Breakfast, lunch (closed Sun). Average main course: $12.*

☺ **Honey 1 BBQ** The Adams family's style of 'cue employs real wood (rather than gas) to impart smoky flavor on slow-cooked slabs. The father and son–run joint has about 50 tables in the simple dining area, so patrons no longer have to call ahead two hours to request ribs. (That was the case at the duo's last take-out spot.) The turnover means the Adamses are smokin' around the clock. *2241 N Western Ave between Lyndale St and Belden Ave (773-227-5130). El: Blue to Western. Bus: 49 (24hrs), X49, 56, 74. Lunch, dinner (closed Mon). Average main course: $9.*

BYOB ☺ **Lagniappe** This amazin' Cajun spot is primarily a carryout and catering operation, but we'll squeeze into the handful of tables to dig in on the spot. Smoky gumbo is thick with spicy roux base, white rice, baby shrimp and chunks of andouille sausage. Jambalaya is rich with tomato and bright with herbs; collard greens have heat and smoke from flecks of smoked turkey; and the shrimp po' boy is unforgettable. End with a slice of warm pineapple-caramel bread pudding. *1525 W 79th St at Justine St (773-994-6375). Bus: 9 (24hrs), X9, 79 (24hrs), 169. Lunch and dinner (closed Sun, Mon). Average main course: $8.*

☺ **Lem's BBQ** As the best barbecue joints on the South Side do, Lem's requires that you order through bulletproof glass and then take your ribs elsewhere to be devoured (it's take out only). But it would take much more than that to scare away devotees of these spare ribs and rib tips, which have a thin, vinegary sauce heavy with spice, and charred outer edges that hide pink, juicy pork. Honestly, the only truly scary thing here is arriving to find the line snaking out the door. *311 E 75th St between Calumet & Prarie Aves (773-994-2428). El: Red to 79th. Bus: 3, 4 (24hrs), 75. Lunch, dinner (closed Tue). Average main course: $7.*

✳ **Maple Tree Inn** The menu reads like an eclectic tribute to Southern, Cajun and Creole cooking, and the kitchen consistently nails the classics (gumbo, fried green tomatoes, shrimp Creole). There's an oddball spin on some dishes, but it mostly works, particularly with the crawfish étouffée risotto and "loafs" (a.k.a. po' boys) drizzled with melted Brie. The barbecue shrimp served on grits should satiate most Southern

cravings. The restaurant's mantra, "sit long, talk much," translates into long waits on weekend nights, but quick bar service keeps the cold Abita beers coming, so time flies. *13301 Old Western Ave, Blue Island (708-388-3461). Bus: Pace 349. Dinner (closed Wed-Sat). Average main course: $17.*

Merle's Smokehouse The term "barbecue joint" usually brings to mind a hole-in-the-wall with a pitmaster. Not Merle's. With big-screen TVs, an ample bar, and images of Elvis, the ambiance is closer to Applebee's than authentic. What it lacks in atmosphere, it makes up for with decent barbecue at a decent price in a location with decent public transportation and parking. Tables are set with rolls of paper towels so you can get to work on the finger-lickin' meat of your choice. *1727 Benson Ave, Evanston (847-475-7766). El: Purple to Davis. Bus: 201 Central/Ridge (24hrs). Pace 208, Pace 250. Lunch (Sat, Sun), dinner. Average main course: $11.*

☺ **Pearl's Place** Whoever you are, Pearl, thank you. You must be pretty special to have inspired this Creole-influenced soul food restaurant in your name. We've learned the hard way to be patient with the long waits. The fried chicken is so damn juicy and sealed in a crunchy, pepper-flecked exterior; the collard greens so tender and flavorful with pork bits; and the sweet-potato pie so fragrant with cinnamon and nutmeg (fluffy near the middle and caramelized where the filling meets the flaky crust) that we'd wait forever. *3901 S Michigan Ave at Pershing Rd (773-285-1700). El: Green to Indiana. Bus: 1, 29, 39. Breakfast, lunch, dinner. Average main course: $8.*

✳ ☺ **Ribs 'n' Bibs** Ribs—the hickory-smoked variety, to be specific—are the specialty of this Hyde Park house. Choose from "The Boss" (a whole slab) or smaller portions such as the "Ranch Hand" and "Jr. Ranch Hand"—which each come with fries, coleslaw and bread. For a little variety, opt for one of the Chuck Wagon Combos—the "chix 'n' ribs" combo gives you two pieces of fried or barbecued chicken and a half-order of ribs for less than $11. *5300 S Dorchester Ave at E 53rd St (773-493-0400). Bus: 55 Garfield (24hrs), X55 Garfield Express. Lunch, dinner. Average main course: $10.*

(✳ **The Smoke Daddy** *2007 Eat Out Award, Readers' Choice: Best barbecue* Gluttony grabs hold in this kitschy kitchen, and it doesn't let go until the band plays its last bluesy rockabilly note. So skip the brisket, ignore the chicken and resist filling up on the addictive sweet-potato fries: You need to reserve your hunger for "The Rib Sampler." It's a huge plate of baby back ribs, spare ribs and rib tips—a pile so big it might intimidate you. But don't worry: The pink, smoky meat pulls off the bone, so you'll have no trouble cleaning your plate. *1804 W Division St between Wood and Honore Sts (773-772-6656). El: Blue to Division. Bus: 9, X9, 50, 70. Lunch, dinner. Average main course: $15.*

★ **BYOB Smoque BBQ** *2007 Eat Out Award, Critics' Pick: Best butt in town (smoked pork butt)* The Northwest Side finally got its meat hooks on some great barbecue. St. Louis spareribs are near-perfect—juicy, pull-apart tender, with subtle smokiness that doesn't overwhelm the tangy spice rub clinging to the sticky, crunchy exterior. Pillow-soft chicken's slick, seasoned skin gives way to meat that's partially pink from smoke and fully flavorful, but if you must add more oomph, go with the thinner, vinegary sauce of the two options. Don't miss the pork-and-beans or the creamy mac and cheese, which gets a simple crust of bread crumbs. *3800 N Pulaski Rd between Grace St and Avondale Ave (773-545-7427). El: Blue to Irving Park. Bus: 53, 80, X80. Metra: Union Pacific NW to Irving Park. Lunch, dinner. Average main course: $12.*

Finger-lickin' good Have the wipes ready when you dig into The Smoke Daddy's ribs.

⊖ **Soul Queen** You won't need the photographic history on the walls to tell you that this restaurant has been around since the '70s—the decor will tip you off right away. The heavily chandeliered dining room and the crowns on the servers' heads make it clear that owner Helen Maybell Anglin takes the title "Soul Queen" seriously. Once you hit the buffet of sweet corn-bread muffins, tender short ribs, fried chicken and peach cobbler, you'll gladly bow down to the throne. *9031 S Stony Island Ave between 90th and 91st Pls (773-731-3366). Bus: 26, 95E, 100. Lunch, dinner. Average buffet: $7.75.*

⊖ **Soul Vegetarian East** See Vegetarian for review

South Water Kitchen See Contemporary American for review.

❋ **Sweet Baby Ray's** You might be surprised to find a real barbecue joint out past O'Hare, but if you're looking for the type of 'cue that typically gets passed through a bulletproof window served instead at a sit-down restaurant, this is your best bet. There's no skimping on smoke when it comes to the meaty baby back ribs. Skip the blah brisket in favor of molasses-rich baked beans, creamed corn and andouille-packed gumbo. *249 E Irving Park Rd, Wood Dale (630-238-8273). Lunch, dinner. Average main course: $12.*

B ⊖ **Sweet Maple Café** Most weekends you'll find a crowd spilling onto this breakfast spot's sidewalk, watching servers carry plates toppling from the weight of sweet-milk biscuits and bone-in ham. The reward with is housemade muffins; vegetable hash with copious amounts of sautéed onions and peppers; and pancakes with sweet pockets of banana. Don't miss the Southern-inspired dishes like the fried catfish, grits and compact, crispy salmon cakes, all of which are served up on the weekends only. *1339 W Taylor St between Ada and Loomis Sts (312-243-8908). El: Pink, Blue (rush hrs) to Polk. Bus: 7, 60 (24hrs). Breakfast, brunch (Sat, Sun), lunch (Mon–Fri). Average main course: $5.*

♨ **TABLE fifty-two** See Classic American $16 and up for review.

⊖ **TailGators BBQ Smokehouse** You know a 'cue joint means business when giant napkin dispensers are affixed to the walls beside the tables. Expect to get deliciously messy while chowing down on lean but tender Texas-style brisket, hickory-smoked pulled pork, and pink and juicy baby back ribs about which Bobby Flay has raved. The sauce is not housemade (it's Sweet Baby Ray's), but we're still licking our lips and dipping the crispy sweet-potato fries right in it. *6726 N Northwest Hwy between Oshkosh and Oliphant Aves (773-775-8190). Bus: 68 Northwest Hwy, Pace 209. Metra: Union Pacific NW to Edison Park. Lunch (Mon–Sat), dinner (Mon–Fri). Average main course: $9.*

B ⊖ **Wishbone** Southern staples such as real grits and biscuits can be hard to come by in these parts. But this enormous West Loop eatery has made it its mission to bring "mornin' hon" hospitality to the heartland, especially at brunch. We can get down with fruit pancakes and savory corncakes (with some hot sauce), the buttery biscuits, and the spicy (but not hot) andouille chicken sausage. *1001 W Washington Blvd at Morgan St (312-850-2663). Bus: 8, 20 (24hrs), X20. Breakfast, brunch (Sat, Sun), lunch, dinner (Tue–Sat). Average main course: $10. · Additional location at 3300 N Lincoln Ave (773-549-2663).*

★ ⊖ **Uncle John's** *2007 Eat Out Award, Critics' Picks: Best reason to carry Handi Wipes (rib tip–hot links combo)* Arkansas-native Mack Sevier, formerly of Barbara Ann's, is smokin' some of the best stuff in town at this Park Manor spot. Go for the rib tips and hotlinks combo: The rib tips are smoky, extremely juicy and crisp around the edges. The hot links are not for the heatphobic, with searing bits of red chili and smoky, porky, sage-packed flavor—like a spicy breakfast sausage. *337 E 69th St at Calumet Ave (773-892-1233). El: Red to 69th. Bus: 3, 30, 67, 71. Lunch, dinner (closed Sun). Average main course: $9.* ∎

Spanish

See also: *Caribbean, Latin American, Mexican, South American*

Arco de Cuchilleros The trend of cutting-edge Spanish cooking hasn't yet reached this tapas bar, which serves up small plates that are tried-and-true. Chicken croquettes have a hot, crisp crunch that gives way to a creamy center; slices of *tortilla española* are tall and savory; and monkfish flakes apart in its delicious broth. There are some weird dishes on the menu—a cold noodle salad topped with crispy duck—but when the weather is warm and you're sitting in the garden slowly draining a pitcher of sangria, it's easy to let a little misstep slide. *3445 N Halsted St between Newport and Cornelia Aves (773-296-6046). El: Red to Addison. Bus: 8, 22 (24hrs), 36, 152. Dinner (closed Mon). Average small plate: $7.*

Azucar Be prepared to grab a margarita next door at El Cid while you wait for a seat to open at this tapas joint—there's almost always a wait, and the bar remains packed throughout the night. While you're sipping, remind yourself what you're waiting for: spice-rubbed pork with a crunchy sprinkling of pistachio; cheese-and-mushroom–stuffed red peppers plated on a creamy chickpea puree; and a *crema catalana* packed with cinnamon. Resist that second margarita if you can—these are tapas you'll want to remember the next day. *2647 N Kedzie Ave between Milwaukee and Schubert Aves (773-486-6464). El: Blue to Logan Square. Bus: 56 Milwaukee, 76 Diversey. Dinner (Wed–Sun). Average small plate: $7.*

B Bravo Tapas and Lounge This trilevel tapas spot is perfect for sipping sangria and people-watching. Head upstairs for a lofty lounge feel, downstairs for a clubby vibe, or the sidewalk patio if the weather's nice. Tapas like the ultratender grilled calamari, chorizo-studded dates wrapped in bacon, and crispy eggplant sprinkled with sesame seeds, fresh mint and lavender honey are among the best bets. We're not sure the loud music and sparkly topped patrons translate under daylight for brunch and lunch. *2047 W Division St between Damen and Hoyne Aves (773-278-2727). El: Blue to Division. Bus: 49 (24hrs), 50, 70. Brunch (Sat, Sun), dinner. Average small plate: $9.*

Café Ba-Ba-Reeba! Lincoln Park loves its tapas joints, and this is the granddaddy of them all, packing in crowds for a somewhat T.G.I. Tapas feel. The ingredients are fresh and good quality: zesty Manchego, full-bodied olive oil, tangy anchovies and spicy chorizo fill the menu. Thick bacon is wrapped around juicy dates and roasted, and sherry tomato sauce tops tiny, tender meatballs. We can't find a thread of saffron in our paella, but most of the loud, sangria-filled patrons don't seem to mind. *2024 N Halsted St between Armitage and Dickens Aves (773-935-5000). El: Brown, Purple (rush hrs) to Armitage. Bus: 8 Halsted, 73 Armitage. Lunch (Sat, Sun), dinner. Average small plate: $6.*

Café Iberico It's kind of like riding the El: The wait at this always-packed tapas joint can be long and annoying, but once you get inside, things go pretty quickly. Cheap plates of *patatas bravas* (soft, habit-forming cubes of potatoes immersed in a spicy tomato sauce) and *croquetas de pollo* (creamy chicken and ham fritters) arrive at the table almost immediately, dropped like afterthoughts by overworked servers. A plate of Manchego and a pitcher of sangria to tide

you over, and you won't even notice the wait. *737 N LaSalle St between Superior St and Chicago Ave (312-573-1510). El: Brown, Purple (rush hrs), to Chicago. Red to Chicago/State. Bus: 22 (24hrs), 66 (24hrs), 156. Lunch, dinner. Average tapa: $5.*

Emilio's Tapas Bar and Restaurant The namesake chef behind this 12-year-old restaurant knows a thing or two about tapas—the Spaniard was the opening chef for Café Ba-Ba-Reeba!, Chicago's first tapas spot. The classics still rule the show: salty-sweet bacon-wrapped dates in roasted red-pepper sauce, killer garlic potatoes, crusty bread topped with tangy tomatoes and whisper-thin *jamón serrano*, and perfectly grilled shrimp in garlic butter. Skip the too-rich goat cheese–eggplant rolls and the oversauced spicy potatoes, but don't miss the velvety flan. *444 W Fullerton Pkwy at Clark St (773-327-5100). El: Brown, Purple (rush hrs), Red to Fullerton. Bus: 22 (24hrs), 36, 74. Dinner. Average small plate: $7.*

1492 Tapas Bar If we have to explain to you how this place got its name, it's time to go back to school. But if it's tapas you want an education on, the 48 varieties here should be a good primer. Excellent imported meats include smoky links of chorizo. Goat cheese croquettes (fried sans batter) are paired with sticky, sweet balsamic. Paella looks and tastes lackluster, so ignore it. But don't skip dessert. We know, desserts aren't the strong point of tapas joints, but the luscious *creme catalana*? Let's just say it schooled us. *42 E Superior St at Wabash Ave (312-867-1492). El: Red to Chicago. Bus: 36, 66 (24hrs), 143, 144, 145, 146, 147, 148, 151 (24hrs). Lunch, dinner. Average small plate: $7.*

People There's no shortage of small plates in Wicker Park, but this tapas spot has something going for it that the others don't: a vibrant bar scene. It's completely fitting that this place looks more like a tavern than a traditional restaurant because the food is best eaten with a beer in your hand. Crispy *patatas bravas*, simple *tortilla española* and herbal, earthy mushrooms wouldn't wow you if you were sober. But paired with a couple of drinks, they provide you with the nourishment you require. *1560 N Milwaukee Ave between North Ave and Honore St (773-227-9339). El: Blue to Damen. Bus: 50, 56, 72. Dinner. Average small plate: $7.*

Read 'em & eat

al ajillo (ahl ah-HEE-yo) with olives and garlic

al jerez (ahl hehr-EZ) cooked in sherry

albóndigas (ahl BON-dee-gas) meatballs

gambas shrimp or prawns

pintxos (peen-CHO) tapas in Basque

Small but mighty Flavors pop from the tapas at People.

Tapas Barcelona The Spanish *tortilla*? It's great, the oniony egg-and-potato wedge is tender but not mushy. The *pincho de pollo*, chunks of chicken on a skewer? Very nice, especially when slathered with cumin mayo. The cinnamony pudding is a delicious way to end. Yet the real reason to visit this popular Evanston haunt is the patio, an idyllic spot to put away some sangria, and—because it butts up against the patio of a retirement home—maybe even get some sage advice from an elder. *1615 Chicago Ave, Evanston (847-866-9900). El: Purple to Davis. Bus: 201 Central/Ridge (24hrs), 205 Chicago/Golf. Metra: Union-Pacific N to Davis. Lunch (Mon–Sat), dinner. Average small plate: $7.*

B Twist You'd have a hard time doing any twisting in this dark, narrow tapas joint. And you'll have a hard time fitting everything you want to try on your table, so ask your server to bring plates out in waves. On the "twisted" portion of the menu (tapas influenced by other cuisines), skip over the dry ahi tuna and try the punchy jalapeño gnocchi. Of the more traditional tapas, the *tortilla española* is full of salty potatoes and onions; and the stuffed chicken breast oozes with goat cheese and roasted red pepper. *3412 N Sheffield Ave between Roscoe and Clark Sts (773-388-2727). El: Red to Addison. Bus: 22 (24hrs), 77 (24hrs), 152. Brunch (Sat, Sun), dinner. Average small plate: $6.* ■

Steakhouses

See also: *Classic American, Italian/Pizza, South American*

A cut above Steaks are ready for the grill at Smith & Wollensky.

✳ **Carmichael's Chicago Steak House** It doesn't hold up to the big name steakhouses more centrally located in higher-rent districts, but Carmichael's is a good choice if you're on your way to the United Center. On-the-ball service and a warm bread basket with a crock of cheddar cheese help balance out cuts of beef that tend to be more chewy than melt-in-your-mouth. Sides like garlic mashed potatoes are worth saving room for, but be prepared for a bit of sticker shock when all those yummy add-ons are added up. *1052 W Monroe St between Morgan St and Racine Ave (312-433-0025). El: Blue to Racine. Bus: 8, 20 (24hrs), 126. Lunch (Mon–Fri), dinner. Average main course: $25.*

Chicago Chop House This century-old brownstone is a quintessential Chicago steakhouse in every sense of the word. Conventioneers and local businessmen with fat expense wallets head upstairs for white-tablecloth service, pricey wines and 48- or 64-ounce porterhouses fit for a king. We prefer the subterranean piano bar, where every inch of wall is covered with vintage photos of Capone and crew and the high wooden tables are packed with loud storytellers, unapologetic smokers and uncompromising carnivores. *60 W Ontario St between Dearborn and Clark Sts (312-787-7100). El: Red to Grand. Bus: 22 Clark (24hrs), 125 Water Tower Exp. Lunch (Mon–Fri), dinner. Average main course: $30.*

✳ **Chicago Firehouse** Some believe the privilege of dining in a beautiful building rich with history is worth any price. Despite this 1904 fire station location, we still don't understand why the cedar-planked Dover sole with browned butter costs forty bucks. The rest of the menu is fair enough: The CF 104 Tower, tender prosciutto encasing three sprigs of asparagus and mascarpone, is a heavenly start; the hearty pot roast falls apart with the touch of a fork; and a juicy rib-eye is topped with a luscious mixture of shallots and blue cheese. *1401 S Michigan Ave at 14th St (312-786-1401). El: Green, Orange, Red to Roosevelt. Bus: 1, 3, 4 (24hrs), 62 (24hrs). Lunch (Mon–Fri), dinner. Average main course: $25.*

★ ✳ **B Custom House** We're constantly going back and forth on which meal this restaurant does best, and the ever-changing seasonal menus make the decision even more difficult. If only all of our favorite dinner haunts could give us a great breakfast buffet, wonderful lunch and splurgeworthy dinner. Chef Shawn McClain is no slouch with high-quality steaks and chops, but we're smitten with specials like Ahi tuna drizzled with caper-raisin vinaigrette; Hawaiian marlin with littleneck clams, housemade bacon and sweet corn chowder; and seasonal sides such as baby summer squash. *500 S Dearborn St at Congress Pkwy (312-523-0200). El: Brown, Orange, Pink, Purple (rush hrs) to Library, Red to Harrison. Bus: 6, 29, 36. Breakfast (Mon–Sat), lunch (Mon–Fri), brunch (Sun), dinner. Average main course: $24.*

★ **B David Burke's Primehouse** Has star chef David Burke given Chicago a steakhouse like no other? Well, we've definitely never come across a crab cake quite so deliciously unique (the impeccable meat is shaped like a maki roll), and the popovers that stand in for bread are a nice twist. And while desserts are creative (fill your own doughnuts), over-the-top desserts are de rigueur at steakhouses. So is it different? Yes. But not so different that your parents won't like it. Which is good, because you'll want them to take you here again and again. *616 N Rush St at Ontario St (312-660-6000). El: Red to Grand. Bus: 36, 125, 151 (24hrs). Breakfast, brunch (Sat, Sun), lunch (Mon–Fri), dinner. Average main course: $33.*

Drake Bros. This unsung steakhouse doesn't exactly reinvent the wheel, but that's no sin when the steaks are this incredible. Great steaks come at a price, but you won't mind the hefty tab after tasting the smooth, smoky, dry-aged New York strip, which just might be the best steak we've ever eaten. Not far behind is the butter-soft, marrow-encrusted sirloin, so rich it could double for dessert. Ask for the housemade mashed potatoes and chipotle-spiked corn on the side, and a prime table by the window. *140 E Walton Pl at Michigan Ave (312-932-4626). El: Red to Chicago. Bus: 10, 66, 143, 144, 145, 146, 147, 148, 151 (24hrs), 157. Breakfast, brunch (Sun), lunch, dinner (Tues–Sun). Average main course: $40.*

♨ **EJ's Place** Half Italian steakhouse, half North Woods supper club, EJ's Place offers the perfect combination of upscale Chicago and laid back Wisconsin to its North Shore clientele. Old school bartenders and waiters give the place a genuine feel. The menu is a collection of entirely predictable steakhouse plates prepared with the least amount of fuss. *10027 Skokie Blvd, Skokie (847-933-9800). Bus: 201 Central/Ridge, 205 Chicago/Golf, Pace 422. Dinner. Average main course: $27.*

(✴ ♨ **Erie Café** Businessmen fill every seat and corner of this hidden West Loop restaurant, where they grab bottles of Chianti with one hand and thick cigars with the other. It's not the most conducive setting for eating dinner, but if you must, ignore the flavorless housemade ravioli and make a meal out of the baked clams and a steak. The meat comes completely unadorned, but it's juicy and as big as your plate—and if you're a real man, that's exactly the way you'll like it. *536 W Erie St at Larrabee St (312-266-2300). Bus: 65 Grand, 66 Chicago (24hrs). Mon–Sat 11am–11:30pm; Sun 3–11pm. Average main course: $30.*

✴ **Fulton's on the River** *2007 Eat Out Award, Readers' Choice: Best outdoor dining* Levy Restaurants' latest contribution to Chicago's culinary scene is as much about the view as it is about the food. Fortunately, both are worth a visit. The menu—equal parts seafood and steak—is nothing out of the ordinary, but everything is of exquisite quality. King crab legs from the extensive raw bar are fresh and sweet, filet mignon is tender, and a side dish of roasted butternut squash with pumpkin butter and goat cheese is so decadent you can skip dessert. Make your trip worth the price, ask for a window seat. *315 N LaSalle St at the Chicago River (312-822-0100). El: Brown, Purple (rush hrs) to Merchandise Mart. Bus: 22 (24hrs), 125, 156. Lunch (Mon–Fri), dinner. Average main course: $25.*

Gene & Georgetti Since 1941 this old school steakhouse has been serving diners steaks and Italian classics in a dark, cozy atmosphere. The murals on the walls are as appealing as the menu and impeccable service. Of course, a hearty, juicy steak is the obvious: go for the filet mignon or loin steak. Tasty non-steak options include veal Vesuvio and even an eggplant Parmigiana (for vegetarians). This family-run spot is a Chicago classic that runs circles around its chain competitors. *500 N Franklin St at Illinois St (312-527-3718). El: Red to Grand. Bus: 65 Grand, 125 Water Tower Express. Lunch, dinner (closed Sun). Average main course: $27.*

....
Side dish
....

Tending to your hunger
Eating at the bar isn't just for loners.

Power bar The upstairs bar at Le Colonial is just as classy as the main dining room.

Forget your hang-ups about dining at the bar: Chances are you'll eat quicker, cheaper and with less fuss. All good things, right? Some bars are better than others, though; here, a list of some that will treat you right.

The bar The upstairs at **Le Colonial** *(937 N Rush St between Walton and Oak Sts, 312-255-0088)* is just like the downstairs: classy, dim and full of wicker and painted wood.
The bites Try the artichoke and crabmeat salad, sesame beef over rice noodles, or the steamed Vietnamese ravioli with chicken and mushrooms.

The bar Directly outside the main dining room at **Moto** *(945 W Fulton Market between Sangamon and Morgan sts, 312-491-0058)* you'll find a lounge with a row of low tables and stools that maintain the restaurant's minimalist design and futuristic feel.
The bites Chef Homaro Cantu doesn't limit his signature items to the main dining room. In addition to the *kajiki served with spicy mayo on a crispy nori chip,* he lets you finish your night with one of his whimsical desserts, like the "nachos": "all the visual and textural components of nachos but in dessert form."

The bar Not too many people are hip to the sleek, curvaceous bar at **Naha** *(500 N Clark St at Illinois St, 312-321-6242),* where you can get great service and and heavy pours from the bartenders.
The bites You can't go wrong here: the golden calamari is served with saffron aioli, the lamb kebabs are juicy and flanked by a chunky Greek salad, and "our mother's own" feta turnovers are so good you'll try to finagle ways to join Nahabedian's clan.

The bar The long, ornately-carved wood bar at **The Grill at Smith & Wollensky** *(318 N State St between Wacker Dr and Kinzie St, 312-670-9900)* is full of regulars.
The bites This bar menu is full of classics like shrimp cocktails and chicken BLTs. But it's their hamburger that'll make you pull up a stool.

Gibsons Bar & Steakhouse *2007 Eat Out Award, Readers' Choice: Best steakhouse* Gibsons may be named after the bling (you know, the one with the onion on top), but it really is all about the steak. Whether it is the 24-ounce porterhouse or the bone-in filet, you'll be enjoying your tender-as-butter cuts of meats with the city's movers-and-shakers. Hearty eaters will also wolf down the larger lobster tail. Don't be surprised if you hear the "happy birthday" refrain multiple times. Gibson's is a special occasion kind of place. *1028 N Rush at Bellevue Pl (312-266-8999). Bus: 36, 70, 145, 147, 151 (24hrs). Lunch, dinner. Average main course: $37.*

(**Grotto on State** The ultra-serious waiters here will recommend "stayks and chawps," but it's better to just stick with the chops. The steaks have a nice peppery crust but can be fatty. The tender lamb chops, however, arrive in a puddle of salty pan juices so delicious you'll use the entire bread basket to soak them up. Sides and desserts like the garlic mashed potatoes, tangy green bean salad with red onion and garlic, and the fresh ricotta cheesecake will send you away happy. *1030 N State St between Oak and Maple Sts (312-280-1005). El: Red to Chicago. Bus: 22 (24hrs), 36, 70. Dinner (closed Sun). Average main course: $25.*

❋ **Harry Caray's** See Italian/pizza for review.

Joe's Seafood, Prime Steaks and Stone Crab See Seafood for review.

(❋ ❹ **Keefer's Restaurant** If you listen closely, you can hear Modest Mouse seeping softly through the dining-room speakers here—the first sign of many that this isn't your grandfather's steakhouse. Chef John Hogan, previously of Savarin, inflects the menu with an inescapable French sensibility. A perfectly poached egg tops the country salad of crisp frisée dotted with lardons and Dover sole meunière gets a classic tableside presentation. The half-dozen cuts of steaks arrive perfectly cooked and gushing with juices. Now if we could only get the staff to turn up the music. *20 W Kinzie St at Dearborn St (312-467-9525). El: Red to Grand. Bus: 29, 36, 65. Lunch (Mon–Fri), dinner (closed Sun). Average main course: $30.*

❋ **Kinzie Chophouse** Don't be alarmed by the guys in the corner wearing jeans and T-shirts; unlike a lot of steakhouses around town, it's perfectly acceptable to dress down here. As for the rest of the typical steakhouse formula, everything is pretty much in place: Apps include all the usual suspects, including oysters Rockefeller generously topped with barely wilted spinach. Choose from several cuts of savory steaks presented on a tray before your meal, and juicy herb-crusted lamb chops fill in for those who aren't in the mood for beef. *400 N Wells St at Kinzie St (312-822-0191). El: Brown, Purple (rush hrs) to Merchandise Mart. Bus: 125 Water Tower Express, 156 LaSalle. Lunch (Mon–Fri), dinner. Average main course: $30.*

Morton's the Steakhouse The way food is touted here—by wheeling over a cart of uncooked meats, including a live lobster—can be a little off-putting (not everybody wants to witness their dinner being wheeled off to its death). But there are reasons why Morton's is so famous: the classic Chicago steakhouse interior, tailor-made for sealing the deal (business or pleasure); crab cakes; and barely seasoned steaks that stand out for their flavor, their tenderness or both. *65 E Wacker Pl between Garland Ct and Wabash Ave (312-201-0410). El: Brown, Green, Orange, Purple (rush hrs), Red to State/Lake. Bus: 29, 36, 144, 145, 146, 148. Lunch (Mon–Fri), dinner. Average main course: $41.*

▽ ❋ **Myron & Phil's** If you're under 50 and don't belong to a North Shore synagogue, you may feel a little out of place at this throwback steakhouse. But don't let that stop you from indulging in the splendor of the chopped liver with bits of hard-boiled egg, fresh challah rolls brought to the table when you sit down, iceberg-lettuce salad with green goddess dressing and the famous skirt steak with burnt onions. It's all well worth the heartburn. *3900 W Devon Ave, Lincolnwood (847-677-6663). Bus: 11 Lincoln. Lunch (Tue—Fri), dinner (closed Mon). Average main course: $25.*

★ **Nine** This trendy steakhouse hasn't lost its sparkle—mirrored tiles, pro athletes, and a neon-glowing Champagne and caviar bar are as posh as the menu. Lobster dots mashed potatoes, steaks (reputedly cooked at 1,200-degrees Fahrenheit) are prime, and catch-of-the-day dishes are well prepared and over-the-top. Ditto for excessive desserts like the pouf of cotton candy studded with candy and ice cream. And don't head for the loungey Ghost Bar upstairs to spot celebs; bathroom stalls are fitted with a tiny TV. *440 W Randolph St between Canal and*

Read 'em & eat

dry-aged beef that has been stored at near-freezing temperatures for several weeks, which gives it a richer flavor and more tender texture

flanken a long, thin strip of beef taken from the chuck end of the short ribs. A Jewish dish, usually boiled and served with horseradish, is named after this cut

grass-fed beef more lean, dense beef from cattle that grazes on grass instead of corn or grain and has been treated with fewer or no antibiotics

hanger steak a chewy cut from the muscles behind the ribs

porterhouse a cut from the large end of the tenderloin, including meat from the top loin muscle and a T-shaped portion of the backbone (T-bone)

prime rib a common misnomer for the rib roast, which is the large section of meat along the rib cage

rib eye the most tender cut, from the center of the rib roast

shell steak a cut of the short loin with the tenderloin cut off

sirloin a cut that lies between the short loin and the round, and includes part of the backbone, hip bone and tenderloin

skirt steak the boneless top-loin muscle, also known as New York strip steak

T-bone a T-shaped portion of the backbone cut from the center of the short loin

New-fangled angle
Steakhouse classics are
served with a fresh
approach at ristorante we.

Orleans Sts (312-575-9900). El: Green to Clinton. Bus: 14, 20 (24hrs), 56, 127. Lunch (Mon–Fri), dinner (Mon–Sat). Average main course: $30.

✳ **The Palm** A chain steakhouse inside a hotel isn't the first place that comes to mind to satisfying carnivorous cravings in this town. But if you've got a taste for old-fashioned indulgence, it would be a shame to overlook this spot that does wonders with monstrous cuts of USDA Prime, gargantuan lobsters and classic artery-clogging add-ons like creamed spinach and French-fried onions. Add a martini or two, and you'll be partying like it's 1959. *Swissotel, 323 E Wacker Dr at Columbus Dr (312-616-1000). El: Brown, Green, Orange, Pink, Purple (rush hrs) to State. Red to State/Lake. Bus: 4 (24hrs), X4, 29, 36, 60 (24hrs), 146, 151 (24hrs). Lunch, dinner. Average main course: $30.*

✳ **Phil Stefani's 437 Rush** No run-down rooms, no grumpy old-school service, no cigar puffing at the tables. In the world of steakhouses, Phil Stefani's slick, cosmopolitan version is as refreshing as shrimp cocktail. Expect expertly prepared porterhouses, with well-seasoned crust hiding tender flesh. But if it's lighter fare you're after, dig into the roasted red king salmon, which balances the textures and flavors of the firm fish, Yukon potato puree and ten-year balsamic. *437 N Rush St between Hubbard and Illinois Sts (312-222-0101). El: Red to Grand. Bus: 2, 3, X4, 10, 26, 29, 65, 125, 143, 144, 145, 146, 147, 151 (24hrs), 157. Lunch (Mon–Fri), dinner (closed Sun). Average main course: $24.*

ristorante we Steakhouses—if you've been to one, you've been to them all, right? Well, no, but if you've ever felt that way, ristorante we's take on beef should prove refreshing. Ignore the ho-hum salmon and order a steak, which comes plated on a pile of arugula and crusted in your choice of Parmesan, Gorgonzola or roasted garlic. You can also forgo a crust in favor of four sauces (we fell pretty hard for the horseradish cream), but why not just order both? *172 W Adams St in the W Chicago City Center (312-917-5608). El: Brown, Orange, Purple (rush hrs) to Quincy. Bus: 1, 7, 28, 126, 151 (24hrs), 156. Lunch, dinner (closed Sun). Average main course: $25.*

(✳ **Rosebud Steakhouse** Relax—this isn't the touristy red-sauce joint on Rush Street. Instead, this bustling, low-lit room is full of dark wood and red leather, lending it an old-school feel. If you can get a seat (be sure to make a reservation), you'll be told about the specialty, a bone-in fillet: It's soft as pudding. The perfectly pink Norwegian salmon is offered with an optional wasabi glaze, which you should get for the additional depth and heat. And if you're on a budget, grab the burger. It's thick, juicy and great with blue cheese. *192 E Walton St between Michigan Ave and Mies van der Rohe Way (312-397-1000). El: Red to Chicago. Bus: 36, 66 (24hrs), 143, 144, 145, 146, 147, 148, 151 (24hrs). Lunch (Mon–Fri), dinner. Average main course: $27.*

Saloon Steakhouse Often overlooked in the classic Chicago steakhouse scene, this spot hits every element with consistency—white coats on the waiters, autographed baseballs along the walls and butter-soft steaks. The bone-in filet is as flavorful as any we've ever had, and the house specialty, the Wagyu (the American Kobe) filet was incredibly tender. The ahi tuna nachos had a welcome, surprising kick, but the beef is really where it's at on this menu, and sometimes you just want a nice, juicy steak. *200 E Chestnut St at Mies van der Rohe Way (312-280-5454). El: Red to Chicago. Bus: 125, 143, 144, 145, 146, 147, 151 (24hrs). Lunch, dinner. Average main course: $35.*

Perfect symmetry
Tramonto Steak & Seafood serves surf and turf in slick digs.

✳ **Smith & Wollensky** The riverside location of this steak-and-chops joint is such a big part of Chicago's vibe that it may surprise you to learn it's not a Windy City original (the chain started in New York). Nevertheless, it's still a local favorite thanks to dishes including creamy and slightly smoky split-pea soup; an all-American wine list; and, of course, those big, fat steaks, all of which are consistently cooked to perfection. *318 N State St between Kinzie St and Hubbard St (312-670-9900). El: Red to Grand; Brown, Purple (rush hrs) to Merchandise Mart. Bus: 22 (24hrs), 29, 36. Lunch, dinner. Average main course: $40.*

✳ **Sullivan's Steakhouse** You'd think a chain steakhouse would get lost in the shuffle in a city that takes its steak pretty seriously, but this spot distinguishes itself with nightly live jazz and a dedicated cigar bar with private humidor lockers. There's also an extensive wine list to sip from while you work your way through the signature 20-ounce bone-in Kansas City strip. Though the menu is standard—steaks, chops and seafood are joined by mandatory hearty starters (oysters Rockefeller) and sides (creamed spinach, onion rings the size of your hand)—it's reliable. *415 N Dearborn St at Hubbard St (312-527-3510). El: Red to Grand. Bus: 22 (24hrs), 29, 36, 65. Lunch (Mon–Fri), dinner. Average main course: $30.*

Tramonto Steak & Seafood With their upscale, four-restaurant food court in the Westin Hotel, Rick Tramonto and Gale Gand have upped the ante for dining in Wheeling. This traditional steakhouse is the most traditional (and expensive) option, offering a solid menu of all the usual steak and seafood suspects. The steaks are fine and all, but we prefer the braised-beef short ribs, with their luscious layers of buttery fat. For dessert, you'll want to go equally simple: We suggest the Brooklyn Blackout. *601 N Milwaukee Ave, Wheeling (847-777-6575). Dinner. Average main course: $30.* ∎

Thai

See also: *Pan Asian*

Delectable dish Thai
Avenue's *sup naw mai* with
pickled bamboo shoots is a
house specialty.

Amarind's Chef Rangsan Sutcharit's Thai creations
draw faithful crowds to his charming eatery on the border
of Oak Park and Chicago. Panang curry is the perfect
balance of spice and tang. Noodles such as the *pad kee mao*
("drunken man's noodles") are tender and flavorful. Best of
all, the chef isn't shy with the presentation skills he
perfected during nine years turning vegetables into works
of art at upscale Arun's. Once you become a regular, you
can call ahead and make off-menu requests. Amarind's has
kid-friendly plates and utensils. *6822 W North Ave, Oak
Park (773-889-9999). El: Green to Oak Park. Bus: 72
North, Pace 311. Lunch (Tue–Sat), dinner (closed Mon).
Average main course: $10.50.*

▼ **Arun's** Chef Arun Sampanthavivat opened this
legend two decades ago, and it has since become the first
Thai restaurant in America to nab four Mobil stars, a AAA
award and a James Beard for Best Chef in the Midwest.
These days, brilliant Thai food is more prevalent, and you
can get some of this elsewhere for a smaller bill, if not with
such service, ambiance and wine pairings. For $85, you'll
get a 12-course tasting of excellent food, including delicate
beef panang curry, ethereal lemongrass crab cake and
perfectly steamed, curry-drizzled lobster. *4156 N Kedzie
Ave between Warner and Berteau Aves (773-539-1909).
Bus: 80 Irving Park, X80 Irving Park ExpEl: Brown Line to
Kedzie. Dinner (closed Mon). Average degustation: $85.*

◉ **Ma & I** We don't understand why the cooks at this
Thai spot are shy with spice. Maybe they figure the nearby
condo dwellers can't handle the heat, but when you can
wipe your eyes with the papaya salad, even Grandma
would be bored. Doctor up the handful of dishes that show
potential—crispy salmon-basil rolls (request peanut
sauce), shrimp noodle panang curry (ask to add veggies)
and "tiger smiling," marinated grilled beef tenderloin cubes
on a bed of watercress. If you don't mind being *that* diner,
you'll end up with some pretty good eats. *1234 S Michigan
Ave between Roosevelt Rd and 13th St (312-663-1234). El:
Green, Orange, Red to Roosevelt. Bus: 1, 3, 4 (24hrs), 12,
29, 62 (24hrs). Lunch, dinner. Average main course: $10.*

◉ **Mama Thai** Mama Thai offers dependable versions
of classics (papaya salad, green curry) that shun less
accessible flavors of funky fish sauce and fermented rice. If
you're a fan of "secret Thai menus," you're setting yourself
up for a let-down; if you're fine with fresh food prepared
Ameri-Thai style with restrained use of authentic
ingredients, you may have found yo Mama. *1112 W
Madison St, Oak Park (708-386-0100). Lunch, dinner
(closed Mon). Average main course: $8.*

◉ **Opart Thai House** Sick of sandwiches for lunch?
Head south of the Loop for your midday meal, and you can
get a pretty tasty dose of Thai instead. All of the standards
are dependable, but we recommend the charred-squid
salad and the *miang sa-wan*—a sweet mess of dried pork,
ginger and peanuts meant to be wrapped in lettuce leaves.
To feed a fish craving, try the crispy catfish tossed with
Thai eggplant and green beans in red-curry paste. If your
idea of curry involves tons of creamy coconut milk, try the
yellow gari with sweet potatoes. *1906 S State St between
Archer Ave and Cullerton St (312-567-9898). El: Red to
Cermak/Chinatown. Bus: 21, 24, 29, 62 (24hrs). Lunch,
dinner. Average main course: $8.* • *Additional location at
4658 N Western Ave (773-989-8517).*

▼ **B P.S. Bangkok** As pleasant and sunny as this
dining room is, purists should steer clear. The rest of us,
however, may be able to appreciate the "Heavenly Tofu"
(tossed with peanuts, chile peppers and soy sauce to sweet-
hot results) and "Bite Size Delights" (tiny lettuce rolls with
dried shrimp, ginger and coconut) for the Americanized
Thai food it is. On Sunday mornings there's a brunch
buffet, and if there's a better cure for hangovers than
unlimited banana fritters and "Dreamy, Creamy, Crispy
Crab" (a.k.a. crab rangoon), we've yet to find it. *3345 N
Clark St between Buckingham Pl and Roscoe St (773-871-
7777). El: Brown, Purple (rush hrs), Red to Belmont. Bus:
8, 22 (24hrs), 77 (24hrs), 152. Brunch (Sun), lunch, dinner
(closed Mon). Average main course: $11.*

◉ **Rosded** If you happen to blink while on your way for
a dose of Germanic oompah in Lincoln Square, you might
just miss one of the better Thai restaurants in town. The
range of "safe" bets and authentic eats is vast, but all are
tasty. Don't miss the tangy "waterfall" beef salad tossed
with roasted rice powder, the earthy "boat" noodles with
pork, the spicy-sour Isaan-style soup and the crispy catfish

steaks smothered in pasty red curry sauce. *2308 W Leland Ave at Lincoln Ave (773-334-9055). El: Brown to Western. Bus: 11, 49 (24hrs), X49, 81 (24hrs). Lunch, dinner (closed Mon). Average main course: $7.*

⊙ **Royal Thai** When you sit down at this eight-table spot, you'll be given two menus: the standard and the vegetarian. Both offer more than one restaurant's worth of options, allowing Royal Thai to hold its own. A Chinese influence finds its way into some of the dishes, like the Chinese flowering cabbage soup, with soft wontons. Classic dishes, like pad thai, are sauced just right. Soups are among the strengths. Try the *tom kha pla* (tilapia in spicy coconut milk broth) or the *potak*, which is chock-full of shrimp, mussels and squid. *2209 W Montrose Ave between Lincoln and Bell Aves (773-509-0007). El: Brown to Western. Bus: 11, 49 (24hrs), X49, 78. Lunch, dinner. Average main course: $7.*

⊙ **Silver Spoon** This Thai spot is the sister restaurant of Lincoln Square's outstanding Spoon Thai, and being right next to the Thai Consulate, we figured the food would be far from Americanized stuff. Surprisingly, the fare is decidedly tame, even for Gold Coast tastes. This isn't necessarily a bad thing (and could be a good jumping off point for Thai-food novices) because what it does, it does well. Chive dumplings get things off to a good start, the *somtum* (papaya salad) is fiery and flavorful, and the panang beef curry is perfectly balanced, with manageable heat. *710 N Rush St between Superior and Huron Sts (312-944-7100). El: Red to Chicago. Bus: 3, 4 (24hrs), X4, 10, 26, 66 (24hrs), 145, 146, 147, 151 (24hrs). Lunch, dinner. Average main course: $7.*

★ ⊙ **Spoon Thai** If you stick to the basics here, you'll miss out on the best stuff. Get adventurous with *kung chae naam plaa*, raw shrimp marinated with lime juice, fish sauce, garlic and chile—a Thai take on ceviche. The Isaan-style pork and rice sausage is almost as addictive as the *naem khao thawt*, a crunchy, salty, tangy salad of fried rice, tiny ham bits and flecks of cilantro. Curry fans should try

the *kaeng som kung sot*, a slightly sour, shrimp-dotted tamarind curry, or call ahead to request special fish balls doused with green curry. *4608 N Western Ave between Wilson and Eastwood Aves (773-769-1173). El: Brown to Western. Bus: 11, 49 (24hrs), X49, 78, 81 (24hrs). Lunch, dinner. Average main course: $7.*

★ ⊙ **Sticky Rice** What we love about this unassuming storefront is that it keeps our interest with new concoctions every couple of weeks. Tried-and-true favorites include housemade spicy fermented pork sausage, probably the best *gang hung lay* (pork in sweet, garlicky, ginger-laden curry) in town, and *khua kae*, a stir-fry of chicken, baby corn, eggplant, shredded lime leaves and roasted rice powder that has a gingery citrus tang. Translations of the Thai-language menu courtesy of "Erik M" are available for adventurous eaters, as well as a vegetarian menu for leaf-eaters. *4018 N Western Ave between Irving Park Rd and Cuyler Ave (773-588-0133). Bus: 49 (24hrs), X49, 80, X80. Lunch, dinner. Average main course: $5.*

Sweet Tamarind True to its name, this charming spot injects dishes with sweet tamarind every chance it gets: Light and fresh cilantro, mint and basil–packed spring rolls get a sweet tamarind dipping sauce, and the crispy rice noodles in the *mee krob* are flavored with tamarind, green onion and egg. But even when the signature ingredient is omitted, dishes still stand out: Crispy catfish arrives in a red curry with a lot of kick, and a cakey pumpkin custard makes for a sweet, tamarind-free ending. *1408 W Diversey Pkwy between Southport and Janssen Aves (773-281-5300). El: Brown to Diversey. Bus: 9, 11, 76. Dinner (closed Mon). Average main course: $9.*

★ ⊙ **TAC Quick Thai** The once-tiny Thai joint at the top of many Chicagoans' favorites list has more than doubled in size. Luckily the kitchen isn't having any trouble keeping up with the crowds that flood the simple, minimalist room. Standouts are still found on the translated Thai-language menu, with never-fail flavor

Read 'em & eat

khao (also kow or khow) rice

....

massaman curry (also known as Muslim curry) a rich sauce, made from coconut, potatoes and peanuts

....

nam sod ("nahm sahd") cold ground pork, mint and ginger salad with chili peppers, lime and fish sauce

....

pad stir-fry

....

panang a dry, aromatic curry made with chilies, coriander, shrimp paste, lime, lemongrass, cilantro, ginger and shallots

....

prik chili; *prik pon* is red-chili powder

....

som tum (sahm tuhm) grated-green-papaya salad with green beans, red chili peppers, crushed peanuts and salted crab or dried shrimp, tossed in a lime juice and fish-sauce dressing

Thrilla from Manila Clams in Chili Sauce keep the crowds coming to TAC Quick Thai.

explosions such as tart and smoky pork-and-rice sausage; ground chicken with crispy basil and preserved eggs; wrap-ready pork meatballs served with rice papers, fierce chilies, garlic cloves, fresh basil and mint, diced banana and apple; and the best beef noodle dish in town, the brisket-packed "boat noodles." *3930 N Sheridan Rd at Dakin St (773-327-5253). El: Red to Sheridan. Bus: 36, 80, 145, 151 (24hrs). Lunch, dinner (closed Tue). Average main course: $8.*

⊙ **Thai Aree** This tidy Thai joint has unpredictable hours, but the loyalists who flock here don't seem to mind making a quick phone call before heading out. The inconvenience-worthy eats include gingery ground pork with peanuts (*nam sod*) and the grilled shrimp with lemongrass. The perfectly balanced "kang" green curry is packed with bamboo, eggplant, basil and your choice of meat or tofu and will leave you satisfied. Most of the salads have the sour-salty-spicy kick for which Thai food is known. *3592 N Milwaukee Ave at Addison St (773-725-6751). Bus: 53, 56, 152. Dinner (closed Sun). Average main course: $8.*

★ ⊙ **Thai Avenue** Located on a strip of Broadway known for its Vietnamese spots, the cuisine shifts to Thai at this simple storefront. Anglo favorites abound but the gems of the menu are the authentic eats. Start with *yum woonsen*, a spicy glass noodle salad with shrimp and ground chicken, and *namtok*, a pork salad with cilantro, red onion, peanuts and roasted rice powder. For more tangy-spicy-salty, go for the *name klug*, deep-fried rice with ham, peanuts, chilies and plenty of lime. Sweet sticky rice with mango or chilled lychee are perfect, simple endings. *4949 N Broadway at Argyle St (773-878-2222). El: Red to Argyle. Bus: 36, 81 (24hrs), 92, 147, 151 (24hrs). Lunch, dinner. Average main course: $6.*

EdaMAme Dip soy beans and more at Ma & I.

▼ ⊙ **Thai Classic** Vegetarians know that just because a dish doesn't have a hunk of pork doesn't mean it's animal-free. This Anglo favorite caters to those phobic of fish sauce, going so far as to omit oyster sauce when a tofu version of noodle or rice classics is ordered. "Drunk noodles" are among the best around, stir-fried in spicy soy with onions, tomatoes, straw mushrooms, bell peppers and hunks of tofu. Pescetarians should go for the gingery steamed tilapia, while meat-eaters should just take a day off; beef is standard at best. *3332 N Clark St between Belmont Ave and Roscoe St (773-404-2000). El: Brown, Purple (rush hrs), Red to Belmont. Bus: 8, 22 (24hrs), 77 (24hrs). Lunch, dinner. Average main course: $8.*

★ BYOB ⊙ **Thai Elephant (formerly The Elephant)** At first glance, the menu at this little BYOB Thai joint seems standard, but superfresh ingredients make standard dishes sing, and up on the chalkboard you'll find specials that make it worthy of your gas cash. From the latter, try the spicy tilapia with globe-shaped eggplants and the beefy "boat" noodles, a brisket-studded soup. From the regular menu, don't miss the crispy basil-wrapped shrimp starter or the roasted duck curry packed with grapes, tomatoes and pineapple chunks. Grab dessert to go from the small counter of imported cookies and candies. *5348 W Devon Ave between Central and Minnehaha Aves (773-467-1168). Bus: 85A, Pace 225, Pace 226. Lunch, dinner (closed Sun). Average main course: $7.*

⊙ **Thai Grocery** As the name states, this is primarily a grocery store, but the array of authentic take-out options in the back of this jam-packed treasure trove makes it worth a visit. A half-dozen classics like fish balls in green curry, crispy catfish, five-spice duck and pad thai are dished up by the pound. At the end of one aisle, stacks of clear containers hold freshly made pastries and sweets—don't miss the golden, flaky curry puffs filled with sweet-and-savory curried potato. *5014 N Broadway St at Argyle St (773-561-5345). El: Red to Argyle. Bus: 36, 81 (24hrs), 92, 147, 151 (24hrs). Average main course: $3.*

BYOB ▼ ⊙ **Thai Lagoon** True, this long-standing Thai spot is an Anglo favorite that isn't going to whip out ant-egg omelettes and fermented pork sausages to impress the authenticity police. But we like the fact that we can visit for an inexpensive dinner with friends who aren't adventurous eaters, bring a bottle of wine and settle into the low-lit room for consistent, tasty eats. Green-curry tofu with green eggplants and basil is rich and fragrant. *Tom kha* soup packs plenty of lime punch, as well as a garden of vegetables. *2322 W North Ave at Claremont Ave (773-489-5747). El: Blue to Damen. Bus: 49 Western (24hrs), 72 North. Dinner. Average main course: $7.*

⊙ **Thai Pastry & Restaurant** As the name suggests, dessert is not to be missed at this bright café: Moist miniature chocolate cakes and swan-shaped cream puffs end the meal on a perfectly sweet note. But don't discount the savories. Spring rolls wrapped in thin pastry (as opposed to rice paper) are superfresh; roasted duck salad is a heavenly combination of rich duck, cool cilantro, sharp green onion and a hint of chile pepper; and panang curry is sweet. *4925 N Broadway St between Ainslie and Argyle Sts (773-784-5399). El: Red to Argyle. Bus: 36, 92, 147, 151 (24hrs). Lunch, dinner. Average main course: $8.*

⊙ **Thai Village** Sometimes you want straight-up Thai. None of that authentic, secret-translated-menu stuff; you want pad thai, *lad nar* and crab-and-cream-cheese–filled wontons. Then, this spot's for you. The crispy roll appetizer is oddly addictive: fried, cigar-shaped rolls of paper-thin rice wrapper holding in threads of vermicelli noodle, ground chicken and sprouts. The peanut-vinegar sauce shines in the fried tofu starter, as does the tangy, spicy lime dressing for both the papaya and the char-broiled sliced beef salad with big chunks of tomato. Pad thai is tasty enough; a better bet is eggplant basil or the spinach and pork in tamarind curry. *2053 W Division St between Damen and Hoyne Aves (773-384-5352). El: Blue to Division. Bus: 49 (24hrs) X49, 50, 70. Lunch, dinner (closed Mon). Average main course: $7.*

☉ **Thai Wild Ginger** Americanized Thai restaurants are a dime a dozen, so why is this successful? Two reasons: It's across from Webster Place theater and the affable chef-owner Tommy is revered by regulars as the nicest guy around. When he's not in the dining room kissing babies, he's in the kitchen turning out Thai standards. The crispy shrimp and the lime-dressed chicken salad are good starters, and the duck or the garlic-lemongrass shrimp are tasty entrées. Vegetarians will be happy with nearly a dozen meat-free dishes. *2203 N Clybourn Ave at Webster Ave (773-883-0344). El: Brown, Purple (rush hrs), Red to Fullerton. Bus: 9 Ashland, 74 Fullerton. Lunch, dinner. Average main course: $9.*

☉ **Tiparos** Having so many great Thai restaurants in the city makes it tough to decide where to head when your craving kicks in. This reliable spot serves up spicy beef skewers that are like awesome jerky with a tangy chili sauce. *Tod mun pla*, fried spicy fish cakes, are flavored with lemongrass and come with a tasty sweet dipping sauce with chunks of cucumber and ground peanuts. Curries are good, too, from mild yellow with peas to the decadent mussaman made with chunks of potatoes, pineapples and tomato, in coconut milk-curry gravy. *1540 N Clark St between Burton Place and North Blvd (312-712-9900). El: Red to Clark/Division; Brown, Purple (rush hrs) to Sedgwick. Bus: 22 (24hrs), 36, 72, 156. Lunch, dinner. Average main course: $6.50.*

▼ ✳ **VTK** So you're interested in trying Thai food, but you're spice-phobic or have kids in tow. Relax and let the servers at this spot—a collaboration between celeb chef Jeanes Georges Vongerichten and Lettuce Entertain You—be your guides. When the crunchy Rocket Roll appetizer is delivered to your table, you're instructed to wrap lettuce leaves around it and dip it in garlic sauce. Order the panang curry noodles and you'll be warned it's medium spicy," but when you dig in to the giant dish of rich, creamy curry and wide rice noodles, your palate will only register a hint of heat. Think of this as Thai cuisine 101. *6 W Hubbard St at State St (312-644-8664). El: Red to Grand. Bus: 22 (24hrs), 36, 65.. Lunch (Mon–Sat), dinner. Average main course: $16.*

BYOB ☉ **Yes Thai** This neighborhood favorite is a bright, sunny spot on an otherwise plain strip of Damen Avenue. Standouts from the menu of typical Thai fare include plump green mussels in a soy-fish broth flecked with green onions, green chilies and basil, and the rama special—crunchy steamed broccoli and fresh ginger served over rice with a yummy housemade peanut sauce. A weekday dine-in lunch special offers an appetizer and entrée for just $6.50. Added bonus: There's free lunchtime wireless Internet access every day except Sunday. *5211 N Damen Ave between Farragut and Foster Aves (773-878-2487). El: Brown to Damen. Bus: 50 Damen, 92 Foster. Lunch, dinner. Average main course: $7.* ■

Prince of Thais

Translated menus offer authentic eats.

A few years ago, a local foodie who goes by the cryptic name "Erik M." dug into the world of Thai-language menus with the goal of making real-deal Thai dishes available to the dining public. In his translator travels, Erik found Thai-language menus at almost a dozen Chicago restaurants. He has deciphered half of them and turned over photocopies of the finished products to the restaurants. Here are some of his favorite truly Thai restaurants, and recommended dishes for more adventurous eaters.

TAC Quick Thai Kitchen *(3930 N Sheridan Rd at Dakin St, 773-327-5253)*
Kra-phrao krawp khai yiaw mua (stir-fried minced chicken and crispy holy basil leaves over preserved eggs)
Khao khaa muu (braised pork leg on rice)
Pha low (Chinese-style braised pork belly with tofu and hard-boiled egg)

Spoon Thai *(4608 N Western Ave at Wilson Ave, 773-769-1173)*
Tom khlong plaa chawn (spicy, herbaceous stew with mudfish)
Naam phrik plaa thuu (shrimp paste "dip" with fried mackerels and crudites)
Naem khao thawt (housemade Thai "pressed ham" with crispy rice)

Sticky Rice *(4018 N Western Ave at Irving Park Rd, 773-588-0120)*
Phak bung fai daeng (stir-fried water spinach with yellow bean sauce)
Phat kra-phrao khaa muu (stir-fried pork leg with basil)
Ehn tun (spicy beef-tendon soup)

Aroy Thai *(4654 N Damen Ave between Eastland and Leland Aves, 773-275-8360)*
Kaeng som plaa thawt (sour curry with crispy fish—no coconut milk)
Laap khua (Northern Thai–style minced-pork salad)
Sup naw mai (pickled bamboo-shoot salad with roasted-rice powder)

Vegetarian

See also: *Indian/Subcontinental, Korean, Kosher, Middle Eastern, Thai*

Small wonder Baby heirloom tomatoes are paired with olive oil, toast and fresh herbs at Green Zebra.

▼ ☺ **Alice & Friends' Vegetarian Café** This place is packed with as many meat-eaters as vegheads, all Zenned out by the loopy lavender walls and the Korean spiritual guru video playing on the front room TV. We don't know exactly what's in the crispy "unchicken" drumsticks slathered in tangy barbecue sauce, but we can't taste the faux meat under the sauce. Steamed veggie dumplings are delicious, if you whisk some chili paste into the soy sauce. Noodle lovers should try the the glass noodles made from sweet potato starch. *5812 N Broadway St between Ardmore and Thorndale Aves (773-275-8797). El: Red to Bryn Mawr. Bus: 36, 84, 147. Lunch (Sat), dinner (Mon–Sat), (closed Sun). Average main course: $8.*

▼ ☺ **Amitabul** Like a Zen koan shocking the mind into enlightenment, this Korean vegan restaurant is an awakening—for vegans, vegetarians and carnivores alike—to how delicious a meatless, eggless, dairy-free meal can be. Employing "Zen meditation cooking energy," chefs whip up everything from vegan dumplings, organic veggies and noodle soups to spicy curry and tofu dishes. Several flavors of vegan ice cream like cappuccino, green tea and plum are available in warmer months. *6207 N Milwaukee Ave between Huntington and Raven Sts (773-774-0276). Bus: 56A North Milwaukee, Pace 270. Lunch, dinner (closed Sun, Mon). Average main course: $8.*

▼ ☺ **Ankh** We were surprised to stumble upon this soulful kiosk in the LaSalle Blue Line stop. The real draw is the delicious, healthful, meat-free eats. Bright tabouli gets a dose of finely diced carrots, lemon juice and parsley. Nuts, fresh fruit and Medjool date jam are layered to create "paradise pie." Potato salad goes Caribbean thanks to yellow curry powder. The jambalaya pâté stands out with a blend of pecans, sun-dried tomatoes, onions and carrots. *LaSalle Blue Line station, 50 W Congress Pkwy (312-834-0530). El: Blue to LaSalle. Mon–Fri 8am–5pm. Average main course: $4.*

▼ ☺ **Blind Faith Café** A vegetarian restaurant in a college town is like a Hooters by the airport: It's a sure thing. Among the NU students at this Evanston institution you'll find plenty of thirtysomething couples, septuagenarians and families eating their way through the meatless menu. Start with the tofu "crab" cakes, two moist crumbly tofu patties in creamy red-pepper sauce. We may miss the sizzling skillet, but we don't long for meat while making fajitas with black beans, guac, seitan, red peppers, salsa and brown rice. Be sure to try a decadent dessert from the attached bakery. *525 Dempster St, Evanston (847-328-6875). El: Purple to Dempster. Bus: Pace 205 Chicago/Golf, Pace 250 Dempster. Breakfast, brunch (Sat, Sun), lunch, dinner. Average main course: $10.*

★ ▼ ✱ **B Chicago Diner** *2007 Eat Out Award, Readers' Choice: Best vegetarian restaurant* Even non-vegetarians know Chicago Diner. The vibe is normal, everyday diner, albeit with soy milk, tofu and tempeh on the giant menu. Waits for weekend brunch can get painful (even though the menu is served daily), but patient non–

meat-eaters are rewarded with dense (and fairly flaky) soy margarine biscuits and sweet blueberry-lemon muffins made with vegan egg substitute. French toast is a little soggy and lackluster—but after all, this *is* diner food. The back patio is an outdoor oasis. *3411 N Halsted St between Roscoe St and Newport Ave (773-935-6696). El: Brown, Purple (rush hrs), Red to Belmont. Bus: 8, 22 (24 hrs), 77 (24hrs). Brunch, lunch, dinner. Average main course: $11.*

▼ ✪ **Chowpatti** If you're the vegetarian who hates the condescending, "Well, I guess we could take the bacon off the cobb salad," this place will be your nirvana. The 26-page, global, meatless menu takes awhile to navigate, with choices inspired from cuisines of America, Italy, Mexico, the Middle East and, most notably, India. Given that the owners of this decades-old veg haven are Indian, we suggest sticking to the filled delicious *dosas*, the rice-lentil pancakes dubbed *uttapam*, any of the veggie-packed curries and the addictive crunchy-sweet-spicy *bhel chaats*. *1035 S Arlington Heights Rd, Arlington Heights (847-640-9554). Bus: Pace 694. Lunch, dinner (closed Mon). Average main course: $10.*

BYOB ▼ ✪ **Cousin's I.V.** Raw foodists are rejoicing that chef Mehmet Ak is making 100% raw, 100% vegan and mostly organic renderings of Turkish and American classics. But they're not the only ones who will enjoy his delicious "pizza"—a flaxseed cracker topped with garlicky tomato sauce, fresh avocado and marinated mushrooms—and his lively marinated spinach. The nutty "zoom" burger and sprout-heavy tabouli, on the other hand, are probably easier to swallow for raw foodists, if only because, for them, there aren't many other options. *3038 W Irving Park Rd between Whipple St and Albany Ave (773-478-6868). Bus: 80 Irving Park, X80 Irving Park. Lunch, dinner. Average main course: $12.*

▼ BYOB **Dharma Garden** See Pan Asian for review.

★ ▼ **B Green Zebra** Shawn McClain's moss-colored, minimalist house of Zen is the only upscale dining experience Chicago vegetarians can truly call their own. The menu's classed-up brunch classics include German-style pancakes with Granny Smith apples and caramelized–banana crêpes with ricotta and Wisconsin honey. The superseasonal dinner menu is always updated. Depending on when you visit, you may find *agnolotti* with stinging nettles, snap peas, baby squash and mascarpone; chilled arugula soup; and roasted halibut with fingerlings, fennel and asparagus. Many menu items are adapted from other Chicago chefs. *1460 W Chicago Ave between Bishop St and Greenview Ave (312-243-7100). El: Blue to Chicago. Bus: 9 Ashland (24 hrs), 66 Chicago (24hrs). Brunch (Sun), dinner. Average main course: $11.*

▼ (✳ **Heartland Café** See Classic American $16 and up for review.

▼ ✳ **Karyn's Cooked** Karyn Calabrese is known for her 100% organic, 100% vegan and 100% raw (i.e. uncooked) cuisine (see: Karyn's Fresh Corner). But here she turns up the heat…these dishes are still vegan and organic, but appeal to those who aren't ready for raw. Try hummus, pizza, salads and entrees made with fake meats. The restaurant serves organic wines and beer and yummy Sunday brunch, with a "conscious comfort food" vibe. Remember: in addition to meatless, vegan means no dairy or refined sugar. *738 N Wells St between Superior St and Chicago Ave (312-587-1050). El: Brown, Purple (rush hrs)*

to Chicago. Bus: 66 Chicago (24hrs). Lunch, dinner. Average main course: $12.

▼ **BYOB** ✳ **Karyn's Fresh Corner** Karyn Calabrese's menu is 100% organic, 100% vegan and 100% raw (i.e. uncooked), so you probably have to be a vegan raw-foodist to appreciate what she's doing. But some dishes taste good no matter what your eating habits are. The stuffed-mushrooms starter is superbly fresh and garlicky, and the "seaweed dim sum," a dumplingesque appetizer, is filled with a creamy mixture of avocado and kalamata olives. Unfortunately the "pasta primavera," which uses thin slices of zucchini in place of pasta, is flavorless enough to send us even deeper into carnivorism. Take out is available. *1901 N Halsted St at Wisconsin St (312-255-1590). El: Brown, Purple (rush hrs) to Armitage; Red to North/Clybourn. Bus: 8, 72, 73. Breakfast (café only), lunch, dinner. Average main course: $20.*

▼ ✪ **Kopi, A Traveler's Café** See Bakeries/cafés for review.

▼ ✪ **Lake Side Café** Adjacent to Inner Meditation University, this spot is a great postyoga fuel-up, offering a nearly all-organic menu. Meat-eaters won't be fooled by the Chicago Polish—the spicy tofu dog is missing the requisite snap of an encased meat. But thanks to heaps of mustard, sauerkraut and relish, you'll hardly care. The Winter Salad—with its huge chunks of creamy feta, carrots, walnuts, cashews, dried cranberries and green onions—is mealworthy, and the veggie-packed, crispy-crust Organic Garden pizza makes junk food seem healthy. *1418 W Howard St at Sheridan Rd (773-262-9503). El: Purple, Red, Yellow to Howard. Bus: 22 (24hrs), 97, 147, 151*

A cook who doesn't "cook" Cousin's IV chef Mehmet Ak creates dishes that are 100 percent raw and vegan.

Sizzle without the steak
Tofu and seitan take the place of meat in Chicago Diner's fajitas.

Vegetarian

(24hrs), 201 (24hrs), 205, 206, Pace 215, Pace 290. Lunch (Sat only), dinner (closed Mon). Average main course: $7.

▼ ☺ **Mysore Woodlands** Come hungry to this South Indian vegetarian spot, because the portions are enormous. Start with *rasam*, a spicy cilantro-and-tamarind soup that's hotter than a Bikram-yoga session (*rasa vada*—lentil doughnuts served with an array of chutneys—temper the heat). A delicious variety of breads—including *poori* (think fluffy and fried) and a fantastically crispy, record album-size *dosai* rice cake—complement the curries of the Royal Thali sampler. *2548 W Devon Ave between Maplewood Ave and Rockwell St (773-338-8160). Bus: 49B Western, 155 Devon. Lunch, dinner. Average main course: $9 .*

▼ ☺ **New Life Vegetarian Restaurant and Health Food Store** For years New Life Vegetarian Restaurant has changed owners and names, but always served up dependable meatless dishes. Find all the standard vegetarian fare, like veggie burgers and "Stakelet" sandwiches. We come early to fill up on a breakfast of veggie sausage, tofu eggs, brown rice and scalloped potatoes. Save room for lemon icebox pie and banana pudding. *3141 W Roosevelt Rd between Troy St and Kedzie Ave (773-762-1090). El: Blue (Forest Park branch) to Kedzie-Homan. Bus: 7, 12, 52, 94. Breakfast, lunch, dinner (closed Sun). Average main course: $6.*

▼ ☺ **Royal Thai** See Thai for review.

▼ ☺ **Soul Vegetarian East** In a family atmosphere for vegans looking to escape boring lentil hell, the "BBQ Twist" sandwich (made from wheat gluten) is as close to real barbecue pulled pork as vegetarians will get, and

somehow the fried cauliflower tastes like chicken. Come for the full Sunday dinner: salad with tangy house dressing, fake chicken potpie, collard greens, corn and potatoes. The vegan apple or peach pie that follows may not be healthy, but that was never the point of soul food. *205 E 75th St at Indiana Ave (773-224-0104). El: Red to 79th. Bus: 3, X3, 75. Breakfast, lunch, dinner. Average main course: $7.*

☺ **Udupi Palace** See Indian/Subcontinental for review.

▼ ☺ **Vegetarian Fun Foods Supreme** The utilitarian booths, bright orange walls and beach shack–style menu board don't look like much. But looks are deceiving. These are some of the tastiest vegan eats in the city. We love the veggie chicken submarine and the spinach pizza, both made with homemade baked goods. Wash them down with honey lemonade (provided, of course, you are not a vegan who eschews honey) and save room for the fresh daily desserts. You won't break a $10 spot. *1702 E 87th St at East End Ave (773-734-6321). Bus: 87 87th. Mon-Sat 10am -9 pm. Average main course: $6.50.*

▼ B ☺ **Victory's Banner** There's an interesting distraction during the long wait for a table at this sunny brunch spot: A TV shows Indian guru Sri Chinmoy (of whom every employee is a follower) lifting heavy things—a crew of firemen, a helicopter, a plane. Impressive, but we're bigger believers in the thick French toast slathered i peach butter and maple syrup, or the pesto-laden, free-range scrambled eggs in the Satisfaction Promise. *2100 W Roscoe St at Hoyne Ave (773-665-0227). Bus: 50, 77 (24 hrs), 152. Breakfast, brunch, lunch (closed Tues). Average main course: $7.50.* ∎

Vietnamese

See also: *Pan Asian*

★ ⊕ **Ba Le** When the French controlled Vietnam, baguettes crossed cultures, and one of the best things that resulted was the *banh mi* sandwich. They're plentiful in the Argyle Street area, but this bakery creates most of the bread the other restaurants use, so go try the source. We like the barbecue pork and the Ba Le special, which piles housemade pâté, headcheese and pork onto a baguette with tangy carrot and daikon slivers, cilantro and jalapeño. Shrimp spring rolls, flaky croissants and canned coffee drinks are must-trys. *5018 N Broadway St between Argyle St and Winnemac Ave (773-561-4424). El: Red to Argyle. Bus: 22 (24hrs), 36, 81 (24hrs), 92. Breakfast, lunch, dinner. Average sandwich: $3.*

⊕ **Fan Si Pan** Susan Furst gives Vietnamese staples a makeover at this cute, mostly take-out shop. Supersized spring rolls are stuffed with sweet-and-salty hoisin-marinated "five star beef"; *banh mi* have contemporary fillings like lime-tinged chicken and mango; and the salads can be dressed up with Furst's family's line of Terrapin Ridge sauces. The best bet, though, is something she didn't mess with: The classic ham-and-pâté *banh mi* is a heavenly contrast of creamy and crunchy, salty and spicy. Chase it with Furst's honeydew limeade and you'll never swear off fast food again. *1618 W Chicago Ave between Ashland and Marshfield Aves (312-738-1405). Bus: 9 (24hrs), X9, 66 (24hrs). Lunch, dinner. Average main course: $5.*

⊕ **Hai Yen** This bastion of solid, authentic Vietnamese eats nails consistency and flavor. We like to start with the beef sausages wrapped in *la lot* leaves (#1), as well as lotus root salad (#18), a mix of crunchy lotus root and *rau ram*. Entrées like catfish in a clay pot (#72) and chicken taro yellow curry (#62) match with stir-fried water spinach. Wash it down with *chanh* (housemade limeade soda). *1055 W Argyle St between Kenmore and Winthrop Aves (773-561-4077). El: Red to Argyle. Bus: 36, 81 (24hrs), 147, 151 (24hrs). Lunch, dinner (closed Wed). Average main course: $7.* ● *Additional location at 2723 N Clark St (773-868-4888).*

★ ●▼ **Le Colonial** There are few Vietnamese joints in the city with a room as pleasant, sophisticated or stylish as the dining room here. But plenty prepare their traditional Vietnamese dishes the same way, at a smidgen of the price. The difference is that this date hot spot spares no expense on impeccably fresh seafood and meat, and some dishes gain from French-colonial-Vietnam flair. Your duck will be lean yet juicy, marinated in ginger and glazed similar to traditional duck à l'orange, and your shrimp will come in a fat, crispy beignet. *937 N Rush St between Walton and Oak Sts (312-255-0088). El: Red to Chicago. Bus: 36 Broadway. Dinner. Average main course: $19.*

⊕ **Nha Trang** The sweet Vietnamese couple that runs this little gem moved it from Little Saigon to Logan Square, but kept the authentic cuisine. The casual room, doting hosts and home-style food make the experience seem like eating in someone's home, only *this* someone churns out barbecue shrimp and sprout–packed Vietnamese pancakes; rice noodle bowls brimming with barbecue pork, crispy egg rolls and peanuts; tangy, spicy lemon shrimp; and restorative, delicate chicken broth–based soups. *3711 W Belmont Ave between*

Lawndale and Ridgeway Aves (773-588-9232). El: Blue to Belmont. Bus: 56, 77 (24hrs), 82. Lunch, dinner . Average main course: $8.

▼ ⊕ **BYOB Nhu Lan Bakery** This bakery makes about 1,000 crusty loaves of bread daily, providing the canvas for eight different *banh mi*. Pig out on the "seasoning pork," which layers pork belly atop a slather of housemade pâté. Grab sides like dried shrimp sticky rice with Chinese sausage. *2612 W Lawrence Ave between Rockwell St and Talman Ave (773-878-9898). El: Brown to Rockwell. Bus: 49 (24hrs), X49, 81 (24hrs). Breakfast, lunch, dinner (closed Tue). Average sandwich: $2.25.*

Pho 777 The main event at this Vietnamese hole-in-the-wall is, of course, the steaming bowls of *pho*, a perfect elixir on a cold and snowy Chicago day. The fairly crummy surroundings can hardly be called decor, but it's worth braving the dingy atmosphere to slurp down the hot, flavor-packed broth, along with slices of beef and vegetables. *1065 W Argyle St between Kenmore and Winthrop Aves (773-561-9909). El: Red to Argyle. Bus: 36, 81 (24hrs), 151 (24hrs). Lunch, dinner (closed Tue). Average main course: $11.*

★ ⊕ **Pho Xe Tang** Known as Tank to Anglos, this spot is the answer for indecisive diners. For Vietnamese-food pros, authentic picks are done well; for novices, the staff has suggestions. Lotus root salad (#5) is limey and minty with shrimp, crunchy peanuts and a subtle chili kick. Pho broth is rich and complex, with all of the right accompaniments. Creamy coconut milk chicken curry (#92) gets oomph from both sweet and new potatoes; and garlic-fish sauce-marinated "shaking beef" (#176) is flash-seared and served with vinegar-laced watercress. *4953-55 N Broadway St at Argyle St (773-878-2253). El: Red to Argyle. Bus: 36, 81 (24hrs), 151 (24hrs). Breakfast, lunch, dinner (closed Wed). Average main course: $7.*

⊕ **Tien Giang** See Pan Asian for review. ■

Read 'em & eat

banh mi (bahn MEE) French bread sandwich traditionally stuffed with pâté, headcheese, cilantro, jalapeños, mayo, jicama and/or carrots

banh xeo (bahn SEE-oh) crêpelike rice-flour omelette filled with pork or shrimp, mushrooms and bean sprouts

chao tom shrimp paste wrapped around sugarcane, then grilled

nuoc nam (noo-AHK NAHM) fermented fish sauce

pho (FUH) rice noodles in beef broth

Bars & Lounges

Live to drink Joie de Vine brings joy to the neighborhood.

Bars & Lounges

Northwest Side

Bim Bom Thanks to a metal-clad exterior that sticks out like a *Clockwork Orange* thumb in this ho-hum stretch of west Belmont Central, this hot, young Polish haunt is impossible to miss. Less Weed Street nightclub and more Exit metal dude hangout, the bar has an interior covered with intricate, high-quality metalwork from a local Polish artist. Add pool and foosball tables, a great jukebox and cheap drinks, and you might just start checking out real estate in the area. *5226 W Belmont Ave between Laramie and Lockwood Aves (773-777-2120). Bus: 77 Belmont (24hrs), 85 Central. Sun–Fri noon–2am; Sat noon–3am. Average beer: $3.*

Byron V's Remember when Goldschlager was big? If you want to go retro, you'll find no fewer than six bottles of the stuff on the back bar here. Speaking of gold, the jukebox plays golden oldies interspersed with some classic country. Try a Grape Bomber, grape-flavored vodka and Red Bull for the nice price of $2.50. *4342 N Elston Ave at Pulaski Ave (773-736-3303). El: Blue to Montrose. Bus: 53 Pulaski (24hrs), 78 Montrose. 10am–2am. Average beer: $2.*

(Christina's Place The windowless front door isn't exactly a welcome mat, but once inside Christina's compact, cozy digs (and after an insanely cheap $2 Guinness) you'll feel right at home. The football pennants hanging over the bar and baseball on several TVs scream sports bar, but the Talking Heads and '60s-era Stones on the juke combined with the bartender's Iggy and the Stooges shirt say otherwise. *3759 N Kedzie Ave between Waveland Ave and Grace St (773-463-1768). El: Blue to Kedzie. Bus: 80, 82, 152. Mon–Wed 5pm–4am; Thu 3pm–4am; Fri 11am–4am; Sat 11am–5am; Sun 11am–4am. Average beer: $3.*

Club Euro Way out west but looking east, Club Euro fills with Eastern Europeans during live rock and dance parties. Singles sweat it out on the dance floor in their swank duds, scoping the scene for kindred spirits. The banging techno nights bring in a more diverse cross-section of beat lovers. *5415 W Irving Park Rd between Long and Linder Aves (773-545-2224). Bus: 80, X80, 85. Wed–Thu 8pm–1am; Fri 8pm–2am; Sat 8pm–3am (closed Sun–Tue). Average cocktail: $5.*

✕ Fifth Province Pub In addition to its library and museum packed with historical acquisitions, the Irish American Heritage Center boasts a cozy weekends-only pub with free live music (Irish, of course) and Guinness-absorbing classics like fish and chips. If everyone were as beer-minded as the Irish, cultural institutions would be flooded with the thirsty and eager to learn. *4626 N Knox Ave between Wilson and Leland Aves (773-282-7035). El: Blue to Montrose. Bus: 54A, 78, 81 (24hrs). Fri 4pm–1am; Sat 5pm–1am. Average beer: $4.*

Fuller's Pub II Small touches of Irish bric-a-brac—a leprechaun napkin holder and an Erin Go Bragh flag—are the only concessions to the Old Sod. Otherwise, this shot-and-beer tap room is heavy on local sports teams past and present, with its framed pics of faded Bears heroes. Beer selections are standard American brews, including Sam Adams and Bud

longnecks, but still, it's an accommodating 18-seat bar and a good dark room to duck into when it's blazing hot outside. *3203 W Irving Park Rd at Kedzie (773-478-8060). Bus: 80 Irving Park, 82 Kimball-Homan. Sun–Fri 11am–2am; Sat 11am–3am. Average beer: $3. Cash only.*

✕ ♦ Galvin's Public House Expect to walk into a rambunctious and cheerful open room that oozes goodwill and Irish charm. Bartender Claire will serve your Magner's hard cider with ice, and the black and tan is poured so beautifully you'd swear you were at the Temple Bar in Dublin. A stone fireplace adds an authentic Irish cottage–like ambience, even though the menu includes some British fare. Live bands pep up the joint even more on the weekends. *5901 W Lawrence Ave at Marmora Ave (773-205-0570). Bus: 81 Lawrence (24hrs), 91 Austin. Sun–Fri 11am–2am; Sat 11am–3am. Average beer: $4.*

Grace's Kind of a cross between *Cheers* and the bar in "The Iceman Cometh," where the "foolosopher" in residence is 75-year-old regular Mikey Voss ("The one thing I know is I know nothing…"), this shot-and-beer joint seems much-loved by the regulars. Perhaps it's the diplomacy on display. The northernmost TV has Cubs games on, while the southernmost TV airs Sox games. Is everybody happy? A few more cheap beers and tunes from the online jukebox, and you will be. *5219 W Diversey Ave between Laramie and Lockwood Aves (773-622-2420). Bus: 76, 77 (24hrs), 85. Sun–Fri 11am–2am; Sat 11am–3am. Average beer: $2.50.*

Grealy's Pub This neighborhood tap room used to be called the Jefferson Pump, but its new name suits it like a fine Irish tweed cap. Ready at the front of the bar station is a bottle of Powers whiskey, and you don't have to remind amiable bartender Valerie to bring the water back. There's an authentic dartboard for the Irish steel darters who assemble here, and the band Finbar Fagan's plays on weekends. *5001 W Lawrence Ave at Lavergne Ave (773-736-5400). El: Blue to Jefferson Park. Bus: 81 Lawrence (24hrs). Sun–Fri 11am–2am; Sat 11am–3am. Average beer: $3.*

✲ Ham Tree Though the name is a head-scratcher, this no-frills pub is a friendly Jefferson Park retreat. A faded mural promises 101 beers, but even though that number has dwindled to a modest 15, the regulars—middle-aged dudes and their frosted-hair babes—probably couldn't care less. The trees in the adjacent beer garden don't bear any ham, but they will make for a shady spot in the summertime. *5333 N Milwaukee Ave between Central and Parkside Aves (773-792-2072). El: Blue to Jefferson Park. Bus: 56, 81 (24hrs), 85. Mon–Fri 10am–2am; Sat 11am–3am; Sun 11am–2am. Average beer: $3.*

✲ Happy Cracovia Lounge This modest Northwest Side shot-and-beer joint takes its name from the first capital of Poland—an indicator of the clientele and serving staff. Vodka's big here, and you can get a generous ice-cold pour for $3.25 and pretend it's a very dry martini (vermouth is overrated anyway). There's a full-color photo of Polish hero and international icon Pope John Paul II on the back bar, several Elvis CDs on the jukebox and an old-fashioned cigarette machine dispensing smokes at retro prices. *2025 N Cicero Ave between Armitage and McLean Aves (773-637-*

6787). Bus: 54 Cicero, 73 Armitage. Sun–Fri 11am–2am; Sat 11am–3am. Average beer: $3.

Harry's All those Elvis, railroad-train and fire-helmet decanters of booze along the back bar have been amassed over the 50 years this dingy, informal bar has been around. Bartender Ralph, who sports 21 years of history here himself, is happy to pour you a $1.25 draft or grab you a $2.25 bottle of beer and let you throw peanut shells on the floor. Ask nicely and he'll even fix you up with a bag of microwave popcorn. *5943 N Elston Ave at Mason Ave (773-774-4166). Bus: 56 Milwaukee, 91 Austin. Sun–Fri 10am–2am; Sat 10am–3am. Average beer: $2.*

✕ ✳ **Hops & Barley** Neighborhood bars are as rampant as drunks in Wrigleyville, right? So why make this one your hangout? Because your current 'hoodie doesn't have exposed wood beams and brick walls, wrought-iron chandeliers, or a downstairs lounge with leather banquettes and a black-felt pool table. The menu alone, which offers a good selection of nicely presented salads, sandwiches and steaks, is well worth becoming a regular. *4359 N Milwaukee Ave between Pensacola and Montrose Aves (773-286-7415). Bus: 54, 56, 78. Sun–Fri 11am–2am; Sat 11am–3am. Average beer: $4.*

✕ **Independence Tap** On one hand, this Cubs-friendly bar is just the kind of blue-collar, man's-man bar that would make Jim Belushi proud. Regulars sit a few stools apart and, after a few drinks, muse about finding "a word or phrase for waking up the next morning and still being drunk." On the other hand, the hefty selection of worldwide brews (like Staropramen and Löwenbräu) and friendly bartenders make its old-timey air more distinctive. *3932 W Irving Park Rd at Harding Ave (773-588-2385). El: Blue to Irving Park. Bus: 54A North Cicero/Skokie Blvd. Mon–Fri 4pm–2am; Sat 11am–3am; Sun 11am–2am. Average beer: $4. Cash only.*

✳ **J & L Lounge** The bartender, Victoria, is happy to brighten up this dark and musty bar by pouring old-fashioned cocktails like the Tequila Sunrise, Harvey Wallbanger or Sea Breeze. This place used to be the G&L Lounge (in fact, that name is still on the sign outside) although George (the "G") is no longer in the picture. There's a comfortable, aging lounge feel that makes for a good neighborhood bar experience, this free pool Monday through Thursday. *3402 N Cicero Ave at Roscoe St (773-286-0447). Bus: 54 Cicero, 152 Addison. Sun–Fri 7am–2am; Sat 7am–3am. Average beer: $3.*

Janina's Lounge Under framed pictures of smiling customers, a sweet old bartender pours you cheap PBR ($5 pitchers, $1.50 glasses) and asks how you've been. And next to you, a college kid visits with his old neighbor. Nice, right? It's easy to relax at this homey spot (the retro bowling game was the clincher for us), which feels as comforting as your grandparents' basement—with the added perk of booze. *3459 N Milwaukee Ave at Newport Ave (773-685-6676). Bus: 53 (24hrs), 56, 152. Sun–Fri noon–2am; Sat noon–3am. Average beer: $2.25.*

✕ **Jesse's Shortstop Inn** It may be named after a crucial infield position, but the night we were there, *Wife Swap* was on instead of the Cubs game—on all seven TV's! And this—on Belmont? That may be due to the feisty female bartender ("No martinis, no margaritas, no nothing but what I know how to make!"). Take your chance on gratis pretzels that look like they remember the Reagan era and tack up any complaints to the community-friendly bulletin board. *5425 W Belmont Ave at Lotus Ave (773-545-4427). Bus: 77*

Belmont (24hrs), 85 Central. Mon–Fri 7am–2am; Sat–Sun 11am–2am. Average beer: $3.

Jet's Public House Bar owner Michael Jettner has done everything right at this Gladstone Park pub. He stocks a dozen beers on tap (Blue Moon, Woodchuck Cider, etc.), nearly twice that number by the bottle, and keeps on hand all the requisite extras like darts, digital jukebox and a half-dozen TVs. Thankfully, none of it distracts from the floor-to-ceiling brick and exposed beams (not that the malecentric crowd really cares). *6148 N Milwaukee Ave at Hyacinth St (773-792-2440). Bus: 56A Milwaukee. Mon–Fri 4pm–2am; Sat 11am–3am; Sun 11am–2am. Average beer: $4.*

Kennedy's Newcomers can expect the same hairy-eyeball treatment we received upon entering this working-class bar. ("Waiting on a Metra train, are ya?" was the Irish-accented owner-bartender's greeting.) Once his right eyebrow lowered and the $1 MGD drafts started flowing, though, we felt almost as welcome as any of the regulars watching the game and enjoying well-deserved whiskey shots after quitting time. *3734 N Milwaukee Ave at Kostner Ave (773-736-1010). El: Blue to Irving Park. Bus: 54, 56, 80, 152. Mon–Fri noon–midnight; Sat, Sun noon–2am. Average beer: $2.50. Cash only.*

✕ **Kildare's Liquors and Restaurant** This place is split into three equally sooty parts, so you must pass through the liquor store to get to the restaurant and then keep going to hit the mile-long bar. Picture the not-so-glitzy side of a Vegas dive with weekend karaoke, live bands performing regularly and a meat-heavy menu featuring respectable tavern fare. *4300 W Lawrence Ave between Lowell and Kildare Aves (773-777-7033). El: Brown to Kimball. Bus: 53 (24hrs), 54A, 81 (24hrs). 11am–2am. Average cocktail: $3.50.*

▼ **Lost & Found Lounge** With its gigantic metal chandeliers, leaded glass cabinetry and old-time lever-operated cash register, this bar has a turn-of-the-century feel (the one before last) that may just make you feel a little transported. Prices aren't quite pre-Prohibition, but you will find generously poured mixed drinks for five bucks, $3 bottled domestic beer (no drafts available) and friendly people (sometimes overly friendly, if you're a gal's gal). *3058 W Irving Park Rd between Whipple St and Albany Ave (773-463-7599). Bus: 80 Irving Park, 82 Kimball/Homan. Sun–Fri 7pm–2am; Sat 7pm–3am. Average beer: $3. Cash only.*

Martini Club Polish Pride abounds at this swank and low-lit cocktail lounge: Artful black-and-white photos of Krakow's Wawel (historic center) adorn the walls, sugar-sweet Euro pop trickles from the loudspeakers and the spirit of choice is vodka. The booths are comfy and the crowd is friendly, but who cares about that when everything we tried from the impressive martini list was so irresistible? *4933 N Milwaukee Ave at Gale St (773-202-9444). El: Blue to Jefferson Park. Bus: 56A, 68, 81 (24hrs), 85, 85A, 91, 92, Pace 225, Pace 226, Pace 270. Sun–Fri 4pm–2am; Sat 4pm–3am. Average cocktail: $7.*

✳ **Mike's Ale House** If "ale" is part of your name, you'd better stock up on a few decent ones. Hopheads beware—you won't find a plethora of tap brews, but if you're looking for a sizable burger or flamin' wings, there are a dozen varieties to choose from. Now, if they could just add that same kind of variety to the ale selection, we'd happily enjoy our tater tots in this bright, airy bar and grill with something other than Goose Island. *5134 W Irving Park Rd at Leamington Ave (773-685-2260). Bus: 80, X80, 85. Sun–Fri 11am–2am; Sat 11am–3am. Average beer: $5.*

Nothing but blue skies
Taking advantage of
horsehoes is half the point
of going to Montrose Saloon.

Some people go around the corner for smokes.

We go to the ends of the earth.

FOUR CORNERS

An additive-free blend drenched in dark, mouthwatering notes from African Burley and lush, woodsy accents from the Turkish Coast. It's just one in our expansive portfolio of small batch, hand-crafted cigarettes, made with the world's rarest, most interesting tobaccos.

MARSHALL M^CGEARTY
TOBACCO ARTISANS

1553 No. Milwaukee Avenue
1 800 665 9271 . mmsmokes.com*

*LOUNGE AGE RESTRICTED (21+).
CALLS AND WEBSITE RESTRICTED
TO LEGAL AGE TOBACCO CONSUMERS.

13 mg. "tar", 1.2 mg. nicotine av. per cigarette by FTC method. Actual amount may vary depending on how you smoke. For T&N info, visit www.rjrttarnic.com.

Four Corners

Our first additive-free artisan blend. Perfectly balanced, beautifully smooth.

No additives in our tobacco
does **NOT** mean a safer cigarette.

SURGEON GENERAL'S WARNING: Smoking By Pregnant Women May Result in Fetal Injury, Premature Birth, And Low Birth Weight.

✳ Montrose Saloon This ideal neighborhood dive is somehow still an overlooked gem. The wood paneling is balanced out by exposed brick, a fantastic tin ceiling and stained-glass lamps hanging over the bar. The giant outdoor patio is one of this area's best-kept secrets—toss horseshoes, play the bean-bag game, or just drink and smoke. And don't mind the new condo-dwellers across the street complaining about the noise; they'll either move soon or come down to join you. *2933 W Montrose Ave at Richmond St (773-463-7663). Bus: 78 Montrose. Mon–Thu 2pm–2am; Fri, Sun noon–2am; Sat noon–3am. Average beer: $3.*

Three Counties This neighborhood bar is so cozy, it used to be called Snuggles Pub (no joke). But even after inheriting Irish-accented bartenders and a Guinness tap, it remains a popular homecoming hang for Gladstone Park thirtysomethings. The circular bar promotes camaraderie, '90s music is still alive in the jukebox and we got so many "Find the Third Boob" photo-hunt games out of a single dollar that we wore out our right index finger. *5856 N Milwaukee Ave between Moody and Medina Aves (773-631-3351). Bus: 56A, 68, 91. Mon–Fri 11am–2am; Sat 11am–3am; Sun 11am–2am. Average beer: $4. Cash only.*

Far North Side

✕ ✳ Bel Ami If you've ever been to a smoky back-alley café in Europe, this Bosnian coffeehouse/bar/restaurant will bring back memories of the old country. The rabid soccer fans pack the patio slugging martinis and mind-blasting coffee drinks, while ripping into platters of juicy meat specialties; think skinless sausages, thick meat patties and skewers of tender beef. *5530 N Lincoln Ave between Maplewood Ave and Rockwell St (773-878-2808). Bus: 11, 84, 93. 9am–2am. Average cocktail: $5. Cash only.*

Bruno and Tim's Lounge and Liquor Store Note to Loyola kids: If you're old enough, you can drink here. Given that it's just across the street from campus, we're really surprised the gritty space isn't crawling with students. Then again, maybe the locals here could go without hearing phrases like "Thirsty Thursday," "Wasted Wednesday" and "Sloshed Saturday." *6562 N Sheridan Rd between Loyola and Albion Aves (773-764-7900). El: Red to Loyola. Bus: 147, 151 (24hrs), 155. Mon–Fri 9am–2am; Sat 9am–3am; Sun 11am–2am. Average beer: $3.*

✕ Buffalo Bar Skip the mediocre food and the worse service at the Heartland Café and head straight to the bar inside this Rogers Park institution. If the extensive selection of $4 import beers—including Hoegaarden's perfect-for-summer white ale—is too overwhelming, the bartender is happy to make recommendations. It's enough to overlook the constantly wafting incense. Eh, hippies. *7000 N Glenwood Ave at Lunt Ave (773-465-8005). El: Red to Morse. Bus: 22 (24hrs), 147, 155. Sun–Fri 7pm–2am; Sat 7pm–3am. Average beer: $4.*

✕ Candlelite Chicago For most of you, this place isn't worth the hike. But for you Far North Siders out there, it's an oasis in your own backyard. This 60-year-old gem offers three-dozen beers (including La Fin du Monde, Delirium Tremens and Smithwicks), cracker-thin "Chicago bar–style" pizza and herb-flecked garlic fries that have quite the loyal local following. Our only hope is that someone fixes the schizo jukebox that's been playing Hall and Oates every other song. *7452 N Western Ave between Birchwood and Fargo Aves (773-465-0087). Bus: 49B, 97, 201. Sun-Fri 11am–2am, Sat 11am–3am. Average cocktail: $6.*

Cary's Lounge Smack in the middle of Indo/Pak territory, this tiny German-style hideaway has been plugging away since '72 and embraces its location with a complimentary Indian food buffet featuring various samosas and kebabs. Bartenders flip the TV channels back and forth between basketball games and *The Simpsons*, but if that doesn't interest you, there's free pool, karaoke on random nights and a stash of frisky regulars to keep you occupied. *2251 W Devon Ave between Oakley and Bell Aves (773-743-5737). Bus: 22 (24hrs), 49B, 155. Mon–Fri 10am–2am; Sat 9am–3am, Sun 11am–2am. Average beer: $2.50.*

Claddagh Ring It looks like the owners have sunk a fair amount of dough into this spiffy Irish pub and saloon. A digital juke hangs on the wall, flat-screen TVs abound and the comfy seating makes the place feel lounge-y. Though there are plenty of gimmicks (Wednesday, for example, is "Get hammered and nailed" night, which includes a cocktail and manicure for $12), most people are happiest just chilling out with a beer. *2306 W Foster Ave at Oakley Ave (773-271-4794). Bus: 49 (24hrs), X49, 49B. Mon–Fri 10am–2am; Sat 7am–2am; Sun 11am–2am. Average beer: $4.*

Cunneen's Newspaper articles declaring the end of Prohibition hang on the walls and the clock is graced with Mayor Daley's mug…the *first* Mayor Daley. So it's no surprise that this place is as friendly, neighborly and comfortable as bars used to be back in the day, you know, before velvet ropes and vodka Red Bulls. *1424 W Devon Ave between Glenwood and Newgard Aves (773-274-9317). El: Red to Loyola. Bus: 22 (24hrs), 36, 155. Sun–Fri noon–2am; Sat noon–3am. Average beer: $3.50. Cash only.*

Dino's Liquors Every family has a creepy uncle, and we just found his hangout. Part liquor store, part bar—this oddly-lit (fluorescent AND incandescent lights?), worn-out corner tap has managed to rope in a small but loyal contingent of whiskery, sunken-faced older men. Some of them come to smoke hands-free and pump money into the Cherry Masters game, while the other smarmy fellers shoot pool waiting to ogle the one unfortunate woman that accidentally walks in here every decade. *6400 N Clark St at Devon Ave (773-743-8282). El: Red to Loyola. Bus: 22 (24hrs), 36, 151 (24hrs), 155. Mon–Fri 7am–2am; Sat 7am–3am; Sun 11am–2am. Average beer: $3.*

✕ Emerald Isle This Far North Side Irish hangout answers the question, "Are fiftysomething men still horny?" They are, at least according to the middle-aged working gals who are relentlessly being hit on at the bar. On the other hand, the place boasts a killer jukebox, expansive seating, cheap pub food, an outdoor patio and a clientele that will gladly make a cigarette run for everyone in the room. *2537 W Peterson Ave at Maplewood Ave (773-561-6674). Bus: 49B Western, 84 Peterson. Mon–Fri 11am–2am; Sat 11am–2am; Sun 11am–midnight. Average beer: $3.50. Cash only.*

☾ ▼ Jackhammer A construction theme dominates this Rogers Park gay bar, where a grab bag of leather dudes, street-tuff trannies and Boystowners out for adventure cram the dance floor on weekend nights. If you can lure yourself away from the constant porn, a beautiful outdoor patio beckons with a psychic on hand to predict that the guy you're about to take home is probably not the same one you'll be introducing to your parents one day. *6406 N Clark St at Devon Ave (773-743-5772). Bus: 22 Clark (24hrs). Mon–Thu 4pm–4am; Fri 4pm–5am; Sat 2pm–5am; Sun 2pm–4am. Average beer: $3.*

Get down The disco ball makes every night boogie night at Star Gaze.

Jarheads Sarge did two tours in Vietnam, and this Rogers Park bar, which he's owned for 17 years, is a shrine to his Marine Corps roots. He's plastered military pictures, flak jackets, packs and other paraphernalia on the walls, while camouflage netting hangs from the ceiling and above the pool table. After buying you a shot of "jungle juice," Sarge will pull up a stool and fill your ear with stories about chasing "Charlies" and keeping out the Rogers Park riffraff. Semper fi! *6973 N Clark St between Morse and Lunt Aves (773-973-1907). El: Red to Morse. Bus: 22 Clark (24hrs). Tues-Sun 4pm–"til everyone leaves" (closed Mon). Average beer: $3. Cash only.*

✗ **Karaoke Restaurant** Want to reenact the karaoke scene from *Lost in Translation* but can't afford the ticket to Tokyo? This Korean joint in a West Rogers Park strip mall will do the trick. Several private karaoke rooms can be reserved (hourly rates range from $45 to $60, depending upon the size of your group) and are outfitted with room-service buttons so you can have your Korean-style popcorn chicken and soju delivered while you do your best "Brass in Pocket." *6248 N California Ave between Granville and Rosemont Aves (773-274-1166). Bus: 93 California/Dodge, 155 Devon. 5pm–3am. Average beer: $3.*

Lamp Post Tavern This Rogers Park corner bar is a lesson in—well—a neighborhood corner bar: sports on the TVs, cold beer on tap and a bunch of dudes flapping their jaws about their favorite teams. For those allergic to sports, picture windows look out over the street, and we have to admit that watching traffic and sipping a beer isn't a bad way to spend a Sunday afternoon. *7126 N Ridge Blvd at Touhy*

Ave (773-465-9571). Bus: 49B Western, Pace 290. Sun–Fri noon–2am; Sat noon–3am. Average beer: $4.

✳ **Leadway Bar and Gallery** As in a middle-school art classroom, you'll find row upon row of paintings on butcher paper covering the bar's bronze-plated, mosaic-tile walls. 'Hood-dwelling thirtysomethings are free to venture over to the easel and, with in-house supplies, create a work of their own twisted genius. Whether it's Surrealist, Abstract, Cubist or Impressionist, the more you drink, the better it will look. *5233 N Damen Ave at Farragut Ave (773-728-2663). Bus: 50 Damen, 92 Foster. Sun–Fri 4pm–2am; Sat 4pm–3am. Average beer: $4.*

◖ ✗ **Mark II Lounge** Dimly lit—probably to hide the many blemishes it has acquired over its half century in business—and teetering on the edge of town between the Loyola and Northwestern campuses, this cozy, low-ceilinged dive is home to a bevy of Far North Side comrades (i.e., smarmy old men) and students who trek off-campus for the cheap pool, cheap darts and even cheaper beer. *7436 N Western Ave at Fargo Ave (773-465-9675). Bus: 49B Western, 96 Lunt. Mon–Fri 5pm–4am; Sat 7pm–5am; Sun 7pm–4am. Average beer: $3.*

✗ **Mullen's Bar and Grill** This Far North Side chapter of the Mullen's fraternity is for those who want their bench-pressed, score-obsessed sports bar, but don't want to jockey for a set in the jockstrap that is Wrigleyville. With eight TVs and an abundance of booths, there's plenty of sight lines and legroom for the medley of postgame softball leaguers and dart-lobbing locals, who all enjoy a more civilized type of testosterone. *7301 N Western Ave at Chase Ave (773-465-2113). Bus: 49B North Western, 96 Lunt. Sun–Fri 11am–2am; Sat 11am–3am. Average Beer: $3.*

✗ **One Galaria** If high cheekbones, scantily clad babes and sultry, late-night grinding are your thing, check out this Serbian hot spot. Those in the know go on ladies night (Thursday), when all three (plus kamakazi shots) are in full effect. Stay tuned for the kitchen to start tossing out more than the meze platter, which for now serves its purpose as party fuel. *5130 N Western Ave at Winona St (773-275-1430). El: Brown to Western. Bus: 49B, 81 (24hrs), 92. 6pm–2am. Average cocktail: $5.*

Poitin Stil It's pronounced "poo-cheen still" (Gaelic for "moonshine"), but take the bartenders' cue and call it "the Stil." This Rogers Park pub is the antithesis of its former inhabitant, Charmers, the city's oldest, grittiest and emptiest gay bar: It's bright and bustling, there's often live music and friendly bartenders pour a proper Guinness. Rest assured, nostalgists: Charmers' beautiful Art Deco bar remains intact. *1502 W Jarvis Ave at Greenview Ave (773-338-3285). El: Red to Jarvis. Bus: 22 (24hrs), 147, 151 (24hrs). 3pm–2am. Average beer: $4. Cash only.*

Red Line Tap Just around the corner from the Heartland Café, this Rogers Park hangout wears many hats: On any given night, the place could be packed with hippies, punks or hipsters depending on who's playing on the stage. If you don't dig, say, the bluegrass band wailing away, sidle up to the adjoining bar area for a more laid-back evening. *7006 N Glenwood Ave between Lunt and Greenleaf Aves (773-338-9862). El: Red to Morse. Bus: 22 (24hrs), 96, 147, 151 (24hrs). Mon–Fri 3pm–2am; Sat 2pm–3am; Sun 2pm–2am. Average cocktail: $4.*

Smilin' Jim's Saloon This spotless bar has been a Rogers Park fixture for ten years, and we're thinking it's due

Bars & Lounges

to the free barbecue doled out 5–8pm daily during the summer and the $1.25 drafts. Don't be surprised to see a blue-collar regular stroll in with 20 pounds of raw chicken and commence grilling—it's just a help-yourself kinda joint. *6306 N Western Ave between Rosemont and Devon Aves (773-973-7422). Bus: 49B Western, 155 Devon. Mon–Fri 2pm–2am; Sat 10am–3am; Sun 11am–2am. Average beer: $1.75.*

(▼ **Touché** Among the city's collection of gay leather bars, this dimly lit establishment—free of the usual blinding lights and techno beats—is perhaps the most laid-back and conversation-friendly of them all. Muted porn videos play on four out of seven TVs, while an older crowd drinks cheap beers (50-cent drafts on Sundays). Don't fret if you happen to waltz in on a day when your leathers are at the cleaners: Jeans and a T-shirt are just as common here as chaps and a vest. *6412 N Clark St between Devon and Schreiber Aves (773-465-7400). El: Red to Loyola. Bus: 22 (24hrs), 36, 151 (24hrs), 155. Mon–Fri 5pm–4am; Sat 3pm–5am; Sun 3pm–4am. Average beer: $3.*

Andersonville/Edgewater/Uptown

▼ ✗ ✳ **Big Chicks** Don't let the name fool you. It's practically all guys in here and calling them "big" could get you bitch-slapped. Andersonville's queer den mother Michelle Fire decks out her bar with choice selections from her impressive art collection, a good back-up plan in case there's a lack of other eye candy. *5024 N Sheridan Rd between Argyle St and Carmen Ave (773-728-5511). El: Red to Argyle. Bus: 151 Sheridan (24hrs). Mon–Fri 4pm–2am; Sat 3pm–3am; Sun 11am–2am. Average cocktail: $4. Cash only.*

✗ **Carol's Pub** A honky-tonk in Sheridan Park with $1.50 Busch bottles, country western karaoke on Thursdays and the house band Diamondback on weekends, featuring sassy little Reba singin' and strummin' rhythm with a darn good gee-tar picker on lead. A pool table in back, greasy grill turning out late-night burgers and Hank-filled jukebox round out the grit fest. *4659 N Clark St between Wilson and Leland Aves (773-334-2402). El: Red to Wilson. Bus: 22 Clark (24hrs), 145 Wilson/Mich Exp. Mon, Tue 9am–2am; Wed–Sun 11am–4am. Average beer: $2.50. Cash only.*

▼ ✗ ✳ ♨ **Charlie's Ale House** Like a gay Cheers, everybody knows everybody's name at the Andersonville outpost of this local mini-chain. A long winding bar, amber lighting, dark wood and green leather booths make for a tavern-y spot to sip one of the gajillion beers or two dozen wines by the glass. TVs show sports, but older locals are focused on their grilled chicken Caesars, and the lesbians are too busy flirting to notice. *5308 N Clark St between Berwyn and Summerdale Aves (773-751-0140). El: Red to Berwyn. Bus: 22 (24hrs), 50, 92. Sun–Fri 11:30am–1am; Sat 10:30am–2am. Average beer: $4. · Additional location at Navy Pier, 700 E Grand Ave (312-595-1440). Go to charliesalehouse.com for suburban locations.*

(▼ **Chicago Eagle** Thanks to proprietor and activist Chuck Renslow and competitions like International Mr. Leather (which is headquartered here), fetish bars enjoy a pretty mainstream status. That doesn't mean this one is for the faint of heart. The front room is dimly lit with Tom of Finland–esque artwork (i.e., well-endowed dudes in various erotic poses) while a dress-code enforced backroom is so dimly lit we can only describe it as dungeonesque. *5015 N Clark St between Argyle St and Winnemac Ave (773-728-*

0050). Bus: 22 Clark (24hrs), 92 Foster. Sun–Thu, 8pm–4am; Sat 8pm–5am. Average cocktail: $5.

Clark's on Clark Sometimes we forget about the gay bars for the older (read: over 25), T-shirt-and-jeans set. But after a night of pool with the lusty normal-Joes at this dark, seedy Uptown joint we don't think we'll ever forget. The drink menu is nothing to scream about, but the porn they show definitely is. *5001 N Clark St at Argyle St (773-728-2373). El: Red to Argyle. Bus: 22 Clark (24hrs). Mon–Fri 2pm–4am; Sat noon–5am; Sun noon–4am. Average beer: $3. Cash only.*

County Pub We've bellied up to many Irish pubs, but we've never seen anything quite as striking as this sporty, well-worn pub's wall filled with Irish coats of arms. Tacked up against a green backdrop, those decorations bring an old-world Ireland feel to the place, so it's all the more puzzling that there's zero Guinness on tap and not one Irish lad in sight. *6341 N Clark St between Highland and Devon Aves (773-274-0499). El: Red to Loyola. Bus: 22 (24hrs), 36, 151 (24hrs), 155. Mon–Fri 8am–2am; Sat 11am–3am; Sun 11am–2am. Average beer: $3.*

▼ ✗ ✳ **Crew Bar and Grill** Whether you're hungry for baseball, football, rugby or just beer, this straight-friendly gay sports bar will definitely work. Forty beers on tap (75 total), tasty (and even healthy) pub grub, lots of TVs and a rah-rah decor make this a fun place to cheer for your team, whatever team you're on. *4804 N Broadway between Lawrence Ave and Gunnison St (773-784-2739). El: Red to Lawrence. Bus: 22 (24hrs), 36, 81 (24hrs), 151 (24hrs). Mon–Fri 11:30am–2am; Sat 11am–3am; Sun 11am–2am. Average beer: $4.*

Getting in the Moody's
Beers and burgers are the stuff of romance at Moody's Pub.

Side dish

This Bud's for you
No matter the weather, there's a beer bar with a light on for you.

Slainte There is never a shortage of St. Patrick's Day green at Cork & Kerry.

Few pastimes are more Chicago than kicking back a cold one. In the brief warm-weather months, locals do this at one of the many bars with beer gardens: outdoor oases for sipping suds. A good beer garden requires both a decent beer list and a comfy spot for soaking up the city's short summer.

The Beverly neighborhood, home of the South Side Irish, is also home to **Cork & Kerry (10614 S Western Ave between 106th and 107th Sts, 773-445-2675),** where high beer-garden fences and leafy trees afford some privacy, and Guinness and Harp are mainstays. The original **Charlie's Ale House** in Lincoln Park (1224 W Webster Ave between Racine and Magnolia Aves, 773-871-1440), with its inviting ivy-covered patio, is an institution with the college crowd. Roscoe Village's **Village Tap (2055 W Roscoe St between Hoyne and Seeley Aves, 773-883-0817)** pours 26 draft selections and puts up sports tarps for when it rains. **Sheffield's** (3258 N Sheffield Ave between School St and Belmont Ave, 773-281-4989) has an enormous shaded beer garden with plenty of picnic-style seating. **Ten Cat** (3931 N Ashland Ave between Irving Park Rd and Byron St, 773-935-5377) is decorated with antique patio furniture, orange fencing and Christmas lights.

Even without a garden, a few serious beer bars draw hopheads year-round with stellar lists. Among the best is Bucktown's **Map Room** (1949 N Hoyne between Armitage Ave and Homer St, 773-252-7636), highly regarded for its 25 beers on tap and more than 150 bottled selections. It also teaches "beer school" classes for novices. **Quenchers** (2401 N Western Ave at Fullerton Ave, 773-276-9730), a long-standing corner tavern–turned–craft-brew mecca, offers discerning drinkers 165 selections. Quaff down more than 40 beer selections at **Kuma's Corner** (2900 W Belmont Ave at Francisco Ave, 773-604-8769), followed by some of the city's best burgers.

Serious craft-beer fans know that **Hopleaf** (5148 N Clark St between Foster Ave and Winona St, 773-334-9851) is the epicenter of Chicago beer-geek mania. Hopleaf offers more than 40 drafts, at least three times as many bottles, and surprisingly upscale bistro-style pub fare.

Driftwood Inn It may be nestled in a new condo monolith, but there's a casual working class neighborhood bar hiding beneath the surface. The bartenders are friendly types who pour with a heavy hand, and while the bar is a case study in Uptown's gentrification, everybody gets along fine over a drink. The pool table and darts provide nice diversions, and two little seating alcoves offer the feeling of a private party. *1021 W Montrose Ave at Broadway (773-975-3900). El: Red to Wilson. Bus: 36, 78, 151 (24hrs). Sun–Fri 5pm–2am; Sat 5pm–3am. Average cocktail: $6.*

✗ **The Edgewater** This smoky bar on the edge of Andersonville offers a homey menu that's good enough to snap you out of that chicken-wing trance you've been lulled into. Nightly specials like Fried Chicken Sundays and Sloppy Joe Thursdays are mighty good. The excellent beer and wine selection and chummy staff will pleasantly surprise you. *5600 N Ashland Ave at Bryn Mawr (773-878-3343). Bus: 22 (24hrs), 50, 92. Sun–Fri noon–2am; Sat noon–3am. Average beer: $4.*

Farragut's Quite possibly the straightest bar in Andersonville, this place gets packed on the weekends with breeders who stop by to drink Goose Island 312, shoot pool, watch some sports, and, sometimes, get drunk by themselves near the patio doors and yell things at passersby. *5240 N Clark St between Farragut and Berwyn Aves (773-728-4903). Bus: 22 (24hrs), 50, 92. Sun–Fri 3pm–2am; Sat 3pm–3am. Average beer: $3.*

▼ **The Granville Anvil** On weekends, the small crowd at this dodgy, dimly lit man's bar can make it feel downright convivial. Otherwise the faded watering hole is surely where Edgewater's gentrification will hold its last stand. Lonely? Drop a few quarters in the jukebox and pour your heart out along with Dolly as she begs Jolene not to take her man. *1137 W Granville Ave at Winthrop Ave (773-973-0006). El: Red to Granville. Bus: 147, 151 (24hrs), 155. Mon–Sat 9am–2am; Sun 11am–2am. Average cocktail: $5.*

▼ ✗ ✳ **Joie de Vine** A wine bar this charming has no business being hidden on a quiet residential street. The location might be why you'll often have the place to yourself. The wine list has some tasty values (both New and Old World) and the small-plates menu has bites like artisan cheeses and charcuterie to offset a nasty wine hangover. *1744 W Balmoral Ave between Paulina St and Ravenswood Ave (773-989-6846). Bus: 22 (24hrs), 50, 92. Sun–Fri 5pm–2am; Sat 5pm–3am. Average glass of wine: $7.*

▼ **Kitty Moon** Owner Dave Miller is a classically trained musician who has transformed this neighborhood tavern into a cozy, low-key venue for those of his kind. With the Art Deco–accented barroom, expanded beer selection and nightly performances of jazz, bluegrass, rock and even opera, music makers and music admirers can grab a pint and oscillate between *fortissimo* and *pianissimo* all night long. *6237 N Clark St at Thome Ave (773-856-6667). El: Red to Granville. Bus: 22 Clark (24hrs), 155 Devon. Sun–Fri 6pm–2am; Sat 6pm–3am. Average cocktail: $5.*

✗ **Konak Pizza & Grill** A tasty pie in a laid-back atmosphere is the specialty of this Andersonville joint. We recommend the house pizza, a unique combo of eggplant, jalapeño peppers and garlic on a crispy (but thankfully not cracker-thin) crust. And if you're just in it for the booze, grab a Delirium Tremens and a seat at one of the couches in the back that surround a big-screen TV. But don't try bringing back munchies; like at home, there's a no-eating rule in the living room. *5150 N Clark St between Winona St and Foster Ave*

Is it hot in here? Warm up with a hottie under the heated patio at Fireside.

773-271-6688). Bus: 22 (24hrs), 36, 92. Sun–Fri 4pm–
am; Sat 4pm–3am. Average beer: $3. Cash only.

▼ ❋ **Marty's** This upscale Andersonville martini lounge
as been burning through olives and vermouth faster than a
teakhouse since it opened. But don't expect to rub elbows
rith homos all night. Straight folk tend to show up first for a
redinner cocktail, and the gay crowd comes later. Like
entrification, but in reverse. *1511 W Balmoral Ave at Clark
't (773-561-6425). El: Red to Berwyn. Bus: 22 (24hrs), 36,
0, 92. 5pm–2am. Average cocktail: $10.*

Max's Place Max is actually a woman (Maxine) and her
ptown establishment is a seminar in Dive Bar 101: the pours
re dangerously strong, the drinks are ridiculously cheap, the
artenders are gloriously mulleted, and the regulars are, uh,
on't sit in anyone's seat and keep those eyes on the bottom of
nat Old Style. *4621 N Clark St between Wilson and Leland
ves (773-784-3864). El: Red to Wilson. Bus: 22 (24hrs), 36,
45. Mon–Sat 7am–2am; Sun 11am–2am. Average beer: $3.*

✕ ❋ ♦ **Moody's Pub** In summer, this beer garden is one
f the best in Chicago, but only if you can deal with ass-to-
lbow crowds. We prefer this beer-and-burger haven in
rinter, when we can snag a table by the fireplace and get cozy
rith our date. Just remember to bring a flashlight to read the
nenu; the place is dark enough that you could carry on an
ffair while your spouse is sitting across the room. *5910 N
roadway between Rosedale and Thorndale Aves (773-275-
696). El: Red to Thorndale. Bus: 36 Broadway, 84 Peterson.*

Mon–Fri 11:30am–1am; Sat 11:30am–2am; Sun noon–
1am. Average beer: $3. Cash only.

Nick's on Wilson Nick Novich (the proprietor of Nick's
Uptown and the original Nick's in Wicker Park) must view
his newest bar as a long-term investment, but we see it as yet
another sign of the inevitable Uptown renaissance. The
bartenders admit the place hasn't yet caught on (weary
Truman professors being the exception), but with its exposed
brick walls, bright red bar, and chic, lofty atmosphere, it's
only a matter of time before it's packed. *1140 W Wilson Ave
between Clifton and Racine Aves (773-271-1155). El: Red to
Wilson. Bus: 22 (24hrs), 36, 145. Mon–Fri 3pm–2am; Sat
3pm–3am; Sun 3pm–2am. Average beer: $4.*

✕ **Ole St Andrew's Inn** With its high-backed wooden
chairs, collection of sabers and, allegedly, a drunken ghost
roaming about, this tavern has a distinctly medieval aura
about it. Even though we haven't spotted any ghosts here,
we're believers: Some of the patrons look like they're on their
last legs and are ready to haunt any day now. *5938 N
Broadway at Thorndale Ave (773-784-5540). El: Red to
Thorndale. Bus: 36 Broadway. Mon–Fri 3pm–2am; Sat
noon–3am; Sun noon–2am. Average beer: $4.*

Ollie's Even at 10am you'll find a loyal clientele of grizzled
late-shifters raising glasses of Old Style to making it through
a night at the factory, buying cigarettes and Snickers from the
same vending machine, and then taking a sixer to go. In other
words, everyone bellying up to the vinyl-padded bar at this
'50s-era gem is a royal cut-up. *1064 W Berwyn Ave between*

Time Out Chicago Eating & Drinking **187**

Kenmore and Winthrop Aves (773-784-5712). El: Red to Berwyn. Bus: 92, 136, 146, 151 (24hrs). Mon–Sat 10am–11pm; Sun 11am–9pm. Average beer: $3.

✗ **Pressure Billiards & Café** Sinking the eight ball without scratching and the siren song of a second biscotto are perhaps the only real pressures at this Edgewater café. Because the only shots this place serves up are espresso, it has a neighborhood rec-center vibe. But when you consider the open nine-ball tournament on Tuesdays, stand-up comedy on Saturdays and free Wi-Fi, you won't miss the booze. 6318 N Clark St at Highland Ave (773-743-7665). El: Red to Granville. Bus: 22 Clark (24hrs), 36 Broadway. 10am–2am. Average coffee: $3.

✗ 🍺 **The Pumping Company** This warm, casual Edgewater hangout (formerly known as Sizzle on Broadway) is a great place to cozy up to a fireplace with a brewski and a plate of cheese fries during the winter months, but the beer garden also packs 'em in during the dog days. And despite the hard-rock vibe of the '80s soundtrack, the eclectic clientele—whose attire during our last visit ranged from chunky glasses and pompadours to jerseys and Afros—is refreshingly chill. 6157 N Broadway between Hood and Granville Aves (773-465-9500). El: Red to Granville. Bus: 36, 136, 147, 151 (24hrs). Mon–Thu 3pm–2am; Fri, Sat 11am–3am; Sun 11am–2am. Average beer: $4.

✳ 🍺 **Ravenswood Pub** This is the cleanest hole-in-the-wall we've ever seen—and one of the friendliest, too. Within your first hour of arrival, you'll rule the digital jukebox, become best friends with the bartender, and be a dozen quarters into a heated match of NTN Trivia. We've just found our home away from home. 5455 N Ravenswood Ave between Foster and Bryn Mawr Aves (773-769-6667). Bus: 50 Damen, 92 Foster. Sun–Fri 11am–2am; Sat 11am–3am. Average beer: $3.50.

Sheridan "L" Lounge and Delicatessen If you've been searching for a hideout, this shadowy, windowless bar crammed between the Sheridan Red Line station and a liquor store is virtually invisible. There's no deli to speak of, so the scant, mostly Latino clientele divide their attention between the pool table in the back and the shrill telenovelas playing on the TV at the bar. Invisibility has its price. 3944 N Sheridan Rd between Dakin St and Irving Park Rd (no phone). El: Red to Sheridan. Bus: 80, X80, 151 (24hrs). Noon–1am. Average beer: $3. Cash only.

Sherry's Bar Across the street from Rosehill Cemetery and wedged between two auto shops, this place is easy to miss. In truth, Sherry's is not to be missed. Inside, Sherry's creates a nice balance: plenty of Bears memorabilia for the sports fans, and dark red walls and retro photos for the cozy-seeking set. And who doesn't like huge burgers served by an old dude who blasts the Clash? In truth, Sherry's is not to be missed. 5652 N Western Ave between Bryn Mawr and Hollywood Aves (773-784-2143). Bus: 49 Western (24hrs), 84 Peterson. Mon–Sat 11am–2am, Sun 11am–midnight. Average beer: $3.

▼ 🍺 **Simon's Tavern** If you're lucky, you can snag a couch by the fireplace where you can take in the cool vintage bar (built in the '30s to resemble a bar on the U.S. Normandy), sip seasonal glögg and check out the friendly neighborhood crowd (equal mix of gay and straight). 5210 N Clark St between Foster and Farragut Aves (773-878-0894). El: Red to Berwyn. Bus: 22 (24hrs), 50, 92. Sun–Fri 11am–2am; Sat 11am–3am. Average cocktail: $4. Cash only.

The Sovereign Many a North Side hipster calls this friendly, laid-back bastion of bargain booze a second home. Little here is touched by time: The '50s-era sign still hangs outside, a jukebox is packed with British Invasion gems, and it's one of the few places where you can still grab a six-pack on your way out the door. 6202 N Broadway at Granville Ave (773-274-0057). El: Red to Granville. Bus: 22 (24hrs), 36, 136, 147, 151 (24hrs), 155. Sun–Fri noon–2am; Sat noon–3am. Average beer: $3. Cash only.

✗ **The Spot** With its three distinct barrooms, this Uptown oasis is custom-made for the indecisive patron. An imposing wine rack and wafting surf-and-turf scents give the ground floor an air of fine dining. But we recommend heading upstairs for all the fun: Mondays' martini and a manicure in the lounge, Thursdays' improv competition, and Fridays' '80s-themed burlesque revue. 4437 N Broadway between Montrose and Sunnyside Aves (773-728-8933). El: Red to Wilson. Bus: 36. Sun–Fri 11am–2am; Sat 11am–3am. Average cocktail: $7.

▼ **Star Gaze** The mirrored wall, prehistoric disco ball and battered, industrial furniture make this Andersonville girls bar feel like an Elk lodge. That is, when there aren't a couple of women pressed up against the bar, grinding into each other so maniacally that their softball caps fall off. 5419 N Clark St between Balmoral and Rascher Aves (773-561-7363). El: Red to Berwyn. Bus: 22 Clark (24hrs), 92 Foster. Tue–Fri 5pm–2am; Sat 5pm–3am; Sun 1pm–2am. Average cocktail: $4.

▼ ✗ 🍺 **T's** The girls and boys at this Andersonville bar and grill may smile politely at each other, maybe mumble a hello, but usually they're in separate rooms. The lesbians flirt in the clubbier back room, the guys hang out in front and the straight people wander back and forth, trying to figure out where they are. Occasional live theater performances in the back attract a more mixed crowd. 5025 N Clark St at Winnemac Ave (773-784-6000). El: Red to Argyle. Bus: 22 Clark (24hrs), 92 Foster. Mon–Thurs 5pm–2am; Fri 3pm–2am; Sat 11am–3am; Sun 11am–2am. Average cocktail: $5.

Tropico Across the street from the Sheridan Red Line station, this place packs in Latino pool enthusiasts looking for cheap MGD to chase even cheaper tequila shots. A tiled floor in front of the entrance says "Elks," which makes sense given that the spacious, woody surroundings—filled with dusty two-tops and chairs—look like they're straight out of a '70s Elks lodge. 3933 N Sheridan Rd at Dakin St (no phone). El: Red to Sheridan. Bus: 36, 80, 151 (24hrs). 1pm–1am. Average beer: $3.

Uptown Lounge In the late-night/early-morning hours, Lawrence Street can often resemble an urban ghost town. But behind the tinted windows of this surprisingly chic, minimalist lounge, pretty people sit on comfy couches and in tall-backed booths under red lighting, sipping martinis. DJs (Wed–Sat) and karaoke (Sun) are a plus, but the late-night liquor license keeps us stumbling back, again and again. 1136 W Lawrence Ave at Clifton Ave (773-878-1136). El: Red to Lawrence. Bus: 36, 81 (24hrs), 151 (24hrs). Sun–Fri 4pm–4am; Sat 4pm–5am. Average cocktail: $6.

Lincoln Square/Ravenswood

◖ **Big Joe's** There's nothing particularly inventive about this corner tap, both levels of which are usually inhabited by your run-of-the-mill, shaggy-haired, middle-aged whiskey sippers—nothing, that is, unless you're here on a Friday

Pin head There are beers to spare at Lincoln Square Lanes.

night. That's when the place fills up with a mix of yuppies, hipsters and everybody in between for a few friendly rounds of turtle racing. (Sounds like a euphemism, we know, but we assure you it's not.) *1818 W Foster Ave at Honore St (773-784-8755). Bus: 50 Damen, 92 Foster. Mon–Fri 1pm–2am; Sat noon–3am; Sun noon–2am. Average beer: $3.*

✕ **Bowman's Bar & Grill** Lincoln Square was apparently starved for a big, classic sports bar—the kind of place that you can stumble into at 1am and find it so boisterous that you get your second wind by osmosis. It's so packed you can barely eat a french fry without getting ketchup on a stranger's shirt, but don't worry—chances are they've had too many beers to notice. *4356 N Leavitt St at Lincoln Ave (773-478-9999). El: Brown to Western. Bus: 11, 49 (24hrs), X49, 50, 78. Mon–Wed 4pm–2am; Thu, Fri, Sun 11am–2am; Sat 11am–3am. Average beer: $5.*

✕ ✳ **Cafe Bourbon** A smoky throwback to the Eastern Bloc (circa '71), this Serbian stomping (and chowing) ground comes decked out with an old-school synth player, glowing blue lights and a randy atmosphere. If it weren't for the cute, heavy-accented waitresses, you'd swear you were back in high school, sweatin' out the hangover shakes in your parents' basement. *4768 N Lincoln Ave at Lawrence Ave (773-769-3543). El: Brown to Western. Bus: 49 (24hrs), X49, 81 (24hrs). 10am–2am. Average cocktail: $5.*

Carola's Hansa Clipper If the heavy weekend traffic of thirtysomethings at Huettenbar ain't your thing, check out this less refined German spot just down the block. The bare-bones setting makes for a laid-back, chatty evening of drinking drafts of König Ludwig or Warsteiner Dunkel. True, the decorative Christmas lights and homemade $6 Jäger

bombs $6 sign scream tackiness, but there's something refreshing about a place that looks like it hasn't changed since 1975. *4659 N Lincoln Ave at Leland Ave (773-878-3662). El: Brown to Western. Bus: 11, 49 (24hrs), 81 (24hrs). Mon–Fri 10am–2am; Sat 10am–3am; Sun noon–2am. Average beer: $5. Cash only.*

❨ ✕ ♦ **Fireside** Ravenswood locals flock to this bar for its namesake's warmth (everyone loves the covered, heated patio) and coziness. Bartenders tend to pour heavy here—we ordered a Scotch on the rocks and found ourselves drinking from a full highball glass—so some food from the adjoining restaurant will be in order to soak it all up. *5739 N Ravenswood Ave between Olive Ave and Rosehill Dr (773-561-7433). El: Red to Bryn Mawr. Bus: 22 (24hrs), 36, 50. Mon–Fri 11am–4am; Sat 11am–5am; Sun 10am–4am. Average beer: $3.*

42 Degrees N. Latitude This Lincoln Square spot is never crowded, and we can't figure out why. The ambience (exposed brick and chocolate hues) is classy, the drinks are strong enough and the food (typical pub grub) fills us up, but for some reason 42 just doesn't pack 'em in. Come to think of it, we kind of like having the big space all to ourselves. *4500 N Lincoln Ave at Sunnyside Ave (773-907-2226). El: Brown to Western. Bus: 11, 49 (24hrs), 78. Mon–Fri 5pm–2am; Sat 11am–3am; Sun 11am–midnight. Average beer: $4.*

✕ **Gio's Sports Pub and Grill** The owners behind this tiny corner tavern must've taken a class called "Friendly Neighborhood Bar 101" because they've nailed down all the requisite perks. There's a brand-spankin'-new digital jukebox on the exposed brick wall, several TVs, cheap pub fare, daily drink specials, ladies night (Tuesday), karaoke

night (Saturday), dart competitions and free pool on Sundays. Pour us another. *4857 N Damen Ave at Ainslie St (773-334-0345). El: Brown to Damen. Bus: 50 Damen, 81 Lawrence (24hrs). Mon–Fri 4pm–2am; Sat noon–3am; Sun noon–2am. Average beer: $3.*

🍴 **The Grafton** Owner Malcolm Molloy has that fresh-off-the-boat brogue that could charm the pants off your own mother. But please don't take this for one of your run-of-the-mill McIrish pubs. Bluegrass bands pluck away and locals might lift a Cosmo just as soon as a pint. So compared with most other pubs laying claim to the Emerald Isle, it's a sea of tranquility. *4530 N Lincoln Ave between Sunnyside and Wilson Aves (773-271-9000). El: Brown to Western. Bus: 11 Lincoln, 78 Montrose. Mon–Fri 5pm–2am; Sat 11am–3am; Sun 11am–2am. Average beer: $5.*

◖ **Hidden Cove** Young and old, dregs and misfits, singers and drunkards—all break out their best shower voice at this Ravenswood spot for karaoke seven nights a week. You're as likely to hear Young MC's "Bust a Move" as you are Sinatra's "It Was a Very Good Year." The same kind of juxtaposition puts watermelon shots next to Manhattans on the weekly specials board. Deee-lish. *5336 N Lincoln Ave between Summerdale and Balmoral Aves (773-275-6711). Bus: 11 Lincoln. 7am–4am. Average beer: $3.*

Huettenbar This charming Lincoln Square "cottage bar" offers a huge selection of German drafts. Sadly, most of the traditional German tunes on the jukebox are gone, but couples still slow-dance to classic pop. Check out the fetching portrait of Irma, the owner, behind the front bar. *4721 N Lincoln Ave between Leland and Lawrence Aves (773-561-2507). El: Brown to Western. Bus: 11, 49 (24hrs), X49, 81 (24hrs). Mon–Fri 2pm–2am; Sat noon–3am; Sun noon–2am. Average beer: $4.50.*

✕ ✱ **Jury's** For one of the best tavern burgers in town (try the blue cheese, medium-rare) and a classy beer garden, this is the spot. Umbrella-topped tables, a wooden privacy fence, ivy-covered brick, friendly service and a superbly stocked bar complete the package. *4337 N Lincoln Ave between Pensacola and Montrose Aves (773-935-2255). Bus: 11, 50, 78. Mon–Fri 11am–10pm; Sat 11:30am–11pm; Sun 2pm–9pm. Average beer: $4.*

K's Dugout In a bar with NASCAR plaques on the walls and baseball and *Cop Land* on the TVs, we were more than surprised to hear Jewel's tolerance anthem "Pieces of You" coming through the speakers. But this place is all about coexistence—sports nuts, pool-playing Replacements fans and those dudes slumped over their PBRs are all somehow able to get along at this little pub. *1930 W Foster Ave at Winchester Ave (773-561-2227). El: Brown to Damen. Bus: 49 (24hrs), X49, 50, 92. Mon–Fri 7am–2am; Sat 7am–3am; Sun 11am–2am. Average beer: $3.50.*

Lincoln Square Lanes Screws and nuts below, bowling pins above. This second-story bowling alley/dive bar—which sits above a hardware store—used to be one of the best hidden gems in the city. Now that the masses have caught on, you can bide your time while waiting for a lane by downing cheap beer, heckling ball-tossers and doing your best Dude impersonation. *4874 N Lincoln Ave at Ainslie St (773-561-8191). El: Brown to Western. Bus: 11, 49 (24hrs), X49, 81 (24hrs). Thu 4pm–2am; Fri 2pm–2am; Sat 2pm–3am, Sun 1pm–2am. Average beer: $2.50.*

Margie's Pub "If assholes could fly, this place would be an airport," declares the sign behind the bar. We didn't find it

to be true, but with two pool tables, a handful of arcade games and three taps of Old Style, we can see how things might get out of hand. *4145 N Lincoln Ave between Warner and Berteau Aves (773-477-1644). El: Brown to Irving Park. Bus: 11 Lincoln, 80 Irving Park. Mon–Fri 11am–2am; Sat 11am–3am; Sun 11am–8pm. Average beer: $2.*

✕ ✱ 🍴 **The Rail** How did one of the best sports bars in town end up in Ravenswood? A dozen beers on tap, almost that many plasma screens (42 inches, and size does matter) and 20-cent wings on Mondays—beats the sticky floors and drunken screaming at your current spot. *4709 N Damen Ave between Leland Ave and Giddings St (773-878-9400). El: Brown to Damen. Bus: 50 Damen, 81 Lawrence (24hrs). Mon–Thu 4pm–2am; Fri 10am–2am; Sat 10am–3am; Sun 10am–2am. Average cocktail: $4.*

Ricochet's With its gaudy mishmash of faux Frank Lloyd Wright stained glass, wood paneling and crumbling Euro-style urinals, this corner tavern seems a likely candidate for *Extreme Makeover: Bar Edition*. Otherwise, this is a perfectly likable corner tavern with a stellar jukebox where single women sip Cosmos out of frosted martini glasses while old men huddle in the corner swilling beer and whiskey. *4644 N Lincoln Ave at Eastwood Ave (773-271-3127). El: Brown to Western. Bus: 11, 49 (24hrs), 81 (24hrs). Mon–Thu 2pm–2am; Fri 1pm–2am; Sat 11am–3am; Sun 11am–2am. Average cocktail: $3.50.*

✕ ✱ **Rockwell's Neighborhood Grill** If you're the type of parent who includes your bambino in your extracurricular activities, we've got the quintessential neighborhood bar for you. Enjoy superb pub grub, killer Bloody Marys, $10 weekend breakfast buffets and a cheerful patio, all while watching your kiddies tumble on the beer-stained floor. *4632 N Rockwell St between Leland and Eastwood Aves (773-509-1871). El: Brown to Rockwell. Bus: 49 (24hrs), X49, 81 (24hrs). Mon–Thu 4–10pm; Fri 4–11pm; Sat 10am–11pm; Sun 10am–10pm. Average cocktail: $6.*

▼ **Scot's** Ties may be loosened and the blazers may come off, but it's still pretty much business class during the week at this Ravenswood boy's room. Hanging plants and holiday-themed decorations add to the office-party vibe, but make no mistake: These guys are champion softball players, so they know how to play the game. *1829 W Montrose Ave between Honore St and Wolcott Ave (773-528-3253). Bus: 50 Damen, 78 Montrose. Mon–Fri 3pm–2am; Sat 11am–3am; Sun 11am–2am. Average cocktail: $5. Cash only.*

▼ ✱ **SoFo** With its friendly staff and polished beer garden, it's a shame that such a nice bar is experiencing an identity crisis. No matter what, this place doesn't want to be called a gay bar. But with a high preponderance of single men getting acquainted with each other, divalicious videos playing on the TVs and bundles of neatly stacked queer magazines, it's not really giving us a lot of leeway to call it anything else. *4923 N Clark St at Ainslie St (773-784-7636). El: Brown to Damen. Bus: 22 Clark (24hrs), 92 Foster. Mon–Fri 5pm–2am; Sat 3pm–3am; Sun noon–2am. Average cocktail: $5.*

▼ **Spyners Pub** This unmarked hole-in-the-wall is the kind of neighborhood spot you'd easily pass by until someone in-the-know introduces you to its discreet charms: old-school matrons working the bar, cheap drink specials and weekend karaoke jamborees. FYI, it's also an unofficial hangout for same-sex-loving ladies. *4623 N Western Ave at Wilson Ave (773-784-8719). El: Brown to Western. Bus: 11, 49 (24hrs), 81 (24hrs). Sun–Fri 11am–2am; Sat 11am–3am. Average cocktail: $4.*

Sunnyside Tap Most great dives look as though they haven't seen so much as a Pledge-soaked rag since the end of World War II. With that in mind, this little, bottles-only (despite its name) tavern is oddly modern. Its scant decor—beer promo posters of bikini-clad women with 'dos straight out of a hair-metal video and an aging jukebox with tunes to match—appears to have been updated as recently as the end of the Cold War. *4410 N Western Ave between Montrose and Sunnyside Aves (no phone). El: Brown to Western. Bus: 11, 49 (24hrs), X49, 78. 10am–1am. Average beer: $3.25.*

✗ **Windy City Inn** Thank your lucky stars if you roll into this no-frills, blue-collar Irish pub on a night the endless fount of entertainment known as Crazy Kerry is slinging drinks. Born and raised in Chicago, this funny, tough-talking gal has seen it all, including deadbeats stumbling in without any cash, so don't be offended if she wants to see some dough before she slides a LaCrosse down the bar. *2257 W Irving Park Rd at Bell Ave (773-588-7088). El: Brown to Irving Park. Bus: 11, 50, 80, X80. Sun–Fri 11am–2am; Sat 11am–3am. Average beer: $3.*

Lakeview/Roscoe Village/ Wrigleyville

✗ **Agave Bar and Grill** Tequila gets the respect it deserves at this lounge, where the impressive agave-based list and the handsome room set the scene for some sophisticated sipping. Purists will drink their tequila straight, but cocktails are no afterthought: Drinks like the rich black-cherry margarita allow the tequila to shine. *3115 N Lincoln Ave between Barry and Belmont Ave (773-404-1800). El: Brown to Paulina. Bus: 9, 11, 77 (24hrs). Sun, Mon, Wed, Thu 5pm–midnight; Fri, Sat 5pm–1am. Average cocktail: $7.*

Out and about The Closet proves that Boystown isn't just for the boys.

✗ ☀ **The Ashland** Sure, it might look like any other neopub replete with a half-dozen flat-screens, more than ten brewskies on tap (including the much ballyhooed Holy Grail Ale) and Golden Tee for the armchair-athlete set. But look past that for the friendly vibe coming from the barkeep and crispy wings and cheese curds coming from the kitchen. And no one from this 'hood's gonna argue with $5 Jäger Bombs. *2824 N Ashland Ave at Wolfram St (773-883-7297). Bus: 9 Ashland, 76 Diversey. Mon–Fri 5pm–2am; Sat 11am–3am; Sun 11am–2am. Average beer: $5.*

▼ ✗ **Avenue Tavern** It's got the requisite menu of fried food and burgers, televisions in every corner and a shot-and-beer–loving clientele. But the surroundings—stone walls, glass facade—lend this Lakeview sports bar a sensibility so laid-back and inviting that even the least sports-enthusiastic people can get into it. *2916 N Broadway at Oakdale Ave (773-975-7000). El: Brown, Purple (rush hrs) to Diversey. Bus: 22 (24hrs), 36, 76. Mon–Fri 3pm–2am; Sat 11am–3am; Sun 11am–2am. Average beer: $4.*

✗ **The Bar on Buena** To the delight of bar-starved Uptown residents, this cozy spot offers 18 beers on tap, 15 wines by the glass, comfortable couches, a Sunday brunch buffet, a large-screen TV that folds away, and garage door-style front windows that separate social drinkers from cracked-out crazy-asses. *910 W Buena between Broadway and Sheridan Rd (773-525-8665). El: Red to Sheridan. Bus: 36, 80, X80, 151 (Express). Mon–Fri 4pm–2am; Sat 11:30am–3am; Sun 11:30am–2am. Average beer: $5.*

✗ **Beat Kitchen** As the name suggests, Beat Kitchen slings out above-average bar nosh (sandwiches, pizzas, salads, killer tortilla soup), and the back room hosts regional rock bands nightly for a cover that averages $8. Comedian-musician Pat McCurdy belts out such classic tunes as "Thankless Bastard" and "Big Porno Hair" Monday nights for a $6 cover. *2100 W Belmont Ave at Hoyne Ave (773-281-4444). El: Brown to Paulina. Bus: 49 (24hrs), X49, 50, 77 (24hrs). Mon–Fri 11am–2pm; Sat noon–3am, Sun noon–2am. Average beer: $4.*

✗ **Belly's** The name conjures images of college dudes gleefully showing off their extra pounds to each other, and, admittedly, there is plenty of masculinity in the air. But for a sports bar (there are about a dozen flat screen TVs), the spacious and refined setup makes for a classier environment. Then again, if you're looking to hook up with that guy with the Fighting Irish tattoo, your chances are pretty high. *. 3210 N Lincoln Ave between Melrose St and Belmont Ave (773-525-3632). Bus: 9, 11, 77 (24hrs). Mon–Fri 5pm–2am; Sat 11am–3am; Sun 11am–midnight. Average beer: $4.*

(▼ **Berlin** This freak-friendly dance destination in Lakeview built its reputation back in the mid-'80s with a mix of German new-wave music, art installations and even transvestite shows. These days, it's still quirky but more retro, with Prince-tribute, disco and '80s nostalgia nights. Goths and gays are extra welcome, but the scene here is made up of almost everyone. *954 W Belmont Ave between the El tracks and Sheffield Ave (773-348-4975). El: Red, Brown, Purple (rush hrs) to Belmont. Bus: 22 Clark (24hrs), 77 Belmont (24hrs). Sun–Mon 8pm–4am; Tue–Fri 5pm–4am; Sat 5pm–5am. Average cocktail: $4.50.*

(✗ **Big City Tap** Looking for an after-hours hetero hookup? When Wrigleyville's bars begin to close, every inch of this cavernous, woody space attached to 1000 Liquors teems with an eager twentysomething crowd looking to maintain a domestic-beer buzz, down a couple $1 Jell-O shots

(Fridays and Saturdays) and make that last-ditch effort to take home a hottie. Big City's rowdy rep belies its late-night kitchen that serves better-than-average bar fare till 3am. *1010 W Belmont Ave between Sheffield and Kenmore Aves (773-935-9229). El: Brown, Purple (rush hrs), Red to Belmont. Bus: 22 Clark (24hrs), 77 Belmont (24hrs). Sun–Fri 11pm–4am; Sat 11am–5pm. Average cocktail: $4.*

🍴 **Black Rock** On the weekends, this polished Roscoe Village hangout is filled with local singles awkwardly trying to get some, and it's sort of like watching a too-good-to-be-true episode of *Blind Date*. Go during the week when there's nary a horndog in sight. Sampling the extensive list of Irish beers and whiskeys is best done in the back—a cool, open space with couches, a fireplace and old-school board games. *3614 N Damen Ave at Addison St (773-348-4044). Bus: 50 Damen, 152 Addison. Mon–Thu 5:30pm–2am; Fri 5pm–2am; Sat noon–3am; Sun noon–2am. Average beer: $4.*

✗ **Blarney Stone** You can gussy up an evening out however you want—with sequined tubetops and plush private rooms, for example—but sometimes you just wanna get hammered. Thankfully, this subdued corner pub offers the cheapest beer and greasy drunk food around. The younger crowd chats with everyone—so come if you want to discuss, at the top of your lungs, how many shots you've done tonight. *3424 N Sheffield Ave at Newport Ave (773-348-1078). El: Brown, Purple (rush hrs), Red to Belmont; Red to Addison. Bus: 22 (24hrs), 77 (24hrs), 152. Mon–Fri 5pm–2am; Sat 11am–3am; Sun 11am–2am. Average beer: $2.50.*

◖ **Bluelight** A friendly late-night joint is hard to find. One where off-duty cops, dolled-up hipsters and sporty types drink together in harmony, like this one, is even harder. Inside, the exposed brick wall and candlelit bar makes for a cozy atmosphere. Add some fine picks by the DJ and two of the nicest bartenders around, and you'll definitely be back for seconds. *3251 N Western Ave between Melrose and School Sts (773-755-5875). Bus: 49 (24hrs), X49, 77 (24hrs). Sun–Fri 6pm–4am; Sat 6pm–5am. Average beer: $4.*

▼ **Bobby Love's** When it comes to trendy gay bars, this crowd has been there, done that, so there's less cruising and more drinking here. During the week, the jukebox features pop, country and oldies, but weekends are all about karaoke. Expect to hear "I Will Survive" at least twice a night. *3729 N Halsted St at Bradley Pl (773-525-1200). El: Red to Addison. Bus: 8, 36, 152. Mon–Fri 3pm–2am; Sat noon–3am; Sun noon–2am. Average cocktail: $5.*

✗ **Bourbon** This bar is earthy, inviting and yet still seductive, much like the Scotches, Irish whiskies and bourbons lining the bar. Owner Peter Mitchell and chef Michael Artel have teamed up to create a loungey vibe and a late-night menu featuring tasty Southern treats like bite-size gator and sweet-potato chips tailor-made for tumblers of the namesake "water of life." *3244 N Lincoln Ave at Melrose St (773-880-9520). El: Brown to Paulina. Bus: 9, 11, 77 (24hrs). Sun–Fri 4pm–2am; Sat 4pm–3am. Average cocktail: $8.*

▼ **Brendan's Pub** Reflections is no more, and its Lakeview storefront space has undergone a minor face-lift. Fish tanks and romance novels have been replaced with exposed brick, new ceilings and a fresh paint job, though the loyal clientele stuck around just the same. The bar has also added two more flat-screen TVs, but it'll show *The Simpsons* or PBS over sports any day of the week. *3169 N Broadway between Belmont Ave and Briar Pl (773-929-2929). El:*

Fine wining

Find a wine bar to match any mood.

Belly up to the bar And order 36 wines by the glass at bin wine café.

Whether you're looking to get a wine education, a good meal or just a good buzz, Chicago has a wine bar that pairs well with your intended purpose. A romantic night out calls for **Webster's Wine Bar** *(1480 W Webster Ave between Clybourn Ave and Dominick St, 773-868-0608)*. One of its dark wood, candle-lit tables is the ideal place for you and your sweetie to share bedroom eyes over a bottle of vino.

Another date destination is **404 Wine Bar** *(2856 N Southport Ave between Wolfram and George Sts, 773-404-5886)*, a sophisticated spot with exposed brick, leather armchairs, hardwood floors, jazz music on the stereo and fireplaces that invite smooching as much as sipping. Still looking for love in all the wrong places (i.e., boisterous neighborhood bars)? Look no further than the nicely finished space of **Vintage Wine Bar** *(1924 W Division between Winchester and Damen Aves, 773-772-3400)*, where laid-back GenYers with taste come to get acquainted fireside. Likewise, the stone fireplace at **D.O.C. Wine Bar** *(2602 N Clark St between Wrightwood Ave and Drummond Pl, 773-883-5101)* is certainly a draw, but the real appeal is that each varietal on the list is explained in detail, so even those green to the grape can chose with confidence.

If you want a little dine with your wine, Bucktown haunt **Meritage Café and Wine Bar** *(2118 N Damen Ave at Charleston St, 773-235-6434)* offers eclectic American cuisine and 150 wines. Alongside the 36 wines available by the glass, **bin wine café** *(1559 N Milwaukee Ave between Honore St and North Ave, 773-486-2233)* dishes out irresistible globally influenced fare and seasonal specials.

The fantastic wines aren't the only reason to lose track of time at the cozy, dimly lit **Tasting Room** *(1415 W Randolph St at Washington Blvd, 312-942-1313)*. Its selection of crispy, delicious pizzas and crave-worthy cheeses and small plates are as good an excuse as any to while away the night.

To just plain get away from it all, head to the minimalist space of **Joie de Vine** *(1744 W Balmoral Ave between Paulina St and Ravenswood Ave, 773-989-6846)*. If its location on a quiet street in the lovely, low-key Andersonville neighborhood doesn't make you feel far enough removed from rush-rush city life, we're sure there is a glass on the list that can.

Brown, Purple (rush hrs), Red to Belmont. Bus: 22 (24hrs), 36, 77 (24hrs). Mon–Fri 10am–2am; Sat 10am–3am; Sun 11am–2am. Average beer: $3.50.

✗ ☀ **Brownstone** Sure, the Tiffany-style light fixtures and Victorian-era decor are classy, and the drinks are just fine. But the real reason to keep coming back here—despite the weekend crowds of former frat bros and their penchant for Def Leppard—is the sugar-coma–inducing cookie skillet. 3937 N Lincoln Ave between Irving Park and Grace Sts (773-528-3700). El: Brown to Irving Park. Bus: 11, 50, 80. Mon–Thu 5pm–2am; Fri 11am–2am; Sat 11am–3am; Sun 11am–2am. Average beer: $4.

▼ ✗ ☀ **Buck's Saloon** There aren't many outdoor options in Boystown, so if the chic upper deck at Sidetrack isn't your thing, try this more peaceful patio. Weave through the front of the joint (with, yes, dead animal heads on the walls) to emerge on the back porch where, except for the bar, it feels just like you're hanging out at an older gay guy's backyard barbecue with beer guzzlers in frayed jean-shorts. 3439 N Halsted St between Roscoe St and Cornelia Ave (773-525-1125). El: Brown, Purple (rush hrs only), Red to Belmont. Bus: 8, 22 (24hrs), 77 (24hrs). Mon–Fri noon–2am; Sat noon–3am; Sun 11am–2am. Average beer: $4.

🍸 **Bungalow Loungebar** A cozy orange glow and horizontal lines inspired by Frank Lloyd Wright draw a hip, laid-back Lakeview crowd. Formerly a dive with urinals chained to the wall, the hot spot now boasts a trendy vibe with DJ-delivered music and an intriguing selection of brew/martinis—seasonal cocktails might include a phenomenal Pumpkintini. 1622 W Belmont Ave between Lincoln and Paulina Sts (773-244-0400). El: Brown to Paulina. Bus: 9, 11, 77 (24hrs). Mon–Fri 6pm–2am; Sat 6pm–3am; Sun 6pm–2am. Average beer: $4.50.

✗ ☀ **Casey Moran's** Can't snag a bleacher seat at the Friendly Confines? Don't fret. Bathed in dark woods and brimming with beer, burgers, apps and wraps, this surprisingly friendly bar just a stone's throw north is the next-best place to park your tush on game day. With 25 HD plasma-screen TVs, you'll catch every angle without catching a single harmful UV ray. 3660 N Clark St between Addison St and Waveland Ave (773-755-4444). El: Red to Addison. Bus: 8, 22 (24hrs), 152. Mon–Fri 10am–2am; Sat 10am–3am; Sun 10am–2am. Average beer: $5.

✗ 🍸 **Celtic Crown Public House** This large Irish pub's marquee announces its daily specials to the neighborhood. Time your visit based on the signage and you may find yourself with a bill for $1 burgers or 25-cent wings. Even at full price, Celtic Crown is still worth a visit for better-than-average bar food. As you'd expect at an Irish pub, the corned-beef sandwich is satisfying, as is the barbecue-rib plate (note to true 'cue fans: They're baked, not smoked), and you can indulge your inner grammar-school student with tater tots. 4301 N Western Ave at Cullom Ave (773-588-1110). El: Brown to Western. Bus: 49 (24hrs), X49, 78. Sun–Fri 11am–2am; Sat 11am–3am. Average beer: $5.

✗ **Central** The guys behind Grand Central and Union Park won't quit: Their new bar, described as "Grand Central's little sister" opened on the first baseball game of the season, and it was definitely not a coincidence. With 20 plasma screens and a emphasis on domestic beer, they're hoping to be the next home-away-from-home for Cubs fans. 3466 N Clark St between Newport and Cornelia Ave (773-880-2222). El: Red to Addison. Bus: 8, 22 (24hrs), 152. Sun–Fri 11am–2am; Saturday 11am–3am. Average beer: $4.

✗ **Clarke's After Dark** Clarke's diner used to be the place you'd go after the party was over, the place to sober up with some pancakes, a burger or a cup of coffee after striking out. But with this Miami Vice–esque lounge and bar area—dominated by silver high-backed leather booths and neon lights—Clarke's is giving you a second at bat with your side of fries. 930 W Belmont Ave at Wilton Ave (773-348-5988). El: Brown, Purple (rush hrs), Red to Belmont. Bus: 8, 22 (24hrs), 77 (24hrs). 7am–3am. Average cocktail: $6.

☾ ▼ **The Closet** This is one of the only girl bars in Boystown, so you'd think the clientele here would be more interested in each other. But in fact, the main attraction seems to be the Silver Streak bowling video game. Think you're any good? These girls are definitely up to the challenge. 3325 N Broadway between Aldine Ave and Buckingham Pl (773-477-8533). El: Brown, Purple (rush hrs), Red to Belmont. Bus: 8, 36, 77 (24hrs). Mon–Fri 2pm–4am; Sat noon–5am; Sun noon–4am. Average beer: $5. Cash only.

▼ **Cocktail** Oh, you wittily named gay bars, with your bartenders who look like the beefy, tattooed biker version of Susan Powter, and, in summer, a plethora of fabulous beach balls (Balls? Get it?) hanging from the ceiling in summertime. Will your winking and nudging ever stop? We hope not, 'cause we love it. But girl, your beers are way too expensive. 3359 N Halsted St at Roscoe St (773-477-1420). El: Red to Addison. Bus: 8, 36, 152. Mon–Fri 4pm–2am; Sat 2pm–3am; Sun 2pm–2am. Average beer: $5.

☀ **Cody's** The slogan says it all: no peeing, no crapping, no barking—and that goes for the dogs, too. Needless to say, this bar is dog-friendly, inside and out. But what really clinches it as one of Chicago's best are the real English darts and the $2 bottles of Schlitz, Pabst, Old Style and Huber. 1658 W Barry Ave between Ashland Ave and Paulina St (773-528-4050). El: Brown to Paulina. Bus: 9, 11, 77 (24hrs), 152. Mon–Fri 2pm–2am; Sat 11am–2am; Sun 11am–2am. Average beer: $3. Cash only.

The Cork Lounge It's just a local watering hole where the bartenders know everybody sitting at the long, battered bar and playing pool in the back. Apparently, they also know the patrons' kids: In the front of the room is one of those claw games, which kids use to dig for stuffed animals while Mommy and Daddy get plowed. 1822 W Addison St between Ravenswood and Wolcott Aves (773-549-9645). Bus: 9, 11, 152. Sun–Fri noon–2am; Sat noon–3am. Average beer: $3.

✗ **Crabby Kim's** This self-proclaimed bikini bar could best be described as a poor man's Hooters, but instead of having an owl as a mascot, it's chosen (egads!) a crab. Surprisingly, it isn't as tawdry as you'd expect, although it could stand to lose the plethora of beer-company swag hanging from every inch of the place. If you don't have the balls to go to a real strip club but still want to ogle some ladies, you could do worse. And with the thin crowd most nights, you're highly unlikely to be spotted by anyone you know. 3655 N Western Ave between Addison and Waveland Aves (773-404-8156). Bus: 49 Western (24hrs), 152 Addison. Mon–Fri 11am–2am; Sat 11am–3am; Sun 11am–midnight. Average cocktail: $4.

✗ **The Cubby Bear** Considering its proximity to Wrigley Field, it's the next-best thing to being in the stands. Cubs fans pack the sticky floor before and during the game, but it's postgame that people are packed in this place like sardines in a tin can. If you're feeling flush, you can spring for a private room overlooking Wrigley to take in a game. When baseball's not center stage, the 30,000-square-foot behemoth still packs

So far, so good Everyone's welcome to kick back a cold one at SoFo.

Sight lines Don't get sidetracked by the rooftop garden: there's plenty of action inside at Sidetrack.

in crowds who come to see bands like the Gin Blossoms and Widespread Panic. *1059 W Addison St at Clark St (773-327-1662). El: Red to Addison. Bus: 22 Clark (24hrs), 152 Addison. During Cubs home games: Mon–Sat, 10am–2am; Sun 11am–1am. All other times: Mon–Fri 4pm–2am; Sat 11am–3am; Sun 11am–2am. Average beer: $4.*

Dram Shop Don't let the fact that they're all sitting four stools apart deceive you: The guys who are hanging out in this tiny, dingy Lakeview gem are hanging out together. You may feel like an outsider at first, but it's worth sticking around to hear them make fun of the people on *Wheel of Fortune. 3040 N Broadway between Barry and Wellington Aves (773-549-4401). El: Brown, Purple (rush hrs), Red to Belmont. Bus: 36, 76, 77 (24hrs). Mon–Fri 7am–2am; Sat 7am–3am; Sun 11am–2am. Average beer: $3.50.*

✕ ✳ **Duke of Perth** You'll never know how relaxing Celtic music can be until you spend an afternoon at this Scottish ale house. Listen closely as you hang out on the serene outdoor patio, eating fish and chips (they're all you can eat on Wednesdays and Fridays) and drinking from one of the best Scotch whiskey lists in the city—soon you'll be humming along. *2913 N Clark St between Surf St and Oakdale Ave (773-477-1741). El: Brown, Purple (rush hrs) to Diversey. Bus: 8, 22 (24hrs), 76. Mon 5pm–2am; Tue–Thu noon–2am; Fri, Sat noon–3am; Sun noon–2am. Average beer: $5.*

✕ ✳ **Fearon's Public House** There is a time and a place for nearly everything; it's just too bad that the time and place for Fearon's is in the rearview mirror by about 10 years. Can we please stop relying on the McIrish pub mold, people? Guinness on tap? Check. Dark wood tones and plasma-screen

TVs? Check. "Juke Box Hero" on the juke and a barmaid that sits on the other side of the bar instead of asking about your next one? WTF?! *3001 N Ashland Ave at Wellington Ave (773-248-0990). Bus: 9, 76, 77 (24hrs). Sun–Fri 11am–2am; Sat 11am–3am. Average beer: $4.50.*

✕ **Finley Dunne's Tavern** Locals descend upon "The Dunne's" from their new condos in Roscoe Village's Pencil Factory, soaking up the sports theme dominated by support for Boston College and Dayton. Golden Tee has succumbed to Silver Lanes for entertainment, and the camaraderie among the regulars would make Finley Peter Dunne (columnist for the *Chicago Evening Post* in the late 1800s) proud. *3458 N Lincoln Ave at Newport Ave (773-477-7311). El: Brown to Paulina. Bus: 9, 11, 77 (24hrs). Mon–Wed 2pm–2am, Thu 4pm–2am, Fri 1pm–2am; Sat 11am–3am, Sun 11am–2am. Average beer: $4.*

✕ ✳ **Fizz Bar and Grill** Just like every other Lakeview bar, this one caters to the young professional crowd; hence, the menu is full of better-than-typical pub food, including a grilled tuna-steak sandwich and filet mignon. But it isn't until the warmer months, when the outdoor beer garden is opened, that Fizz really starts sizzling. *3220 N Lincoln Ave at Belmont Ave (773-348-6000). El: Brown to Paulina. Bus: 9, 11, 77 (24hrs). Mon–Fri 4pm–2am; Sat noon–3am; Sun 10am–1am. Average beer: $5.*

Foley's The sign out front has a shamrock where the apostrophe is supposed to be, hinting that it's an Irish dive bar where locals linger and the bartender is loose with free shots. If that's not compelling enough, you could always come here for inspiration for your next novel, *Shooting the Shit in Chicago. 1841 W Irving Park Rd between Wolcott and*

Ravenswood Aves (773-929-1210). El: Brown to Irving Park. Bus: 9, 50, 80. Mon–Fri 7am–2am; Sat 10am–3am; Sun 11am–2am. Average beer: $3.

✗ **Four Moon Tavern** A wood-paneled ceiling, pool table, Texas longhorn skulls, scattered vintage beer memorabilia and a jukebox stocked with jazz, standards and bluegrass make for a nice spot to rest your heels in Roscoe Village. Well-made cocktails and regional beers like Goose Island's awesome 312 are the norm. Staff and patrons dabble in theater, so look for local play postings. *1847 W Roscoe St between Wolcott and Ravenswood Aves (773-929-6666). El: Brown to Paulina. Bus: 11 Lincoln, 50 Damen. Mon–Thu 5pm–2am; Fri noon–3am; Sat 10am–2am; Sun 10am–2am. Average cocktail: $4.*

Four Treys Pub Six days a week, this Roscoe Village standby's got a Northwoods Wisconsin feel (think cluttered walls spotlighting the owner's fishing triumphs and an authentic Old Milwaukee wooden beer tap) and is chock-full of the 'hood's youth. But on Saturdays, karaoke distracts from the usual conversational buzz, and brings with it the not-so-sorely missed Lincoln Park party-boy contingent. *3333 N Damen Ave at Henderson St (773-549-8845). Bus: 50, 73, 152. Mon 5pm–2am; Tue-Fri noon–2am; Sat noon–3am; Sun noon–2am. Average beer: $4. Cash only.*

✗ ✳ **404 Wine Bar** You've heard of beer gardens, but a wine garden? Comfortable and classy, with a menu of upscale pizzas, global wine flights and cheese plates to match, this spot is a favorite among young professionals discussing their new condo purchases and their favorite lines from Sideways. *2856 N Southport Ave between Wolfram and George Sts (773-404-5886). El: Brown, Purple (rush hrs) to Wellington. Bus: 9, 11, 76. Mon–Fri 5pm–2am; Sat noon–3am; Sun noon–midnight. Average glass of wine: $7.50.*

🍴 **Friar Tuck** Merry ol' England this ain't, but it's tough to find a sports hub this inviting along Broadway. In the front, kegs are stacked next to a pinball machine; near the back, a disco ball is suspended over the jukebox; and Cubs signs are peppered throughout the narrow space. Yeah, there are some odd decorating choices, but any place where the off-duty bartender buys us a free shot gets our vote. *3010 N Broadway between Wellington and Barry Aves (773-327-5101). El: Brown, Purple (rush hrs) to Wellington; Red to Belmont. Bus: 22 (24hrs), 36, 77 (24hrs). Sun–Fri 2pm–2am; Sat 2pm–3am. Average beer: $4. Cash only.*

🍴 **Full Shilling Public House** There's nothing really special about this Wrigleyville spot, but the daily deals draw us in like flies. With $1 domestic drafts on Mondays and $1 burgers on Thursdays (and plenty of other specials in between), it's no wonder why this cozy place is always packed. *3724 N Clark St between Waveland Ave and Grace St (773-248-3330). El: Red to Addison. Bus: 22 Clark (24hrs), 152 Addison. Mon–Fri 4pm–2am; Sat, Sun 11am–2am. Average beer $4.*

🍴 **G&L Fire Escape** Criticism of our country probably isn't wise inside these wood-paneled, firehouse-themed walls. With all the pro-America posters and flags, there's more patriotism in here than in the White House and the Pentagon combined. Join the crowd of old firemen on a Sunday, when they usually grill outside. No one will understand your "commie talk" if you've got a brat stuffed in your mouth. *2157 W Grace St at Leavitt St (773-472-1138). Bus: 49 (24hrs), 50, 80, 152. Mon–Fri 7am–2am; Sat 7am–3am; Sun 11am–2am. Average beer: $2.50. Cash only.*

✗ **Gannon's Pub** There's nothing fancy going on here, just a welcoming neighborhood bar with regulars who wouldn't have it any other way. The camaraderie is a bit *Cheers*-ish, but the extended fam seems amiable to welcoming newbies to the group. Keep the burgers and beer coming—we've just found our new hangout. *4264 N Lincoln Ave at Cullom Ave (773-281-1007). El: Brown to Western. Bus: 11 Lincoln, 78 Montrose. Mon–Fri 4pm–2am; Sat 11am–3am; Sun 11am–2am. Average beer: $4.*

▼ **Gentry** Honey, things don't get much bitchier than this. It doesn't matter how well you're dressed or how dark the corner you're sitting in is: Between his sets of '70s medleys and show tunes, pianist Khris Francis will hunt you down and call you out. And you know what? You're gonna love it. *3320 N Halsted St between Aldine Ave and Buckingham Pl (773-348-1053). El: Brown, Purple (rush hrs), Red to Belmont. Bus: 8, 22 (24hrs), 77 (24hrs). Mon–Thu 6pm–2am; Fri 4pm–2am; Sat 4pm–3am; Sun 4pm–2am. Average cocktail: $5.*

✗ **Ginger's Ale House** Catch this dark-wood Irish pub on an off night (as in, a nonsoccer night) and the place is fairly desolate, save for a few locals pounding Smithwick's. However, the bar hasn't been rated the country's No. 1 soccer bar by USSoccer.com for nothing—when game day rolls around, football fanatics from all over the city (and some out-of-towners) line up as early as 6:30am. *3801 N Ashland Ave at Grace St (773-348-2767). Bus: 9, 80, 152. Mon–Fri, Sun 11am–2am; Sat 11am–3am. Average beer: $3.*

Gingerman Tavern The two coin-op pool tables suck, and you'll be lucky if there are an even number of striped and solid balls. But the Gingerman, the best Wrigleyville bar for the meathead-avoider, is still a great place to play pool. The talent varies widely, from journeyman players who run the table to apprentice drinkers who struggle to hold a cue, which means you have an excellent chance of actually getting to play. *3740 N Clark St between Waveland Ave and Grace St (773-549-2050). El: Red to Sheridan. Bus: 22 (24hrs), 80, X80. Mon–Fri 3pm–2am; Sat noon–3am; Sun noon–2am. Average beer: $3. Cash only.*

✗ **The Globe Pub** Brits have taken over the former Lyon's Den in North Center, cleaned it up and added plenty of dark-wood high tables; a menu of U.K. pub grub; a digital jukebox with thousands of tunes; a couple dozen bitter-style drafts; and a small stage in back for Monday-night improv comedy. *1934 W Irving Park Rd between Wolcott and Damen Aves (773-871-3757). El: Brown to Irving Park. Bus: 50, 80, X80. Sun–Fri 10am–2am; Sat 10am–3am. Average beer: $4.*

Goldie's A tasteful renovation has replaced the creepy stonework facade, but Goldie's still remains strangely unknown. The cork dartboards and pool table offer better distraction than the sports-tuned TVs that are jammed into the rest of the 'hood, and the affordable beer selection ($1 PBR and $3 Guinness drafts) is a refreshing back-to-basics approach to inebriation. *3835 N Lincoln Ave between Berenice Ave and Byron St (no phone). El: Brown to Irving Park. Bus: 11, 50, 80, X80. Mon–Fri 2pm–2am; Sat 2pm–3am (closed Sun). Average beer: $2.*

🍴 **Gunther Murphy's** A facelift transformed the façade of Gunther Murphy's into one reminiscent of a true Irish pub, and bartenders (occasionally from the old country) do pour a mean pint of Guinness. The bare-bones backroom has a definite '70s basement feel, with a stage that spotlights comedy, open-mike nights and local bands for a nominal cover. *1638 W Belmont Ave between Lincoln and Paulina Sts*

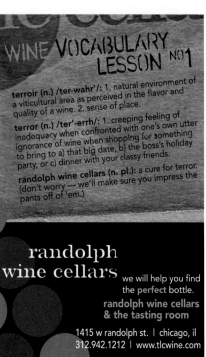

(773-472-5139). El: Brown to Paulina. Bus: 9, 11, 77 (24hrs). Mon 5pm–2am; Tue–Fri 3pm–2am; Sat 2pm–3am; Sun 2pm–2am. Average beer: $4.

✗ **Guthries Tavern** The twentysomethings in the back room playing board games are missing out. The real action is at the bar, where silver-haired ladies flirt with ex-frat boys and the occasional indie-rock couple. It's tough to find a place in Wrigleyville where worlds collide and all are welcome for a mildly drunken "Kumbaya vibe." *1300 W Addison St at Lakewood Ave (773-477-2900). El: Red, Purple (rush hour only) to Addison. Bus: 152 Addison. Mon–Fri 5pm–2am; Sat, Sun 2pm–2am. Average beer: $4.50.*

✗ **Harrigan's Pub** There's an electronic countdown to St. Patrick's Day and a bar made out of Irish pennies. Do we really need to spell out for you what this place is all about? On Sunday nights it's as sleepy as an Irish hamlet, but on Fridays and Saturdays it's as raucous as Dublin. *2816 N Halsted St between Diversey Pkwy and Wolfram St (773-248-5933). El: Brown, Purple (rush hrs) to Diversey. Bus: 8 Halsted, 76 Diversey. Mon–Thu 1pm–2am; Fri 11am–2am; Sat 11am–3am; Sun 11am–2am. Average cocktail: $4.*

✗ **Higgins' Tavern** Dim and vaguely tinted green (likely due to the Michigan State Spartan memorabilia that covers nearly everything), this worn, yet welcoming, Lakeview watering hole boasts more than 30 bottled beers. It's the kind of simple tavern where the bartender won't hesitate to "top off" your drink a couple times just for ordering some of the tasty pub grub. *3259 N Racine Ave between Melrose and School Sts (773-281-7637). El: Brown, Purple (rush hrs), Red to Belmont. Bus: 22 Clark (24hrs), 77 Belmont (24hrs). Mon–Fri 7am–2am; Sat 7am–3am; Sun 10am–2am. Average beer: $3.*

✗ **Hi-Tops** Kitty corner from the Friendly Confines, this gigantic bar (drinking arena, actually) sports more TVs than any place we've come across. And when the games are over, expect the brahs here to tilt their heads slightly toward the dolled-up girlies. We were pretty impressed with its bottle collection, considering Miller Lite is almost exclusively consumed. *3551 N Sheffield Ave between Addison St and Cornelia Ave (773-348-0009). El: Red to Addison. Bus: 8 Halsted, 152 Addison. Mon–Fri 3:30pm–2am; Sat 10am–3am; Sun 10am–2am. Average beer: $4.*

✗ **Holiday Club** The shiny awning and glittery old-Hollywood sign outside may draw us into this Lakeview bar, but the photo booth keeps us staying much later than planned. The '50s diner ambiance is swanky, the food is decent and the bar boasts a friendly crowd—so friendly that you may get back your photo strip and spot an unknown face. *4000 N Sheridan at Irving Park Rd (773-348-9600). El: Red to Sheridan. Bus: 80 Irving Park, 151 Sheridan (24hrs). Mon–Fri 4pm–2am; Sat 4pm–3am; Sun 10am–2am. Average beer: $4.50.*

✗ **Houndstooth Saloon** It's easy to get caught up in Southern pride when Alabama alums holler "Roll Tide" at the flat screens with a Lone Star in one hand and a pulled-pork hoagie in the other. The familiar Old Style lettering glows out front, lest you forget the bar's Chicago roots. *3438 N Clark St at Newport Ave (773-244-1166). El: Red to Addison. Bus: 22 (24hrs), 77 (24hrs), 152. Mon–Fri 5pm–2am; Sat 11am–3am; Sun 11am–2am. Average beer: $3.75.*

Hungry Brain This converted theater kept its artsy charm with thrift-store finds galore. An old piano, couches and a coffee table sit on the small stage (which gets occasional

use for one-night shows). Art-school dropouts flank the Ms. Pac-Man/Galaga game and great jukebox and friendly bartenders serve up cheap beers with a smile. *2319 W Belmont Ave between Oakley and Western Aves (773-935-2118). El: Brown to Paulina. Bus: 49 (24hrs), X49, 77 (24hrs). Tue–Sun 9pm–2am. Average beer: $2.50. Cash only.*

The Irish Oak Every Irish bar in the city claims maximum authenticity, but this one has the goods to prove it: The vibe is a nice mix of traditional and contemporary Irish pub culture, the bar was designed and built in Ireland, and most of the waitstaff are real live Irish folks (or just really good at faking accents). *3511 N Clark St at Cornelia Ave (773-935-6669). El: Red to Addison. Bus: 22 Clark (24hrs), 152 Addison. Sun–Thurs 11:30am–12:30am; Fri, Sat 11:30am–2:30am. Average beer: $4.50.*

✗ ✳ ♦ **Jack's Bar and Grill** Couples and small groups flock to this dimly lit Lakeview spot (situated next to 404 Wine Bar; they're connected inside) to cozy up by the fireplace or in one of the überhigh, black leather booths. That's not to say you can't go alone—just be prepared to sip your Sam Smith up at the bar. *2856 N Southport Ave between Wolfram and George Sts (773-404-8400). El: Brown, Purple (rush hrs) to Diversey. Bus: 9, 11, 76. Mon–Fri 5pm–2am; Sat 5pm–3am (closed Sun). Average beer: $4.*

▼ **Jacqueline's** Is it a gay bar? Is it straight? Do we care? Scattered about this sexually ambiguous bar—where a long list of bottles makes up for the lack of beer on tap—are decorations from holidays long gone (a witch and her broomstick hangs overhead). The old relics are like the regulars—they'll stick around as long as they can. *3420 N Broadway at Roscoe St (773-404-5149). El: Brown, Purple (rush hrs), Red to Belmont. Bus: 36, 77 (24hrs), 152. Sun–Fri 11am–2am; Sat 11am–3am. Average beer: $4.*

Jake's Pub We're still not sure what's more extensive at this friendly, narrow watering hole: the beer selection or the jukebox. The 50 bottled beers (including several Belgians) should satisfy even the fussiest bargoer, but with every Uncle Tupelo album at your fingertips and lots of Dylan and Stones to pick through, your inner DJ might tempt you to invest your bucks in a killer soundtrack instead. *2932 N Clark St at Oakdale Ave (773-248-3318). Bus: 8, 22 (24hrs), 36, 76. Mon–Fri 3pm–2am; Sat noon–3am; Sun noon–2am. Average beer: $4.*

Joe's on Broadway Just a few blocks from the testosterone-fueled Wrigleyville hangouts, this might be our favorite dive in the neighborhood: sparsely occupied, gritty and completely relaxing. When we were here last, the bartender noted that our choice of Leinie's Red was "classy" and also gave us props for playing all of the Stones' *Sticky Fingers* on the jukebox. *3563 N Broadway between Addison St and Brompton Ave (773-528-1054). El: Red to Addison. Bus: 36 Broadway, 152 Addison. Sun–Fri 11am–2am; Sat 11am–3am. Average beer: $3.*

John Barleycorn When young college grads move to the city, this Wrigleyville sports bar/dance club is their first stop. The TVs blasting sports, greasy bar food and weekend dancing upstairs can rival any campus bar on a good Thursday night. In fact, the only thing missing is the line for keg stands. *3524 N Clark St between Addison St and Sheffield Ave (773-549-6000). El: Red to Addison. Bus: 22 Clark (24hrs), 152 Addison. Mon–Fri 5pm–2am; Sat 3:30pm–3am; Sun 3:30pm–2am. Average beer: $4.50.*

The dark side Avoid the big city's bright lights in the dark corners of L&L Tavern.

Johnnie's Yes, the rumors are true: To get into this old-timey watering hole, Johnnie has to buzz you in. Once admitted, it's nostalgia central: a '60s jukebox, retro beer posters, Christmas decorations from way back when, old newspapers lying in the corner. Better still, if the longtime proprietor digs talking to you, he'll keep the beer flowing past closing time. *3425 N Lincoln Ave at Roscoe St (773-248-3000). El: Brown to Paulina. Bus: 9, 11, 77 (24hrs), 152. 9am–2am. Average beer: $3.*

❋ ♦ ✕ **Johnny O'Hagan's** The best of this bar's details—a stone fireplace, stained-glass windows and the dark wood bar itself—were imported from Ireland. It also gets points for serving a killer burger with "champ" (mashed potatoes and green onions), but loses points for its unfortunate seating arrangements. Hard, wooden booths, with accompanying low tables, are barely padded; daddy longlegs will be in pain. *3374 N Clark St between Aldine Ave and Roscoe St (773-248-3600). El: Brown, Purple (rush hrs), Red to Belmont. Bus: 11, 22 (24hrs), 36, 77 (24hrs). Sun–Fri 11am–2am; Sat 11am–3am. Average beer: $4.50.*

❋ **June's Inn** Quintessential Chicago, this narrow 30-year-old storefront is a perfect pit stop on the other type of pub crawl. You know, the one where you just want cheap liquor ($2.50 bottles of beer), cool jukebox tunes (the bartender will happily match you dollar for dollar) and sassy regulars (everyone's raving about the new condom dispenser). *4333 N Western Ave between Pensacola and Montrose Aves (773-463-3122). El: Brown to Western. Bus: 49 (24hrs), X49, 78. Mon–Sat 10am–2am; Sun 11am–2am. Average beer: $2.50.*

✕ **Katerina's** We are in love with Katerina. Like any good lover, it's the little things that keep us infatuated: her

signature cocktails like the sour cherry martini, the eclectic roster of bands (jazz, funk, traditional Greek), the candlelit loungelike space, and her Southern European menu (calamari, sautéed shrimp, *spanokopita*). In between checking IDs and pouring cocktails, it's common for Katerina to quip that "cigarettes make your breasts firmer" or break into song and croon for the love-struck regulars. *1920 W Irving Park Rd at Wolcott Ave (773-348-7592). El: Brown to Irving Park. Bus: 11, 50, 80, X80. Mon–Fri 5pm–2am; Sat 5pm–3am. Average cocktail: $7.*

✕ ❋ ♦ **Kirkwood Bar and Grill** This sporty-chic hot spot is hardly recognizable as the location that for so long housed Pops for Champagne. Even though the left side of the dual bar setup may be packed with loud, flat-screen–focused Colts and Hoosiers fans, the earth-tone stained-glass lighting and large windows in front give the surroundings a calm, open feel. If that's still too much to handle, the clientele on the less-rowdy right side is (just slightly) older, better dressed and wants to know more about your tastes than just your sports loyalties. *2934 N Sheffield Ave at Oakdale Ave (773-770-0700). El: Brown to Wellington. Bus: 8, 76, 77 (24hrs). Mon–Fri 5pm–2am; Sat 11am–3am; Sun 11am–2am. Average beer: $4.50.*

L & L Tavern The Clark and Belmont 'hood is a unique mix of runaway trannnies, wasted Cubs fans and local renters who love a bargain. This no-frills Lakeview tavern keeps the madness at bay in favor of friendly bartenders who buy rounds during afternoon *Jeopardy*, a $2 beer-of-the-month and a great collection of two-dozen Irish whiskeys. *3207 N Clark St between Belmont and Aldine Aves (773-528-1303). El: Brown, Purple (rush hour only), Red to Belmont. Bus: 77 Belmont (24hrs).*

Mon-Fri 2pm–2am; Sat noon–3am; Sun noon–2am. Average beer: $3. Cash only.

✕ ✳ **Lakeview Broadcasting Company** Okay, there are '80s-style boom boxes on the walls, a shag-carpeted, glass-walled room where models hang out (supposedly), and the boys behind the bar look straight out of the band Good Charlotte. Can somebody please tell us what the hell is going on here? *3542 N Halsted St between Brompton Ave and Addison St (773-857-2444). El: Red to Addison. Bus: 8, 36, 152. Tue–Fri 5pm–2am; Sat 5pm–3am; Sun 5pm–2am. Average cocktail: $7.*

Lange's At first glance, this square, low-lit bar seems a little too unkempt for the typical Southport crowd. But squint through the cigarette smoke and you might find a group of girls leaning against the bar. They're leaning because they're drunk, and they're here because unlike some of the other bars on this strip, nobody's going to cut them off. *3500 N Southport Ave at Cornelia Ave (773-472-6030). 11 Lincoln, 76 Diversey. Mon–Fri 2pm–2am; Sat noon–3am, Sun noon–2am. Average cocktail: $4.*

✕ **Lennox Lounge** *Au courant* bands like Bloc Party provide the soundtrack at this posh Lakeview spot, where martinis are made with Hendrick's gin and sipped while lounging in big, circular, black leather booths. The vibe is class without attitude, and we can't for the life of us figure out why it's not packed. *3032 N Lincoln Ave between Wellington and Barry Aves (773-281-9900). El: Brown, Purple (rush hrs) to Wellington. Bus: 9, 11, 77 (24hrs). Sun–Fri 5pm–2am; Sat 5pm–3am. Average cocktail: $6.*

Lincoln Tap Room Downstairs from the fictitious pool hall in *The Color of Money*, this joint keeps it real with Hamms in cans, two dozen taps, free pool on Wednesdays and an old-school photo booth. A laid-back, dark and funky vibe attracts an indie-rock crowd clad in bowling shirts. *3010 N Lincoln Ave at Wellington and Southport Sts (773-868-0060). El: Brown, Purple (rush hrs) to Wellington. Bus: 9 (24hrs), 11, 77 (24hrs). Sun–Tue 6pm–2am; Wed–Fri 3pm–2am; Sat 3pm–3am. Average beer: $4.*

✕ 🍸 **Lion Head Pub** DePaul students, hospital staff and neighborhood urban professionals alike belly up at this combo spot. Decent bar food, foosball, pool and darts dominate downstairs at the Lion Head, where it's impossible not to find yourself facing one of the two dozen plasma and big-screen TVs. Upstairs, the Apartment sports a corny (yet comfy) club atmosphere with its beds, couches and recliners, which get plenty of use on weekends when the place is packed assholes-to-elbows with singles. *2251 N Lincoln Ave between Webster and Belden Aves (773-348-5100). El: Brown, Purple (rush hrs), Red to Fullerton. Bus: 8, 11, 74. Mon–Fri 3pm–2am; Sat 3pm–3am; Sun 3pm–2am. Average beer: $5.*

The Long Room Of all the neighborhood bars trying to make the area around rambling Ashland Avenue feel more homey, this gem is among the homiest. Art Deco touches abound, live music kicks up a little dust on the weekends and the mood is consistently upbeat, chatty and sociable. The twenty/thirtysomething regulars live on the cusp—they're not quite Lakeview and not quite Ravenswood, which suits us just fine. *1612 W Irving Park Rd at Ashland Ave (773-665-4500). El: Brown to Irving Park. Bus: 9 Ashland, 80 Irving Park Rd. Mon–Fri 5pm–2am; Sat 5pm–3am; Sun 7pm–2am. Average cocktail: $4.*

▼ **Lucky Horse Shoe Lounge** Gay men and straight women can create their own luck by popping into this

pleasant Boystown stalwart. After all, it's easy to get lucky at a place where go-go boys dance in the middle of the horseshoe-shaped bar. Just bring enough dollar bills. *3169 N Halsted St between Briar Pl and Belmont Ave (773-404-3169). El: Brown, Purple (rush hrs), Red to Belmont. Bus: 8, 22 (24hrs), 77 (24hrs). Mon–Fri 4pm–2am; Sat 2pm–3am; Sun 2pm–2am. Average cocktail: $5.*

✕ **Mad River Bar and Grille** At first glance, there's much to like about this Lakeview newcomer: an understated decor straight out of the Ralph Lauren catalog, loftlike high ceilings and spacious booths that can fit you and seven of your mates. But if the dance floor in the back beckons, beware of "that guy"—the one who's going to drop his pants and blind you with his sparkling white ass. *2909 N Sheffield Ave between George St and Oakdale Ave (773-935-7500). El: Brown to Diversey. Bus: 8 Halsted, 22 Clark (24hrs). Sun–Fri 11am–2am; Sat 11am–3am. Average beer: $4.*

✕ ✳ 🍸 **Matisse** Like a secret underground community of sexy, friendly people and cheap drinks (specials include $2 sangria on Tuesdays, $3 chocolate martinis on Wednesdays and half-price drinks on Thursdays), this dim and cavernous basement bar seems to attract people you'd actually want to get to know. *674 W Diversey Pkwy between Clark and Orchard Sts (773-528-6670). El: Brown, Purple (rush hrs) to Diversey. Bus: 22 (24hrs), 36, 76. Mon–Fri 4pm–2am; Sat 11am–3am; Sun 11am–2am. Average cocktail: $5.*

✕ **Merkle's Bar and Grill** There's something endearing about a bar named for a 1908 New York version of Steve Bartman; Fred Merkle wrecked a victory for the New York Giants by failing to touch base in a playoff game against the Cubs. Not surprisingly, this watering hole bleeds true Cubby blue, complete with pennants and pics of old-time ballplayers. The taps lack heartier brews, focusing on the lighter lagers for drink-'em-down sports fans. The best deal is the $2 Honey Weisse "Leinies" on Thursdays. *3516 N Clark St between Cornelia Ave and Eddy St (773-244-1025). El: Red to Addison. Bus: 8, 22 (24hrs), 152. Sun–Fri 4pm–2am; Sat 11am–3am. Average beer: $4.*

Miller's Tap and Liquor Store From open to close, this combination dark bar/liquor store serves a slow trickle of flushed old war vets and tipsy early-morning barflies looking to keep their buzz going. Loaded as the chain-smoking crowd is, it's a jolly bunch, and anyone who loves a cold one is treated like family. *2204 W Roscoe St between Bell and Leavitt Aves (773-472-1821). El: Brown to Paulina. Bus: 49 (24hrs), X49, 50. Mon–Thu 7am–2am; Fri–Sat 7am–3am; Sun 11am–1am. Average beer: $2.25.*

▼ ✕ **minibar** Calling yourself "mini" isn't going to get you very far in Boystown, which may be why this slick, sophisticated bar is refreshingly free of beefcake and has been attracting a hetero clientele. But let's be clear: While the boys may be happy to share the house-infused vodkas with you, the lotion in the bathroom is all theirs. *3341 N Halsted St between Buckingham Pl and Roscoe St (773-871-6227). El: Brown, Purple (rush hrs), Red to Belmont. Bus: 8, 22 (24hrs), 77 (24hrs). Sun–Fri 5pm–2am; Sat 5pm–3am. Average cocktail: $7.*

✕ ✳ **Monsignor Murphy's** We can't figure out how this sports bar got such a revered name, but trust us, it doesn't quite fit. Not that it's not nice—it's just that the beer garden is a little campy (very Florida Keys) but nonetheless lovely on a warm day. Those who eschew kitsch can try the patio in front. *3019 N Broadway between Wellington and Barry Aves (773-348-7285). El: Brown, Purple (rush hrs), Red to Belmont.*

Size matters Neither the drinks nor the attitude are small at minibar.

Bus: 36, 76, 77 (24hrs). Mon–Fri 2pm–2am; Sat noon–3pm; Sun 2pm–2am. Average beer: $3.

✕ ✱ **Mullen's on Clark** This bilevel Wrigleyville joint draws a strange crowd: a mix of ball-capped football fans paying full attention to the wall-size TV behind the bar and aspiring improv comics from nearby I.O. who love to rehash favorite bits and revel in their ironic choice of destination. No group pays any heed to the other, particularly when the orders of tater tots arrive. *3527 N Clark St between Cornelia Ave and Eddy St (773-325-2319). El: Brown, Purple (rush hrs) to Belmont; Red to Addison. Bus: 8, 22 (24hrs), 77 (24hrs), 152. Mon–Wed 5pm–2am; Thu, Fri 11am–2am, Sun 11am–2am; Sat 11am–3am. Average beer: $3.50.*

Mulligans Public House The bartender, Kevin, is a bowling man himself, but the dart team is always looking for players, so he may encourage you to join. Other than that, the only pressure you'll feel at this Roscoe Village sports bar is deciding which of the 14 TV screens to look at if you're not back in the tournament-quality dart room. *2000 W Roscoe St at Damen Ave (773-549-4225). El: Brown to Paulina. Bus: 50, 77 (24hrs), 152. Mon–Fri 3pm–2am; Sat noon–3am; Sun noon–2am. Average beer: $3.50.*

✱ ◖✕ **Murphy's Bleachers** Function trumps form and comfort at this woody, yet cavernous Cubbie corral and outdoor stable, er, patio behind the Friendly Confines. The former frat-brother and sorority-sister clientele want their alma mater's game on the TV and they want it now—not a problem considering the prevalence of flat screens. *3655 N Sheffield Ave between Addison St and Waveland Ave (773-281-5356). El: Red to Addison. Bus: 8, 22 (24hrs), 152. Mon–Sun 11am–2am. Average beer: $4.*

✕ ✱ **Mystic Celt** The interior—dominated by earth tones, comfy brown leather armchairs and a forest's worth of wood tables and stools—is neither mystical nor particularly Celtic. The clientele of unmarried, quickly aging yuppies— the type of pint-pounding bros and broads who still passionately sing along to "Since You've Been Gone" but are starting to get teary-eyed every time Springsteen's "Glory Days" comes on—are on the prowl. *3443 N Southport Ave between Newport and Cornelia Aves (773-529-8550). El: Brown to Southport. Bus: 9 Ashland. Sun–Fri 11am–2am; Sat 11am–3am. Average beer: $4.50.*

✕ ✱ **Newport Bar and Grill** No, you're not imagining things: This bar is attached to a laundromat. And the proprietors definitely cater to those looking to piss away some time while the rinse cycle finishes (you can choose from board games such as Clue or Trivial Pursuit). The brew selection leans heavily on the domestic side, and the menu isn't anything to write home about, but beer and suds? We like any bar that gives an excuse to show up wearing sweats. *1344 W Newport Ave at Southport Ave (773-325-9111). El: Brown to Southport. Bus: 9, 152, 154. Mon–Fri 11am–2am; Sat 10:30am–3am; Sun 10:30am–2am. Average beer: $4.*

◖ **Nick's Uptown** When Wrigleyville singles hear the phrase last call at their neighborhood bar, their next concern is getting to this late-night drunken den. The building's Art Deco details (including a vaulted ceiling) are impressive (albeit a little difficult to appreciate with glazed, half-closed eyes), and the setup of four pool tables and two bars seems a sympathetic nod to the fact that intoxicated and impatient go hand in hand. *4015 N Sheridan Rd between Irving Park Rd and Cuyler Ave (773-975-1155). El: Red to Sheridan. Bus: 36, 80, 151 (24hrs). Sun–Fri 4pm–4am; Sat 4pm–5am. Average cocktail: $6.*

▼ **The North End** This low-key sports hangout is one of several Boystown bars far enough off the strip to avoid the parade of stand-and-model party boys that stink up the intersection of Halsted and Roscoe with too much cologne and hair product. Instead, the North End attracts its steady share of regulars looking for solid baseball coverage, a good pool table and an alternative place to cruise on Saturday night. *3733 N Halsted St at Waveland Ave (773-477-7999). El: Brown, Purple (rush hrs), Red to Addison. Bus: 8 Halsted, 152 Addison. Mon–Fri, 3pm–2am; Sat noon–3am; Sun noon–2am. Average beer: $3.*

✕ **O Lounge** The music here gets our hips moving, but the dance floor is small and awkwardly shaped (due to stairs smack-dab in the middle). Pricey cocktails are the drink of choice, but come in plastic, er, glasses. The glowing platform, for the most liquid-courageous of dancers, looks like a giant version of the memory game Simon. In the end, this is a bar with a weak club facade—but judging by the massive line outside, for some, that might be enough. *3140 N Lincoln Ave between Barry and Belmont Aves (773-248-2988). Bus: 9, 11, 77 (24hrs). Wed–Fri 9pm–2am; Sat 9pm–3am. Average cocktail: $8.*

▼ ✕ ✱ **O'Donovan's** The corner where this North Center tap sits has been a neighborhood hot spot since Prohibition: The former Schulien's featured a basement speakeasy and a house magician. The 'hood has changed—today's O'Donovan's operates as a laid-back hangout for younger couples and small groups—but the tableside magic shows (and the occasional balloon sculptist) remain on weekends. Escape the crowds by grabbing a seat on the ample sidewalk café or in the tucked-away beer garden. *2100 W Irving Park Rd at Hoyne Ave (773-478-2100). El: Brown to Irving Park. Bus: 11, 80, X80. Mon–Fri 11am–2am; Sat 11am–3am; Sun 10am–2am. Average beer: $4.*

◖ ✕ **Oakwood 83** The glowing neon signs in the windows of this middlebrow supper club proclaim: steak, ribs and fish. But after 2am, they could just as easily declare transvestites, Eastern European mafia and drunken frat boys. That all of these demographics and more can comfortably mingle is a testament to the friendly staff, a surprisingly good jukebox and the shared belief that the first eight vodka tonics just weren't enough. *1959 W Montrose Ave between Winchester St and Damen Ave (773-327-2785). Bus: 11, 50, 78. 11am–4am. Average cocktail: $4.*

O'Lanagan's The museum of antiquated taverns needs to add this place to its collection. It has wall-to-wall original wood paneling, a pool table with matted and faded felt, and a vague race-car theme that seems like it was lovingly put together some 30 years ago. The patrons here look like they showed up in their youth and never left, but they all seem to like the friendly bar matron who smokes Newports in the most desultory fashion. *2335 W Montrose Ave at Claremont Ave (773-583-2252). El: Brown to Western. Bus: 49 Western (24hrs), 78 Montrose. 11am–2am. Average cocktail: $4.*

Parrots Bar and Grill Looking to play pool, remain anonymous and buy a beer from a bartender who isn't snobby but isn't looking to become your best friend? Head here, where groups of post-college friends relax and split time between glancing up at the game and choosing between Prince and David Allen Coe on the juke. *754 W Wellington Ave at Halsted St (773-281-7878). El: Brown, Purple (rush hrs) to Diversey. Bus: 8, 22 (24hrs), 36, 76. Sun–Fri 11am–2am; Sat 11am–3am. Average beer: $3.50.*

✗ **Red Ivy** This sports spot is just blocks away from Wrigley Field, but we think the view of the Cubs is better from the bar. Movie-size projections of the games flicker behind the surprisingly good lineup of liquor, getting you a lot closer to the action than those scalped tickets will. And the food here—Palermo's pizza—beats Wrigley's hot dogs any day. *3525 N Clark St between Cornelia Ave and Eddy St (773-472-0900). El: Red to Addison. Bus: 8, 22 (24hrs), 152. Sun–Fri 11am–2am; Sat 11am–3am. Average cocktail: $6.*

✗ **Redder** A policy of pouring generously means that the cocktails you get at this new hangout will be smooth and potent. But more than that, it keeps this generic—albeit bright, casual and friendly—hangout from getting lost in Southport's waves of homogeny. *3417 N Southport Ave between Roscoe St and Newport Ave (773-472-5300). El: Brown to Southport. Bus: 9 Ashland, 22 Clark (24hrs). Mon–Thu 4pm–midnight; Fri 4pm–2am; Sat noon–3am; Sun 2–10pm. Average cocktail: $4.50.*

✗ ✳ **Redmond's** This sporty bar is too far from Wrigley for the raucous fieldside tomfoolery, but it's still close enough to put up Cubs logos here and there. The result? We can actually move around, hear the game and keep our clothes relatively spill-free. Sounds like it's time to defect from the intense Cubby Bear regime. *3358 N Sheffield Ave at Roscoe St (773-404-2151). El: Brown, Purple (rush hrs), Red to Belmont. Bus: 22 Clark (24 hrs), 77 (24hrs), 152. Mon–Fri 11am–2am; Sat 11am–3am; Sun 11am–midnight. Average beer: $5.*

Roscoe Village Pub As one bartender told us from her sounding post at the long wooden bar's apex: "This is not a place where you'll find the pointy-shoe, popped-collar crew." As the neighborhood skews younger, things might change. But for now the space stays true to its homely roots with an old-fashioned jukebox and a back area cluttered with '70s furniture and unused office supplies. *2159 W Addison St at Leavitt St (773-472-6160). Bus: 49 (24hrs), 50, 152. Mon–Thu 2pm–2am; Fri noon–2am; Sat noon–3am; Sun noon–2am. Average beer: $4.50. Cash only.*

Rose's Lounge Any of this spot's divey iniquities can be forgiven with the $1 mugs of Old Style. Rose—the cute, old Eastern European owner-bartender—hasn't changed a thing since the '70s: A shingled awning hangs over the back of the bar, wood paneling lines the walls and plenty of eclectic grandma knickknacks mingle with the bottles of liquor. And at seven plays for a buck, not even the jukebox prices have changed over the years. *2656 N Lincoln Ave between Wrightwood Ave and Diversey Pkwy (773-327-4000). El: Brown, Purple (rush hrs), Red to Fullerton. Bus: 11, 74, 76. Noon–2am. Average beer: $2.*

Sally's Lounge This worn-around-the-edges watering hole is the last place you'd expect to find old men gathered around a horseshoe bar, glued to reruns of *Will & Grace*. Then again, weird sightings are de rigueur here: Dearly departed Sally herself allegedly shows up (in ghost form) near the jukebox every now and again. But when a bar is this minimal—the only eye candy here is an attractive female bartender standing against a background of Christmas lights and wood paneling—patrons are happy for something new to look at. *3759 N Western Ave between Grace St and Waveland Ave (773-463-7120). Bus: 49 Western (24hrs), 80 Irving Park. Mon–Thu 1pm–midnight; Fri 1pm–2am; Sat 1pm–3am (closed Sun). Average cocktail: $3.50. Cash only.*

✳ **Sheffield's** *2007 Readers' Choice: Best beer garden* During warmer months this huge beer garden turns into a laid-back college reunion on weekend nights, with baseball-

capped dudes and spaghetti-strapped chicks flanking the outdoor bar for $2 "Bad Beers of the Month" (Old Milwaukee and Stroh's, recently). There's also a grill, but it's charcoal, so bring coals with your grub. Inside, the railroad apartment-style layout means there's a place for everyone, from pool players to folks who just want to hang by the fire with a brew. *3258 N Sheffield Ave between Belmont Ave and School St (773-281-4989). El: Brown, Purple (rush hrs), Red to Belmont. Bus: 8 Halsted, 77 Belmont (24hrs). Mon–Fri 3pm–2am; Sat noon–3am; Sun noon–2am. Average beer: $4.*

✗ **Side Street Saloon** When is a bar *truly* a neighborhood bar? When it also serves as a library, as does this charming, wallpapered-like-Grandma's-house bar. Regulars come by to drop off old books, borrow new ones and discuss the merits of both over beers, burgers and fried mozzarella sticks. *1456 W George St between Southport and Greenview Aves (773-327-1127). Bus: 9, 11, 76. Mon, Tue 4pm–2am; Wed–Fri, Sun 11am–2am; Sat 11am–3am. Average beer: $4.*

▼✳ **Sidetrack** If size matters, there's no better bar in Boystown than this well-hung hot spot. Six big rooms—we like the smoke-free Glass Bar—are all packed with cute, frisky boys distracting themselves with the same three things: the videos on the wall, the drink in their hand and the ass in your jeans. Gay and straight come out in droves to sing along together to show tunes from movie musical clips shown on giant screens several nights a week. *3349 N Halsted St between Buckingham Pl and Roscoe St (773-477-9189). El: Brown, Purple (rush hrs), Red to Belmont. Bus: 8 Halsted. Sun–Fri 3pm–2am, Sat 3pm–3am. Average cocktail: $4.*

Silvie's Lounge Even when there's no show scheduled this place is still poised to rock. The bartender keeps a guitar strapped to her back (weird, but true) and you'll find indie kids lounging on the couches talking shop. In a separate room, you'll find old career drinkers reminiscing about rock gone by. *1902 W Irving Park Rd at Wolcott Ave (773-871-6239). El: Brown to Irving Park. Bus: 11, 50, 80. Tue–Fri 4pm–2am; Sat 4pm–3am. Average beer: $4.*

✗ ✳ **Sopo Lounge & Grill** Okay, so this place isn't as trendy as the name (short for Southport) might suggest, but we wouldn't have it any other way. The drinks are strong and the crowd is fun. And with drink and food specials ($2 burgers, $3 drafts on Mondays, for example) every day of the week, it's possible to leave the bar feeling richer than when you went in. *3418 N Southport Ave between Roscoe St and Newport Ave (773-348-0100). El: Brown to Southport. Bus: 77 Belmont (24hrs), 152 Addison. Mon–Fri 4pm–2am; Sat 10am–3am; Sun 10am–2am. Average beer: $4.*

✗ **Southport Lanes & Billiards** It should be no surprise that this bar, decked out in rich wood tones and old chandeliers, comes complete with a billiards room and old-school bowling lanes. But what is surprising is the clientele, which is a hell of a lot less obnoxious than other fratastic bars on this strip. (No, seriously—this is tame for Southport.) *3325 N Southport Ave at Henderson St (773-472-6600). El: Brown to Southport. Bus: 9, 11, 152. Mon–Fri noon–2am; Sat noon–3am; Sun noon–1am. Average beer: $4.*

▼ **Spin** No, it's not a gym, but it might as well be. The boys at this Boystown veteran look like stars of their spinning classes, and there's even a shower room. Every other Friday a handful of contestants dance under the spray for the chance to win $100 while cuties sipping Long Island iced teas hoot and holler. *800 W Belmont Ave at Halsted St (773-327-7711). El: Brown, Purple (rush hrs), Red to Belmont. Bus: 8,*

Get a cue Action on the felt at Ten Cat Tavern.

22 (24hrs), 77 (24hrs). Mon–Fri 4pm–2am; Sat 2pm–3am; Sun 2pm–2am. Average cocktail: $4.

Sports Corner If you're having a severe case of Wrigleyville sports bar déjà vu, this place won't cure what ails you. But if you're near the Friendly Confines and just looking for an exponentially more laid-back version of Hi-Tops, this is your place. The large, dimly lit, concrete-and-tile space may not be any more comfortable, but the slightly older, less annoyingly boisterous crowd is more interested in the score of the game than scoring. *956 W Addison St at Sheffield Ave (773-929-1441). El: Red to Addison. Bus: 8, 22 (24hrs), 152. Sun–Fri 10am–2am; Sat 10am–3am. Average beer: $4.*

Spot 6 We're not sure how to peg this place. At times it feels like a neighborhood bar, yet with a loungey vibe. Factor in the pool table and cheap drinks, and you have an ambitious hole in the wall. Bands play weekends, so maybe it's a live music venue. Whatever the case may be, this spot has something for everyone. We're not complaining. *3343 N Clark St at Roscoe St (773-388-0185). El: Red to Addison. Bus: 22 Clark (24hrs), 152 Addison. Tue–Fri 5pm–2am; Sat 5pm–3am. Average beer: $3.50.*

T. Mellon's Hye Bar This woody bar has the same investment banker–look-alike clientele and beer selection as every other Irish-tinged sports bar on this strip of Southport, but a few curiosities remain. The sepia-toned photos of the bar's namesake, circa early 20th century, posing victorious in a wide variety of sports (conquering a steep mountainside on skis; winning an auto race) is puzzlingly humorous, while the large aquarium behind the bar—full of water and coral, yet entirely fish-free—is just plain puzzling. *3707 N Southport*

Ave between Waveland Ave and Grace St (773-244-4102). El: Brown to Southport. Bus: 152 Addison. Mon–Fri 4pm–2am; Sat noon–3am; Sun noon–2am. Average beer: $4.

(Tai's Til 4 We heard rumors that this late-night hookup haven gets packed with sweaty grinders around 1am, so we settled on a more mellow afternoon drink instead. Which turned out to be just fine. The chatty bartender helped us pick from the dozen beers on tap, the pool table was open and despite our best efforts, nobody hit on us. Once area bars close down, however, it's a seedier story. *3611 N Ashland Ave between Addison St and Waveland Ave (773-348-8923). Bus: 9 Ashland, 152 Addison. Mon–Fri 5pm–4am; Sat 5pm–5am; Sun 11am–4am. Average beer: $4.*

✕ ✹ **Take Five** Lured by the promise of cheap eats (everything on the menu rings in at a mere five bones), drinks, small groups of Southport-strip regulars populate this boxy, bricky space. Tableside flat screens and a strange, curtained-off corner (um…VIP?) mean people keep mostly to themselves—the exception being *Grey's Anatomy* and *24* viewing parties on Thursdays and Mondays, respectively. *3747 N Southport Ave between Waveland Ave and Grace St (773-871-5555). El: Brown to Southport. Bus: 9, 22 (24hrs), 80, 152. Mon–Fri 11am–2am; Sat 11am–3am; Sun 5pm–2am. Average beer: $3.50.*

Tavern 33 With JT Collins having gone the way of the dodo, Tavern 33 has established itself as the new local for Roscoe Villagers and other wandering souls, both during the week and as weekend starter bar. The tavern features a warm atmosphere thanks to the lively regulars, bartenders happy to drink with you, and old sepia photographs of North Lincoln Avenue. *3328 N Lincoln Ave between School and Henderson*

Sts (773-935-6393). El: Brown to Paulina. Bus: 9, 11, 77 (24hrs). Mon–Fri 5pm–2am; Sat noon–3am, Sun noon–2am. Average beer: $3.50.

⚓ Ten Cat Tavern Drinking here is like getting into the DeLorean and traveling back to 1955—sort of like when you're just drunk enough at Green Mill to think it's the '40s. Eclectic, mismatched furniture and an old blues-heavy jukebox set the mood for kicking back or rackin' 'em up at the two vintage pool tables. Just be careful, McFly: The bartenders will not hesitate to embarrass you on the felt. *3931 N Ashland Ave between Byron St and Irving Park Rd (773-935-5377). El: Brown to Irving Park. Bus: 9 Ashland, 80 Irving Park. Sun–Fri 3pm–2am; Sat 3pm–3am. Average beer: $3.*

▼ 3160 Owned by the folks behind bachelorette-party bar Baton Show Lounge, this likable venue (formerly Annex 3) is now a piano bar similar to Gentry (think cabaret cuties and the 40-and-older crowd who loves them). Recent nights were a bit barren, but the flickering candles, fresh-cut flowers, friendly staff and quality entertainment should bring in the crowds once the word's out. *3160 N Clark St at Fletcher St (773-327-5969). El: Brown, Purple (rush hrs), Red to Belmont. Bus: 8, 22 (24hrs), 77 (24hrs). Mon–Fri 3pm–2am; Sat noon–3am; Sun noon–2am. Average cocktail: $6.*

✕ Toon's Bar This sleeper on the edge of Wrigleyville draws in neighbors for billiards and shuffleboard, televised sports with a cheering crowd, pulled pork sandwiches and po' boys, and a dose of New Orleans-style hospitality. Hard-to-find Abita beer on tap and sunny sidewalk tables make it even more irresistible. *3857 N Southport Ave between Grace and Byron Sts (773-935-1919). El: Brown to Irving Park. Bus: 9, 22 (24hrs), 80, X80. Sun–Fri 11:30–2am; Sat 11:30–3am. Average beer: $4.50.*

Town Hall Pub In case you couldn't guess, this bare-bones dive, known for its constant stream of live bands and for being one of the oldest bars on Halsted, is for breeders. And as the only straight bar in this stretch of increasingly hetero Boystown, it'll only get busier. *3340 N Halsted St between Buckingham Pl and Roscoe St (773-472-4405). El: Brown, Purple (rush hrs), Red to Belmont. Bus: 8, 22 (24hrs), 77 (24hrs). Sun–Fri 6pm–2am; Sat 6pm–3am. Average cocktail: $5.*

The Trace The coolest and sleekest of Wrigleyville bars can handle spillover from any Metro show, no matter who's been playing. That's no easy task, but the look and feel of this place—exposed brick walls littered with slick flat-screen TVs and paintings of jazz musicians—is as welcoming to Atmosphere die-hards as Sufjan Stevens fans. *3714 N Clark St between Waveland Ave and Grace St (773-477-3400). El: Red to Addison. Bus: 22 (24hrs), 36, 152. Sun–Fri 5pm–2am; Sat 5pm–3am. Average cocktail: $5.*

✕ ✷ Trader Todd's Pop into any bar boasting seven days of karaoke and you're likely to hear more than your fair share of Bon Jovi. Thankfully, this Lakeview parrot-head hangout offers ample patio space (heated in the winter) to escape juiced-up choruses of "Sweet Caroline." This place is good for satiating drunk *American Idol* desires, but bad for house cocktails. Stick to your beer of choice over Todd's odd concoctions. *3216 N Sheffield Ave at Belmont Ave (773-975-8383). El: Brown, Purple (rush hrs), Red to Belmont. Bus: 8, 22 (24hrs), 77 (24hrs). Mon–Thu 4pm–2am; Fri 11am–2am; Sat 10am–3am; Sun 10am–2am. Average beer: $3.50.*

✕ Tre Is this a sports bar? Kind of—it's close enough to Wrigley Field that on game days the crowd will be in full Cubs regalia. But with only three TV screens, this is a sports bar of a different kind—that is, it's a bar where you can grab a booth with your friends and actually hear yourselves as you talk about the game or (and this is the truly different part) anything else. *3330 N Clark St at Buckingham Pl (773-281-6463). El: Red to Belmont. Bus: 8, 22 (24hrs), 77 (24hrs). Sun–Fri 4pm–2am; Sat 4pm–3am. Average beer: $4.*

✕ ✷ Uberstein Although the German beer hall design is respectable, the fratesque Wrigleyville clientele works against its authenticity. There was plenty of imported Hofbrau to fill our mugs, but we couldn't shake the feeling we were on the abandoned set of *The Man Show*. If you're looking a spot to escape those Kimmelesque "ziggy zaggy" chants, we'd recommend the more tolerable, appropriately-named "biergarten." *3478 N Clark St between Newport and Cornelia Aves (773-883-0300). El: Red to Addison. Bus: 22 Clark (24hrs), 152 Addison. Sun–Fri 3pm–2am; Sat 3pm–3am. Average beer: $6.*

❨ Underbar Tucked away in the shadow of the Western Avenue bridge, this cozy, candlelit bar seems (at least early in the night) like a good place to write your long-awaited debut novel while nursing one of 40 eclectic, hard-to-find beers. Just don't get too comfy, Hemingway: The rowdy, late-night rush is this establishment's bread and butter. So stay and spot the subject of your next broken-heart tale. *3243 N Western Ave at Melrose St (773-404-9363). Bus: 49 Western (24hrs), 77 Belmont (24hrs). Sun–Fri 4pm–4am; Sat 4pm–5am. Average beer: $4.50.*

Underground Lounge Not to be confused with the Underground, the much buzzed-about River North bunker bar, this no-less-subterranean spot is more about the stage than the scene. Thursday through Saturday, local and touring acts of all musical stripes—from jazz to punk—take the small, barely elevated stage, and on the off nights, there's always pool. *952 W Newport Ave between Halsted St and Sheffield Ave (773-327-2739). El: Red to Addison. Bus: 8, 22 (24hrs), 152. Sun–Fri 7pm–2am; Sat 7pm–3am. Average cocktail: $7.*

✕ Vaughan's Pub Its rowdy neighbor Mad River Bar & Grille has bargoers queueing up for entry, but this friendly watering hole is worth giving up your spot in line. Dim and narrow, the pub sports candlelit tables, sociable regulars and enough pockets of space to accommodate everyone. Translation: No line...at least not yet. *2917 N Sheffield Ave between George St and Oakdale Ave (773-281-8188). El: Brown, Purple (rush hrs) to Wellington. Bus: 8, 11, 76. Mon–Fri 1pm–2am; Sat 10am–3am; Sun 11am–2am. Average beer: $3.*

✕ Vida The giant video screen hints cheesy club and the location might suggest yuppie crowd, but don't be fooled: Vida is a nuevo-Latino lounge serving tapas and signature martinis for all your sassy-drink needs. And if the spirit ever moves you to learn tango and salsa dancing, then Thursday's your night and this is your place. *1248 W George St between Lincoln Ave and Lakewood St (773-935-5700). El: Brown, Purple (rush hrs) to Diversey. Bus: 11 Lincoln, 76 Diversey. Tue–Fri 5pm–2am; Sat 5pm–3am; Sun 5pm–2am. Average cocktail: $7.*

✕ ✷ ⚓ Village Tap Roscoe Village has gentrified over the last few years, and the same goes for its watering holes, especially this one. These days it's yuppie central, but it's still one of the best places in town to grab a beer from the extensive list, chat with the friendly bartenders and test your alcohol-addled vocabulary with a game of Scrabble. Burgers are better than the average bar fare. *2055 W Roscoe St at Hoyne Ave (773-883-0817). Bus: 50, 77 (24hrs), 152 Addison. Mon–Thu 5pm–2am; Fri, Sat 3pm–3am, Sun noon–10pm. Average beer: $3.50.*

✕ ✻ **Waterhouse** Simple formula, really: Draw in the honeys with fruity, Red Bull–infused cocktails and watch the boys follow. Add indiscernible house beats, muted reds, oversize booths, minichandeliers, appetizers that go one step further than pub grub, and a Golden Tee, and you've pretty much got the idea. *3407 N Paulina St at Lincoln Ave (773-871-1200). El: Brown to Paulina. Bus: 9, 11, 77 (24hrs). Mon–Thu 4pm–2am; Fri noon–2am; Sat noon–3am; Sun noon–2am. Average cocktail: $6.*

Wellington's The most distinctive quality of this rather typical Lakeview bar is its shuffleboard table, a distraction hard to find in the big city. Otherwise, it has everything you could expect from a cozy hangout on a condo-lined street: standard liquor lineup, seven beers on tap, lots of dark wood, Golden Tee and a handful of lovey-dovey, brother and sister–type heterosexual couples. *1300 W Wellington Ave between Racine and Lincoln Aves (773-524-1111). El: Brown, Purple (rush hrs) to Wellington. Bus: 11, 76, 77 (24hrs). Mon–Fri 5pm–2am; Sat Noon–3am; Sun Noon–2am. Average cocktail: $8.*

✕ **Wild Goose Bar & Grill** The paint's chipping off the walls here and there, the bathroom is a claustrophobe's nightmare, and if it's busy you might be forced to belly up to a folding table. Then again, this surprisingly spacious bar is filled with so many flat-screen and projection TVs and fills up with enough yummy bar food that we almost didn't notice. Pretty, friendly waitresses don't hurt either. *4365 N Lincoln Ave between Hutchinson St and Cullom Ave (773-281-7112). Bus: 11, 50, 78. Mon–Fri 11am–2am; Sat noon–3am, Sun noon–1am. Average beer: $3.*

The Wild Hare Even though it's in Wrigleyville, this place feels miles—even hours—away from the baseball scene. But what's lacking in pendants and face-painted fans is made up for with reggae paraphernalia and lots of rum punch and Red Stripe, so it's no wonder that Jamaicans all over the city call this joint their second home. *3530 N Clark St at Addison St (773-327-4273). El: Red to Addison. Bus: 22 Clark (24hrs), 152 Addison. Mon–Fri, Sun 8pm–2am; Sat 8pm–3am. Average cocktail: $5.*

✕ ✻ **Will's Northwoods Inn** Escape to the great outdoors Wisconsin-style with your Leinenkugel, Point or Sprecher and shoot the breeze under the watchful eye of the giant moose that stands sentry. Friends meet at picnic tables, tunes float out from the jukebox (Phish and fowl with "Free Bird" represented) and the occasional neighborhood Labrador mingles with the regulars. *3030 N Racine Ave at Nelson St (773-528-4400). El: Brown, Purple (rush hrs) to Wellington. Bus: 11, 76, 77 (24hrs). Sun–Fri 11am–2am; Sat 11am–3am. Average beer: $3.50.*

▼ ✕ **winebar** It takes balls for a wine bar to put a bottle from Ohio on its opening list, but as an extension of Boystown favorite minibar, balls are exactly what this bar will be full of. It's not that the beautiful, dimly lit room is something only gay guys can appreciate—rather, it's the puppy-dog eyes of the bartender that will pack them in. *3339 N Halsted St between Buckingham Pl and Roscoe St (773-871-6227). El: Brown, Purple (rush hrs), Red to Belmont. Bus: 8, 22 (24hrs), 77 (24hrs). Mon–Wed 5–11pm; Thu, Fri, Sun 5pm–2am; Sat 5pm–3am. Average glass of wine: $10.*

Wrigleyville North Stretching the boundaries of Cubbie territory nearly to Irving Park Road, this dive-among-dives has only one thing characteristically Wrigleyville about it: its name. The first sign: the bartender's missing her four front teeth. The second sign: the low, garage band–ready stage with cowboy hats atop the amplifiers. The final clue: the refreshing absence of loud, red-faced bros and their stumbling Botox broads. *3900 N Sheridan Rd at Byron St (773-929-9543). El: Red to Sheridan. Bus: 36, 80, 151 (24hrs). Sun–Fri 11am–2am; Sat 11am–3am. Average beer: $3.*

✕ ✻ **Xippo** This North Center joint may look like a upscale lounge at first glance, but it's really just a friendly neighborhood bar. Locals get cozy in the sleek, red decor while electro-pop is piped from the sound system and VH1 plays on the televisions. Food is served, but hungry patrons should arrive early to eat because the kitchen's closing hours can be unpredictable. *3759 N Damen Ave between Grace St and Bradley Pl (773-529-9135). Bus: 50 Damen, 152 Addison. Mon–Fri 3pm–2am; Sat 11am–3am; Sun 11am–2am. Average beer: $5.*

❨ ✕ **Yak-Zies Bar & Grill** Although the descent is only about a half-dozen steps, the low ceilings, scant decor and dim, smoky environs make this so-called sports bar feel more like the most subterranean of all dives. It's not necessarily a bad thing, especially if you really dug hanging out in your dad's rec room in the early '80s. And the late-night fried food (think cheese fries and chicken wings) pairs well with being a good 4am bender drunk. *506 W Diversey Pkwy at Pine Grove Ave (773-327-1717). El: Brown, Purple (rush hrs) to Diversey. Bus: 22 (24hrs), 36, 76, 151 (24hrs). Sun–Fri 11am–4am; Sat 11am–5am. Average beer: $4.50.*
● *Additional location at 3710 N Clark St (773-525-9200).*

✕ ✻ **The Yard** Although this recently opened bar in the former Pepper Lounge space doesn't stray too far from the Wrigleyville mold, its dark woods, exposed brick and sports-memorabilia deficiency seem classier than many of the surrounding drunk dens. The bar's namesake half-yard glass can be filled with more than a dozen draft brews and trotted out to the rear beer garden which sports three old horse stables the owners say will eventually become semiprivate nooks for small groups. *3441 N Sheffield Ave between Newport and Cornelia Aves (773-477-9273). El: Red to Addison. Bus: 8, 22 (24hrs), 152. Mon–Fri 5pm–2am; Sat 11am–3am; Sun 11am–3am (opens at 11am on Cubs game days). Average beer: $5.*

Humboldt Park/Logan Square

❨ **Alice's Lounge** This long wooden bar is helmed by a few middle-aged women who, on Sundays, mix huge batches of kamikazes and sell them for $2 a pop—but the real draw here is karaoke. If you get there and the door's locked, don't get discouraged. Just ring the bell over and over again (sometimes the bartenders can't hear it over yet another version of "Don't Stop Believin'"). *3556 W Belmont Ave at Central Park Ave (773-478-5975). El: Blue to Belmont. Bus: 56, 77 (24hrs), 82. Mon–Fri 3pm–4am; Sat noon–5am; Sun noon–4am. Average beer: $2.*

Archie's This inconspicuous bar is equal parts after-work dive and *Antiques Roadshow*. Amid dusty knickknacks and bric-a-brac, the family who runs the place will pour you a stiff drink and then try to sell you a Civil War–era revolver, a set of buffalo-themed shotglasses or anything else lying around—anything except for the patriarch's wall-mounted marlin and the Hamm's sign hanging out front. *2600 W Iowa Ave at*

Quench your thirst
Whatever your poison,
winebar's got it.

Bars & Lounges

History repeats The 100-year-old bar at The Continental has heard many good stories.

Rockwell St (no phone). Bus: 49 Western (24hrs), 66 Chicago (24hrs). 11am–2am. Average beer: $3.

Bob Inn Nothing brings together the hip kids and blue-collar Chicagoans better than cheap alcohol—and this no-frills Logan Square dive across from Fireside Bowl is living proof. Watch as the earnest mustaches of Blackhawks and Sox fans mingle amiably with ironically bearded Black Keys and White Stripes fans. And if that gets dull, just head to the back for a 75-cent game of pool. *2555 W Fullerton Ave at Rockwell St (no phone). El: Blue to California. Bus: 49 (24hrs), X49, 74. Sun–Fri 11am–2am; Sat 11am–3am. Average cocktail: $4.*

Cafe Lura On a corner of lonesome desolation lies this neo-gothic den of inequity. Is it a moody, clean-as-a-whistle lounge or a haunt for I-coulda-been-Bo-Bice metal heads? Early, this low-key nightclub spills out sweet European tunes, and then right at dusk, watch out: Here come the Polish head-bangers. *3184 N Milwaukee Ave between Davlin Ct and Belmont Ave (773-736-3033). El: Blue to Belmont. Bus: 56, 77 (24hrs), 82. Sun–Fri 5pm–2am; Sat 5pm–3am (closed Mon). Average cocktail: $6.*

California Clipper The Clipper is just a photo booth away from exhibiting the same shabby-chic hipster cool as Wicker Park dives like Goldstar or the Rainbo Club. If you can cut through the wall of smoke, you may just see a jazz trio playing in the corner. Slide into one of the gorgeous booths on a Monday night for a tongue-and-cheek version of bingo. *1002 N California Ave at Augusta Blvd (773-384-2547). Bus: 52, 66 (24hrs), 70. Sun–Fri 8pm–2am; Sat 8pm–3am. Average cocktail: $5.*

Celina's Place It's probably only going to be you, whomever you bring and the owner, Celina, in this place. S gal, but she doesn't speak much English, so she'll hand over your $2 beer and leave you to soak up the wood paneling, year-round Christmas lights, video-game slots and pool table in solitude. *900 N Western Ave at Iowa St (773-486-8737). El: Blue to Chicago. Bus: 49 (24hrs), 50, 66 (24hrs). Noon–midnight. Average beer: $2. Cash only.*

❨ **Cindy's Our Place** This no-frills, carpeted bar is spacious enough to host even the surliest of late-night crowds, especially those in the mood for cut-rate martinis and all-around cheap booze. It's loaded with poker machines, electronic darts and a pool table, but it's the back-talking bartenders who really liven things up. *3534 W Belmont Ave between Drake and Central Park Aves (773-588-4390). El: Blue to Belmont. Bus: 56, 77 (24hrs), 82. Noon–4am. Average cocktail: $3.50.*

❨ **The Continental** In its past life as Hiawatha (a.k.a. Pizza Lounge), the only thing you'd pick up here was a six-pack of cheap beer to lug next door for a chicken dinner at Feed. Now, the 100-year-old dive has transformed into a slick little enclave for the late-night crowd to scope each other out and suck down the last liquor of the night while the tunes of the DJ's all-rock repertoire play on. *2801 W Chicago Ave at California Ave (773-292-1200). Bus: 52 Kedzie/California, 66 Chicago (24hrs). Sun–Fri 3pm–4am; Sat 3pm–5am. Average cocktail: $5.*

Domino It's tough to get more authentic than this Polish bar, where if there's not a soccer game on, then surely the jukebox is playing some ditty from the homeland. The gritty space is so authentic, in fact, that regulars might get caught off-guard when you speak English, but only for a second. And besides, really cheap beer, ping-pong and pool are things every ethnicity can embrace. *3905 W Belmont Ave at Milwaukee Ave (773-725-0267). El: Blue to Belmont. Bus: 53, 56, 77 (24hrs). Mon–Sat 7pm–2am; Sun 11am–2am. Average beer: $2.*

✗ **Green Eye Lounge** Named after the light that gives El trains the go-ahead, this Logan Square bar is nestled under the tracks at the Western stop. Friendly service, Goose Island draft and that prime spot right next to the Blue Line makes this place easy to add into your daily routine. *2403 W Homer St at Western Ave (773-227-8851). El: Blue to Western. Bus: 49 Western (24hrs). Mon–Fri 3pm–2am; Sat 12pm–3am; Sun 12pm–2am.. Average beer: $4.*

Nacional treasures
Bartenders at Nacional 27
want to get fresh with you.

Perfect pour The bartenders at Weegee's Lounge are experts at mixing classic cocktails.

reign—save for one or two quiet barflies—over the pool table and digital juke, and enjoy the bartender's full attention. And although we got a puzzled look when we asked for a PBR, the small selection of tasty Polish beers made us forgive and (eventually) forget. *3394 N Milwaukee Ave between Karlov Ave and Roscoe St (773-286-4482). El: Blue to Irving Park. Bus: 56 Milwaukee. Sun–Fri 5pm– 4am; Sat 5pm–5am. Average beer: $3. Cash only.*

Nelly's Saloon Pearls? Check. Cigarettes? Check. Bright pink lipstick? Check. All of owner Nelly's essentials are in order and she's officially open for business. Expect handsome, loaded Romanian imports chowing down on the earthy cuisine of their homeland: platters of *mititei* (grilled sausages); fried kraut with bits of bacon fat; heaping bowls of polenta with feta; and pan-fried chicken wings. Other than weekends when there's live music or anytime a soccer game's on, it's likely to be just you and Nelly, the queen of amaretto stone sours. *3256 N Elston Ave between Belmont Ave and Henderson St (773-588-4494). El: Blue to Belmont. Bus: 77 (24hrs), 82, 152. Mon–Sat 10am–2am; Sun Noon–2am. Cash only.*

✗ **Stadium West** Someone stood up in the bar on our last visit and declared it "dude night" because of the dearth of ladies in the crowd. It's this sort of good-natured conviviality that sends local thirtysomethings here in droves. Chill out on a couch, shoot a game of pool in the back or check out one of the live bands that perform on the tiny stage several nights a week. *3188 N Elston Ave at Belmont Ave (773-866-2450). Bus: 52 California, 77 Belmont (24hrs). Sun–Fri 5pm–2am; Sat 5pm–3am. Average cocktail: $3.50.*

✗ 🍴 **Streetside Café** The DJs here alternate between spinning house and indie rock, but either way, it doesn't change the vibe. When you combine two fireplaces, plenty of room to spread out, a handful of weary Logan Square locals and a Ms. Pac Man game, everything's nice and chill. *3201 W Armitage Ave at Kedzie Ave (773-252-9700). Bus: 73 Armitage, 82 Kimball-Homan. Sun–Fri 11:30am–2am; Sat 11:30am–3am. Average cocktail: $4.*

The Tap Room The pervasive red lighting and long bar might recall *Mean Streets*, but don't fret: Your chances of getting offed by the mob are slim to none here. Locals tend to huddle in groups of two or three, nursing bottled beers and chatting about sports, their wives, etc. Considering how a lot of Western Avenue bars fill up with younger, hipper and louder clientele, the relaxed vibe is a nice change of pace. *2218 N Western Ave between Palmer and Lyndale Sts (773-489-3622). El: Blue to California. Bus: 49 Western (24hrs). Sun–Fri 10am–2am; Sat 10am–3am. Average beer: $4. Cash only.*

Tini Martini This low-tech Logan Square hangout is too good to keep secret any longer. DJs trade nights spinning hip-hop, reggae, techno and house to a mixed crowd in a space that resembles everyone's dream loft. If the music isn't enough, fall back on killer martinis like the Krispy Kreme or the Astro Pop. *2169 N Milwaukee Ave at Talman Ave (773-269-2900). El: Blue to California. Bus: 56, 73, 74. Sun–Fri 9pm–2am; Sat 9pm–3am. Average cocktail: $7.*

✳ **Weegee's Lounge** Ten years from now, when this strip of Armitage is populated with coffee shops and vintage clothing stores, this old-school, soul-record– playing, classic-cocktail–mixing bar will be overrun with hipsters vying for their turn in the photo booth. Start

Helen's Two Way Lounge Scenesters haven't ruined this honky-tonk Logan Square joint—named for its dual entryways—yet. That's why when you see those banjos and fiddles above the bar and witness the ladies square-dancing with each other to the tunes of Johnny Cash and Hank Williams, you can bet this shit ain't ironic. *2928 W Fullerton Ave at Milwaukee Ave (773-227-5676). El: Blue to California. Bus: 52, 56, 74. Sun–Fri 9am–2am; Sat 7am–3am. Average beer: $3. Cash only.*

✗ **Hotti Biscotti Café** This Logan Square hangout began life as a coffeehouse, but has emerged in recent years as a hip live music venue for emerging artists (i.e., twentysomethings with keyboards). Now it keeps bar hours and serves dirt-cheap beer, cocktails and in an odd twist, milk shakes. Capacity is around 50, so you can probably fit close to 75 skinny hipsters. *3545 W Fullerton Ave at Drake Ave (773-292-6877). El: Blue to Logan Square. Bus: 74 Fullerton, 82 Kimball. Tue–Sat 5pm–2am. Average beer: $2.*

The Mutiny By day it's home to dedicated regulars, by night it's packed with rock & rollers drinking $5 half pitchers and nodding to free live bands. Pool, darts and Golden Tee are all free, and so is the chance to mark your territory by painting a ceiling tile. If you hate smoke, this place is not for you. But if you're in search of (semitarnished) gold, this is your treasure. *2428 N Western Ave between Montana and Altgeld Sts (773-486-7774). El: Blue to California. Bus: 49 (24hrs), X49, 74. Mon 1pm–2am; Tue–Fri 11am–2am; Sat 8am–3am; Sun noon–2am. Average beer: $2.50.*

🍸 **My Place on Milwaukee** This forgotten Polish bar is usually so empty that shortly after arriving you'll feel like you and your friends own the place. Bask in your uncontested

hanging out here now so you can say you knew it in the good old days. *3659 W Armitage Ave at Lawndale Ave (773-384-0707). Bus: 53 (24hrs), 73, 82. 5pm–2am. Average cocktail: $6.*

Whirlaway Lounge This Logan Square watering hole glows with charm—or is it the string of Christmas lights behind the bar? Either way, retired rock stars put away beers next to their disciples under the soft lights, snapshots of regulars and the warm smile of the maternal owner-bartender, Maria. *3224 W Fullerton Ave between Kedzie Blvd and Sawyer Ave (773-276-6809). El: Blue to Logan Square. Bus: 74 Fullerton, 82 Kimball-Homan. Sun–Fri 4pm–2am; Sat 4pm–3am. Average beer: $3. Cash only.*

✕ ✳ **Winds Café** This bar's location in the heart of Logan Square and its Caribbeanish comfort grub (jibaritos, jerk chicken) help it maintain its refreshingly diverse clientele. Exposed brick walls display colorful local art, which sets the scene for drinking Mexican Pacifico beer to a soundtrack of trance-inducing dub reggae with live bongo accompaniment. *2657 N Kedzie Ave at Milwaukee Ave (773-489-7478). El: Blue to Logan Square. Bus: 56 Milwaukee, 76 Diversey. Mon, Tue 2pm–midnight; Wed–Sat 11am–2am; Sun 11am–10pm. Average beer: $3.50.*

Bucktown/Wicker Park

Beachwood Inn No hipsters, no yuppies, no class-drawing lines here—just regular neighborhood folks in this one-room watering hole taking turns on the pool table or playing games like Scrabble and Connect Four. The scatterbrained decor (old movie posters, sports crap, beer memorabilia) is as random as the jukebox, which offers pre-'90s tunes from the Pretenders to Michael Jackson. *1415 N Wood St at Beach Ave (773-486-9806). El: Blue to Division. Bus: 9, 56, 72. Mon–Fri 4pm–2am; Sat 3pm–3am; Sun 3pm–2am. Average cocktail: $5. Cash only.*

✕ **Blue Line Club Car** The theme at this cozy Wicker Park diner is old-school railroad dining car, which is fitting considering it's underneath the Damen stop on the Blue Line. And although the menu has plenty of choices (pork chops, mussels, burgers), don't blow your money on dinner. Opt for a snack and keep the drinks coming. *1548 N Damen Ave between Pierce and North Aves (773-395-3700). El: Blue to Damen. Bus: 50, 56, 72. Mon–Thu 5pm–1am; Fri 4pm–2am; Sat 4pm–3am. Average cocktail: $6.*

boutique Considering that this place is financially backed by a hip-hop entrepreneur, it should come as no surprise that the hip-hoppers who hang out at the former Dragon Room are hustling in everything from the music to fashion biz. The Zen monastery–inspired decor makes a chic backdrop, but a good portion of the club is often given over to VIP areas. *809 W Evergreen Ave between Dayton and Halsted Sts (312-751-2900). El: Red to North/Clybourn. Bus: 8 Halsted, 72 North.*

✳ **Bucktown Pub** At first glance it didn't seem any different from other dark-wood neighborhood taverns. But then we noticed the psychedelic posters lining the walls, the bottomless baskets of free popcorn and the old man in the corner laughing his ass off at nothing. Is this bar high? *1658 W Cortland St between Marshfield Ave*

and Paulina St (773-394-9898). Bus: 9, 50, 73. Sun–Fri 3pm–2am; Sat 3pm–3am. Average beer: $4.

✕ ✳ **Cans** Cheap beer fast. What's not to like about that? As its name suggests, Cans serves canned beer, nearly three dozen varieties. Waitresses take your order with a Palm Pilot, but that's about the only thing advanced here. If Greek (a.k.a. frat talk) ain't your speak, the pool table (one of Bucktown's best) and the '80s soundtrack are draws. *1640 N Damen Ave between North and Wabansia Aves (773-227-2277). El: Blue to Damen. Bus: 50, 56, 72. Mon–Fri 4pm–2am; Sat 10am–3am; Sun 10am–2am. Average beer: $5.*

✕ **Celebrity** Chicago is known for a lot of things. Paris Hilton sightings are not one of them. But Wicker Park gets its bling on nonetheless with yet another one of these not-quite-a-bar-not-quite-a-club joints. The crowd's as diverse as the drinks, which range from cans of Old Style to bottles of Cristal. But if you're not into DJs and graffiti art, forget about it, you're in the wrong 'hood to begin with. *1856 W North Ave between Honore St and Wolcott Ave (773-365-0091). El: Blue to Damen. Bus: 50 Damen, 72 North. Tue–Fri 7pm–2am; Sat 7pm–3am; Sun 9pm–2am. Average cocktail: $5.*

The Charleston Will the hipsters, yuppies, freaks, dirty old men and bluegrass bands that pack this tchotchke-ridden corner tap—easily one of Bucktown's favorites—lose any of their charm now that the place is officially smoke-free? Not really—they'll just smell better. None of the above descriptors fit your personality? No worries. Between the piano, the pool table, the board games or Wi-Fi, you'll find

Natural selection Opting for a burger to go with your beer is an easy choice at Darwin's.

Board silly Board games are served up with the brews at the Charleston.

something that suits. *2076 N Hoyne Ave at Charleston St (773-489-4757). El: Blue to Western. Bus: 50 Damen. Mon–Fri 3pm–2am; Sat–Sun 2pm–2am. Average beer: $4. Cash only.*

The Corner The bar here, a huge Art Deco affair, is the only design element in this place. Otherwise it's a no-frills watering hole, with a dog splayed on the floor, locals filling up the tables and a jukebox playing lonely, heartbroken Tom Waits tunes. *2224 N Leavitt St at Palmer St (773-235-9279). Bus: 50 Damen, 74 Fullerton. Mon–Fri 9am–2am; Sat 9am–3am; Sun 11am–2am. Average beer: $3.*

Cortland's Garage The decor of this bar's former tenant, the kitschy Leopard Lounge, has been stripped down to inoffensive exposed-brick walls and high-top tables. But that just means there's less distraction when you're listening to the Top 40 remixes and hypnotized by the bright-blue martinis—or, more likely, the people holding them. *1645 W Cortland St between Marshfield Ave and Paulina St (773-862-7877). Bus: 9 Ashland, 73 Armitage. Mon–Thu 6pm–2am; Fri 4pm–2am; Sat 4pm–3am. Average cocktail: $5.*

Danny's Tavern The floors of this converted Bucktown house shake so much from the weight of hot-footed trendsetters you'd think the place is seconds from caving in. Most of the dancing is set to a mix of hip-hop, electro and rock on the weekends (and the insanely popular first-Wednesday-of-the-month funk party called Sheer Magic), but there are plenty of nooks and crannies to sit back, relax and people-watch. *1951 W Dickens Ave between Damen and Winchester Aves (773-489-6457). El: Blue to Damen. Bus: 50 Damen, 73 Armitage. Sun–Fri 7pm–2am; Sat 7pm–3am. Average cocktail: $4.*

✕ **Darwin's** In keeping with its name, this Bucktown institution proved that evolution is possible: After being closed for "renovations," it re-opened with a new coat of paint and the same sense of sarcasm. Stay away from the "Ha Ha We're Back" brew, aimed at those who doubted their re-emergence (unless you crave a PBR); stick with the Walking Fish Amber Ale instead. *1935 N Damen Ave between Cortland St and Armitage Ave (773-252-8530). El: Blue to Western. Bus: 50 Damen, 73 Armitage. Sun–Fri 5pm–2am; Sat 5pm–3am. Average beer: $3.50.*

✕ **Debonair Social Club** Early in the evening at this bilevel hangout, the video art on the wall is the room's main source of light, giving off a sultry cocktail-lounge vibe. But it's the calm before the storm: When celebrity DJs stop by, the place gets packed with clubby scenesters and frantic bass lines—so if you're here for the quiet, enjoy it while you can. *1575 N Milwaukee Ave between Honore St and North Ave (773-227-7990). El: Blue to Damen. Bus: 50, 56, 72. Tue–Fri 8pm–2am; Sat 8pm–3am; Sun noon–6pm. Average cocktail: $7.*

✕ **D'Vine** After a few hours of hustling to überambient, bass-heavy hip-hop and tossing back martinis in plush high-back booths with your loyal entourage, you'll stop comparing this dark, cavernous lounge to D'Vine's former life as a restaurant and welcome the scene that now is. *1950 W North Ave at Damen Ave (773-235-5700). El: Blue to Damen. Bus: 50, 56, 72. Sun–Fri 9pm–2am; Sat 9am–3am (closed Tue). Average cocktail: $10.*

Ed and Jean's It's not that this old Bucktown standby feels like somebody's living room; it's that it basically is one. Jean's been here for more than 50 years, and in that time she's accumulated more knickknacks than a flea market. It's her second home, and after a few minutes chatting with her over a cheap bottle of beer, it starts feeling like yours, too. *2032 W Armitage Ave between Damen and Hoyne Aves (no phone). El: Blue to Western. Bus: 49 (24hrs), 50, 73. 11am–11pm. Average beer: $2.50. Cash only.*

Empire Liquors Black walls, wiry chandeliers and more guyliner than a My Chemical Romance concert make this place the angstiest addition to Matt Eisler's trifecta of bars. The scene can get a little overwhelming in front, but if you can snag a seat in the private(ish) room in back you'll be golden— or at least as golden as a goth kid can get. *1566 N Milwaukee Ave between Honore St and North Ave (773-278-1600). El: Blue to Damen. Bus: 50, 56, 72. Wed–Fri 8pm–2am; Sat 8pm–3am. Average cocktail: $8.*

(**Estelle's** Not feeling Subterranean's music for the night? Can't take the hipper-than-thou crowd at Rainbo? Well, then head to this low-key sanctuary in the otherwise oft-pretentious Milwaukee-North-Damen intersection. No one's trying to out-cool anyone here (though late at night, they're definitely trying to pick each other up), so feel free to strike up a conversation with a stranger over some tasty late-night bar eats, served till 3am. *2013 W North Ave at Milwaukee Ave (773-782-0450). El: Blue to Damen. Bus: 50, 56, 72. Sun–Fri 7pm–4am; Sat 7pm–5am. Average cocktail: $5.*

Gallery Cabaret Perhaps one of the most active and random stages in the city can be found at this eclectic, art-filled corner tavern, where nightly performances can range from poetry readings and jam bands to a musical tribute to a famous deceased racehorse (seriously). More reliable is the beer menu: 17 bottles and 16 draft beers, including the venerable Three Floyds Alpha King. *2020 N Oakley Ave between Armitage and McLean Aves (773-489-5471). El: Blue to Western. Bus: 56, 73, 49 (24hrs), X49. Sun–Fri 5pm–2am; Sat 5pm–3am. Average beer: $4.*

✕ ✳ **Handlebar Bar & Grill** The multiple bike racks out back are packed with every kind of two-wheeler imaginable no matter the time of year at this biker bar (and by biker, we mean bicycle-r sense). Eco-minded folks chat over tasty vegan fare (the 'shroom caps and barbecue sandwich are great), check out each other's rides and sample from the ample list of diverse drafts. *2311 W North Ave between Oakley and Claremont Aves (773-384-9546). El: Blue to Damen. Bus: 49 (24hrs), 50, 72. Mon–Thu 11am–midnight; Fri 11am–2am; Sat 10am–2am; Sun 10am–midnight. Average beer: $3.50.*

✳ **Hideout** A ramshackle, roadside house of country-rock in an industrial stretch of the city wouldn't be complete without a few characters hanging out on the porch no matter the weather. Longtime local acts like Kelly Hogan and Devil in a Woodpile play inside, but the music can still be heard over the cracking of PBR cans out front. It can be difficult to reach this juke joint via public trans, but it is worth it for the cheap beer, live local country-rock and DJs dropping nostalgia from Prince to Devo. *1354 W Wabansia Ave between Willow and Ada Sts (773-227-4433). Bus: 72 North. Tue 7pm–2am; Wed–Fri 4pm–2am; Sat 7pm–3am; Sun, Mon (open select days 7pm–2am). Average beer: $2.*

innjoy The bartender has a pompadour and a pistol tattooed on his arm, Old Styles are $2, Sloppy Joes are on the menu and DJs are indie-rock happy. But this spot is far from being too cool for school; there's a nice mix of locals from the neighborhood and industry folk from Division's Restaurant Row who head for the downstairs pool room after work. *2051 W Division St between Damen and Hoyne Aves (773-394-*

2066). El: Blue to Division. Bus: 50 Damen, 70 Division. Mon–Fri 5pm–2am; Sat noon–3am; Sun noon–2am. Average beer: $3.

✕ **Jun Bar** This bright, sleek, minimalist space brings a cool, collected and slightly clubby option to Division Street. Expect design-types in chunky eyewear drinking gin and discussing the merits of Mies. And keep in mind that if things get too heady, the rowdier (and slightly less intellectual) crowd is right across the street. *2050 W Division St between Damen and Hoyne Aves (773-486-6700). El: Blue to Division. Bus: 49 (24hrs), X49, 50, 70. Mon–Fri 4pm–2am; Sat 11am–3am; Sun 11am–2am. Average cocktail: $6.*

Lemmings Don't take the name literally: There's a nice crowd here, but the joint isn't packed with followers, so you can usually find a seat to soak up the comforting vibe. We want to keep this beloved place low-key, and were almost hesitant to tell you about it, but we're running out of competition on the Ms. Pac-Man and the pool table. *1850 N Damen Ave between Moffat and Cortland Sts (773-862-1688). El: Blue to Damen. Bus: 50, 56, 73. Mon–Fri 4pm–2am; Sat noon–3am; Sun noon–2am. Average beer: $3.*

✕ **Lincoln Tavern** Step into this Bucktown corner tap (the "tavern" half of the bar/restaurant combo, that is) and you'll feel like you've stumbled upon a small-town rural watering hole: The service is patient, the chatter is minimal and the TVs are tuned to local news. Pace your evening accordingly, but don't be too late—the bar tends to shut down early on slow evenings. *1858 W Wabansia Ave between Honore St and Wolcott Ave (773-342-7778). El: Blue to Damen. Bus: 50, 56, 72. Mon–Sat 10:30am–1am (closed Sun). Average beer: $4.*

Lottie's Pub So you're wondering how a sports bar with a crowd of screaming coeds and an impressive list of drinkable "bombs" (when Jäger alone just won't cut it anymore) found its way into Bucktown. But you're sucking down the Lunar Bombs like they're holy water and hogging the pool table, so the frat-mentality invasion can't be all that bad. *1925 W Cortland St between Wolcott and Winchester Aves (773-489-0738). El: Blue to Damen. Bus: 9, 50, 73. Sun–Fri 11am–2am; Sat 11am–3am. Average cocktail: $5.*

The Map Room You couldn't fit another beer on the killer list or another Bucktown local around the pool table here, especially on Tuesdays, a.k.a. "International Night." This weekly party brings in food from a different ethnic spot around town—plates are free with an order of two drinks. If you're a more low-key drinker, but like the vibe, stop by in the a.m. when the Map Room functions as a coffee house. *1949 N Hoyne Ave between Homer St and Armitage Ave (773-252-7636). El: Blue to Western. Bus: 50 Damen, 73 Armitage. Mon–Fri 6:30am–2am; Sat 7:30am–3am; Sun 11am–2am. Average beer: $4.*

✕ **Marshall McGearty Tobacco Lounge** Don't be intimidated by the looming threat of lingering smoke; the ventilation system at this quirky nest for nicotine fiends recycles the air every six minutes. Part tobacco emporium touting hand-rolled cigarettes, part café and part bar adds up to a cool retro basement vibe. *1553 N Milwaukee Ave between North Ave and Honore St (773-772-8410). El: Blue to Damen. Bus: 50, 56, 72. Sun-Thu 11am-mid; Fri-Sat 11am-2am. Average cocktail: $4.*

(✳ **Nick's Beergarden** The rumble of the train drowns out your conversation in the beer garden every five minutes, but that's a small price to pay for a laid-back day sipping beer

in the sun (or, in case of a sudden downpour, under the covered portion of the garden). Servers are attentive, and the crowd outside is pretty chill—the only shit-talking going on is at the Golden Tee or at the pool table. That is until the rest of the neighborhood's bars close at 2 and the line waiting outside gets unruly. *1516 N Milwaukee Ave between Honore St and Damen Ave (773-252-1155). El: Blue to Damen. Bus: 50, 56, 72. Sun–Fri 4pm–4am; Sat 4pm–5am. Average beer: $5.*

✕ ❋ **Northside Bar and Grill** Part garden patio, part sidewalk cafe, the outdoor space at this stalwart is a visual reminder of Wicker Park's shifting population. Artsy musician types and new parents rub elbows early, but once the sun sets, it's prime territory for picking up virtually any kind of local. The surprisingly tasty pub grub is served late, and regardless of the Golden Tee and sports-tuned TVs, the meathead quotient remains low. *1635 N Damen Ave between North and Wabansia Aves (773-384-3555). El: Blue to Damen. Bus: 50, 56, 72. Sun–Fri 11am–2am; Sat 11am–3am. Average beer: $4.*

✕ ❋ **Phyllis' Musical Inn** One of Wicker Park's first spots for live music refuses to go the way of cover bands, instead booking local acts that play original rock. They're not always great, but the garden patio is. A scrappy mix of chairs and tables, a basketball hoop and groups of friends shooting the shit over cheap drinks makes for a classic summer night. *1800 W Division St at Wood St (773-486-9862). El: Blue to Division. Bus: 70 Division. Mon–Fri 3pm–2am; Sat 3pm–3am; Sun 2pm–2am. Average beer: $3. Cash only.*

Pint The name makes it pretty clear: This is a simple joint where you can grab a cool pint of your favorite brew while cheering for your favorite team. The awesome flat screens and big screen are being put to good use with satellite TV tuned in to games around the globe. Add some of the coldest brews around served up by the cuties behind the bar, and they might have finally scored. *1547 N Milwaukee Ave between Honore and Damen Sts (773-772-0990). El: Blue to Damen. Bus 50, 56, 72. Sun–Fri 11am–2am; Sat 11am–3am. Average beer: $4.*

✕ ❋ **Pontiac Cafe** It's impossible to be in the Wicker Park triangle and not hear the din from this converted gas station's patio. Aside from the insanely popular Friday-night live-band karaoke, DJs and bands fill the air with music, while an anything-goes crowd gawks at passersby, custom bicycles and shiny motorcycles. *1531 N Damen Ave between Wicker Park and Pierce Aves (773-252-7767). El: Blue to Damen. Bus: 50, 56, 72. Sun–Fri 11am–2am; Sat 11am–3am. Average beer: $3.50. Cash only.*

Quencher's Saloon This 25-year-old beer bar sitting on the Bucktown/Logan Square border has one of the most diverse crowds in town. The well-heeled eye each other on weekends, local beer nerds meet to taste the 200 choices on weeknights and drunk punks wander in whenever. Luckily they peacefully co-exist in two spacious rooms, all in the name of beer. Daytime crowds enjoy the laid-back vibe, thanks for free popcorn and comfy couches. *2401 N Western Ave at Fullerton Ave (773-276-9730). El: Blue to California. Bus: 49 Western (24hrs), 74 Fullerton. Sun–Fri 11am–2am; Sat 11am–3am. Average beer: $4. Cash only.*

✕ ❋ **Small Bar** Actually, this welcoming neighborhood joint is far from small—it's a decent-sized, airy space that opens up onto a sidewalk patio. If it's literal names they wanted, maybe Beer Bar (named for the 90-beer-strong list), Scenester Bar (it's not Rainbo, but close) or Cash Bar (obscure beer ain't cheap, kids) would have been

Is it drafty in here? You'll find a lengthy, diverse list of beers on tap at Handlebar.

more accurate. *2049 W Division St between Damen and Hoyne Aves (773-772-2727). El: Blue to Division. Bus: 49 (24hrs), 50, 70. Mon–Fri 4pm–2am; Sat 11am–3am; Sun 11am–2am. Average beer: $4.*

✕ ❋ **Swig** This amber-tinted lounge is certainly chic and a bit upscale, but somehow lacks the stuffiness usually associated with other upscale spots. Its restaurant-worthy menu is enhanced by the attentive, conversational staff and colorful paintings by local artists that dot the bar's exposed brick walls. The result is a laid-back atmosphere that draws an eclectic mix of artists and nine-to-fivers. *1469 N Milwaukee Ave between Evergreen Ave and Honore St (773-384-1439). El: Blue to Damen. Bus: 50, 56, 72. Mon–Thu 5pm–2am; Fri 4pm–2am; Sat, Sun noon–2am. Average cocktail: $6.*

✕ **The Violet Hour** This cocktail lounge in the old del Toro space is exactly what you'd expect from a bar named after a line of T.S. Eliot poetry: pristine (the carefully constructed cocktails are excellent), pretentious (you won't find a sign on the door—just look for the long lines) and, ultimately, completely and inarguably gorgeous. *1520 N Damen Ave between Le Moyne St and Wicker Park Ave (773-252-1500). El: Blue to Damen. Bus: 50, 56, 72. Sun–Fri 8pm–2am; Sat 8pm–3am. Average cocktail: $11.*

The Web Our favorite part of this Bucktown corner dive is Dawn, the superfriendly bar maid and confidant. She can effortlessly toss out Leinies Honey Weiss and get the day's gossip handed down from her faithful barflies. When you hop in to wind the evening down with some not-so-competitive darts, be sure to say hi. *2026 W Webster Ave between Seeley* and Damen Aves (773-276-3411). Bus: 50, 73, 74. Mon–Fri 11am–2am; Sat 11am–3am; Sun 1pm–2am. Average beer: $3. Cash only.

(Wicker Park Tavern Like Borderline before it, this Wicker Park bar attracts late-night, beer-goggled types. The multiple plasma screens blasting sports may get drinkers in a little earlier than the 2am prime time of the past. A jukebox means your cash, rather than a DJ, drives the sounds. *1958 W North Ave at Damen Ave (773-278-5138). El: Blue to Damen. Bus: 50, 56, 72. Sun–Fri 4pm–4am; Sat 4pm–5am. Average beer: $4.*

Zakopane If you're lucky, you'll stumble in on a night when the Anna Kournikova look-alike bartender is working, pouring vodka drinks with a heavy hand. But any night will do at this wood-paneled, Polish-owned watering hole. The old drunks are quick to challenge you at pool, and the young Poles are obsessed with the jukebox that spits out Polish versions of early-'90s American chart toppers. *1734 W Division St between Hermitage Ave and Wood St (773-486-1559). El: Blue to Division. Bus: 9, 50, 70. Mon–Sat 7am–2am; Sun 11am–2am. Average cocktail: $4. Cash only.*

Lincoln Park

B.L.U.E.S. The music—blues provided by live bands every night—is too loud to talk over, but you're not *supposed* to talk over it. You are supposed to drink, and if you want to have an easier time getting served, be nice to the ladies behind the bar—they don't take any bullshit. *2519 N Halsted St between Altged St and Lill Ave (773-528-1012). El: Brown, Red, Purple (rush hrs) to Fullerton. Bus: 8 Halsted, 74 Fullerton. Sun–Fri 8pm–2am; Sat 8pm–3pm. Average beer: $4.*

Bacchus Appropriately named after the Roman god of wine, this crowded, clubby Lincoln Park nightspot serves as a den of debauchery for DePaul's scantily clad student body. Columns, marble and other generic Roman decor dominate the first-floor lounge area, while Thursday through Saturday DJs lay down beats upstairs (though we're guessing these kids would happily slap bodies without any music at all). *2242 N Lincoln Ave between Webster and Belden Aves (773-477-5238). El: Brown, Purple (rush hrs), Red to Fullerton. Bus: 8, 11, 74. Mon–Fri 8pm–2am; Sat 8pm–3am (closed Sun). Average cocktail: $8.*

✗ Barleycorn Sports Bar You're not going to be impressed by this John Barleycorn spin-off unless you're a sports fan. Because for nonsports fans the ten beers on tap, the pizza-and-burgers menu, and the weekly drink specials aren't anything new. So expect the 180 seats here to be filled with jocks, who only care about the 32 flat-screen TVs, which will show every type of sports game in which one can compete. *2142 N Clybourn Ave between Wayne and Southport Aves (773-348-0414). El: Brown, Purple (rush hrs) to Armitage. Bus: 73 Armitage, 74 Fullerton. Sun–Fri 11am–2am; Sat 11am–3am. Average beer: $4.*

(✗ Beaumont There's tons of room to spread out in this standard Lincoln Park pub, whether it's to down some Stella in a booth or play some darts. Space is harder to come by at around 10pm, when the DJ inspires ass-slapping and groin-grinding—you'll either have to make a quick escape or join in. *2020 N Halsted St between Armitage and Dickens Aves (773-281-0177). El: Brown, Purple (rush hrs) to Armitage. Bus: 8 Halsted, 73 Armitage. Mon–Fri 6pm–4am; Sat 3pm–5am. Average beer: $5.*

✗ Bird's Nest It's a sure thing: There will always be games to be watched, wings to be eaten and pitchers to be drunk. Here's your spot for cheapo food and nightly drink specials. Darts, billiards and video games rule the spacious front room, and behind the curtain in back, local crooners love the weekly acoustic open mike night and karaoke. *2500 N Southport Ave between Altgeld and Lill Aves (773-472-1502). El: Brown, Purple (rush hrs), Red to Fullerton. Bus: 9, 11, 74. Mon–Fri 5pm–2am; Sat 11am–3am; Sun noon–2am. Average beer: $3.50.*

✗ Burwood Tap We can't resist a bartender who occasionally wears a cowboy hat and hands out Buttery Nipples like they're candy. And apparently neither can the neighborhood locals, who gather here to watch the game, eat pizza or let the messages on the LCD screen (e.g., "Bill Clinton, we miss you") incite heated debates. *724 W Wrightwood Ave at Burling St (773-525-2593). El: Brown, Purple (rush hrs) to Diversey. Bus: 8, 22 (24hrs), 77 (24hrs). Sun–Fri 11am–2am; Sat 11am–3am. Average beer: $4.*

✗ ✹ Charlie's on Webster Sometimes one of those grumpy old-timers takes a seat among the younger Lincoln Park buttoned-down crowd here. Once the geezers settle into plush leather booths, chat with the impeccable bartender and sip a beer, even they can't stay in a bad mood. *1224 W Webster Ave at Magnolia Ave (773-871-1440). El: Brown, Purple (rush hrs), Red to Fullerton. Bus: 73 Sedgwick, 74 Fullerton. Mon noon–2am; Tue–Thu 5pm–2am; Fri noon–2am; Sat 11am–3am; Sun 11am–2am. Average beer: $4.*

Clark Bar There are no beautiful couples snuggling in the corner here, and no artisanal beer list—and that's exactly how the clientele of this no-frills Lincoln Park neighborhood joint likes it. The only polished thing about this place is the sweet, motherly bartender, so grab a bottle and pick up a pool stick. *2116 N Clark St between Dickens and Webster Aves (773-327-3070). El: Brown, Purple (rush hrs) to Armitage. Bus: 11, 22 (24hrs), 36. Mon–Fri 4pm–2am; Sat 3pm–3am; 3pm–2am. Average beer: $4.*

✗ ✹ ♦ Clybar Located on a fairly blah strip of Clybourn Avenue, Clybar's standard clientele gets younger and younger as new condo developments spring up along Fullerton Parkway. If any more condos get built, the bar might need to start worrying about fake IDs—at this point, recent college grads occupy most of the plush couches, wall-side booths and patio. The place fills up fast, so best to send a scout early to snag a cocktail table for later. *2417 N Clybourn Ave between Terra Cotta Pl and Wrightwood Ave (773-388-1877). Bus: 9, 74, 76. Sun–Fri 5pm–2am; Sat 3pm–3am. Average cocktail: $6.*

The Copa Wood paneling behind the bar, intricate tile work behind the leather wrap-around booths...this lounge has retro style to burn, we just don't know what era they're in. This is a martini type of place, and they make a mean one, but it's the Budweiser in nifty vintage cans that get our money. *1637 N Clybourn Ave between North Ave and Concord Pl (312-642-3449). El: Red to North/Clybourn. Bus: 8 Halsted, 72 North. Mon–Fri 5pm–2am; Sat 6pm–3am; Sun 7pm–2am. Average cocktail: $6.*

✗ ♦ D.O.C. Wine Bar This cozy wine bar is a sibling of next door's Dunlays on Clark, a casual bar/restaurant, but the incredible high ceilings here give it some kind of urban barnyard feel. The bottle selection is excellent (though we wish there were more glass options), and you won't find even the slightest whiff of pretension, despite the mostly yuppie clientele. *2602 N Clark St between Wrightwood Ave and*

All-star lineup The beer menu at the Map Room is full of global favorites.

Drummond Pl (773-883-5101). El: Brown, Purple (rush hrs), Red to Fullerton. Bus: 11, 22 (24hrs), 36. 5pm–2am. Average glass of wine: $9.

❨ **Deja Vu** This rock & roll–themed, late-night Lincoln Park spot is known simply as "the Vu" to the DePaul students and other liquored-up twentysomethings who can be found queued up outside after 2am. Inside, you'll find lighting ranging from eclectic to gaudy, comfy armchairs and couches, checkerboard floors, and all manner of rock swag (from guitars to a gigantic framed Sgt. Pepper's–era Beatles poster hanging on the walls. *2624 N Lincoln Ave between Sheffield and Kenmore Aves (773-871-0205). El: Brown, Purple (rush hrs), Red to Fullerton. Bus: 11 Lincoln. 9pm–4am. Average cocktail: $6.*

Delilah's One of the city's best spots for rock & roll doesn't even have a stage. Instead, this Lincoln Park favorite has one of the best jukeboxes in town for the main room (so you can play DJ Fridays and Saturdays) and hires DJs for Sunday through Thursday who know their Buzzcocks from their Bullocks. Add an insane whiskey selection, more than 200 beers (Belgian, microbrews, seasonals) and frequent free movie nights, and you have a bar to call home. *2771 N Lincoln Ave between Schubert Ave and Diversey Pkwy (773-472-2771). El: Brown, Purple (rush hrs) to Diversey, Bus: 11 Lincoln, 76 Diversey. Sun–Fri 4pm–2am; Sat noon–3am. Average beer: $4.*

✕ 🍴 **Duke's Bar & Grill** With its come-as-you-are attitude and hefty selection of 20 eccentric burgers (Hawaiian, Truffle, Garbage, etc.), Duke's is built to last a lot longer than the building's previous tenants, who cycled through like Elizabeth Taylor's husbands. Extensive woodwork on the

walls and a "trickling" waterfall scene mounted above the bar make it kinda like hanging out in a tricked-out tree house. *2616 N Clark St at Wrightwood Ave (773-248-0250). El: Brown to Diversey. Bus: 22 (24hrs), 36, 76. Tue–Fri, Sun 5pm–2am; Sat 5pm–3am (closed Mon). Average beer: $5.*

✕ **Durkin's** This bar certainly leans toward frat-tastic, but its patrons seem oddly subdued. Perhaps the spot's three-room layout provides ample high-top tables and bartenders to avoid the usual drink-order clamor. Or maybe the sociable crowd hates abrasiveness, too. Whatever the case may be, this is one frat party that won't leave you feeling like you're in a scene in *Revenge of the Nerds. 810 W Diversey Pkwy between Halsted and Dayton Sts (773-525-2515). El: Brown, Purple (rush hrs) to Diversey. Bus: 8, 22 (24hrs), 36, 76. Mon–Fri 4pm–2am; Sat 11am–3am; Sun 11am–2am. Average beer: $4.*

Fieldhouse This overlooked Lincoln Park hangout is noted for its mellow vibe, in contrast to the many meatmarkets surrounding it. The bartenders are friendly, the flat-panels numerous and the patrons toss peanut shells onto the floor while trying to spot their alma mater from a banner display that would make the United Nations jealous. *2455 N Clark St at Arlington Pl (773-348-6489). El: Brown, Purple (rush hrs), Red to Fullerton. Bus: 11, 22 (24hrs), 36. Mon–Fri 4pm–2am; Sat 2pm–3am; Sun 2pm–2am. Average beer: $4.*

✕ **Flounder's** A simple, friendly neighborhood sports bar is nothing to sniff at, especially when you can gorge yourself Wednesday nights on all-you-can-eat beer-battered fish and garlic fries, or 15-cent wings on Mondays. The place puts up pennants from a slew of schools, but don't let that fool you: The drinkers here pledge allegiance to Wisconsin and

Space and light You can sit and watch the world go by from the bar at Pops for Champagne.

Nebraska. *2201 N Clybourn Ave between Webster and Greenview Aves (773-472-9920). El: Brown, Purple (rush hrs), Red to Fullerton. Bus: 9 Ashland, 74 Fullerton. Sun–Fri 11am–2am; Sat 11am–3am. Average beer: $4.*

✕ **Four Shadows** The great thing about a neighborhood bar is that a good one reveals just what kind of people live on the block. This rehabbed corner tavern is inhabited by a loosened-tie Lincoln Park crowd in their post–frat boy years and the ladies who love them. The look and feel is of a polished pub, and the killer jukebox will take you from *The Greatest* by Cat Power to *The Greatest Hits of Hall & Oates* in one short trip. *2758 N Ashland Ave at Diversey Ave (773-248-9160). Bus: 9 Ashland, 76 Diversey. Mon–Fri 4pm–2am; Sat 11am–3am; Sun 11am–2am. Average cocktail: $5.*

❨ **Frank's** This cocktail lounge is named after Sinatra, so it only makes sense that Ol' Blue Eyes' songs show up in the jukebox and Rat Pack photos line the walls. But customers feel more like packed rats as this after-hours spot fills up; the crowded room is so narrow that claustrophobic drinkers might only last one round. *2503 N Clark St between St James and Demming Pls (773-549-2700). El: Brown, Purple (rush hrs), Red to Fullerton. Bus: 22 (24 hrs), 36, 76. Sun–Fri 11am–4am; Sat 11am–5am. Average beer: $4.50.*

✕ ❋ **Galway Arms** There's a lot more Gaelic cheer at this bar than just the Guinness on tap. The yummy pub grub is authentic, most of the staff is actually Irish and it's never too crowded to nab a table (choose between the vintage woodwork inside and the expansive, open-air patio). Just don't spread the word too much—we'd hate to wind up ass-to-elbow like at most Lincoln Park McPubs. *2442 N Clark St at Arlington Pl (773-472-5555). El: Brown, Purple (rush hrs), Red to Fullerton. Bus: 22 (24hrs), 36, 74. Mon–Thu 5pm–2am; Fri 5pm–2am; Sat 11am–2am; Sun 11am–midnight. Average beer: $4.*

Galway Bay At this garden-level watering hole, the leather couches and bar-side high chairs are where young locals plop down, whereas the pure-blooded Irish set up camp over by the back bar and its adjacent pub games. The line between crowds gets blurrier when overloads of Harp and U2 are thrown into the mix—two things on which both crowds can agree. *500 W Diversey Pkwy at Pine Grove Ave (773-348-3750). El: Brown to Diversey. Bus: 22 (24hrs), 36, 76. Sun–Fri 1pm–2am; Sat 1pm–3am. Average beer: $4.50.*

✕ ❨ **Gamekeepers** At this garden-level watering hole, the leather couches and bar-side high chairs are where young locals plop down, whereas the pure-blooded Irish set up camp over by the back bar and its adjacent pub games. The line between crowds gets blurrier when overloads of Harp and U2 are thrown into the mix—two things on which both crowds can agree. *345 W Armitage Ave at at Lincoln Ave (773-549-0400). El: Brown, Purple (rush hrs) to Armitage. Bus: 11, 22, 36, 73. Mon–Fri 5pm–4am; 11am–5am; Sun 11am–4am. Average beer: $3.50.*

Glascott's From the standard look of the place you'd never suspect this bar's anything special. But we call it "McGee's Lite" for a reason: For those who raged when they were younger but can't hack it anymore, this (supposedly) Irish joint perfectly walks the fine line between chill neighborhood spot and rowdy sports bar. *2158 N Halsted St between Webster and Dickens Ave (773-549-5999). El: Brown, Purple (rush hrs), Red to Fullerton. Bus: 8, 73, 74. Mon–Fri 10am–2am; Sat 10am–3am; Sun 11am–2am. Average beer: $4.*

❋ **Goodbar** One look at the "aqua lounge" rooftop garden here and it seems like the people at Goodbar took the term watering hole literally. The turquoise paint treatment is meant to give the effect of shimmering blue water to the hoards of barely dressed boys and girls who crowd the place to whet their whistles. *2512 N Halsted St between Lincoln and Lill Aves (773-296-9700). El: Brown, Purple (rush hrs), Red to Fullerton. Bus: 8, 11, 74. Tue, Wed 7pm–2am; Thu, Fri 6pm–2am; Sat 6pm–3am. Average beer: $4.*

The Gramercy This place is so white. Literally. The upholstery, the curtains, the floor, the ceiling—all of it stark white. Thankfully, the college-age clientele is sufficiently diverse and good-looking (if you're into nighttime Ray-Ban wearers and Tyra Banks look-alikes), and the Euro-trash house music is so pounding that you won't mind the blinding decor. If the whiteness disorients, just remember to make like the ironic mullet you'll spot here on occasion—stay close to the front bar if you want to chat, and party down in the back. *2438 N Lincoln Ave between Montana St and Fullerton Ave (773-477-8880). El: Brown, Purple (rush hrs), Red to Fullerton. Bus: 8, 11, 74. Tue–Fri and Sun 7pm–2am; Sat 7pm–3am. Average cocktail: $6.*

✕ **The Grand Central** As its name implies (and its location next to the El tracks underscores), the feel here is that of a bar inside a Depression-era train station. Stained-glass ceiling lights emit an amber glow; fringe dangles from the faux smoke-stained lampshades; and small black-and-white ceramic tiles line the floor. But the centerpiece—despite the prevalence of flat-screen TVs and crazy-drunk locals on weekends—is the piano that sits on a round stage behind the long front bar. *950 W Wrightwood Ave between Wilton and Sheffield Aves (773-832-4000). El: Brown, Purple (rush hrs), Red to Fullerton. Bus: 11 Lincoln. Mon–Fri 4pm–2am; Sat 11am–3am; Sun 11am–midnight. Average beer: $4.*

Halligan Bar Nearly every square inch of wall space at this fireman-themed, triangle-shaped corner pub is plastered with surprisingly arresting black-and-white photographs of burning houses and heroic rescues, antique fire alarms, vintage axes and several flat-screen TVs with a Fighting Irish bias. Daily discounts, including "half-price everything" on Tuesdays, make this an attractive option for down-and-out DePaul kids. *2274 N Lincoln Ave between Webster and Belden Aves (773-472-7940). El: Brown, Purple (rush hrs), Red to Fullerton. Bus: 8, 11, 74. Mon 6pm–2am; Tue–Fri 5pm–2am; Sat 11am–3am; Sun 11am–2am. Average beer: $3.*

❧ **The Hidden Shamrock** Laying claim to being Lincoln Park's oldest Irish pub isn't what made us fall for this bar. Instead, it was the charming, airy space with exposed brick, roaring fireplace and original artwork. Of course, having 17 taps (two dedicated to Guinness) on hand didn't hurt either. If you can, pop in on a slower night when the joint isn't overrun with Trixies. *2723 N Halsted St at Schubert Ave (773-883-0304). El: Brown to Diversey. Bus 8 Halsted, 76 Diversey. Mon–Thu 4pm–2am; Fri 10:30am–2am; Sat 10:30am–3am; Sun 11am–2am. Average beer: $5.*

✕ **Hog Head McDunna's** There's a serious contingent of regulars calling this bar home, including newly legal DePaul students who pack the place late at night. But it serves our purposes perfectly for an early spot to grab a beer and catch the game. We get 20 screens all to ourselves? Score. *1505 W Fullerton Ave between Greenview and Bosworth Aves (773-929-0944). El: Brown, Purple (rush hrs), Red to Fullerton. Bus: 9 Ashland, 74 Fullerton. Sun–Fri 11–2am; Sat 11am–3am. Average beer: $4.*

✕ **Kelly's Pub** Didn't you see the sign? This is DePaul country, dude! So don't come up in this piece with your Northwestern gear on or talking smack about the Blue Demons tennis team. The best move is to just try and blend in; wear a baseball cap and chug some beers and you'll do just that. *949 W Webster Ave between Bissell St and Sheffield Ave (773-281-0656). El: Brown, Purple (rush hrs), Red to Fullerton. Bus: 73 Armitage, 74 Fullerton. Sun–Fri 11am–2am; Sat 11am–3am. Average beer: $4.*

✕ **Kincade's** With checkerboard floors, as much dark wood as an Oak forest and more than two dozen sports-centric TVs, this is a quintessential neighborhood bar with some serious ball—basketball, baseball and football, that is. While Kansas University alums are busy gulping Miller Lite and downing burgers with their former frat brothers, the ladies who love them do a fine job standing by—some looking pretty and bored, and some just pretty bored. *950 W Armitage Ave at Sheffield Ave (773-348-0010). El: Brown, Purple (rush hrs) to Armitage. Bus: 8 Halsted, 73 Armitage. Sun–Fri 11am–2am; Sat 11am–3am. Average beer: $3.*

✕ **Kelly's Pub** Didn't you see the sign? This is DePaul country, dude! So don't come up in this piece with your Northwestern gear on or talking smack about the Blue Demons tennis team. The best move is to just try and blend in; wear a baseball cap and chug some beers and you'll do just that. *949 W Webster Ave between Bissell St and Sheffield Ave (773-281-0656). El: Brown, Purple (rush hrs), Red to Fullerton. Bus: 73 Armitage, 74 Fullerton. Sun–Fri 11am–2am; Sat 11am–3am. Average beer: $4.*

✕ **Leila Jane's** This isn't your typical Armitage Avenue bar. Churchlike stained-glass windows, a close-up painting of Elvis's face and a huge gothic chandelier loom over the misfit clientele, most of whom have come to this wheels-friendly spot on skateboards or bicycles to drink beer, play cards and lounge on the antique furnishings. *1008 W Armitage Ave between Sheffield and Kenmore Aves (773-665-7885). El: Brown, Purple (rush hrs) to Armitage. Bus: 8 Halsted, 73 Armitage. Wed–Fri 6pm–2am; Sat 6pm–3am; Sun 4pm–2am. Average beer: $3.*

The Liar's Club Are we a bunch of suckers or what? The hours here are completely undependable, the crowd's a crapshoot (punks on the weekdays, prepsters on weekends) and there's no sink in the men's room. But something about this place (and the signage) charms our socks off. But only during the week. We're not about to pay a cover—we'd rather spend our money in the photo booth. *1665 W Fullerton Ave between Clybourn Ave and Wood St (773-665-1110). Bus: 74 Fullerton. Sun–Fri 8pm–2am; Sat 8pm–3am. Average beer: $4. Cash only.*

Lilly's This easy-to-miss, former blues bar's interesting architecture makes up for its lackluster liquor lineup and crummy toilet. The uneven brick floor leads to a dizzying arrangement of green stucco walls and archways that yield several opportunities for private tables. The balcony's ragtag but comfy chairs offer the best view of Tuesday night's open mike. *2513 N Lincoln Ave between Altgeld St and Lill Ave (773-525-2422). El: Brown, Purple (rush hrs), Red to Fullerton. Bus: 8, 11, 74. 4pm–2am. Average beer: $3.*

✕ **Lincoln Station** It's not every night that you can get crazy with a bunch of DePaul students, each one a little louder, a little drunker and a little more scantily dressed than the one before. Well, actually, at this rowdy and friendly

sports bar you can do that every night—and maybe get in a few rounds of pool, too. *2432 N Lincoln Ave between Fullerton Ave and Montana St (773-472-8100). El: Brown, Purple (rush hrs), Red to Fullerton. Bus: 8, 11, 74. Sun–Fri 11am–2am; Sat 11am–3am. Average beer: $5.*

✕ **Local Option** Nestled on a tree-lined street in Lincoln Park, this watering hole is the epitome of neighborly drinking. (It is named for the laws that allow neighbors to decide how communities sell alcohol.) A friendly bartender will chat you up and introduce you to the locals as he mixes your Hendrick's and tonic. But he knows when to shut up and let you listen to Ryan Adams's cover of "Wonderwall." Head to the restaurant in the back to pad your stomach with good Cajun-themed grub. *1102 W Webster Ave between Seminary and Clifton Aves (773-348-2008). El: Brown, Purple (rush hrs), Red to Fullerton. Bus: 73 Armitage, 74 Fullerton. Sun–Fri noon–2am; Sat noon–3am. Average beer: $4.*

(▼ ✳ **Manhandler** Lest you think the name of this place is a joke, a sign on the door announcing the bar's "one drink minimum" reveals its true nature: Guys aren't really coming here to drink. But don't let that keep you from ordering a cocktail from the friendly bartender, especially if you prefer watching your leatherdaddy porn while listening to the jukebox tunes of Elvis Costello. *1948 N Halsted St between Wisconsin St and Armitage Ave (773-871-3339). El: Brown, Purple (rush hrs) to Armitage; Red to North/Clybourn. Bus: 8, 72, 73. Sun–Fri noon–4am; Sat noon–5am. Average cocktail: $4. Cash only.*

Marquee Lounge It's nestled on a corner in the heart of Lincoln Park, but this isn't your typical trixie spot. It's a casual, sophisticated space that's low-key and laid back, and filled with folks who are a couple years past frequenting spots where a 22-year-old vomiting Jager on their shoes is commonplace. Dogs are welcome. *1973 N Halsted St at Armitage Ave (312-988-7427). El: Brown, Purple (rush hrs) to Armitage. Bus: 8, 11, 73. Mon–Fri 4pm–2am; Sat noon–3am; Sun noon–2am. Average cocktail: $5.*

✕ **Matilda** What do you get when you put a sign on your door stating that nobody under the age of 23 can enter? A lot of college kids pissed off that they can't hang out on the mod furniture under the faux stars, listening to the sing-along-friendly soundtrack of Prince and Lenny Kravitz. *3101 N Sheffield Ave at Barry Ave (773-883-4400). El: Brown, Purple (rush hrs) to Wellington. Bus: 8, 76, 77 (24hrs). Tue–Fri 6pm–2am; Sat 6pm–3am (closed Sun, Mon). Average beer: $4.*

(**Maxbar** Thankfully, this isn't the big, thumping club we expected the boys who founded crobar to unveil. Instead, the front room is a well designed bar (think typical Irish pub meets Nate Berkus). The clubbing thing happens in the back, but you can't hear or see it from the front, leaving you free to enjoy your gin and tonic in peace. *2247 N Lincoln Ave between Webster and Belden Aves (773-549-5884). El: Brown, Purple (rush hrs), Red to Fullerton. Bus: 8 Halsted, 11 Lincoln. Sat–Thu 7pm–4am; Fri 5pm–4am. Average cocktail: $8.*

✕ **McGee's Tavern** Hold on to your Bud Light as tight as you can at this enormous, quintessential Lincoln Park sports bar. There will always be lots of drunken screaming, drunken tumbles, drunken hugs and drunken tongues in your drunken mouth. *950 W Webster Ave between Bissell St and Sheffield Ave (773-549-8200). El: Brown, Purple (rush hour only), Red to Fullerton. Sun–Fri 11am–2am; Sat 10am–3am. Average beer: $3.*

Breathe deep and relax Enjoy your wine in plush surroundings at D.O.C. Winebar.

✗ ✳ **Mickey's** If it's too nippy to make use of the stellar sidewalk café, head inside where the diner look has yielded to blue suede booths and flat panel TVs. Mojitos and the house version of Sliders are the specialties, and nostalgia for Wrigley Field is induced upon every visit to the metal trough in the men's room. *2450 N Clark St at Arlington Pl (773-435-0007). El: Brown, Purple (rush hrs), Red to Fullerton. Bus: 11, 22 (24hrs), 36. Mon–Fri 11am–2am; Sat 9am–3am; Sun 9am–2am. Average cocktail: $5.*

✗ **The Other Side Bar** "Dude, are you working on Friday night? Because we're coming back here and totally getting sloshed," we overheard one "dude" say to his friend at this bar attached to the Pasta Bowl restaurant. And that's what happens here. College kids get wasted and eat cheap bar food while Franz Ferdinand and the Killers blast from the jukebox. *2436 N Clark St between Arlington Pl and Fullerton Pkwy (773-525-8238). El: Brown, Purple (rush hrs), Red to Fullerton. Bus: 22 (24hrs), 36, 151 (24hrs). Mon–Fri 3pm–2am; Sat 11am–3am, Sun 11am–2am. Average beer: $4.*

✗ ✳ **Pops for Champagne** *2007 Eat Out Award, Readers' Choice: Best new wine bar* Pops is sleeker, shinier and more grown-up than its old Lincoln Park location, and that's a good thing for their older, jazz-loving crowd (the intimate, nonsmoking jazz club in the basement should please those folks, too). The young Lincoln Parkers who used to stop by for a glass of wine may be out of luck, however. Not only is this not their crowd anymore— it's also out of their price range. *601 North State St at Ohio St (312-266-7677). El: Red to Grand. Bus: 22 (24hrs), 36, 65. Sun–Fri 6pm–2am; Sat 8pm–3am. Average glass of wine: $15.*

☾ ✳ **Raven's** The one thing that sets this place apart from every other Lincoln Park Golden Tee–hosting, free popcorn–offering, Black Crowes–blasting, post–frat-boys-high-fiving hangout is *The Dark Crystal* playing on the TVs. But as far as 4am spots on this strip goes, we'd rather get loaded on the $3 beer-of-the-month drafts here than deal with the unbearable heaviness of Neo. *2326 N Clark St between Belden Ave and Fullerton Pkwy (773-348-1774). Bus: 22 (24hrs), 36, 74. Mon–Fri 3pm–4am; Sat noon–5am; Sun noon–4am. Average beer: $4. Cash only.*

✗ ✳ **Red Lion Pub** British ales and imported Scotches aren't the only spirits served up at this cozy little slice of London; ghost stories are as commonly dished out (as are baskets brimming with fish and chips). If you ask nicely, the pub's silver-tongued owner, Colin Cordwell, might break from carefully eyeing DePaul students' IDs to brag about all the spooked former employees of his supposedly haunted haunt. *2446 N Lincoln Ave between Fullerton Ave and Altgeld St (773-348-2695). El: Red, Brown, Purple (rush hrs) to Fullerton. Bus: 11 Lincoln, 74 Fullerton. Mon–Fri noon–2am; Sat 2pm–3am, Sun 2pm–2am. Average cocktail: $5.*

✗ **River Shannon** At first glance, this 60-year-old establishment seems cast from the same mold as every other neighborhood Irish pub. After all, it has about a dozen Irish whiskeys, an antique wooden bar and photos of the South Side from the early 1900s hanging on its walls. It's the theme nights that separate this spot from the rest of the Notre Dame flag–waving pack. Our favorites are Sundays (free hotdogs from noon to 6pm), Mondays ("party with your pooch") and Tuesdays (board games). *425 W Armitage Ave between Sedgwick St and Hudson Ave (312-944-5087). El: Brown, Purple (rush hrs) to Armitage. Bus: 8, 11, 22 (24hrs), 36, 73.*

Neighborhood treasure
Gold Star Bar's a hit with the
locals in Ukrainian Village.

Mon–Wed, Fri 3pm–2am; Thu 1pm–2am; Sat noon–3am;
Sun noon–2am. Average beer: $5.

✗ ✹ **Rocks Lincoln Park** A more appropriate name for
this cozy neighborhood tavern might be simply "Rock,"
because that's exactly what you're given when you order a
drink on ice: one enormous cube. We found the pours here to
be very generous, which might explain why everybody was
kissing the bartender as they left. 1301 W Schubert Ave at
Lakewood Ave (773-472-7738). El: Brown, Purple (rush hrs)
to Diversey. Bus: 11 Lincoln, 76 Diversey. Mon–Fri 5pm–
2am; Sat 11am–3am; Sun 11am–2am. Average cocktail: $6.

✗ **Sedgwick's Bar & Grill** On most nights, this cozy
space is an after-work stopover for biz-caz yuppies escaping
their Old Town high-rises. Brews, yummy comfort food and
muted big-screen sports highlights abound. All those things
happen on Tuesdays, too, with a little euchre thrown into the
fold. League play occupies most of the tables, but you'll
always have a seat on those "really don't feel like cooking"
evenings. 1935 N Sedgwick St between Armitage Ave and
Wisconsin St (312-337-7900). El: Brown, Purple (rush hrs) to
Sedgwick. Bus: 11, 22 (24hrs), 36, 73. Mon–Fri 11:30am–
2am; Sat 10am–3am; Sun 10am–2am. Average beer: $3.

✗ ✹ **Southport City Saloon** Tucked away behind the
main dining room of the restaurant, the outdoor space
handles overflow diners and then turns into a beer garden at
around 9:30pm, complete with its own cabana-style bar. On
Mondays, margaritas are five bucks, and on Thursdays,
Corona bottles go for $3.50. There's one TV outside, but more
are rolled out for big games. More inclement weather makes
the bar in front of the restaurant a better place for kicking
back a cold one. 2548 N Southport Ave between Lill and

Wrightwood Aves (773-975-6110). El: Brown, Purple (rush
hrs) to Diversey. Bus: 9, 11, 74. Sun–Fri 11:30am–2am; Sat
11:30am–3am. Average beer: $4.

Sterch's Something doesn't add up: If every other Lincoln
Avenue pub is packed sweaty ass to sweaty crotch, why is it
that Sterch's pulls in only a handful of drinkers? It must suck,
right? Well, given this venerable bar (in its forties) is inviting
to newbies, loyal to its regulars (old photos on the wall, house
bowling leagues, etc.) and plenty spacious for the two to
mingle, that's probably not the case. Be thankful this friendly
drinking relic is still around. 2238 N Lincoln Ave between
Webster and Belden Aves (773-281-2653). El: Brown, Purple
(rush hrs), Red to Fullerton. Bus: 8, 11, 74. Mon–Fri, Sun
3:30pm–2am; Sat 3:30pm–3am. Average beer: $3.50.

(**The Store** A dark, smoky room. A long wooden bar. A
couple of middle-aged guys playing video trivia in the corner.
A staff who couldn't care less. Who would guess there'd be
lines around the corner to get in here come 2am? Guess that's
what a 4am license gets ya. 2002 N Halsted St between
Armitage and Dickens Aves (773-327-7766). El: Brown,
Purple (rush hrs) to Armitage. Bus: 8, 11, 73. Mon–Thu
5pm–4am; Fri 3pm–4am; Sat 5pm–5am; Sun noon–4am.
Average beer: $3.50.

Ta'Too Hot, underdressed girls and the guys who
follow them pack this Lincoln Park bar, where, miraculously,
the staff gets friendlier as the crowds grow thicker. If there's a
game on, they'll be playing it, but you won't hear a thing over
the blaring radio hits. 1365 W Fullerton Ave between Wayne
and Southport Aves (773-525-2739). El: Brown, Purple (rush
hrs), Red to Fullerton. Bus: 74 Fullerton. Sun–Fri 4pm–2am;
Sat 4pm–3am. Average beer: $4.

Tin Lizzie All the usual suspects of a Lincoln Park sports bar are in place here: a pool table, jukebox and wings on the menu. But the only thing really criminal about the place is the collection of celebrity mug shots on the wall. The bar favors Michigan State, so expect to watch anything in which the school is competing. *2483 N Clark St at Arlington Pl (773-549-1132). El: Brown, Red to Fullerton. Bus: 22 (24hrs), 36, 76. Mon–Fri 5pm–2am; Sat 11am–3am; Sun 11am–2am. Average beer: $4.50.*

The Tonic Room Because this lounge hasn't fallen prey to the sporty, fratty trappings of most DePaul-area bars, it has become the place for the mellow, martini-sipping Lincoln Park set to find a mate. Deep red walls and dim crimson lighting surround moveable black leather blocks and a small stage that plays host to acoustic guitarists on Mondays, a jazz trio on Tuesdays, rock bands on Wednesdays and DJs the rest of the week. *2447 N Halsted St between Fullerton Pkwy and Lill Ave (773-248-8400). El: Brown, Purple (rush hrs), Red to Fullerton. Bus: 8 Halsted, 74 Fullerton. Sun–Fri 5pm–2am; Sat 5pm–3am. Average cocktail: $8.*

✕ ⚬ **Trinity** Peg Leg Sullivan's has morphed from a grungy Lincoln Park chug fest into a three-story mecca of dark polished wood and working fireplaces. But the changes don't stop there: A no-smoking policy will likely draw some of the older locals out of their condos, where they'll have to fight the frat boys (body-shot contest, perhaps?) for a seat. *2721 N Halsted St between Schubert Ave and Diversey Pkwy (773-880-9293). El: Brown, Purple (rush hrs) to Diversey. Bus: 8, 74, 76. Mon 6pm–2am; Tue–Fri 5pm–2am; Sat 11am–3am; Sun 11am–2am. Average beer: $4.*

✕ ✳ **Tripoli Tavern** You'd never know it, but there are tomatoes growing in the garden and lobsters in the kitchen of this Lincoln Park watering hole. That doesn't keep out the kids who are just here to watch the game and ogle the waitresses. But it also doesn't keep out a more refined crowd looking for a bar with restaurant-quality food. *1147 W Armitage Ave between Clifton and Racine Aves (773-477-4400). El: Brown, Purple (rush hrs) to Armitage. Bus: 8 Halsted, 73 Armitage. Sun–Fri 11am–2am; Sat 11am–3am. Average beer: $5.*

✕ ✳ **Twisted Lizard** Nothing's better than kickin' back at this spot with a potent pitcher of margaritas and baskets of thick chips and homemade salsa. If it weren't for the big, fat Starbucks sign next door, you might even think you were in a roadside cantina in the Mexican outback. Think tender, flame-grilled steak fajitas, with piles of warm tortillas and a stack of limes; Baja-style beer-battered fish tacos, with tangy chipotle–sour cream sauce; and sides of firm black beans and chewy Mexican rice, peppered with little bits of veggies. *1964 N Sheffield Ave between Armitage and Maud Aves (773-929-1414). El: Brown to Armitage. Bus: 8 Halsted, 73 Armitage. Sun–Wed 11am–10pm, Thu 11am–11pm, Fri, Sat 11am–midnight. Average cocktail: $6.*

✕ **Victory Liquors** With 25 plasma screens strategically arranged throughout these two wood-rich rooms, there's absolutely no place to escape the game. That's good if you're a Notre Dame fan; if you're not, you'd better go on a night when the Irish aren't fighting. Or just go when the games are over—it's a better time to turn your game on anyway. *2610 N Halsted St between Wrightwood Ave and Diversey Pkwy (773-348-5600). El: Brown, Purple (rush hrs) Red to Fullerton. Bus: 8, 74, 76. Wed–Fri 4pm–2am; Sat, Sun noon–2am. Average beer: $4.*

✕ ✳ ⚬ **Webster's Wine Bar** We've missed many a movie because we stopped by this funky wine bar next to Webster Place theater for a pre-show cocktail. When tasting pours are this affordable (and interesting), we pretend it's for educational purposes and stay all night, soaking up the dark, Bohemian vibe and munching on tasty cheese plates. We'll catch the movie on Netflix. *1480 W Webster Ave between Clybourn Ave and Dominick St (773-868-0608). Bus: 9 Ashland. Mon–Fri 5pm–2am; Sat 4pm–3am; Sun 4pm–2am. Average glass of wine: $7.*

Wise Fools Pub Posters of Muddy Waters and other music legends speak to this bar's history as a former blues club, but these days you're more likely to hear a DePaul student strumming a Jason Mraz–ish version of Radiohead's "Fake Plastic Trees" than anything with Delta roots. Disappointed? Then stay close to the long, unpolished bar and try to drown out the collegiate crooners with nightly beer specials like $3 Berghoff bottles. *2270 N Lincoln Ave at Orchard St (773-929-1300). El: Brown, Purple (rush hrs), Red to Fullerton. Bus: 8, 11, 74. Mon–Fri 7pm–2am; Sat 7pm–3am; Sun 7pm–2am. Average beer: $4.*

✕ **Witt's** Remember that jock in high school who smoked pot and listened to *Dark Side of the Moon*? Yeah, well, he now hangs out at this sporty slacker bar. There are plenty of games on the flat screens and classic rock on rotation, as well as an inexpensive, surprisingly good menu (try the juicy blue-cheese burger) to quell those munchie attacks. *2913 N Lincoln Ave between George St and Wellington Ave (773-528-7032). Bus: 9, 11, 76, 77 (24hrs). Sun–Fri 11am–2am; Sat 11am–3am. Average beer: $3.50.*

The Wrightwood Tap It's amazing what a difference an hour or two makes at this corner tap. Before 11pm, conversational buzz and the sounds of the Cure dominate, but the place gets packed as soon as midnight strikes—picture some sort of reverse-Cinderella story—and the music begins a transition into upbeat territory. Those first few minutes are the most entertaining for people-watching, as cramped, confused bargoers struggle to get down to "Just Like Heaven." *1059 W Wrightwood Ave between Lincoln and Seminary Aves (773-549-4949). El: Brown, Purple (rush hrs), Red to Fullerton. Bus: 11 Lincoln. Mon–Fri 4pm–2am; Sat 11am–3am; Sun 11am–2am. Average beer: $4.*

✳ ⚬ **Zella** Singles looking for a classy spot love getting spiffed up in their slinkiest summer gear for a night here, where there's always going to be plenty of green: on the outdoor patio and in their wallets. Pink martinis are de rigueur for the ladies, while the guys go for cocktails and the occasional Jager shot to work up the nerve to chat up the hotties. *1983 N Clybourn Ave at Racine Ave (773-549-2910). Bus: 9, 11, 76, 77 (24hrs). El: Brown, Purple (rush hrs) to Armitage. Bus: 8 Halsted, 73 Armitage. Sun–Fri 5pm–2am; Sat 5pm–3am Average cocktail: $7.*

Ukrainian Village/West Town

Alfredo's Bar Literally overshadowed by its neighbor, the popular restaurant Hacienda Tecalitlan, it's easy to miss this bare-bones Mexican hangout. An open bar stool is tough to come by, but thankfully there are a few tables scattered throughout and pool and foosball to keep you busy. If you're not up for bar sports, here's a game: Count whether there are more posters displaying Mexican pride or women in bikinis. *826 N Ashland Ave between Chicago Ave and Pearson St (312-733-9873). Bus: 9 Ashland (24hrs), 66 Chicago (24hrs). Sun–Fri 6pm–2am; Sat 6pm–3am. Average beer: $3.*

(Betty's Blue Star Lounge The black-on-black decor here is only interrupted by streaks of blue neon, a look so '80s that you'll expect RoboCop to walk in at any moment. Early in the night, local boozehounds have the place to themselves, but around 2am, the spillover from early-to-bed clubs squeezes in to sweat to hip-hop and house beats. *1600 W Grand Ave at Ashland Ave (312-243-1699). El: Green to Ashland. Bus: 9 Ashland (24hrs), 65 Grand. Sun–Fri 7pm–4am; Sat 7pm–5am. Average cocktail: $5.*

✕ ✳ ♣ Black Beetle DJs here know their crowd. Doses of hip-hop come in indie, underground and funky, while rock ranges from '70s stoner to modern garage. All can be heard from the sidewalk tables, where drinking pints of Goose Island's 312 blurs the boring view of a wood palette lot. *2532 W Chicago Ave at Maplewood Ave (773-384-0701). Bus: 49 (24hrs), X49, 66 (24hrs). Mon–Fri 11:30am–2am; Sat noon–3am, Sun noon–2am. Average beer: $3.50.*

Blind Robin The crew behind Green Eye and Underbar purchased the former Bar Vertigo space and gave it a bit of a face lift, and, seemingly overnight, it was packed. The Art Deco back bar from the old Lava Lounge space is squeezed into these new narrow digs, but the real eye candy is the never-ending parade of tattooed hipsters who seem to travel in packs to this bar family's watering holes. *853 N Western Ave between Rice and Iowa Sts (773-395-3002). Bus: 49 Western (24hrs), 66 Chicago (24hrs). Mon–Fri 4pm–2am; Sat noon–3am; Sun noon–2am. Average beer: $4.*

Chipp Inn Vodka Collins? No. Margarita? Sorry. Apple martini? Not a chance. Better just grab a beer or a shot of whiskey and sit down. The history of this blue-collar watering hole is told through the fliers and newspaper clippings that clutter the walls. From what we can tell, looks like the place hasn't changed much over the years. *832 N Greenview Ave at Fry St (312-421-9052). El: Blue to Chicago. Bus: 9 Ashland (24hrs), 66 Chicago (24hrs). Sun–Fri 1pm–2am; Sat 1pm–3am. Average beer: $3.75. Cash only.*

Club Foot Fans of VH1's *I Love the '80s* will be in heaven surrounded by walls plastered with vintage concert tees and glass cases jam-packed with every collectible toy created in that era. During the week there's room to take it all in, but weekends get crammed with locals rocking white belts playing pool to a DJ's mix of punk, indie rock and occasional polka. Yes, polka. After all, it is the Ukrainian Village. *1824 W Augusta St between Wood and Honore Sts (773-489-0379). El: Blue to Division. Bus: 50 Damen. Sun–Fri 8pm–2am; Sat 8pm–3am. Average beer: $2. Cash only.*

✕ DeLux A mere sidestep from the expanding Milwaukee/Grand/Halsted late-night hub, DeLux has more exposed ductwork, raw brick walls and industrial-grade metal tables than even your rich friend's "Hey, look! I live in a former meat locker!" condo. Belly up to the prominent dark-wood bar at night or nurse your hangover at the spot's weekend boozy Effen Brunch—the lights are dim, the TVs subdued and the "tater smash" (basically mashed-up tater tots and onions) plenty greasy. *669 N Milwaukee Ave at Ancona St (312-850-4008). El: Blue to Grand. Bus: 8, 56, 65. Mon–Fri 4pm–2am; Sat 10am–3am; Sun 10am–midnight. Average beer: $4.*

(Exit Thursday is fetish night and Monday it's punk rock, but pretty much any night you stumble upon this haunt for the black-clad you'll see that the freaks indeed do come out at night. Like any clique, it tends to have an insider feel, but brave souls looking for their Ministry and PBR fix have to start somewhere. Beware: There's a $5 cover on weekends. *1315 W North Ave between Ada and Throop Sts (773-395-2700). El: Red to North/Clybourn. Bus: 9 Ashland (24hrs), 72 North. Sun–Fri 9pm–4am; Sat 9pm–5am. Average beer: $3.*

EZ Inn Those not paying attention risk stumbling past the subtle neon signage and buzzer-protected door of this Ukrainian Village dive. To feel like a regular inside, simply nab a Miller Lite, lend an ear at the bar stools and shamelessly belt Van Halen's "Top of the World" between dart tosses. A tip to the wanna-be sharks: Pool is taken very seriously. *921 N Western Ave between Iowa and Walton Sts (773-384-9682). Bus: 49 (24hrs), 50, 66 (24hrs). Sun–Fri 11am–2am; Sat 11am–3am. Average beer: $2.50.*

✕ Five Star Bar *2007 Eat Out Award, Readers' Choice: Best new bar* There goes the neighborhood. Once sleepy and under-appreciated, this raucous spot has single-handedly turned up the volume in West Town. It's packed with tanned, gelled and button-downed dudes devil-horning to old Metallica and gawking at chicks in shirts that look like they've been mauled by tigers. So far, the locals haven't called the cops with noise complaints, but the fashion police should be on their way any minute. *1424 West Chicago Ave at Bishop St (312-850-2555). El: Blue to Chicago. Bus: 9 (24hrs), 56, 66 (24hrs). Mon–Fri 4pm–2am; Sat noon–3am; Sun noon–2am. Average cocktail: $8.*

Gold Star Bar Truly a neighborhood hangout, this tried-and-true East Village bar is frequented by those who appreciate Claudio the tamale guy, a jukebox that stocks both white-hot jazz and doom metal, a cheap pool table, equally cheap drinks and a crowd who could care less if you show up in sweats. *1755 W Division St between Wood St and Hermitage Ave (773-227-8700). El: Blue to Division. Bus: 70 Division. Mon–Fri 4pm–2am; Sat 3pm–3am; Sun 3pm–2am. Average beer: $3. Cash only.*

✕ ✳ Happy Village A gurgling goldfish pond, endless picnic tables and lush greenery all around is the scene at this West Town dive. But when it rains (or at 11pm, when the garden closes), it's back inside, where cigarette smoke mingles with the smell of whiskey and cheap beer, and the jukebox coughs out the Cars and Madonna. *1059 N Wolcott Ave at Thomas St (773-486-1512). El: Blue to Division. Bus: 50 Damen, 70 Division. Mon–Fri 4pm–2am; Sat 3pm–3am, Sun 4pm–11pm. Average beer: $3.*

✕ High Dive This well-lit bar doesn't have any beers on tap but serves ahi tuna. In short, it will never truly be a dive. But we don't care, because we feel at home among the concert posters on the walls and the red-velvet booths. And if we're going to drink out of bottles, it might as well be from this 27 beer–strong selection. *1938 W Chicago Ave between Winchester and Damen Aves (773-235-3483). Bus: 50, 65, 66 (24hrs). Mon–Fri 4pm–2am; Sat 3pm–3am; Sun 11:30am–2pm. Average beer: $4.*

Inner Town Pub Smoky as hell and with more clutter than your eccentric aunt's house, this former speakeasy in Ukie Village serves up cheap booze (all shots are $3) and warm salted nuts in true dive fashion. Indie-rockers on their way to Empty Bottle shows take advantage of free pool, while a smattering of toothless old-timers keep it gritty with war stories and phlegmy coughs. *1935 W Thomas St at Winchester Ave (773-235-9795). El: Blue to Division. Bus: 50 Damen, 70 Division. Sun–Fri 3pm–2am; Sat 3pm–3am. Average beer: $3. Cash only.*

Franks a lot Five Star Bar won the 2007 Eat Out Awards Readers' Choice for best new bar.

✕ **La Manzanilla Lounge** Named after the owner's hometown in Mexico, this informal cantina has a homey feel—an aunt makes tamales on holidays and snacks on weekends. There's Spanish music on the jukebox, and Tecates are three bucks a pop. Just don't try anything too fancy (they're often out of margarita mix), and make like the regulars—they seem quite happy with their *cerveza frias* and tequila with a side of Squirt. *1958 W Huron St between Wolcott and Damen Aves (312-666-6020). Bus: 50, 65, 66 (24hrs). Sun–Fri 11am–2am; Sat 11am–3am. Average beer: $3. Cash only.*

Lava Lounge The once-divey Ukie Village DJ bar has been reborn as a compact, high-design club in Wicker Park. The Suhail-conceived concrete bar contrasts with a glowing red ceiling panel, and removable modular seating means more dance space for bigger gigs. The owners (also of SmallBar) promise low or no cover, and have kept the diverse roster of resident DJs. The style upgrade doesn't mean a neglected beer list: Look for more than a dozen boutique labels on the bottle list. *1270 N Milwaukee Ave at Ashland Ave (773-342-5282). El: Blue to Division. Bus: 9 (24hrs), 50, 72. Sun–Fri 7pm–2am; Sat 7pm–3am. Average beer: $5.*

✕ **Loop Tavern** If 9:30pm seems a little early for alcohol-fueled antics—and by "antics" we mean a drunken regular named James who'll likely hit you up (twice) for a dollar "for the jukebox"—keep in mind that this slashy closes at 11pm. And it's clear that everybody's got a lot of beer drinking, chips eating and lottery-ticket scratching to do before then. *1610 W Chicago Ave between Ashland and Marshfield Aves (312-226-6740). Bus: 9 Ashland (24hrs), 66 Chicago (24hrs). Mon–Thu 7am–11pm; Fri, Sat 7am–1am; Sun 11am–7pm. Average beer: $2. Cash only.*

✳ **Matchbox** If the thought of being crammed in this tiny boxcar of a bar makes you nervous, relax. The patio practically doubles the capacity of the place, and it's the perfect spot to throw back one of its margaritas, made with fresh lemon and lime juice, top-shelf liquors and powdered sugar, and poured with a heavy hand. *770 N Milwaukee Ave between Carpenter St and Ogden Ave (312-666-9292). El: Blue to Chicago. Bus: 56 Milwaukee, 66 Chicago (24hrs). Sun–Fri 3pm–2am; Sat 3pm–3am. Average cocktail: $5.*

Nilda's Place When we strolled into this endearingly tacky Latino holdout tucked into a gentrifying residential block, a tipsy twentysomething swiveled his stool our way, raised his hands to the sky and gleefully announced to the four other people in the place: "Finally! You're here." It was drunk talk all right, but this stranger summed up exactly how this bewitching bar makes you feel: Like it's been waiting for you to become a regular all these years. *1858 W Iowa St at Wolcott Ave (773-486-4720). El: Blue to Division. Bus: 9 (24hrs), 50, 66. 4pm–2am. Average beer: $2. Cash only.*

Ola's Liquor Catering to those who "work" odd hours (read: unemployed indie filmmakers) and a ragtag troupe of friendly regulars, this tiny bar–cum–liquor store is the perfect final destination for raucous night. Doors open at the crack of dawn and Ola, the Polish live wire who owns the joint, has been known to unlock earlier if properly coerced. *947 N Damen Ave between Augusta Blvd and Walton St (773-384-7250). El: Blue to Division. Bus: 50 Damen, 70 Division. Mon–Sat 7am–2am; Sun 11am–2am. Average cocktail: $3.50.*

Rainbo Club The bittersweet reality of great little dives is that they often lose charm when overrun by masses of clingers-on. Somehow, this Ukrainian Village spot has managed to remain an underground favorite. The local artists and musicians who frequent it hold on to terra firma with cheap drink in hand, awaiting a turn in the photo booth while nodding to everything from Aesop Rock to Black Sabbath. *1150 N Damen Ave between Haddon Ave and Division St (773-489-5999). El: Blue to Division. Bus: 70 Division. Sun–Fri 4pm–2am; Sat 4pm–3am. Average cocktail: $4. Cash only.*

Rite Liquors If you're not familiar with the glorious convenience of "the slashy" (a.k.a. liquor store/bar), this old-man haunt is a good introduction. Sure, it looks like your average corner store: Cases of beer, liquor and cheap wine surround retail shelves stocked with junk food in a fluorescent-lit room. But wander toward the dimly lit back of the store and you'll find yourself in bar country wondering whether or not you should have a couple before heading home with a fresh six-pack. *1649 W Division St at Marshfield Ave (773-486-6257). El: Blue to Division. Bus: 9 (24hrs), 56, 70. 7am–1am. Average beer: $3.*

Stella's Tap This spot's a typical, charming, pool-table dive distinguished by its namesake: the tiny woman who pours the drinks. Certain nights can be a real sausage fest, including some baldies from Chicago's Finest, and every one of them gives her a huge bear hug. Tip Stella right and you might start getting hugs, too. *935 N Western Ave at Walton St (773-384-0077). El: Blue to Chicago. Bus: 49 (24hrs), 50, 66 (24hrs). Sun–Fri 9am–2am; Sat 9am–3am. Average beer: $3.*

✕ ✳ **Tuman's** Okay, so it's not the hipster shithole it used to be when it was called Tuman's Alcohol Abuse Center. But just because it's a little shinier, a little cleaner and a little friendlier doesn't mean this Ukie Village classic isn't still a good clubhouse for locals looking to waste a Sunday away with some Jameson and the local news. *2159 W Chicago Ave at Leavitt St (773-782-1400). Bus: 50, 66 (24hrs), 70. Mon–Fri 3pm–2am; Sat noon–3am; Sun noon–2am. Average beer: $3.*

✕ ✳ **Twisted Spoke** When you begin brunch by showing your ID at the door, you know you're in the right place for a Bloody Mary. Spicy and sweet, garnished with salami and completed with a beer back, it's practically a meal in itself. Don't let that distract you from the food, however. Breakfast tacos are a good way to spice up your egg intake. And the Spoke's signature "fatboy" burgers are thick, juicy and perfectly tender. *501 N Ogden Ave at Grand Ave (312-666-1500). El: Blue to Grand. Bus: 8, 9 (24hrs), 65. Mon–Fri 11am–2am; Sat 9am–3am; Sunday 9am–2am. Average beer: $4.*

Old Town/River North

Blue Frog It's all about game-playing here. No, not those kinds of normal games people play. Blue Frog is stocked with childhood faves like Operation and Scrabble, not to mention almost two dozen kinds of beers. *676 N LaSalle St between Erie and Huron Sts (312-943-8900). El: Red to Grand. Bus: 156 LaSalle. Mon–Thu 11:30am–midnight; Fri 11:30am–2am; Sat 6pm–3am (closed Sun). Average cocktail: $6.50.*

(✕ ✳ **The Boss Bar** Guys, don't even bother. This River North hangout has plenty of tables to nosh on a burger and a big, circular bar with plenty of stools to put down your pints. But after work it's crowded three-suits-deep with men trying to flirt with the gorgeous bartenders, so only a woman could

get lucky here. *420 N Clark St at Hubbard St (312-527-1203). El: Red to Grand. Bus: 22 (24hrs), 36, 65. Sun–Fri 11am–4am; Sat 11am–5am. Average cocktail: $5.*

✕ ✳ **Brehon Pub** Rumor has it that crooked politicians were busted for taking bribes at this Irish pub in the late '70s, but as far as we can tell, these days the unpretentious spot is packed with the law-abiding and superfriendly. The homey, neighborhood joint has survived a couple dozen St. Patrick's Days and probably twice as many Irish impersonators. *731 N Wells St at Superior St (312-642-1071). El: Brown to Chicago. Bus: 66 Chicago (24hrs), 156 LaSalle. Mon–Fri 11am–2am; Sat noon–3am; Sun noon–2am. Average beer: $4.*

(✕ **Burton Place** These four levels of 4am debauchery in the heart of Old Town yield exactly the kind of crowd you would expect on the weekends: young, loud and drunk, with shots spilled on their shirts. But on weeknights it's a gathering spot for older gentlemen hoping to grab a Scotch, a good seat to watch the game and possibly a little bit of that weekend energy. *1447 N Wells St at Burton Pl (312-664-4699). El: Brown, Purple (rush hrs) to Sedgwick. Bus: 72 North, 156 LaSalle. Sun–Fri 11am–4am; Sat 11am–5am. Average beer: $4.*

(✕ **Butch McGuire's** Even when it gets packed with the typical Division Street crowd, this Irish pub has an old soul. Antique beer paraphernalia and model ships hang from the ceiling, framed paintings of Chicago's past dot the walls and beers are served in frosted glass mugs. When its patriarch passed away a few years ago, the wake made front-page headlines. *20 W Division St between State and Dearborn Sts (312-337-9080). El: Red to Clark/Division. Bus: 36 Broadway, 70 Division. Sun–Fri 11am–4am; Sat 8am–5am. Average beer: $5.*

(**Buzz** River North's Buzz is a bit of a chameleon, catering to salsa, house and hip-hop crowds on almost every day of the week. Latin beats rule on Thursdays and a promoter caters to a predominantly Asian crew of nightclubbers on Fridays for a blend of house and hip-hop. But because it's within walking distance to the other River North hot spots, there's a crazy cross-section of partyers letting loose. *308 W Erie St at Franklin St (312-475-9800). El: Brown to Chicago. Bus: 66 Chicago (24hrs), 156 LaSalle. Mon–Fri 10pm–4am; Sat 10pm–5am; Sun 7pm–2am. Average cocktail: $10.*

▼ **Cabaret Cocktail Boutique** *Moulin Rouge* meets *Casino* meets thirtysomething scenesters at this lounge/club (cover ranges from $10 to $20) in River North, where servers wear tasseled corsets…and that's all. Since the place has little to do with the musical of the same name, theater queens will have to get their kicks around the corner at Gentry. *15 W Hubbard St between State and Dearborn Sts (312-245-3100). El: Red to Grand. Bus: 29, 36, 65. Wed–Fri 8pm–2am; Sat 8pm–3am; Sun 9pm–2am. Average cocktail: $10.*

♨ **Celtic Crossings** It usually takes nothing but a four-leaf-clover cut out of construction paper to make a bar "Irish," but this tchotchke-filled River North pub is different. It's certified by the James Joyce Society and full of real, live Irish people. So throw down that Guinness (or Boddingtons) with confidence: This is the real thing. *751 N Clark St between Superior St and Chicago Ave (312-337-1005). El: Brown, Purple (rush hrs) to Chicago. Bus: 22 Clark (24hrs), 66 Chicago (24hrs). Sun–Fri 2pm–2am; Sat 2pm–3am. Average beer: $3.*

✕ **Chi Bar** An extreme makeover rendered this bar, nestled riverside in the Sheraton Hotel, a lot hipper than the

Lift your spirits Try a classic cocktail like the Singapore Sling at The Motel Bar.

rest of the hotel would suggest. The cocktails follow suit: "The 'L'" mixes vodka, Chambord, guava juice and fresh sour mix to sweet-and-tart perfection. The tourist clientele doesn't always match the contemporary vibe, but the drinks make the trade-off worth it. *301 E North Water St at Columbus Dr (312-755-2227). Bus: 2, 29, 65, 66 (24hrs), 124. Mon–Fri 5pm–2am; Sat, Sun 11am–2am. Average cocktail: $11.*

Clark Street Ale House We've seen people at this dim, homey, Near North pub hang out without ever ordering a drink, but we just can't follow suit. We envy the friendly neighbors who drop onto wooden stools just to chat up the bartender. But when we spy two dozen beers on tap—mostly domestic gems like Great Lakes Brewing Company's Elliot Ness—we feel like settling in and getting our drink on. *742 N Clark St between Superior and Chicago Sts (312-642-9253). El: Red to Chicago. Bus: 22 Clark (24hrs). Sun–Fri 4pm–4am, Sat 4pm–5am. Average beer: $4.*

✕ **Coogan's** A few blocks from Lyric Opera and just off the river, this beautifully setup bar is a primo spot if you need a little "you" time after dark. Stop by around 9pm, when most of the after-work crowd has headed home. When scarcely populated, the polished wood and brass decor, high ceilings and old-time photographs evoke a Chicago-of-yesteryear feel that's hard to find. *180 N Wacker Dr between Lake St and Couch Pl (312-444-1134). El: Brown, Green, Orange, Purple (rush hrs), Pink, Blue to Clark/Lake. Mon–Fri 11am–10:30pm; Sat–Sun noon–6pm. Average beer: $5.*

✕ ✳ **Corcoran's** As a sibling of Mystic Celt and Vaughan's Pub, this popular Old Town pub knows how to get Irish. On any given night, you'll find the place packed with pre- and post–Second City fans digging on pints of beer,

Color your world Warning: The minute you step into the Rainbo Club, you're officially a hipster.

greasy pub grub, and a mix of Lou Reed and Guns N' Roses blaring from the outdoor speakers. *1615 N Wells St between North Ave and Concord Ln (312-440-0885). El: Brown, Purple (rush hrs) to Sedgwick. Bus: 72 North, 156 LaSalle. Sun–Fri 11am–2am; Sat 11am–3am. Average beer: $4.*

❨ **Crobar** The original cro in the dance-club franchise (there are now outposts in Miami, New York and South America) was remodeled a few years ago with a South Beach–meets–industrial materials look. These days, the club hosts everything from a midweek Latin night to visits from big-name techno, house and trance DJs. But a typical weekend night features residents hammering with au courant dance tracks while girls on platforms demonstrate the finer points of deca dancing. *1543 N Kingsbury Ave between Eastman and Weed Sts (312-266-1900). El: Red to North/Clybourn. Bus: 8 Halsted, 72 North. Wed 10pm–4am; Fri 10am–4pm; Sat 10pm–5am. Average cocktail: $9.*

✕ **Fadó Irish Pub** We know it's a chain, but we like it. All three floors of this dark, wood-filled, slightly over-stylized Irish pub are packed with young professionals getting sloshed and loosening their ties and tongues. After trying the "black velveteen," a smooth and sweet blend of Guinness and cider, we're inclined to join them. *100 W Grand Ave at Clark St (312-836-0066). El: Red to Grand. Bus: 22 Clark (24hrs), 65 Grand. Sun–Thu 11:30am–2am; Fri, Sat 11:30am–3am. Average beer: $5.*

✕ **Garret Ripley's** This is one friendly bar. We always intend to have one after-work drink, but there's something about this place that keeps us ordering round after round. The welcoming staff, vintage photo–filled interior and upscale Irish pub grub make this Garret one talented Mr. Ripley. *712 N Clark St between Huron and Superior Sts (312-642-2900). El: Brown, Purple (rush hrs), Red to Chicago. Sun–Fri 11am–2am; Sat 11am–3am. Average beer: $5.*

✕ **Green Door Tavern** If you're into slick, minimalist lounges or enormous, bass-heavy clubs, you may find it hard to believe that this River North stalwart has anything to offer you. But poke around and you'll find a nice dining room to the side, a pool room in the back and a jukebox that caters to any taste. *678 N Orleans St between Erie and Huron Sts (312-664-5496). El: Brown, Purple (rush hrs) to Chicago. Bus: 66 Chicago. Mon–Fri 11:30am–2am; Sat 11:30am–3am; Sun noon–8pm. Average beer: $5.*

✕ **Hogs and Honeys** So your parents wouldn't send you to Texas A&M because they were afraid the state with the bull-size party rep would eat up all your self-control along with all their tuition money? No use crying over being stuck at UIC—this beer-and-babes spot has that Texas party thing down pat, complete with wasted, tan blonds gyrating on a mechanical bull and big-boobed bartenders jumping up on the bar every now and then to do synchronized dances that rival Xtina's pre–glam-girl days. *1551 N Sheffield Ave between Weed St and North Ave (312-377-1733). El: Red to North/Clybourn. Bus: 8 Halsted. 72 North. Wed–Fri 9pm–2am; Sat 9pm–3am. Average beer: $3.*

✕ **J. Patrick's Irish Bar & Grill** The conflicting vibes (and Irish name) confused the hell out us. With a crunchy guitar duo belting acoustic versions of Radiohead and waitresses in short, plaid skirts, we didn't know if we were at summer camp or a Britney Spears concert. It ain't Irish but it ain't all that bad. *1367 W Erie St between Ada and Noble Sts (312-243-0990). El: Blue to Chicago. Bus: 9 Ashland (24hrs), 66 Chicago (24hrs). Mon–Fri 11am–2am; Sat 11am–3am, Sun 11am–midnight. Average beer: $5.*

Jet Vodka Lounge By serving more than 130 vodkas, this Weed District bar aims to make the transparent spirit as revered as wine. If your pockets aren't deep, don't even think about trying to keep up with this bottle-service crowd. And drinkers who fear flying may want to take caution (or Xanax). The stark-white, somewhat minimalist settings are inspired by the interior of a 777. *1551 N Sheffield Ave between Weed St and North Ave (312-730-4395). El: Red to North/Clybourn. Bus: 8 Halsted, 72 North. Wed–Fri 8pm–2am; Sat 8pm–3am; Sun 8pm–2am. Average cocktail: $10.*

✗ **Joe's on Weed** Even with 120 TV screens, it's mind-boggling that this quintessential sports bar manages to pack all 20,000 feet of its warehouselike space with people—on nights when the Illini are playing, you can't even move. When the game's not on, musical acts (Tone-Loc is considered music, right?) and an outdoor patio keep the place buzzing. *940 W Weed St between Fremont St and Sheffield Ave (312-337-3486). El: Red to North/Clybourn. Bus: 8 Halsted, 72 North. Mon–Thu 5pm–2am; Fri 5pm–4am; Sat noon–5am; Sun varies (call ahead). Average beer: $4.*

✗ **The Kerryman** A little older and a little wiser, the after-work crowd here doesn't have the patience for the plastic cups of beer and sticky floors of other area bars. So patrons pack this slick, contemporary version of an Irish pub to flirt with fellow classy pint-drinkers. *661 N Clark St at Erie St (312-335-8121). El: Red to Grand. Bus: 22 (24hrs), 36, 65. Sun–Fri 11am–2am; Sat 11am–3am. Average beer: $5.*

(✗ ✦ **Martini Ranch** A martini hideaway? Sounds like an oxymoron, but this River North spot manages to marry the two into a union of after-work debauchery. After the nine-to-fivers roll it up on weeknights, industry folks (local bartenders and waitstaff) saddle up a martini and ride off into the dawn. On weekends, the Ranch becomes a hitching post—DJs spin house and urbanites try to make room to grind by the pool table. *311 W Chicago Ave between Orleans and Franklin Sts (312-335-9500). El: Brown, Purple (rush hrs) to Chicago. Bus: 66 Chicago (24hrs). Sun–Fri 5pm–4am; Sat 5pm–5am. Average cocktail: $9.*

✗ **McCormick & Schmick's Scratch Bar** Scratch likes to think of itself as a "saloon," and that means you get bartenders who care a lot about the way they make your cocktail. The bar is loaded with fresh fruit used in making your drink—no syrup mixes here. There's a long list of wines by the glass, craft beers and more than 35 whiskeys. *41 E Chestnut St at Wabash Ave (312-397-9500). El: Red to Chicago. Bus: 146, 147, 151 (24hrs). Mon–Thu 11:30am–1am; Fri, Sat 11:30am–2am; Sun 11:30am–midnight. Average cocktail: $9.*

✗ ✳ **The Motel Bar** The boys behind Division Street restaurant Mas are also the guys to thank for this low-lit, earth-toned lounge. It's nothing like motels we've checked into, but we dig the throwback classic cocktails, the "room service" comfort food menu and eclectic jukebox in lieu of a DJ turning it into a club. *600 W Chicago Ave at Larrabee St (312-822-2900). Bus: 66 Chicago (24hrs). Sun–Fri 3:30pm–2am; Sat 3:30pm–3am. Average cocktail: $6.*

(✗ **Mother Hubbard's** We absolutely love the idea of a slightly scuzzy bar being surrounded by uppity, polished, tourist-filled restaurants. The winding bar area is occupied by loners watching the big screen, but near the surrounding checkered-tablecloth–topped tables is the more gregarious set. And in the back, three pool tables are ripe for a good game. *5 W Hubbard St between State and Dearborn Sts (312-828-*

You got a mother thing coming Get a shot for a penny with every drink you buy at Mother's Too.

0007). El: Red to Grand. Bus: 29, 36, 65. Sun–Fri 11am–4am; Sat 11am–5am. Average beer: $3.50.

Mother's Too Are times tough for River North bars or something? This Division Street legend gives away a shot for a penny with every drink you buy, possibly to make you forget that when you walked in here they were blasting Billy Joel, but also to give you the confidence to talk to that honey you have your eye on. *14 W Division St between State St and Dearborn St (312-266-7444). El: Red to Clark/Division. Bus: 36 Broadway, 70 Division. Sun–Fri 11am–2am; Sat 11am–3am. Average beer: $4.*

(✗ **O'Callaghan's** It's just your normal Irish pub with a few topless women carved into the wooden bar. But to anybody who's looking for a clean, casual place to drink until 4am in River North, it's an oasis of Jameson, Guinness and a late-night menu of jalapeño poppers and nachos. *29 W Hubbard between State and Dearborn Sts (312-527-1180). El: Red to Grand. Bus: 29, 36, 65. Sun–Fri 11am–4am; Sat 11am–5am. Average beer: $4.*

(**Old Town Ale House** *2007 Eat Out Award, Readers' Choice: Best dive bar* Among the framed drawings of regulars cluttering the wooden walls of this saloon-style staple are posters boasting that you're in "le premiere dive bar" of Chicago. We don't know where this place gets off speaking French, but it's been around since 1958, so we'll grant it bragging rights. *219 W North Ave at Wieland St (312-944-7020). El: Brown, Purple (rush hrs) to Sedgwick. Bus: 72 North, 156 LaSalle. Sun–Fri noon–4am; Sat noon–5am. Average beer: $4. Cash only.*

✗ ✳ **Players Bar and Grill** Louder, bigger and more in-your-face than the view any stadium seat can

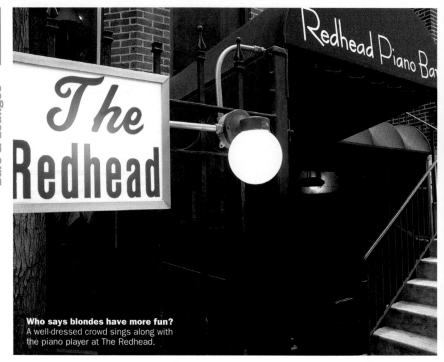

Who says blondes have more fun?
A well-dressed crowd sings along with
the piano player at The Redhead.

give you, experiencing the game at this new River West sports bar is second only to actually being in the game—or, if you're in front of the 120-inch screen, even better. Only instead of hot dogs and nachos, the menu here features burgers and, um, goulash. *551 N Ogden Ave between Grand Ave and Ohio St (312-733-2121). Bus: 65 Grand. Mon–Fri 4pm–2am; Sat 10am–3am; Sun 11am–midnight. Average beer: $4.*

(**The Redhead** For the piano-bar fiend who likes his joints a little more Grace than Will, this smoky underground spot should hit all the right notes. But even though the guys here aren't gay, they're at least dressed well: Bouncers inspect outfits as well as your ID, and flip-flops and T-shirts don't get through the door. *16 W Ontario St between State and Dearborn Sts (312-640-1000). El: Red to Grand. Bus: 22 (24hrs), 36, 125. Sun–Fri 7pm–4am; Sat 7pm–5am. Average cocktail: $6.*

(✕ **Roadhouse** The name might remind you of the rough-and-tumble bar in that Patrick Swayze flick. On the weekends, you'd probably be correct. But during the week, this sports bar filled with car paraphernalia is quiet and laid-back. Sit on the stools—with all that debauchery, you never know what's hidden in those plush velvet car seats. *1653 N Wells St between Concord Ln and Eugenie St (312-440-0535). El: Red to North/Clybourn. Bus: 72 North, 156 LaSalle. Mon–Fri 4pm–4am; Sat 11am–5am; Sun 11am–4am. Average beer: $5.*

✕ ✱ **Rock Bottom Brewery** Just a drunken stumble from the Grand Red Line station, this sporty brewpub offers six house-brewed beers to sip while watching your team on more than a dozen TVs. The menu features signatures like jambalaya with Red Ale rice and

meatloaf in either Brown Ale mushroom sauce or Stout tomato sauce. The fare is fine, but the beer is so tasty we'd just as soon head up to the rooftop beer garden with a pint. *1 W Grand Ave at State St (312-755-9339). El: Red to Grand. Bus: 22 (24hrs), 29, 36, 65. 11am–2am. Average beer: $5.*

Rossi's Like a secret chamber of debauchery, the red door to this State Street bar reveals no sign of what's inside. Turns out it's a dark cabinish space with a mixed crowd of lewd yuppies and bitter locals. Pissed off? Up to no good? You'll fit in just fine. *412 N State St between Kinzie and Hubbard Sts (312-644-5775). El: Red to Grand. Bus: 29, 36, 65. Mon–Fri 7am–2am; Sat 7am–3am, Sun 11am–2am. Average beer: $3.50. Cash only.*

✕ ✱ **Shamrock Club** It's a tiny space and it's packed with Merch Mart employees looking to drink their workday away, so it might take the luck of one of the four-leaf clovers that decorate the place to get a seat. Strangers are regarded with suspicion here, so keep away from the regulars until you become one yourself. *210 W Kinzie St between Wells and Franklin Sts (312-321-9314). El: Brown, Purple (rush hrs) to Merchandise Mart. Bus: 65 Grand, 125 Water Tower Exp. Mon–Sat 11am–2am (closed Sun). Average beer: $3.75.*

✕ **Snickers** Could anything be more perfect? It's a deli. It's a bar. It's your new favorite pit stop. Spend your mornings at the dinerlike counter with an egg-and-cheese, stop by for a gyro and a beer for lunch and return after work for cocktails. You may never go home again. *448 N State St between Hubbard and Illinois Sts (312-527-0437). El: Red to Grand. Bus: 29, 36, 65. Mon–Fri 7am–2am; Sat 7am–3am; Sun 8am–2am. Average cocktail: $5.*

✗ **Stone Lotus** This bilevel, spa-theme lounge is decorated with carefully lit cherry blossoms and a steady sheet of water cascading down the walls. Allegedly, it's the most luxurious, upscale spot in town. So why is every guy dressed like he's at a Cubs game? And why are all the ladies dressed like Fly Girls? We like the cocktails (even the balsamic-and-mozzarella–spiked "Caprese"), but come on, people: You may have finagled your way past the doorman, but you can at least *look* like you belong. *873 N Orleans St between Chestnut and Locust Sts (312-440-9680). El: Brown, Purple (rush hrs) to Chicago. Bus: 66 Chicago (24hrs). Tue–Fri 8pm–2am; Sat 8pm–3am. Average cocktail: $14.*

✳ **Suite Lounge** Leather booths with flowing privacy curtains, perky servers with tight T-shirts and a pimped-out "penthouse" room: When a place drips with this much sex, it takes work not to get some. Got no game? That's cool—a list of creative champagne cocktails and martinis will soothe your sexually frustrated soul. *1446 N Wells St between Schiller St and North Ave (312-787-6103). El: Brown, Purple (rush hrs) to Sedgwick; Red to North/Clybourn. Mon–Fri 7pm–2am; Sat 7pm–3am. Average cocktail: $7.*

✗ **Swirl Wine Bar** Because drinking on an empty stomach is a one-way ticket to drunk-dialing your ex, falling asleep in the bathroom or other drama, this wine bar thankfully puts just as much focus on the food. The housemade empanada hides earthy mushrooms inside its flaky crust; hefty crab cakes get a golden exterior of panko crumbs; a caprese salad gets a twist by using blue cheese instead of mozz; and a pizza topped with caramelized onions and pears goes perfectly with an off-dry riesling. *111 W Hubbard St between Clark St and LaSalle Blvd (312-828-9000). El: Brown, Purple (rush hrs) to Merchandise Mart; Red to Grand. Bus: 22 (24hrs), 36, 62 (24hrs), 65. Tue–Fri 5pm–2am; Sat 7pm–3am. Average glass of wine: $10.*

10 Pin If drinking at a bowling alley seems a little too *Roseanne* for a posh crew like yours, you obviously haven't been to lanes like these before. The rambunctious singles crowd seems more interested in each other (and the neon-bright martinis and enormous screens playing larger-than-life music videos) than they do actually picking up a bowling ball. One way or another, you'll probably score. *330 N State St between Upper Wacker Dr and Kinzie St (312-644-0300). El: Red to Grand; Brown, Purple (rush hrs) to Merchandise Mart. Bus: 22 Clark (24hrs), 36 Broadway. Sun–Thu 11am–1am; Fri 11am–2am; Sat 11am–3am. Average cocktail: $8.*

✗ ✳ **Weed's Tavern** Dozens of bras hang from the ceiling inside, but the rustic, fenced-in beer garden has a vibe all its own, with its covered gazebo and its funky yellow lightbulbs hanging overhead. If you're new to the bar, and owner Sergio Mayora notices you, be prepared for a free shot of tequila. *1555 N Dayton St at Weed St (312-943-7815). El: Red to North/Clybourn. Bus: 8 Halsted, 72 North. Mon–Fri 4pm–2am; Sat 7am–3am (closed Sun). Average beer: $3.*

Wells on Wells Who knew a respite of dignified drinking existed on this somewhat trashy stretch of Wells? The cool beige interior with soft lighting and softer (but good) music offers up a lounge feeling, minus the snobbery and obscene prices. This basically guarantees the only fratness you'll get will be a random howl from the neighboring bars. *1617 N Wells St between North Ave and Concord Ln (312-944-1617). El: Brown, Purple (rush hrs) to Sedgwick. Bus: 72 North, 156 LaSalle. Mon 5pm–2am; Tue–Fri 11am–2am; Sat 10am–3am; Sun 10am–2am. Average cocktail: $5.*

✗ **Y Bar** This long, modern room is decked out with sleek, low-lying furniture, and is the perfect spot for bottle service and canoodling with other Euro-minded audiophiles. Guys would be smart to wait until Thursday to drop by, though—that's when models get in for free. If you're going to press your luck, it might as well be with a model. *224 W Ontario St between Wells and Franklin Sts (312-274-1880). El: Brown, Purple (rush hrs) to Chicago. Bus: 66 Chicago (24hrs), 125 Water Tower Express. Tue–Fri 9pm–2am; Sat 9pm–3am. Average cocktail: $10.*

Gold Coast/Mag Mile/ Streeterville

✗ **The Bar at Peninsula Hotel** Escort a date to the Peninsula's dark, clubby cocktail bar and you won't go home alone. All the manly bases have been covered—a glowing fireplace, a stogie-stocked humidor and high-backed bar stools or cozy couched conversation nooks. Sip well-crafted cocktails, bubbly by the glass or whiskeys from obscure distillers. *108 E Superior St, fifth floor, between Michigan Ave and Rush St (312-573-6766). El: Red to Chicago. Bus: 3, 66 (24hrs), 145, 146, 147, 151 (24hrs). 3pm–1am. Average martini: $13.*

✗ **Basil's** There are two types of people who drink in this classic bar, which is full of dark wood and brass: tourists staying in the Talbott Hotel who don't know anywhere else to drink, and locals who know that anywhere else isn't half as classy. *20 E Delaware Pl between State St and Wabash Ave (312-944-4970). El: Red to Chicago. Bus: 36, 66 (24hrs), 143, 144, 145, 146, 147, 151 (24hrs). Sun–Thu 8am–11pm; Fri, Sat 8am–2am. Average cocktail: $7.*

❨ **Bootleggers** The Prohibition era-meets–New Orleans theme sets the scene for one big bachelorette party. Girls go wild with dance contests to pop and '80s hits, and while Mardi Gras beads start the night dangling around animal heads hung on the walls, they eventually end up around the necks of drunken revelers. *13 W Division St between State Pkwy and Dearborn St (312-266-0944). El: Red to Clark/Division. Bus: 29 State, 70 Division. Sun–Fri 7pm–4am; Sat 7pm–5am. Average beer $4.50.*

✗ **Boston Blackie's** With its classic wooden bar and gritty location under Michigan Avenue, this bar has a Casablanca-era feel about it. But we never saw Bogart take down a huge burger, so we're inclined to skip the bland, preformed patties that it's "famous" for and stick with whiskey instead. *164 E Grand Ave at St. Clair St (312-938-8700). El: Red to Grand. Bus: 2, 3, 4 (24hrs), X4, 10, 26, 29, 65, 143, 144, 145, 146, 147, 151 (24hrs), 157. Mon–Sat 11am–11pm; Sun noon–9pm. Average beer: $3.*

❨ ✗ **Dublin's** Despite its name, this Viagra Triangle spot is no more Irish than a string of green lights and its corned beef and cabbage. It is, however, a low-key destination for hearty (but pricey) late-night grub; the menu boasts a plethora of chicken, seafood and steak dishes. The bar itself occupies most of the interior real estate, but allows for a stool-side view of the neighborhood regulars and the open-style kitchen. *1050 N State St at Maple St (312-266-6340). El: Red to Clark/Division. Bus: 22 (24hrs), 36, 70, 156. Sun–Fri 11am–4am; Sat 11am–5am. Average beer: $5.*

✗ ✳ **Elephant and Castle** This bar is as close as any to Northwestern's downtown campus, but if you're here to pick up a med student, think again. However, if you're here to hang out with a boisterous motley crew of eccentric Gold Coasters, chatty international tourists and seen-it-all bartenders, take a seat and have a pint. *160 E Huron St between Michigan Ave and St. Clair St (312-440-1180). El: Red to Chicago. Bus: 3, X3, 4 (24hrs), X4, 10, 26, 143, 144, 145, 146, 147, 151 (24hrs). 6:30am–midnight. Average beer: $5.*

Elm Street Liquors The Gold Coast meat market has evolved. Board of Trade types here are hot, single and ready to splurge for bottle service. Not your thing? The crowd does mix up, making it almost as likely to find cute left-brainers coughing up cash for one of a dozen pro martinis. *12 W Elm St between State and Dearborn Sts (312-337-3200). El: Red to Clark/Division. Bus: 36 Broadway, 70 Division. Mon–Fri 6pm–2am; Sat 6pm–3am. Average cocktail: $6.*

✗ **Eno** It's harder to pair wine and cheese than you think—so stop thinking about it and let the people at this sophisticated wine-cheese-chocolate bar do it for you. Experts flutter around the warm, dark wood–ridden room, expounding on the carefully handled wines and artisanal cheeses. It's the kind of service (and diet) a person could really get used to—if it weren't so damn expensive. *Hotel InterContinental, 525 N Michigan Ave at Illinois Ave (312-321-8738). El: Red to Grand. Bus: 3, 4 (24hrs), X4, 10, 26, 29, 36, 65, 125, 143, 144, 145, 146, 147, 151 (24hrs), 157. Sun–Fri 4pm–midnight; Sat 3pm–1am. Average glass of wine: $15.*

❨ ✗ **Finn McCool's** As its name suggests, McCool's is an Irish-style pub, but as its location suggests, the emphasis is on flash rather than authenticity. Not that there's anything wrong with that, especially if you're looking for a big crowd where fake brogues can go unnoticed, plus cheaper drinks than the surrounding spots. *15 W Division St between State and Dearborn Sts (312-337-4349). Bus: 22 (24hrs), 36, 70. El: Red to Clark/Division. Mon–Wed 11:30am–2am; Thu–Fri 11:30am–4am; Sat 11am–5am, Sun 3pm–2am. Average beer: $5.*

❨ **The Hangge-Uppe** As soon as you walk into this place it's obvious that everyone has had enough drinks to consider you their best friend—and they know every single lyric to every single song. The first floor caters to the hip-hop/Top-40 crowd, while the lower level gives you sing-a-long '80s rock. If you can maneuver your way through the late-night dancing crowd, you'll agree: This place always delivers a good time. *14 W Elm St between State and Dearborn Sts (312-337-0561). El: Red to Clark/Division, Bus: 22 (24hrs), 36, 70, 156. Sun–Thu 7pm–4am; Fri 5pm–4am; Sat 5pm–5am. Average cocktail: $6.*

✗ **J Bar** Two slick rooms awash in shiny mirrored tile and video art, martinis garnished with olive-blue-cheese lollipops, and a clientele of only the richest, prettiest, most accomplished Chicagoans. No wonder this hot spot is in the James Hotel; the place is so packed you're going to have to stay overnight to get a seat. *616 N Rush St at Ontario St (312-660-7200). El: Red to Grand. Bus: 36, 125, 151 (24hrs). 6pm–2am. Average cocktail: $10.*

Jilly's Too Go ahead and take your friends who don't dig piano bars: This subterranean sequel to the original Jilly's is so slick (bars backlit with a glowing, red light; mod leather furniture; plenty of hidden rooms to get purposely lost in) that nobody's really paying attention to the musicians anyway. *1009–11 N Rush St between Oak St and Bellevue Pl (312-664-0009). El: Red to Clark/Division. Bus: 36 Broadway, 70 Division. Wed–Fri 8pm–2am; Sat 8pm–3am. Average cocktail: $7.*

✗ ♦ **Le Bar** Ooh-la-la, this fancy bar in the Sofitel Hotel is a sensual sipping spot for travelers and locals alike. Plush leather bar stools, a cool-to-the-touch chrome bar and well-made (and incredibly expensive) cocktails give this place its cosmopolitan vibe, but it's the bad techno that gives it that European edge. *20 E Chestnut St at Wabash Ave (312-324-4000). El: Red to Chicago. Bus: 36, 66 (24hrs), 143, 144, 145, 146, 147, 151 (24hrs). Sun–Wed 3pm–1am; Thu–Sat 3pm–2am. Average cocktail: $9.*

❨ ✗ ♦ **Leg Room** Less of a frat-boy-meets-tourist scene than many Rush and Division bars, Leg Room is the classiest place on this strip to get a drink. But don't expect a low-key neighborhood bar. You'll get animal-print stools, a free-floating bar and a free jukebox with your martinis. *7 W Division St between State Pkwy and Dearborn St (312-337-2583). El: Red to Clark/Division. Bus: 22 (24hrs), 36, 70. Sun–Fri 7pm–4am; Sat 7pm–5am. Average cocktail: $6.*

✗ ✳ ♦ **Lizzie McNeill's** Your parents are moving back into the city. If you don't believe us, visit this River East Irish pub and notice the preponderance of Baby Boomers reclining at the outdoor patio with a Guinness in one hand and a Reuben in the other. This may sound too unhip for you, but Lizzie's is spitting distance from the Chicago River, a nice diversion on a sunny day. *400 N McClurg Ct at North Water St (312-467-1992). Bus: 2, 29, 65, 66 (24hrs), 124. Sun–Fri 11am–2am; Sat 11am–3am. Average beer: $4.*

The Lodge Time stands still in this log-cabinish tavern... or at least the patrons wish it did. Whereas every other bar on this strip is packed with freshly waxed twentysomethings, this place seems to be popular with the older, wistful Division Street crowd, the ones who are past their prime but just can't let go. Little do they know that their sullen whiskey-drinking makes this the most interesting bar on the strip. *21 W Division St between State and Dearborn Sts (312-642-4406). El: Red to Clark/Division. Bus: 22 (24hrs), 36, 70, 156. Mon–Thu 2pm–4am; Fri noon–4am; Sat noon–5am; Sun noon–4am. Average cocktail: $5.*

✗ ♦ **Lucky Strike Lanes** The L.A. Lucky Strike is a fave on *Entourage*. Chicago's branch is less celeb. Still, you can feel like one of the beautiful people downing drinks and munching better-than-you'd-expect grub in the wine bar. Or make it more casual by playing pool or bowling while you quaff a cold one. *322 E Illinois St between Fairbanks and McClurg Cts (312-245-8331). Bus: 65 Grand, 66 Chicago (24hrs). 11am–2am. Average cocktail: $8.*

✗ **Martini Bar at the Millennium Knickerbocker Hotel** Instead of tucking away its bar to the side, this hotel ingeniously puts it in the middle of the lobby. So the first thing guests see when they walk into the place, so they head right to the stools, creating a scene that, sure, *looks* like a hotel lobby, but feels like a happening hot spot. *163 E Walton Pl between Mies Van Der Rohe Way and Michigan Ave (312-751-8100). El: Red to Chicago. Bus: 36, 66 (24hrs), 143, 144, 145, 146, 147, 151 (24hrs). 11:30am–1:30am. Average cocktail: $8.*

❨ ✗ ♦ **McFadden's Restaurant and Saloon** There are no other words that describe the clientele here better than dudes and chicks. Similarly, there's nothing that can describe the bar, with its plethora of flatscreens and loud (but good) sound system blaring football, other than sports pub. And when it's 3am on Saturday night and the dudes and chicks are still wide awake, this 5am bar is the go-to, if only because it's one of the few places in the 'hood still serving. *1206 N State Pkwy at Division St (312-475-9450). El: Red to Clark/*

Come and knock on our door
The vibe at The Reagle Beagle is unabashedly early '80s.

Division. Bus: 22 (24hrs), 36, 70, 156. Sun–Fri 11am–4am; Sat 11am–5am. Average beer: $5.

✕ ✳ **Melvin B's Truck Stop** Once the lobby bar for the Cedar Hotel, this place lives for summer, with the beer garden making up almost the entire establishment. The postwork crowd is completely shit-faced by 10pm, so when the college-age jeans-and-short-skirt crowd hits this spot, it's a cacophony of bad jokes and even worse pick-up lines. It's Cancún in Chicago. *1114 N State St between Cedar and Elm Sts (312-751-9897). El: Red to Clark/Division. Bus: 22 (24hrs), 36, 70. Sun–Fri 11am–2am; Sat 11am–3am. Average beer: $5.*

✕ **Palm Court at The Drake** Tell your friends you went to this Gold Coast spot just to make fun of the old rich people all you want. But the truth is you can't sit among the sparkling fountain and oversized flower arrangements, slowly sipping your perfectly shaken martini, without thinking that your mom was right all along: You are special. *140 E Walton Pl between Michigan Ave and Mies van der Rohe Way (312-787-2200). El: Red to Chicago. Bus: 143, 144, 145, 146, 147, 151 (24hrs). Mon–Fri 1:30pm–midnight; Sat, Sun 1pm–midnight. Average cocktail: $8.*

(✕ ✳ **Pippin's Tavern** Who the hell are all these people? Late at night, this place attracts a curiously diverse pack of frat boys, cowboys, corporate suits and the occasional hippie. It's a far cry from the upper-crust crowd we'd expect, which is precisely why we like this Gold Coast rebel. *806 N Rush St between Chicago Ave and Pearson St (312-787-5435). El: Red to Chicago. Bus: 3, X4, 10, 26, 66 (24hrs), 125, 143, 144, 145, 146, 147, 151 (24hrs). Sun–Fri 11am–4am; Sat 11am–5am. Average beer: $5.*

✕ **The Reagle Beagle** Yes, this is really happening: You're sitting in a cheesy lounge, on ugly office furniture, and you're listening to the theme from *The Love Boat*. The televisions really are showing programs (and commercials) from the early '80s, and your drink truly is called the "Tony Danza Extravaganza." We know, we know—it feels like you're in some bad, early '80s sitcom. But you're not. You're simply in a bar dedicated to them. *160 E Grand Ave between Michigan Ave and St. Clair St (312-755-9645). El: Red to Grand. Bus: 2, 29, 65, 66 (24hrs), 124. 4pm–2am. Average cocktail: $7.*

✕ **Ritz-Carlton Bar** This bar sits high above Michigan Ave, just north of the fountain and atrium in the 12th-floor lobby of the Ritz-Carlton Hotel. And as could be expected from a bar inside one of the city's most luxurious hotels, this place is old-school swanksville. Chairs upholstered in soft leather, ribbed corduroy and plush velvet surround ornate tables in a copper-tinted room that, after a couple martinis, you'll never want to leave. *160 E Pearson St between Michigan Ave and Mies van der Rohe Way (312-573-5223). El: Red to Chicago. Bus: 3, 4 (24hrs), X4, 10, 26, 125, 143, 144, 145, 146, 147, 151 (24hrs). Noon–2am. Average cocktail: $12.*

✕ **Season's Lounge** Cloth napkins, linen doilies and exceptional cocktails like the ginger martini (with fresh ginger shavings collected at the bottom of the glass): Would you expect anything less from the Four Seasons? And would you expect to pay anything less than ten bucks per drink? Good. Then be prepared to have your expectations met. *120 E Delaware Pl between Ernst Ct and Michigan Ave (312-280-8800). El: Red to Chicago. Bus: 36, 143, 144, 145, 146, 147, 148, 151 (24hrs). Sun–Thu*

Sweet relief Butterfly
Social Club's menu of
nonalcoholic drinks
includes the cocoa elixir.

11:30am–11:30pm; Fri, Sat 11:30am–2am. Average cocktail: $10.

▼ **Second Story Bar** You wouldn't believe the brand of tie-loosened debauchery that happens at this fantastic dive on a nightly basis. Unless, of course, you climb the carpeted stairway—following the thumping bass and uninhibited laughter coming from behind the heavy, unmarked door—and step inside. Once you see this place, you'll believe anything. *157 E Ohio St between St. Clair St and Michigan Ave (312-923-9536). El: Red to Grand. Bus: 2, 3, 10, 26, 125, 143, 144, 145, 146, 147, 148, 151 (24hrs), 157. Sun–Fri noon–2am; Sat noon–3am. Average cocktail: $4. Cash only.*

✕ **676 Bar** If you can ignore the chain-mail curtains on the windows, we highly recommend this Omni Hotel lounge for their cocktails. The Cucumber Gimlet (sweetened with a house-made lime cordial) and pink grapefruit cosmo are both delicious—and strong enough that you'll cease to care that they cost twice the amount they should. *676 N Michigan Ave at Huron St (312-944-7676). El: Red to Grand. Bus: 65, 145, 146, 147, 151 (24hrs). Sun–Thu noon–11:30pm; Fri–Sat noon–12:30pm. Average cocktail: $12.*

✕ **Streeters Tavern** When we asked our waitress at this dimly lit basement bar if there were any specialty beers on tap, she looked awfully confused. Despite its wide selection, it's a question that doesn't get asked a lot. Instead, regulars (a youngish, button-down crowd) suck down $3 Coors bottles, listen to the classic rock–fueled jukebox and play table tennis, pool and foosball. Stop by during the week when frat boys are nowhere to be found. *50 E Chicago Ave between Wabash Ave and Rush St (312-944-5206). El: Red to Chicago. Bus: 3 (24hrs), 10, 66 (24hrs). Sun–Fri 11am–4am; Sat 11am–5am. Average beer: $5.*

✕ **Taps Lounge** Venturing into the famous "Tip Top Tap" building (a.k.a. the Allerton Hotel), we expected to find a bar that hearkens back to the "good old days": jazz quintets doing Armstrong, flappers dancing the Charleston...that sort of thing. But in fact, this is a quiet, sophisticated spot where one can have a cocktail by himself, and if not relive the old days, at least think about them in peace. *701 N Michigan Ave at Huron St (312-440-1500). El: Red to Chicago. Bus: 3, 4 (24hrs), X4, 10, 26, 125, 143, 144, 145, 146, 147, 148, 151 (24hrs). Sun–Thu 3pm–midnight; Fri, Sat 3pm–12:30am. Average cocktail: $10.*

(✕ **Timothy O'Toole's** In one corner of this subterranean sports bar you'll find frat boys flirting with the bartenders. In another, you'll see an entire accounting department downing beers and watching various games on the 50 screens. And somewhere there's a table of Northwestern med students—but they're just trying to relax, so leave the questions about your gallbladder for your doctor. *622 N Fairbanks Ct at Ontario St (312-642-0700). El: Red to Grand. Bus: 2, 3, 66 (24hrs), 157. 11am–3am. Average beer: $4.*

✕ **Winners Lounge** Well, "winners" might be a stretch, but we're certainly not going to call the folks who sit at the green Formica counter in this windowless Holiday Inn lobby bar losers. Besides, we're right there with them, watching the television in silence and slowly sipping our beers with satisfaction, knowing that nobody's going to find (much less bother) us here. *300 E Ohio St at Fairbanks Ct (312-787-6100). El: Red to Grand. Bus: 2, 3, 66 (24hrs), 157. Mon–Sat 11:30am–2am; Sun noon–midnight. Average beer: $5.*

The Zebra Lounge Around the corner from Division Street's jack-ass bar scene is this cozy one-room saloon tucked inside the Canterbury Court Hotel. Singles, socialites, cigar smokers and even sexagenarians pack themselves in on busy weekends. The zebra theme is a bit reckless, but distinctive. The ultrared lighting, on the other hand, makes you wonder if students from the Art Institute are going to emerge from behind the bar with developed film. A nightly piano player keeps the Zebra refreshingly unhip with old-school faves like "Do You Know the Way to San Jose." *1220 N State Pkwy at Division St (312-642-5140). El: Red to Clark/Division. Bus: 22 (24hrs), 36, 70. Mon–Fri 5pm–2am; Sat 5pm–3am; Sun 6pm–2am. Average cocktail: $6.*

Loop/West Loop

Aria Bar A surprising number of locals hang at this hotel bar in the Fairmont Chicago thanks to its hip-but-not-trying-too-hard atmosphere. Unlike so many bars, there are plenty of comfy places to sit: the tiny tables in the middle of the room, on bar stools with backs on them or in leather booths. *200 N Columbus Dr at Lake St (312-444-9494). Bus: 4 (24hrs), 20 (24hrs), 60 (24hrs). Sun–Thu 10:30am–1am; Fri–Sat 10:30am–2am. Average cocktail: $9.*

✕ ✳ **Beer Bistro** Doing its part to keep the West Loop from succumbing to all the glitz and glamour of Randolph Street is this tavern, which carries upward of 100 beers, including Dogfish Head 60 Minute IPA and Lindemans' Framboise lambic on draft—both of which you can witness guys downing during Sunday-afternoon football. *1061 W Madison St between Morgan and Aberdeen Sts (312-433-0013). Bus: 8, 19, 20 (24hrs). Sun–Fri 11am–2am; Sat 11am–3am. Average beer: $4.50.*

✕ ✳ **The Big Downtown** This place claims it serves "Chicago's best Bloody Mary," and as famed pitcher Dizzy Dean said, "It ain't braggin' if you can back it up." The Big Downtown can. Said drink comes with a theatrical garnish of a leafy stalk of celery, pickled asparagus spear and *haricot vert*, a jumbo olive and a sweet gherkin. The rim is powdered with celery salt, and the secret spicy tomato mix blends nicely with top-shelf vodka. *Palmer House Hilton, 124 S Wabash Ave at Monroe St (312-917-7399). El: Brown, Green, Orange, Pink, Purple (rush hrs) to Adams. Sun–Fri 6:30am–2am; Sat 1am–3am. Average cocktail: $8.*

Butterfly Social Club Take the aesthetic of Rain Forest Cafe, throw in some "jungle beats" and hire a crew of skinny, modern-day hippies to run the place, and you might have something resembling this sister bar to Funky Buddha Lounge. Concerned with your overall wellness as much as your level of inebriation, the alcohol here is all organic. But you may as well order one of the delicious nonalcoholic drinks (such as the milk shake–like cocoa elixir)—you won't need a drink to feel trippy in here. *726 W Grand Ave between Union and Milwaukee Aves (312-666-1695). El: Blue to Grand. Bus: 8, 56, 65. Tue–Sat 9pm–2am. Average cocktail: $10.*

✕ **Cactus Bar** Traders fight frat boys for a seat at this expansive Loop watering hole, where the beach-bum decor makes them feel like they've died and gone to spring break. Cigars, Coronas and shots of tequila add to the Cancún vibe, but don't expect to see any girls in bikinis. *404 S Wells St at Van Buren St (312-922-3830). El: Brown, Purple (rush hrs), Orange to LaSalle. Mon–Fri 11am–midnight; Sun 4pm–midnight (closed Sat). Average beer: $5.*

In the spirit Pippin's Tavern has the oldest liquor license on Rush Street.

✕ **Cal's Liquors** Cal himself slings insults and Old Style at this Loop dive bar (under the El), where a handful of stools are warmed by bike messengers, construction workers and the occasional gritty punk coming to check out bands like Urinal Mints and Rabid Rabbit that bang out music from a tiny corner of the room. *400 S Wells St at Van Buren St (312-922-6392). El: Brown, Orange, Purple (rush hour only) to LaSalle. Mon–Thu 7am–7pm; Fri 7am–2am; Sat 7pm–2am. Average beer: $3.*

✕ ✱ **Crocodile Lounge** Crikey! A late-night lounge in the financial district? Quite a find. Once the after-work crowd has thinned, this spot turns into a hip-hop grind fest. The exposed brick gives the space its industrial panache, and nighttime bar nosh offers fuel to keep your mack game up. *221 W Van Buren St between Wells and Franklin Sts (312-427-9290). El: Brown, Pink, Purple (rush hrs), Orange to LaSalle/Van Buren. Mon 5pm–2am; Tue–Thu 11am–2am; Fri 11am–4am; Sat 10pm–5am (closed Sun) (hours subject to change). Average cocktail: $10.*

(✕ **Dugan's Pub** Who knew the Irish and the Greeks got along so well? Early in the evening, this friendly watering hole seems to be filled with people waiting for a table at Greek Islands. Later, off-duty cops start filing in, not so much to keep the peace, but to grab a beer and a handful of free popcorn. *128 S Halsted St between Washington Blvd and Randolph St (312-421-7191). El: Green to Clinton. Bus: 8, 20 (24hrs), 126. Mon–Sat 2pm–4am; Sun noon–4am. Average beer: $4.*

✕ **Emerald Loop Bar & Grill** It's quite an accomplishment for a place this huge to look full. But we certainly understand why this new bar is packed with suits

after quitting time. The tall bay windows allow for a fantastic view of the city, there are plenty of beers on tap, and the menu is an expansive collection of better-than-average pub grub. Just don't come expecting old-school Dublin; it's more like an upscale sports lounge, Chicago-style. *216 N Wabash Ave between Haddock Pl and Lake St (312-263-0200). El: Brown, Green, Pink, Purple (rush hrs), Orange to State. Mon–Fri 7am–2am; Sat 11am–3am; Sun 11am–2am. Average beer: $4.50.*

✕ **Emmit's** Of course it's crazy on the weekends, but even on weekend afternoons, regulars gather at this bilevel, wood-heavy pub to watch the game and—judging from the bottles of Jameson suspended upside-down above the bar (all the easier to pour)—drink a lot of Irish whiskey. *495 N Milwaukee Ave at Grand Ave (312-563-9631). El: Blue to Grand. Bus: 8, 56, 65. Mon–Thu 4pm–2am; Fri 3pm–2am; Sat 11am–3am; Sun 11am–2am. Average beer: $5.*

✕ **Exchequer Restaurant & Pub** Banking on its building's supposed history as a former Capone speakeasy, this Loop joint draws its share of hungry tourists who—along with their beer, burger and fries—get a lunchtime eyeful of Chicago history via the photos and newspaper clippings plastered on the walls. Its downtown location situated beside the elevated tracks also makes this a great place for a little heel kicking and tie loosening after work. *226 S Wabash Ave between Jackson Blvd and Adams St (312-939-5633). El: Brown, Green, Orange, Pink, Purple (rush hrs) to Adams. Mon–Thu 11am–11pm; Fri, Sat 11am–midnight, Sun noon–9am. Average beer: $3.*

✕ **14 Karat Lounge** Despite the name, the after-work crowd that loosens their ties and slides up to the bar here sport very little bling. Instead, it's the slew of eccentric characters this place (attached to Ada's Deli) attracts—both bartenders and barflies alike—that makes this place a diamond in the rough. *14 S Wabash Ave between Madison and Monroe Sts (312-214-4282). El: Blue, Red to Monroe; Brown, Green, Orange, Purple (rush hrs) to Madison. Sun–Fri 6am–2am; Sat 6am–3am. Average beer: $5.*

✕ ♦ **Fulton Lounge** Saturday nights at this Fulton warehouse district hot spot are packed, so expect to wait to get in and again at the bar. Opt for a weekday when there's space to take in the charming bookshelves, exposed brick walls and diverse crowd. Now you can see what all the fuss is about. *955 W Fulton St at Morgan St (312-942-9500). Bus: 65 Grand. Mon–Fri 4pm–2am; Sat 4pm–3am. Average cocktail: $8.*

G Cue Billiards and Restaurant The menu boasts 30 martinis, but don't be surprised when the bartender thumbs through Mr. Boston's crib sheets to concoct them. The "Mag Mile Manhattan" features smoky and silky 18-year-old Elijah Craig bourbon, but beware the heavy-handed buzzkill of sweet vermouth. More than two-dozen professional pool tables fill the bilevel space, and the jukebox is packed with crooners—Sinatra, Dino and Darin—lending an old-school vibe. *157 N Morgan St between Randolph and Lake Sts (312-850-3170). El: Green, Pink to Clinton. Bus: 20 Madison (24hrs). Mon–Fri 11am–2pm; Sat 5pm–3am; Sun 5pm–2am. Average cocktail: $10.*

✕ **Globe Bar** Although it has such a prime Chicago location—the windows look out on Michigan Avenue—it's hard to think of this bar inside China Grill as "global." Even the enormous half globe that hovers above diners in the bar doesn't do it. But then you'll get the steep bill for all those delicious cocktails (we like the Orange Blossom mojito) and you'll get it: It's the prices that are out of this world. *230 N Michigan Ave between Lake St and Wacker Pl (312-334-6700). El: Brown, Green, Orange, Purple (rush hrs), Red to State/Lake. Bus: 2, 3, 10, 26, 143, 144, 145, 146, 147, 151 (24hrs), 157. Sun–Thu 11:30am–10:30pm; Sat, Sun 11:30am–11pm. Average cocktail: $12.*

The Grillroom If Sinatra and steakhouses are your scene, try this Loop chophouse-wine bar. Poised professionals line the mahogany bar, sipping their way through a list of 40 (mostly domestic) wines by the glass while Rat Pack standards play in the background. *33 W Monroe St between State and Dearborn Sts (312-960-0000). El: Blue, Red to Monroe; Brown, Green, Orange, Purple (rush hrs) to Madison. Mon–Fri 11:30am–12am; Sat 5pm–12am; Sun 5pm–11pm. Average glass: $8.*

✕ ✳ **Hawkeye's Bar and Grill Chicago** Come for the pitchers, stay for the pizza—or something like that. Hawkeye's doesn't really impress in either department (unless you like your Miller lite and your pies plain), but when you're rolling deep in a pack of Phi Kappa Psis out on the prowl and you've managed to catch the eye of one of the well-endowed waitresses, it doesn't really matter what she's carrying to your table, now does it? *1458 W Taylor St between Bishop and Laflin Sts (312-226-3951). El: Blue to Racine. Bus: 7, 9, 12, 60. Sun–Fri 11am–2am; Sat 11am–3am. Average beer: $3.*

✕ **Jak's Tap** If you're wondering what sets this friendly West Loop bar and grill apart from every other pub that's packed tightly with graduate- and law-school types, it's the selection of 40 draught beers (including three tasty styles from our Hoosier faves Three Floyds). The large food menu goes beyond the average pub, with eats like baby back ribs, a hummus platter and an assortment of salads. *901 W Jackson Blvd at Peoria St (312-666-1700). El: Blue to UIC-Halsted. Bus: 8, 20 (24hrs), 126. Mon–Wed 11am–midnight; Thu, Fri 11am–2am; Sat noon–2am; Sun noon–1am. Average beer: $4.*

✕ ✳ ◖ **Jefferson Tap** This bar looks like a familiar North Side baseball-crazed, watered-down pub (and if transplanted above Division Street, we're sure the endless flat screens would serve it well) but feels a lot friendlier. The vibe's got less to do with sports and more to do with West Loopers chasing their work blues with pint upon pint, hella-delicious bar fare and downloaded jukebox tunes. *325 N Jefferson St at Wayman St (312-648-0100). El: Green, Blue, Pink to Clinton. Bus: 8, 20 (24hrs), 56. Sun–Wed 11am–2am; Thu, Fri 11am–4am; Sat 11am–5am. Average beer: $4.*

✕ **Lake & Union Grill & Tap** When the whistle blows, this West Loop hideout turns from desolate dive to serious unwinding joint. The peanuts might be complimentary, but the lap dancers sure aren't ($10 a pop, Tuesdays and Thursdays from 5 to 8pm). What these fly-by-night amateurs lack in youthfulness, they overcompensate for with changes of clothes. It's worth it just to chat up a working stiff with a, well, you get it. *666 W Lake St between Desplaines St and Union Ave (312-559-0036). El: Green, Pink to Clinton. Bus: 8, 14, 20 (24hrs), 56. Mon–Fri 11am–9pm; Sat 11am–2pm (closed Sun). Average beer: $3.*

◖ ✕ **Miller's Pub** Whether it's lunchtime or late at night, this steak-and-a-beer standby captures a classic Chicago feel in a far more subtle manner than most. It could be the bartender with his slick vest and tie or the towering walls of signed photos from satisfied Chicago sports and entertainment celebs. But we like to think that classic-ness is

mainly due to the straight-talking clientele who like their whiskey on the rocks and their ties loose. *134 S Wabash Ave at Adams Sts (312-645-5377). El: Brown, Green, Orange, Purple (rush hrs) to Adams; Blue, Red to Monroe. 11am–2am. Average beer: $4.*

Monk's Pub For more than 30 years, this cavernous Loop tavern has cornered the market on medieval dives. Beyond the heavy doors that seem to hide a monastery, you'll find an after-work crowd of mostly suits and occasional skirts downing beer and adding to the piles of peanut shells littering the floor. *205 W Lake St between Wells and Franklin Sts (312-357-6665). El: Blue, Brown, Green, Orange, Purple (rush hrs) to Clark. Mon–Fri 9am–2am. Average cocktail: $5.*

✕ **Old Timers Restaurant and Lounge** We'd never advocate being crocked while you're on the clock, but if you must get your breakfast buzz, nuzzle up to the bosom of this well-worn, wood-paneled bar/diner in the Loop. Seating choices include the sliced-up stools or one of many vinyl booths. The grizzled waitresses have more than an ounce of attitude and won't think twice about dropping a little more Hennessy in your coffee as you scarf down a Denver omelette. *75 E Lake St at Garland Ct (312-332-3561). El: Brown, Green, Purple (rush hrs), Orange, Pink to State. Mon–Fri 6am–2am; Sat 7am–1am (closed Sun). Average beer: $3.*

✕ **Poag Mahone's** The burger here has been exclaimed by *GQ* magazine as one you have to try before you die. We tried it and…well, let's just say we prefer this Irish hangout as a place for a few pints of Bass. And if we're really craving a burger, we'll order one at night—during the day this place is too packed to enjoy anything. *333 S Wells St between Jackson Blvd and Van Buren St (312-566-9100). El: Brown, Orange,*

High note Cocktails get the diva treatment at Aria Bar.

Purple (rush hrs) to Quincy. Mon–Fri 10am–9pm (closed Sat, Sun). Average beer: $5.

Richard's Bar A bistro in France it ain't, but curiously enough, this tidy, dark dive takes a few traditions from across the Atlantic. The bartender—a skinny, older gentleman—dresses in an immaculately crisp white button-down, and you can buy hard-boiled eggs for 75 cents. The larger-than-life posters of De Niro on the wall, however, are completely American. *725 W Grand Ave between Halsted St and Union Ave (312-421-4597). El: Blue to Grand. Bus: 8, 56, 65. Mon–Fri 7:30am–2am; Sat 9am–3am, Sun noon–2am. Average beer: $3.*

✕ **17 West** What used to be the Berghoff bar is now essentially a cleaner version of its former self (with a frilly martini list to boot). The room is a little airier since the wall between restaurant and bar has been taken down, the century-old German pub was always about that gorgeous, room-length bar. And the mix of tourists, after-work suits and afternoon men won't notice the renovations when they're bellying up to that wooden monolith. *17 W Adams St between State and Dearborn Sts (312-427-3170). El: Blue, Red to Monroe. Mon–Thu 11am–9pm; Fri, Sat 11am–10pm (closed Sun). Average beer: $5.*

(✕ **Spectrum Bar** Greektown is home to a shady character or two, and at first it may seem like they'd congregate here. But if you ignore the eerie, Coen brothers–esque neon-red glow of the place and focus on the cheap drinks, cheap bar grub and electronic darts, you'll melt into the scene just fine. *233 S Halsted St between Adams St and Jackson Blvd (312-715-0770). El: Blue to UIC-Halsted. Bus: 8 Halsted, 126 Jackson. Sun–Fri 11am–4am; Sat 11am–5am. Average cocktail: $6.*

✕ **Third Rail Tavern** West Loop residents have this comfy place to escape their condos, lofts and loft-condos. The owners say they're trying to capture "old-school Chicago," which to them means 14-foot exposed-brick walls, warm lighting, a beautiful antique bar and well-dressed clientele—not rusty Old Style signage and sepia-toned photos from the 1893 World's Fair. *1133 W Madison St at May St (312-432-9107). Bus: 20 Madison (24hrs). Mon–Fri 3pm–2am; Sat 11am–3am; Sun 11am–2am. Average beer: $5.*

✕ **Villains Bar and Grill** Though this bar would undoubtedly like to think of itself as badass, we found nothing villainous about it. In fact, considering its proximity to the Loop, their penchant for playing good music (such as low-key indie-rockers the Good Life), and impressive eye for decor (note the Andy Warhol wallpaper), we thought this place was pretty sweet. *649 S Clark St between Harrison and Polk Sts (312-356-9992). El: Blue to LaSalle, Red to Harrison. Bus: 12, 24, 36, 127. Mon–Fri 5pm–2am; Sat 5pm–3am (closed Sun). Average beer: $4.*

Whiskey Blue The bar at the Loop's W Hotel-City Center attracts local and visiting scenesters alike. Expect lounge-worthy leather chairs, models moonlighting as waitresses and sexed-up singles looking to clink Cosmos. And while the well-stocked bar lives up to its name with dozens of whiskeys, bartenders also make mean martinis and Manhattans for the nostalgic set. *172 W Adams St between LaSalle and Wells Sts (312-782-4933). El: Brown, Orange, Purple (rush hrs) to Quincy. 4pm–2am. Average cocktail: $8.*

Windsor's Lounge Carpeting and cigar bars don't usually mix, and this ornate lobby bar at the Palmer Hilton is a good example why. Even though it smells like your great-

uncle's armchair, you can't beat the scenery here: marble walls, grand chandeliers, a beautiful domed ceiling and countless questionable (and entertaining) fashion choices from tourists. *17 E Monroe St at State St (312-726-7500). El: Blue, Red to Monroe; Brown, Green, Pink, Purple (rush hrs), Orange to Madison. 3pm–1am. Average cocktail: $9.*

South Loop

✕ **Billy Goat III** An artery-clogging breakfast can be found at any greasy spoon, but this South Loop outpost of the Billy Goat (brighter and not as historically charming as the original) specializes in slinging drinks alongside plates of steak and eggs. Purists may be shocked to see fries being served, an act that flies in the face of the original tavern's famous "No fries, chips" mantra. But it's nothing another beer can't soothe. *330 S Wells St between Van Buren St and Jackson Blvd (312-554-0297). El: Brown, Pink, Purple (rush hrs) Orange to LaSalle. Mon–Fri 6am–2am; Sat 8am–4am (closed Sun). Average beer: $3.*

✳ **Cork & Kerry** Hang with the Beverly crowd at this Far South Side institution, where Irish brogues are the norm and the staff is among the friendliest in town. The fenced-in deck has a homey, antique decor (i.e., wagon wheels and hanging plants), along with two bars that serve $1 domestic drafts during Sox and Cubs home games. *11610 S Western Ave between 116th and 117th Sts (773-445-2675). Bus: 49A, 103, Pace 349. Mon–Fri 2pm–midnight; Sat noon–3am; Sun noon–2am. Average beer: $2.75.*

✕ **Cullinan's Stadium Club** Whether you play sports or just watch them on TV, this Beverly institution has got you covered. You'd probably have to become a die-hard regular to join the bar-sponsored rec teams, but if you're just looking to play some darts and catch the game, everyone's welcome—so long as you don't start talking smack about the Sox. *10614 S Western Ave between 106th and 107th Sts (773-445-5620). Bus: 49A, 119, Pace 349. Sun–Fri 11am–2am; Sat noon–3am. Average beer: $3.50.*

End Zone Not to be confused with ESPN Zone, this cozy South Side spot banks on real sports fans and loyal locals rather than tourists and buffalo wings. You can still catch just about any major pro or college game on one of the tubes, and if you get bored with the game, you can roam the room, checking out the vintage photos and clippings of sports legends from an era that predates bling-teeth. *10034 S Western Ave between between 100th and 101st Sts (773-238-7969). Bus: 49A, 103, Pace 349. 1 Sun–Fri 1pm–2am; Sat 1pm–3am. Average beer: $3.*

(**George's Lounge** Though old George has been bellying up to the big bar in the sky for decades, his small tavern survives untouched, save the digital juke. A true dive, within these smoke-stained, wood-paneled walls, the beer's mostly canned and on-tap suds are limited to Bud and Bud Light. Not exactly what we would call a selection, but the construction crews who frequent George's like it just fine. *646 S Wabash Ave between Harrison St and Balbo Dr (312-427-3964). El: Brown, Green, Orange, Pink, Purple to Madison. 11am–4am. Average beer: $3. Cash only.*

✕ **Grace O'Malley's** You'll consider staying in the South Loop forever just to make this place your local hangout, so make sure you have some time on your hands before you belly up to the beautiful, shiny wood bar. And be prepared for some drooling when the guy next to you orders a burger on one of the soft pretzel buns. *1416 S Michigan Ave between*

Puttin' on the Ritz
Imbibe in swanky style
at the Ritz-Carlton Bar.

14th and 16th Sts (312-588-1800). El: Green, Orange, Red to Roosevelt. Bus: 1, 4 (24hrs), 12. Mon–Fri 11:30am–2am; Sat 9am–3am; Sun 9:30am–midnight. Average cocktail: $6.

✗ ✳ **Hackney's** Pity the Printer's Row outpost of this local pub. In the suburbs Hackney's gets so much more respect—people are constantly drooling over the famous "Hackneyburger." Its lone city outpost isn't given as much acclaim, but it's nonetheless a warm, inviting, friendly place to get a drink. And they seem to be grooming other Chicago legends: The drinks menu features local beers, vodkas and gins. *733 S Dearborn St between Harrison and Polk Sts (312-461-1116). El: Red to Harrison. Bus: 2, 6, 22, 36, 62. Mon–Wed 10:30am–11pm; Thu 10:30am–midnight; Fri, Sat 10:30am–1am; Sun 10:30am–11pm. Average beer: $5.*

✗ ✳ **Kasey's Tavern** The people-watching at Kasey's is almost as good as it is from the benches around the Printer's Row fountain, but this popular watering hole's got beer. And pizza. Advantage: Kasey's. You'll recognize the same Irish-English-pub vibe from up north, and you may spy a frat rat, but generally the crowd—like the bookish, lofty-artsy neighborhood—is definitely mixed, especially when it comes to baseball loyalties. *701 S Dearborn Ave between Harrison and Polk Sts (312-427-7992). El: Red to Harrison. Bus: 22 (24hrs), 36, 62. Sun–Fri 11am–2am; Sat 11am–3am. Average beer: $3.*

Kitty O'Shea's There are endless Irish pubs in the city to choose from, and this one, with its dark wood interior and menu of typical pub grub (fish and chips, corned beef and cabbage) blends in with the rest of them. So why patronize this one over the others? Because it's in the

Chicago Hilton. You never know when a visiting Irishman from the Old Country is going to walk inside. *720 S Michigan Ave at Balbo Dr (312-294-6860). El: Red to Harrison. Bus: 1, 2, 3, 4 (24hrs), 6, 10, 14, 26, 127, 146. 11am–2am. Average beer: $4.50.*

M Lounge One step inside this sleek, cool and narrow South Loop bar and you'll be convinced that the *M* stands for mellow. Plush velvet chairs, slick leather couches, a soft jazz soundtrack and easygoing cocktails like the Orange Crush martini attract locals of every type—except for those who can't keep their cool. *1520 S Wabash Ave between 14th Pl and 16th St (312-447-0201). El: Green, Orange, Red to Roosevelt. Bus: 1, 4 (24hrs), 12, 29, 62 (24hrs). Mon–Thu 4pm–midnight; Fri, Sat 4pm–2am (closed Sun). Average cocktail: $10.*

Manhattan's Bar Succeeding in the bar biz often requires hooch hucksterism, like daily drink specials and karaoke. This small, steps-from-the-Loop bar isn't immune, but at the end of the workday, the crowd of lawyers, law students and traders applaud the basics: decent prices, no-frills munchies and a killer soundtrack (think old Bowie) played loud enough to appreciate but low enough to talk over. *415 S Dearborn Ave between Congress Pkwy and Van Buren St (312-957-0460). El: Blue, Red to Jackson; Brown, Orange, Purple (rush hrs) to Van Buren. Bus: 21, X21, 22 (24hrs), 62 (24hrs). Mon–Fri 11am–2am; Sat 1pm–2am. Average cocktail: $5.*

❨ ✗ **South Loop Club** South Loop Boy's Club is more like it. This is the place where local bachelors and jocks from surrounding universities come to get hammered on one of the

80 kinds of beer, scarf down a pile of greasy food, watch the game and, of course, bug the waitress for her phone number. *701 S State St at Balbo Dr (312-427-2787). El: Red to Harrison. Bus: 2, 6, 29, 36, 62 (24hrs). Sun–Fri 11am–4am; Sat 11am–5am. Average beer: $4.50.*

Tantrum The only downside to this sophisticated South Loop lounge is its ridiculous name, which doesn't do the low-lit, laid-back vibe here a bit of justice. But sitting in one of the plush booths and sipping one of the signature martinis, you'll be way too relaxed to be up in arms. *1023 S State St between 9th and 11th Sts (312-939-9160). El: Green, Orange, Red to Roosevelt. Bus: 12, 29, 62 (24hrs). Mon–Thu 5pm–2am; Fri 2:30pm–2am; Sat 5pm–3am (closed Sun). Average cocktail: $9.*

✕ **Wabash Tap** Put your money to good use (i.e., for something other than beer) at this popular, no-frills after-work joint. Every Wednesday night, a guest (i.e., amateur) bartender gets behind the bar, slinging drinks for a cause (all tips go to his or her charity of choice). So drink up, but skip the mediocre bar food—nobody needs to be that generous. *1233 S Wabash Ave between Roosevelt Rd and 13th St (312-360-9488). El: Green, Orange, Red to Roosevelt. Bus: 1, 3, 4 (24hrs), 12, 29, 62 (24hrs). Sun–Fri 11:30am–2am; Sat 11:30am–3am. Average beer: $4.*

✕ **Weather Mark Tavern** We could have sworn the days of sailor bars were over, but this cheery, nautically themed bar (full-size sails divide the long room into distinct canoodling areas) brought it back, South Loop style. In other words, think sun-kissed yuppie boaters, not pirates. No boat of your own? Refreshing cocktails—like the lemongrass-spiked "Almost Stormy"—do a decent job of sailing you away. *1503 S Michigan Ave between 14th and 16th Sts (312-588-0230). El: Green, Orange, Red to Roosevelt. Bus: 1, 4 (24hrs), 12. Mon–Fri 11:30am–2am; Sat 10:30–3am; Sun 10:30–midnight. Average cocktail: $5.*

Bridgeport

✕ **Bertucci's Corner** This place is primarily a restaurant, but we like just stopping in for a Peroni at the bar. You'll probably rub elbows with old Italian locals who remember Chinatown before it was Chinatown. The joint's been around since '33, and the regulars whose mugs hang from the ceiling are long gone, but they're immortalized in a dusty photo hanging behind the bar. Hungry? Hearty pastas or sausage and peppers will work. *300 W 24th St at Princeton Ave (312-225-2848). El: Red to Cermak-Chinatown. Bus: 21, 24, 44. Mon–Fri 11am–2am; Sat 4pm–3am; Sun 3pm–2am. Average beer: $3.*

Mitchell's Tap The Sox sign over the door and the Bridgeport address should clue you in that this ain't no yuppie bar. Still, newcomers are welcomed by the friendly bartender (who upholds the area's third-round's-on-us custom) and a good selection of beers like Delirium Tremens and Tetleys. *3356 S Halsted St between 33rd Pl and 34th St (773-927-6073). Bus: 8 Halsted. Sun–Fri 11am–2am; Sat 11am–3am. Average beer: $3.*

✕ **Red-I** So you're sounding pretty good in the shower these days, huh? Well it's almost as if the people behind this new Chinatown lounge heard you singing, because the focus of their all-red space is the karaoke machines. Show the entire bar your skills, or simply reserve a VIP room and show off your latest Beyoncé rendition for your friends. *2201 S Wentworth Ave at Cermak Rd (312-927-7334). El: Red to Cermak-Chinatown. Bus: 21 Cermak, 62 Archer (24hrs). Sun–Fri 5pm–2am; Sat 5pm–3am. Average cocktail: $5. Cash only.*

✕ **Schaller's Pump** There's no better place to cheer on the Sox than this down-home, blue-collar institution that's been serving up cold ones since 1881. Arrive at least a half hour before game time if you're planning on eating—and you should definitely plan on eating. Just-like-Mom-made classics include crispy pork tenderloin smothered in perfect pan gravy and greaseless fried chicken. Add doting servers, cheap beer and a living room–like atmosphere, and you've got the best sports experience short of front-row tickets. *3714 S Halsted St between 37th and 38th Sts (773-376-6332). El: Red to Sox-35th. Bus: 8 Halsted, 35 35th. Mon–Fri 11am–2am; Sat 4pm–3am; Sun 4pm–9pm. Average beer: $2.50. Cash only.*

South Side

BeviAmo Wine Bar Draped in more fabric than a *Project Runway* rerun and with more incense in the air than a Logan Square yoga studio, this place doesn't really scream "Italian wine bar" to us. Neither do the DJs, who turn what would otherwise feel like drinking in a Moroccan tent into some sexy and sultry sipping. *1358 W Taylor St at Loomis St (312-455-8255). El: Blue to Racine. Bus: 12 Roosevelt, 60 Blue Island/*

Shaken, not stirred Indulge in fancy cocktails at The Big Downtown.

Smooth sailing A nautical theme sets the tone at the Weather Mark Tavern.

26th (24hrs). Mon–Fri 5:30pm–2am; Sat 5:30–3am; Sun 6:30pm–2am. Average glass of wine: $6.

✗ **The Drum and Monkey** This cozy, immaculately detailed Irish pub (formerly Four Corners) might be the last thing you'd expect on the spaghetti strip of Taylor Street, but soon it'll be first on your "places to swig pints and shovel eats from across the pond" list. Just ask any of the UIC doctors who are regulars. *1435 W Taylor St at Bishop St (312-563-1874). El: Blue to Polk. Bus: 12 Roosevelt. Sun–Fri 11am–2am; Sat 11am–3am. Average beer: $5.*

✗ **Fifty Yard Line Bar and Grille** Waitresses in white dress shirts adhere to a dress code, so you better follow suit: no sneakers, jeans or ball caps after 9pm. The rule keeps out what the owner deems as "riffraff," while the DJ's smooth jazz and "Quiet Storm" style of soul brings in the steppers. Novices better brush up before jumping on the floor, or sit back with a drink and watch the silk-suited shimmy. *69 E 75th St between Wabash and Michigan Aves (773-846-0005). El: Red to 79th. Bus: 24, 29, 75, 79 (24hrs). 3pm–2am. Average cocktail: $4.*

✗ **Illinois Bar & Grill** One could do a lot worse than grabbing a bucket of beer and a cheeseburger as big as a sofa cushion at this sports pub—especially when said burger comes with grilled onions and hand-cut fries. This is the flagship joint (one of three locations in and around Chicago), and it's a comfortable spot, with an old-fashioned tin ceiling, brick walls and plenty of flirty UIC students. Now if the bartenders could just learn to pour a beer with a decent head on it, we'd be all set. *1421 W Taylor St between Loomis and*

Bishop Sts (312-666-6666). El: Blue to Polk. Bus: 9 Ashland (24hrs), 12 Roosevelt. 8am–2am. Average beer: $4.

✗ ☀ **Junior's Sports Bar** You can take the sports fan out of the sports bar and put him in this sophisticated University Village lounge. But even couches covered in faux suede and slick flat screens in each booth won't take the sports bar out of the fan. For that we're thankful because despite the swankiness, this college spot from the folks behind Cans and Four doesn't have an ounce of attitude. *724 W Maxwell St between Union Ave and Halsted St (773-276-7582). Bus: 8 Halsted, 12 Roosevelt. Sun–Fri 10am–2am; Sat 10am–3am. Average beer: $5.*

❲ **New Apartment Lounge** Every Tuesday night, jazz legend Von Freeman attracts a crowd of admirers from all over the city, along with a cabal of eager beaver instrument-toting youngsters who hope to get in on the end-of-the-show jam session. The rest of the week, the crowd thins to a group of neighborhood regulars. *504 E 75th St at Eberhart Ave (773-483-7728). Bus: 75 74th-75th. Sun–Fri 2pm–4am; Sat 2pm–5am. Average beer: $3.*

✗ **Skylark** This speakeasy-esque space—a vacuous room, lined with booths and sprinkled with tables and chairs—is a nightly respite for local artists. The Tater Tots are a greasy must-have—wash 'em down with a $2 Pabst. Don't miss the photo booth tucked in the back corner. *2149 S Halsted St between 21st and 22nd Sts (312-948-5275). Bus: 8 Halsted, 21 Cermak. Sun–Fri 4pm–2am; Sat 4pm–3am. Average beer: $3. Cash only.* ∎

Subject Index

RESTAURANTS

BYOB

Subject Index

Subject Index

Subject Index

Neighborhood Index

Northwest Side

Al Khayameih 142
4748 N Kedzie Ave between
Leland and Lawrence Aves.
Middle Eastern

Amitabul 174
6207 N Milwaukee Ave between
Huntington and Raven Sts.
Vegetarian

Angelica's 153
3244 N Milwaukee Ave between
Belmont Ave and School St.
Polish

Arun's 170
4156 N Kedzie Ave between
Warner and Berteau Aves.
Thai

Beograd Meat Market 69
2933–39 W Irving Park Rd at
Richmond St. *Eastern European*

Brisku's Bistro 39
4100 N Kedzie Ave between
Belle Plaine Ave and Irving
Park Rd. *Classic American $15
and under*

Caponies Trattoria 102
3350 N Harlem Ave between
School and Roscoe Sts.
Italian/Pizza

Carthage Café 144
3446 W Foster Ave between
Bernard St and St. Louis Ave.
Middle Eastern

Chiyo 119
3800 W Lawrence Ave at Hamlin
Ave. *Japanese and Sushi*

**Chocolate Shoppe
Ice Cream** 89
5337 W Devon Ave at Minnehaha
Ave. *Ice Cream and Sweets*

Cousin's I.V. 175
3038 W Irving Park Rd between
Whipple St and Albany Ave.
Vegetarian

Cuban Island 25
3446 W Peterson Ave between
Bernard St and St. Louis Ave.
Caribbean

Dharma Garden 149
3109 W Irving Park Rd between
Albany Ave and Troy St.
Pan Asian

★ **Edgebrook** 42
Coffee Shop
6322 N Central Ave between
Caldwell and Devon Aves.
*Classic American $15
and under*

El Potosi 134
3710 N Elston Ave between
Kimball and Christina Aves.
Mexican

Gale Street Inn 35
4914 N Milwaukee Ave between
Gale St and Higgins Ave. *Classic
American $16 and up*

Golden Crust 106
Italian Pizzeria
4620 N Kedzie Ave between
Wilson and Eastwood Aves.
Italian/Pizza

Hagen's Fish Market 155
5635 W Montrose Ave at
Parkside Ave. *Seafood*

Halina's Polish Delights 153
5914 W Lawrence Ave between
Marmora and Mason Aves.
Polish

Hong Huah 29
5924 W Fullerton Ave between
Marmora and Mason Aves.
Chinese

★ **Hot Doug's** 44
3324 N California Ave between
Henderson and Roscoe Sts.
Classic American $15 and under

★ **Kangnam** 126
4849 N Kedzie Ave between
Lawrence Ave and Ainslie St.
Korean

Kebab House (formerly 145
Sahar Pita)
4835 N Kedzie Ave between
Lawrence Ave and Ainslie St.
Middle Eastern

Kouks Vintage Café 20
5653 N Northwest Hwy between
Seminole St and Merrimac Ave.
Bakeries/Cafés

La Brasa Roja 131
3125 W Montrose Ave at Troy St.
Latin American

La Humita 131
3466 N Pulaski Rd between
Cornelia and Newport Aves.
Latin American

La Pena 131
4212 N Milwaukee Ave between
Berteau Ave and Hutchinson St.
Latin American

Latin Sandwich Café 157
4009 N Elston Ave between
Irving Park Rd and Ridgeway
Ave. *South American*

Marie's Pizzeria 109
& Liquors
4127 W Lawrence Ave between
Karlov and Kedvale Aves.
Italian/Pizza

Mirabell 86
3454 W Addison St between
Bernard St and St. Louis Ave.
German

Mitad del Mundo 132
2922 W Irving Park Rd at
Richmond St. *Latin American*

Nonno Pino's 110
6718 N Northwest Hwy between
Oshkosh and Oliphant Aves.
Italian/Pizza

★ **Noon O Kabab** 145
4661 N Kedzie Ave between
Eastwood and Leland Aves.
Middle Eastern

Paradise Japanese 151
2916 W Montrose Ave between
Francisco Ave and Richmond St.
Pan Asian

Sabatino's 114
4441 W Irving Park Rd between
Kenneth and Kilbourn Aves.
Italian/Pizza

Salam 146
4636 N Kedzie Ave between
Eastwood and Leland Aves.
Middle Eastern

Semiramis 146
4639 N Kedzie Ave between
Eastwood and Leland Aves.
Middle Eastern

Shiraz 146
4425 W Montrose Ave between
Kenneth and Kostner Aves.
Middle Eastern

Smak-Tak Restaurant 154
5961 N Elston Ave between
Mason and Austin Aves.
Polish

★ **Smoque BBQ** 160
3800 N Pulaski Rd between
Grace St and Avondale Ave.
Southern

★ **Superdawg Drive-In** 50
6363 N Milwaukee Ave at Devon
Ave. *Classic American $15 and
under*

Susie's Drive-In 92
4126 W Montrose Ave between
Elston and Keokuk Aves. *Ice
Cream and Sweets*

Taboun Grill 127
6339 N California Ave between
Devon and Rosemont Aves.
Kosher

TailGators BBQ 161
Smokehouse
6726 N Northwest Hwy between
Oshkosh and Oliphant Aves.
Southern

Tel Aviv Kosher Pizza 127
6349 N California Ave between
Devon and Rosemont Aves.
Kosher

Thai Aree 172
3592 N Milwaukee Ave at Addison
St. *Thai*

★ **Thai Elephant** 172
(formerly "The Elephant")
5348 W Devon Ave between
Central and Minnehaha Aves.
Thai

Trattoria Porretta 115
Ristorante & Pizzeria
3656 N Central Ave between
Waveland and Patterson Aves.
Italian/Pizza

Tre Kronor 77
3258 W Foster Ave between
Sawyer and Spaulding Aves.
Eclectic

Zia's Trattoria 117
6699 Northwest Hwy at Oliphant
Ave. *Italian/Pizza*

Far North Side

A & T Restaurant 39
7036 N Clark St at Greenleaf Ave.
Classic American $15 and under

Adobo Express 149
5343 N Lincoln Ave between
Summerdale and Balmoral Aves.
Pan Asian

Afghan Restaurant 142
2818 W Devon Ave between
California Ave and Mozart St.
Middle Eastern

African Harambee 15
7537 N Clark St between
Birchwood Ave and Howard St.
African

Arya Bhavan 95
2508 W Devon Ave between
Campbell and Maplewood Aves.
Indian/Subcontinental

Bhabi's Kitchen 95
6352 N Oakley Blvd between
Devon and Rosemont Aves.
Indian/Subcontinental

Café Suron 142
1146 W Pratt Ave between
Sheridan Rd and the lake. *Middle
Eastern*

Chopal Kabab & Steak 95
2240 W Devon Ave between Bell
and Oakley Aves. *Indian/
Subcontinental*

Dagel & Beli 41
7406 N Greenview Ave between
Jarvis and Fargo Aves. *Classic
American $15 and under*

Dairy Star 91
3472 W Devon Ave at St. Louis
Ave. *Ice Cream and Sweets*

★ **Deta's Pita** 69
7555 N Ridge Blvd between
Birchwood Ave and Howard St.
Eastern European

Ghareeb Nawaz 95
2032 W Devon Ave at Seeley Ave.
Indian/Subcontinental

Good To Go 25
1947 W Howard St between
Damen and Winchester Aves.
Caribbean

Grande Noodles and 149
Sushi Bar
6632 N Clark St at Wallen Ave.
Pan Asian

Gulliver's 107
2727 W Howard St between
Washtenaw and California Aves.
Italian/Pizza

Hae Woon Dae 126
6240 N California Ave between
Granville and Rosemont Aves.
Korean

Heartland Cafe 44
7000 N Glenwood Ave at Lunt Ave.
Classic American $15 and under

★ **Hema's Kitchen** 95
6406 N Oakley Ave at Devon Ave.
Indian/Subcontinental

Indian Garden 95
2548 W Devon Ave between
Maplewood Ave and Rockwell St.
Indian/Subcontinental

Jamaica Jerk 25
1631 W Howard St between
Paulina and Marshfield Aves.
Caribbean

★ **Katsu** 121
2651 W Peterson Ave between
Talman and Washtenaw Aves.
Japanese and Sushi

★ **Khan B.B.Q.** 97
2401 W Devon Ave at Western
Ave. *Indian/Subcontinental*

La Cazuela 136
6922 N Clark St between Farwell
and Morse Aves. *Mexican*

★ **La Unica** 26
1515 W Devon Ave between
Bosworth and Greenview Aves.
Caribbean

Lake Side Café 175
1418 W Howard St at Sheridan Rd.
Vegetarian

★ **Las Islas Marias** 137
6635 N Clark St between Wallen
and North Shore Aves. *Mexican*

Mazza BBQ 97
2226 W Devon Ave at Bell St.
Indian/Subcontinental

Mekato's Colombian 20
Bakery
5423 N Lincoln Ave between
Rascher and Balmoral Aves.
Bakeries/Cafés

Morseland 74
1218 W Morse Ave between
Glenwood Ave and Sheridan Rd.
Eclectic

Mysore Woodlands 176
2548 W Devon Ave between
Maplewood Ave and Rockwell St.
Vegetarian

Neighborhood Index

Neighborhood Index

Neighborhood Index

Neighborhood Index

Neighborhood Index

Alphabetical Index

RESTAURANTS

A

A & T Restaurant **39**
7036 N Clark St at Greenleaf Ave
(773-274-0036). Bus: 22 (24hrs), 96,
155. Metra: Union Pacific North to
Rogers Park.

A La Turka **142**
3134 N Lincoln Ave between
Barry and Belmont Aves (773-935-
6101). El: Brown to Paulina. Bus: 9
(24 hrs), 11, 77.

A Taste of Heaven **17**
5401 N Clark St at Balmoral Ave
(773-989-0151). El: Red to Berwyn.
Bus: 22 (24hrs), 36, 50, 92.

A Tavola **99**
2148 W Chicago Ave between
Hoyne Ave and Leavitt St (773-
276-7567). Bus: 49 (24hrs), 50, 66
(24hrs). Metra: Milwaukee North
Line to Western Ave.

★ **Addis Abeba** **15**
1322 Chicago Ave, Evanston (847-
328-5411). El: Purple to Dempster.
Bus: 201 (24hrs) Central/Ridge, 205
Chicago/Grl.

Adesso **99**
3332 N Broadway at
Buckingham Pl (773-868-1516).
El: Brown, Purple (rush hrs),
Red to Belmont. Bus: 36, 77
(24hrs), 145, 146, 152.

Adobo Express **149**
5343 N Lincoln Ave between
Summerdale and Balmoral Aves
(773-293-2362). Bus: 11, X49, 49
(24hrs), 92.

★ **Adobo Grill** **133**
2005 W Division St at Damen
Ave (773-252-9990). El: Blue to
Division. Bus: 50 Damen, 70
Division.

Afghan Restaurant **142**
2818 W Devon Ave between
California and Mozart St
(773- 262-8000). Bus: 93 California/
Dodge, 155 Devon.

African Harambee **15**
7537 N Clark St between
Birchwood Ave and Howard
St (773-764-2200). El: Purple,
Red, Yellow to Howard.
Bus: 22 (24hrs), 97, 147,
151 (24hrs), 201 (24hrs), 205,
Pace 215, Pace 290.

Agami **119**
4712 N Broadway at Leland
Ave (773-506-1854). El: Red to
Lawrence. Bus: 22 (24hrs), 36, 78,
81 (24hrs).

Aigre Doux **53**
230 W Kinzie St between Wells
and Franklin Sts (312-329-9400).
El: Brown, Purple (rush hrs)
to Merchandise Mart. Bus: 65,
125, 156.

Al Khayameih **142**
4748 N Kedzie Ave between
Leland and Lawrence Aves
(773-583-0999). El: Brown
Line to Kedzie. Bus: 81 Lawrence
(24hrs).

Al's Italian Beef **39**
169 W Ontario St between Wells

St and LaSalle Blvd (312-943-
3222). El: Brown, Purple (rush hrs)
to Chicago; Red to Grand. Bus: 22
(24hrs), 125, 156.

Aladdin's Eatery **142**
614 W Diversey Pkwy between
Clark St and Lehman Ct (773-
327-6300). El: Brown, Purple
(rush hrs) to Diversey. Bus: 22
(24hrs), 36, 76.

Alhambra Palace **142**
1240 W Randolph St between
Racine Ave and Elizabeth St (312-
666-9555). El: Green to Ashland.
Bus: 20 Madison (24hrs).

Alice & Friends' **174**
Vegetarian Café
5812 N Broadway between
Ardmore and Thorndale Aves
(773-275-8797). El: Red to Bryn
Mawr. Bus: 36, 84, 147 .

★ **Alinea** **53**
1723 N Halsted St between North
Ave and Willow St (312-867-0110).
El: Red to North/Clybourn. Bus: 8
Halsted, 72 North.

Aloha Eats **71**
2534 N Clark St between Deming
and St James Pls (773-935-
6828). El: Brown, Purple (rush
hrs), Red to Fullerton. Bus: 11,
22 (24hrs), 36.

Amarind's **170**
6822 W North Ave, Oak Park
(773-889-9999). El: Green to Oak
Park. Bus: 72 North, Pace 311.

Amelia's Bar and Grill **133**
4559 S Halsted St between 45th
and 46th Sts (773-538-8200). El:
Red to 47th. Bus: 8, 44, 47.

Amira **142**
455 N Cityfront Plaza between
Water and Illinois Sts (312-923-
9311). El: Red to Grand. Bus: 2, 3, 4
(24hrs), X4, 10, 26, 29, 65, 143, 144,
145, 146, 147, 148, 151 (24hrs), 157.

Amitabul **174**
6207 N Milwaukee Ave between
Huntington and Raven Sts
(773-774-0276). Bus: 56A North
Milwaukee, Pace 270.

Andalous **142**
3307 N Clark St between Aldine
Ave and Buckingham Pl (773-
281-6885). El: Brown, Purple (rush
hrs), Red to Belmont. Bus: 22 Clark
(24hrs), 77 Belmont (24hrs).

Andies Restaurant **142**
5253 N Clark St between Berwyn
and Farragut Aves (773-784-8616).
Bus: 9, 22 (24hrs), 92.

Andrzej Grill **153**
1022 N Western Ave between
Augusta Blvd and Cortez St (312-
489-3566). El: Blue to Division.
Bus: 49 (24hrs), X49, 66, 70.

★ **Angel Food Bakery** **17**
1636 W Montrose Ave at Paulina
St (773-728-1512). Bus: 22 (24hrs),
50, 78.

Angelica's **153**
3244 N Milwaukee Ave between
Belmont Ave and School St (773-
736-1186). El: Blue to Belmont.
Bus: 56, 77 (24hrs), 82.

Angelina **99**
3561 N Broadway between
Brompton Ave and Addison St
(773-935-5933). El: Red to Addison.
Bus: 36, 146, 151 (24hrs), 152.

Ankh **174**
LaSalle Blue Line station, 50 W
Congress Pkwy (312-834-0530). El:
Blue to LaSalle.

Ann Sather **71**
929 W Belmont Ave between
Sheffield Ave and Clark St
(773-348-2378). El: Red to Belmont.
Bus: 8, 22 (24hrs), 77 (24hrs).

Anna Held Florist **89**
& Fountain Café
5557 N Sheridan Rd between
Catalpa and Bryn Mawr Aves
(773-561-1940). El: Red to Bryn
Mawr. Bus: 84, 136, 147, 151
(24hrs).

Anna Maria Pasteria **99**
4400 N Clark St at Montrose
Ave (773-506-2662). Bus: 22
(24hrs), 78, 145, 148.

Annette's Homemade **89**
Italian Ice
2011 N Bissell St at Armitage
Ave (773-868-9000). El: Brown,
Purple (rush hrs) to Armitage.
Bus: 8 Halsted, 73 Armitage.

Anteprima **99**
5316 N Clark St between Berwyn
and Summerdale Aves (773-506-
9990). Bus: 22 Clark (24hrs), 92
Foster.

Apart Pizza **101**
2205 W Montrose Ave at
Lincoln Ave (773-588-1550).
El: Brown to Western. Bus: 11,
49 (24hrs), 78.

Arco de Cuchilleros **162**
3445 N Halsted St between
Newport and Cornelia Aves
(773-296-6046). El: Red to Addison.
Bus: 8, 22 (24hrs), 36, 152.

Argo Tea **17**
16 W Randolph St between
State and Dearborn Sts
(312-553-1550). El: Blue, Red
to Washington; Brown, Green,
Orange, Purple (rush hrs) to
Randolph. Bus: 14, 20, 22 (24hrs),
29, 36, 56, 60 (24hrs), 124, 127, 147,
151 (24hrs), 157.

Aria **71**
200 N Columbus Dr at Lake St
(312-444-9494). Bus: 4 (24hrs), 20
(24hrs), 60 (24hrs).

Army & Lou's **159**
422 E 75th St between King Dr
and Vernon Ave (773-483-3100).
El: Red to 79th. Bus: 3, X3, 75.

The Art of Pizza **101**
3033 N Ashland Ave at Nelson
St (773-327-5600). El: Brown
to Paulina. Bus: 9, X9, 11, 77
(24hrs).

Artist's Café **39**
412 S Michigan Ave between
Van Buren St and Congress
Pkwy (312-939-7855). El:
Brown, Green, Orange,
Purple (rush hrs) to Adams.
Bus: 1, 3, 4 (24hrs), X4, 7, 26,
X28, 126, 127, 145, 147, 148,
151 (24hrs).

Artopolis Bakery, **17**
Café, & Agora
306 S Halsted St at Jackson
Blvd (312-559-9000). El: Blue to
UIC-Halsted. Bus: 7, 8, 60 (24hrs),
126, 156, 157.

Arun's **170**
4156 N Kedzie Ave between

Warner and Berteau Aves
(773-539-1909). El: Brown Line to
Kedzie. Bus: 80 Irving Park, X80
Irving Park Exp.

Arya Bhavan **95**
2508 W Devon Ave between
Campbell and Maplewood Aves
(773-274-5800). Bus: 49B Western,
155 Devon.

Ashkenaz Deli **65**
12 E Cedar St between State St
and Lake Shore Dr (312-944-5006).
El: Red to Clark/Division. Bus:
22, 36, 70.

Athena **88**
212 S Halsted St at Adams St
(312-655-0000). Bus: 8 Halsted, 20
Madison (24hrs).

Athenian Room **88**
807 W Webster Ave between
Halsted and Dayton Sts (773-
348-5155). El: Brown, Purple
(rush hrs), Red to Fullerton. Bus:
8, 11, 22, 74.

Atwater's **33**
Herrington Inn, 15 S River Ln,
Geneva (630-208-8920).

Atwood Café **33**
1 W Washington St at State St
(312-368-1900). El: Blue, Red to
Washington. Bus: 56, 60 (24hrs),
124, 127, 157.

Augie's **39**
5347 N Clark St between
Summerdale and Balmoral Aves
(773-271-7868). El: Red to Berwyn.
Bus: 22 (24hrs), 36, 50, 92.

★ **Avec** **53**
615 W Randolph St between
Jefferson and Desplaines Sts (312-
377-2002). El: Green to Clinton.
Bus: 56 Milwaukee, 125 Water
Tower Exp.

★ **Avenues** **53**
108 E Superior St between
Rush St and Michigan Ave
(312-573-6754). El: Red to
Chicago. Bus: 3, X3, 4 (24hrs),
X4, 10, 26, 125, 144, 145, 146,
147, 151 (24hrs).

Azucar **162**
2647 N Kedzie Ave between
Milwaukee and Schubert Aves
(773-486-6464). El: Blue to Logan
Square. Bus: 56 Milwaukee, 76
Diversey.

B

★ **Ba Le** **177**
5018 N Broadway between
Argyle St and Winnemac
Ave (773-561-4424). El: Red to
Argyle. Bus: 22 (24hrs), 36, 81
(24hrs), 92.

Bacchanalia Ristorante **101**
2413 S Oakley Ave between
24th and 25th Sts (773-254-
6555). El: Blue (rush hrs), Pink
to Western (54th and Cermak).
Bus: 49 (24hrs), X49, 60.

★ **Backstage Bistro** **53**
180 N Wabash Ave between
Benton Pl and Lake St (312-
777-7800). El: Brown, Green,
Orange, Pink, Purple (rush hrs)
to Randolph. Bus: 3, 4 (24hrs),
X4, 10, 26, 143, 144, 145, 146, 147,
151 (24hrs).

C

Café 28   **23**
1800 W Irving Park Rd at
Ravenswood Ave (773-528-2883).
El: Brown to Irving Park. Bus: 9,
11, 50, 80.

Café Absinthe   **55**
1954 W North Ave between
Winchester and Damen Aves
(773-278-4488). El: Blue to Damen.
Bus: 50, 56, 72.

Café Aorta   **73**
2002 W 21st St at Damen
Ave (773-738-2002). El: Pink
to Damen. Bus: 21 Cermak,
50 Damen.

Café Ba-Ba-Reeba!   **162**
2024 N Halsted St between
Armitage and Dickens Aves (773-
935-5000). El: Brown, Purple (rush
hrs) to Armitage. Bus: 8 Halsted,
73 Armitage.

Café Bernard   **80**
2100 N Halsted St at Dickens
Ave (773-871-2100). El: Brown,
Purple (rush hrs) to Armitage.
Bus: 8, 73, 74.

Café Bionda   **11**
1924 S State St at Archer Ave
(312-326-9800). El: Red to Cermak/
Chinatown. Bus: 21, 29, 62.

Café Blossom   **119**
608 W Barry Ave at Broadway
(773-935-5284). El: Brown,
Purple (rush hrs), Red to
Belmont. Bus: 8, 22 (24hrs), 36,
77 (24hrs), 156.

Café Bolero   **23**
2252 N Western Ave between
Lyndale St and Belden Ave (773-
227-9000). El: Blue to Western.
Bus: 49 Western (24hrs), 74
Fullerton.

Café Central   **23**
1437 W Chicago Ave at Bishop St
(312-243-6776). El: Blue to Chicago.
Bus: 9 Ashland (24hrs), 66 Chicago
(24hrs).

Café Ciao   **102**
939 W Madison St at Sangamon
St (312-850-2426). Bus: 8, 19, 20
(24hrs).

Café con Leche   **23**
2714 N Milwaukee Ave
between Spaulding and
Sawyer Aves (773-289-4274).
El: Blue to Logan Square.
Bus: 56, 74, 76, 82.

Café des Architectes   **80**
20 E Chestnut St at Wabash
Ave (312-324-4000). El: Red
to Chicago. Bus: 36, 66 (24hrs),
143, 144, 145, 146, 147, 148, 151
(24hrs).

Café Effe   **69**
2030 W Montrose Ave between
Damen and Seeley Aves (773-334-
3436). Bus: 11, 50, 78, 145.

Café Iberico   **162**
737 N LaSalle St between
Superior St and Chicago
Ave (312-573-1510).
El: Brown, Purple (rush hrs)
to Chicago. Bus: 22 (24hrs), 66
(24hrs), 156.

Café Laguardia   **23**
2111 W Armitage Ave between
Hoyne Ave and Leavitt St (773-
862-5996). El: Blue to Western.
Bus: 50, 56, 73.

Café las Delicias   **128**
4300 W Montrose Ave at
Spaulding Ave (773-293-0656).
El: Brown to Western. Bus: 78
Montrose, 82 Kimball.

Café Le Coq   **80**
734 Lake St, Oak Park (708-848-
2233). El: Green to Oak Park. Bus:
N20, 309, 311, 313.

Café Luigi   **102**
2548 N Clark St at Deming Pl
(773-404-0200). El: Brown, Purple
(rush hrs) to Diversey. Bus: 8, 22
(24hrs), 36, 76.

Café Matou   **80**
1846 N Milwaukee Ave between
Bloomingdale Ave and Moffat
St (773-384-8911). El: Blue to
Western. Bus: 49 (24hrs), X49,
56, 73.

Café Orchid   **142**
1746 W Addison St at Hermitage
Ave (773-327-3808). Bus: 9, 11,
50, 152.

Café Penelope   **41**
230 S Ashland Ave between
Adams St and Jackson Blvd (312-
243-6655). Bus: 9, 20 (24hrs), 126.

Café Selmarie   **17**
4729 N Lincoln Ave between
Leland and Lawrence Aves
(773-989-5595). El: Brown to
Western. Bus: 11, 49 (24hrs), X49,
81 (24hrs).

Café Simone   **80**
546 N Wells St between Grand
Ave and Ohio St (312-467-0546).
El: Brown, Purple (rush hrs) to
Merchandise Mart. Bus: 65 Grand,
125 Water Tower Exp.

Café Spiaggia   **102**
980 N Michigan Ave between Oak
St and Walton Pl (312-280-2750).
El: Red to Clark/Division. Bus: 143,
144, 145, 146, 147, 151 (24hrs).

Café Suron   **142**
1146 W Pratt Ave between
Sheridan Rd and the lake (773-465-
6500). El: Red to Loyola or Morse.
Bus: 96, 147, 155.

Café Too   **55**
4715 N Sheridan Rd between
Lakeside Pl and Leland Ave (773-
275-0626). El: Red to Lawrence.
Bus: 81 (24hrs), 145, 151 (24hrs).

CaféNeo   **19**
4655 N Lincoln Ave at Leland
Ave (773-878-2233). El: Brown to
Western. Bus: 11, 49 (24hrs) X49,
78, 81 (24hrs).

Caliente   **133**
3910 N Sheridan Ave between
Dakin St and Sheridan Rd (773-
525-0129). El: Red to Sheridan.
Bus: 36, 80, 151 (24hrs).

Caliterra   **57**
633 N St. Clair St between Ontario
and Erie Sts (312-274-4444). El:
Red to Grand. Bus: 2, 3, X4, 10,
26, 65, 143, 144, 145, 146, 147, 151
(24hrs), 157.

Calo Ristorante   **102**
5343 N Clark St between
Summerdale and Balmoral Aves
(773-271-7725). Bus: 22 (24hrs),
50, 92.

Calumet Fisheries   **155**
3259 E 95th St between Chicago
and Ewing Aves (773-933-9855).
Bus: 26 South Shore Exp. Metra:
Electric Line to 93rd/South
Chicago.

Calypso Café   **102**
5211 S Harper Ave between 52nd
Pl and E 52nd St (773-955-0229).
Bus: 2, 15, 158.

Campagnola   **102**
815 Chicago Ave, Evanston (847-
475-6100). El: Purple to Main. Bus:
205 Chicago/Golf.

★ **Canady Le Chocolatier**   **89**
824 S Wabash Ave between 8th

and 9th Sts (312-212-1270). El: Red
to Harrison. Bus: 1, 3, 4 (24hrs), 29,
62 (24hrs).

Caoba Mexican   **133**
Bar & Grill
1619 N Damen Ave between North
Ave and Concord Pl (773-342-
2622). El: Blue to Damen. Bus:
50, 56, 72.

Cape Cod Room   **155**
140 E Walton Pl at Michigan
Ave (312-787-2200). El: Red to
Chicago. Bus: 3, X4, 10, 26, 66
(24hrs), 125, 143, 144, 145, 146,
147, 151 (24hrs).

Caponies Trattoria   **102**
3350 N Harlem Ave between
School and Roscoe Sts
(773-804-9024). Bus: 77
(24hrs), 90, 152.

Carmichael's Chicago   **165**
Steak House
1052 W Monroe St between
Morgan St and Racine Ave
(312-433-0025). El: Blue to Racine.
Bus: 8, 20 (24hrs), 126.

Carnivale   **128**
702 W Fulton St at Union Ave
(312-850-5005). Bus: 8 Halsted,
65 Grand.

Caro Mio   **102**
1827 W Wilson Ave between
Ravenswood and Wolcott Aves
(773-275-5000). El: Brown to
Damen. Bus: 50 Damen, 145
Wilson/Mich Exp.

Carolina Caramel   **19**
1511 S State St between 15th and
16th Sts (312-922-5007). El: Green,
Orange, Red to Roosevelt. Bus: 12,
24, 21, 29, 62 (24hrs).

Carthage Café   **144**
3446 W Foster Ave between
Bernard St and St. Louis Ave
(773-539-9004). El: Brown
to Kimball. Bus: 81 (24hrs),
82, 92.

Catedral Café   **73**
2500 S Christiana Ave at 25th St
(773-277-2233). Bus: 52 Kedzie/
California, 60 Blue Island/26th
(24hrs).

Cedars Mediterranean   **144**
Kitchen
1206 E 53rd St at Woodlawn Ave
(773-324-6227). Bus: 2, 6, 15, 28, 55,
X55, 171, 172.

Chalkboard   **33**
4343 N Lincoln Ave between
Cullom and Montrose Aves
(773-477-7144). El: Brown to
Western. Bus: 11, 49 (24hrs),
X49, 50, 78.

★ **Charlie Trotter's**   **57**
816 W Armitage Ave between
Halsted and Dayton Sts (773-
248-6228). El: Brown, Purple (rush
hrs) to Armitage. Bus: 8 Halsted,
73 Armitage.

Chef's Station   **57**
915 Davis St, Evanston (847-570-
9821). El: Purple to Davis. Bus:
93, 205, 206, Pace 208, Pace 212,
Pace 213.

Chen's   **149**
3506 N Clark St between Cornelia
Ave and Eddy St (773-549-9100).
El: Red to Addison. Bus: 8, 22
(24hrs), 152.

Chez Joël   **80**
1119 W Taylor St at May St (312-
226-6479). El: Blue to Racine. Bus:
7, 12, 60 (24hrs).

CHIC Café   **57**
Cooking and Hospitality
Institute of Chicago, 361 W
Chestnut St at Orleans St (312-

873-2032). El: Red to Chicago.
Bus: 66 Chicago (24hrs).

Chicago Bagel Authority   **41**
953 W Armitage Ave
between Bissell St and
Sheffield Ave (773-248-9606).
El: Brown, Purple (rush hrs)
to Armitage. Bus: 8 Halsted,
73 Armitage.

Chicago Brauhaus   **86**
4732 N Lincoln Ave between
Leland and Lawrence Aves
(773-784-4444). El: Brown to
Western. Bus: 11, 49 (24hrs),
X49, 81 (24hrs).

Chicago Chop House   **165**
60 W Ontario St between
Dearborn and Clark Sts (312-
787-7100). El: Red to Grand.
Bus: 22 Clark (24hrs), 125 Water
Tower Exp.

★ **Chicago Diner**   **174**
3411 N Halsted St between
Roscoe St and Newport Ave
(773-935-6696). El: Brown, Purple
(rush hrs) to Belmont. Bus: 8,
22 (24 hrs), 77 (24hrs).

Chicago Firehouse   **165**
1401 S Michigan Ave at 14th St
(312-786-1401). El: Green, Orange,
Red to Roosevelt. Bus: 1, 3, 4
(24hrs), 62 (24hrs).

Chicago Pizza and Oven   **104**
Grinder Co.
2121 N Clark St between
Dickens and Webster Aves
(773-248-2570). El: Brown,
Purple (rush hrs) to Armitage.
Bus: 11, 22 (24hrs), 36.

China Grill   **27**
230 N Michigan Ave between
S Water and Lake Sts (312-334-
6700). El: Red to Lake. Bus: 2, 3,
X4, 6, 10, 26, 29, 143, 144, 145, 146,
147, 151 (24hrs), 157.

Chiyo   **119**
3800 W Lawrence Ave at Hamlin
Ave (773-267-1555). El: Brown
to Kimball. Bus: 53 (24hrs), 81
(24hrs), 82.

★ **Cho Sun Ok**   **126**
4200 N Lincoln Ave at Berteau
Ave (773-549-5555). El: Brown
to Irving Park. Bus: 11, 50, 78,
80, X80.

Chocolate Shoppe   **89**
Ice Cream
5337 W Devon Ave at Minnehaha
Ave (773-763-9778). Bus: 84
Peterson, 85A North Central.

Chopal Kabab & Steak   **95**
2240 W Devon Ave between
Bell and Oakley Aves (773-
338-4080). Bus: 49B Western,
155 Devon.

Chowpatti   **175**
1035 S Arlington Heights Rd,
Arlington Heights (847-640-9554).
Bus: Pace 694.

Cid's Ma Mon Luk   **149**
9182 W Golf Rd, Niles (847-803-
3652). El: Blue to Jefferson Park.
Bus: Pace 270, Pace 208 .

CJ's Eatery   **159**
3839 W Grand Ave at Avers Ave
(773-292-0990). Bus: 53, 65, 70.

Clarke's   **41**
2442 N Lincoln Ave between
Fullerton Pkwy and Montana St
(773-472-3505). El: Brown, Purple
(rush hrs), Red to Fullerton. Bus:
8, 11, 74.

Club Lago   **104**
331 W Superior St at Orleans St
(312-337-9444). El: Brown, Purple
(rush hrs) to Chicago. Bus: 66
Chicago (24hrs).

Alphabetical Index

Alphabetical Index

Alphabetical Index

Alphabetical Index

Alphabetical Index

Tsuki 125
1441 W Fullerton Ave between
Janssen and Greenview Aves
(773-883-8722). Bus: 9 Ashland,
74 Fullerton.

Tsunami 125
1160 N Dearborn St at
Division St (312-642-9911).
El: Red to Clark/Division.
Bus: 22 (24hrs), 36, 70.

Tucci Benucch 116
900 N Michigan Ave at
Walton St (312-266-2500).
El: Red to Chicago. Bus: 3, X4,
10, 26, 66, 125, 143, 144, 145,
146, 147, 151 (24hrs).

Tufano's Vernon Park 116
Tap
1073 W Vernon Park Pl
between Carpenter and Aberdeen
Sts (773-733-3393). El: Blue to
Racine. Bus: 7, 12, 60.

★ **Turkish Cuisine and** 147
Bakery
5605 N Clark St between Bryn
Mawr and Olive Aves (773-878-
8930). El: Red to Bryn Mawr. Bus:
22 Clark (24hrs), 50 Damen.

Turquoise Café 147
2147 W Roscoe St between
Hamilton Ave and Leavitt St
(773-549-3523). El: Brown to
Paulina. Bus: 49 (24hrs), X49, 50,
77 (24hrs), 152.

Tuscany 116
3700 N Clark St at Waveland Ave
(773-404-7700). El: Red to Addison.
Bus: 8, 22 (24hrs), 36, 152.

★ **Tweet** 37
5020 N Sheridan Rd between
Carmen and Argyle Sts (773-728-
5576). El: Red to Argyle. Bus: 81
(24hrs), 92, 151 (24hrs).

Twin Anchors 37
1655 N Sedgwick St between
Concord Pl and Eugenie St (312-
266-1616). El: Brown, Purple (rush
hrs) to Sedgwick. Bus: 72 North,
156 LaSalle.

Twist 163
3412 N Sheffield Ave between
Roscoe and Clark Sts (773-388-
2727). El: Red to Addison. Bus: 22
(24hrs), 77 (24hrs), 152.

Twisted Lizard 141
1964 N Sheffield Ave between
Armitage and Maud Aves (773-
929-1414). El: Brown to Armitage.
Bus: 8 Halsted, 73 Armitage.

★ **Twisted Spoke** 51
501 N Ogden Ave at Grand Ave
(312-665-1500). El: Blue to Grand.
Bus: 8, 9, 65.

U

U Lucky Dawg 93
6821 N Western Ave between
Pratt Blvd and Farwell Ave (773-
274-3652). Bus: 49B, 96, 155.

★ **Udupi Palace** 98
2543 W Devon Ave at Maplewood
Ave (773-338-2152). Bus: 49B
Western, 155 Devon.

★ **Uncle John's** 161
337 E 69th St at Calumet Ave
(773-892-1233). El: Red to 69th.
Bus: 3, 30, 67, 71.

Uncommon Ground 64
3800 N Clark St at Grace St (773-
929-3680). El: Red to Addison. Bus:
22 (24hrs), 80, 152.

Usmania 98
2253 W Devon Ave between Bell
and Oakley Aves (773-262-1900).
Bus: 49B Western, 155 Devon.

V

V.I.C.E. 77
840 W Randolph St between Green
and Peoria Sts (312-733-3379). El:
Green to Clinton. Bus: 8 Halsted,
20 Madison (24hrs).

★ **Va Pensiero** 116
1566 Oak Ave, Evanston (847-475-
7779). El: Purple to Davis. Bus: 93,
201 (24hrs), 205, 213.

Vegetarian Fun Foods 176
Supreme
1702 E 87th St East End Ave (773-
734-6321). Bus: 87 87th.

Vella Café 22
1912 N Western Ave between
Cortland and Homer Sts (773-489-
7777). El: Blue to Western. Bus: 49
(24hrs), X49, 56, 74.

Ventoso 117
540 N Michigan Ave between
Grand Ave and Ohio St (312-836-
6336). El: Red to Grand. Bus: 2, 3,
X4, 10, 26, 29, 65, 125, 143, 144,
145, 146, 147, 151 (24hrs), 157.

Ventrella's Caffé 22
4947 N Damen Ave between
Argyle and Ainslie Sts (773-506-
0708). El: Brown to Damen. Bus:
50, 81 (24hrs), 92, 145. Metra:
Union Pacific N to Ravenswood.

Vermilion 98
10 W Hubbard St between State
and Dearborn Sts (312-527-4060).
El: Red to Grand. Bus: 22 (24hrs),
29, 36, 65.

Via Carducci 117
1419 W Fullerton Ave between
Janssen and Southport Aves
(773-665-1981). El: Brown, Purple
(rush hrs), Red to Fullerton. Bus:
9, 11, 74.

Via Carducci la Sorella 117
1928 W Division St between
Wolcott and Damen Aves (773-
252-2244). El: Blue to Division.
Bus: 9, 56, 70.

Via Veneto 117
6340 N Lincoln Ave at Drake Ave
(773-267-0888). Bus: 11, 82, 155.

Viand 77
155 E Ontario St between
Michigan Ave and St. Clair St
(312-255-8505). El: Red to Grand.
Bus: 65, 146, 147, 151 (24 hrs).

Victory's Banner 176
2100 W Roscoe St at Hoyne Ave
(773-665-0227). Bus: 50, 77 (24
hrs), 152.

★ **Vie** 64
4471 Lawn Ave, Western Springs
(708-246-2082). Metra: Burlington
Northern Santa Fe to Western
Springs.

Viet Bistro and Lounge 152
1344–46 W Devon Ave between
Wayne and Glenwood Aves (773-
465-5720). Bus: 22 (24hrs), 36, 147,
151 (24hrs), 155.

The Village 117
71 W Monroe St between Clark
and Dearborn Sts (773-332-7005).
El: Blue, Red to Monroe. Bus: 1, 2,
6, 7, 10, 14, 20, 22 (24hrs), 24, 28,
29, 36, 56, 60 (24hrs), 62, 124, 126,
127, 144, 146, 151 (24hrs), 156, 157.

Vinci 117
1732 N Halsted Ave between
North Ave and Willow St (312-266-
1199). El: Red to North/Clybourn.
Bus: 8 Halsted, 72 North.

Vines on Clark 117
3554 N Clark St at Eddy St (773-
327-8572). El: Red to Addison. Bus:
8, 22 (24hrs), 77 (24hrs), 152.

Vintage Wine Bar 64
1942 W Division St between
Winchester and Damen Aves (773-
772-3400). El: Blue to Division.
Bus: 50 Damen, 70 Division.

Vito and Nick's 117
8433 S Pulaski Rd at 84th Pl
(773-735-2050). Bus: 53A Pulaski,
87 87th.

Vive la Crêpe 83
1565 N Sherman Ave, Evanston
(847-570-0600). El: Purple to Davis.

Vivere 117
71 W Monroe St between Clark
and Dearborn Sts (312-332-7005).
El: Red, Blue to Washington;
Orange, Brown, Green, Purple
(rush hrs) to Adams. Bus: 1, 7,
X28, 126, 151.

Vivo 117
838 W Randolph St between Green
and Peoria Sts (312-733-3379). El:
Green to Clinton. Bus: 8 Halsted,
20 Madison (24hrs).

Volo 64
2008 W Roscoe St between Damen
and Seeley Aves (773-348-4600).
Bus: 50, 77 (24hrs), 152.

VTK 173
6 W Hubbard St at State St (312-
644-8664). El: Red to Grand. Bus:
22 (24hrs), 36, 65.

W

★ **Wakamono** 125
3317 N Broadway between
Aldine Ave and Buckingham
Pl (773-296-6800). El: Brown,
Purple (rush hrs), Red to
Belmont. Bus: 36, 77 (24hrs), 152.

Wave, 77
W Chicago Lakeshore
644 N Lake Shore Dr
between Ontario and Erie
Sts (312-255-4460). Bus: 134,
135, 136.

Weber Grill 37
539 N State St at Grand
Ave (312-467-9696). El: Red to
Grand. Bus: 22 (24hrs), 36, 65.

★ **West Town Tavern** 37
1329 W Chicago Ave at
Throop St (312-666-6175).
El: Blue to Chicago. Bus: 9 (24hrs),
56, 66 (24hrs).

Wholly Frijoles 141
Mexican Grill
3908 W Touhy Ave,
Lincolnwood (847-329-9810).
Bus: 11 Kedzie, Pace 290.

The Wiener's Circle 51
2622 N Clark St between
Wrightwood Ave and
Drummond Pl (773-477-
7444). El: Brown, Purple
(rush hrs) to Diversey. Bus: 22
(24hrs), 36, 76.

Wildfire 37
159 W Erie St between
LaSalle and Wells Sts (312-
787-9000). El: Blue, Brown,
Orange, Pink, Purple (rush hrs) to
LaSalle. Bus: 1, 7, 22 (24hrs), 24,
X28, 125, 151 (24hrs).

Windy City Sweets 93
3308 N Broadway at Aldine
Ave (773-477-6100). El: Brown,
Purple (rush hrs), Red to Belmont.
Bus: 8, 22 (24hrs), 36, 77 (24hrs).

Winston's Market 51
Everyday
3440 N Southport Ave
between Roscoe St and Newport
Ave (773-327-6400). Bus: 9
Ashland, 152 Addison.

Wishbone 161
1001 W Washington Blvd
at Morgan St (312-850-2663).
Bus: 8, 20 (24hrs), X20.

Wolfy's 51
2734 W Peterson Ave at
Fairfield Ave (773-743-0207).
Bus: 84, 84, 93.

Woo Chon 126
5744 N California Ave between
Ardmore and Lincoln Aves
(773-728-8001). Bus: 11, 84, 93.

Wow Bao 152
Water Tower Place, 835 N
Michigan Ave between
Pearson and Chestnut Sts
(312-642-5888). El: Red to
Chicago. Bus: 66 (24hrs), 143, 144,
145, 146, 147, 148, 151 (24hrs).

X

★ **Xni-Pec** 141
5135 W 25th St, Cicero (708-652-
8680). El: Blue (54th/Cermak) (rush
hrs), Pink to Cicero. Bus: 54 Cicero,
54B South Cicero.

Y

Yassa 16
716 E 79th St between
Evans and Langley Aves
(773-488-5599). El: Red to 79th St.
Bus: 3, 4 (24hrs), 79.

Yes Thai 173
5211 N Damen Ave between
Farragut and Foster Aves (773-
878-3487). El: Brown to Damen.
Bus: 50 Damen, 92 Foster.

Yoshi's Café 64
3257 N Halsted St at Aldine Ave
(773-248-6160). El: Brown, Purple
(rush hrs), Red to Belmont. Bus: 8
Halsted, 77 Belmont (24hrs).

Z

Zacatacos 141
6224 W Cermak Rd, Berwyn (708-
484-8443). Bus: 21 Cermak. Pace
304, 315, 322.

★ **Zad** 147
3112 N Broadway between Briar
Pl and Barry Ave (773-404-3473).
El: Red, Brown, Purple (rush hrs)
to Belmont. Bus: 8, 22 (24hrs), 36,
76, 77 (24hrs).

★ **Zapatista** 141
1307 S Wabash Ave at 13th St
(312-435-1307). El: Green, Orange,
Red to Roosevelt. Bus: 1, 4 (24hrs),
29, 62 (24hrs).

★ **Zealous** 64
419 W Superior St between
Sedgwick and Kingsbury Sts
(312-475-9112). Bus: 66 Chicago
(24hrs).

Zia: A New Mexican Café 77
340 W Armitage Ave between
Orleans and Sedgwick Sts (773-
525-6959). Bus: 11, 22 (24hrs), 36,
73, 151 (24hrs), 156.

Zia's Trattoria 141
6699 Northwest Hwy at Oliphant
(773-775-0808). Metra: Union
Pacific NW to Edison Park. Bus:
68 Northwest Hwy.

Zocalo 141
358 W Ontario St between Orleans
and Kingsbury Sts (312-302-9977).
El: Brown, Purple (rush hrs) to
Chicago. Bus: 65 Grand, 125 Water
Tower Exp.

BARS

A

Alphabetical Index

Alphabetical Index

Green Eye Lounge   **210**
2403 W Homer St at Western
Ave (773-227-8851). El: Blue
to Western. Bus: 49 Western
(24hrs).

The Grillroom   **239**
33 W Monroe St between
State and Dearborn Sts
(312-960-0000). El: Blue,
Red to Monroe; Brown, Green,
Orange, Purple (rush hrs) to
Madison.

Gunther Murphy's   **197**
1638 W Belmont Ave
between Lincoln and Paulina
Sts (773-472-5139). El: Brown to
Paulina. Bus: 9, 11, 77 (24hrs).

Guthries Tavern   **199**
1300 W Addison St at
Lakewood Ave (773-477-
2900). El: Red, Purple (rush
hour only) to Addison.
Bus: 152 Addison.

H

Hackney's   **241**
733 S Dearborn between Harrison
and Polk Sts (312-461-1116). El:
Red to Harrison. Bus: 2, 6, 22,
36, 62.

Halligan Bar   **221**
2274 N Lincoln Ave between
Webster and Belden Aves
(773-472-7940). El: Brown, Purple
(rush hrs), Red to Fullerton. Bus:
8, 11, 74.

Ham Tree   **179**
5333 N Milwaukee Ave between
Central and Parkside Aves (773-
792-2072). El: Blue to Jefferson
Park. Bus: 56, 81 (24hrs), 85.

Handlebar Bar & Grill   **215**
2311 W North Ave between
Oakley and Claremont Aves (773-
384-9546). El: Blue to Damen. Bus:
49 (24hrs), 50, 72.

The Hangge-Uppe   **234**
14 W Elm St between State and
Dearborn Sts (312-337-0561). El:
Red to Clark/Division, Bus: 22
(24hrs), 36, 70, 156.

Happy Cracovia Lounge   **179**
2025 N Cicero Ave between
Armitage and McLean Aves
(773-637-6787). Bus: 54 Cicero, 73
Armitage.

Happy Village   **226**
1059 N Wolcott Ave at Thomas
St (773-486-1512). El: Blue to
Division. Bus: 50 Damen, 70
Division.

Harrigan's Pub   **199**
2816 N Halsted St between
Diversey Pkwy and Wolfram St
(773-248-5933). El: Brown, Purple
(rush hrs) to Diversey. Bus: 8
Halsted, 76 Diversey.

Harry's   **180**
5943 N Elston Ave at Mason
Ave (773-774-4166). Bus: 56
Milwaukee, 91 Austin.

Hawkeye's Bar   **239**
and Grill Chicago
1458 W Taylor St between Bishop
and Laflin Sts (312-226-3951). El:
Blue to Racine. Bus: 7, 9 (24hrs),
12, 60.

Helen's Two Way Lounge 212
2928 W Fullerton Ave at
Milwaukee Ave (773-227-5676). El:
Blue to California. Bus: 52, 56, 74.

Hidden Cove   **191**
5336 N Lincoln Ave between
Summerdale and Balmoral Aves
(773-275-6711). El: 11 Lincoln.

The Hidden Shamrock   **221**
2723 N Halsted St at Schubert
Ave (773-883-0304). El: Brown
to Diversey. Bus 8 Halsted, 76
Diversey.

Hideout   **215**
1354 W Wabansia Ave
between Willow and Ada Sts
(773-227-4433). Bus: 72 North.

Higgins' Tavern   **199**
3259 N Racine Ave between
Melrose and School Sts
(773-281-7637). El: Brown,
Purple (rush hrs), Red to
Belmont. Bus: 22 Clark (24hrs),
77 Belmont (24hrs).

High Dive   **226**
1938 W Chicago Ave between
Winchester and Damen Aves
(773-235-3483). Bus: 50, 65, 66
(24hrs).

Hi-Tops   **199**
3551 N Sheffield Ave
between Addison St and
Cornelia Ave (773-348-0009).
El: Red to Addison. Bus: 8
Halsted, 152 Addison.

Hog Head McDunna's   **221**
1505 W Fullerton Ave
between Greenview and
Bosworth Aves (773-929-0944).
El: Brown, Purple (rush hrs),
Red to Fullerton. Bus: 9 Ashland,
74 Fullerton.

Hogs and Honeys   **230**
1551 N Sheffield Ave between
Weed St and North Ave
(312-377-1733). El: Red to
North/Clybourn. Bus: 8 Halsted.
72 North.

Holiday Club   **199**
4000 N Sheridan at Irving
Park Rd (773-348-9600).
El: Red to Sheridan.
Bus: 80 Irving Park, 151
Sheridan (24hrs).

Hops & Barley   **180**
4359 N Milwaukee Ave
between Pensacola and
Montrose Aves (773-286-
7415). Bus: 54, 56, 78.

Hotti Biscotti Café   **212**
3545 W Fullerton Ave at
Drake Ave (773-292-6877).
El: Blue to Logan Square.
Bus: 74 Fullerton, 82 Kimball.

Houndstooth Saloon   **199**
3438 N Clark St at Newport
Ave (773-244-1166). El: Red to
Addison. Bus: 22 (24hrs), 77
(24hrs), 152.

Huettenbar   **191**
4721 N Lincoln Ave between
Leland and Lawrence Aves
(773-561-2507). El: Brown to
Western. Bus: 11, 49 (24hrs),
X49, 81 (24hrs).

Hungry Brain   **199**
2319 W Belmont Ave between
Oakley and Western Aves
(773-935-2118). El: Brown to
Paulina. Bus: 49 (24hrs), X49,
77 (24hrs).

I

Illinois Bar & Grill   **243**
1421 W Taylor St between
Loomis and Bishop Sts (312-666-
6666). El: Blue to Polk. Bus: 9
Ashland (24hrs), 12 Roosevelt.

Independence Tap   **180**
3932 W Irving Park Rd at
Harding Ave (773-588-2385).
El: Blue to Irving Park. Bus: 54A
North Cicero/Skokie Blvd.

Inner Town Pub   **226**
1935 W Thomas St at Winchester
Ave (773-235-9795). El: Blue to
Division. Bus: 50 Damen, 70
Division.

innjoy   **215**
2051 W Division St between
Damen and Hoyne Aves (773-394-
2066). El: Blue to Division. Bus: 50
Damen, 70 Division.

The Irish Oak   **199**
3511 N Clark St at Cornelia
Ave (773-935-6669). El: Red to
Addison. Bus: 22 Clark (24hrs),
152 Addison.

J

J & L Lounge   **180**
3402 N Cicero Ave at Roscoe St
(773-286-0447). Bus: 54 Cicero, 152
Addison.

J Bar   **234**
616 N Rush St at Ontario St (312-
660-7200). El: Red to Grand. Bus:
36, 125, 151 (24hrs).

J. Patrick's Irish   **230**
Bar & Grill
1367 W Erie St between Ada
and Noble Sts (312-243-0990). El:
Blue to Chicago. Bus: 9 Ashland
(24hrs), 66 Chicago (24hrs).

Jack's Bar and Grill   **199**
2856 N Southport Ave between
Wolfram and George Sts (773-404-
8400). El: Brown, Purple (rush hrs)
to Diversey. Bus: 9, 11, 76.

Jackhammer   **183**
6406 N Clark St at Devon Ave
(773-743-5772). Bus: 22 Clark
(24hrs).

Jacqueline's   **199**
3420 N Broadway at Roscoe St
(773-404-5149). El: Brown, Purple
(rush hrs), Red to Belmont. Bus:
36, 77 (24hrs), 152.

Jak's Tap   **239**
901 W Jackson Blvd at Peoria St
(312-666-1700). El: Blue to UIC-
Halsted. Bus: 8, 20 (24hrs), 126.

Jake's Pub   **199**
2932 N Clark St at Oakdale Ave
(773-248-3318). Bus: 8, 22 (24hrs),
36, 76.

Janina's Lounge   **180**
3459 N Milwaukee Ave at
Newport Ave (773-685-6676). Bus:
53, 56, 152.

Jarheads   **184**
6973 N Clark St between Morse
and Lunt Aves (773-973-1907).
El: Red to Morse. Bus: 22 Clark
(24hrs).

Jefferson Tap   **239**
325 N Jefferson St at Wayman
St (312-648-0100). El: Green,
Blue, Pink to Clinton. Bus: 8, 20
(24hrs), 56.

Jesse's Shortstop Inn   **180**
5425 W Belmont Ave at Lotus
Ave (773-545-4427). Bus: 77
Belmont (24hrs), 85 Central.

Jet Vodka Lounge   **231**
1551 N Sheffield Ave between
Weed St and North Ave (312-730-
4395). El: Red to North/Clybourn.
Bus: 8 Halsted, 72 North.

Jet's Public House   **180**
6148 N Milwaukee Ave at
Hyacinth St (773-792-2440). Bus:
56A Milwaukee.

Jilly's Too   **234**
1009–11 N Rush St between Oak
St and Bellevue Pl (312-664-0009).
El: Red to Clark/Division. Bus: 36
Broadway, 70 Division.

Joe's on Broadway   **199**
3563 N Broadway between
Addison St and Brompton
Ave (773-528-1054). El: Red to
Addison. Bus: 36 Broadway, 152
Addison.

Joe's on Weed   **231**
940 W Weed St between Fremont
St and Sheffield Ave (312-337-
3486). El: Red to North/Clybourn.
Bus: 8 Halsted, 72 North.

John Barleycorn   **199**
3524 N Clark St between Addison
St and Sheffield Ave (773-549-
6000). El: Red to Addison. Bus: 22
Clark (24hrs), 152 Addison.

Johnnie's   **200**
3425 N Lincoln Ave at Roscoe
St (773-248-3000). El: Brown to
Paulina. Bus: 9, 11, 77 (24hrs), 152.

Johnny O'Hagan's   **200**
3374 N Clark St between Aldine
Ave and Roscoe St (773-248-3600).
El: Brown, Purple (rush hrs), Red
to Belmont. Bus: 11, 22 (24hrs), 36,
77 (24hrs).

Joie de Vine   **186**
1744 W Balmoral Ave between
Paulina St and Ravenswood Ave
(773-989-6846). Bus: 22 (24hrs),
50, 92.

Jun Bar   **215**
2050 W Division St between
Damen and Hoyne Aves (773-486-
6700). El: Blue to Division. Bus: 49
(24hrs), X49, 50, 70.

June's Inn   **200**
4333 N Western Ave between
Pensacola and Montrose Aves
(773-463-3122). El: Brown to
Western. Bus: 49 (24hrs), X49, 78.

Junior's Sports Bar   **243**
724 W Maxwell St between
Union Ave and Halsted St
(773-276-7582). Bus: 8 Halsted, 12
Roosevelt.

Jury's   **191**
4337 N Lincoln Ave between
Pensacola and Montrose Aves
(773-935-2255). Bus: 11, 50, 78.

K

K's Dugout   **191**
1930 W Foster Ave at Winchester
Ave (773-561-2227). El: Brown
to Damen. Bus: 49 (24hrs), X49,
50, 92.

Karaoke Restaurant   **184**
6248 N California Ave between
Granville and Rosemont Aves
(773-274-1166). Bus: 93 California/
Dodge, 155 Devon.

Kasey's Tavern   **241**
701 S Dearborn Ave between
Harrison and Polk Sts (312-427-
7992). El: Red to Harrison. Bus: 22
(24hrs), 36, 62.

Katerina's   **200**
1920 W Irving Park Rd at Wolcott
Ave (773-348-7592). El: Brown to
Irving Park. Bus: 11, 50, 80, X80.

Kelly's Pub   **222**
949 W Webster Ave between
Bissell St and Sheffield Ave
(773-281-0656). El: Brown, Purple
(rush hrs), Red to Fullerton. Bus:
73 Armitage, 74 Fullerton.

Kennedy's   **180**
3734 N Milwaukee Ave at Kostner
Ave (773-736-1010). El: Blue to
Irving Park. Bus: 54, 56, 80, 152.

The Kerryman   **231**
661 N Clark St at Erie St (312-335-
8121). El: Red to Grand. Bus: 22
(24hrs), 36, 65.

Alphabetical Index

Alphabetical Index

Alphabetical Index

Ritz-Carlton Bar 235
160 E Pearson St between
Michigan Ave and Mies
van der Rohe Way (312-573-
5223). El: Red to Chicago.
Bus: 3, 4 (24hrs), X4, 10,
26, 125, 143, 144, 145, 146,
147, 151 (24hrs).

River Shannon 223
425 W Armitage Ave
between Sedgwick St and
Hudson Ave (312-944-5087).
El: Brown, Purple (rush hrs) to
Armitage. Bus: 8, 11, 22 (24hrs),
36, 73.

Roadhouse 232
1653 N Wells St between
Concord Ln and Eugenie St
(312-440-0535). El: Red to
North/Clybourn. Bus: 72 North,
156 LaSalle.

Rock Bottom Brewery 232
1 W Grand Ave at State St
(312-755-9339). El: Red to
Grand. Bus: 22 (24hrs), 29, 36, 65.

Rocks Lincoln Park 224
1301 W Schubert Ave at
Lakewood Ave (773-472-
7738). El: Brown, Purple
(rush hrs) to Diversey.
Bus: 11 Lincoln, 76 Diversey.

Rockwell's 191
Neighborhood Grill
4632 N Rockwell St between
Leland and Eastwood
Aves (773-509-1871).
El: Brown to Rockwell. Bus:
49 (24hrs), X49, 81 (24hrs) .

Roscoe Village Pub 204
2159 W Addison St at Leavitt St
(773-472-6160). Bus: 49 (24hrs),
50, 152.

Rose's Lounge 204
2656 N Lincoln Ave between
Wrightwood Ave and
Diversey Pkwy (773-327-
4000). El: Brown, Purple
(rush hrs), Red to Fullerton.
Bus: 11, 74, 76.

Rossi's 232
412 N State St between
Kinzie and Hubbard Sts
(312-644-5775). El: Red to
Grand. Bus: 29, 36, 65.

S

Sally's Lounge 204
3759 N Western Ave
between Grace St and
Waveland Ave (773-463-7120).
Bus: 49 Western (24hrs), 80
Irving Park.

Schaller's Pump 242
3714 S Halsted St between
37th and 38th Sts (773-376-
6332). El: Red to Sox-35th.
Bus: 8 Halsted, 35 35th.

Scot's 191
1829 W Montrose Ave
between Honore St and
Wolcott Ave (773-528-3253).
Bus: 50 Damen, 78 Montrose.

Season's Lounge 235
120 E Delaware Pl between
Ernst Ct and Michigan
Ave (312-280-8800). El: Red
to Chicago. Bus: 36, 143, 144,
145, 146, 147, 148, 151 (24hrs).

Second Story Bar 237
157 E Ohio St between St.
Clair St and Michigan
Ave (312-923-9536). El: Red
to Grand. Bus: 2, 3, 10, 26,
125, 143, 144, 145, 146, 147,
148, 151 (24hrs), 157.

Sedgwick's Bar & Grill 224
1935 N Sedgwick St
between Armitage Ave and
Wisconsin St (312-337-7900).
El: Brown, Purple (rush hrs)
to Sedgwick. Bus: 11, 22 (24hrs),
36, 73.

17 West 240
17 W Adams St between
State and Dearborn Sts
(312-427-3170). El: Blue,
Red to Monroe.

Shamrock Club 232
210 W Kinzie St between
Wells and Franklin Sts
(312-321-9314). El: Brown,
Purple (rush hrs) to Merchandise
Mart. Bus: 65 Grand, 125 Water
Tower Exp.

Sheffield's 204
3258 N Sheffield Ave between
Belmont Ave and School St
(773-281-4989). El: Brown,
Purple (rush hrs), Red to
Belmont. Bus: 8 Halsted, 77
Belmont (24hrs).

Sheridan "L" Lounge 188
and Delicatessen
3944 N Sheridan Rd between
Dakin St and Irving Park Rd
(no phone). El: Red to Sheridan.
Bus: 80, X80, 151 (24hrs).

Sherry's Bar 188
5652 N Western Ave
between Bryn Mawr and
Hollywood Aves (773-784-
2143). Bus: 49 Western (24hrs),
84 Peterson.

Side Street Saloon 204
1456 W George St
between Southport and
Greenview Aves (773-327-
1127). Bus: 9, 11, 76.

Sidetrack 204
3349 N Halsted St between
Buckingham Pl and Roscoe
St (773-477-9189). El: Brown,
Purple (rush hrs), Red to
Belmont. Bus: 8 Halsted.

Silvie's Lounge 204
1902 W Irving Park Rd at
Wolcott Ave (773-871-6239). El:
Brown to Irving Park.
Bus: 11, 50, 80.

Simon's Tavern 188
5210 N Clark St between
Foster and Farragut Aves
(773-878-0894). El: Red to
Berwyn. Bus: 22 (24hrs), 50, 92.

676 Bar 237
676 N Michigan Ave at
Huron St (312-944-7676).
El: Red to Grand. Bus: 65, 145,
146, 147, 151 (24hrs).

Skylark 243
2149 S Halsted St between 21st
and 22nd Sts (312-948-5275). Bus:
8 Halsted, 21 Cermak.

Small Bar 217
2049 W Division St between
Damen and Hoyne Aves
(773-772-2727). El: Blue to
Division. Bus: 49 (24hrs), 50, 70.

Smilin' Jim's Saloon 184
6306 N Western Ave between
Rosemont and Devon Aves
(773-973-7422). Bus: 49B
Western, 155 Devon.

Snickers 232
448 N State St between
Hubbard and Illinois Sts
(312-527-0437). El: Red to
Grand.Bus: 29, 36, 65.

SoFo 191
4923 N Clark St at Ainslie
St (773-784-7636). Bus: 22
Clark (24hrs), 92 Foster.

Sopo Lounge & Grill 204
3418 N Southport Ave
between Roscoe St and
Newport Ave (773-348-0100).
El: Brown to Southport. Bus: 77
Belmont (24hrs), 152 Addison.

South Loop Club 241
701 S State St at Balbo Dr
(312-427-2787). El: Red to
Harrison. Bus: 2, 6, 29, 36,
62 (24hrs).

Southport City Saloon 224
2548 N Southport Ave
between Lill and Wrightwood
Aves (773-975-6110). El:
Brown, Purple (rush hrs) to
Diversey. Bus: 9, 11, 74.

Southport Lanes 204
& Billiards
3325 N Southport Ave at
Henderson St (773-472-6600).
El: Brown to Southport.
Bus: 9, 11, 152.

The Sovereign 188
6202 N Broadway at
Granville Ave (773-274-0057).
El: Red to Granville. Bus: 22
(24hrs), 36, 136, 147, 151
(24hrs), 155.

Spectrum Bar 240
233 S Halsted St between
Adams St and Jackson Blvd
(312-715-0770). El: Blue to UIC-
Halsted. Bus: 8 Halsted,
126 Jackson.

Spin 204
800 W Belmont Ave at
Halsted St (773-327-7711).
El: Brown, Purple (rush hrs),
Red to Belmont. Bus: 8, 22
(24hrs), 77 (24hrs).

Sports Corner 206
956 W Addison St at
Sheffield Ave (773-929-1441).
El: Red to Addison. Bus: 8, 22
(24hrs), 152.

The Spot 188
4437 N Broadway between
Montrose and Sunnyside
Aves (773-728-8933). El: Red to
Wilson. Bus: 36.

Spot 6 206
3343 N Clark St at Roscoe
St (773-388-0185). El: Red to
Addison. Bus: 22 Clark (24hrs),
152 Addison.

Spyners Pub 191
4623 N Western Ave at
Wilson Ave (773-784-8719).
El: Brown to Western.
Bus: 11, 49 (24hrs), 81 (24hrs).

Stadium West 212
3188 N Elston Ave at
Belmont Ave (773-866-2450).
Bus: 52 California, 77 Belmont
(24hrs).

Star Gaze 188
5419 N Clark St between
Balmoral and Rascher Aves
(773-561-7363). El: Red to
Berwyn. Bus: 22 Clark (24hrs),
92 Foster.

Stella's Tap 228
935 N Western Ave at
Walton St (773-384-0077).
El: Blue to Chicago. Bus: 49
(24hrs), 50, 66 (24hrs).

Sterch's 224
2238 N Lincoln Ave between
Webster and Belden Aves
(773-281-2653). El: Brown,
Purple (rush hrs), Red to
Fullerton. Bus: 8, 11, 74.

Stone Lotus 233
873 N Orleans St between
Chestnut and Locust Sts
(312-440-9680). El: Brown,

Purple (rush hrs) to Chicago. Bus:
66 Chicago (24hrs).

The Store 224
2002 N Halsted St between
Armitage and Dickens
Aves (773-327-7766). El: Brown,
Purple (rush hrs) to Armitage.
Bus: 8, 11, 73.

Streeters Tavern 237
50 E Chicago Ave between
Wabash Ave and Rush St
(312-944-5206). El: Red to
Chicago. Bus: 3 (24hrs), 10, 66
(24hrs).

Streetside Café 212
3201 W Armitage Ave at
Kedzie (773-252-9700).
Bus: 73 Armitage, 82
Kimball-Homan.

Suite Lounge 233
1446 N Wells St between
Schiller St and North Ave
(312-787-6103). El: Brown,
Purple (rush hrs) to Sedgwick;
Red to North/Clybourn.

Sunnyside Tap 192
4410 N Western Ave between
Montrose and Sunnyside
Aves (no phone). El: Brown to
Western. Bus: 11, 49 (24hrs),
X49, 78.

Swig 217
1469 N Milwaukee Ave
between Evergreen Ave and
Honore St (773-384-1439). El:
Blue to Damen. Bus: 50, 56, 72.

Swirl Wine Bar 233
111 W Hubbard St between
Clark St and LaSalle Blvd
(312-828-9000). El: Brown,
Purple (rush hrs) to Merchandise
Mart; Red to Grand. Bus: 22
(24hrs), 36, 62 (24hrs), 65.

T

T. Mellon's Hye Bar 206
3707 N Southport Ave between
Waveland Ave and Grace St (773-
244-4102). El: Brown to Southport.
Bus: 152 Addison.

T's 188
5025 N Clark St at Winnemac Ave
(773-784-6000). El: Red to Argyle.
Bus: 22 Clark (24hrs), 92 Foster.

Ta'Too 224
1365 W Fullerton Ave between
Wayne and Southport Aves
(773-525-2739). El: Brown, Purple
(rush hrs), Red to Fullerton. Bus:
74 Fullerton.

Tai's Til 4 206
3611 N Ashland Ave between
Addison St and Waveland Ave
(773-348-8923). Bus: 9 Ashland,
152 Addison.

Take Five 206
3747 N Southport Ave between
Waveland Ave and Grace St (773-
871-5555). El: Brown to Southport.
Bus: 9, 22 (24hrs), 80, 152.

Tantrum 242
1023 S State St between 9th and
11th Sts (312-939-9160). El: Green,
Orange, Red to Roosevelt. Bus: 12,
29, 62 (24hrs).

The Tap Room 212
2218 N Western Ave between
Palmer and Lyndale Sts (773-489-
3622). El: Blue to California. Bus:
49 Western (24hrs).

Taps Lounge 237
701 N Michigan Ave at Huron St
(312-440-1500). El: Red to Chicago.
Bus: 3, 4 (24hrs), X4, 10, 26, 125, 143,
144, 145, 146, 147, 151 (24hrs).

Alphabetical Index

Tavern 33 206
3328 N Lincoln Ave between School and Henderson Sts (773-935-6393). El: Brown to Paulina. Bus: 9, 11, 77 (24hrs).

Ten Cat Tavern 207
3931 N Ashland Ave between Byron St and Irving Park Rd (773-935-5377). El: Brown to Irving Park. Bus: 9 Ashland, 80 Irving Park.

10 Pin 233
330 N State St between Upper Wacker Dr and Kinzie St (312-644-0300). El: Red to Grand; Brown, Purple (rush hrs) to Merchandise Mart. Bus: 22 Clark (24hrs), 36 Broadway.

Third Rail Tavern 240
1133 W Madison St at May St (312-432-9107). Bus: 20 Madison (24hrs).

3160 207
3160 N Clark St at Fletcher St (773-327-5969). El: Brown, Purple (rush hrs), Red to Belmont. Bus: 8, 22 (24hrs), 77 (24hrs).

Three Counties 183
5856 N Milwaukee Ave between Moody and Medina Aves (773-631-3351). Bus: 56A, 68, 91.

Timothy O'Toole's 237
622 N Fairbanks Ct at Ontario St (312-642-0700). El: Red to Grand. Bus: 2, 3, 66 (24hrs), 157.

Tin Lizzie 225
2483 N Clark St at Arlington Pl (773-549-1132). El: Brown, Red to Fullerton. Bus: 22 (24hrs), 36, 76.

Tini Martini 212
2169 N Milwaukee Ave at Talman Ave (773-269-2900). El: Blue to California. Bus: 56, 73, 74.

The Tonic Room 225
2447 N Halsted St between Fullerton Pkwy and Lill Ave (773-248-8400). El: Brown, Purple (rush hrs), Red to Fullerton. Bus: 8 Halsted, 74 Fullerton.

Toon's Bar 207
3857 N Southport Ave between Grace and Byron Sts (773-935-1919). El: Brown to Irving Park. Bus: 9, 22 (24hrs), 80, X80.

Touché 185
6412 N Clark St between Devon and Schreiber Aves (773-465-7400). El: Red to Loyola. Bus: 22 (24hrs), 36, 151 (24hrs), 155.

Town Hall Pub 207
3340 N Halsted St between Buckingham Pl and Roscoe St (773-472-4405). El: Brown, Purple (rush hrs), Red to Belmont. Bus: 8, 22 (24hrs), 77 (24hrs).

The Trace 207
3714 N Clark St between Waveland Ave and Grace St (773-477-3400). El: Red to Addison. Bus: 22 (24hrs), 36, 152.

Trader Todd's 207
3216 N Sheffield Ave at Belmont Ave (773-975-8383). El: Brown, Purple (rush hrs), Red to Belmont. Bus: 8, 22 (24hrs), 77 (24hrs).

Tre 207
3330 N State St at Buckingham Pl (773-281-6463). El: Red to Belmont. Bus: 8, 22 (24hrs), 77 (24hrs).

Trinity 228
2721 N Halsted St between Scubert Ave and Diversey Pkwy (773-880-9293). El: Brown, Purple (rush hrs) to Diversey. Bus: 8, 74, 76.

Tripoli Tavern 225
1147 W Armitage Ave between Clifton and Racine Aves (773-477-4400). El: Brown, Purple (rush hrs) to Armitage. Bus: 8 Halsted, 73 Armitage.

Tropico 188
3933 N Sheridan Rd at Dakin St (no phone). El: Red to Sheridan. Bus: 36, 80, 151 (24hrs).

Tuman's 228
2159 W Chicago Ave at Leavitt St (773-782-1400). Bus: 50, 66 (24hrs), 70.

Twisted Lizard 225
1964 N Sheffield Ave between Armitage and Maud Aves (773-929-1414). El: Brown to Armitage. Bus: 8 Halsted, 73 Armitage.

Twisted Spoke 228
501 N Ogden Ave at Grand Ave (312-666-1500). El: Blue to Grand. Bus: 8, 9 (24hrs), 65.

U

Uberstein 207
3478 N Clark St between Newport and Cornelia Aves (773-883-0300). El: Red to Addison. Bus: 22 Clark (24hrs), 152 Addison.

Underbar 207
3243 N Western Ave at Melrose St (773-404-9363). Bus: 49 Western (24hrs), 77 Belmont (24hrs).

Underground Lounge 207
952 W Newport Ave between Halsted St and Sheffield Ave (773-327-2739). El: Red to Addison. Bus: 8, 22 (24hrs), 152.

Uptown Lounge 188
1136 W Lawrence Ave at Clifton Ave (773-878-1136). El: Red to Lawrence. Bus: 36, 81 (24hrs), 151 (24hrs).

V

Vaughan's Pub 207
2917 N Sheffield Ave between George St and Oakdale Ave (773-281-8188). El: Brown, Purple (rush hrs) to Wellington. Bus: 8, 11, 76.

Victory Liquors 225
2610 N Halsted St between Wrightwood Ave and Diversey Pkwy (773-348-5600). El: Brown, Purple (rush hrs) Red to Fullerton. Bus: 8, 74, 76.

Vida 207
1248 W George St between Lincoln Ave and Lakewood St (773-935-5700). El: Brown, Purple (rush hrs) to Diversey. Bus: 11 Lincoln, 76 Diversey.

Village Tap 207
2055 W Roscoe St at Hoyne Ave (773-883-0817). Bus: 50, 77 (24hrs), 152 Addison.

Villains Bar and Grill 240
649 S Clark St between Harrison and Polk Sts (312-356-9992). El: Blue to LaSalle, Red to Harrison. Bus: 12, 24, 36, 127.

The Violet Hour 217
1520 N Damen Ave between Le Moyne St and Wicker Park (773-252-1500). El: Blue to Damen. Bus: 50, 56, 72.

W

Wabash Tap 242
1233 S Wabash Ave between Roosevelt Rd and 13th St (312-360-9488). El: Green, Orange, Red to Roosevelt. Bus: 1, 3, 4 (24hrs), 12, 29, 62 (24hrs).

Waterhouse 208
3407 N Paulina St at Lincoln Ave (773-871-1200). El: Brown to Paulina. Bus: 9, 11, 77 (24hrs).

Weather Mark Tavern 242
1503 S Michigan Ave between 14th and 16th Sts (312-588-0230). El: Green, Orange, Red to Roosevelt. Bus: 1, 4 (24hrs), 12.

The Web 217
2026 W Webster Ave between Seeley and Damen Aves (773-276-3411). Bus: 50, 73, 74.

Webster's Wine Bar 225
1480 W Webster Ave between Clybourn Ave and Dominick St (773-868-0608). Bus: 9 Ashland.

Weed's Tavern 233
1555 N Dayton St at Weed St (312-943-7815). El: Red to North/Clybourn. Bus: 8 Halsted, 72 North.

Weegee's Lounge 212
3659 W Armitage Ave at Lawndale Ave (773-384-0707). Bus: 53 (24hrs), 73, 82.

Wellington's 208
1300 W Wellington Ave between Racine and Lincoln Aves (773-524-1111). El: Brown, Purple (rush hrs) to Wellington. Bus: 11, 76, 77 (24hrs).

Wells on Wells 233
1617 N Wells St between North Ave and Concord Ln (312-944-1617). El: Brown, Purple (rush hrs) to Sedgwick. Bus: 72 North, 156 LaSalle.

Whirlaway Lounge 213
3224 W Fullerton Ave between Kedzie Blvd and Sawyer Ave (773-276-6809). El: Blue to Logan Square. Bus: 74 Fullerton, 82 Kimball-Homan.

Whiskey Blue 240
172 W Adams St between LaSalle and Wells Sts (312-782-4933). El: Brown, Orange, Purple (rush hrs) to Quincy.

Wicker Park Tavern 218
1958 W North Ave at Damen Ave (773-278-5138). El: Blue to Damen. Bus: 50, 56, 72.

Wild Goose Bar & Grill 208
4365 N Lincoln Ave between Hutchinson and Cullom Ave (773-281-7112). Bus: 11, 50, 78.

The Wild Hare 208
3530 N Clark St at Addison St (773-327-4273). El: Red to Addison. Bus: 22 Clark (24hrs), 152 Addison.

Will's Northwoods Inn 208
3030 N Racine Ave at Nelson St (773-528-4400). El: Brown, Purple (rush hrs) to Wellington. Bus: 11, 76, 77 (24hrs).

Winds Café 213
2657 N Kedzie Ave at Milwaukee Ave (773-489-7478). El: Blue to Logan Square. Bus: 56 Milwaukee, 76 Diversey.

Windsor's Lounge 240
17 E Monroe St at State St (312-726-7500). El: Blue, Red to Monroe; Brown, Green, Pink, Purple (rush hrs), Orange to Madison.

Windy City Inn 192
2257 W Irving Park Rd at Bell Ave (773-588-7088). El: Brown to Irving Park. Bus: 11, 50, 80, X80.

winebar 208
3339 N Halsted St between Buckingham Pl and Roscoe St (773-871-6227). El: Brown, Purple (rush hrs), Red to Belmont. Bus: 8, 22 (24hrs), 77 (24hrs).

Winners Lounge 237
300 E Ohio St at Fairbanks Ct (312-787-6100). El: Red to Grand. Bus: 2, 3, 66 (24hrs), 157.

Wise Fools Pub 225
2270 N Lincoln Ave at Orchard St (773-929-1300). El: Brown, Purple (rush hrs), Red to Fullerton. Bus: 8, 11, 74.

Witt's 225
2913 N Lincoln Ave between George St and Wellington Ave (773-528-7032). Bus: 9, 11, 76, 77 (24hrs).

The Wrightwood Tap 225
1059 W Wrightwood Ave between Lincoln and Seminary Aves (773-549-4949). El: Brown, Purple (rush hrs), Red to Fullerton. Bus: 11 Lincoln.

Wrigleyville North 208
3900 N Sheridan Rd at Byron St (773-929-9543). El: Red to Sheridan. Bus: 36, 80, 151 (24hrs).

X

Xippo 208
3759 N Damen Ave between Grace St and Bradley Pl (773-529-9135). Bus: 50 Damen, 152 Addison.

Y

Y Bar 233
224 W Ontario St between Wells and Franklin Sts (312-274-1880). El: Brown, Purple (rush hrs) to Chicago. Bus: 66 Chicago (24hrs), 125 Water Tower Express.

Yak-Zies Bar & Grill 208
506 W Diversey Pkwy at Pine Grove Ave (773-327-1717). El: Brown, Purple (rush hrs) to Diversey. Bus: 22 (24hrs), 36, 151 (24hrs).

The Yard 208
3441 N Sheffield Ave between Newport and Cornelia Aves (773-477-9273). El: Red to Addison. Bus: 8, 22 (24hrs), 152.

Z

Zakopane 218
1734 W Division St between Hermitage Ave and Wood St (773-486-1559). El: Blue to Division. Bus: 9 (24hrs), 50, 70.

The Zebra Lounge 237
1220 N State Pkwy at Division St (312-642-5140). El: Red to Clark/Division. Bus: 22 (24hrs), 36, 70.

Zella 225
1938 N Clybourn Ave at Racine Ave (773-549-2910). Bus: 9, 11, 76, 77 (24hrs).

Maps

Place of interest and/or entertainment ....
Railway stations ....
Parks ....
Hospitals/universities ....
Neighborhood .... **LOOP**
Metra Station .... ◆M◆
CTA Station ....Clark ═══
(color designates line)

Chicago Overview

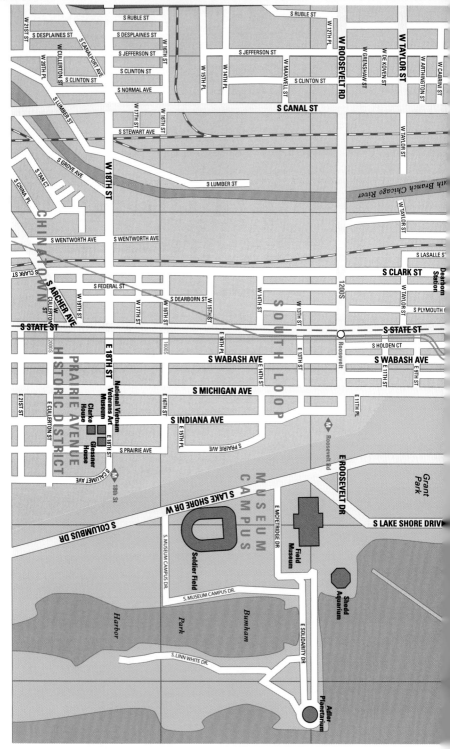

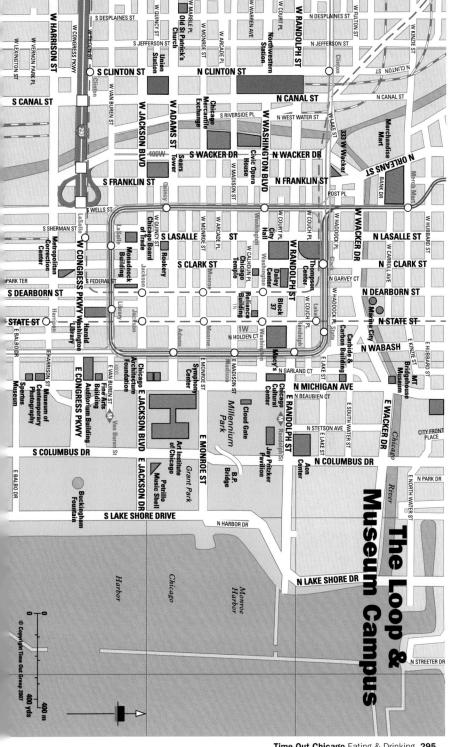

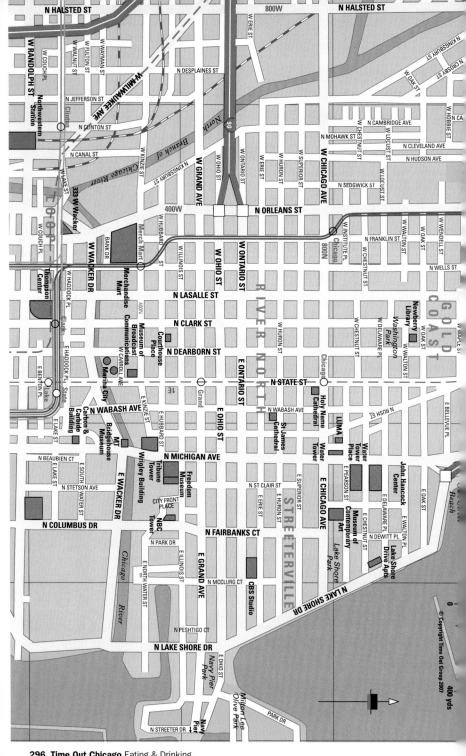

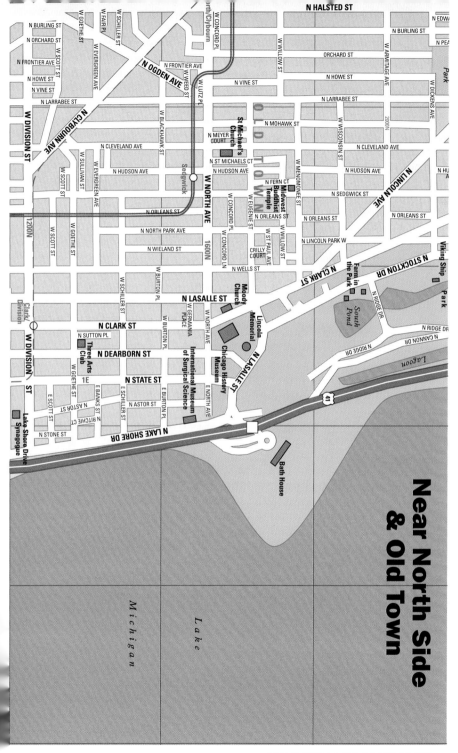

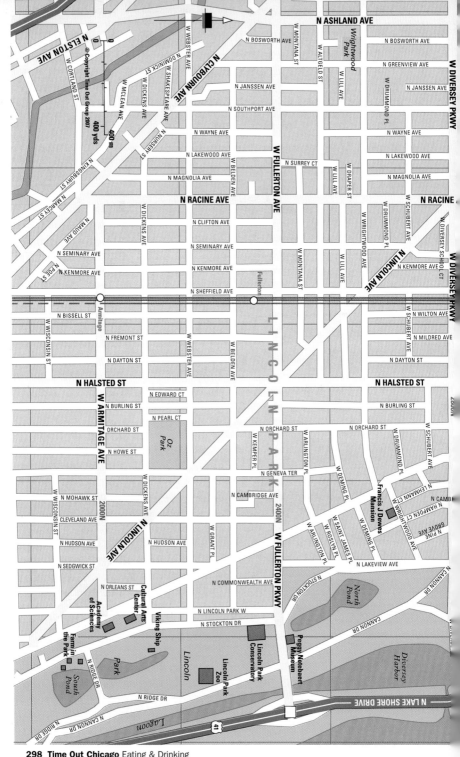

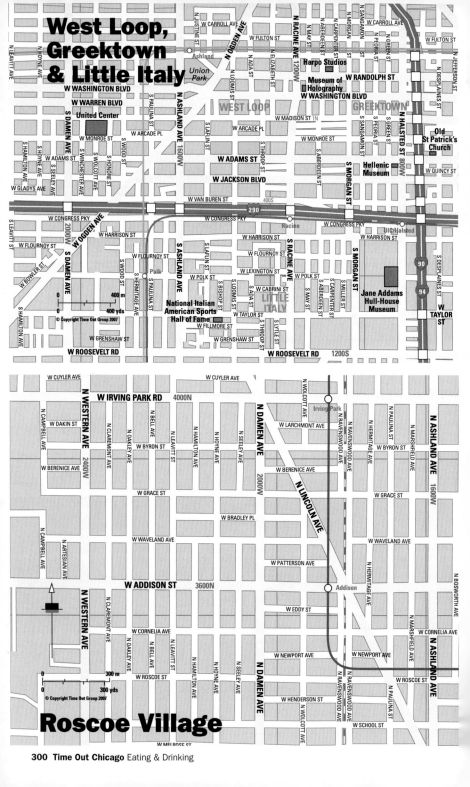

West Loop, Greektown & Little Italy

WEST LOOP

GREEKTOWN

LITTLE ITALY

Union Park

United Center

Harpo Studios

Museum of Holography

Old St Patrick's Church

Hellenic Museum

National Italian American Sports Hall of Fame

Jane Addams Hull-House Museum

UIC/Halsted

Ashland

Racine

Polk

© Copyright Time Out Group 2007

0   400 m
0   400 yds

Roscoe Village

Irving Park

Addison

© Copyright Time Out Group 2007

0   300 m
0   300 yds

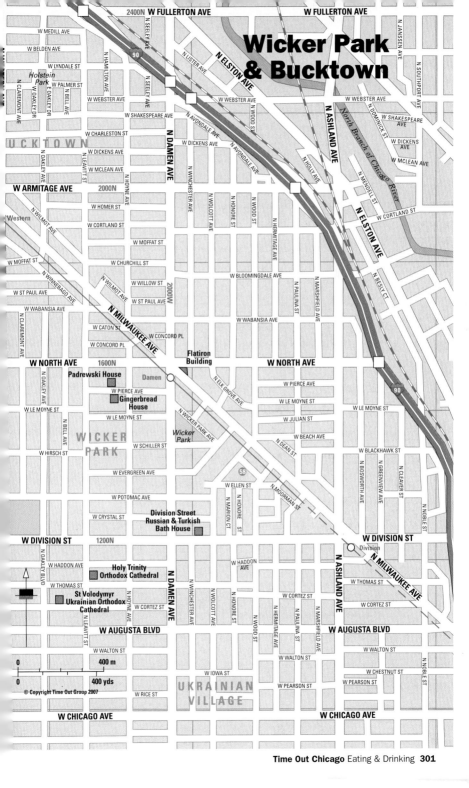

Wicker Park & Bucktown

Chicago Neighborhoods

© Copyright Time Out Group 2007

0   2 km

0   1 mile

IRVING PARK &
ALBANY PARK

LINCOLN SQUARE
& RAVENSWOOD

ANDERSONVILLE,
EDGEWATER
& UPTOWN

W FOSTER AVE 5200N

W LAWRENCE AVE 4800N

W MONTROSE AVE 4400N

W IRVING PARK RD 4000N

W ADDISON ST 3600N

LAKEVIEW,
WRIGLEYVILLE
& ROSCOE VILLAGE

W BELMONT AVE 3200N

AVONDALE

W DIVERSEY AVE

W DIVERSEY PKWY 2800N

Belmont
Harbor

Lake

Michigan

LOGAN SQUARE

Lincoln
Park

W FULLERTON AVE 2400N

LINCOLN
PARK

W ARMITAGE AVE 2000N

WICKER PARK
& BUCKTOWN

OLD
TOWN

W NORTH AVE 1600N

HUMBOLDT
PARK

Humboldt
Park

GOOSE
ISLAND

W DIVISION ST 1200N

RIVER
NORTH

GOLD
COAST

W CHICAGO AVE 800N

UKRAINIAN VILLAGE
& WEST TOWN

W CHICAGO AVE

MAGNIFICENT MILE
& STREETERVILLE

GARFIELD PARK

W LAKE ST

Garfield
Park

W MADISON ST 1N

THE
LOOP

To Oak Park →

Grant
Park

WEST LOOP,
GREEKTOWN &
LITTLE ITALY

W ROOSEVELT RD 1200S

Douglas
Park

W 16TH ST 1600S

W OGDEN AVE

W 15TH PL

W 18TH ST

PILSEN

THE SOUTH
LOOP &
CHINATOWN

W CERMAK RD 2200S

LAWNDALE

W 26TH ST 2600S

HEART OF
CHICAGO

W 31ST ST 3100S

W 31ST ST

E 31ST ST

BRONZEVILLE

BRIDGEPORT

W 35TH ST

MCKINLEY PARK

S ARCHER AVE

To Hyde Park ↓

CTA Rail System

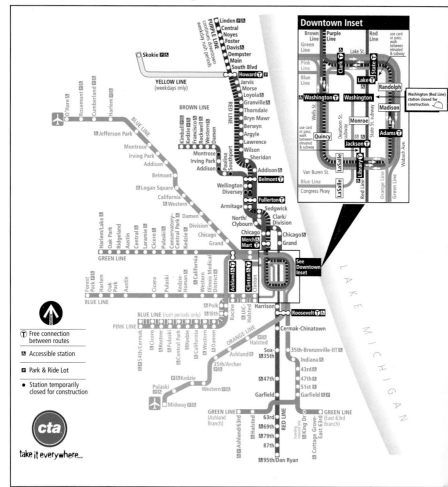

Note: Washington (Red Line) subway station is temporarily closed for construction until 2008.